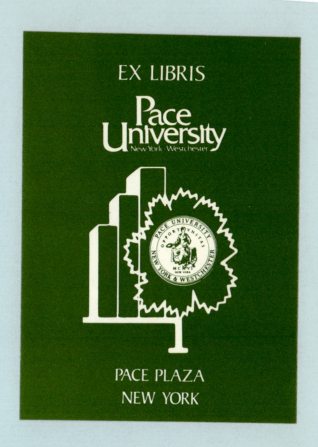

THE
GLADSTONE
DIARIES

Gladstone in the late 1860s

THE GLADSTONE DIARIES

WITH
CABINET MINUTES
AND
PRIME-MINISTERIAL
CORRESPONDENCE

VOLUME VII
JANUARY 1869–JUNE 1871

Edited by
H. C. G. MATTHEW

CLARENDON PRESS · OXFORD
1982

Oxford University Press, Walton Street, Oxford OX2 6DP

London Glasgow New York Toronto
Delhi Bombay Calcutta Madras Karachi
Kuala Lumpur Singapore Hong Kong Tokyo
Nairobi Dar es Salaam Cape Town
Melbourne Auckland
and associate companies in
Beirut Berlin Ibadan Mexico City

Published in the United States by
Oxford University Press, New York

British Library Cataloguing in Publication Data

Gladstone, W. E.
   The Gladstone diaries with cabinet minutes
   and Prime-Ministerial correspondence
   Vol. 7: 1869–June 1871.
   1. Gladstone, W. E.
   I. Title   II. Matthew, H. C. G.
   941.081′092′4   DA563.4

   ISBN 0-19-822638-1

Library of Congress Cataloging in Publication Data (Revised)

Gladstone, William Ewart, 1809–1898.
   The Gladstone diaries.

   Vols. 5–   edited by H. C. G. Matthew.
   CONTENTS: v. 1. 1825–1832.—v. 2. 1833–1839.—[etc.]—
v. 7. 1869–June 1871.
      1. Gladstone, William Ewart, 1809–1898.   2. Great
Britain—Politics and government—1837–1901.   3. Prime
ministers—Great Britain—Biography.   I. Foot, Michael
Richard Daniel, ed.   II. Title.
   DA563.A34   941.081′.092′4 [B]   68–59613
   ISBN 0-19-822638-1   AACR1

Set by Anne Joshua Associates (Oxford)
Printed in Great Britain
at the University Press, Oxford
by Eric Buckley
Printer to the University

PREFACE

The reader will see at a glance that the scope of the material included in volumes seven and eight is very considerably wider than that of previous volumes. In addition to the daily text of Gladstone's personal journal, these two volumes include all of his extremely important and hitherto unpublished Cabinet Minutes and an extensive selection of over eight hundred of the letters which he wrote as Prime Minister in his first administration.

The effect of this is greatly to increase the political content and importance of *The Gladstone Diaries*, and to offer by far the fullest documentary account of a British administration in peacetime. Volumes covering his three subsequent administrations will follow the same pattern.

Gladstone preserved detailed notes of almost every Cabinet meeting at which he presided, and all of these for his first government are printed in these two volumes. Their content and significance is discussed in the Introduction.

Correspondence was a primary preoccupation of Gladstone's prime ministerial life, as his daily diary shows. A wide-ranging selection from it is included in these volumes, interleaved with the daily diary and the Cabinet Minutes. Copies of virtually all of his letters on political topics were made by him or by his secretaries, and the starting point for the selection has been the record he assembled of his correspondence in these years. Wherever possible, the holograph of the letter has been traced and is the version printed below. The selection of letters attempts to include all the important political letters which Gladstone wrote during his first administration, and also to give a fair representation of his quasi-political activities and his religious and literary correspondence. Limitations of space have been the only curtailing factor. Letters in the series already published—to his wife, to the Queen, to Lord Granville, and to Arthur Gordon—have not been duplicated. A selection of the letters to the evangelical ex-courtesan, Laura Thistlethwayte, an important preoccupation in these years, is printed in an Appendix in volume VIII. A note about the technical aspects of the editing of these letters will be found below, at the start of the List of Correspondents.

The Archbishop of Canterbury is again to be thanked for permission to publish the diary and extracts from the ancillary material

owned by him. Similar thanks are due to Sir William Gladstone for
permission to publish material from the British Library and St.
Deiniol's Library collections, for his generous assistance with illustrations, and for his help to the project over the years.

The editor continues to receive essential support and assistance
from the *ad hoc* committee which superintends the publication of
this edition. Lord Blake continues to be its chairman; its other members are Mr. E. G. W. Bill, Lord Bullock, Dr. J. F. A. Mason, Mr. C. H.
Stuart, and Mr. A. F. Thompson. Mr. R. Denniston and Dr. I. Asquith
of the Oxford University Press have in turn acted as its secretary, and
its finances have been watched over by Dr. A. B. Tayler of St. Catherine's College (the project's academic sponsor). The editor would like
to express his thanks to all these for their encouragement and wise
advice.

Finance for the research for these volumes has been provided by
the Archbishop of Canterbury, by the Gladstone Memorial Trust,
and especially by the Rhodes Trust which has provided the bulk of
the funds. The committee and the editor are particularly grateful to
the Rhodes Trustees for making the continuation of the edition
possible, and to the British Academy for a generous grant towards
the costs of the publication of volumes seven and eight.

The diaries continue to be edited in Christ Church, Oxford, in the
rooms which the diarist occupied as an undergraduate. This provision
of accommodation next to Christ Church's own splendid library, and
near to the Bodleian, has been of incalculable advantage and inspiration to the editor.

The expansion of the scope of the content of these two volumes
has naturally posed many problems and difficulties. Mrs. Francis
Phillips has provided many of the answers. She has undertaken much
of the work of the transcription of the correspondence, and most of
the bibliographic research. The day-to-day progress of the edition has
depended on her energy and competence. Mrs. Jean Gilliland has
freed Mrs. Phillips and myself from many extremely time-consuming
chores involved in the preparation of material for the Press and has
assisted in research at the British Library and the Public Record
Office. The editor and the edition have been extremely fortunate to
have been assisted by two persons with such enthusiasm and resource.

The librarian and assistant librarian of Christ Church (Dr. John
Mason and Mr. John Wing) and of Lambeth Palace (Mr. Geoffrey Bill)
and their staffs have been most helpful, as have those of St. Deiniol's
Library, and the Bodleian. Mr. Daniel Waley and his staff at the Students' Room of the British Library eased the progress of the edition
at a number of important moments. Mr. Geoffrey Veysey and Mr.

Christopher Williams of the Clwyd Record Office at Hawarden have continued to place at the edition's disposal their unrivalled knowledge of the Gladstone and Glynne family papers which are deposited at St. Deiniol's Library at Hawarden.

Thanks are also due to Sir Robert Mackworth-Young, Keeper of the Royal Archives, to Mrs. Marion Stowell, Miss Anne Abley and their staff at the History Faculty Office and Library at Oxford, to the staffs of the Public Record Office, the National Library of Scotland, the Record Offices of Glamorgan and Somerset, and to the many other librarians and county archivists who have responded so generously to the editor's cries for help.

The manuscript diaries have been on temporary deposit in the Bodleian Library, where special arrangements were most helpfully made for them. Access to the unpublished Lambeth diary and to its ancillary papers remains restricted to the editor. Addenda, corrigenda, and enquiries should be sent to him at Christ Church, Oxford.

Many colleagues have shown willingness and even enthusiasm when faced by the sometimes bewildering obscurity of Gladstone's more cryptic journal notes, abbreviations and references. Editorial skill consists partly, perhaps even largely, in knowing where to look. The editor soon learnt that somewhere in Oxford, someone always knows the answer; Mr. Peter Parsons has usually been that person. Dr. Alban Krailsheimer and Dr. John Mason have often given me the benefit of their eclectic knowledge. It was my privilege to hold many conversations with the late Mr. Colin Macleod on nineteenth-century classical scholarship. Professor H. W. Lawton's transcript of the daily journal has been of particular value for its bibliographical erudition. Dr. David Steele, Dr. Theo Hoppen, Dr. Kenneth Morgan, Mr. Murney Gerlach, Dr. Adrian Cook, Dr. Brian Harrison, and Mr. Jonathan Parry have assisted me with information on Ireland, Wales, the United States, and other topics of the period. Mr. Mark Curthoys has placed at the edition's disposal his wide knowledge of the popular politics and industrial relations of the period, and Mr. Peter Ghosh has done the same for finance; their comments, and those of Lord Blake, Dr. Boyd Hilton, Dr. Ross McKibbin, and Mr. A. F. Thompson, on the draft of the Introduction, led to substantial improvements. I remain responsible for its deficiencies and for any errors in the edition. I am most grateful to all those mentioned above for their generosity with their time, their knowledge, and their opinions. I am most grateful also to the Governing Body of St. Hugh's College, Oxford, for allowing me a Sabbatical term during which the Introduction was written, and to the Senior and Junior Members there who have borne with patience, enthusiasm, and good nature such a Gladstonian incursion.

Anyone working on this period would be happy to recognise two debts which are in a class of their own: John Morley, whose long analysis of Gladstone's first administration, deficient though certain aspects of it may now seem, charted the way with far more understanding, detail, and argument than is to be found for a comparable period in any other political biography by a contemporary, and Agatha Ramm, whose edition of the Gladstone–Granville correspondence set a classic standard of editorial achievement. It is a pleasure to be able to acknowledge these debts, a sadness not to be able to repay them more fully.

'It is a work that enchains when once begun' Gladstone remarked of his classical studies on 6 April 1874, and the same has proved the case with the editing of his journal. An editor's task is mostly slog, slog, slog. When the author being edited is Gladstone, and when the text is as long as that of his diaries, any slacking can be made to seem some form of moral delinquency, and, certainly, the more one knows of Gladstone and his kind, the more one wonders, how did they do it all? The utterly unVictorian *insouciance* of my family—Sue, David, Lucy, and Oliver—has discouraged brooding and has prevented, I hope, excessive self-absorption in so powerful a personality. I owe my chief thanks to them.

COLIN MATTHEW

Oxford
November 1981

CONTENTS

VOLUME VII

VOLUME VIII

LIST OF ILLUSTRATIONS

ABBREVIATED CHRISTIAN AND SURNAMES

in diary text of Volumes VII and VIII

(*prefixed or suffixed to a name in a footnote indicates an article
in the *Dictionary of National Biography*)

A.	Agnes Gladstone, *daughter, or* the duke of Argyll
A., D. of	duke of Argyll
Agnes	Agnes Gladstone, *daughter*
A.G.	*the same*
A.K.	A. Kinnaird
Arthur	A. Gordon
Arthur, Ld	Clinton
B., Miss	Miss Browne, *governess*
B., Lord	Lord Brougham
B., Count	Count Bernstorff
B., Mrs.	Mrs. Bennett, *cousin*
B. & B.	Bickers & Bush, *booksellers*
C.	Catherine Gladstone, *née* Glynne, *wife*
C., Ld	Lord Clarendon
C., Ld F.	Lord Frederick Cavendish
C., Lucy	Lady Frederick Cavendish, *née* Lucy Lyttelton
C.E.T., Sir	Sir Charles Trevelyan
C.G.	Catherine Gladstone
C.N.G., Lady	Lady Charlotte Neville Grenville
D.	B. Disraeli
D., Aunt	*wife of next*
D., Uncle	David Gladstone *or* Divie Robertson
D., Ld	Lord Derby
D.G.	David Gladstone *or deo gratia*
D. of N.	fifth or sixth duke of Newcastle
E.	Elizabeth Honoria Gladstone, *née* Bateson, *sister-in-law*
E., Lord and Lady	Lord and Lady Ellesmere
E.C.	Edward Cardwell *or* Elizabeth Collins *or* Emma Clifton
E.K., Sir	Sir E. Kerrison

F., Sir T.	Sir T. Fremantle
F., Mr.	W. E. Forster
F.E., Ld or Ly	Lord *or* Lady F. Egerton
F.C., Ld	Lord Frederick Cavendish
Ff., Archd.	Archdeacon Ffoulkes
F.H.D.	Sir F. H. Doyle
F.L.	Frank Lawley
Frank	*the same*
G.	George Lyttelton, *wife's brother-in-law, or* Lord Granville
G.A.S.	(Bishop) G. A. Selwyn
Gertrude	Gertrude Glynne
G.L.	George Lyttelton
G., Lady	Lady Glynne, *mother-in-law*
H.	(Bishop) W. K. Hamilton *or* Helen Jane Gladstone, *sister*
H., Lord	Lord Hardinge
H., Lady	Lady Herbert of Lea
H., Mr. and Mrs.	Mr. and Mrs. Hampton, *the butler and his wife*
Harry	Henry Neville Gladstone, *son*
Helen	Helen Jane Gladstone, *sister, or* Helen Gladstone, *daughter*
Henry	Henry Glynne, *brother-in-law*
Herbert	Herbert John Gladstone, *son*
H.G.	Helen Jane Gladstone, *sister*
H.J.G.	*the same*
Hs., the two	Herbert and Harry, *sons*
J.	John Neilson Gladstone, *brother, or* Johnnie Gladstone, *nephew*
J.L. & co.	Johnson, Longden & Co., *stockbrokers*
J., Lord	Lord John Russell
J.M., Lord	Lord John Manners
J.M.G.	James Milnes Gaskell, *or* John Murray Gladstone, *cousin*
J.M.G. (R.)	J. M. G. Robertson, *cousin*
J.N.G.	John Neilson Gladstone, *brother*
John	*the same*
Johnnie	John Gladstone, *nephew*
J.R.	J. M. G. Robertson, *cousin*
J.S.H., Sir	Sir J. S. H. Forbes
J.S.W.	James Stuart-Wortley

K.	A. Kinnaird *or* Lord Kimberley
Kate *or* Katie	Catherine Glynne, *wife's niece,* *or* Katherine Gladstone, *niece*
L.	Lyttelton *or, occasionally* Marquis of Lorne
L., Lord	Lord Lansdowne
Lavinia	Lavinia Glynne, *née* Lyttelton, *wife's sister-in-law*
Lena	Helen Gladstone, *daughter*
L.L.	Lucy Lyttelton
Ln	Lord Lyttelton *or, occasionally* W. H. Lyttelton
Louisa	Louisa Gladstone, *née* Fellowes, *sister-in-law*
L.R.	L. Rumpff
Lucy	Lady Frederick Cavendish, *wife's niece*
M.	Meriel Sarah Lyttelton, *wife's niece*
M., Dr.	Dr. Moffatt
Mary Ellen	Mrs. Robertson Gladstone, *née* Jones, *sister-in-law*
May	Mary Lyttelton, *wife's niece*
Mazie *or* Mary	Mary Gladstone, *daughter,* *or* Mary Lyttelton, *wife's niece*
M.E.	Mrs. Robertson Gladstone, *sister-in-law*
Meriel	Meriel S. Lyttelton, *wife's niece*
M.G., Mrs.	Mrs. Milnes Gaskell
Molly	Mary Glynne, *wife's niece*
M.S.	M. Summerhayes, *rescue*
Murray, John	John Murray Gladstone, *cousin*
N., D. of	duke of Newcastle
N.	N. G. Lyttelton, *wife's nephew*
Neville	*the same*
Nina	Helen Gladstone, *daughter*
Nora	Honora Glynne, *wife's niece*
P., Col.	Col. Ponsonby
R.	Robertson Gladstone, *brother*
R., Lord	Lord Ripon *or* Lord Russell
R.G.	Robertson Gladstone, *brother*
Rn (G.)	*the same*
Robn	*the same*
Ronald	Ronald Leveson-Gower
R.P.	Robert Phillimore *or* Roundell Palmer

S.	Summerhayes, *rescue*
S. of A.	Lord Stanley of Alderley
S.E.G.	Stephen Gladstone, *son*
S.G.	*the same*
S.R.G.	Sir Stephen Glynne, *brother-in-law*
Stephy	Stephen Gladstone, *son*

T.	(Sir) Thomas Gladstone, *brother*
T., Mrs. *or* Th., Mrs.	Laura Thistlethwayte
T.G.	Sir Thomas Gladstone, *brother*
Tom	*the same*
T.S.G.	T. S. Godfrey

W.	William Henry Gladstone, *son*
W., Lady	Lady Wenlock
W., Lord	Lord Ward
Willy	William Henry Gladstone, *son*
Winny	Lavinia Lyttelton, *wife's niece*
W.H.L.	William Lyttelton
W.L.	*the same*
W.W., Sir	Sir Watkin Williams Wynn

| Xt | Christ |

ABBREVIATED BOOK TITLES, ETC.

Used in Volumes VII and VIII

Aberdare MSS | Papers of H. A. Bruce, Lord Aberdare, in the Glamorgan Record Office

Acton-Simpson Correspondence | *The correspondence of Lord Acton and Richard Simpson*, edited by J. L. Altholz, D. McElrath and J. C. Holland, 3v. (1971–5)

Add MS(S) | *Additional Manuscript(s), British Library*

Argyll | Eighth duke of Argyll, *Autobiography and memoirs*, 2v. (1906)

Autobiographica | J. Brooke and M. Sorensen, eds., *The prime minister's papers: W. E. Gladstone*. I–III (1971–8)

Bassett | A. Tilney Bassett, ed., *Gladstone to his wife* (1936)

Bassett, *Speeches* | A. Tilney Bassett, ed., *Gladstone's speeches: descriptive index and bibliography* (1916)

Battiscombe | Georgina Battiscombe, *Mrs Gladstone* (1956)

BFSP | *British and Foreign State Papers*

Blake | Robert Blake, *Disraeli* (1966)

Brand MSS | Papers of H. B. W. Brand, Lord Hampden, in the House of Lords Record Office

Buckle | W. F. Monypenny and G. E. Buckle, *Life of Benjamin Disraeli*, 6v. (1910–20)

Buxton, *Finance and Politics* | Sydney Buxton, *Finance and politics: an historical study, 1783–1885*, 2v. (1888)

CAB | Prime Minister's letters to the Queen on film in the Bodleian Library

Cambridge University Library | Papers of Sir J. D. Acton, first Baron Acton, in the Cambridge University Library

Carlingford MSS | Papers of C. P. S. Fortescue, Lord Carlingford, in the Somerset County Record Office

Chatsworth MSS | Papers of Lord Hartington at Chatsworth House

Clapham, *Bank of England* | Sir J. H. Clapham, *The Bank of England: a history*, 2v. (1944)

Clarendon MSS | Papers of George Villiers, Lord Clarendon, in the Bodleian Library

Cook, *Alabama Claims* | A. Cook, *The Alabama Claims* (1975)

Denison, *Journal*	J. E. Denison, Viscount Ossington, *Notes from my journal when Speaker of the House of Commons* (1899)
DLFC	J. Bailey, ed., *Diary of Lady Frederick Cavendish*, 2v. (1927)
DNB	*Dictionary of National Biography*, 71v. (1885–1957)
EHR	*English Historical Review* (from 1886)
Elliot	A. R. D. Elliot, *Life of G. J. Goschen*, 2v. (1911)
Fitzmaurice	Lord E. Fitzmaurice, *Life of Earl Granville*, 2v. (1905)
F.O.C.P.	Foreign Office Confidential Prints, PRO.
F.R.U.S.	*Foreign Relations of the United States*
Gardiner	A. G. Gardiner, *Life of Sir William Harcourt*, 2v. (1923)
Gleanings	W. E. Gladstone, *Gleanings of past years*, 7v. (1879)
Guedalla, *Q*	P. Guedalla, ed., *The Queen and Mr Gladstone*, 2v. (1933)
H	*Hansard's Parliamentary Debates*, third series (1830–91)
Hammond	J. L. Hammond, *Gladstone and the Irish Nation* (1938)
Harrison, *Drink and the Victorians*	B. H. Harrison, *Drink and the Victorians* (1971)
Hawn P	Hawarden Papers (deposited in St Deiniol's Library, Hawarden)
Hickleton MSS	Papers of Lord Halifax on film in Cambridge University Library
Holland	B. Holland, *Life of Duke of Devonshire*, 2v. (1911)
Houghton MSS	Papers of Lord Houghton in Trinity College, Cambridge
Hughenden MSS	Papers of B. Disraeli in the Bodleian Library
Juventus Mundi	W. E. Gladstone, *Juventus Mundi, the Gods and Men of the Heroic Age* (1869)
Jenkins, *Dilessi Murders*	R. J. H. Jenkins, *The Dilessi Murders* (1961)

Kent Record Office   Papers of E. H. Knatchbull-Hugessen, first Baron Brabourne, in the Kent Record Office

Kimberley, *Journal*   *A Journal of Events during the Gladstone Ministry 1868-1874, by John, first Earl of Kimberley*, edited by E. Drus, *Camden Miscellany*, vol. XXI (1957)

Knaplund, *Imperial policy*   P. Knaplund, *Gladstone and Britain's imperial policy* (1927)

Lathbury   D. C. Lathbury, *Correspondence on church and religion of W. E. Gladstone*, 2v. (1910)

LQV   A. C. Benson, Viscount Esher, and G. E. Buckle, *Letters of Queen Victoria*, 9v. (1907-32) in three series 1837-61; 2 s., 1862-85; 3 s., 1886-1901

Magnus   Sir Philip Magnus, *Gladstone* (1954)

Marsh, *Victorian Church*   P. T. Marsh, *The Victorian Church in decline* (1969)

Masterman   C. F. G. Masterman, ed. and abridged J. Morley, *Life of Gladstone* (1927)

Matthew, 'Vaticanism'   H. C. G. Matthew, 'Gladstone, Vaticanism and the question of the East' in D. Baker, ed., *Studies in Church History*, xv (1978)

Matthew, 'Budgets'   H. C. G. Matthew, 'Disraeli, Gladstone and the politics of mid-Victorian Budgets', *Historical Journal* (1979)

Max Müller MSS   Papers of F. Max Müller in the Bodleian Library

Maxwell   Sir H. Maxwell, *Life of the Earl of Clarendon*, 2v. (1913)

Millman   R. Millman, *British foreign policy and the coming of the Franco-Prussian War* (1965)

Morgan, *Wales in British Politics*   K. O. Morgan, *Wales in British Politics 1868-1922* (1963)

Morley   J. Morley, *Life of William Ewart Gladstone*, 3v. (1903)

Mundella MSS   Papers of A. J. Mundella in Sheffield University Library

Newman   *The Letters and Diaries of John Henry Newman*, edited by C. S. Dessain and T. Gornall (1961ff.)

N.L.S.   National Library of Scotland

Norman, *The Catholic Church*	E. R. Norman, *The Catholic Church and Ireland in the Age of Rebellion* (1965)
Ornsby	R. Ornsby, *Memoirs of J. R. Hope-Scott*, 2v. (1884)
Perry, *Forbes*	W. Perry, *Alexander Penrose Forbes* (1939)
Phillimore MSS	Papers of Sir R. I. Phillimore in Christ Church Library, Oxford
Ponsonby	A. Ponsonby, *Henry Ponsonby* (1943)
PP	*Parliamentary Papers*
PRO	Public Record Office
Purcell	E. S. Purcell, *Life of Cardinal Manning*, 2v. (1896)
Purcell, *De Lisle*	E. S. Purcell, *Life of A. Phillipps de Lisle*, 2v. (1900)
R.A.	Royal Archives, Windsor Castle
Ramm, I	Agatha Ramm, *Political Correspondence of Mr Gladstone and Lord Granville 1868–1876*, 2v. (1952)
Reid, *F*	(Sir) T. Wemyss Reid, *Life of . . . William Edward Forster*, 2v. (1888)
Reid, *G*	Sir T. Wemyss Reid, ed., *Life of W. E. Gladstone* (1899)
Selborne MSS	Papers of R. Palmer, Lord Selborne, in Lambeth Palace Library
Selborne, I	Earl of Selborne, *Memorials family and personal*, 2v. (1896)
Selborne, II	Earl of Selborne, *Memorials personal and political*, 2v. (1898)
Steele, *Irish Land*	E. D. Steele, *Irish Land and British Politics. Tenant-Right and Nationality 1865–1870* (1974)
Studies on Homer	W. E. Gladstone, *Studies on Homer and the Homeric Age*, 3v. (1858)
Tait MSS	Papers of A. C. Tait in Lambeth Palace Library
T.A.P.S.	*Transactions of the American Philosophical Society*
VCH	*Victoria History of the Counties of England*

Walpole	S. Walpole, *Life of Lord John Russell*, 2v. (1889)
Ward	W. R. Ward, *Victorian Oxford* (1965)
Wilberforce	A. R. Ashwell and R. G. Wilberforce, *Life of the rt. rev. Samuel Wilberforce*, 3v. (1881)
Wilberforce MSS	Papers of S. Wilberforce in the Bodleian Library
Wolf, *Ripon*	L. Wolf, *Life of the first Marquess of Ripon*, 2v. (1921)

OTHER ABBREVIATIONS

ab.	about
abp.	archbishop
acct.	account
aft(n).	afternoon
agst. *or* agt.	against
amdt.	amendment
appt.	appointment
apptd.	appointed
arr.	arrived
b.	book *or* born *or* brother
B.	board of trade
bart.	baronet
Bd.	board of trade
B.I.R.	board of inland revenue
bkfst.	breakfast
B.N.A.	British North America
B. of T.	board of trade
bp.	bishop
br.	brother
B.S.	Bedford *or* Berkeley Square
B.T.	board of trade
ca.	*circa*
cd.	could
C.G.	Carlton Gardens
Ch.	church *or* Chester
Ch. of Exchr.	Chancellor of the Exchequer
C.H.T.	Carlton House Terrace
C.O.	colonial office
co.	county
Col. Ch.	Colonial Church
commee.	committee
commn.	commission
cons.	conservative
cp.	compare
cr.	created
ctd.	continued

cttee.	committee
cum	with
d.	died
da.	daughter
deb.	debate
deptn. *or* dpn.	deputation
dft.	draft
div.	division
do.	ditto
Dowr.	Dowager
Dr.	doctor *or* dowager
E.	earl
E.C.	ecclesiastical courts
eccl.	ecclesiastical
ed.	edited *or* edition *or* editor *or* educational
E.I.	East Indies *or* East Indian
Ep.	epistle
evg.	evening
f.	father *or* folio
F.	father *or* Fasque
fa.	father
ff.	folios *or* following
F.O.	foreign office
1°R	first reading
G. & co.	Gladstone and company
gd.	granddaughter
gf.	grandfather
Gk.	Greek
gm.	grandmother
govt.	government
gs.	grandson
G.W.R.	Great Western Railway
H.C.	holy communion
Hn.	Hawarden
Ho.	house of commons
H.O.	home office
H. of C.	house of commons
H. of L.	house of lords
H.S.	holy scripture

Ibid.	*ibidem*, in the same place
J.S.	joint stock
k.	killed
l.	letter
Ld.	lord
lect.	lecture
lib.	liberal
Ln.	London
Lpool.	Liverpool
Ly.	lady
m.	married *or* mother, *or, with figures*, mille (a thousand)
M.D.R.	Metropolitan and District Railway
mem.	memorandum
mg.	morning
Nk.	Newark
N.S.	National Society
N.S.W.	New South Wales
nt.	night
n.y.n	not yet numbered
N.Z.	New Zealand
No. 11	11 Carlton House Terrace
No. 15 G.S.	15 Grosvenor Square (Mrs. Thistlethwayte)
O.F.	Oak Farm
O. and W.R.R.	Oxford, Worcester, Wolverhampton Railway
p., pp.	page(s)
P.O.	post office
pr. *or* priv.	private
pt.	part
rec(d).	receive(d)
ref(s).	reference(s)
resp.	respecting
Rev(d).	reverend
R.R.	railway

2°R	second reading
S.	son *or* series *or* sister
Sact.	sacrament
S.B.	Savings Banks
Sec. Euch.	Secreta Eucharistica
sd. *or* shd.	should
soc.	society
Sol. Gen.	solicitor-general
sp.	speech
S.P.G.	Society for the Propagation of the Gospel
succ.	succeeded
T.	Treasury
tel.	telegram
3°R	third reading
tr.	translated *or* translation
Univ.	university
v.	verso *or* very *or* volume
V.C.	vice-chancellor
Vicar, the	Henry Mackenzie
vol.	volume
vss.	verses
vy.	very
w.	wife
wd.	would
wh.	which
W.I.	West Indies
W.L.	Wine Licences
Xtn	Christian
yesty.	yesterday

Signs used by the diarist

X	rescue work done this day
+	prayer, usually when on a charitable visit
ɱ	million

Signs inserted into the text editorially

[R]	follows names of subjects of diarist's rescue work
⟨ ⟩	words written by diarist and then deleted

INTRODUCTION

'Truth, justice, order, peace, honour, duty, liberty, piety', these are the objects before me in my daily prayers with reference to my public function, which for the present commands (and I fear damages) every other: but this is the best part of me. All the rest is summed up in 'miserere'.[1]

And so falls the curtain on another anxious and eventful year [1872]: probably the last of the present cares, and coming near the last of all.[2]

The year ends as it were in tumult. My constant tumult of business makes other tumult more sensible. Upon me still continued blessings rain: but in return I seem to render nothing except a hope that a time may come when my spirit instead of grovelling may become erect, and look at God. For I cannot, as I now am, get sufficiently out of myself to judge myself, and unravel the knots of being and doing, of which my life seems to be full.[3]

I

That Gladstone regarded the premiership which began in December 1868 as his last as well as his first, can hardly be doubted by any reader of his journal. Anticipation of retirement is perhaps the most frequently reiterated theme in moments of recorded private reflection and in hints in private correspondence. The foreknowledge of the dramas of subsequent decades should not warp the reader's perspective on Gladstone's attitude of mind as he kissed hands as First Lord of the Treasury for the first time in December 1868.

Politically, Gladstone's view was consistent. For the previous two decades he had seen politics and policies from the perspective of the Treasury. As Chancellor of the Exchequer he had been the codifier, legislator, and guardian of the canons of Peelite finance. Under his suzerainty the Treasury had become the guarantor of the 'minimalist' State.

No industrial economy can have existed in which the State played a smaller role than that of the United Kingdom in the 1860s. Government had appeared to forswear responsibility for fiscal and economic management and it had abolished virtually all tariffs, save those non-protective duties required for revenue purposes. As yet, government responsibility for education existed only through its relationship with the Established Church and its schools and universities, and through small grants to non-established denominations. Government involvement in industrial relations and legislation was largely confined

---

[1] 29 Dec. 72.   [2] 31 Dec. 72.   [3] 31 Dec. 73.

to labour relations in the royal dockyards and to the inspectorate created by the Factory Acts. The concept of social welfare in the twentieth-century sense did not exist. Government grudgingly accepted a 'last resort' responsibility in the specific areas of public health and pauperism, but this was a responsibility to prevent disease in the first case and death in the second, not a responsibility for any positive concern in the welfare of individuals.

Gladstone's part in the construction of this model had been self-conscious and deliberate. His Chancellorship had had as its first aim 'to complete the construction of a real department of Finance'[1] and this had been achieved. There remained outstanding items,[2] aspects of the great plan of 1856[3] which had not yet been executed, but their absence did not detract from the fundamental success of the plans of the 1850s and 1860s.'

Even by the 1860s, the 'minimalist' State in Britain was under attack, both directly and by attrition. It was already clear that neither the Established Church nor voluntaryism could meet the demand for education. Gladstone himself had introduced, in direct and controversial competition with the friendly societies, state-guaranteed annuities which, although self-financing, voluntary, and in practice ineffective, pointed the way to National Insurance.

As a good Peelite, Gladstone had always accepted that the reserve powers of the executive must be retained. He did not accept constitutional devices which would impede executive spending should the policy for such spending be agreed upon, and his criticism of the Bank Act of 1844 was not that it was monopolistic, but that it was inefficient. One of his Cabinet's first acts was to consolidate the preceding Tory Government's nationalisation of the telegraph system. Gladstone's religion, his Peelism, and his innate political and executive activism prevented him from ever being a thoroughgoing *laisser-faire* Liberal. Indeed, there was always a strong *étatiste* element in Gladstone which lay ambivalently and uneasily side-by-side with his fiscal liberalism. For he certainly looked to free trade as providing, in the realm of secular affairs, what he regarded as a second-order political morality, his own first-order concept of a confessional, Anglican State having been set aside in the 1840s, though not wholly abandoned.

There were, therefore, always substantial qualifications both in Gladstone's mind and in the minds of most mid-Victorians to the

[1] See 20 Feb. 56.
[2] See letter to Lowe, 10 Jan. 69. References to those of Gladstone's letters which are printed in the text below are given in this form.
[3] See 16 and 20 Feb. 56.

view that minimal 'interference' was the best government. It is probably the case that, although the minimalist State was achieved in
Victorian Britain in the fullest form compatible with the social
requirements of an industrialised population, none the less, in these
qualifications were contained the assumptions which were to lead to
its gradual disintegration. But the consequences of these qualifications
upon the minimalist State were as yet faint and ill-perceived. Though
many of the measures of Gladstone's first administration prepared
the ground for future developments, these were not intentionally
pursued, at least at Cabinet level. For this was a Cabinet, not just a
Prime Minister, in deadly earnest about retrenchment. In one area at
least—that of the poor law now supervised, from 1871, by the new
Local Government Board under Goschen—the administration could
claim spectacular success in enforcing a dramatic reduction in supposedly sentimental and unsystematic outdoor poor relief, and in
making, in cooperation with the Charity Organization Society (1869),
the most sustained attempt of the century to impose upon the working classes the Victorian values of providence, self-reliance, foresight,
and self-discipline.[1]

Looking at the architecture of the State in the late 1860s, Gladstone saw the grand design largely fulfilled. The odd cornice remained
to be completed, but the foundations and superstructure were built.
Gladstone saw his first Government not as the new dawn of thoroughgoing liberalism emancipated by democracy, but as the setting of the
sun at the end of the day of the building of the mid-century edifice.
The long-term implication of the household suffrage was, no doubt,
the destruction of this creation. But it must be remembered that
Gladstone had not sought the household suffrage of 1867, had resisted
it until it was forced upon him, and had promoted limited franchise
reform in 1866 as a means of consolidating the mid-century order of
State, Party, and politics, not of undermining it.

Unlike 1859, Gladstone came into office in 1868 with no overall
legislative programme. He entered office intent on making the existing structure of government work, improving it at the margin, and
legislating on Ireland. No great lists of topics to be tackled were drawn
up, and apart from the Irish Church, the programme for the first session ('Bankruptcy—Middle Schools—Scotch Education—Irish
railways—Rating clauses')[2] was modest. It was not, of course, the
case that a government would play all its cards in its first session—

[1] See M. E. Rose, 'The crisis of poor relief in England 1860–1880' in W. J. Mommsen,
ed., *The emergence of the Welfare State in Britain and Germany* (1981) and C. L. Mowat,
The Charity Organization Society 1869–1913 (1961); Gladstone was associated with its first
Report in 1870, ibid., p. 19.
[2] 22 Dec. 69.

and the Cabinet in 1868 could theoretically expect the norm of six years of office—but there seems little evidence that Gladstone in December 1868 had a clear view of the overall legislative future of his administration.

Of course, there was nothing unusual in this. Peel had been exceptional among Prime Ministers in being seen as the originator of many of the legislative measures of his administration. It would not have occurred to Melbourne, Aberdeen, or Palmerston that his duty as Prime Minister was personally to stimulate, far less personally to draw up, bills for Parliament, or that his Government should be judged by legislative achievement. Russell's view in 1848 had characterised the epoch between the first two Reform Acts: 'It is not the sole or principal duty of a government to introduce legislative measures or to carry them through Parliament.'[1]

It was Gladstone's problem that his career had hitherto been unusually associated with great legislative successes, and that many of his supporters expected legislation of a dramatic sort to follow the 1867 Reform Act and the great electoral victory of 1868. Allied to this was Gladstone's view of the minimalist State, which was primarily fiscal. Fiscal policies for Gladstone always implied moral principles: he never took a narrow or mechanistic view of fiscal questions, but rather regarded them as being the political and administrative expression of a comprehensive set of moral beliefs. But the form of this expression was fiscal, a general Peelite emphasis, intensified for Gladstone by his long tenure of the Chancellorship of the Exchequer. The curious dislocation of early Victorian politics had meant that fiscal liberalism had been achieved while political liberalism had been barely begun. Such had indeed been the Peelite objective: to show that fiscal liberalism was possible without political reform; equality of opportunity should be the gradual consequence of fiscal measures, not the result of deliberately pursued programmes of social and political reform. Gladstone by no means shared the view that free trade in tariffs should be mirrored by free trade in religion, or that the Burkean social structure of England should be disrupted save by the slow consequences of economic competition. He had arrived in the 1840s at a theoretically pluralistic view of religion in the State, a fact of which he reminded his supporters through the publication of 'A Chapter of Autobiography' at the end of the election campaign in 1868,[2] but in practice his interest in disestablishment was confined to Ireland. A politician might perceive a result to be politically probable, without having an onus personally to promote it. Indeed Gladstone seems in the late 1860s more sceptical about the value of

[1] *H* ci. 669 (30 August 1848).   [2] See above, v. lii, and 23 Nov. 68.

political liberalism generally than he had been in the days of readjustment of theoretical questions of Church and State in the late 1840s.

Not so his supporters. Buoyed up by the great Nonconformist revival of the 1860s, Dissenters saw the victory of 1868 as the occasion
for an assertion of the political priorities of Nonconformity: general
disestablishment, abolition of university tests, a Burials Bill. The disestablishment of the Anglican Church would lead to social and political equality in the same way that Peelite finance had led to fiscal and
economic equality. Allied to these proposals were those of the intel-
lectuals, especially demanding educational reform, the abolition of
university tests, the ballot, and equality of opportunity in entrance
to the Civil Service. Most of these Gladstone regarded with caution,
and some with hostility. He particularly disliked the complete repeal
of university tests, which he succeeded in avoiding in its extreme
form.[1] He also regretted the introduction of the ballot which he
came to see as unavoidable but with a 'lingering reluctance',[2] and
whose various delays he contemplated with some satisfaction, partly
because the issue helped to hold the Party together in 1871 and
1872.[3] Certainly the days were over when, as in the later years of
Palmerston, Gladstone had been regarded by many, not least by
Palmerston himself, as almost a Radical. Given the completion of his
radical fiscal programme, this was not surprising, but it came to surprise many who had seen in Gladstone's espousal of Irish disestablishment early in 1868, the implication of his general espousal of the
Radical political programme.

The problems of Gladstone's personal relationship with Radicalism
worked themselves out against the canvas of the electorate and constituencies created by the 1867-8 Reform measures. The picture on
this canvas was as yet like a preliminary charcoal sketch, of which
only the vague outline was apparent. The household suffrage in the
boroughs had expanded the electorate, more than Gladstone had
wished, in practice less than many had expected. The 1868 election
had taken place in considerable bureaucratic confusion, with registers
hastily and often imperfectly drawn up, and constituency boundaries
so new as to make identification with the candidate on the part of
the elector difficult and confusing. It was certainly not clear that
Conservative resurgence was to be a chief consequence of the Act.
Acton's observation that 'by sinking a shaft through the Democratic
drift they would come to a Conservative substratum'[4] was coming

---

[1] To Coleridge, 4 Dec. 70; see also Ward, *Victorian Oxford*, ch. xi and letters to Liddell,
3 Feb. and 24 Mar. 70. [2] 27 June 70.
[3] See B. Kinzer, 'The 1872 Ballot Act and the Politics of Cabinet-Making'; I am much
obliged to Dr Kinzer for showing me his as yet unpublished paper.
[4] In a deb. on the Elections Bill: *H* ccviii. 1272 (10 August 1871).

to be understood in many an individual constituency, not least in Gladstone's own constituency of Greenwich; but its implications for the Liberal Party at a national level were only slowly grasped. Indeed the Party in a national, organisational sense, barely existed. It had no framework save the moderate discipline that the whips could exercise through the distribution of patronage and small sums of money; it had no permanent structure in many constituencies; and it had no membership. No lead from the centre was given throughout this period of government as to how these problems could be solved. Glyn and A. W. Peel, successively the chief whips of the ministry, had nothing to contribute to the development of the Liberal Party in an extended electorate. They saw their roles in strictly traditional terms.[1] Gladstone had no John Gorst, nor did he look for one.[2] Neither was it the duty of the Cabinet to consider the Party, save at moments of crisis. Though it was the only forum for joint discussion that the Liberals had, the Cabinet did not attempt to deal with the structure of the Party; 'Party' only intruded into its discussions when that structure had, in the Commons, disintegrated. Initiative, when it came, came from the provinces, and especially from Birmingham. Confusion in the constituencies and mismanagement and ill-discipline in the Commons were distinctive features of the administration, and the latter came to be predominant.

The dismantling of the patronage system in the previous fifty years meant that the party in power had little of the 'pork-barrel' left to offer its followers save honours; as Gladstone correctly reminded Lowe in 1869, when the latter urged Cabinet discussion of the topic, the opening of the Civil Service to competition would critically change some of the functions of the whip's office: 'the change would affect more or less the basis of his [Glyn's] office, his *quid pro quo*'.[3] Patronage in the Civil Service had been almost the last '*quid pro quo*' left of the old system of familial government; there remained after 1870 only the odd Lord Lieutenancy, the Church, the colonies, and the Justices of the Peace. For Nonconformists, the first was as yet beyond their aspirations, the second impossible by definition, the third inimical and expensive, the fourth the preserve of a Lord Chancellor almost certain to be an Anglican. To the eighteenth-century Lord Chesterfield, patronage had been the 'pasture for the

---

[1] For the moderate advances that had been made, see A. F. Thompson, 'Gladstone's Whips and the General Election of 1868', *E.H.R.* lxiii. 195 (1948).

[2] The historian of Gladstone's own constituency (until 1880) observes: 'the Greenwich electoral register between 1870 and 1900 was largely a creation of the Conservative Party'; G. Crossick, *An Artisan Élite in Victorian Society* (1978), 213.

[3] To Lowe, 8 Dec. 69. The change in the 'basis' of the whips' functions as a result of open competition merits further exploration.

beasts we feed'; for Gladstone, the process of legislation became the sustenance of his followers, and he promised more of it in his election address in 1874.[1]

But if legislation was the primary expectation of the backbenchers and Party workers, it was by no means the only concern of the incoming premier. Indeed, the advantage of the Irish Church Bill was that it ensured at least a session of relative concord within the Party. Unanimously supported at least as to its principle of disestablishment by the Party before the election, confirmed by the electors, admitted as in some form legitimate by the Opposition, opposed in full only by the Anglican establishment in Ireland, but certain to provoke severe infighting in Commons and Lords on details, the Irish Church Bill offered a sure means of stabilising the majority and preventing the dreadful disintegration which had followed victory in the 1865 general election. The future for the first Session could not but be bright in the main.

II

But if the mass of the Party looked to legislative achievement, the Prime Minister's immediate duties were more traditional: the making of a Cabinet and the management of the Court. The two were closely related. The Cabinet as formed in December 1868 had fifteen members; the Whigs predominated as a group with seven: Hatherley, Clarendon, Granville, Fortescue, Hartington, Kimberley, and Argyll (a Peelite/Whig); three Whigs, Halifax, Russell, and Sir George Grey had declined to serve. There were two Peelites, Gladstone and Cardwell (Roundell Palmer, a Peelite, declined to serve), one Radical quasi-Peelite, de Grey (from 1871, Ripon),[2] two contrasting Radicals, Lowe and Bright, and three Liberals, Childers, Goschen, and Bruce. All were nominally Anglicans, save Bright, a Quaker; only ten of the fifteen had been to university (four to Christ Church, Oxford, three to Trinity College, Cambridge), most were substantial landowners, and one, Bright, had some direct experience of industrial management. All, save Bright, had held at least minor office before, but, surprisingly, in view of the long predominance of Whig–Liberal Governments, only just over half (eight) had sat in Cabinet before: Gladstone, Cardwell, Clarendon, Granville, Argyll, de Grey (Ripon), Goschen, and Hartington. The refusal of the three old Whigs to serve

---

[1] 'I fear that the time has not yet come when you can anticipate a diminution in the calls for legislative labour . . .'; *The Times*, 24 January 1874, 18b.

[2] Ripon is hard to categorise; having been a Christian Socialist, and a supporter of Palmerston in 1857, he was not an orthodox Peelite; having been born in 10 Downing Street during the premiership of his Tory father, 'Prosperity' Robinson, Lord Goderich, he was certainly not a Whig.

gave the Cabinet a fresh look—indeed five of its members were still in Cabinets in the mid-1890s, and one, Ripon, lived to sit in Campbell-Bannerman's Cabinet of 1905.

Before discussing the details of the Cabinet minutes, correspondence, and decisions which form so much of the material printed below, and which were one of Gladstone's chief preoccupations as Prime Minister, a general point about the assumptions of the Cabinet may be made. That the future government of Britain and the Empire was to lie with the 'Box and Cox' alternation of Liberals and Tories was by no means clear to contemporaries. 'The swing of the pendulum', as politicians at the end of the century came to call it, lay in the future: there may be a case for saying it began to swing in 1874, though 1880 or 1886 may be seen as its true start; in practice its arc was almost always irregular. 1868 may seem in retrospect to be the start of 'modern' party politics, but it was not seen as such then. The Cabinet represented a ruling political coalition whose only absence from office had been the result of internal disputes: since 1846, the Whig-Liberal-Peelite alliance had occasionally lost office, but never power. The Cabinet thus worked very much within assumptions to which it anticipated no serious challenge save that of spasmodic obstruction; it did not expect the reversal of policy or legislation, and it gave electoral considerations a low priority.

The assumption of most Liberals was that the worst that could follow the first Gladstone Government would be another minority Tory administration, which would allow time for the party of progress to regroup and then again take power. That the Tories would replace the Gladstone Government with a substantial majority in the Commons was beyond expectation; that the Tories would begin their administration in 1874 by reversing Liberal legislation was a precedent for the twentieth century, not a precept of the nineteenth. After losing the election of 1874, Gladstone complained about a Tory bill: 'This is the first instance on record, so far as I have been able to ascertain, of any deliberate attempt being made by a Ministry of retrogression.'[1] Adversary politics were on the doorstep, but the

---

[1] The Endowed Schools Amendment Act; it is worth having Gladstone's exposition (*H* ccxx. 1707): 'This is a Bill for undoing part of the work of the last Parliament. It is in that respect unusual. I do not wish to deny or to qualify or weaken the fact that the party which sits opposite possesses, after having been many years in a minority, a large majority. What I wish to point out is this, that the history of our country for the last 40 or 50 years, presents to us, as a general rule, this remarkable picture: The initiative of policy in almost every instance—I do not know of even one exception—both of administrative and legislative, was supplied by the Liberal party, and subsequently adopted in prudence and in honesty by the party which is called Conservative. Take the financial—take the colonial—take any of the Departments; and I venture to say that you will find that this is a true description of the

door was still closed. In certain respects, therefore, ministers simply did not think in those terms of party which were soon to become dominant. In other words, ministers were closer to the eighteenth than to the twentieth century in the way they saw their role.

Considering its obvious importance, and the place which Bagehot assigned it as the central and coordinating element of the British constitution, the Victorian Cabinet has been remarkably little studied. In part this has been the consequence of poor documentation. The documentation of Gladstone's Cabinets is far more thorough than that of any other Prime Minister until records began to be officially kept in 1916. For most Cabinets before 1916, the Prime Minister's letter reporting its transactions to the monarch is the chief regular source.[1] But these letters have obvious and severe limitations, especially when they describe the affairs of a Cabinet to which the monarch was hostile. Gladstone's letters to the Queen were intended to instruct, Disraeli's to entertain; neither attempted to describe the details of Cabinets often lasting several hours. Gladstone's method was to tell the Queen of important decisions which the Cabinet had made, particularly in those areas of foreign and colonial policy which especially interested her. Cabinet discussions on prospective policy, on details of domestic policy, and on Party matters and Commons business, are rarely alluded to. To take a random example: the letter reporting the Cabinet of 8 July 1871 only mentions the first of the five items discussed by the Cabinet, the state of play in the row about abolition of purchase.[2]

Gladstone is unique among Victorian Prime Ministers in keeping systematic records of his Cabinets, all of which, for his first administration, are published with the diary text and correspondence in these volumes. These records provide, at the least, a comprehensive guide to topics discussed. The Cabinet usually had a weekly meeting during the Parliamentary Session, several meetings in the autumn for the discussion of the Estimates and of business accumulating during the Recess, and several meetings for planning the work of the Session

---

history of which we have all been witnesses. When the Conservative Government came into power in 1834, and again in 1841, after the first Reform Act had been the subject of a long dispute and much contention, there was absolute security in the mind of the country and full conviction that the party coming into office would not be so unwise and so unpatriotic as to retrace the steps taken by their Predecessors.'

[1] See S. Roskill, *Hankey—Man of Secrets* (1970), i. 340–1.
[2] See Guedalla, *Q*, i. 286, which concludes: 'There was no other subject treated by the Cabinet to-day which it is necessary for him to bring before Your Majesty'; the other subjects discussed were proposals for a Law University, the cumulative vote in School Board elections; bishops' resignations, and Contagious Diseases Acts.

and the preparation of the Queen's Speech; crises, political and foreign, required extra meetings as occasion demanded. The average number of Cabinet meetings for each year between 1869 and 1873 was about fifty. Gladstone's minutes provide information on almost all of these. Exceptions are those meetings at which he was absent through illness, in which case Granville presided,[1] meetings held hurriedly in the Commons during great crises, such as the deadlock over the abolition of army purchase in 1871, and occasional meetings held in odd places, such as that of 21 March 1871, when the Cabinet met in a G.W.R. railway carriage, 'to consider the Telegram on the U.S.', as its members returned from Windsor. Very occasionally, a Cabinet held in normal circumstances has no surviving minutes.[2] Although kept entirely on Gladstone's initiative, these minutes had some official standing, or could be used officially, for Granville wrote to General Schenck, the American Minister in London during the crisis over the Alabama negotiations, of a Cabinet decision on Alabama 'as recorded in a minute by Mr. Gladstone'.[3] Gladstone's minutes are almost always brief; they are in fact a combination of topics for discussion and consequent decisions for implementation. In most cases the agenda was listed before the meeting began, and the decisions filled in on the same sheet. From time to time the reports show that the order of discussion was altered at the last moment, with certain urgent topics being promoted.[4]

Sometimes Cabinets have an agenda with ticks in the margin opposite each or most items: in most cases this indicates that the item was discussed: some items are left unticked, or have 'postponed' written against them, or have a lack of discussion indicated by a circle in the margin.[5] Items which are left without a tick or a circle were clearly not necessarily undiscussed: sometimes they clearly were discussed, for the decisions taken are listed against the item.[6] Some Cabinets have no ticks or circles but appear to be in every other respect normal. Gladstone consistently recorded Cabinets, but he was not consistent in the way he recorded them. Ticks, circles, and 'postponed' clearly have some positive meaning, but their absence probably means mere inconsistency or negligence on Gladstone's part. It would be unwise to infer a negative: the absence of a tick should not be taken to mean

---

[1] Minutes of these sometimes survive; see 24 July 69.

[2] See 19 Dec. 71. See 4 Apr. 71 for 'a quasi Cabinet'. Records also survive for some 'conclaves' (see, e.g., 9 Apr. 69); a 'conclave' was a meeting with non-Cabinet members present, usually for the purpose of discussing a specific problem or emergency, such as the Irish Church Bill's progress, or the state of the Alabama negotiation.

[3] Granville to Schenck, 20 March 1872, *F.R.U.S.*, 1872, ii. 440, referring to the cabinet held on 14 Dec. 71.

[4] See, e.g., 20 Feb., 6 Mar. 69.   [5] See 1 July 71.   [6] 17 Apr. 69; 15 Dec. 71.

that the item was not discussed, or even that no decision was reached: *quandoque dormitat,*[1] as Gladstone was fond of remarking.

Gladstone's aim seems to have been to list the topics for discussion and the decisions taken or not taken, as concisely as possible. His minutes rarely reveal the content or flavour of the discussion and only on the odd occasion its participants, other than the name of the Minister responsible for beginning the discussion. His records are therefore an essential guide to the chronology and *acta* of the administration; they do not, by themselves, often offer a commentary on its quality, tone, or state of morale.

This baldness is not to be explained merely by shortage of time. Gladstone had little interest in the gossip of politics. In all of his vast correspondence it would be hard to find a single letter, outside those dealing with family affairs, which could be called gossipy. The odd pleasantry from time to time occurs at the end of a letter, but it is rarely *ad hominem*, and never malicious. The spirit of futility about the usefulness or success of democratic politics which usually characterises letters of political gossip was entirely lacking in Gladstone. His minutes and letters carry the same assumption of self-confident purpose.

This is not to say that Gladstone was naive about the content of much of political life. Commenting on an obituary of the fourteenth Earl of Derby, Gladstone observed:

> Politics are at once a game and a high art; he allowed the excitement of the game to draw him off from the sustained and exhausting efforts of the high art. But this was the occasional deviation of an honourable man, not the fixed mental habit of an unprincipled one.[2]

Whether or not this description is true of Lord Derby, it is certainly the case that Gladstone saw politics as 'at once a game and a high art'. Much of their fascination for him sprang from the problems posed in working out the detailed consequences of great principles in the context of Cabinet and Parliament. Gladstone saw the process of politics as inseparable from its principles; nothing delighted him more than the evolving of a policy which was both internally coherent and at the same time outflanked the enemy. This combination of gamesmanship and morality gave Gladstone much of his power. He was as alert to political manoeuvring as the most formidable of his opponents, as flexible and resourceful at defending or exploiting a position, and

---

[1] 'Sometimes even good Homer nods.'

[2] Morley, ii. 244; the passage deplores the translation of 'leichtsinnig' in Stockmar's *Memoirs* as 'frivolous'; Gladstone regarded 'lightminded' as both correct and fundamentally different in implication.

more than a match in stamina for any of his contemporaries when it came to a pitched battle. On the other hand, he appeared to act within a general context of moral objectives which allowed him to personify the moral imperatives of Victorian Liberal politics.

With respect to politics as a game, Gladstone's first ministry was in one sense not dramatic, for many of the players at Cabinet level were remarkably unambitious. Gladstone's position as Prime Minister was unassailable and unassailed, and his role as Party coordinator was essential. None of the other Cabinet members made any persistent attempt to act as an alternative focus of power or influence within the Cabinet, save on certain specific issues: for example, the Whigs on Ireland and foreign policy, Bright on education.

It may surprise the reader of these diaries, with their record of persistent tug and tussle, that Gladstone looked back in 1897 on this ministry as 'a Cabinet easily handled'.[1] This was not rose-tinted nostalgia, for what Gladstone meant was that, despite the arguments, personal relationships within the Cabinet were easy: the presence of 'several members who were senior to myself' facilitated business. These older Whigs were unambitious but not embittered; they fought on policies much more than on personalities. Gladstone's happy relationship with Granville is well-known, but he believed he also came to be on good terms with Clarendon (who died in June 1870), with Halifax (once the Charles Wood of the disastrous budget of 1851) and, to a lesser extent, with Kimberley, the leader of the younger Whigs. These Whigs were inclined to find 'Merrypebble', as Clarendon nicknamed Gladstone, in principle almost ridiculous, with his Tractarianism and his moralising, but during the first ministry their personal relationships with him remained amiable, though they fought tooth-and-nail on policies. While their doubts about Gladstone's restlessness and unpredictability increased, these were, at Cabinet level, still doubts fairly easily contained within the existing structure of politics. When Kimberley believed the Government was at an end after the defeat on the Irish University Bill in March 1873, he noted in his journal a judgement clearly relative to his experience of administrations since 1852: 'We have been wonderfully harmonious during our four years of office and power.'[2]

The Whigs were a first and particular worry for Gladstone. Though a diminishing force in the country, they remained essential for government. They controlled the Foreign and Colonial Offices almost as by right, and with their great landholdings they dominated the Irish offices. They were an essential link between Court and premier (here the appointment of Halifax as Lord Privy Seal in July

---

[1] Morley, ii. 414; *Autobiographica*, i. 96.   [2] Kimberley, *Journal*, 37.

1870 was a shrewd move, creating a buffer between Queen and Prime Minister and taking some of the weight off the overworked Granville), and the support of the Whigs in the Lords was all the Liberals had. Disaffection among the leading Whigs would therefore bring rapid disaster; disaffection among some Whigs there certainly was, as will be shown below, but at Cabinet level the Whigs cooperated sufficiently to maintain the unity of the ministry. It is a moot point whether Russell outside the Cabinet was more trouble than he would have been inside it; Gladstone went to considerable lengths, especially in 1869-70, to keep him in touch, but he came to regard Russell's supposedly failing powers as irremediable.

At the other end of the Cabinet stood John Bright, ill, ineffective in administration, perhaps rather idle, but still a dominant force in non-official Liberalism, or at least regarded as such by Gladstone. Bright represented in Cabinet the old Liberalism of the Anti-Corn-Law League but also something of the new Liberalism of the 1860s, the complex clutch of reforming urges round which Radicalism had clustered in the constituencies. To lose Bright, especially before the Education Bill was passed, would be to isolate official Liberalism, that body of men which formed the executive, still essentially the Aberdonian coalition of Whigs and Peelites, from the new enthusiasts.

Gladstone's letters to Bright testify to his persistence and, on the whole, to his success. He encouraged Bright by offering 'early friendly and confidential communication on subjects of great public interest';[1] he flattered him by praising his 'Herculean efforts';[2] he arranged for Bright to remain a Cabinet member though unable to attend for several months;[3] he succeeded in delaying Bright's resignation, promised for late 1870, until January 1871, when the worst of the crisis of the Franco-Prussian war was over.[4] In October 1871 Gladstone returned to the pursuit with flattery ('those who have official responsibility must ever feel a natural anxiety to arm themselves with the best assistance and advice'),[5] arranging a visit by Bright to Hawarden,[6] informing him of Cabinet details once he had ceased to be a member,[7] and eventually succeeding in bringing him back into the Cabinet in September 1873 to strengthen the Government after the sundry crises of the spring and summer of that year.

[1] 22 May 69.

[2] 31 July 69; encouragement of this kind, to cabinet colleagues, especially in such enthusiastic terms, is rarely to be found in Gladstone's letters.

[3] 16 Mar. 70; this illness was most fortuitous for Gladstone, as Bright was not attending Cabinets while the Education Bill was proceeding.

[4] 4, 8, 10 Aug. 70; 16, 19, 28 Nov. 70; 11, 16 Dec. 70. Even at the last stage, Gladstone proposed a form of Cabinet association, dangling the Alabama arbitration and defence retrenchment as a carrot; see 11 Dec. 70.

[5] 24 Oct. 71.   [6] 13-15 Nov. 71.   [7] 25 Nov. 71.

Next to the Queen, no-one was more cossetted than John Bright. Whereas Lowe received a very sharp analysis of the attributes of his character,[1] Bright's executive deficiencies passed without hostile comment, evoking merely sympathetic understanding. Gladstone began his brutally frank comments on Lowe's political failings by observing that 'I always hold that politicians are the men whom as a rule it is most difficult to understand i.e. understand completely; and for my own part, I never have thus understood or thought I understood above one or two, though here and there I may get hold of an isolated idea about others.'[2] Gladstone's handling of Bright shows he had understood a good deal of the sentimental side of Victorian Radicalism.

In cossetting Bright, Gladstone cossetted Nonconformity; he was much more successful with the particular than the general. He ended with Bright back in the Cabinet but with Nonconformity at best apathetic, at worst openly hostile. Cabinet cohesion was a window-dressing which was intended to mask disintegration in the constituencies. Bright balanced the Cabinet, and allowed Gladstone to appear in a more central and less exposed position than would have been the case with Bright absent: Bright had therefore a function *vis-à-vis* the Whigs and the Court as well as *vis-à-vis* the Nonconformists and constituency Radicals.

It was Court and Whig departmental business which formed the first course of the Cabinet's staple diet. Discussion of foreign and colonial business—especially the former—was the regular business of the Cabinet, and was usually discussed as the first or second item of the agenda. The second regular function of the Cabinet was agreement on and supervision of the legislative programme. Third, particularly at certain times of the year, the Cabinet discussed finance and the Estimates. It also, naturally, dealt with miscellaneous problems as and when they occurred.

It is not the aim of this introduction to assess or examine the overall achievement of the 1868–74 Liberal Government, though the materials below constitute the first source for such an assessment, but rather to examine the part which Gladstone played in that administration, to discuss those issues in which he involved himself, or was necessarily particularly involved by the nature of his office. Of course, as Prime Minister and Leader of the Commons, papers dealing with every aspect of the ministry's activities came before him, as they also came before the Queen. But some subjects, of importance for the ministry and its subsequent fate, such as legislation on the drink trade, largely passed him by, and are thus not discussed below.

[1] 13 Aug. 73.   [2] Ibid.

It will be convenient to discuss Gladstone's involvement as Prime Minister under the headings outlined above: foreign and colonial policy; the legislative programme; the Court; the economy.

III

First, foreign and colonial policy. Gladstone had not previously been directly and persistently involved in the making of foreign policy, though he had been Colonial Secretary in 1845–6. However, as Chancellor of the Exchequer, he had seen many Foreign Office despatches, and he had of course been in Cabinet during both the Crimean and Schleswig-Holstein crises, and throughout the American Civil War. He had therefore been privy in general to the making of much of British foreign policy since 1852, and the Anglo-French Cobden Treaty of 1860 had been more his achievement than that of any other member of Palmerston's Government.

For a utopian and out-and-out free trader, foreign policy might seem in principle unnecessary: international free trade was to lead to international harmony which would replace the need for bargains between governments. But the way that British free trade had developed had not in fact been that of unilateral tariff abolition. Britain by the late 1860s was related to most European countries by a complex series of trade treaties, most of them most-favoured-nation treaties, a process which was still not completed.[1] It was not until the Continental abrogation of freer trade in the 1870s that British free trade existed quite independently of Continental attitudes. By the late 1860s the framework of the free trade treaty structure was built. Gladstone, as one of its architects, now looked to its defence; while happy to extend the system, he did not come to office with any intention of fundamentally changing it. His objective in the long negotiations over the renewal of the French Commercial Treaty after the 1870 war was essentially to save what he could of the 1860 Treaty; he stressed his 'unchanged adherence to the principles and objects of 1860 whatever force there may be in the consideration that the application of such principles must be subject to considerations of time, place, & circumstance'.[2]

The same can be said of Gladstone's attitude to foreign policy generally. His acute sense of organic and historicist nationality exemplified in *The State in its Relations with the Church* meant that the acceptance of nationality was his starting point. Foreign policy was not, as it was for the Radicals, corrupt dealings between landed

---

[1] See, e.g., letter on proposed tariff treaty with Spain; 27 Dec. 69.
[2] To M. Chevalier, 14 Oct. 72.

castes,[1] but rather the means by which European nations communicated for the public good. It was, therefore, desirable and potentially beneficial. Amongst these nations Gladstone discerned a developing awareness of civic progress, based on the acknowledgement of mutual interests, through 'treaties of mutual benefit with every nation of earth; treaties not written on parchment, but based on the permanent wants and interests of man, kept alive and confirmed by the constant play of the motives which govern his daily life'.[2] It was the function of the British 'to found a moral empire upon the confidence of the several peoples'. His article in the *Edinburgh Review*, anonymously written and published at the height of the Franco-Prussian war, was intended to give public airing to views which could not be given an official imprimatur: 'the silence of a Government need not be copied by those who, not invested with authority, aim at assisting the public mind and conscience by discussion'. It concluded with an interesting and optimistic statement which is both retrospective and admonitory:

> Certain it is that a new law of nations is gradually taking hold of the mind, and coming to sway the practice, of the world; a law which recognises independence, which frowns on aggression, which favours the pacific, not the bloody settlement of disputes, which aims at permanent and not temporary adjustment; above all, which recognises, as a tribunal of paramount authority, the general judgment of civilised mankind. It has censured the aggression of France; it will censure, if need arise, the greed of Germany. '*Securus judicat orbis terrarum.*'[3] It is hard for all nations to go astray. Their ecumenical council sits above the partial passions of those, who are misled by interest, and disturbed by quarrel. The greatest triumph of our time, a triumph in a region loftier than that of electricity and steam, will be the enthronement of this idea of Public Right, as the governing idea of European policy; as the common and precious inheritance of all lands, but superior to the passing opinion of any. The foremost among the nations will be that one, which by its conduct shall gradually engender in the mind of the others a fixed belief that it is just. In the competition for this prize, the bounty of Providence has given us a place of vantage; and nothing save our own fault or folly can wrest it from our grasp.

This passage exemplifies Gladstone's expectations and hopes for foreign policy. Its tone is certainly not thoroughgoingly Radical: the central quotation, St. Augustine's famous maxim which drove J. H. Newman to Rome, resurrects the image of a Christian, homogeneous

---

[1] Gladstone seems to have felt no particular irritation at the exemption of the foreign office from entry by competition, and he raised few complaints about the quality of the predominantly whiggish British envoys abroad.

[2] 'Germany, France, and England', *Edinburgh Review*, October 1870, reprinted in *Gleanings*, iv, begun on 1 Sept. 70, the day of the battle of Sedan. Attempts to keep authorship 'absolutely secret' fairly quickly failed, see letters to H. Reeve, the *Edinburgh's* editor, 26 Aug., 23, 26, 30 Sept., 3 Nov. 70.

[3] 'The verdict of the whole world is conclusive.'

Europe. The comity of nations was to mirror the ecumenical councils of the Church.

This introduction of ecumenism at so vital a point reflects Gladstone's personal religious preoccupations of recent years. It also refers to his major preoccupation in foreign affairs in the first year of his ministry: the preparations for the Vatican Council and for the declaration of Infallibility. Gladstone's case against Infallibility was both personal and general: it ruined ecumenism in England, and it cast in doubt the civic allegiance of all Roman Catholic populations. It was 'civic individuality' which gave European nations the right to claim superiority in world affairs, and it was 'civic individuality' which was the guarantor of liberty both personal and national: 'Nothing can compensate a people for the loss of what we may term civic individuality. Without it, the European type becomes politically debased to the Mahometan and Oriental model.'[1] Ultramontanism struck straight at 'civic individuality'; Gladstone's hope was that 'a combined action of the Governments' would strengthen 'the more moderate & right minded Bishops' and consequently either prevent or moderate a declaration of Infallibility; 'there may be an opportunity of helping to do what the Reformation in many things did: to save the Pope and the Roman Church from themselves'.[2]

Gladstone's difficulty was first that Britain had no official diplomatic representation at Rome, thus finding it difficult to take the lead, and second, that the Whiggish and world-weary Clarendon, though thoroughly Erastian and anti-Papal, did not invest the controversy with the same ideological significance or urgency as his Prime Minister. The conscience of Europe stirred twice, in the Bavarian initiative of the spring of 1869, and in the French initiative of March 1870. Britain was not included in the Bavarian initiative, and only marginally in the French initiative. In the latter case, Clarendon persuaded the Cabinet, against Gladstone's wishes, to respond to the French appeal verbally, rather than by a note.[3] The voice of Europe, when it spoke, fell on deaf ears, despite the fulfilment of Gladstone's wish that 'Pope & Ecclesiastics' should not be able 'to say with truth that they never received a friendly warning'.[4]

The appeal of the Concert had been spectacularly unsuccessful in the case of the Roman Catholic Church. Its failure called into question Gladstone's hope that 'the general judgment of civilized mankind'

[1] *Gleanings*, v. 235.   [2] To Clarendon, 21 May 69.
[3] 17 Mar. 70: 'Ecumenical Council: conversation on concurrence in possible French move. H.M. Govt. to stand in 2d rank.'
[4] To Clarendon, 24 Aug. 69; I have discussed these negotiations in more detail in 'Gladstone, Vaticanism and the Question of the East' in K. D. Baker, ed., *Studies in Church History*, xv (1978).

would act as the guarantor of the European order. Gladstone realised this; once the Council was under way he hoped that the French would threaten to withdraw their troops, using the threat of leaving the Papacy at the mercy of the Italian Government as a means of containing the Pope's theological ambitions. He also felt this negative use of troops to be the only way of bringing effective pressure to bear: 'withdrawal of the troops is the only measure within the power of France to take which the Pope and his myrmidons care about . . . it is by threats and threats alone that the Court of Rome, as to its Roman & Church policy, is influenced: its whole policy is based in the rejection of reason'.[1]

The success of Ultramontanism seemed to Gladstone to mark a major crisis in the progress of 'civic individuality' in Europe, as well as in its effect on Anglican-Roman relations in England and on the Irish situation. It would be going only just too far to say that he regarded it as a worse blow than the Franco-Prussian war, which ended the Council peremptorily but with the French troops staying in Rome long enough to allow a declaration of Infallibility to be rushed through. He returned to the theme frequently in correspondence and speeches, and his attempt to include in his election manifesto in 1874 a passage admonishing vigilance to prevent the effects of Ultramontanism on 'civil rights and equality of all' was only struck out at the last moment by the demands of the other members of the Cabinet.[2] His response to Ultramontanism was to be the obsession of his quasi-retirement and the occasion of his return to public dispute with the publication of *The Vatican Decrees* in November 1874.[3]

Gladstone had intervened as enthusiastically as he could to stimulate the Concert to action on Ultramontanism. He had been held back partly by Clarendon's reluctance but mainly by Britain's weak position: no official envoy in Rome, the lack of Roman Catholic representation in the official classes, and the unfortunate fact that the leader, whip, and wire-puller of the Ultramontanists, 'the madmen of the Council',[4] was his former intimate, the apostate H. E. Manning, Archbishop of Westminster, whose cooperation was thought central to the management of the Irish bishops and Liberal M.P.s and thus to the success of the Government's Irish legislation. In such circumstances Britain was relatively uninfluential: 'I agree with you', Gladstone told Clarendon, 'that Dr. Döllinger expects far too much from anything we could say.'[5]

[1] To Clarendon, 13 Mar. 70. He felt the French 'have made a wretched mess of it: & the Pope has snubbed & trampled on that Govt. most relentlessly, as he was certain to do, the moment he knew the troops would not be recalled'; 24 Mar. 70.
[2] See 23 Jan. 74.
[3] See, e.g., 30 Sept. 74, 20 Oct. 74.
[4] To Clarendon, 15 June 70.
[5] To Clarendon, 24 Mar. 70.

Was this to be the case with the 'deluge of events' in the second half of 1870, the war between Prussia and France which 'unset, as it were, every joint of the compacted fabric of Continental Europe'?[1] Starting from the assumption that 'the nations of Europe are a family', Gladstone saw British involvement in the quarrel as wholly natural: England's 'hand will not be unready to be lifted up, on every fit and hopeful occasion, in sustaining the general sense of Europe against a disturber of the public peace'.[2]

Here he differed sharply from traditional Mancunian isolationism embodied in the Cabinet by John Bright.[3] In addition to the precept of intervention, he supported a traditional priority of the 'national interest' view of Continental affairs. Right at the start of his ministry, he told Clarendon: 'A war between France and Germany would be sad but the compulsory or fraudulent extinction by annexation of the Free State of Belgium would be worse.'[4] The careful qualifications characteristic of any Gladstonian letter show that he did not at that stage regard Belgium as an absolute commitment, and he soon made it clear that British interest was not in itself sufficient: 'I for one believe, but do not know, that the true public opinion of Belgium is possessed with a sense of nationality, & is resolved to struggle for its maintenance. That is the only possible standing point I apprehend for permanent resistance.'[5] The 'dirt in the sky'[6] which Gladstone saw early in 1869 was in large measure lost sight of as the immediate crisis of the Belgian railways passed.

'What pretext has he [Bismarck] for interfering in Bavaria?', Gladstone asked Clarendon in February 1870.[7] By the summer, Bismarck had his pretext, and Gladstone made no complaint about Prussia's conduct in the outbreak of the war, but blamed France's 'folly, inconsistency, and temerity'.[8] His analysis of French politics shows an understanding of the dynamic and unstable nature of the Second Empire, which the Cobden Treaty, in his view, had been intended, but had had insufficient time, to stabilise. He also showed an understanding of the internal dynamics of German nationalism and Prussian politics but made no direct link between them and the events of the first half of 1870. Gladstone could not object to the formation of 'our Teutonic cousins' into a single political nation. It is striking that he assumed that 'Germany' was what Bismarck made it: that is,

[1] *Gleanings*, v. 197–8. [2] Ibid., 248.
[3] See D. M. Schreuder, 'Gladstone as "troublemaker" ', *Journal of British Studies*, xvii. 125 and 'The Gladstone–Max Müller debate on nationality and German unification', *Historical Studies*, xviii. 561.
[4] To Clarendon, 30 Jan. 69. [5] To Clarendon, 18 Feb. 69.
[6] To Clarendon, 30 Jan. 69. [7] To Clarendon, 16 Feb. 70.
[8] *Gleanings*, iv. 217.

'Germany' for Gladstone meant the *Kleindeutsch* solution, and Prussia's policy was thus in his view teleologically directed and justified: 'the aggrandisement of Germany by consolidation from within her own frontiers, is not a matter of which other countries are entitled to take any hostile cognisance'.[1]

Officially, Gladstone and the British Government maintained a strictly neutral position, arranging the guarantee of Belgian neutrality by treaty. Privately, Gladstone acted quickly to make the War Office 'study the means of sending 20,000 men to Antwerp',[2] while strongly resisting the use of the occasion for a general increase in military strength, which was 'the extreme susceptibility, on one side of the case, of some members of the Cabinet'.[3] Gladstone seems to have had no personal doubt about the maintenance of Belgian and consequently British neutrality, for when Consols fell he bought £2,500 at 90 on 18 July.[4]

The defence of Belgium was achieved without the dual priorities of British national interest and the rights of peoples having to be disentangled by members of the Cabinet. The same was not the case with Alsace and Lorraine. Gladstone differed from his colleagues in the vehemence of his hostility to Bismarck's annexation. He discussed the question simultaneously with his old friend, the French free-trader Michel Chevalier, and with Friedrich Max Müller, the peregrinating philologist and apologist for German nationalism who was in 1870 a professor in Oxford. To Chevalier, he blamed the French for making their case against annexation on the basis of erecting 'the inviolability of soil into an abstract principle';[5] to Max Müller, he complained at the absence of 'previous proof' that 'the inhabitants generally are favourable' and that annexation was militarily necessary to Germany and that Germany would not use Alsatian fortifications against France.[6] Unilateral annexation and lack of general discussion on the terms of the peace would, Gladstone believed, mean 'that Germany, crowned with glory & confident in her strength, will start on her new career . . . without the sympathies of Europe', a mistake as 'ruinous' in its consequences as 'our going, or Mr. Pitt's going, to war in 1793'.[7]

Gladstone was not opposed to flexibility of boundaries; what he required was legitimation of their change. An advance upon the 'old and cruel practice of treating the population of a civilised European

---

[1] Mem. at 23 Nov. 70.

[2] To Cardwell, 16 July 70. He soon back-tracked on the implications of this suggestion, see 24 July 70.

[3] To Cardwell, 24 July 70.   [4] Bank Book 1870, Hawn P.   [5] 14 Sept. 70.

[6] 9 Oct. 70; see also 29 Dec. 70, 30 Jan., 24–8 Feb., 1 Mar. 71. See also Schreuder, 'The Gladstone–Max Müller debate', op. cit.

[7] 30 Jan. 71.

country as mere chattels'[1] had been achieved by references to local opinion in plebiscites or votes of assemblies; Gladstone proposed 'military neutralization'[2] as an alternative to annexation in the case of Alsace-Lorraine, and requested the Cabinet's agreement for an appeal to other neutral nations for support. The Cabinet supported Granville's more anodyne suggestion,[3] and a second attempt was drowned by the Gortchakoff circular on the Black Sea clauses of the 1856 Paris Treaty.[4]

In neither the Vatican question nor the Franco-Prussian war had 'the mind of Europe' been as clearly or as forcefully expressed as Gladstone would have liked. His differences with his Cabinet should not, however, be exaggerated. In neither case was Gladstone suggesting more than verbal initiatives, and in both cases his initiatives were intended as homilies which would inform the Cabinet and, if accepted there, the civilised world, what ought to be done, rather than as policies which Gladstone believed had any real chance of success. He did not think that either the Papacy or Bismarck would change course; he felt that neither should be allowed to go against what he saw as the standards of civilisation without remonstrances which might act as precedents for the future.

In both these great crises of the mind and shape of Europe, Britain's intervention depended on the attitude of other members of 'the family'. In neither case were the relatives likely to be cooperative, and in the Franco-Prussian war Russia showed that she at any rate would use a family row to take what she could get. In the case of British–American relations, however, only America and the British Empire were involved, and it was thus easier for Gladstone to stiffen the will of his Cabinet at the vital moment.

The problem of the *Alabama* claims involved not only questions immediately arising from damage done to Northern shipping during the Civil War by the *Alabama* and similar ships, but also the 'indirect claims' (i.e. the claim that the United States should be compensated not only for damage done directly by ships sold to the South during the war by British shipbuilders, but also for the indirect losses suffered—at their most extreme, all the losses caused by the delay in the ending of the war) in settlement of which the United States at one stage suggested the cession of Canada—it had just bought Alaska. The 'claims' also raised the question of security of the Canadian border and the Fenian raids across it, and outstanding Canadian-American disputes on tariffs and fisheries. Much detail will be found below on these questions.

[1] *Gleanings*, iv. 242.   [2] 25 Sept. 70.
[3] See 30 Sept. 70.   [4] 10 Nov., 23 Nov. 70.

Gladstone was also personally involved, in the sense that his notorious Newcastle speech of October 1862, which could be easily and most obviously construed as a recognition of Confederate right to secede, was a severe embarrassment to him and to the Government. For most of 1869, following the rejection of arbitration by the Senate in the form proposed in the Johnson–Clarendon treaty of January 1869,[1] Gladstone made little attempt to do more than encourage Clarendon on American questions, sometimes complaining at the 'submissiveness' which the weakness of the Canadian frontier forced upon Britain.[2] The appointment of the historian J. L. Motley as American minister in London severely embarrassed Gladstone personally, for Motley had attacked Gladstone's 1862 speech as a 'consummate work of art', comparable to Mark Antony's burial speech.[3] Gladstone's reaction to Motley's appointment was to demand withdrawal of the phrase; elaborate arbitrations followed, successful only by the time that Motley had lost his own government's confidence.

For Gladstone, unlike radical pro-Northerners in Britain, did not see the developments leading up to the arbitration at Geneva in 1872 as 'righting a wrong'. He saw the process as exemplifying the means by which two civilised nations could settle differences, without either having to admit being in the wrong. In the autumn of 1869 he began to take a more perceptive view than Clarendon of the highly complex position of Hamilton Fish, the American Secretary of State, to defend Fish against Clarendon's scorn,[4] and to suggest that 'the two countries should set about the consideration of a good prospective system, and should thereafter, in the light of principles thus elucidated, reconsider the matter of arbitration, or any other mode of proceeding in the Alabama case'. Even when Fish revived the demand for the annexation of Canada in exchange for the settlement of the Claims, Gladstone counselled maintaining 'our present composed temper'.[5] The proposal of 'a good prospective system' was embodied in the Treaty of Washington of 1871 whose articles' general significance was in Gladstone's view 'to become rules for international law for the future'.[6]

The successful conclusion of the Washington Treaty seemed to mark the end of the affair, bar the settling of the details. But the American claim, made in their 'Case' of December 1871 prepared for submission to the arbitration tribunal, that the question of the 'indirect claims' was still open, astonished and appalled the British.

[1] So called, but effectively negotiated by 15th Earl of Derby when Foreign Secretary under Disraeli in 1868.
[2] To Clarendon, 30 Mar. 69.   [3] 22 Mar., 1 Apr. 69.
[4] 23, 25 Oct. 69. For Fish's difficulties, see Cook, *The Alabama Claims*, ch. 5.
[5] 24 Jan. 70.   [6] To Northcote, 3 Apr. 71.

Gladstone responded with a vigorous denunciation in the Commons of American behaviour,[1] which was both genuinely felt and politically convenient. He then short-circuited the cumbersome channels of communication, by which his own views reached the Americans only *via* Granville, the Foreign Office, and Thornton, the ambassador in Washington. He proposed to Granville that direct communication between himself and Schenck, the new American minister, should be the first means of negotiation.[2] As Gladstone was already on terms with Schenck, this would give him more personal control and initiative. His first use of this direct access to Schenck was to be the delivering of a vast letter justifying his own record during the Civil War, and replying to the sections of the American 'Case' which seemed to impugn it. In this, he was overruled by the Cabinet, led by Granville.[3] His urge for self-justification was linked to a strong intention to make the negotiation succeed within the terms of the Treaty of Washington and to show that its terms were not ambiguous.[4]

The extraordinary contortions through which, between March and June 1872, both British and Americans eventually contrived to make the Treaty work can be traced in detail below. Gladstone's role was to push forward negotiations whenever possible and, when a breaking point seemed almost to have occurred, to rally his Cabinet, especially Halifax, Kimberley, and Cardwell, the chief dissenters, behind the larger view. 'My determination upon it is now firmly rooted & tested by all the mental effort I can apply.'[5] The strategy prevailed and, greatly assisted by the common sense of Charles Adams, the American arbitrator, the arbitration proceeded without consideration of the 'indirect claims'. Both the Treaty of Washington and the arbitration could be offered to the world as the path for the future. So also, eventually, could Gladstone's self-justification. His vast letter to Schenck—really a political pamphlet, and the longest single item written by Gladstone during this government—was eventually sent to Schenck, against Granville's advice,[6] in November 1872 and was later published in *Harper's New Monthly Magazine* (it is reprinted below).[7] Gladstone had felt throughout that he and the British position during the Civil War had subsequently been hard done by. He had urged Clarendon to get someone such as Merivale to publish a defence of it.[8] His letter to Schenck was his version of that defence

---

[1] 6 and 7 Feb. 72.   [2] To Granville, 25 Feb. 72, Ramm I, ii. 312.
[3] 26 Feb.–2 Mar. 72.   [4] To Blachford, 9 Mar. 72.
[5] 13 June 72.   [6] Ramm I, ii. 364–5.   [7] 28 Nov. 72.
[8] 19 May 69; Gladstone also felt that his proposal 'early in the war' for rules to govern prospective cases such as the *Alabama* had been neglected, by implication by Russell; but he could make no allusion publicly to this, for Russell was already very touchy on the question of his record as Foreign Secretary; ibid.

and marked the start of that assiduous cultivation of American liberal opinion which was to be so marked a characteristic of the rest of his life.

Gladstone's initiatives in some areas of foreign policy thus found him on occasion in disagreement with his Cabinet, and, on the whole, the Cabinet prevailed. Gladstone's concept of an 'ecumenical council' of civilised opinion appealed neither to the Whigs, who preferred the discreet bargains of the closet, nor to the Radicals, who saw in it sinister implications of Continental involvement.

Allied to foreign policy, in that it was traditionally a Whig preserve and the subject of routine Cabinet discussion occasioned by the arrival of despatches, was colonial policy. Of India, the Cabinet heard little. Gladstone's letters to Argyll, the Secretary for India, were largely about British questions. Gladstone's own 'desires' for India's future were that 'nothing may bring about a sudden, violent, or discreditable severance; that we may labour steadily to promote the political training of our fellow-subjects; & that when we go, if we are to go, we may leave a clear bill of accounts behind us'.[1] This vision would have startled many of his contemporaries, but he made no moves to encourage its realisation. Indian security was a more immediate problem. On the question of Russian expansion in Turkestan, he followed Granville in a policy of issuing general cautions combined with concessions.[2]

'Colonial policy' for the most part meant the relationship of Britain to her colonies of European descent. Granville's Colonial Secretaryship in 1869 and 1870 was marked by the withdrawal of British troops from New Zealand and preparations for their withdrawal from Canada.[3] This was part of a long-standing and systematic attempt on the one hand to force the colonists to act responsibly, on the other to help to reduce defence costs at home, which accounted for about a third of the British budget. As Colonial Secretary in 1845-6, Gladstone had moved towards self-government in New Zealand as quickly as possible[4] and, as he reminded Granville in 1869, one of his first actions as Peel's Colonial Secretary had been to instruct the new Canadian Governor-General 'that we did not *impose* British connection upon the Colony, but regarded its goodwill and desire as an essential condition of the connection'.[5]

Even before the 1867 Canada Act, Gladstone had been most reluctant to accept a Vote for Canadian fortifications.[6] As Palmerston's

---

[1] To Northbrook, 15 Oct. 72.   [2] e.g. 10 Dec. 72, 2 Jan. 73.

[3] See C. C. Eldridge, *England's Mission* (1973), ch. 3.

[4] See introduction above, iii. xxxv.

[5] Ramm I, i. 24. See 20 Jan. 46ff.   [6] See mem. at 19 Jan. 65.

Chancellor, he had played a leading role in the 'Conferences on Canadian Defence' with Canadian politicians which had negotiated the agreement essential to the making of the 1867 Canada Act.[1] Gladstone's readiness to support troop withdrawal was therefore consistent with his position over many years. Considering army reform in 1870, at the height of the Franco-Prussian war, he anticipated getting 'rid of all drafts upon the regular army for Colonial purposes, in ordinary circumstances, except in the four cases of Malta-Gibraltar-Halifax-Bermuda'.[2] But these withdrawals were only to continue in peacetime conditions: where Britain was 'satisfied as to the cause whether Canada were independent of us or not, such [armed] assistance . . . would only be limited by our means'. The 'whole power of the Empire' should be used to sustain 'a political connection' as long as Canada wanted one.[3]

Gladstone thus assumed that the 'union of heart and character'[4] would continue as long as it was desired by both sides, and that it would be a union supported by arms if necessary. How little he anticipated unilateral action by colonies is shown by his astonished reaction to the Australian demand for differential tariffs in 1871. 'Do I understand . . . that New Zealand (for instance) may admit free shoes made in Sydney and tax at any rate she pleases shoes made in Northampton?' He thought this 'advance . . . brings us near the *reductio ad absurdum* of colonial connection, & the people of this country should have an opportunity of passing an opinion on it'.[5] 'Astounding' though this might seem, the British Cabinet was forced to acknowledge there was little they could do about it, despite the fact that it upset all the delicately balanced trade treaties which Britain had concluded with European states in the name of the British Empire as a whole. Reserved powers of commercial treaty-making turned out, to Gladstone's regret more than Kimberley's, to be nonexistent, the pass being finally sold by Lisgar, the Governor-General of Canada (whose confusions in Ionia Gladstone had been sent out to right in 1858), who without consultation with London gave the Royal Assent to a Canadian Bill establishing differential tea and coffee duties with America.[6]

The movement towards an Empire less formally integrated constitutionally and administratively was thus significant, but it was a movement based on localised fiscal and protectionist priorities, unencouraged and reluctantly conceded by London. The speed with

---

[1] See 19 May–10 June 65.   [2] 13 Oct. 70.
[3] 19 Jan. 70. Granville was more cautious, see ibid., note.
[4] See supra, iii, xxxv.   [5] To Kimberley, 16 May 71; see also 22 May 71.
[6] To Kimberley, 29 Dec. 71, 25 Jan., 9 Feb., 14 Oct. 72.

which colonies made use of the legislative freedom which the previous twenty years of imperial policy-making had given them, clearly came as a shock to Gladstone, who seems to have thought that responsible government and support for free trade would go hand in hand. The enthusiasm for colonial development which he had shown in the 1840s was absent; a co-founder of the Canterbury settlement in New Zealand, he gave no encouragement to the various lobbies of similar feeling in the 1870s.[1] Undoubtedly this was a mistake from the point of view of domestic politics: failure to present the positive side of the emotional 'kin beyond the sea' view of colonial relationships and a readiness to rely on an understanding by the electorate of the technical details of long-established policies, made it all the easier for the opposition to link patriotism with Conservatism and claim that 'there has been no effort so continuous, so subtle, supported by so much energy, and carried on with so much ability and acumen, as the attempts of Liberalism to effect the disintegration of the Empire of England'.[2]

In Cabinet, Gladstone had found himself more cautious than Granville on imperial questions, and differing with Kimberley on the importance of the colonial tariff question. On questions of colonial expansion, he found himself on the defensive. A long rearguard action on the annexation of Fiji, conducted with Gladstone's usual resourcefulness, succeeded in delaying a decision, despite powerful pressures from the anti-slavery lobby, but in the Gold Coast, Gladstone was reluctantly persuaded by the combined action of the Colonial Office and the War Office, to concede the sending of a military force under Sir Garnet Wolseley in the autumn of 1873. He threatened Kimberley with a recall of Parliament, the implied revolt of Bright, the refusal of the Cabinet to defend the expedition in the Session expected in 1874, but it was all to no avail.[3] 'I am not master of the facts', Gladstone told Kimberley,[4] and the War Office saw to it that this remained the case; Gladstone had to rely on newspaper reports for information about the preparation of Wolseley's force, and understandings about Cabinet supervision of the stages of its progress were simply ignored.[5] 'The pressure of the three Departments, with a view to military preparations', Gladstone told Bright, 'has gone beyond what I feel competent to deal with & beyond the mere execution of the orders

[1] See 3 Feb. 70, and H. L. Malchow, *Population Pressures: emigration and government in late nineteenth-century Britain* (1979), 32.
[2] Disraeli at the Crystal Palace, 24 June 1872, in Buckle, v. 194. Dr. Eldridge rightly draws attention to the government's failures of presentation, op. cit., p. 91. See also Gladstone's rather lame reference of the imperialist Macfie to Hugessen's 1871 speech, 30 Apr. 72.
[3] See 14 Aug., 30 Aug., 4 Sept., 20 Nov., 16 Dec. 73.
[4] 30 Aug. 73.   [5] To Cardwell, 5 Sept., 15 Sept., 17 Sept. 73.

of the Cabinet'.[1] The Gold Coast question illustrated the weakness both of Gladstone as Prime Minister, and of the office as such. Cardwell and Kimberley effectively prepared and despatched the expedition on their own authority; the Prime Minister had no constitutional way of stopping them. By the time the Cabinet met, the expedition was on its way. However, the military conduct of the expedition, once launched, on the whole met with Gladstone's approval. It was well organised, cheap and quick, and stood out favourably in all respects in comparison to the Tories' Abyssinian adventure of 1867–8. Gladstone lauded Wolseley's conduct in an interesting letter which may represent, in part, an attempt to repair the generally poor relations between the Liberal party and the army.[2]

The discovery of the diamond field at Kimberley in 1869 and the anarchic allegiances of uncontrolled prospectors threatened British informal control of the non-colonised areas of southern Africa. The Cabinet decided in principle to annex the 'Cape Diamond Fields' in May 1871,[3] and the stresses within southern Africa thus provoked, prepared the way for the decision to give 'a general encouragement' to 'South African Federation'.[4] However, in the complex maze of southern African relationships and the difficulties of communication with London, the Governor of the Cape, Barkly, on his 'own Act', annexed the Diamond Fields to Cape Colony, regardless of the federation plans—a classic example of action by 'the man on the spot'.[5] Gladstone had warned Kimberley 'that in opening the door to the re-incorporation of the Boer States in the Empire you will (as is your wont) take due precautions against extension of the responsibility of the H[ome] Government'.[6] However, he made no attempt to influence in detail the development of an area which, when he returned to power in 1880, was to prove one of his chief external preoccupations. Neither the Cabinet nor the Prime Minister had any consistent control over imperial expansion, nor, except in the case of Fiji, did Gladstone attempt to intervene decisively in it. 'No objection taken' was the laconic record in the Cabinet minutes of Barkly's initiative.[7]

IV

The second of the chief areas of concern within which it is convenient to discuss the business of the Cabinet was its coordination and supervision of the form and content of the Government's legislative programme. In Gladstone's first ministry this was a major task,

[1] To Bright, 26 Sept. 73.   [2] To Wolseley, 22 Feb. 74.
[3] 13 May 71.   [4] 6 Nov. 71.   [5] 14 Dec. 71.
[6] 26 Oct. 71.   [7] 14 Dec. 71.

for the programme was exceptionally dense, partly because of the Prime Minister's predilection, partly because of the great volume of bills promoted by the various government departments, and partly, as has been suggested above, because the expectations of the ministry's supporters—to call them a Party is to suggest too coherent a description—required that they be kept sweet, or at least supportive, by legislative proposals whether expected to pass or not.

Each legislative proposal must have its own history, its own relationship to government departments and to pressure groups, and will be shaped within the context of a long series of precedents, legal conventions, and departmental preparations. Normally, by the time the proposal reaches the Cabinet, the room for manoeuvre is severely constricted. That elaborate and often impenetrable process by which certain measures emerge as the questions of the day can hardly be dealt with in general here. The history of government departments is usually the key to the analysis of this process; but Gladstone had no department, nor did he, except on very rare occasions, deal with departments save through their Cabinet representatives.[1] He did on several occasions, however, act as a one man department in the sponsorship of legislation, and it will be convenient first to discuss those bills in which he took a particular personal or leading interest.

The Sessions of 1869 and 1870 had Irish legislation as their centrepiece. The Irish Church Bill of 1869 was, and the Irish Land Bill of 1870 became, very much Gladstone's own bills. The Irish Church Bill he prepared himself, in consultation with selected advisers and Thring, the parliamentary draftsman. The Land Bill was prepared in a partnership of varying balance between the Prime Minister and Chichester Fortescue, the Irish Secretary and author of the failed Irish Land Bill of 1866. Not since Peel's Bank Act of 1844 had the Prime Minister been seen as the almost single-handed architect of a major piece of legislation, apart from the unique circumstances of the Reform Bills.

Ireland was for Gladstone a preoccupation, not an interest, an embarrassment, not an intellectual attraction. Clearly, Ireland had not progressed, but Gladstone showed little intellectual curiosity about this anomalous corner of the 'workshop of the world'. His aim in his Irish policy was simply stated: 'our purpose & duty is to endeavour to draw a line between the Fenians & the people of Ireland, & to make the people of Ireland indisposed to cross it'.[2] Institutional

---

[1] A chief exception to this is E. Hammond of the foreign office.

[2] To General C. Grey, 28 Mar. 69, discussing the release of Fenian prisoners. He admitted, under pressure from Earl Grey, that Fenians in Ireland and England 'have had a very important influence on the question of the time for moving upon great questions of policy for Ireland'; 27 and 28 Apr. 69.

reform (the Irish Church Bill) and social and economic reform (the Land Bill) were intended to have a political effect. Gladstone seems to have believed that if the Irish were shown the Westminster Parliament redressing their grievances by spectacular acts of legislation, then this would encourage their adherence to the existing political structure, both as to institutions and political parties.

The disestablishment of a part of the Anglican Church was, naturally, a formidable political and technical undertaking, an assault on the formal structure of the establishment as dramatic in principle as anything achieved between 1689 and the present day. Gladstone felt that he had sufficient political impetus to maintain his bill in principle in the Commons despite 'a possible development of *minor* schism in the Liberal body'[1] over details of the Bill affecting Roman Catholics, and indeed this proved correct. In the crisis over the bill in June and July 1869, he was able to use the Liberal majority in the Commons against both the Lords and opponents of his approach in the Cabinet. Almost from the start, he saw the Lords as 'the most formidable stumbling block'.[2]

His bill was predominantly negative in tone: that is, it concentrated on disestablishment, and did not attempt to use the occasion for the more positive incorporating approach which the policy of concurrent endowment implied.[3] As he told Archbishop Tait, in the Commons 'there is not that distinction between the question of disestablishment and disendowment which exists in Your Grace's mind',[4] and, he might have added, in the minds of many Erastians, both Conservative and Whig. Concurrent endowment (i.e. the endowment of the Roman Catholic Church in Ireland side by side with the Anglican) went against all Gladstone's principles. If an established church could not represent 'religious nationality', he favoured the opposite extreme of voluntaryism. The notion of the State being involved in the support of various denominations which were doctrinally irreconcilable he profoundly abhorred, and the ending of the Maynooth grant in 1869 was probably one of the most satisfactory consequences of disestablishment for him personally. Gladstone successfully warded off concurrent endowment, favoured by Lord John Russell in his pamphlets of 1868–9, and by some other Whigs, as well as by many Conservatives.

---

[1] To E. Sullivan, 7 Jan. 69.   [2] Ibid.
[3] i.e. the distribution of the assets of the Anglican Church in Ireland between the three chief Irish denominations, Anglican, Roman Catholic, and Presbyterian; the Roman Catholics and the Presbyterians up to disestablishment received state subsistence through the Maynooth Grant and the Regium Donum respectively. These grants were ended with compensation from the Anglican endowments, though they had been a charge on the Imperial Exchequer, not on the Irish establishment.
[4] 3 June 69.

It is hardly likely that the Roman Catholic hierarchy would have accepted it if it had been offered.

The bill was rapidly drawn up at Hawarden with the advice of Archdeacon Stopford, and with Granville and Acton in attendance. Gladstone returned to London on 1 February 1869 and by 9 February the Cabinet 'completed the heads of the Irish Church measure to my great satisfaction'.[1] Complex negotiations, 'conclaves', and discussions changed some of the details of the bill,[2] but its substance emerged unscathed, and the bill was given a first reading on 1 March 1869.

Gladstone had made one major change from the plan he drew up in December 1868:[3] originally, the disestablished church was to have kept its glebe houses, and some of their 'immediately annexed lands'.[4] Under pressure from Roman Catholics, Presbyterians, and John Bright, this continuation of the endowment was drastically reduced. The concession proved fortuitous for, when the clash with the Lords came in July 1869, the dispute centred on three chief questions: concurrent endowment; the glebe lands and other property, and the related question of compensation for curates; and the threat to delay the date of operation of the Act. Gladstone absolutely ruled out any concession on the first, and on 26 June 1869 carried the Cabinet with him: 'Discussion on concurrent Endowment. Govt. do not entertain it.' The Tories might try to keep the issue alive, but, with the Queen wanting a settlement, the issue came down to cash, a bargain to be struck between the two Houses: 'All that remains is to say to the majority of the H. of C. *such and such a sum* is not worth the quarrel and the postponement. This sum must be moderate.'[5] Gladstone's low offer on the glebe lands gave room for manoeuvre: Disraeli wanted one sum, Tait a second, Cairns a third and highest.

Under the strain and excitement of the negotiations, not least for him, Gladstone had the first of those short illnesses which often punctuated all his ministries at times of major crisis. Clearly something more than what today would be called a 'diplomatic illness'— nervous exhaustion would seem to have been the cause—it was none the less extremely convenient, for, rather than the slightly frenetic, Tractarian Prime Minister, it left the composed Erastian Granville to conduct the final negotiations, in which the Opposition's hostility

[1] 9 Feb. 69.
[2] These are clearly analysed in D. H. Akenson, *The Church of Ireland: ecclesiastical reform and revolution, 1800–1885* (1971), ch. 4.
[3] 18 Dec. 68.
[4] Ibid., and Akenson, op. cit., 256. The plan of 18 Dec. 68 anticipated something of this possibility in the phrase, 'if Parliament shall be indisposed to this course . . .'.
[5] 19 July 69.

swiftly collapsed and a compromise unexpectedly favourable to the Liberals' demands was reached. The favourable issue left Gladstone, upstairs on his sofa, 'almost unmanned, in the reaction from a sharp and stern tension of mind'.[1]

Gladstone believed Ireland had provided the momentum for the party in 1868 and 1869, and his policy of disestablishment without concurrent endowment had satisfied not only himself, but his Roman Catholic and Nonconformist supporters. This policy had been 'the basis on which the late remarkable cooperation of the Liberal majority has been founded . . . the question whether any other basis would be abstractedly better is a question, at this moment, for Debating Societies'.[2]

On the question of Irish land, Gladstone was at first cautious— 'the Church is enough for today'[3]—but, following Bright's outright commitment to a major land bill at the end of April, Gladstone—at least from May 1869—had come to see the pace set by the drafting and passing of the Irish Church Bill as being matched by a Land Bill, although this would involve 'both more difficulty and less support', for 'if we succeed with the Church, & fail with the Land, we shall have done less than half our work';[4] 'we must lay our first parallel the moment we are out of the Church'.[5] Irish land had little of the mandate which it was hard to deny the electorate had conferred upon Irish disestablishment; within the Liberal Party it alarmed the Whigs, not only those with Irish land or connections, like Clarendon, but also great Scottish magnates like the Duke of Argyll; it raised by implication exactly that attack on property generally of which opponents of the household suffrage had warned.

On the other hand, Irish land reform was supported by Irish middle-class opinion represented by the *Freeman's Journal* and Sir John Gray, and by the Irish Liberal M.P.s in the Commons, opinion which, since the start of Fenianism and the Ribbon Men, had come to be regarded in England as relatively respectable and moderate, limited in its aims to a type of demand which the imperial Parliament might feel itself able to go some way to meeting. The Tenant League, which embodied these demands, already called for the 'Three Fs' which were eventually granted in the 1881 Land Act.

Just as Gladstone had declined to see Irish disestablishment as

---

[1] 22 July 69.

[2] To Manning, 13 July 69; Manning was the channel for Gladstone's personal information about the support of Cullen for the original bill and against concurrent endowment; see 12 July 69. He also worked to persuade Roman Catholic M.P.s when they wavered on aspects of the Church Bill; 13 July 69.

[3] To Spencer, 28 Apr. 69.   [4] To Bright, 22 May 69.

[5] To Manning, 3 June 69.

necessarily implying English, Scottish, or Welsh disestablishment, so
he tried to isolate the Irish land question from the general question
of British social and economic relationships. A simple change in the
law of contract was therefore undesirable, as was the intervention of
'a public authority' to determine prices and consequently rent, for
this would be a 'principle essentially imperial', 'no less applicable to
England & Scotland, than it is to Ireland'.[1] The solution offered by
George Campbell, an ex-Indian judge, had in this context an immediate appeal for Gladstone. Campbell's solution, read by Gladstone
on 11 August 1869, was, crudely stated, to use the tradition of the
Ulster tenant right[2] as a way to recognise customary rather than con-
tractual land relationships in Ireland generally. Campbell's solution,
if it could be carried through into law, fitted splendidly into Gladstone's political preoccupations. Because its intention was to recognise customary relationships, it could be presented as a conservative
measure; because it used a particularly Irish form of customary tenure
as its basis, its 'imperial' implications would be much reduced.

It was clearly not the 'Three Fs', but it could be offered to the
Irish as reform on indigenous principles, offering both security and
compensation to the tenant, ending 'wanton eviction' and, consequently, also ending 'demands for *unjust* augmentations of rent'.[3]
The problem was that the simplicity of the 'Three Fs' could not be
matched by the bill: 'the circuitous road is really the only one practicable, & is to be much preferred to scaling and descending precipices'.[4]
But that depended on how quickly the travellers were determined to
reach their destination, particularly if they were not worried about
injuries on the way.

For Gladstone as Cabinet coachman, the responsibility was to
reach the end of the road; when he tried to take what his passengers
saw as the dangerous short cut *via* the generalisation of Ulster tenant
right, he was forced to change course. The Whigs led by Fortescue
would not stand for so bold a measure, which implied an end of landlord initiative. Fortescue's solution—compensation for disturbance
—implied that disturbance, that is, eviction, was to continue, eased
by a legislative mechanism. Ironically, this made the question of a
precedent for England the more likely. By December 1869 Gladstone
found himself faced with the fact that a Land Bill supported by his
present Cabinet could not be a tenant-right bill; rather than abandon

---

[1] To J. F. Maguire, 20 Sept. 69.
[2] The right to bestow or sell the right of occupancy—much more valuable than the
English right of compensation for improvements made by the tenant; see Steele, *Irish Land*,
5–15.
[3] To Manning, 16 Feb. 70.   [4] Ibid.

the bill altogether, he fell back on tenant right for Ulster, compensation for disturbance for the rest.

The process by which the Cabinet lurched along this 'circuitous road' is already the subject of a classic study of the making of an Act,[1] and the complex negotiations can be followed in the mass of letters included below for the months of August 1869 to January 1870.

The Irish Land Act was conceived and passed in the light of what Gladstone saw to be the requirements in Ireland for social and consequently political stability. The plan for some form of State purchase or sponsorship of Irish railways, which he originally intended to accompany the Land Bill to assist in the economic development of this stabilised peasantry, was not pressed. The immediate political objectives of the legislation can be seen in the acute interest Gladstone showed in the reception of the bill in Ireland,[2] and by his attempt to accompany it by the liberation of Fenian prisoners, which the Whigs prevented throughout 1869 until late in 1870, when Gladstone wore down Dublin Castle and obtained 'the very early liberation of all those who can be regarded as purely political offenders'.[3]

The Irish Church Act and the Land Act were intended to stabilise Ireland as it was, not to restructure Ireland for the future. The latter would have involved incorporation of the largely hostile Irish Roman Catholic clergy by concurrent endowment, wholesale evictions, and forced emigration of surplus tenantry, and an agricultural tariff; in other words it would have required the British Government to live out of its time, to treat Ireland as the norm and the rest of the United Kingdom as an anomaly.[4] In the British context, Ireland was an anomaly,[5] but, in political terms, anomalous treatment could not be taken far; the best that could be done was to hope that marginal social adjustment could produce political tranquillity. 'Right relations' between landlord and tenant might also, in time, encourage economic growth.

Politically, the Land Bill was in trouble from the start. As soon as

[1] Steele, *Irish Land.*   [2] To Argyll, 16 Feb. 70, to Spencer, 17 Feb. 70.
[3] To Bright, 16 Nov. 70; see also to Spencer, 3 and 14 Sept. 70.
[4] Dr. Barbara Solow argues that the Act was 'well designed to cure the evils it assumed', i.e. deter evictions and deter landlords from raising rents on tenant improvements, but that it attacked the wrong problems: 'The real problem in Ireland was not the division of a given pie, but the provision of a larger one.' But this is merely to highlight the anomalous position of Ireland in a United Kingdom where growth was spontaneous, considerable, and completely independent of direct government stimulus. B. Solow, *The Land Question, and the Irish Economy, 1870–1903* (1971), 50, 88.
[5] Bright's demand (see 4 Dec. 69) for simultaneous bills for English and Scottish land, though considered reluctantly by the Cabinet, came to nothing in practice; Steele, *Irish Land*, 219.

it was known that a government measure was in the making, expectations and demonstrations rose in Ireland. By November 1869 it was
clear that the bill could not meet these expectations. Gladstone attempted to douse them with a letter to Sir John Gray.[1] The Cabinet
would not allow the release of Fenian prisoners, and the Prime Minister was unable to avoid having to accompany his Land Bill with a
Coercion Bill. In March 1870, Roman Catholic bishops came out for
the 'Three Fs', and, in the Irish context, the Land Bill emphasised
the inability of the imperial Parliament to meet Irish demands, rather
than the political integration for which Gladstone had initially hoped.
Publicly, the Land Bill was marked by alarm among the propertied
classes, privately it was one of the two great defeats of Gladstone by
the Whigs in Cabinet, the other being the defeat over Alsace-Lorraine
a year later.

Irish affairs of church and land had thus dominated Gladstone's
attention in 1869 and early 1870: 'until it is disposed of, it seems to
engross and swallow up my whole personal existence', he told Manning,[2] and certainly no legislative topic, except perhaps the Irish university question, so engaged his attention between 1871 and 1874.

Gladstone had drawn up the Church and Land Bills, and especially
the former, as if he were still a department minister. But at the same
time, in addition to being First Lord, he was also Leader of the House
of Commons. As such, he had responsibility for the details as well as
the general strategy of the Government's legislative programme, and as
such he was expected to be in the Commons to supervise the smooth
running of the daily, and nightly, progress of the legislation. It was in
this capacity that he was remembered by many backbenchers as
responsible in the debacle of 1865-6, when a large Government
majority disintegrated over parliamentary reform. Gladstone had, not
surprisingly, an acute memory of that crisis in which his political
career came near to foundering.[3] The Irish Church Bill held the party
together: 'the House has moved like an army', he told Manning, but
adding with ominous implication, 'an army where every private is his
own general'.[4] The Irish Land Bill passed the Commons, but only
after major amendments from Radicals (W. Fowler), and Peelites (Palmer) had been avoided with difficulty, and in the face of the outright
opposition of a number of Irish M.P.s, including Sir John Gray. However, Gladstone's personal authority, and the assumption amongst
Liberals outside the Cabinet that the contents of the bill were his,
prevented disastrous disruptions on Irish land.

[1] 28 Nov. 69. The Fenian O'Donovan Rossa had won Tipperary the previous day.
[2] 16 Apr. 70.
[3] See, e.g., to Clarendon, 22 Apr. 70.   [4] 3 June 69.

This was not to be the case with Irish education, 'the redemption of our last Irish *pledge*',[1] to which Gladstone in August 1870 moved after the Land Bill, though without the same insistent urgency as he had moved in 1869 from church to land. He prodded Fortescue into action without 'violent hurry'[2] and implied to him that he could expect much the same prime ministerial involvement in the preparation of the measure as he had suffered with respect to the Land Bill: 'It seems to me that in the main we *know* what we ought to give them whether they will take it or not.'[3]

The lack of haste and the didacticism were deliberate. The subject was fraught with complexity[4] and possible disaster from the start: 'a difficult & probably a dangerous one for the Government, as there is no more doubtful point in the composition & tendencies of the Liberal party than its disposition to extremes in the matter of unsectarianism as it is called'.[5] A solution could not be reached by negotiation or general discussion. The problem was compounded by events within Ireland, and within Europe. In Ireland, the Keogh judgement of June 1872[6] infuriated the Roman Catholics, and the O'Keeffe[7] case seemed to confirm fears of the civic consequences of ultramontanism. In Europe, the 1870 Vatican Council encouraged a general wave of anti-Popery. Added to this was the great debate about science, religion, and the future role of Christianity in schools and universities. As Broad Church empiricism conquered the English universities, many, and not only Roman Catholics, looked to the Irish experiment as a chance for a fresh start through what to others was an anti-intellectual reaction. All these elements worked together to raise the exceptionally intricate details of the Irish university arrangements to the highest level of political significance. Nothing illustrates the tone and central concerns of Victorian politics more clearly than that the Government of the British Empire should resign after a narrow defeat on what to the twentieth-century mind might seem, at least at first glance, to be a mere bill about a provincial university.

Some consideration of the details of this complex problem is therefore necessary.

[1] To Russell, President of Maynooth, 2 January 1873, quoted in Norman, *The Catholic Church*, 447.

[2] To Fortescue, 15 Aug. 70.   [3] To Fortescue, 19 Aug. 70.

[4] Emphasised by the progress made by the solution of the English secularist Liberals led by Fawcett—the abolition of remaining tests at Trinity, Dublin; see L. Stephen, *Life of Henry Fawcett* (1886), ch. vi.   [5] To Manning, 28 July 71.

[6] Judge Keogh's judgment in the Galway by-election petition, powerfully condemned clerical excesses in the election campaign; Norman, *The Catholic Church*, 423-4.

[7] Father Robert O'Keeffe's suspension for taking successful civil action against other Roman Catholic clergy was upheld by the Commissioners of National Education; O'Keeffe then brought a series of civil actions, winning one against Cardinal Cullen; ibid., 431-6.

Experience had shown that no plan of general educational reform in Ireland could succeed until disputes about the apex of the system —the university—had been resolved, and it appears to have been assumed from the start by ministers that Irish university legislation would be both first and separate in Irish educational legislation.

Gladstone, through his work on the 1854 Oxford University Bill, was an experienced legislator in such matters, and his view of the question was in part founded on this experience. But an additional precedent for the Irish University Bill was the Scottish Universities Bill of 1858, which he had, though not in office, successfully amended to permit future unification of the various Scottish universities into one national university, the existing universities becoming its colleges. This proposal had not been popular in Scotland, and had cost him the Chancellorship of Edinburgh University in 1868.[1]

The problem in Ireland was religious and financial. The Roman Catholics had set up their own, poorly endowed, Catholic university; the Queen's University, with its 'godless' colleges, set up by Peel and Graham in 1845, had been largely ignored by Roman Catholics; Trinity College, Dublin, was well endowed but Anglican. Thus 'the R.C. grievance . . . is held to consist in this, that an R.C. educated in a college or place where his religion is taught cannot by virtue of that education obtain a degree in Ireland. . . . I think we desire that a portion of the public endowments should be thrown open, under the auspices of a neutral University, to the whole Irish people.'[2] A 'neutral University' was an answer to the Irish demands for a separate, concurrently endowed, Roman Catholic university, existing side-by-side with Trinity College. In the circumstances of the day, quite apart from Gladstone's own antipathy to concurrent endowment, it was probably the only solution with a chance of success, even though Hartington, who reluctantly replaced Fortescue as Irish Secretary in December 1870 under the full weight of Gladstone's moral suasion,[3] pushed his hostility to the 'central university' plan almost to the point of resignation.[4] But a 'neutral University' which incorporated colleges with ancient traditions was hard to translate into a statute. Gladstone drew up the bill with Thring[5] much as he had the Irish Church Bill, at Hawarden, in touch with colleagues only by letter,

---

[1] See above, v. xxxix, 21 Nov. 68n and 5 July 58. As he pointed out to Spencer, Playfair's objection to the Irish University Bill would be along such lines forcing Gladstone to modify his view; see to Spencer, 26 Sept. 72, to Hartington, 26 Oct. 72.

[2] To Spencer, 26 Sept. 72. [3] 30 Dec. 70.

[4] To Hartington, 1 Dec. 72 and Holland, *Devonshire*, i. 109.

[5] Despite its complexities, Thring thought 'the Irish University Bill was incomparably the best bill I ever drew'; Thring to Northbrook, 13 June 1873, India Office MSS Eur. C144/21.

with only scant reference to the Irish officers in his Government, advised on the affairs of Protestant Ireland by a Trinity don, J. K. Ingram, who came over for the purpose.[1] The bill was thus as much his own as the Irish Church Bill had been.

Gladstone's solution[2] was characteristically neat and Burkean, in the sense of restorative conservatism. He made a clear distinction between the University of Dublin, which he showed had existed since the fourteenth century,[3] and Trinity College which had existed since the sixteenth century and had since then effectively subsumed the University within the College. Gladstone proposed to restore the University to its original status, and to allow it to have as colleges Trinity College, the Belfast and Cork Colleges of the Queen's University (which would itself be wound up along with its third college of Galway), and such of the 'voluntary' colleges—Newman's Roman Catholic College in Dublin and the Presbyterian Magee College—as wished to join. Many problems sprang from the restrictive details thought necessary to allow the plan a chance to work: no theology, philosophy or modern history chairs were to be founded, a professor was to 'be punished or reprimanded' for wilfully offending 'the conscientious scruples of those whom he instructs in the exercise of his office', and the legislature was in the early years to exercise much patronage by nominating the members of the University Council.[4]

The comprehensiveness of the plan offered a bold means of solving this vexed question, which was, as Gladstone pointed out, the first stage towards a general plan of Irish education. It was also a frank recognition of sacrifices which would have to be made if partition in education was to be avoided.

Gladstone made it clear in the first sentence of his speech introducing the bill that the proposals were 'vital to the honour and existence of the Government'[5]—that is, it was from its introduction a matter of confidence, a caveat aimed by Gladstone probably more at the 'secularist' English Liberals than at the Irish. That it was a matter of confidence seems to have been largely the result of Gladstone's identification with the bill: Halifax commented dryly, 'Gladstone had to deal with the third branch of the Upas tree, and therefore made a great deal of the University bill, not in itself a measure of such

[1] To Hartington, 14 Dec. 72, to Spencer, 26 Sept. 72; 16 and 22 Jan. 73.

[2] Dr. Norman points out Gladstone's debt to Monsell for the bones of the plan; *The Catholic Church*, 446.

[3] Since Clement V's Bull of 1312; see H. Rashdall, *The Universities of Europe in the Middle Ages* (1895), esp. on 'Paper Universities', and J. H. Newman, *Office and Work of Universities* (1856).

[4] Provisions lucidly explained by Gladstone on 13 Feb. 73, in Bassett, *Speeches*, 426.

[5] Bassett, *Speeches*, 427.

vital importance.'[1] But once this was the case, clearly the Government had to back the second reading absolutely. Thus the ten 'English and Scotch' Liberals, the thirty-five Irish who voted against the bill, and the twenty-two Irish Liberals who abstained, acted in full knowledge of the consequences.[2] Only twelve 'Irishmen' voted with the Government, as opposed to sixty-nine against. The Government was defeated on 11 March 1873 by three votes and, after considering dissolution in the context of Gladstone's poor health and the generally poor state of the Party,[3] resigned, only to be forced back into office by Disraeli in one of the coolest and boldest calculations of British politics—the last occasion on which the Opposition declined to take office when it was offered.[4] Not for the last time in Irish affairs, the appeal to reason and conciliation came to nought. The earlier Irish legislation of the Government had not brought Irish trust in the ability of the Westminster Parliament to act in 'Irish interests'. Indeed, the opposite had happened. Since the 1870 Land Act, the Home Rule Association had made rapid strides, and Irish Liberal members feared for their seats. Thus when Archbishop Cullen denounced the bill, the game was up. The foundations for the maintenance of the Liberal Party in Ireland were already eroded. The University Bill stated what the 1874 general election confirmed: Liberal Ireland was soon to be dead and gone.

Despite the run of home rule successes in by-elections,[5] little of this fundamental shift in Irish politics seems to have been perceived by Gladstone and those around him. During the making of the University Bill, Gladstone had dealt with the Irish hierarchy—as far as he dealt with it at all—through the agency of Manning. Though from the start there had been doubts and caveats, both seem to have expected the bill to pass. Even as late as 1 March, Gladstone assumed that the bishops' Resolutions, which were 'really War to the knife', were the result of mistaken tactics—'how is it possible this should not have been perceived?'[6]—rather than outright hostility. Gladstone saw the defeat first as a stupid rejection of 'boons'[7] offered to the Irish, secondly as a stab in the back by treacherous, ultramontane bishops: 'Your Irish Brethren have received in the late vote of Parlt. the most extravagant compliment ever paid them. *They* have destroyed the measure; which otherwise was safe enough.'[8]

[1] Halifax to Northbrook, 19 March 1873, India Office MSS Eur. C144/21.
[2] See analysis at 11 Mar. 73. [3] See 12–13 Mar. 73.
[4] See 11–19 Mar. 73.
[5] For these, and the partial check to them in 1872, see D. Thornley, *Isaac Butt and Home Rule* (1964), ch. iii.
[6] To Manning, 1 Mar. 73. [7] To Manning, 3 Mar. 73.
[8] To Manning, 13 Mar. 73.

Gladstone's Irish measures had been conceived in the spirit of Edmund Burke. Irish land and the University Bill had been profoundly conservative in presentation—the first based on the Ulster tenant right, a prescriptive right by definition, the second the resurrection of an ancient university, a prescriptive right in effect. The disestablishment of the Irish Church by the author of *The State in its Relations with the Church* had been the acknowledgement of a pluralism which was self-consciously a second best. 'There is nothing that Ireland has asked and which this country and this Parliament have refused', Gladstone said at Aberdeen in 1871, going on to acknowledge the remaining 'single grievance' of university education.[1] By 1873 the Irish themselves were registering their disagreement with this view at by-elections. English 'boons' were not enough. 'I have looked in vain for the setting forth of any practical scheme of policy which the Imperial Parliament is not equal to deal with, or which it refuses to deal with, and which is to be brought about by Home Rule.'[2] The endowed Catholic university was exactly such a scheme, and its Gladstonian alternative of 1873 provided the occasion for the cutting of what Gladstone had called in 1871 'the silken cords of love', to the weaving of which much of his and his ministry's time had been devoted.

The man who disestablished the Irish Church could carry a Land Bill despite the fact that his supporters almost all thought it too little or too much; the essential struggle had been with Cabinet colleagues. The Anglican Tractarian, the former member of the National Society for the Education of the Poor in the Principles of the Established Church, found himself more personally and politically engaged in the great struggle over English education.

The education question had its roots in two royal commissions and two developments of the 1860s; first, the realisation that a combination of voluntaryism and the Established Church could no longer realistically aspire to offer an adequate elementary education in the cities; second, the early stirrings of awareness of the achievements of continental nations in educational and industrial development. It is, of course, a hoary schoolboy myth that the Franco-Prussian war 'caused' the 1870 Education Act—the chronology of 1870 would have to be reversed to allow that—but awareness of the Prussian model certainly existed as a result of Mark Pattison's report for the Duke of Newcastle's Royal Commission in the 1860s. Once the 1870 war began, Gladstone's *Edinburgh Review* article quickly made the

[1] 26 Sept. 71; *The Times*, 27 Sept. 71, 6; see J. R. Vincent, 'Gladstone and Ireland', App. A, *Proc. Brit. Acad.*, lxiii. 232.
[2] Ibid.

connection: 'Undoubtedly the conduct of the campaign, on the German side, has given a marked triumph to the cause of systematic popular education.'[1]

Gladstone had shown little interest in education in the 1850s and 1860s, save for reform of the universities and public schools. In this context, he was personally an unrepentant advocate of the classical curriculum, which many of his essays and books, including *Juventus Mundi* (1869), were intended to justify, and he deplored the fact that the '*low* utilitarian argument . . . for giving it [education] what is termed a practical direction, is so plausible' that it was winning by default.[2] He and the Cabinet declined to give a government grant to Owen's College in Manchester, and Gladstone later used this decision as a precedent for declining aid for the founding of Aberystwyth.[3] Despite the general concern about the strength of technical education in Germany, the Liberal Cabinet, for reasons both of religion and political economy, refused to be drawn into the direct funding of British universities.

Of the Cabinet, Bruce, Forster and de Grey were well known protagonists of popular education. A bill dealing with England could not fail to be controversial, and the Cabinet dealt first with Scottish education in 1869. Discussion in Scotland on education had progressed further than in England, and in Scotland only two interests, the Established Church and the Free Church, were taken into account —the vast spectrum of denominational concern characteristic of the English debate was absent.[4] None the less, Argyll's Scottish Bill, introduced into the Lords in February 1869, was soon in difficulties.[5] The Lords treated it as a precedent for England, where they already disliked the important Endowed Schools Bill, also of 1869, a measure in whose preparation Gladstone seems to have played no part. The Lords amended the Scottish bill so as to destroy the notion of a 'national system', and leave denominationalism as firmly entrenched as possible. By the time the bill reached the Commons in the summer, it had become enmeshed in the crisis of the Irish Church Bill. Gladstone seems to have given no attention to it outside the Cabinet; concessions were made to keep the bill alive, but there was no real prospect of it passing, and it foundered.[6] In October 1869 Gladstone encouraged de Grey and Forster to meet with him 'to lay the foundation

[1] *Gleanings*, iv. 211.

[2] To Lyttelton, 29 August 1861, in Morley, ii. 646.

[3] See 8, 10, 24 Apr. 69 and 14 Apr. 71.

[4] The interests of Roman Catholics and Episcopalians were virtually ignored in Scotland.

[5] See D. J. Withrington, 'Towards a national system, 1867–72: the last years in the struggle for a Scottish Education Act', *Scottish Educational Studies* (1972).

[6] See Cabinets of 10 July, 31 July, 6 Aug. 69.

stone of our Education measure in England'.[1] This suggests that a
vague opinion that there would be an English bill was already forming
(Gladstone in early September already assumed the predominance of
'the two large subjects of Irish Land and Education in England'),[2]
but Gladstone's letter clearly had a stimulating effect, for no preparations seem to have been made hitherto.[3] Why Gladstone encouraged
the question is unclear. Certainly, popular pressure for an English bill
was already considerable. Gladstone may have hoped it would prevent
Irish land becoming overdominant and contentious. The two issues
fed on each other: in Cabinet, land predominated to the extent that
education was discussed only once[4] before the full bill was approved
in Cabinet on 4 February 1870, without any controversy being noted
by Gladstone. In the Commons, Irish land was to some extent subor-
dinated to the great debates on English education.

The Scottish bill had made it clear that the path of a successful
English bill would require careful planning: that the route lay through
a minefield was not immediately apparent. From Gladstone's point
of view, Forster and de Grey's proposals, that the existing system of
denominational schools be supplemented where necessary by school
boards locally elected, was in general satisfactory. He never made any
attempt to modify the general structure of their plan. This was not
surprising as it was the only plan likely to survive the Lords, and it
was one which he could, in general, support. Not only Anglican but
Roman Catholic interests were at stake, as Gladstone recognised in
putting Manning in touch with de Grey at a very early stage.[5]

Following the position that his friend, the High-Churchman Dean
Hook, had championed since the late 1830s,[6] Gladstone focused at
once on the aspect of the bill which particularly concerned him personally: 'the proposal to found the State schools on the system of
the British and Foreign Society would I think hardly do';[7] he made
clear what was to be, with some modification, his consistent preference throughout the ministry: 'Why not adopt frankly the principle
that the State or the local community should provide the secular
teaching, & either leave the option to the Ratepayer to go beyond
this *sine quâ non*, if they think fit, within the limits of the conscience
clause, or else simply leave the parties themselves to find Bible &
other religious education from voluntary sources.'[8] As he told Bright

[1] 2 Oct. 69.   [2] To Bright, 1 Sept. 69.
[3] Forster did not mention the Bill in his diary until 10 October; Reid, *F*, i. 463.
[4] 10 Nov. 69.
[5] 27 Oct. 69, i.e. before the de Grey–Forster proposals reached Cabinet.
[6] W. R. W. Stephens, *Life and letters of W. F. Hook*, i. 443ff. (1878).
[7] The Nonconformist British and Foreign School Society had from 1833 distributed an
Exchequer grant and provided non-denominational religious teaching.   [8] 4 Nov. 69.

retrospectively, 'the application of the Rate to be confined by law to secular teaching only' was the only 'solid and stable ground'.[1]

On this issue, Gladstone found he had the Cabinet, the Anglican Church, and the Dissenters against him.[2] If restriction to secular teaching could not be achieved, Gladstone went to the other extreme. In a long memorandum written on 29 May 1870, after meeting several Nonconformist deputations, he made as strong a case as he could against 'the plan that the Bible be read & explained, while formularies are to be forbidden', though admitting that the proposal had some advantages.[3] The absence of formularies (i.e. of an understanding of the dogma, structure, and teaching of the apostolic church) would be a surrender to latitudinarianism and Nonconformity.

However, the absence of formularies was exactly the solution reached through the Cowper–Temple amendment, agreed by the Cabinet on 14 June 1870. As Gladstone's memorandum of 29 May 1870 recognised, 'the concord of opinion' behind this solution was 'due to a great anxiety to maintain a direct connection between religion and popular education', and in practical political terms it was the only way of reconciling the two. The acceptance of this was a major personal blow for Gladstone. It was not exactly a defeat, in that he had not associated himself systematically with the bill and his usual persistence had not been placed behind his own preference. But it was a personal concession which rankled more deeply than any of the many concessions Gladstone made to hold his ministry together.

The Education Bill was the largest of the Government's legislative measures in whose preparation Gladstone did not involve himself intimately at every stage, though, as we have seen, his interventions and encouragement were at certain moments extremely important. It ran side by side with his Land Bill, and once it was in the Commons Gladstone, the most formidable of the Liberal front bench in procedural manipulation, took over much of the responsibility for its safe passage. Together, the Land and Education Bills brought to a dramatic close the Session of 1870—the last occasion until 1911 when two major, highly controversial bills were run together in a single Session.

Church, Land, and Education were, however, bought at a high legislative price. In June 1869 the Cabinet for the first time considered 'Bills Abandoned',[4] and the midsummer purge of bills proposed but not passed became a distinctive feature of the ministry.[5] The policy of 'filling up the cup', of starting bills which were certain

---

[1] See letter and mem. at 25 Nov. 71.   [2] Ibid.
[3] 29 May 70. He drew special attention to Roman Catholic needs in England.
[4] 26 June 69.   [5] See, e.g., 2 July 70, 15 July 71, 15 July 72.

to run into difficulties and then of not allowing enough time for the resolution of those difficulties, might keep the fissiparous elements within the majority occupied, but it would not necessarily keep them happy.[1] The use of the 'clôture' was considered, but it was not introduced.

The problem was circular: the bringing forward of legislation was a form of party discipline, but an undisciplined party would not support the means by which such legislation might pass the Commons, namely a readiness to subordinate the interests of particular groups to the success of the government legislative programme. That programme was, of course, impeded by the wrecking tactics of the Lords. But since members of the majority in the Commons were often equally vocal in their hostility to aspects of government bills, the Lords could claim to be doing no more than playing their natural role in the constitution. In fact, government homogeneity barely existed outside the government's early Irish legislation. The whips could never be sure when the spirit of 1866 would arise again, and the large majority obtained at the 1868 election had always been expected to produce problems of management.

Gladstone did not blame Glyn, the chief whip. He thought that 'there is something of a tide in politics. At the Election we had an immense impetus & we came back with more than a natural or nominal majority'; by 1871 he saw the tide as turning,[2] and by 1872 he thought 'that our hold over the Constituencies is weakened, & that the Conservatives may begin soon to think of another advent to power'.[3] Disraeli saw the same pattern. He waited until the 'immense impetus' had spent itself, and in 1872 he pounced. Disraeli's strategy was to let the Liberals discredit themselves. Their vast and unprecedented flood of legislation, whether passed or not, was in itself discrediting; the Conservatives appeared conservative simply by sitting silent on their benches.

Despite his position as First Lord and Leader of the House, there was little Gladstone could do. Several of the proposals were personally

---

[1] Gladstone described the process to his constituents: 'such was the state of public expectation and demand with regard to every one of those subjects [Scottish education, licensing, local taxation, mines regulation in 1871], that it was not in our choice to refuse to place our views before Parliament in the form of a bill laid upon the table; and I believe I am within the mark in saying that if we had attempted to avoid incurring that responsibility, either other members of Parliament would themselves have endeavoured to procure—not legislation upon the subject, but at least the production of measures of their own . . .' or resolutions would have been passed demanding government bills; Bassett, *Speeches*, 404. In 1871 a three tier system of ranking bills was adopted, see 25 Jan. 71. The very complex question of the state of government business and the number of bills lost in this Parliament will be clarified when Dr. Ramm's paper on the subject is published.

[2] 23 Aug. 71.　　　　　　　　　　　　　　　　　　　[3] 16 Sept. 72.

repugnant to him; he was reluctant to admit that the preservation of Oxford and Cambridge as national universities required the abolition of religious tests,[1] and he had little enthusiasm for the ballot, necessary corollary of parliamentary reform though he might admit it to be.[2] The Cabinet did not prove to be a suitable body to redeem the situation. Though it oversaw the details of parliamentary business, it does not seem at all to have acted as a body for developing a coherent Party strategy. This may well have been an impossible objective, but Cabinet members do not seem to have thought in terms of a party structure of electoral management. The Cabinet continued to act chiefly as an executive body, distanced and often estranged from the political structure which had placed it in power.

V

Cabinet members received their seals from the Queen, and relationships with the Court were one of their chief preoccupations. Gladstone's daily journal testifies to the vast amount of time, in letter writing, visits, and negotiations, that the leader of a government, and especially of a reforming government, had to spend on the monarchy. Both the Queen and the Prince of Wales seemed major problems. In the heady enthusiasms of post-reform Britain, the relationship of the Court and 'the democracy' was very uncertain.

The absenteeism of the Queen and the blatant profligacy of the Prince created the conditions for the only moment in the history of industrial Britain when it seemed as if republicanism might become a serious political issue. Gladstone took the view that the risk was not worth taking, and that the monarchy must be strengthened by positive action on the part of its members and defenders. He believed that to meet republicanism, Bradlaugh and Dilke, by repression 'would tend to establish rather than end the controversy. What is needed is that we should if possible do or cause something to be done of a nature likely to remove the dissatisfaction, of which the absurd republican cry is an external symptom.'[3]

From the first Cabinet of the ministry, he brought forward a plan to associate the monarchy more closely with Ireland,[4] more particularly suggesting that the Irish Office should be reformed, and that the

---

[1] Gladstone hoped for what the Queen's Speech of 1870 called a 'legislative settlement' —i.e. a compromise saving some of the entrenched Anglicanism of Oxford and Cambridge. He worked to head off 'absolute secularisation' (to Coleridge, 1 and 4 Dec. 70). Morley makes an unusual error in stating the Government only made the question an official measure in 1871; Gladstone bitterly complained to Liddell in 1870 when the latter suggested the Government were bungling the bill's timetable. Morley, ii. 314; to Liddell, 24 Mar. 70; see also 13 Jan., 22 and 25 Apr., 30 June 71.
[2] 11 Dec. 71, 27 July 70.
[3] 4 Dec. 71.
[4] 22 Dec. 68.

Prince of Wales should become Lord Lieutenant, presiding as a constitutional monarch in that country. He urged this pertinaciously, especially after the Prince's involvement in the Mordaunt divorce case.[1] From late in 1870 Gladstone pursued his plan with spasmodic assistance from Granville and Halifax. But the Queen was a match for them, and would not give an inch. Gladstone persistently tried to overcome her refusal to appear in public; when she said she would not open a bridge, he demanded she name a substitute.[2] Gladstone's moment came with the Prince's near-fatal illness in December 1871. He insisted that the Queen should capitalise on the swelling sympathy for the Prince by a public appearance at a thanksgiving service at St. Paul's. He met every argument with a prepared position, and at the crisis of the discussion, when the Queen 'contracted her objection to the length of the service', he trumped her by quoting the '*Annual Register* of 1789 (from which it appears that the Commons set out at 8 a.m., the King and Queen at 10, and their Majesties only returned to the Palace at half past three.)'[3] The Queen gave way, and the service was a great success, especially for Disraeli, who was loudly cheered outside the cathedral.

Gladstone and his Cabinet's battle with the Queen had to be kept a secret within the establishment. The Cabinet could not say what pains they took to save the Queen from herself and from the Radical wing of their own supporters. What had in bygone years been stock patriotic Whig criticism of the Civil List, now, in the context of post-reform politics, could easily be made by the Tories to seem, and in a few cases actually was, open republicanism. Gladstone himself gave away a trick in trying to win over his constituents at Greenwich by quoting an egalitarian parody of the National Anthem from the *Secularist Hymn Book,*[4] 'a questionable book [with] verses which I think contain much good sense'.[5] It was to this sort of incident that Disraeli could refer when he accused Gladstone of alternating 'between a menace and a sigh'.[6] The Whigs were of little help, except individually and behind the scenes. Palmerston and Russell had dissipated the legacy of Melbourne, and Gladstone had failed to capitalise on the resemblance of high-principled earnestness between himself and Prince Albert which in the early 1860s had looked as if it could bear substantial fruit.[7]

[1] 25 June 71; see Magnus, *Edward VII*, 111. This case gave Gladstone a rare moment of utility to Victoria, who asked him 'to speak to the P. seriously'; 22 Feb. 70.
[2] 18 June 69.   [3] 21 Dec. 71.   [4] 24 and 28 Oct. 71.
[5] Bassett, *Speeches*, 423. His secretary, Gurdon, issued a denial that the book had Gladstone's approval; Gurdon to H. R. Taylor, 6 November 1871, published in the *Reformer*, 11 November 1871.
[6] At Manchester, 3 April 1872; Buckle, v. 190.   [7] See ante, v. li.

Undoubtedly Gladstone's overbearing, moralising manner did no good. We have seen in the case of John Bright that he knew how to flatter; in the case of the Queen, he never took up the trowel. In his persistent advocacy of the Prince of Wales' potential usefulness, and in his meetings with the Prince,[1] there are some signs of a Liberal–Marlborough House alliance being formed, but this would have conflicted too much with Gladstone's plans for the public rehabilitation of Victoria for it to emerge as a serious element in politics.

Personal emollience might have helped, but behind the growing private friction lay great public issues. The abolition of purchase in the army seemed an assault as brutal as disestablishment on the internal traditions of the landed class and the Court. First raised by Cardwell in Cabinet in March 1870,[2] the question became, for Gladstone, part of a general plan of reconstruction of the mores of that 'vast leisured and wealthy class'. Prompted by the Franco-Prussian war, and particularly by the 'mechanical perfection' of the Prussians, whose 'most consummate army' was 'put into the field with the greatest expedition, and at the smallest cost ever known',[3] Gladstone wanted 'complete and definite' army reform involving India, the Colonies, the militia, and the training of officers by 'making all our young cadets learn a soldier's business in the ranks', and a complete overhaul of the activities of the peacetime army: 'the greatest difficulty of all in truth is this: to redeem the officer's life from idleness in time of peace'.[4] He consistently urged Cardwell to go beyond abolition of the purchase of commissions,[5] but Cardwell's Army Regulation Bill was primarily a purchase abolition and compensation bill, together with the centralisation of control of the militia.

The bill appeared therefore as an attack on the privileges of a caste, without offering, as Gladstone had wanted, the prospect of its reconstruction in the national interest.[6] That caste constituted the heart of the most privileged section of Victorian society, and its exclusiveness was emphasised by its leader, the Queen's cousin, the Duke of Cambridge, commander-in-chief and colonel of the Horse Guards. The struggle through the summer of 1871 was long and bitter—much more so than that over Irish land or church. Back benchers on both sides of the House defended their interests with a fanatical resolution

[1] See 30 Nov. 72.

[2] 12 Mar. 70. Cardwell's subsequent abortive bill of 1870 did not deal with purchase itself, but with 'over-regulation' by abolishing the junior ranks of cornet and ensign.

[3] *Gleanings*, iv. 210.

[4] 13 Oct. 70; the plan was publicly adumbrated in his *Edinburgh Review* article, in learning 'all we can from the Prussian system'; *Gleanings*, iv. 244–5.

[5] 21, 23 Sept., 4, 8, Oct. 70, 27 May 71.

[6] See T. F. Gallagher, ' "Cardwellian Mysteries": the fate of the British Army Regulation Bill, 1871', *Historical Journal* (1975), 338.

which the Duke of Cambridge did nothing to moderate. With immense difficulty the Queen, who had in the first instance supported the abolition of purchase,[1] was brought to suggest to her cousin that he should support her Government's bill; but the best he would do was to abstain.

The bill wrecked the Government's programme in the Commons and was summarily dismissed in the Lords. Although the proposal was supported in principle by both front benches, the organs of representative government proved unable to abolish the purchase system by legislation. The executive then did what it could have done at any time, effected abolition by Royal Warrant.[2] This was possible because purchase had been made illegal by an Act of 1809, except in those cases in which a Royal Warrant allowed an exception (the 'regulation' price purchase). The Cabinet's Royal Warrant withdrew these exceptions which in fact had spread to cover almost all commissions. This left the officers of the army with the prospect of purchase being ended without the financial compensation which Cardwell's bill provided, and the Lords therefore hastened to pass it.

In Gladstone's view, the defence of purchase represented the failure of the landed class to justify its existence in the modern industrial world. He approved in principle of wealth, the Court, and an hereditary aristocracy. He was cautious about the absorption of the middle class into the aristocracy, despite his own record, telling the citizens of Liverpool, 'I know not why commerce should not have its old families rejoicing to be connected with commerce from generation to generation. . . . I think it is a subject of sorrow, and almost a scandal, when those families which have either acquired or received station and opulence from commerce turn their backs upon it and seem to be ashamed of it. (Great applause.) It is not so with my brother [Robertson] or with me. (Applause.)'[3] He saw the aristocracy as a separate class with its own duties. His views on army reform centred not on the opening of the army to middle class entry, but on efficient promotion and training within the traditional military caste. But he wanted Court and County to follow the middle class values of efficiency, application, and economy. He believed that obsession with wealth was coming to dominate the aristocracy at the expense of duty, especially 'in the Clubs, and in the army'. 'Ploutocracy' he commented in the aftermath of the purchase crisis, produced 'a bastard aristocracy & aristocracy shows too much disposition, in Parliament especially, to join hands with this bastard'.[4]

---

[1] Ibid., p. 340 and 12, 15 July 71. [2] 22 July 71.
[3] Speech at Liverpool College, *The Times*, 23 December 1872, 8c.
[4] To Houghton, 13 Sept. 71.

Gladstone's problems were therefore not confined to the Queen and the Duke of Cambridge; rather, his relationship with the upper echelons of the Court was symptomatic of a general distrust felt for him by landed property, Whigs as well as Tories.

As First Lord, he was responsible for the exercise of the vast range of Crown patronage, from awarding Garters to filling Regius chairs, bishoprics, deaneries, and rectories. Civil Service reform might have reduced the whips' source of patronage but that of the First Lord was by no means diminished. The response to Gladstone's exercise of patronage strikingly illustrates the extent to which landed society was reluctant to associate itself with his administration.

Offers of honours such as the Garter and posts of influence and significance in the localities, such as lord lieutenancies, were rejected on political grounds by erstwhile supporters of Whig–Liberal governments. The Garter was declined on political grounds by the Duke of Leinster[1] in 1869 and the Duke of Norfolk in 1870, the latter despite Gladstone's assurance that 'the public would consider your acceptance of the Garter as implying not by any means a permanent pledge but a present inclination *towards* the party & the Govt.: as indeed they may already have thought from so slight a circumstance as your doing me the favour to drive with me on the celebration of the Queen's birthday.'[2] The failure to secure Norfolk, the youthful leader of the English Roman Catholics, was a particular blow, given the lengths to which Gladstone went to solicit that denomination's support.[3] The Lord Lieutenancy of Staffordshire was offered to Wrottesley, who refused it, to Gladstone's Peelite friend and, in the Oak Farm days, his creditor, Dudley,[4] who refused it, and to Hatherton, who refused it. Wrottesley was eventually persuaded to accept it. Hostility to the ministry and to Gladstone personally was not as marked as it became in the 1880-5 government, but the steady drift of the landed classes away from the Liberal Party had clearly begun, as surely as the Court was finding itself the agent of the Tory Party.

The exercise of church patronage the First Lord shared with the Lord Chancellor; Gladstone tried to ease the demand for parish livings, 'which throw me to despair', by informally linking his patronage lists with those of the Lord Chancellor, and he also sent Hatherley a list of those deserving cathedral preferment.[5] Sharp attention was

[1] To Leinster, 8 Nov. 69.   [2] To Norfolk, 30 Aug. 70.
[3] Norfolk's mistrust of the ministry did not prevent his complaining that Gladstone's letter to Dease, which caused outbreaks of Protestant rage, did not go far enough; see 30 Nov. 70, 6 Feb. 71. Norfolk accepted the Garter from Salisbury in 1886.
[4] Gladstone's offer to Dudley was explicitly political, 'to one not unfavourably disposed towards them as regards the general objects of their political action'; 15 June 71.
[5] To Hatherley, 3 Jan. 70.

paid to the politics of priests receiving promotion, more so than to their position in the theological spectrum. 'No talents, no learning, no piety, can advance the fortunes of a clergyman whose political opinions are adverse to those of the governing party', wrote Lord John Russell in a dictum generally true of the nineteenth century, and true in some measure of Gladstone's patronage, at least in so far as Liberal bishops could be found.[1] He asked the ex-Tory M.P., Sir William Heathcote, a prominent Tractarian, to report to him on 'eminently good' clergymen, but with the significant proviso that Heathcote should include information about their attitude to Irish disestablishment.[2]

The unexpected recovery of Tait from an illness in 1869 removed the excitement of an archiepiscopal appointment. There was a clutch of appointments of bishops in September 1869—Wilberforce from Oxford to Winchester, Temple to Exeter, Hervey to Bath and Wells, Mackarness to Oxford. These were not appointments of mere ecclesiastical significance—each of them was subsequently circularised by Gladstone with an appeal to vote for the Irish Land Bill in the Lords.[3] He also canvassed episcopal support for the Army Bill abolishing purchase in 1871, and for other measures.[4] Liberalism would certainly seem to be the reason for the appointment of Temple to Exeter. Temple was one of the contributors to *Essays and Reviews* (1860), the modernists' manifesto, and his promotion caused outrage in Tractarian circles. Gladstone re-read Temple's essay after appointing him, finding it 'on reperusal . . . crude and unbalanced, but neither heretical nor sceptical'.[5] The episcopal appointment which caused much the most difficulty was the comparatively minor one of St. Asaph, that see whose separate preservation Gladstone had tried to make a condition when first invited to join the Cabinet by Peel in 1843:[6] here Gladstone wished to appoint a Welsh-speaking bishop so as to moderate the appearance of the Anglican Church as an alien element in Welsh culture. Though previously unimpressed by the Welsh language,[7] Gladstone evidently thought that such appointments could

[1] Earl Russell, *An essay in the history of the English government and constitution* (1865 ed.), 309.

[2] To Heathcote, 3 Mar. 69.

[3] To Wilberforce, 20 June 70; other bishops then appealed to were Salisbury, Carlisle, Chichester, Chester, and Manchester (i.e. Fraser, Gladstone's appointment). All of those to whom Gladstone appealed, except apparently Wilberforce, voted with the Government during the Land Bill's committee stage, though Chichester voted against on one clause: *H* ccii. 766, 772, 988. For similar appeals in 1871 and 1872, see D. W. R. Bahlman, 'Politics and Church Patronage in the Victorian Age', *Victorian Studies*, xxii. 262.

[4] See 28 July 71, 12 Feb. 72.

[5] 21 Nov. 69; see also letter to Pusey, 10 Oct. 69.

[6] 13 May 43.

[7] 23 Sept. 55.

affect what he called the 'singularly susceptible population' of the principality.[1] Joshua Hughes was nominated after a 'very laborious though interesting search'.[2] Gladstone's speech to the Eisteddfod at Mold in 1873 emphasised the seriousness with which he had begun to take Welsh affairs.[3]

VI

The last of the areas of routine business with which the First Lord and the Cabinet were necessarily involved was government finance and the economy. By the 1870s, 'finance' appeared to have little to do with the state of the economy. It would not be true to say that the Cabinet had no interest in the working of the economy, but it would be true to say that it took no direct responsibility for it. When Daniel Jones, a miner from Newcastle-under-Lyme, wrote to tell him of his unemployment and to complain of low wages, Gladstone made the classic mid-Victorian reply:

> The only means which have been placed in my power of 'raising the wages of colliers' has been by endeavouring to beat down all those restrictions upon trade which tend to reduce the price to be obtained for the product of their labour, & to lower as much as may be the taxes on the commodities which they may require for use or for consumption. Beyond this I look to the forethought not yet so widely diffused in this country as in Scotland, & in some foreign lands; & I need not remind you that in order to facilitate its exercise the Government have been empowered by Legislation to become through the Dept. of the P.O. the receivers & guardians of savings.[4]

Gladstone was becoming uneasily aware, as were other perceptive observers of the Victorian economy, that the economy worked with a chronic 'enormous mass of paupers',[5] and that: 'Again, and yet more at large, what is human life, but, in the great majority of cases, a struggle for existence? and if the means of carrying on that struggle are somewhat better than they were, yet the standard of wants rises with the standard of means, and sometimes more rapidly. . . .'[6] He was moreover aware that 'great vicissitudes mark the industrial condition of society; and we pass rapidly in a series of cycles from periods of great prosperity to periods of sharp distress'.[7] He suggested to Lowe that what would have amounted to a primitive cost of living index should be drawn up, so that the condition of the working

---

[1] To Thirlwall, 12 Jan. 70.   [2] To Hughes, 11 Mar. 70.
[3] 19 Aug. 73; see Morgan, *Wales in British Politics*, 41.
[4] The letter was clearly intended for publication but I have not found it published.
[5] Budget speech of 1864, in W. E. Gladstone, *Financial Statements* (1864), 519.
[6] Ibid. What exactly Gladstone said on this topic in the 1863 budget is the subject of dispute; see the *résumé* of quotations by Engels in his preface to the fourth German edition of the first volume of *Das Kapital* (1890).
[7] *H* clxxxix. 1004–10 (1 March 1870) quoted in Malchow, *Population Pressures*, 36.

classes in 1832, 1852, and 1872 could be compared, but nothing seems to have come of this.[1]

Gladstone was fortunate in that, in general terms, his first ministry witnessed the emergence of the nation from a period of 'sharp distress' (the beginnings of which occurred in his later years at the Exchequer in the 1860s) into an upward cycle, largely though not wholly stifling the first widely-based murmurings against free trade since the early 1850s. In 1867 and 1868 during Disraeli's Chancellorship, *per capita* net national income had actually fallen slightly to £21.9, but by 1874 it had reached £27.4 at 1900 prices, or risen from £27.2 to £34.6 at current prices.[2] Gladstone saw this spectacular rise as a vindication of the fiscal and institutional reforms of the previous twenty years and of the principle that the maximum freedom of the market and the minimum absorption of its funds by the Government was the best guarantee of the creation of wealth.

This dramatic increase in national prosperity was, of course, not necessarily fully apparent to contemporaries, nor did it benefit all groups or classes equally. Its immediate political consequences are uncertain. Gladstone's administration had to deal with two political problems whose origins lay deep in social reactions to economic change: the problem of trade unions and their status, and the problem of the propertied classes' reaction to taxation. It is hard to judge how much the political expression of these problems was occasioned by economic change. First, change in the form of the uncertainties of the 1866 and 1873 disruptions of the money market. Second, in the end of the gradual inflation which had underpinned growth in the 1850s and 1860s, and which gave way at the end of 1873 to the start of the long deflation of the 1870s, 1880s, and 1890s. Third, in both downswings and upswings of certain sectors of the economy. A further underlying factor was the political opportunity and alarm which the household suffrage encouraged in the working and propertied classes respectively.

The economic problems of the working classes came before the Cabinet in the form of the trade unions. The Trades Union Congress, which first met in 1868, characterised with a new urgency a problem which had been recognised but not solved in the early 1860s: the legal status of unions and their funds. The Gladstone Cabinet offered

---

[1] To Lowe, 20 Dec. 72; the comparison was to be based on the price of lodging, fuel, clothing, food, locomotion, books, and newspapers.

[2] Feinstein's calculations in B. R. Mitchell and P. Deane, *Abstract of British Historical Statistics* (1962), 367; any such estimates have their difficulties, but all indices for 1868–74 show the same trend; e.g. GNP at constant factor cost (1913 = 100) rose from 43.7 in 1870 to 48.9 in 1874; C. H. Feinstein, *National Income Expenditure and Output of the United Kingdom* (1972), table 7.

the first tentative legislative solution to a series of questions which, a century later, remain contentious.

It recognised the legal existence of trade unions and secured their property by allowing them to register their rules with the Registrar of Friendly Societies, and sought to ameliorate those areas of the criminal law specifically affecting the actions of trade union members. This legislation took the form of two Acts, both passed in 1871, the Trade Union Act and the Criminal Law Amendment Act. This simple statement disguises a complex narrative in 1869,[1] when a bill introduced by Thomas Hughes and A. J. Mundella was withdrawn in the light of Government promises of legislation, and prolonged pressure in 1871 when the Government's original single bill finally passed as two separate Acts. The Cabinet's principles were 'to prevent violence; and in all economic matters the law to take no part'.[2] The first phrase revealed the Cabinet's intention to allow peaceful collective bargaining, the second its unwillingness to circumscribe the activities of trade unions on the grounds merely of their alleged violation of the canons of orthodox political economy by combining 'in restraint of trade'.[3] The bills' drafters, however, underestimated the ingenuity of the bench, for the directions to the jury of Mr Justice Brett in the Gas Stokers' Case of December 1872 revealed that the statute had insufficiently protected trade unionists from the operation of the common law of conspiracy,[4] whilst local Justices of the Peace tended to interpret the provisions of the Criminal Law Amendment Act affecting picketing in a more restrictive manner than its originators had intended. As a result, the hostility of a labour movement, swelled both in numbers and in confidence by the exceptional prosperity of the early 1870s, was directed towards the Gladstone Government.

The T.U.C. campaign for amendment of the labour laws led Lowe, the new Home Secretary, to suggest the possibility of some concession[5] and, on the prompting of Bright, Gladstone encouraged Lowe in September 1873 to bring proposals before the Cabinet following 'some rather careful inquiry'.[6] Under Lowe's guidance the Cabinet,

---

[1] See 3 and 10 July 69.   [2] 28 Jan. 71.

[3] Clause 2 of the Trade Union Act 1871 attempted to place unions and their members beyond charges of conspiracy; it was intended that the Criminal Law Amendment Act would do this.

[4] 'It is clear, therefore, that in 1871 the Legislature was passing a statute regulating all the relations between masters and servants; and by those provisions they practically say that there shall be no other offences as between master and servant but the offences detailed in the preceding part of this section'; Mr. Straight's argument defending the Gas Stokers, E. W. Cox, *Reports of cases in criminal law* (1875), xii. 331.

[5] Lowe to Gladstone on the Edinburgh demonstration, 29 August 1873, Add MS 44302, f. 152.

[6] To Lowe, 27 Sept. 73.

with dissensions from Selborne the Lord Chancellor, moved towards fresh legislation which would restore the position in which the Acts of 1871 had sought to place the unions. The Cabinet in November 1873[1] seems to have agreed to the heads of a bill which would have done much of what Disraeli's Cabinet eventually did in the Conspiracy and Protection of Property and the Employers and Workmen Acts of 1875.

Gladstone did not set out directly to involve himself in trade union questions, and the legislation seems to have been largely departmental in inspiration.[2] His role in September 1873 was as coordinator rather than initiator. There is a hint that he played some role in getting the Gas Stokers' sentences reduced.[3] He discouraged the use of troops in the particular case of a farmer who persuaded the army to take over the harvesting to enable him to dismiss unionised labour,[4] but in general Gladstone was characteristic of the ambivalence of the pro-pertied classes towards unions: he recognised their existence and their usefulness in producing order and coherence in industrial relations, but he would not give them the tools they thought they needed to do the job. Thus he encouraged 'the employment of the spare time of soldiers in useful civilian occupations', thinking 'there is always a risk, lest the labouring classes should like other classes be led to exaggerate their own rights in such a matter, so deep does the principle of monopoly lie in human nature'.[5]

As a Flintshire land and coal owner he became involved in a bitter controversy over the closed shop, discussed below. As Prime Minister, he did not encourage a swift restoration of the intentions of his own Government's legislation, and he paid for this politically. The extent of Cabinet agreement in November 1873 was insufficiently wide, or Gladstone was insufficiently interested in the question, for the loss of trust on the part of the unions to be reduced. The snap dissolution of January 1874 occurred during considerable union anger with the Liberals; the election manifesto promised much to the middle classes, but nothing specific to the unions—the plans for restorative union legislation being only hinted at.[6] Not surprisingly some unions and unionists worked for the Tories at the general election, or ran their own candidates.[7]

The reaction of urban ratepayers against government—not

---

[1] See Cabinet minutes and memoranda by Lowe and Selborne at 26 Nov. 73.

[2] I am much obliged to Mr. M. Curthoys for information on these points; his work when published will greatly clarify this complex subject.

[3] To Potter, 15 Jan. 73.   [4] To Cardwell, 5 Nov. 72.   [5] Ibid.

[6] Save for a brief and wholly unspecific mention of 'laws affecting the relations between employers and employed'; *The Times*, 24 January 1874, 8.

[7] See H. Pelling, *A history of British trade unionism* (1972 ed.), 68.

necessarily only Liberal governments—was a marked feature of these years. The State in normal circumstances raised its revenue by two quite separate means: national taxation, requested in the budget and granted in the finance bill, raising in 1868 £67,800,000, and local taxation, assessed and raised locally mainly from the taxation of owners and occupiers of rateable property, raising in 1868 £19,800,000. But the total expenditure of local authorities (the difference being made up by loans, government subventions, and rents and sales of locally owned property) was £30,140,000—nearly half the figure for the national government's income, a total which Goschen described as 'astounding'.[1]

The difficulties involved were various; in the counties the rates were administered by the non-elected Quarter Sessions, in the towns by the corporations elected on the 1835 local franchise; the Tories had argued since the later 1840s that where local administration had to deal with questions which were essentially national, the cost should be borne by the Exchequer and raised by national not local taxation.[2] This was the line of attack which the Tories returned to in 1869 when at the very start of the first Session Sir Massey Lopes called for a royal commission.

Lopes repeated his demands for an amelioration of the rate-payers' burdens at intervals throughout the government, and with considerable success. Goschen's two bills of 1871 (which offered an ambitious attempt to consolidate and standardise, 'to make all hereditaments, both corporeal and incorporeal' liable to rates, while at the same time surrendering the house tax to the relief of local rates) were withdrawn virtually without discussion; they were condemned as being overfavourable to urban dwellers.[3] In April 1872, having previously forced the ministry to withdraw by the device of moving the previous question, Lopes defeated in 259:159 a conciliatory amendment moved by the Liberal Sir Thomas Acland and carried his own resolution that 'it is expedient to remedy the injustice of imposing Taxation for National objects on one description of property only'.[4] The Cabinet's decision had been to 'oppose Lopez [sic] and stand on things already agreed'.[5]

The problem was that the Cabinet could not agree. Gladstone deplored any concession on the part of the Exchequer: 'my judgment is very hostile to taxing the Exchequer for local purposes. Even Sir

---

[1] G. J. Goschen, *Local Taxation* (1872), 5, from which the above figures are taken; the book was published following Gladstone's urging; 18 Sept. 72.

[2] See Matthew, 'Budgets', *passim*.

[3] *H* ccviii. 1115 and 6 May 71. Newdegate (the only speaker apart from Goschen) roundly condemned the tax-burden proposals.

[4] 16 Apr. 72; *H* ccx. 1404.

[5] 13 Apr. 72.

R. Peel went too far in that direction.'[1] When the Cabinet tried to agree on legislation following Lopes' resolution, he told Goschen: 'I seem but very little to see my way towards doing the thing that the H. of C. wants us to do.'[2] The Cabinet had a 'much prolonged . . . general conversation introduced by W.E.G. on the question of Local Taxation'.[3] Some agreement was reached on a bill to standardise assessment and valuation, consolidate the rates and abolish exemptions—that is, to set the existing system on a more regularised basis[4] —but in 1873, despite Tory taunts, no local government bill was introduced, Stansfeld, the new President of the Local Government Board, falling back on a select committee on parish boundaries.[5] The solution that Gladstone had proposed to Goschen in 1869, 'to occupy the ground' by 'a measure for County Boards on the elective principle'[6] was then returned to. At Gladstone's suggestion, Stansfeld drew up plans in November 1873 for county boards;[7] the Cabinet's reaction was uncertain, in general favourable to mixed county boards (i.e. made up partly of elected representatives, partly of J.P.s), but with ominous reservations from Goschen.[8]

Before the Cabinet could meet to discuss a bill, Gladstone had decided on dissolution. In his election address he pointed out that the Government 'have been unable to meet the views of those who appear to have thought that, provided only a large amount of public money could be had in any form to relieve the rates, no great heed need be paid to anything else'. But he recognised the 'very general desire that some new assistance should be afforded to the ratepayers of the country from funds at present under the command of the State', and he promised 'a thorough and comprehensive, not a partial, handling of the question . . . relief coupled with reform of local taxation'; there would be 'relief of rates and other property'.[9]

Gladstone was 'rather uncomfortable'[10] about local taxation, and remained so. He loathed the gradual conflation of imperial and local finance implied by grants-in-aid—'doles' as he called them—but this

[1] To Goschen, 17 Jan. 69.

[2] To Goschen, 18 Sept. 72; see also to Lowe, 24 Sept. 72, 7 Nov. 72.

[3] 14 Oct. 72.

[4] The Cabinet's decision followed the advice of Halifax in a mem. of 4 December 1872 (PRO T 168/82) opposing memoranda for more radical changes by Lowe and Childers (ibid.); Halifax argued for equalisation of assessment, and redrawing of boundaries; he was personally 'not in favour of any radical change'.

[5] *H* ccxi. 1819; see also ibid. 798.   [6] To Goschen, 17 Jan. 69.

[7] Stansfeld's memorandum, 'Local Government in connection with Local Taxation', of 26 November 1873, PRO T 168/82, 'prepared at the suggestion of Mr. Gladstone', circulated to the Cabinet.

[8] Answers of Cabinet members, but not Gladstone's, printed for the Cabinet, 7 January 1874, PRO T 168/82.

[9] *The Times*, 24 January 1874, 8.   [10] To Goschen, 18 Sept. 72.

was a conflation hard to avoid and one which was steadily increasing even before his own Government's Education Act gave to grants-in-aid what was in the long run to be their greatest fillip.[1]

In its dealings with economic questions as manifested by trade unions and the local taxation movement, the Cabinet cannot be said to have had much success. Both ran as festering sores throughout the Parliament, and neither was healed by the time of its dissolution.

The Cabinet also dealt with the economy more directly, through the Estimates, the budget, and the finance bill, all recurring items with an accepted timetable in the Cabinet's year, the Estimates being drawn up in the autumn, the budget in the spring.

Competence in fiscal management was the long, strong suit which the Liberals had played throughout the 1860s, and it was the card Gladstone's defenders could play when he was accused of erratic behaviour in other areas of policy. It was therefore a major blow to the reputation and self-respect of the Government when in 1871 Lowe's budget had to be withdrawn (following powerful opposition to the Estimates and to his proposals for a match tax balanced by change in the succession duties)—the first time this had happened to an established administration since Wood's budget of 1851.

Gladstone had, on the whole, let Lowe have his head.[2] He had sent him a list of measures which he saw as still outstanding from his long Chancellorship,[3] but he had not tried to exercise as close a supervision of the preparation of Lowe's budget as his own experience might have warranted, though the two were, naturally, in very frequent correspondence, as the letters printed below show. Lowe was quite an inventive Chancellor, though without raising any major threat to the framework of fiscal behaviour which Gladstone had established. Gladstone only saw the 1871 budget shortly before it was due to be presented to the Commons. The match tax might be thought to have offended against orthodox Gladstonianism, in that it broadened the basis of indirect taxation, but Gladstone does not seem to have objected to it on that score; nor does he seem to have seen soon enough the political dangers involved, though he advised Lowe to discuss the point with Glyn, the Chief Whip. His main reservations were on the political difficulties of reforming the death duties, though even here he showed no real alarm.[4]

Gladstone's 'list of remnants' sent to Lowe at the start of the

---

[1] Gladstone supported the proposal of Lowe for the change made mid-way through the Education Bill debates, by which the Exchequer grant to denominational schools was increased; to Lowe, 15 June 70; this clarifies the problem raised in Reid, *F*, i. 504.

[2] Lowe's budgets are usefully discussed in J. Winter, *Robert Lowe* (1976), chapters 14 and 15.

[3] To Lowe, 9 Jan. 69.

[4] To Lowe, 11 Apr. 71.

Government referred mainly to minor adjustments and improvements to his own work as Chancellor; no major constructive measures remained, though many of the adjustments were controversial. Gladstone's remnants were: abolition of remaining corn duty, abolition of tea licences, change in probate duty, abolition of conveyance duties save railways, commutation of fire insurance duty, reduction of income tax, reform of malt duty. In his budget of 1869, Lowe dealt with many of these; he abolished the corn duty, repealed the tea duty, abolished the fire insurance duty altogether, against Gladstone's judgement, reduced conveyance duties, and reduced income tax by a penny. Much more of a problem was the question of retrenchment, without whose continuance the whole carefully balanced compromise which Gladstone reached on taxation in the 1850s and 1860s was likely to collapse. Gladstone found Lowe an ineffective ally in his battles with the spending departments.[1]

The Government came into office pledged to further retrenchment, and made much in the electoral campaign of Disraeli's profligacy in his financing of the Abyssinian expedition of 1867–8. Gladstone had spent much of the 1860s in conflict with Palmerston on the question of retrenchment, and especially on the War Office and Admiralty expenditure, which accounted for about a third of Government expenditure.[2] Now Prime Minister, with control of appointments, he should have been in a good position to achieve his ends. After the *débâcle* of Lowe's budget in 1871, and as it became clear that in legislative terms it was going to be very hard to follow the success of the 1869 and 1870 Sessions, he began to look to finance as the unifying element of the domestic programme, as it had been in the 1860s under his own Chancellorship. The routine item of the Estimates was seen as central, 'bearing upon the position of the country, the party and the Government':

> They will be the *key* to our position at the outset of the session. We may announce Bills, but nobody will believe in them (unreasonable as the unbelief will be), except the Ballot; and that is discounted. On the Estimates will depend our chance of a fair start.[3]

Expenditure on defence fell dramatically through retrenchment

---

[1] See 14 Dec. 71.

[2] See table in Matthew, 'Budgets', p. 633. The defence estimates were as follows (Indian establishment excluded):

	1868 (Tory)	1869	1870	1871	1872	1873
Army	14.6	13.5	12.3	15.3	14.7	14.8
Navy	11.2	10.0	9.3	9.8	9.5	9.9

[3] To Cardwell, 9 Sept. 71; see also to Lowe, 30 Aug. 71.

and reorganisation in both army and navy in April 1869 and April 1870, but army expansion following the Franco-Prussian war spoilt the graph, and the abolition of purchase was also expensive, varying from year to year, but around £800,000 per annum. Gladstone hoped to get the figure back as nearly as possible to that of the pre-war Estimates, but, despite considerable savings by Cardwell by the end of 1872, the situation was gloomy: 'we have upon the last Estimates taken back all but some 300,000 of the £2,200,000 saving or thereabouts which in Feb. 71 we had made upon the Estimates of our predecessors'.[1] This was particularly reprehensible in view of the fact that for Gladstone the defeat of France in 1870 had had one great advantage—the disabling by land and sea of 'the only country in Europe that has the power of being formidable to us'.[2]

Gladstone's view of France had been that she was a potential danger that could be slowly neutralised by commercial ties: her neutralisation had now been more decisively achieved by Bismarck. In this sense, the result of the war of 1870 had been a bonus for Britain. The consequence thus ought to be, according to the maxim that 'policy determines expenditure', that naval and military retrenchment should be the easier. But this was not the view of the War Office or the Admiralty, where forces for expansion operated almost independently of the Cabinet ministers responsible for those departments, forces to which historians have as yet paid slight attention. 'Policy determines expenditure' seemed to mean to those departments that policy demanded greater expenditure.

The problem of the Estimates was compounded by inflation, which reached its peak at the end of 1873, and was recognised particularly to affect the Navy.[3] But inflation, and the marked rise in national wealth, also benefited the exchequer: the yield from indirect and direct taxes markedly increased, and splendid surpluses occurred in 1872 and 1873. The opportunity for spectacular budgets was thus created.

In 1873, the major weakening of the Government from its resignation and then resumption of office in March was emphasised by further blows to its fiscal record, when irregularities in the use of the Post Office Savings Banks funds and in the contract for the telegraph to southern Africa[4] were revealed.

The 'scandals' (as Gladstone called them)[5] of the summer of 1873

[1] To Cardwell, 6 Dec. 72.
[2] To Cardwell, 9 Sept. 71. This contrasted markedly with Disraeli's conclusion: 'The balance of power has been entirely destroyed, and the country which suffers most, and feels the effect of this great change most, is England'; Buckle, v. 134.
[3] To Cardwell, 6 Dec. 72.
[4] See 14 June, 12-25 July 73.   [5] 30 July 73.

highlighted a general failing of the administration explicable in part perhaps by Gladstone's absorption in legislation and the legislative process. The falling away of the popularity of the Government was in part the result of a dislike of its tone. For all its administrative achievements, especially in the defence departments, it had become associated with departmental mismanagement and even, in the summer of 1873, with a want of probity. Keen as he was on administrative efficiency in his own department, when he had one, Gladstone rather assumed efficiency in others, and had poor intelligence for gaining early knowledge of when things were going astray. His absence of interest in gossip, written or spoken, and in the small change of politics, perhaps intimidated colleagues and subordinates from keeping him in touch with those small details which signal danger to the acute political eye.[1] Small incidents that go wrong tend to be as much remembered as great legislative achievements that go right. An Opposition leader as witty as Disraeli was well placed to exploit this weakness; he waited for the legislative achievements of 1869–71 to run their course and then moved into the attack in 1872, capitalised upon the unpopularity of aspects of the legislation, set the tone for subsequent Toryism by pillorying the patriotism of the Government, and reaped the reward for abstaining from accepting office in the form of the 'scandals'.

By July 1873 Gladstone found himself the leader of a demoralised government which was almost at the point of breakdown. Only the end of the Session offered some respite. In attempting to come to terms with the situation, Gladstone implied that, individual failings and muddle apart, Lowe's suzerainty of the Treasury was too weak: the implication was that he had failed to see that the Permanent Secretary and the Financial Secretary knew the whole business of their department,[2] and it was, of course, the duty of the Treasury to oversee all such financial details throughout the administration. The canons of Victorian public life put the responsibility for 'the scandals' on the head of the department; however much his subordinates had let him down, Lowe was the man responsible for the fiscal probity of the nation. 'Cardwell broke to Lowe the necessity of his changing his office'[3] and he had, in effect, to resign as Chancellor, being shifted to the Home Office. After a day off at Chislehurst, and 'a very anxious day of constant conversation and reflection',[4] Gladstone wrote to the Queen on 5 August to submit details of the reshuffle,

---

[1] Gladstone's reliance on Granville meant that he was well up on potential crises in foreign policy, but much less so for domestic affairs.

[2] To Lowe, 11 June 73.

[3] 2 Aug. 73; see also Winter, *Robert Lowe*, 294.

[4] 4 Aug. 73.

as a result of which he became Chancellor of the Exchequer: 'he submits this recommendation with extreme reluctance, and greatly in
deference to the wish of his most experienced colleagues'.[1]

Thus it was that on 9 August 1873 Gladstone 'received a third
time the Seals of my old office',[2] and became Chancellor of the Exchequer as well as First Lord of the Treasury. He did so with his
Government in rare and sustained disarray, and by doing so he opened
a Pandora's box of constitutional precedents, as to whether he would
have to stand at the by-election obligatory to those taking an office
of profit under the Crown. He may have accepted the Chancellorship
with 'extreme reluctance' but he immediately plunged into its work
with enthusiasm and apparent forethought. Two days—a Sunday
intervening—after taking the seals, he revealed a daring and dramatic
plan, and then left for Hawarden:

> Saw . . . Mr Cardwell: to whom at the W.O. I told in deep secrecy my ideas of
> the *possible* finance of next year: based upon abolition of Income Tax &
> Sugar Duties with partial compensation from Spirits and Death Duties. This
> *only* might give a chance.[3]

The last sentence of this passage, which Morley omitted when quoting
this day's entry in his biography,[4] revealed the political motivation
which was a central element of the plan—a bold attempt to regain
the initiative within his own Party and in the country generally.
Coupled with the plan outlined to Cardwell, though apparently not
mentioned to him, was a substantial relief of local taxation—in the
order of £800,000 per annum. This was to be done not through further grants-in-aid, which he so much disliked, but by relieving localities in proportion as they paid national taxes such as the house tax
and licensing fees.[5] Gladstone had always looked to the house tax as
preferable to the income tax, but in a budget which set out to relieve
local taxation, which was largely raised on property, the house tax
could hardly be expected to bear all the burden. Gladstone therefore
turned also to the death duties in the form of the legacy and succession duties,[6] though these would have constituted something of a
'tit-for-tat' for the local taxation reforms.

[1] Guedalla, *Q*, i. 420; the Queen's approval was necessary before the Cabinet could be collectively informed. On the undated jottings made about this time, Goschen is mentioned for
the Exchequer; it is unclear whether it was offered to him; he is unmentioned in the journal between 22 July and Gladstone's departure for Hawarden on 11 August.   [2] 9 Aug. 73.
[3] 11 Aug. 73; curiously Gladstone later claimed to Cardwell (18 Sept. 73) that he could
not remember whether he had told him of the plan or not; this may have been a way of re-
minding Cardwell of it and, by implication, of the importance of retrenchment to it.
[4] The entry occurs in two parts: Morley, ii. 465, 478; Morley does, however, quote the
letter to Bright of 14 Aug.; ii. 479.
[5] To Lambert, 2 Jan. 74.   [6] To Stephenson, 12 Aug. 73.

The abolition of the income tax was, of course, not a new idea. Gladstone had always disliked the tax as such and when considered purely on its own terms and not in comparison to other taxes. He disliked it first because of the inequities inherent in it; second, because in the 1860s he had come to see it as encouraging rather than discouraging expenditure because of the ease with which it brought in revenue. In the mid-1860s, looking for ways of encouraging retrenchment, he had considered income-tax abolition before deciding that the enfranchisement of artisans would strengthen the retrenching arm of the Commons.[1]

Abolition rather than reduction of the income tax had not been one of the 'remnants' he had left to Lowe,[2] but in the spring of 1873, that is, well before he had resumed the Chancellorship, he returned to the subject, when Childers raised it with reference to Lowe's budget preparations: 'The idea of abolishing Income Tax is to me highly attractive, both on other grounds & because it tends to public economy. . . .'[3]

The problem, as it had always been since the 1840s for the Peelites, was that the income tax could not be treated in isolation, or considered on its own terms only. It was a central feature of the great compromise between direct and indirect taxation which was the distinguished, and in contemporary European terms, distinguishing achievement of mid-nineteenth-century Britain.[4] Before the 1867 Reform Act Gladstone had seen direct taxation as falling upon those with the vote, indirect upon those without it: the direct tax payers had thus been the 'virtual representatives' of the indirect. After 1867 this was changed: the indirect taxpayers, or some proportion of them, now had the vote—the days of virtual representation in the British political system were thought to be ending, save for women and, as yet, farm labourers. 1867 was widely expected to inaugurate a bid for booty from the working classes, but what in fact it marked was a relaxation of the need for responsibility on the part of the propertied classes.

Before 1867, direct taxation had been an act of self-sacrifice on the part of the propertied classes, for they alone paid it and they alone elected the representatives to the Parliament which imposed it. After 1867, however, direct taxation, unless altered, was thought to be the servant of the extended franchise. This alarmed Gladstone just as it alarmed Lord Salisbury, though for different reasons. Gladstone

[1] See introduction *supra*, v. xxxvii.
[2] 9 Jan. 69; his comment to Lowe was '6. The income tax at 6d., I suppose, presents a forward claim.'
[3] To Childers, 2 Apr. 73.
[4] See Matthew, 'Budgets', for a discussion of this subject.

always feared the ease with which the income tax, in particular, raised
revenue and consequently encouraged expenditure; Salisbury feared
it as a weapon of class vengeance. Abolition of the tax in the new
circumstances thus took on a new urgency for Gladstone as a means
of maintaining the minimalist State. On the other hand, he retained,
as it behoved him as Leader of the Liberal Party to retain, a strong
concern for balance in the incidence of national taxation: income tax
might go, but not at the expense of a shifting of the burden onto the
non-propertied classes who, despite 1867, could hardly be said to be
exerting significant pressure upon the structure of British politics in
the 1870s. 'You cannot provide for the means for abolishing Income
Tax, either in whole or in part, out of new indirect taxation,' he told
Childers, and he wanted 'to go a little beyond this & say that when
the Inc. Tax is abolished *some part* of the means must be got out of
some new impost touching property'.[1] Thus the plan included the
reform of and an increase in the death duties, although this was not
mentioned in Gladstone's election address.[2] Death duties might, in
Salisbury's terms, wreak great havoc, but they were difficult to use
to produce great revenues quickly.

The 1874 budget was intended to ensure retrenchment without
upsetting class relationships. But its presentation in Gladstone's
election address of January 1874 looked like a bid for the middle
class vote. In the short or even medium term this can be seen as a
shrewd enough move, for the battle in British politics in the 1870s
and 1880s was a contest for the support of the middle class.

The budget plan was therefore a bold and comprehensive scheme.
The 1853 and 1860 budgets had launched great governments; the
1874 plan was intended to end one by crowning it in fiscal triumph.
But despite the balancing element of alternative sources of direct
taxation, and of some concessions towards the 'Free Breakfast Table'
being demanded by the Free Trade League, the 1874 budget plans
put their main emphasis on the relief of taxation in the two areas of
principal concern to the propertied classes, income tax and local
rates: the budget would therefore have lacked the wide social vision
which had distinguished the great budgets of 1853 and 1860. In
those years, interlocking plans of vast complexity had been presented
to the nation as major contributions to the solution of the mid-
Victorian problems of political and social integration and order. The
1874 budget would have been narrower in conception and probably
highly divisive within the Liberal Party in the country. Moreover, the

---

[1] To Childers, 2 Apr. 73.
[2] The address reserved the position by mentioning 'judicious adjustments to existing
taxes', *The Times*, 24 January 1874, 8.

abolition of income tax would have placed so inelastic a corset around government spending that it would certainly have quickly snapped. Either the income tax would have been swiftly restored, or the Liberal Party would have found itself defending a fiscal system in which indirect taxation was given an ever-increasing role, and this would have brought to a much earlier grave its attempt at the creation of a non-class-based popular party.

That those developments were anticipated and that the abolition would have been politically controversial within the Party is shown by the reaction of both the Radical *Bee Hive* and Bagehot's *Economist* to Gladstone's election address of January 1874 which outlined his budgetary intentions. The *Bee Hive* argued that the proposal was socially unjust, the *Economist* that it was socially dangerous. James Aytoun in the *Bee Hive* stated that 'To this, as the old consistent advocate of the rights of the working classes we are altogether opposed',[1] and Bagehot, always a moderate direct taxer, argued in the *Economist* that an intense effort ought to be made by 'the best persons of all parties to retain it', for, in addition to the income tax's valuable elasticity, 'there is . . . much more than mere money in this tax. We want in our taxation not only real equality but apparent equality. . . .'[2] That tribune of provincial Radicalism, the people's Joseph, retrospectively drove the point home with characteristic, uncompromising hyperbole: Gladstone's proposals in his election address constituted 'the meanest public document that has ever, in like circumstances, proceeded from a statesman of the first rank. His manifesto was simply an appeal to the selfishness of the middle classes.'[3]

Reaction on the Tory side tended to express alarm that post-1867 British politics was indeed becoming an auction in which the two parties bid for the prize of democratic support. Lord Carnarvon, an extreme case in the sense that he had resigned with Salisbury in protest at the Derby–Disraeli Reform Bill, but none the less rather typical of high Tory reaction, noted in his diary:

All Engd runs in a state of excitement. In a few days the election will begin. I do not like either Gladstone's or Disraeli's addresses. G. offers a bribe of £5,000,000 in the shape of the remission of taxn & D at once caps it. It is

---

[1] *Bee Hive*, 31 January 1874. E. S. Beesly in the same issue argued: 'Mr Gladstone has sacrificed the lower classes, who worshipped him, to the richer classes, who disliked him', but concluded that 'on his past record . . . I do not expect that we shall find him proposing any financial scheme which, as a whole, will amount to relieving the rich at the expense of the poor.'

[2] *The Economist*, 31 January 1874.

[3] J. Chamberlain, *Fortnightly Review*, xxii. 412 (October 1874).

what we said at the passing of the last Reform bill that the constitution wd be put up to auction on each genl election.[1]

But for Gladstone, the plan was the best that could be offered to answer the political problem which had been so clearly defined at the time of the defeat in March 1873 on the Irish University Bill: 'There is now no *cause*. No great public object on wh. the Liberal party are agreed & combined.' His difficulty was that, despite a surplus of about £5 million, and about £2 million anticipated from 'new sources of revenue', in order to abolish the income tax, relieve local taxation, and make remissions on the sugar duties, he still needed about £600,000 more.[2] He wanted the sum to come from retrenchment in the army and navy estimates, especially the latter. Details of the budget proposals were linked with a general statement on 'the pledges of [18]68' and 'the principles of economy'.[3] But Cardwell and Goschen, the two ministers concerned, could not find the economies. Warning shots were fired in the correspondences of the Recess, intermingled with tart exchanges about the purposes and expenses of the Gold Coast expedition. But Gladstone saw no immediate reason to bring the issue to a decision, and he suggested that the question of the Estimates be put off until his return to London early in January.[4] He does not seem to have revealed to Cardwell or Goschen the extent of his demand for further retrenchment in the Estimates.

The legislative programme for the Session of 1874 was agreed upon, as was the custom, at the Cabinets before Christmas in 1873. The Cabinet decided '*Not* to take Co. Suffrage, *not* to take Land Laws'.[5] The county franchise, on which Ripon had resigned though without public fuss in the midst of 'the scandals' in July,[6] and to which Gladstone had given, *via* Forster, general personal approval,[7] was too divisive a topic for the Cabinet to tackle: it threatened a

---

[1] Carnarvon's Diary, 27 January 1877, Add MS, not yet numbered. I am obliged to Mr. M. Curthoys for this reference.

[2] 19 Jan. 74. Mr. P. Ghosh has made the interesting point to me that Gladstone had extra funds up his sleeve from (1) technical adjustments in the accounts; (2) the reluctance of government departments to include allowance for inflation and for the large increments of these years in their calculations which therefore consistently underestimated the revenue. I am much obliged to him for showing me his unpublished paper on the plans for the 1874 budget.

[3] 19 Jan. 74.

[4] To Cardwell, 1 Dec. 73. There was a technical reason for this, revealed in this letter: Gladstone rightly believed that the peak of inflation had been reached, and that prices were now falling: any delay would thus lend support to his argument that the defence departments, and especially the Admiralty, would need less next year.

[5] 21 Nov. 73.

[6] 25 July 73n; even the Queen was told this was 'on account of private affairs'; Guedalla, Q, i. 421.

[7] To Forster, 23 July 73.

rapid return to the fissures of 1866. Local taxation relief was necessary, but not an adequate basis for Party rehabilitation: 'the Tories are completely beforehand with us, secondly they will outbid us if we enter into a competition'.[1]

In Gladstone's view, this left only 'Finance', i.e. the budget, as a focal point round which the Party could rally. The November Cabinets thus confirmed the view that Gladstone had held since 'the scandals' of the summer: only the budget could restore the Party to something like a coherent and companionable body. He spelt out his arguments in a gloomy letter to Granville on 8 January 1874: he considered the subject of dissolution at this time, in the context of the general weakness of the Party and the Government, but concluded: 'Dissolution means either immediate death, or at the best Death a little postponed, and the party either way shattered for the time'.[2] On 16 January 1874 Gladstone returned to London. Cardwell had been sent a copy of the letter to Granville, and the extent of its demands for reduction of the defence estimates had taken him by surprise: 'I have not received from Gladstone any intimation that he considers a further reduction of establishment possible or proper: & I do not see the way of effecting it',[3] he told Granville, with a clear hint of possible resignation. After a conference with Granville and Wolverton, Gladstone found 'the prospects of agreement with the two Depts on Estimates are for the present bad'.[4] Next day, a Sunday, Gladstone returned to thoughts of dissolution:

This day I thought of dissolution. Told Bright of it. In evening at dinner told Granville and Wolverton. All seemed to approve. My first thought of it was as escape from a difficulty. I soon saw on reflection that it was the best thing in itself.[5]

The 'escape from a difficulty' probably meant the Estimates; Gladstone listed the first reason for a dissolution as being 'we gain time, & avoid for the moment a ministerial crisis';[6] the only other subject for a crisis at that time was the county franchise, on which Gladstone reaffirmed his general and personal support to a deputation on 21 January,[7] but it would have taken some time for a ministerial crisis to have developed on that subject, as the Cabinet had already agreed not to introduce a bill. The large amount of reduction in defence estimates that Gladstone wanted—between £1 million and £600,000 —would need much more than marginal adjustments and was bound to produce a major row. Gladstone tried to get Goschen and Cardwell

---

[1] To Granville, 8 January 1874, Ramm I, ii. 439. [2] Ibid.
[3] Cardwell to Granville, 15 January 1874, Add MS 44120, f. 210.
[4] 17 Jan. 74.   [5] 18 Jan. 74.   [6] 20 Jan. 74.   [7] 21 Jan. 74n.

to sign a paper to agree to keep the Estimates question open.[1] The dispute could not be mentioned during the election campaign; but if the Government were returned to office Gladstone could bring further pressures of retrenchment and the pledge to abolish income tax to bear upon the Admiralty and the War Office to return to something like the expenditure levels of February 1870. Further, if a dissolution was to be had within the next three months, it was necessary, because of the constraints of the parliamentary timetable for financial questions, that it be done immediately.

The dissolution was therefore essentially a dissolution against the defence departments. Even combining the offices of First Lord and Chancellor of the Exchequer had not allowed Gladstone to prevail against them. First, their expedition to West Africa was on a scale which Gladstone believed was excessive, second, they were behaving, and seemed likely to behave successfully, as if Palmerston had never died. Only an election victory on the general principles of retrenchment, and the specific pledges to remove the most elastic variable of the Government's revenue, the income tax, and to make remissions of local taxation by central government help, would suffice to crush them.

The disastrous election bore out Gladstone's earlier forecast of the Party 'shattered for the time' rather than the tentative optimism of his notes for the Cabinet: 'I think our victory is as likely in an immediate as in a postponed Dissolution. While we run fewer chances of a crushing defeat.'[2] The long run of by-election losses in 1873 proved no false guide: the 1874 general election ended the pattern of British elections since 1847, that whoever it was that made up the majority in the Commons, it was not the Tories.

VII

Thus ended Gladstone's first administration; he resigned on 17 February 1874 without meeting Parliament. On 19 February he drafted a letter to the chief whip stating 'it is not my intention to assume the functions of Leader of a Parliamentary Opposition in the House of Commons to the new Government'.[3] This letter, clearly intended for publication had it been sent, disclaimed difficulties with the Party as a reason, but Gladstone's personal views became clearer in a series of notes made in March: the electorate had rejected his view about retrenchment, a significant section of the Party differed irreconcilably from him on education; the 'failure of 1866–8' boded ill for his future shadow leadership, especially given the tendency of

[1] 22 Jan. 74.   [2] 20 Jan. 74.   [3] To Peel, 19 Feb. 74; see also 7 Feb. 74.

back-benchers 'of making a career by & upon constant active opposition to the bulk of the party' even when the Party was in office. But the first reason was personal: to accept leadership meant to accept the future presumption of office as well, i.e. a Tory Parliament followed by a Liberal Parliament, the two of which could amount to fourteen years: 'this is not consistent with my views for the close of my life'.[1] Pressed by alarmed colleagues, he accepted a compromise, that he should remain as nominal but inactive leader in the Commons, the position to be reconsidered before the start of the Session of 1875.[2]

Gladstone had spent much of his administration in conflict with his colleagues and with groups in his Party both 'left' and 'right', but when it came to the point, they could not let him go. The Liberal Party aspired to classlessness, but it was riddled with class; it hoped for interdenominationalism but it divided between Erastianism, sectarianism, and secularism; it tried to offer justice to the three kingdoms but it satisfied none. Gladstone stood outside the Cabinet and the Party; his class was indefinable, his religion exceptional; he was an extreme Radical on some questions, an unreconstructed Conservative on others; he was at the same time a chief architect of the mid-nineteenth-century settlement and seen as one of the chief threats to its continuation. Disraeli was self-evidently exotic, but viewed from the perspective of any one of the groups that constituted the Liberal Party, so was Gladstone.

In the decades after the start of household suffrage, British political parties slowly, surprisingly slowly, and in the case of the Liberals only in part, took on those attributes characteristic of a modern party: bureaucracy and caution. But during the transitional phase, exceptional demands were made of their leaders and especially of the leader of the Liberal Party as it struggled to preserve its identity caught between the certainty of a property-based Conservative Party and the uncertainty of developments 'to the left'. The position resulting from the defeat of 1874 was, of course, only the start of a long-drawn-out and ultimately unsuccessful attempt by the Liberals to meet the problem of 'the squeeze', but one thing was already clear: no available Whig could successfully appeal over the horizon of his own constituency to the disparate groups beyond. Much as they were coming to fear Gladstone, the Whigs feared isolation more.

The abrupt dissolution in January 1874 caught the Party as well as the country by surprise. Since the abortive resignation of March 1873, dissolution had been, in general terms, a probability,[3] but

---

[1] 5 and 7 Mar. 74. [2] See Ramm I, ii. 449.
[3] Gladstone made cryptic reference to it a week *before* the abortive resignation in one of his rare extra-parliamentary speeches, which is marked by its elegiac tone; see 5 Mar. 73.

the speed with which events moved in January and February 1874 was unusual; there had not been a dissolution in the Recess without prior announcement since that of 1780. It found Gladstone in considerable embarrassment with respect to his own seat. His election address was written for 'an unnamed constituency',[1] and the decision to stand again for one of the two Greenwich seats was taken at the last moment. The doubts were justified when he came second to 'Boord the distiller . . . more like a defeat than a victory, though it places me in Parliament again'.[2]

Gladstone's relationship with Greenwich had been neither intimate nor amiable. The constituency was a kaleidoscope of advanced Liberals, Republicans, and naval dockyard workers, many of whom were Tories. Retrenchment by both Tory and Liberal Governments had borne heavily on the dockyards, but Gladstone had dealt with the various delegations which waited upon him with homilies on the national need for reduction of government establishments. None of the interest in the unemployed which he had shown in Lancashire in the 1860s was bestowed on the dockyard workers who had lost their jobs. Gladstone's contact with the constituency had been mainly through his colleague as M.P., Alderman Salomons, but Salomons had died in 1873, and the Tories captured his seat at the by-election.[3]

Despite the weakness of the local Liberal organization and its obvious need for leadership, Gladstone went to very considerable lengths to avoid speaking in the constituency. 'You cannot treat Birmingham as I am able to treat Greenwich, & you are I believe to address your constituents shortly', observed Gladstone to Bright at the end of 1869.[4] 'No-one had had so little to do with my now being member for Greenwich as I have myself' he told the chief whip,[5] but he did little to remedy this situation.

He spoke, after prolonged stalling, at the great meeting at Blackheath in October 1871,[6] but even then chiefly because speeches in his son's marginal constituency of Whitby,[7] and in receiving the Freedom of Aberdeen,[8] meant that Greenwich could no longer be ignored. He did not speak there again until the general election, and considered in the meantime other possibilities for a seat, especially his old constituency of Newark, which he had held between 1832 and 1845.[9] The rapid dissolution in January 1874 thus found Gladstone

---

[1] 20 Jan. 74.   [2] 3 Feb. 74.
[3] See G. Crossick, *An Artisan Élite in Victorian Society* (1978), 212, which gives a lively description of this large and complex constituency.
[4] To Bright, 30 Dec. 69.   [5] To Peel, 11 Oct. 73.
[6] 28 Oct. 71.   [7] 2 Sept. 71.   [8] 26 Sept. 71.
[9] To Peel, 31 Dec. 73. He also declined an invitation to stand at a by-election in Kincardineshire, a safe Liberal seat, primarily for 'the family reason'—i.e. his brother Tom's

almost as much a stranger to his constituents as when he first met them; it allowed no time for a change of seat, and little time for campaigning—only three election speeches were made.[1]

The prototype of a new style of popular executive politician which Gladstone had so carefully developed in the 1860s was thus to some considerable extent set aside. There were no great set piece addresses other than the few mentioned above. Appearances at the annual Lord Mayor's banquet were resented and resisted when possible. A half-hearted attempt to rally popular support behind the Irish University Bill was made in March 1873,[2] the odd gathering at railway stations or outside the gates of great houses received a few words, but of 'The People's William' there was little sign.

Of course, there were some good reasons for this. After 1870, any speech was likely to be either evasive or divisive, and Gladstone speechifying would license his opponents within the Cabinet to do likewise—the contents of the Blackheath speech were a matter for Cabinet discussion: 'WEG invited contributions, or cautions.'[3] Even so, Gladstone forfeited one of his major assets, and allowed the shades of the Cabinet and the Party in the Commons to crowd closely around him; it was strange to see an England with Disraeli as the leading demagogue.

Gladstone's strategy of wooing the votes of the propertied classes —exemplified especially in the relief of local taxation proposals— showed the acuteness of his perception of the real implications of the household suffrage, and it may be that this encouraged him to avoid giving hostages to the Tory press in the form of speeches to great crowds. But the nature of much of the rank-and-file following of the Liberal Party was such that deference was no longer enough. Commenting on Gladstone's speech at Whitby attacking the bias of the metropolitan press, Lord Houghton told Gladstone shrewdly: 'there is a Demon not of Demogogism but of Demophilism, that is tempting [you]'.[4] It may be that there was, but Demos personally saw little of it during this government, and was offended.

Gladstone's appearance in the 1860s as a new kind of executive politician had been buttressed by his shrewd use of the press, and especially of the Liberal *Daily Telegraph*.[5] He retained his press

Toryism, Fasque, the family home, being in the constituency; to have resigned his Greenwich seat in mid-Parliament would have been an extraordinary manoeuvre; to Sir T. Gladstone and to W. Alexander, 20 Nov. 72. There were various other offers, including Chester; to Lord Westminster, 3 Jan. 74.

[1] 28 and 31 Jan., 2 Feb. 74.   [2] 5 Mar. 73.
[3] 27 Oct. 71.   [4] See to Houghton, 13 Sept. 71n.
[5] See introduction above, v. xliv. Frank Lawley, his former secretary and informal press contact, almost disappears from the journal, 1868–74.

contacts, but used them much less frequently and more formally. His contacts were mainly with editors, whereas previously they had been mainly with reporters. Thornton Hunt, the *Telegraph* reporter whom he had seen sometimes almost daily when at the Exchequer and during the Reform Bill debates, barely appears in the journal after December 1868; he died in 1873.[1] Contacts with Levy, the owner and editor of the *Telegraph*, were irregular and seem to have been limited to announcements for formal developments, such as the order of government business, the dates of state visits, and the like.[2] Gladstone showed himself willing to use his *Telegraph* contacts to get a 'special' reporter sent to investigate a scandal in Shetland,[3] but he does not seem to have used the *Telegraph*, as he had in 1866, to ventilate his views on Irish policy.

The Times replaced the *Daily Telegraph* as the focus of Gladstone's attentions. Delane, its editor, was kept in touch with the developments of the Irish Church Bill,[4] and to some extent with the preparation of the Irish Land Bill.[5] He was summoned for consultations during the crisis with the Lords in July 1869.[6] When the 1871 Session ran into difficulties, with ballot and army bills being dismembered in the Lords after long struggles in the Commons—both reforms which when passed seemed to general consent both necessary and just— Gladstone singled out the metropolitan press for particular blame:

> A considerable section of the Metropolitan Press had discussed with greater severity the proceedings of Parliament during the last Session than had been the case with the Provincial Press. He was bound to say that he could find reason for that difference in this fact,—the present Government had not hesitated when it thought the public interest required it to make proposals which had been highly offensive to powerful classes in this country (cheers) . . . the effect of that bias was most felt where wealth was concentrated, as in the metropolis, and where . . . the opinions of the Clubs, rather than the opinion of this great nation, were reflected in a considerable portion of the Metropolitan Press.[7]

In this speech Gladstone indicated the extent to which Liberalism was ceasing, despite its majority in the Commons and its hold over certain sections of the Civil Service, to be the Party of 'the establishment'. Whereas in the 1850s the Tories had found themselves bereft of metropolitan newspaper support, the Liberals in the 1870s found

---

[1] *Daily Telegraph*, 30 June 1873, 5. See, however, 9 Dec. 69.
[2] Levy congratulated Gladstone, 19 August 1869, Add MS 44421, f. 253, on the 'grand results of your work'. The strange affair of the Edmunds case (see 6 and 7 Aug. 72) involved the *Telegraph*.
[3] To Bruce, 20 Mar. 70.   [4] To Delane, 3, 4, and 27 Feb. 69.
[5] To Delane, 6 Oct. 69.   [6] To Delane, 19 July 69, 21 June 70.
[7] At Whitby, *The Times*, 4 September 1871, 12.

the balance shifting in the other direction. These developments caused
the Liberals considerable anxiety. Gladstone suggested to Glyn, the
chief whip, that Liberal weakness among the London evening papers
might be countered by *The Echo* having a second edition which
would serve as an evening edition,[1] but he does not seem to have
taken a sustained interest in regaining the initiative for the Liberals.
His outburst at Whitby initiated a tradition of complaint within
Radical circles which was to prove enduring; that he did little behind
the scenes to find a remedy was to be equally characteristic of the
Radical leadership.

This indifference may in part have been because the most popular
and the most influential of the London papers, the *Daily Telegraph*
and *The Times* respectively, remained loyal to Gladstone, if not to
the Liberal Party.[2] Both papers supported the return of the Government, and especially of Gladstone, at the election of 1874. The *Telegraph* did so in its capacity as still almost a Party paper, though already
with qualifications; *The Times* with some reservation after an initially
very favourable reaction to the financial proposals ('the coloured
lights on the stage soon fade'),[3] but none the less quite emphatically:
'there are good chances for a Government which has given proofs of
energy and capacity, and has a magnificent programme ready for the
Session. After all, no one can do Mr Gladstone's work as well as Mr
Gladstone and it is Mr Gladstone's work which the Conservative
Party has now proffered itself to do [by agreeing to income tax abo-
lition].'[4] Both papers were soon to be lost not only to the Liberal
Party but to Gladstone also.

Gladstone did pay attention to publications designed to win the
argument at the highest level. His own article on the Franco-Prussian
war has been discussed above. In 1872 he encouraged, without success,
Cardwell to publish 'in a Pamphlet a full but *popular* account of our
army system as it now is . . . it would help to stereotype a state of
opinion you have well earned'.[5] More successfully, he told Goschen
'I should like to see the whole substance of your Report . . . put out
in the best form, as a great document upon the subject.' This resulted
in Goschen's *Local Taxation* (1872),[6] a work which exemplified the
rationalistic approach to public opinion pursued by the Liberals.

[1] To Glyn, 19 May 69.
[2] See S. Koss, *The rise and fall of the political press in Britain*, i. 197, 201 (1981) and
generally for a thorough treatment of this topic.
[3] *The Times*, 27 January 1874, 9a.
[4] Ibid., 30 January 1874, 9b; 'On the last occasion the watchword was Gladstone and
the disestablishment of the Irish Church; now it is Gladstone alone.'
[5] To Cardwell, 21 Aug. 72. Sir J. Adye, *The British Army* (1875) tried to fulfil this function.
[6] To Goschen, 18 Sept. 72; the book was published at the end of that year.

Few politicians in peacetime can have been more fully stretched than Gladstone in his first ministry. This introduction has tried to indicate the main areas of government activity in which he involved himself. Any reader of the material published below could not but be puzzled by Lord Houghton's view, that Gladstone had a 'one idea at a time faculty', a view which has had an eminent following since.[1] It may be that Gladstone sometimes presented himself as having one idea at a time, and it is certainly the case that a departmental minister, trying to cope with a line of policy in which the Prime Minister was interesting himself, must have felt that he was Gladstone's sole object of attention. But the first ministry shows Gladstone at the height of political awareness, sensitive to the implications of every phrase in every letter on a vast range of topics. Certainly he was more interested in some topics than in others, and he was completely identified with three of the Government's main bills. But even his speeches in the House show the extent of his mastery of the work of the ministry as a whole—indeed he increasingly found himself not merely conducting the orchestra from the piano, but playing most of the other instruments as well.

In a man prone to tension, it is not surprising that this experience was wearing. In January 1874 he had been in office continually since 1859, with the exception of July 1866 to December 1868. The administration was punctuated by Gladstone's illnesses, many of them occurring at moments of crisis. 'Tightness in the chest', fever and diarrhoea removed him from direct political leadership during the crisis over the Irish Church negotiations in 1869, the 'scandals' crisis in July 1873, and the negotiations about the Estimates and dissolution in January 1874.[2] His physician, Andrew Clark, played an important though not quite clearly definable role in the attempted resignation of March 1873.[3] Gladstone also suffered at less politically sensitive moments.[4] These bouts of illness do not seem, however, to have had any lasting effect. He recovered from them with persistent resilience. His handling of the correspondence of both Chancellor and First Lord in the months at the end of the Government certainly does not suggest that he was exhausted either physically or mentally. His walk of thirty-three miles in the rain across the Grampians from Balmoral through Glen Feshie to Drumguish and Kingussie does not suggest a body enfeebled by illness.[5] Reviewing himself on his sixty-fourth birthday, Gladstone found it was inward 'strain and tossing of the spirit' which troubled him—outwardly 'a weaker heart,

---

[1] See Hammond, 184 and D. A. Hamer, *Liberal politics* (1972), 69.
[2] 22-3 July 69, 23-8 July 73, 18-20 Jan. 74.   [3] 12-13 Mar. 73.
[4] e.g. 20 July 70, 29 May-3 June 71.   [5] 1 Sept. 73.

stiffened muscles, thin hairs: other strength still remains in my frame'.[1]

VIII

Resilience was one of Gladstone's most notable features as an executive politician. A minor example, though a telling one, was his regular evening entry in the journal. The entries for the first administration are slightly longer than for the earlier years of the 1860s. There may be some link here with Gladstone's decision no longer to write 'political memoranda' recording the course of important events, save for royal interviews and the occasional crisis. Certainly, the recording of the day's activities, however briefly, was important to him: when he left the little volume behind at Hawarden during a visit to Spencer at Althorp, he immediately asked for it to be forwarded, keeping up the entries on writing paper and sticking it into the volume once regained.[2]

The journal was preserved partly to record a schedule which was, at the least, exacting. Compared to some Presidents and Prime Ministers in the second half of the twentieth century, Gladstone's level of activity, especially if the Recess is included, was not especially severe. But it must be remembered that a Prime Minister before the First World War prepared all his speeches and answers to questions himself, conducted much of his correspondence personally, and had, comparatively, very little in the way of supporting staff. It was for Gladstone himself to check that Cabinet decisions were carried out, and to complain when returns and tables were not produced as requested.

On top of this was the priority given to the affairs of the House of Commons. As Prime Minister, Gladstone regularly sat on the Treasury bench in the Commons for seven hours a day, and attendances of over nine hours occur quite frequently. Hours of attendance in the Commons, together with church services, are always recorded in the diary. Gladstone usually began sitting in the Commons about 2.15 p.m. and often sat, with an hour off for dinner, until after midnight. He did not find these long sittings particularly stressful, for, commenting on a rare bout of insomnia promoted by an evening of unsuccessful attempts to persuade John Bright to rejoin the Cabinet, he noted: 'My brain assumes in the evening a feminine susceptibility, and resents any unusual strain: tho' strange to say, it will stand a debate in the House of Commons.'[3] The morning and, sometimes in the Recess, part of the afternoon also,[4] was given over to correspondence, for Gladstone's inclination was always to proceed by

---

[1] 29 Dec. 73. [2] 5–9 Nov. 73. [3] 14 Nov. 71.
[4] See 2 Sept. 69 for seven hours spent on correspondence.

written argument, whether his colleague was out of London or on his doorstep. The development of policy by social intercourse was not Gladstone's method: in the whole of his first premiership he does not record entering a political club.[1] This personal isolation should not of course be exaggerated. Gladstone saw a very great deal of his colleagues. Political dinners were regularly held at his house in Carlton House Terrace. During the Session, he rarely dined at home. If not entertaining, he dined out, sometimes with members of his Government and Party, sometimes with old Tractarian friends like Sir Walter James and Sir Robert Phillimore, quite frequently with one of his secretaries (often Algernon West), and quite frequently also with Mrs. Thistlethwayte. Gladstone is almost always careful to note in the journal whom his host or hostess was for the dinner, which in the Session was usually an hour long at most. He very rarely notes a political discussion at these dinners. Compared with the Palmerstonian years, Gladstone used the country house weekend sparingly, usually visiting aristocratic relatives, such as the Cavendishes at Chislehurst, rather than touring the great Whig houses.[2] Next to Chislehurst and Granville's refuge at Walmer Castle, Lord Salisbury's Hatfield was, surprisingly, his most frequent weekend visiting place.

Gladstone's outpouring of correspondence was huge. He records each day the most important of the letters written. A selection—and the reader can see for himself its extent—is printed below together with the daily text of the journal and the Cabinet minutes. Gladstone's writing methods merit description. When the post was opened, certain letters were set aside to be answered by the private secretaries. These were usually letters about deputations, invitations to speak, begging letters, and the like. Gladstone personally answered all letters which he lists in the daily diary entry—usually at least five and often many more—and from time to time more letters than he lists. Copies of these letters, save those on family affairs, or to Mrs. Thistlethwayte, were then made by the private secretaries. Gladstone indicated on the holograph how the letter was to be recorded—one tick in the bottom left-hand corner meant that it was to be copied into the letter book, two ticks that it was to be copied onto a separate sheet of paper and filed separately.

The letter books and the separately copied sheets (the latter now to be found in the appropriate volume of the special and general correspondence in the Gladstone Papers), taken together, thus constitute

---

[1] He joined the Reform under strong pressure from Glyn, the chief whip, and resigned in 1874; see 17 May 69n.

[2] 'Where Was He', printed at the end of each volume, lists all weekend visits. Lord Frederick Cavendish was his wife's niece's husband.

an extremely thorough record of the outgoing letters.[1] It is very rare
to find a letter by Gladstone in the papers of his correspondents for
which there is no copy in the Gladstone Papers, and it is not at all
unusual to find that the copies of letters in the Gladstone Papers
considerably outnumber the holographs preserved in the papers of
his colleagues. This recording process operated, unfortunately, only
while Gladstone was in office: systematic recording in the letter
book ceased at the end of February 1874 and on 5 March 1874 Gladstone noted 'tomorrow I encounter my own correspondence single-
handed'.[2] While out of office, he had no secretary, though copies of
letters were sometimes made for him by his wife or children.

Gladstone thus ran an embryonic 'cabinet office', probably more
formally organised and certainly more fully recorded than that of his
predecessors. This went some way to compensating for the absence
of a Prime Minister's department, but the want of any permanent
staff meant that there was no necessary continuity of this practice
when a change of office occurred. The records of his premiership are
much more systematic than those of any of his predecessors, and the
care and attention to recording and filing by both the secretaries and
Gladstone himself reflect not only his awareness of the importance
of records for the smooth running of business, but also his awareness
of his own role as an historical phenomenon. The Peelites were unusually conscious of the use to which private papers might be put—
viz. the rapid and unusual printing in 1856 by Cardwell and Stanhope
of Peel's memoranda of 1845-6, and of the private printing of Aberdeen's papers by his son, Gladstone's erstwhile secretary, Arthur
Gordon, to which endeavour Gladstone as Prime Minister gave very
considerable attention.[3] Gladstone's awareness of his own historical
role, and the part that his letters were to play in it, was heightened by
the death of his close friend of the 1830s and 1840s, James Hope
(-Scott) in 1873. A lengthy appraisal[4] and a sorting of the correspondence followed. Gladstone had reached that stage in his life when his
archives were becoming one of the chief sources for British political
and religious life from the 1830s onwards. He was soon to reach that

---

[1] See Sir E. W. Hamilton, *Mr. Gladstone* (1898), 79–83. The outgoing letters were more
thoroughly recorded than the incoming ones were kept; these are, perhaps surprisingly, quite
often not in place; forwarding to departmental ministers was probably the cause. A useful
résumé of the history of the Gladstone archives will be found in *Autobiographica*, iv. 118ff.

[2] The result of this was that Gladstone dealt himself with the vast correspondence in the
summer of 1874, much of it from well-wishers with no previous direct contact with him;
many of the incoming letters from these have not survived; I have not written 'unidentified'
in footnotes for each of them. The names of such correspondents in 1874 are listed in the
Dramatis Personae at the end of Volume VIII; if there is no note for a correspondent whose
date there is 1874, then he or she is unidentified.

[3] 16 Jan. 71ff.   [4] See 13 Sept. 73.

strange position—starting perhaps with the biography of Samuel Wilberforce (1879)—of seeing himself as a chief actor in the published biographies of the day, and watching the intimate personal and religious crises of his youth replayed before his own and the public's gaze.

Correspondence was, then, together with sitting in the Commons during the Session, the main business of his day; it was the lifeblood of his ministry and the process by which the Cabinet maintained its identity and the Prime Minister his suzerainty. This was particularly the case given Gladstone's quite frequent absences from London, especially in autumn and winter. In 1872, for example, he was away from London between 5 August and 10 October, and between 16 October and 14 November, as well as for many other short absences. These spells of absence were rarely used for directly political purposes. Attendance at Balmoral was unavoidable, but Gladstone did not otherwise devote much time to political week-ending. As already mentioned, most of his weekends away were spent with Lord Frederick Cavendish and his wife (Catherine Gladstone's niece) at Chislehurst, without a house party. Weekends away were, in fact, for relaxation.

There were of course exceptions. Two visits to Chatsworth were clearly politically important, as were several visits to Lord Salisbury at Hatfield. Salisbury and Gladstone shared a quasi-Tractarian, High-Churchmanship and a contempt for Disraeli, but they shared little more. Gladstone felt that these visits, which were not reciprocated, went well ('There are no kinder hosts than here'), and he approved of what he found: 'In few Chapels is all so well and heartily done.'[1] Their shared dislike of Disraeli reflected the intense moral and religious language in which both men expressed their view of politics, but this certainly offered no basis for cooperation, and Salisbury remained one of the ministry's most persistent and effective critics. The two visits to Salisbury's young nephew Arthur Balfour, at his shooting lodge and at Whittinghame,[2] and Balfour's strong friendship —quite how strong is not clear—for Catherine Gladstone's niece, May Lyttelton, had obvious political overtones for both families. But most of Gladstone's visits were to old cronies such as Wolverton, Milnes Gaskell, Edward Ellice and his undergraduate friend Walter Sneyd. Of course, no act by a Prime Minister is without political implications—Gladstone's visit to the Roman Catholic convert Ambrose Phillipps de Lisle at Garendon[3] had implications well beyond the mere observation of de Lisle's monastery—but it is fair to say that Gladstone did not primarily intend these visits to be political in

[1] 7 Dec. 72, 16 July 71.   [2] 3 Oct. 72, 14 Nov. 74.
[3] 7 Oct. 73.

tone, and that his use of them differed from his rather assiduous use of the political weekend in the 1860s.[1]

This readiness to distance himself physically from his colleagues —especially in the Recess—while remaining in touch with them by letter to the extent that he wished to do so, clearly allowed Gladstone to give himself periods of rest and regeneration which his tendency to nervous illness at times of stress and crisis suggests was essential. Most of his creative work—the three Irish bills, and the budget planned in the autumn of 1873—was done at Hawarden, and he returned to London from the country the more eager and the more resourceful politically.

Although Gladstone was throughout these years an intensely active Prime Minister—much more so than Disraeli in the Government which succeeded him—it should not be thought that his energies were wholly devoted to the process and policy-making of Government. As a reading of his daily journal shows, Gladstone organised his routine in such a way as to permit—in all but exceptional crises—a continuation of his habit of extensive reading in an eclectic range of subjects—from a biography of Schleiermacher,[2] through Trollope, Disraeli,[3] and George Eliot to a vast range of pamphlets, periodicals, and tracts, ecclesiastical, classical, and secular. His very demanding attendance at the Commons naturally reduced his reading during the Session, though even then it is rare for a day to pass without some record of reading outside government papers. But in the Recess and on Sundays, the level of reading differs little from that in previous volumes. The reading may be said to be rather more practically directed, in that much of it was intended to provide background information to governmental questions—for example, the first three months of 1869 not surprisingly find Gladstone deep in literature and ephemera on the Irish Church. But he also found time in those same months to read, *inter alia*, Bagehot on money, Baxter on taxation, Giffen's essay on his own finance, Matthew Arnold's *Culture and Anarchy*, Cobbett's *Reformation*, Sedgwick's 'charming book on Cowgill Chapel', Coleridge's *Life of Keble*, J. E. Morgan's 'Town life among the poorest', and the Duke of Argyll's *Primeval Man*,[4] as well as various works on the preparations for the Vatican Council. In those months we also find him correcting the proofs of *Juventus Mundi*, which was published in August 1869. An important example of Gladstone's reading influencing his views on policy is his study of works on Irish land in 1869, in particular his reading of George

---

[1] See above, v. l.   [2] See 22 Sept. 73.   [3] 18 May 70, 27 Feb. 74.
[4] 11 Feb. 69, 22 Jan. 69, 8 Jan. 69, 30 Mar. 69, 26 Mar. 69, 3-4 Feb. 69, 7 Feb. 69, 2 Mar. 69, 21 Mar. 69.

Campbell's pamphlet,[1] which fully bears out the importance which has been attached to it.[2]

As in previous volumes, Gladstone usually records his reading with, at the most, brief comment. From time to time letters give his views of books, as for example those on R. H. Dana's *Two Years before the Mast* and Matthew Arnold's *Culture and Anarchy*,[3] and his parliamentary speeches show a mind hardly ever at a loss for a fact or a reference. Gladstone had nothing of the contemporary trend which he discerned and roundly condemned in a speech at Liverpool College in December 1872—a trend towards 'a scepticism in the public mind, of old as well as young, respecting the value of learning and of culture, and a consequent slackness in seeking their attainment'.[4] This speech, which caused much controversy, including a public exchange with Herbert Spencer,[5] offers an interesting insight into the conclusions Gladstone was drawing from his eclectic gleanings from the contemporary scene, for in it he adumbrated, at a very early stage, what was to become in the hands of others a general critique of Britain's relative economic and cultural decline:

> In the ulterior prosecution of almost any branch of inquiry, it is to Germany and to the works of Germans that the British student must look for assistance . . . a far greater number of her educated class are really in earnest about their education; and they have not yet learned, as we, I fear, have learned, to undervalue, or even to despise, in a great measure, simplicity of life.

Gladstone was alarmed at the 'corroding pest of idleness—that special temptation to a wealthy country'. Yet admire German achievement as he did, he deplored its most prominent ideological trend even more, denouncing the materialism of D. F. Strauss' *The old faith and the new*[6] and with it both those in England who promulgated such opinions theologically, and those who—almost all of them in his own Party—argued for secularism in education. His reflections on the spirit of the age thus showed alarm at the corrosive consequences of wealth, and fear that the 'reconciliation between Christianity and the conditions of modern thought, modern life and modern society' which it had been his life's mission to accomplish,[7] might after all be a sham reconciliation dependent on the surrender of traditional Christianity to scientific materialism. Gladstone's hopes for the Christian future rested first on ecumenism between the apostolic churches, Anglicans, Roman Catholics and Orthodox (with the Non-

---

[1] 11 Aug. 69. [2] Steele, *Irish Land*, 104ff.
[3] 13 Jan. 71; 30 Mar. 69, 7 June 70.
[4] 21 Dec. 72; *The Times*, 23 December 1872. [5] 3 and 13 Nov. 73n.
[6] 1 Dec. 72. [7] To Manning, 16 November 1869, Purcell, ii. 408.

conformists following in an ill-defined theological relationship)—an ecumenism he worked to promote even when Prime Minister[1] and which he now saw failing—and second, on the refutation of ideas of the Straussian sort through the methodology of Joseph Butler, the eighteenth-century Anglican divine and philosopher, whose *'method of handling . . .* is the only one known to me that is fitted to guide life, and thought bearing upon life, in the face of the nineteenth century'.[2] The Vatican Council set the first back by a century, and the onward progress of secular Darwinism rendered victory over the second at best a very long haul.

IX

Correspondence, relaxation, reading, the stress of public life, religion, the conversion of prostitutes, all come together in Gladstone's relationship with Laura Thistlethwayte, the evangelical ex-courtesan. Mrs. Thistlethwayte has already figured quite prominently in the previous volume of these diaries, and some details about her have already been given in volume V, pages lxi–lxv. She had risen from a past at best murky by her relationship with Palmerston's Colonial Secretary, Gladstone's colleague and life-long friend, the fifth Duke of Newcastle.[3] Gladstone had met her in 1865, dined at her house and begun an intermittent correspondence, mostly on religious topics.

However, Gladstone told her in November 1869, 'I have only known you in an inner sense within the last two months.'[4] This intimacy had developed as a result of the manuscript of Mrs. Thistlethwayte's autobiography being sent in instalments to the Prime Minister, and the intensity of his reaction to it. Perhaps anticipating the excitement and quantity of correspondence that a serialised version was likely to cause him, Gladstone requested it 'all at once'—but it was sent in at least twenty-three batches during September and October 1869.

The manuscript has, unfortunately, not survived: the reader can reconstruct something of its quality from Gladstone's comments upon it in the letters quoted in the Appendix. It was accompanied by an outpouring of undated letters written on exotic paper with Eastern symbols in a vast and illegible hand; the scent on the paper still wafts, at least metaphorically, upwards to the reader. The manuscript and letters taken together 'astonished' and tantalised Gladstone: 'duty and evil temptation are there before me, on the right and left'.[5] He was clearly deeply attracted to her, and when a joke

---

[1] See the visit of Abp. Lykourgos to Hawarden, 10 Jan. 70.   [2] 24 Dec. 72.
[3] Her relationship with Newcastle's family clearly continued after his death, for her will left all her effects to Lord Edward Pelham Clinton, Newcastle's second son.
[4] Appendix in Volume VIII, 1 Nov. 69.   [5] 25 and 28 Oct. 69.

in one of his letters was taken as a slight, he was mortified and profoundly disturbed until all was set right.[1]

This tiff—almost a lover's tiff—on paper brought the affair to a
crisis. Laura Thistlethwayte wrote 'a great, deep, weighty word' which
Gladstone in his reply could not bring himself to repeat—apparently
'love'[2]—and she suggested they burn their letters to each other. Gladstone drew back: was she sure the word should be used?—burning
was 'dangerous. It removes a bridle: it encourages levity in thought.'[3]
On the other hand, he admitted she had 'got within my guard'[4]—with
Gladstone something achieved perhaps only by his wife and, years
before, Arthur Hallam and James Hope.

The questions her exotic tale raised, the state of her soul, and the
relationship between them could only be resolved by a lengthy meet-
ing. This took place over a weekend at the Thistlethwaytes' house at
Boveridge whither went Gladstone and Arthur Kinnaird, the Whig
M.P. who with Newcastle had introduced the couple. At Boveridge
'Mrs. Th. came to my rooms aft[ernoon] and at night'.[5]

After this meeting, the affair—for such it must be called—reached
a more balanced state. Letters and meetings, especially the former—
sent in specially marked envelopes to avoid the private secretaries—
continued to be frequent, but without the extreme excitement and
intensity of the months of October to December 1869.

Much of this correspondence reflects the curious ambivalence of
the religious mind. Gladstone's stated urgings were all towards
morality. He accepted Laura Thistlethwayte's protestations of virtue
and defended her against traducers. He urged her towards restoring
relations of every sort with her husband, and suggested to her that
her 'vocation' should be to 'act upon the bitter wintry frosts which
originally cast your wifehood in a mould of ice'.[6] Yet Gladstone's
relationship with her was clearly fraught with danger for him, as is
shown in his correspondence with her and by his frequent use of 'X'
(the sign usually used after a morally dangerous meeting with a prosti-
tute) as a comment on his meetings with her. That willingness to be
tempted, to 'court evil'[7] while doing good, which had played so important a part in his early rescue work, that feeling that he must
expose his soul and body to spiritual danger, clearly in the case of
Laura Thistlethwayte led Gladstone on, for a time, to a point not far
short of infatuation.

However, that point, and the reader will have to locate it for himself, *was* short of infatuation. Gladstone did not use 'the weighty

[1] 20 Oct. 69 and Appendix 19–22 Oct. 69.   [2] Appendix, 27 Oct. 69.
[3] Appendix, 23 Oct. 69.   [4] Ibid., 25 Oct. 69.   [5] 11 Dec. 69.
[6] Appendix, 6 Jan. 70.   [7] 19 July 48.

word' back to Laura Thistlethwayte, and despite all, he maintained some sort of balance.

The affair was, like Gladstone's work with prostitutes, carried on in the full knowledge of the political elite, amongst whom Laura Thistlethwayte was notorious. It occurred at the height of the Cabinet bargaining about the contents of the Irish Land Bill, and of Tory speculation about the balance of power within the Cabinet. The fifteenth Earl of Derby noted in his journal on 11 December 1869:

> Strange story of Gladstone frequenting the company of a Mrs. Thistlethwaite, a kept woman in her youth, who induced a foolish person with a large fortune to marry her. She has since her marriage taken to religion, and preaches or lectures. This, with her beauty, is the attraction to G and it is characteristic of him to be indifferent to scandal. But I can scarcely believe the report that he is going to pass a week with her and her husband at their country house—she not being visited or received in society.[1]

The episode thus added to Gladstone's reputation amongst leading Whigs and Tories for eccentricity and 'madness'[2] and contributed to their underestimation of his self-control and resilience.

Generosity and naivety characterised Gladstone's behaviour. He persistently saw the best—'a sheep or a lamb rather, that had been astray . . . and that had come back to the Shepherd's Fold'[3]—where others had seen mere chicanery, and he largely ignored the dangers to himself, both as to the effect all this might have on his relationship with Catherine Gladstone, and as to the public. He several times reassured Laura Thistlethwayte about the security arrangements for safeguarding her letters and manuscript—'Were it to fall into the hands of some rogue'[4]—but he assumed security and confidentiality on her part.

His confidence was justified. Mrs. Thistlethwayte seems to have made little attempt to capitalise on her new respectability, save to send Gladstone frequent invitations to dinner, which were quite regularly accepted, and she seems to have had few political ambitions, unlike Olga Novikoff, 'the M.P. for Russia', who emerges in 1873 as something of an alternative to Mrs. Thistlethwayte as a female

---

[1] J. Vincent, ed., *Disraeli, Derby and the Conservative Party* (1978), 346.

[2] Carnarvon had earlier reached this view: 'Gladstone seems to be going out of his mind. Northcote has just told me that Gladstone's last passion is Mrs Thistlethwaite. He goes to dinner with her and she in return in her preachments to her congregation exhorts them to put up their prayers on behalf of Mr G's reform bill'; Carnarvon diary, 9 June 1866, Add MS 60896, f. 24; I am much obliged to Mr. Mark Curthoys for this reference.

[3] Appendix, 19 Oct. 69. Laura Thistlethwayte's feelings are hard to determine from the jumbled state of her letters to Gladstone—several hundred, undated and virtually unsortable—but they seem to be genuine enough: 'Oh how madly I love', she docketed Gladstone's letter of 16 March 1871.

[4] Ibid., 25 Oct. 69.

correspondent outside the family, though the intensity of the relationship is in no sense comparable.[1]

'Mrs. Th's' non-political nature may have been part of her appeal (though her Irish origins seem to have played some part in conditioning the tone of Gladstone's expressions about Ireland during the preparation of the Land Act[2]), but her religiosity, constant expressions of suffering and pathetic concern with respectability would seem, in addition to her ' "signal soul clad in a beautiful body" '[3] to have aroused in Gladstone a powerful fellow-feeling and sympathy. Her youthful sufferings had coincided with his great crisis of 1850-1, his 'saddest' year which 'well nigh tore me to pieces'—the height of his self-flagellation at the time of the Gorham Judgement, the apostasy of Manning and James Hope, and the crisis of his rescue work.[4] With Laura Thistlethwayte in the 1870s he felt he could share, at least in retrospect, something of the crisis of the Victorian soul which his wife's serenity could not begin to comprehend: that Tennysonian[5] mixture of religion, sex, and patriotism, each element both stimulating and moderating the others to produce a soul in great tension but in balance—a mixture whose balance Gladstone only just maintained, and which conditioned all his public and private actions and thoughts. The pregnant image of his repeated phrase, 'my country is my first wife' was no convenient or casual platitude;[6] it reflected the emotional and in some ways sexual involvement of Gladstone and his nation.[7]

The Thistlethwayte affair seems to have siphoned off a good deal of the nervous energy which usually accompanied Gladstone's work with prostitutes. This certainly continued regularly while he was Prime Minister, and several of his encounters are marked by the sign 'X', denoting temptation on his part. But the sign is also used after some of his meetings with Mrs. Thistlethwayte, a fact which in itself testified to the ambiguity of her position in Gladstone's mind. Was she friend, or rescue case? When she left for Egypt on doctor's advice in 1872, he noted in his diary: 'It is well for me that she goes.'[8] She was not away for long, and no rescue case took her place as the focal point of Gladstone's extra-marital fixation.

Laura Thistlethwayte was not Gladstone's mistress in the physical sense—the reader may here be reminded of Gladstone's solemn

[1] 14 Feb. 73.   [2] Appendix, 2 Dec. 69.
[3] Ibid., 22 Apr. 70.   [4] See above, iii. xlviff.
[5] Gladstone gave Mrs. Thistlethwayte his annotated copy of Tennyson; see also the Tennyson quotation at 12 Dec. 69, and above, v. lxiv.
[6] Appendix, 22 Oct. 69.
[7] I have tried to develop this theme in Matthew, 'Vaticanism'.
[8] 11 Feb. 72; see 27 Jan. 72.

declaration in 1896 that he had 'never been guilty of the act which is known as that of infidelity to the marriage bed'.[1] But she fulfilled the other functions of that office.

'It embarrasses' was Gladstone's comment on her 'extraordinary claim for sympathy';[2] the reader may well feel the same about the correspondence which Gladstone's children, with a commendable sense of responsibility to posterity, decided not to destroy, but to preserve, side-by-side with their father's daily journal.

Not surprisingly, rescue work exposed Gladstone to danger: there is at least one suggestion reaching the stage of discussion with solicitors of what seems to be a paternity suit—'a "plant" as it is called'—though nothing came of it.[3]

What Catherine Gladstone thought of the Thistlethwayte affair, of the rescue work in this period, or of the meeting with the solicitors can only be guessed at. Gladstone told Freshfield, the solicitor, that his wife 'was wiser than I & said "You are too credulous" '.[4] She may well have thought the same about her husband's relationship with Mrs. Thistlethwayte. Self-reliant though Catherine Gladstone was, it is hard to believe that she was not wounded—though she may have become inured.

Certainly the family life of the Gladstones continued happy, though the closeness of the family was necessarily diminished by the dispersal of the children—Henry Neville to India,[5] Herbert to University College, Oxford, and a Third in Mods, Agnes to be married.[6] But Willy worked closely and now more easily with his father politically, and Stephen became rector of Hawarden on the death of Henry Glynne, Catherine Gladstone's brother.

Much the saddest family event of these years was the death of Sir Stephen Glynne, the other brother, the shy bachelor whose gentle antiquarianism had charmed away alarm at his financial incompetence. His funeral was a great Hawarden occasion, honoured with a full description in the diary.[7] The mourning was intertwined in classic Gladstonian and Victorian fashion with the resettlement of the estate, as Gladstone gave his children 'a sketch of the romance, for such it is, of the financial history',[8] and Willy entered into an inheritance he can hardly have felt was his own.

Stephen Glynne's death also provoked intense conversation on the future between the diarist and his wife: 'the future seemed to clear a little before her. But how greedy I am—not satisfied with the last 22 years, or the last 35!'[9] Immediately after this, the death of his

---

[1] See above, vol. iii. xlvi–xlvii, and 7 Dec. 96.   [2] 27 Feb. 70.
[3] 14 June 73.   [4] Ibid.   [5] 2 Dec. 74.   [6] 27 Dec. 73.
[7] 24 June 74.   [8] 18 June 74.   [9] 26 June 74.

niece Ida, Sir Thomas Gladstone's daughter, required a visit to Fasque, the family house in Kincardineshire, and brought about something of a reconciliation between William and his fiercely Tory elder brother. For William Gladstone it was understandably a nostalgic occasion, this visit to his father's house with its 'old and still dear details'. Ida's coffin was placed in the family vault next to that of his cherished daughter Jessy, and Gladstone's thoughts returned, as so often, to the dreadful, shattering year of 1850-1.[1]

X

Defeat in the general election in January 1874 and retirement from active leadership of his Party placed Gladstone in an unwonted situation. For nearly fifteen years, since 1859, he had been in office or expecting imminently to be in office. Now he was, at his own insistence as well as that of the electorate, responsible largely if not solely to himself. Difficulties at once arose. The first of these was money. 'Expulsion from office' brought to a point of crisis Gladstone's personal finances. The salary of £5000 which he drew as First Lord of the Treasury (he had received the same amount as Chancellor from 1859 to 1866) had provided the chief element of the income necessary for his day-to-day living. With this assured, he had been able to make substantial capital purchases while in public office by borrowing, usually from his bankers, S. Scotts. In terms of his total assets, he was a wealthy man. At the end of his period of office, his accounts stood thus:[2]

Class I	Property in Hawarden Parish	153,000
	Seaforth Estate	37,000
	Lease of 11 Carlton House Terrace	23,500
	Mortgage on Trinity College	2,500
	Outstanding rents etc.	4,000
		220,000
Class II	£8000 5% Preference Metropolitan District Railway at £62½	5,000
	£57,500 Ordinary Metropolitan District Railway at £30	17,000
	£5000 Philadelphia & Reading Mortgage Bonds	5,000
		247,000
Class III	Furniture, books, porcelain etc.	22,100
		£269,100

[1] 30 June 74; he visited Fasque briefly in 1869, see 25 Sept. 69; his brother's Toryism entered into consideration when Gladstone was offered the Kincardineshire seat, see 20 Nov. 72.
[2] Taken from 'Rough Book B', Hawn P.

Against these assets were to be counted debts of £39,000, which included mortgages on 11 Carlton House Terrace (£4,500), on the 'Chester block' Saltney purchase at Hawarden (£9,000), the Aston estate purchase (£12,000),[1] and the loss by Robertson Gladstone of about £6000 of his brother William's share of the Seaforth estate near Liverpool.[2] The Aston Hall purchase, which was made in October 1869 for £57,000,[3] contained two collieries, and was a substantial addition to the Hawarden estate, but it only produced £2069/10/1½ net income in 1873.[4] The net income on Gladstone's Flintshire estates for 1873 was £2695/8/5 (gross £5703/18/8), a return on his assets there of two per cent.

Gladstone's purchases of land in Flintshire were less risky than his holdings of railway stocks and shares. As the above table shows, he was heavily, and in terms of his portfolio, narrowly involved in the Metropolitan District Railway. He had held shares in it for some time, but had increased his holdings at the end of the 1860s, and in 1869, after selling some of its stock, he bought £10,000 more.[5] Unfortunately for him, the company fell into difficulties. Its dividend was passed and its shares fell. It is hard to calculate from Gladstone's records exactly what his losses on this railway were, but they appear to amount to about 50% on about £50,000.[6]

Gladstone's activities in the stock market, both as Chancellor and Prime Minister, were therefore, over a period of a decade, considerable, and known to be so. As mentioned above, he had no qualms about buying Consols when they fell to a favourable 90 when Bismarck invaded France. The *Chester Chronicle* found it necessary to point out that this was not money-making at the public expense and that 'the world of gossip . . . ringing with stories of Mr. Gladstone's pecuniary difficulties' was proved wrong.[7] The *Chronicle*'s report referred to the Aston Hall purchase, but gossip of this sort about Gladstone's share purchases seems to have been quite widely circulated, encouraged, apparently, surprisingly, unjustifiably, and perhaps for personal political ends, by his own stockbroker, James Watson, Lord Provost of Glasgow, whom he knighted in 1874. Lord Derby noted in his diary: 'In singular confirmation of the stories we had heard at Minard, the Lord Provost [i.e. Watson the stockbroker] told Pender, who repeated it to me not an hour afterward, that the

---

[1] Schedule of Account, 1873, Hawn P.   [2] 18 Apr. 74.
[3] 23 Oct. 69.   [4] Schedule of Account, 1873, Hawn P.
[5] On 15 March, at 46¼; Bank Book for 1869, Hawn P. On 10 July 1869 he borrowed £21,000 from Scotts. Ibid.
[6] The Bank Books from 1873–80 are missing in Hawn P; the Metropolitan shares were mostly sold off by 1875.
[7] *Chester Chronicle*, 4 December 1869.

Premier had been very active in stock exchange speculations, and had lately employed him (Watson). Very strange—but what motive had he to invent the story if not true?'[1] This sort of story was a clear exaggeration, and represented that expectation of hyperbole which Gladstone already encouraged among Tories. Gladstone had not been 'very active'; he had made purchases in the Metropolitan District Railway Company over a period of several years which had not paid off. He was at no time in financial difficulty and, with money as cheap as it was in 1869-72, short-term borrowing backed by the sort of assets Gladstone commanded was in no way imprudent.

None the less, Gladstone was short of ready cash, and in 1872 he drew the state of affairs to his wife's attention: 'why and how more pinched'.[2] In 1873 he anticipated having to give up his house in Carlton House Terrace 'at or about the expiry of the present Government'.[3] When his salary ended in February 1874, his immediate position became dramatically worse. He calculated in June 1874 that after 'necessary allowances' for his wife and five of his children, and his usual charitable donations, he had only £1000 'for all general expenditure whatsoever'.[4] The death of his brother-in-law Sir Stephen Glynne, the owner of Hawarden, just after these calculations were made,[5] made little difference for by the arrangement of 1865 the Glynne estates went to Willy Gladstone and anyway produced little net income. The way was thus pointed to the sale of 11 Carlton House Terrace and of some of his art collections as the best means of raising his income, and preparations were made in the last months of 1874 for the sales of these assets in 1875.

The second difficulty about the life of 'mental repose'[6] which Gladstone intended for himself was that, still an M.P., his activities were necessarily subject to persistent scrutiny. Thus his support for the manager of the Aston Hall Colliery in opposing attempts by the miners to impose a closed shop had national as well as local implications: even the life of the country squire exposed him to national attention and controversy.[7]

The Aston Hall controversy was symptomatic of the sort of class tension which Liberalism could never avoid at the constituency level, however integrative its national ideology aspired to be. But far more

---

[1] Derby's journal, 25 September 1872; see also 22 September 1872; I am much obliged to Professor John Vincent for this quotation. Watson's implication that his employment by Gladstone was unusual was quite misleading—they had been in regular correspondence and dealings since 1851. Nothing in the summer of 1872 in the Hawarden account books seems to bear out Watson's tale; there were no changes in the M.D.R. holdings; £3,600 Pennsylvanian and Reading stock was bought.

[2] 2 Sept. 72.   [3] 13 Dec. 73.   [4] 1 June 74.
[5] 17-24 June 74.   [6] 29 Dec. 74.   [7] 9-10 June 74.

dramatically national in implication were to be the religious thoughts which Gladstone retired to Hawarden to contemplate.

Gladstone's religion had always been a complex and indivisible blend of the national and the personal. Intense personal experience related in his personality intimately and inseparably to intense feeling about 'National Religion'. A similar synchronous purpose pervaded his study of Homer which was always justified in terms of his religious view of world history rather than by antiquarianism. Thus his contemplation in his retirement of things of the spirit necessarily led rapidly to public involvement in ecclesiastical controversy. He found both the Anglican Church and Christian Europe threatened—the first by Archbishop Tait, Disraeli, and the anti-ritualists in both parties, and the second by the Papacy. Partly as a reward to what had been a powerful element in their support in the elections, the Conservatives made ecclesiastical bills—the Public Worship Regulation Bill for England and Wales and the Church Patronage Bill for Scotland—the first chief legislative business for their large majority. In a manner reminiscent of his opposition to Palmerston's Divorce Bill in 1857, Gladstone moved Resolutions intended to transform the Public Worship Regulation Bill, and had to withdraw them a week later.[1] His ill-temper shows even through the flatness of the columns of Hansard. But whereas in 1857 he had acted on his own with a few friends to maintain the 'Catholic' position, in 1874 he was still nominally leader of the Liberal Party, which contained a significant body of opinion, exemplified by Sir William Harcourt, hostile to 'Puseyism' and in favour of the bill. The isolation of the Tractarian Liberals within the Party evident in the controversy over education during the Government thus became confirmed in opposition.

The problem of the Vatican Council, and the issues of civil liberty and allegiance which it seemed to raise, had, as has been shown earlier in this introduction, greatly exercised Gladstone's administration, both in its foreign and in its British policy. For Gladstone there was an added element—his longstanding and intense ambivalence about Roman Catholicism. He was drawn by its internationalism and majestic tradition, but repelled by what he saw as its authoritarianism, antiliberalism, and refusal to acknowledge a distinction between secular, civil allegiance on the one hand, and spiritual obedience on the other. 'Temporal power' was the phrase by which Gladstone summed up these deficiencies; he saw the Vatican Decrees of 1870 as the climax of an attempt by the Papacy to regain by ultramontane authoritarianism what it had lost to nationalism. The apostasy of his

---

[1] 9–16 July 74. He also powerfully opposed the Scottish Patronage Bill, but in this he had a substantial part of the Liberal Party with him.

sister in 1845 and of several of his friends in 1851 had provoked the most intense crisis of his life, a disturbance in the balance between religion, sex, and patriotism causing a reaction in all three elements of his personality. Recollecting this, he told Samuel Wilberforce on the occasion of the apostasy of his brother Robert Wilberforce:

> For could I, with reference to my own precious children, think that one of them might possibly live to strike, though in sincerity and thinking he did God service, such a blow, how far rather would I that he had never been born.[1]

It was not merely prudential politics, important though those certainly were, which caused Gladstone to make, on the occasion of her conversion to Roman Catholicism, a 'termination of any literary relations' between himself and his cousin, Mrs. Bennett, his assistant when he translated Farini's *Lo Stato Romano*.[2] Gladstone's public role had involved him in attempts to frustrate the success of the Infallibilists, led by Manning; his private religious contacts had led to links with the Old Catholic movement through his old friend J. J. I. von Döllinger, now excommunicated for his opposition to the decisions of the 1870 Council. Just after leaving office, he dropped a hint that public expostulation might be on the way.[3]

Hostility to developments in both Anglicanism and Roman Catholicism were expressed in Gladstone's signed article, 'Ritualism and Ritual', published in the *Contemporary Review*, and begun in August 1874 when the passing of the Public Worship Regulation Bill was completed.[4] Alarmed by the barriers to Catholic ecumenicalism being erected by both sides, disturbed by the conversion to Roman Catholicism of Lord Ripon, his recent Cabinet colleague,[5] moved by Charlotte Yonge's life of the Tractarian bishop J. C. Patteson which he was reviewing,[6] impressed by the arguments and conferences of the Old Catholics,[7] and stimulated by the appeals for help from Döllinger, whom he was visiting in Munich, Gladstone inserted into the proofs of his article on ritualism a fierce denunciation of British Roman Catholics for their supine reaction to the Vatican Decrees.[8] After further consideration of the Old Catholic position, and with initial encouragement from the anti-Infallibilist Lord Acton, Gladstone 'Wrote on the Papal questions',[9] writing which blossomed into his pamphlet *The Vatican Decrees in their bearing on civil allegiance: a political expostulation*, published on 7 November 1874. Acton,

[1] To S. Wilberforce, 17 October 1854, Wilberforce MS. d. 36, f. 25; see Matthew, 'Vaticanism', 423.

[2] To Mrs. Bennett, 8 June 71.   [3] To Odo Russell, 3 Mar. 74.

[4] 2, 19 Aug. 74.   [5] 21 Aug. 74.   [6] 2, 26 Aug., 19 Sept. 74.

[7] 19, 30 Sept. 74.   [8] 13 Sept. 74.   [9] 20 Oct. 74.

Ambrose Phillipps de Lisle, and Arthur Gordon who were at Hawarden during its preparation were alarmed by its intemperance: 'They all show me that I must act mainly for myself.'[1]

Act for himself Gladstone certainly did. The pamphlet was a remarkable blend of political theory, Protestant anti-Popery and Tractarian *angst*. Beneath the historical and ecclesiastical argument, important in itself and in its political implications, lay a profound sense of anger and betrayal—anger with the 'direct influence' of the Irish Roman Catholic bishops, anger with the Papacy from which much had never been expected, betrayal by Manning who should have known better, and by Newman who should have done more.[2]

The Vatican Decrees showed Gladstone's extraordinary capacity to change direction. He had gone out of office at the start of 1874 after a spirited initiative in national finance; he ended the year as the protagonist of a vast controversy on Church and State whose pamphlets poured as voluminously from presses in America and Europe as they did from those in Britain. But he also confirmed the political direction which he had taken after the defeat of the general election, for on the last day of 1874 he prepared for transmission his letters to Granville resigning as leader of the Liberal Party. The Vatican controversy showed Gladstone's inability to leave the world of affairs; his resignation of even the title of party leader showed his refusal to accept that world's conventional limitations.

The day before revising his letters of resignation, Gladstone finished *Middlemarch*: 'It is an extraordinary, to me a very jarring book.' 'Every limit is a beginning as well as an ending' remarks George Eliot in her 'Finale', and such a 'limit' was 1874 for Gladstone. What George Eliot called 'the home epic—the gradual conquest or irremediable loss of that complete union which makes the advancing years a climax, and age the harvest of sweet memories in common' was for Gladstone an epic written on a national as well as a domestic scale. From his country, his 'first wife', he found himself estranged, rejected by the political nation, at odds with most of the Protestant element of his own Party on Anglican religion and education, and with almost all the Roman Catholic element on the Papacy. Gladstone's career was an extraordinary public epic, and 1874 was an important caesura in it. But that it was a caesura before a long finale and not a conclusion, was not, and could not be, apparent to Gladstone.

---

[1] 30 Oct. 74. Gladstone wrote to Granville, who was abroad, only after the MS went to press; Ramm I, ii. 458.

[2] Much the same sense is expressed in more ecclesiatical form in the three parts of E. B. Pusey's *Eirenicon* (1865–70).

[VOLUME XXVII.] [1]

[The inside front cover contains:—]

Private.

(NO. 27.)

Jan. 1. 69–Sept 20/70.

The sensual and the dark rebel in vain
Slaves by their own compulsion.
S.T.C. [2]

[On a sheet of thin paper folded into 4 and attached to the inside front cover:—]

Hagley.

Frid. Jan. One 1869. Circumcision

Church at 10.30. WHL[yttelton] preached an excellent Sermon. Wrote to Scotts—Bishop of Moray—Lord Spencer—Archdn Churton—Lord Granville—Chancr of Exchr—Mr Headlam—Mr G. Leeman—Ld Amberley—Mr J. Murray—Chancr of Exchr—Mr Maguire —C.A. Wood—Earl Russell—and minutes. Cutting at an *enormous* poplar in the afternoon. Saw the Misses Rogers. Read Canadian Synod on Ritualism. [3] Worked a little on Homer. A merry & large dinner party as usual.

2. Sat. [*Hawarden*]

Wrote to Sir R. Phillimore—Ld Clarendon—Mr Ellice—Mr H.A. Bruce—Rev. R.S. Hunt—Earl Spencer—and minutes. Saw Ld F. Cavendish respecting Representation—Ld L. on Church & other matters. Off at 2.30—Hawarden at 8. Unpacking & arranging. Worked 'some' on Homer. [4] Read [blank].

---

[1] Lambeth MS 1441.
[2] From S. T. *Coleridge's retraction of radicalism in 'France: an ode' (1798).
[3] *The debates on ritualism* (1868).
[4] Preparing *Juventus Mundi* for the printer; see 11 July 67n.

3. 3. S.aft Circ.

Church 11 AM & H.C.—also 6½ P.M. Wrote to Sir J.K. Shuttleworth
—Abp of Canterbury—Mr Hamilton—Archdn Stopford—The
Speaker—Att.Gen for Ireland—Mr Glyn—Earl de Grey—and
minutes. Read Bahamas Disestablishment![1]—Hawkins's Sermon[2]—
Wray on the Bishops Call[3]—Walker's Eirenicon[4]—Union Review[5]
—& other tracts.

4. M.

Church 8¼ A.M. Wrote to Earl Spencer—the Duke of Sutherland—
Ald.Salomons—Sir G.F. Lewis—Rev R W Church—Mr C.C. Prance[6]
—Mr A.E. West—and minutes. Tel. to F.O. Unpacked & stowed Litter,
a precious record. Much rearrangement in Library. Worked a little on
Homer. Read Smith's Account of Surveying[7]—Mr Lawes on Wheat[8]
—Mr Seymour on Synods.[9] Saw Mr Chamberlain.[10]

5. Tu.

Ch. 8½ A.M. Wrote to Dean of Worcester—Rev.Dr Miller—Sir H.
Holland—Rev Presb.Moderator[11]—Ld de Grey—Bp of Salisbury
—The Speaker—J. Watson & Smith—Ld de Grey—Mr G.G. Glyn
—and minutes. Spent the morning on arranging papers relating to
my private affairs, examining securities, and drawing up the annual
sketch of my affairs. Read Modern Ireland[12]—Ffoulkes to Manning.[13] Worked a little on Homer—late at night—as before.

6. Wed. Epiph.

Ch.11 A.M.: C.s birthday. May God bless her, as He has blest her.
Wrote to The Lord Chancellor—Sir R. Phillimore—The Queen—

---

[1] On disestablishment and disendowment there: a precedent for Ireland.
[2] E. *Hawkins, 'Our debts to Caesar and to God' (1868).
[3] C. Wray, 'The Bishop's call to conformity' (1869).
[4] C. Walker, *Pax super Israel. An Irenicon* (1867).
[5] *Union Review*, vii. (January–December 1869).
[6] Courtenay Connell Prance, solicitor in Evesham, had sent his sonnet, 'Gladstone in 1868'; Add MS 44418, f. 3.
[7] J. A. Smith, *A treatise on land surveying in theory and practice* (1869).
[8] J. B. *Lawes, *On the home produce, imports, and consumption of wheat* (1868).
[9] R. Seymour, 'Diocesan Synods' (1867).
[10] Frederick Townshend Chamberlain, curate at Hawarden 1865–73.
[11] Charles L. Morell; copy in Add MS 44418, f. 23.
[12] See 17 Nov. 68.
[13] E. S. Ffoulkes, 'The Church's Creed or the Crown's Creed? A letter to Archbishop Manning' (1869).

Lord Clarendon——Mr Gurdon——Archbp of Canterby——Ld Spencer
——Lord Granville——Mr Roundell[1]——Lord Caithness——Mr Bruce——
Lord Lurgan——Memoranda, & minutes. Worked a little on Homer.
Read Modern Ireland. Finished Ffoulkes's most damaging letter.

To H. A. BRUCE, home secretary, 6 January 1869.   Add MS 44537, f. 89.

It is desirable that there should be no unnecessary delay in our answer to the
Irish Bishops.[2] Will you therefore write or still better telegraph to the Irish
Attorney General for an answer upon the case at the earliest moment they can
contrive unless you see any objection.

I quite agree that you should proceed with the Ritual Commission forthwith.

To LORD CLARENDON, foreign secretary,   Clarendon MSS, c. 497.
6 January 1869.

No wonder that Lord Lyons should be puzzled about his terms when La
Valette spoke so much in the Paulo *post futurum*.[3] I suppose the verdict is not
to be stereotyped beforehand. I enclose a Mem.[4] with such observations as occur
to me: but not as laying much stress upon them.

However, I think that if Russia and Greece play their cards well they will
hitch the Conference into such a position as will bring out the soundness of your
original objection to it as leading too far.

And possibly you might supply a partial remedy if you could devise a paragraph,[5] which, while it gave credit to Turkey for a benevolent and unconciliatory
policy in some noted cases, and pointed out the enhancement of the obligations
to the suzerain thence morally arising, should at the same time convey distinctly
the expectation, by assuming it is not open to doubt, that the Porte will not
only continue in the faithful discharge of engagements but will seize every opportunity of *developing* local liberty under the shadow of its own rights and powers.

It seems so difficult to get off without something: & if this something *can* be
concocted, you are the man to mix the ingredients.

7. Th.

Ch. 8½ AM. Herbert's birthday: God bless his young life. Wrote to
Mr Weld Blundell——Sir C. Trevelyan——Mr West——General Menabrea
——Robn G.——Watson & Smith——G.G. Glyn——Att.Gen. for Ireland
——The Queen——Telegr.to Gen. Grey——Sir F. Rogers——Mr J.B.
Mozley——and minutes. Worked on Homer: revision. A little wood-
cutting. Read Modern Ireland. Dined at the Rectory. Saw Mr Burnett.

[1] C. S. Roundell (see 13 June 68), *Spencer's private secretary.   [2] See 7 Jan. 69n.
[3] Despatch by Lyons sent by Clarendon, 5 January; Add MS 44133, f. 152.
[4] Attached to letter, suggesting two rephrasings.
[5] Proposed paragraph (see Lyons to Clarendon, 8 January 1869, Clarendon MSS, c. 497)
rejected by Charles, marquis de la Valette, 1806-81; French foreign minister 1867-9, London ambassador 1869-70. See M. M. Robson, 'Clarendon and the Cretan question 1868-9',
H.J. iii. 38.

To E. SULLIVAN, Irish attorney general,   Add MS 44418, f. 78.
7 January 1869. 'Private'.

I quite agree with you about Archdeacon Stopford's suggestion.[1] It is quite
wrong. Moreover I am of opinion that any question of a Church influence in the
formation of the plan is a very grave one & I certainly shall do nothing to give
such influences a *locus standi* without much consideration. Still I doubt whether
your letter takes fully into view the great advantage of establishing the *nucleus*
of a party of concession, from among those who have hitherto resisted. *Suppose*
now for argument's sake, that some English Bishops—and among others the
Bishops of Oxford & Peterborough, should take that side at the present juncture
—& suppose that on your side [of] the Channel any similar movement takes
place, possibly in concert with them—I assure you I think it impossible to over-
rate the value of such a diversion with reference to that wh. is the most formidable stumbling block in our way, viz. the possibility that the H. of Lords might
be tempted, partly by the English County elections, partly by a possible development of *minor* schism in the Liberal body, when we come to adjunct details esp.
with ref. to R.C.s—to use its majority by rejecting the Bill. I feel certain I am
right in offering to see Stopford: whether to go further or not will depend (if he
comes)[2] upon *what* I see in him. My impression is that he is now in conference
with Bp. Magee. I am not at all displeased to see a pair of Church meetings held
by separate bodies. And I hope Whiteside will now take an active part: for then
we shall be safe. Please return to me the Archdeacon's letter & inclosure.

[P.S.] I cannot help considering the request of the Bishops to *us* to be allowed
to meet in Synod as a good sign. You will, I dare say, contrive to give an opinion
with dispatch as the question of *power* to permit it. They can never dream we
shld. let them meet except to consider terms & mode of transmission.

[The book proper begins:—]

1869

Hawarden Jan 8. Fr.

Wrote to The Lord Chancellor—Lord Granville—Mr H.A. Bruce—
Mr Hamilton—Ld St German's—Bp of Oxford—M. Bratiano—
Dean of Westmr—Dr Miller—Mr Fortescue—Gen. Grey—Lord
Southesk—Mr Helps—Mr Gurdon—Mr Reeve—Mr Hammond—
Ld Radstock—Telegr. to Mr H.—Sir C. Trevelyan—Mr G.O.
Trevelyan,[3] & minutes. *Two* evening messengers from London:
worked late. Felling a tree in aftn. Church 8½ A.M. Read Giffen on
Finance.[4]

[1] That the govt. should pass special Act to let the Irish clergy meet in Convocation before
disestablishment; see E. Sullivan to Gladstone, 6 January 1869, Add MS 44418, f. 15.
[2] See 14 Jan. 69.
[3] On his supposed rudeness about the Court; see Guedalla, *Q*, i. 150.
[4] Sir R. *Giffen, 'Mr. Gladstone's work in finance' (1869), reprinted in *Essays in finance*
(1880).

9. Sat.

Ch. 8½ A.M. Wrote to Duke of Cambridge—Lord Granville—Mr Glyn—Chancr of Exr—Mr Gurdon—Sec. Eccl.Commn—Mr Bruce —Mr Cardwell—Mr Ouvry—Sir F. Rogers—The Queen—and minutes. Worked on Homer. Long Homeric conversation with Edw. Talbot. We felled a tree in aftn. Read Karcher, Instit.d'Angleterre.[1]

10. 1 S.Epiph.

Ch 11 AM and 6½ P.M. Wrote to Sir C. Trevelyan—Bp of Chester— Mr Reeve—Mr Gurdon—Mr Bruce—Sir R. Palmer—Mr Goschen —The Queen (2)—Dr Moffatt—Chancr of Exr—Mr [M. H.] Foster —and many minutes. Read Archdn Stopford's Pamphlet[2]—Mr Cox's Lecture[3]—The Rector and his friends[4]—Milman's St Paul's.[5]

To R. LOWE, chancellor of the exchequer,   Add MS 44537, f. 93.
10 January 1869.

I have referred to my list of *remnants*; and I will begin with those that I tried in parliament and failed in:——1. Collection of taxes by Queen's officers instead of local officers. 2. Taxation of charities. 3. Bill for restraining, with a view to ultimately abolishing, the Circulation of the Notes of Private Banks. 4. Plan for bringing the Chancery and other judicial accounts under the control of parliament. Here I had a commission (on chancery accounts) but did not dare to go farther. What commonly happened, on cases of this kind, in my time, was as follows. The opposition waited for a development of discontent and resistance among some small fraction of Liberal members. When this was compact in itself, or was at all stimulated by constituencies, they sent out habitually strong party whips; and either beat me, or forced me to withdraw in order to avoid beating, or exposing our men to local disadvantage. This game, I hope, will not be quite so easy now.

The following are subjects which I was not able to take in hand:—
1. Abolition of the remaining duty upon corn; an exceeding strong case. 2. I should be much disposed to abolish the Tea Licences as greatly restrictive of the consumption of a dutiable and useful commodity. I modified them; but am not sure that this was enough. The B.I.R. could throw light on this subject. 3. The probate duty calls, I fear, loudly for change; but I wanted either time or courage to take it in hand. 4. The remaining conveyance duties, apart from railways, I always considered as marked for extinction. On this subject Mr. Ayrton has rather decided antecedents. 5. The fire insurance duty is sure to be further assailed. Though not as bad (relatively to other taxes) as is supposed, it is bad enough to be very hard to defend in an adverse House; and this is one of the questions on which it is not likely that the opposition will help to see fair play.

[1] T. Karcher, *Études sur les institutions politiques et sociales de l'Angleterre* (1867).
[2] E. A. Stopford, 'To clergy and laity' (1868); on disestablishment.
[3] S. *Cox, 'The quest of the chief good' (1868).   [4] See 13 Dec. 68.
[5] H. H. *Milman, *Annals of St Paul's Cathedral* (1868).

The promises that liberal reduction will lead to recovery of anything like the old or previous revenue have always been confidently pressed by irresponsible men, and are in my opinion illusory. The tax is a tax on property: and, as we have too few of these rather than too many, what would seem desirable is to commute it; leaving no more than a penny stamp on the policy. This might perhaps be done, if it were made part of a large Budget. 6. The income-tax at 6d., I suppose, presents a forward claim. 7. The commutation of malt duty for beer duty must always, I presume, be spoken of with respect; but the working objections to it have thus far been found too hard to deal with.

There is always room in detail for amendments of stamp duties, but the great case as among them is the probate. They are of a class which, without any legal knowledge, I found very hard to work through the House of Commons. I do not look upon the Act of 1844, as the *end* of legislation in currency; but this subject is a big one. Scotch and Irish notes would be hard to deal with until the English case is disposed of. I forget whether we have abolished the last of the restrictions on newspapers. If not, they deserve to be taken in hand, according to me. I have always wished to equalize the outgoings of the exchequer as much as possible over the several weeks of the year. Few incomes admit of this advantage in the same degree as the public income. It would make our 'account' much more valuable to our bankers; therefore to us.

These, I think, were the main matters which lay more or less in perspective before me. I must add that I am strongly in favour of paying off the national debt, not only by annual surpluses, but by terminable annuities *sold to the national debt commissioners for securities held by them against deposit monies.* The opponents of this plan were Mr. Hubbard and Mr. Laing. I am satisfied that neither of them had taken the trouble, and it requires some trouble, to understand it. I admit them to be no mean authorities. Terminable annuities sold to others than yourself are quite another matter. I got into the law some power of this kind over post office savings bank monies to be exercised by the chancellor of the exchequer from time to time.

This is all I need trouble you with, and I have endeavoured to keep clear of all idiosyncratic propositions as much as in me lies. Of course such a letter calls for no answer. As this legacy opinion to you takes the form of a donation *inter vivos* it will, I hope, escape duty.[1]

11. M.

Ch. 8.30 A.M. Wrote to Archdeacon Stopford—Irish Att.Gen.—Mr Gurdon—Mr Fortescue—Mr Bright—Mr M'Combie—Watsons—Mr Salisbury—Mr [M. H.] Foster—The Lord Steward—Ld Russell—Ld Clarendon—Mr Leeman—Mr Cardwell—and minutes. Wrote Supplem. Memm on Irish Church.[2] Saw Mr Thompson. Conversation with Archdn Ffoulkes. We felled a large ash, quite ruined by delay. Read Modern Ireland. Worked on Homer.

[1] Part in Morley, ii. 650.
[2] Adding to that of 26 December 1868; Add MS 44757, ff. 23, 66.

To E. CARDWELL, war secretary, 11 January 1869.   PRO/30/48/6, f. 32.

I have read your most interesting letter[1] on the army with great pleasure. It is really like seeing a little daylight after all these years, & a return to reason from what has been everything except reason.

I am not well enough abreast of the facts as to the Volunteers to be able to form an opinion on that part of the plan which is a minor one. On the other hand I hope your retention of the Cadres does not *exclude* the consideration of what I for one consider a great reform (according to my scanty lights) namely reduction of the number of subalterns at any rate in the peace Establishment. But with these secondary observations I really have nothing to do but to say *ditto* to your letter.

Probably you may have a new set of difficulties when you come to consider the Staff but these it is needless to anticipate.

To LORD CLARENDON, foreign secretary,   Clarendon MSS, c. 497.
11 January 1869.

Your 'son'[2] is always most refreshing, and I make a visit to Rome every time that I read one of his letters. But the atmosphere of Antonelli's room stifles me. Every question, Turco-Greek, Italo-French, Anglo-Irish, or be it what it may, means one thing to him and one thing only, the Pope's power & especially his temporal power.[3]

It seems the Queen is quite sensible of her obligations as 'the great Mahometan Power'.

I am much concerned about the withdrawal of the Greek.[4] He loses nothing: and gains a grievance. I think the French have mismanaged this: and I am very glad that you had declared *you* did not stand upon the point. If an Eastern Insurrection is really contemplated, this is a plausible plea (and I do not think it more than plausible) to help it to a justification in the eyes of its own people. We cannot I imagine propose to recede.

General Grey has made upon me, during the late transactions, the impression of a very upright man, not perhaps always thinking broadly, but always thinking honestly, full of loyal sentiment, and not in the least degree desirous to take advantage of his position.

We go to Osborne on the 23d, and I imagine the Queen will then open further the question of the Irish Church.

Lord Spencer sleeps here on Thursday: and it happens that Archdeacon Stopford also comes on the same day.[5]

If I tremble a little at the prospect of any special share in your responsibility for Foreign affairs, it is wholly because I feel the narrowness of my capacity & my knowledge, & from no other cause, for you do everything that man can do to make it both pleasant & easy to me, & I am grateful for it.

We think of offering ourselves to Lord Russell for Sat. 30th to the 1st. Your

---

[1] Of 9 January, Add MS 44119, f. 21, proposing to reduce the army abroad by virtually half, to officer the militia with half-pay army officers, to eradicate inefficient corps in the Volunteers.
[2] i.e. Odo *Russell, Clarendon's son-in-law, letter forwarded by Clarendon, Add MS 44133, f. 157.   [3] See Matthew, 'Vaticanism', p. 428.
[4] From conference on Turkish-Greek difficulties, sitting in Paris: *PP* 1868-9 lxiv.
[5] Rest of letter missing in holograph, copy taken from Add MS 44133, f. 161.

giving him foreign intelligence from time to time will be most soothing to him. When he comes to town I shall try to get sometimes to his house: but Pembroke Lodge is really beyond my reach. I hope you have good accounts of Lady Clarendon, & from her.

[P.S.] Pray advise Mr. Odo Russell in case Cardinal Pentini [asks?] to look after his Capo di Monte China.

To EARL RUSSELL, 11 January 1869.   PRO 30/22/16F, f. 24.

We propose to come to you if it entirely suits you & Lady Russell on the 30th and stay over Sunday. The Cabinet meets on the 26th. Up to this time I need not tell you, we have decided nothing about the Irish Church; nor shall we before the time I propose for seeing you.

The subjects of Rating Clauses—Middle schools—Scotch Education—Bankruptcy—Irish Railways—are more or less in hand: also County Boards, but without final decision on any.

Does it occur to you as possible that Middle schools or Scotch Education could be introduced in the H. of Lords?[1] It will be very hard to get the second reading of an Irish Church Bill before Easter: but I do not despair.

12. Tu.

Ch. 8½ AM. Rose at 5.45 to read papers from the Conference. Wrote to Ld Clarendon—Telegram to Mr Hammond—Lord Chancellor—Mr Bruce—Lord Granville—Mr Dodson—Att.Gen. Ireland—Mr Brand—Chancr of Exchr—Mr Whitmore—Mr Fortescue—Mr Cardwell—Lord Advocate—Mr M'Millan—Watsons—& minutes. Worked among the Trees. Worked on Homer. Conversation with Archd. Ffoulkes. Read Karcher.

To E. CARDWELL, war secretary, 12 January 1869.   PRO/30/48/6, f. 34.

Your letter[2] on Sir C. Trevelyan's paper about competition reminds me of something I omitted yesterday in writing about Army Reforms. It is this: that I daresay you are looking to some plan for making places, of certain ranks, in the Civil Service available for soldiers who have passed through the army: that this will involve in some way or other a diminution of the means of Government by Patronage: & that you will certainly have whatever help I can give you in bringing about that diminution.

13. Wed.

Ch. 8½ A.M. Wrote to Lord Clarendon—Ld Southesk—Mr Helps—Watson & S.—Mr Ouvry—also [blank] and minutes. Tel. to Ld

[1] Russell approved middle school legislation being there introduced, 13 January 1869, Add MS 44294, f. 176.
[2] Of 11 January; Add MS 44119, f. 27; favourable to competition.

Clarendon (2)—Tel. to Mr Gurdon. Wrote out a paper on the plan of the measure respecting the Irish Church, intended perhaps for the Queen.[1] Worked on Homer. We felled a lime. Conversation with Archdn Ff[oulkes] and Mr Cooper[2] on Ritualism.

To LORD CLARENDON, foreign secretary,   Clarendon MSS, c. 497.
13 January 1869.

1. I have thought it best to Telegraph from Chester that as far as I can judge[3] without having the Claims Convention by me we had better proceed at once, the main point viz. the Sovereign being conceded by us.
2. The answers of the Turk about the Enosis, and about the declaration proposed to be made in or after the Conference, seem to be reasonable in themselves.
3. It is really ludicrous as far as I can see that, when for every practical purpose the difference of consultative seat and voting seat is imperceptible, the Conference should break down upon it. But the Greek has this advantage—in asking to be recognised as a Power he will have I think the feeling with him that he asks for what is something to him & hurts nobody. But what ground can there be for sympathy with the Turk's refusal, or what could we lose by the Greek's vote? It really seems as if it were a question between Glyn and Taylor.[4]
   With the prospect we have now before us of the verification of your fears of the working of the Conference, as an event too probable, I cannot help thinking that unless an early change for the better occurs the shortest way out of the affair may be the best. To go on without Russia would be I suppose to prepare the way for very serious dangers in the East. Of that I suppose you could not think: but we might blame everybody: Greece for demanding, Turkey for refusing, Russia for withdrawing. If Russia really agreed to the consultative voice it is most fair to France that this should be placed on record.
4. Mr Erskine's letter which I return seems to me to contain much good sense.
5. I am glad you have been fully on the alert against any idea of a proposal by the Conference to interfere with the Greek Constitution.
6. My telegram includes adhesion to the draft proposed for Lord Lyons.[5]

14. Th.

Ch. 8½ A.M. Wrote to Duke of Cambridge—Ld Clarendon—Ld De Grey—Mr Cardwell (2)—Mr West—Mr Trevelyan—Mr G. Russell —Ld Chichester—D. of Argyll—Sir J. Coleridge—M. Karcher[6]— Archbp of Dublin[7]—Mr Gurdon—Dean of Worcester—Css Castrofiana—& minutes. We felled another tree. Worked on Homer: not

[1] See Morley, ii. 260, and for extracts to 4 February.
[2] Probably James Hughes Cooper, d. 1909, rector of Tarporley 1865-88.
[3] Gladstone's note added here reads: 'I have since writing got the Draft Conv[ention].'
[4] i.e. the liberal and tory whips.   [5] Add MS 44133, f. 176.
[6] Translating 'A chapter of autobiography' into French; Add MS 44418, f. 148.
[7] In *R. C. *Trench: Letters and Memorials* (1888), ii. 73, on Irish bishops' request for a convocation.

much: for in evening came the Spencers[1] & also Archdeacon Stopford, and I had much Irish conversation with them. Read Irish Railway Commn Report.[2]

To the DUKE OF ARGYLL, Indian secretary,   Add MS 44536, f. 97.
14 January 1869.

I return Dufferin's letter.[3] I can very well believe that after the obstinate and
most selfish resistance which has now for so long a time been offered to reasonable measures in relation to the land in Ireland, we shall find it difficult when
the time comes to keep within the limits of a true modification. But I do not
find that anyone connected with the Govt has gone beyond due bounds in
speaking on the Land question: nor do I well see how our Irish authorities can
undertake to rebuke the vagaries of a R.C. Bishop: the more so as I presume
they do not & cannot engage to notice with censure acts & words which may
often deserve it in the opposite sense.
    Your reference to Dufferin's Church patronage is an enigma to me, as I do
not know in what way he can be open to other interference than that of an incessant dunning & pestering, which I now for the first time in my life am called
upon to suffer. I enclose a spare copy of Tupper's homage to the pair; & I offer
my best congratulations on the second marriage which I see has come off. All
good wait upon both.

15. Fr.

Ch. 8½ AM. Wrote to Att.Gen. for Ireland—Ld Clarendon—Mr
Bruce—Att. General—Mr Goschen—Mr Childers—Scotts—Dr
Russell—Sir J. Gray—and minutes. We felled an ash. Three hours
conversation with the Viceroy & Archdeacon. I went over much of
the roughest ground of the intended measure & found the Archdn
able & helpful. Also conversation with the Viceroy: who went before
7. Saw the Bp of Chester [Jacobson] on the Irish Church & on English Ch. preferment. Worked on Homer at night.

To LORD CLARENDON, foreign secretary,   Clarendon MSS, c. 497.
15 January 1869.

1. I think that the dispatch to Alcock and your communications with Burlingame[4]
constitute a real advance towards placing our relations with China, and by parity

[1] *Spencer, the lord lieutenant, came to be informed of the heads of the Irish Church
Bill, already drafted by Gladstone in cahoots with *Fortescue, who had stayed on in Dublin;
see Add MS 44418, f. 4.
[2] Confidential printed paper by M. H. Foster, with Gladstone's annotations, in Add MS
44609, f. 6.
[3] Untraced letter from Dufferin to Argyll on 'Irish "Liberal" Catholic leaders', forwarded
by Argyll on 12 January; Add MS 44101, f. 1.
[4] Clarendon to Alcock, 13 January 1869, and to Anson Burlingame, leading Chinese
diplomatic mission, 28 December 1868, in PP 1868–9 lxiv 11, 15.

of reasoning, with other foreign countries, on a sound footing. As Burlingame has admitted that force may be properly employed 'there & then' for the immediate protection I think he says of life & property, it is not for us to narrow that proposition. But I suggest that as between this Government and its own subjects we are not to be bound to interfere by force, and least of all without the knowledge of the Government at home, at every point where a traveller or merchant or missionary may contrive to plant his foot in China or other foreign countries. I would not admit *as towards British subjects* that the British force is to be employed whenever & wherever within reach as matter of course, & without reference home, for the protection of life & property *in situ*, but only by affording the protection of refuge. If you agree in this you will know what precautions are proper to be taken.

2. The opinion of the Law Officers appears to me modest, but very judicious.

3. I return the papers in their box to Mr. H[ammond] & I am much pleased to hear of the Signature.

PS. Stopford has been here, & has met Spencer. Both of us are struck with him as a ready handy instructed man of business. Spencer sails tonight with Ldy S.

16. Sat.

Ch. 8½ A.M. Wrote to Sir E. Colebrooke—Ld Clarendon—Mr Otway —Sir T. Lloyd—C.A. Wood—Ld Sydney—Watsons—and minutes. Another full conversation with Archdn Stopford, who went away. Worked on Homer. We felled an elm. Read Gallwey on Irish Ch.[1]

To A. J. OTWAY, under secretary, foreign office,   Add MS 44418, f. 158.
16 January 1869.

I should think, with reference to this draft (though I do not at all press it) that it might be practicable to push the French Government a little harder in the direction of further negotiation of their Tariff by putting to them two points. 1. I think our own general experience has established that great as is the advantage of substituting duties for prohibitions, & moderate duties for high ones, the last stage, that of sweeping away duty altogether is by far the most beneficial both to the particular trade which is relieved, and to the general trading purse of the country, and finally through this latter medium to its faculty of consuming dutiable commodities, and thus to the revenue itself, which at first sight appeared to suffer. 2. Experience seems also to have shown under this Treaty that there has been such a revelation to France itself of its own productive energy and power, and the extension of its trade has been so very remarkable, that inasmuch as the Treaty on the French side is but a partial measure, we are justified, without making ourselves judges, in the belief that they will desire to extend the range of an experiment so inviting from its ascertained results.

[1] T. Gallwey, *Short essays on the Irish Established Church* (1869).

17. 2 S.Epiph.

Ch. mg with H.C. and 6.30 Evg. Wrote to Bp of Oxford—Ld Clarendon—Mr Goschen—Mr Cardwell—Mr Bruce—E. Hamilton—Mr
Mozley—Att.Gen. Ireland—Lady Blantyre—& many minutes.
Conversation with Harry and Herbert on the parable of the Talents
& the use of money. Read Mozley on Baptism: the Rector and his
friends.[1]

To G. J. GOSCHEN, president of the poor law board,   Add MS 44536, f. 99.
17 January 1869.

I quite agree with the general views set forth in your letter.[2] We ought if possible
to occupy the ground. Acland makes his proposal in the best spirit. But he will
not be able to controul the spirit you describe. Towards this occupation of the
ground, a measure for County Boards on the elective principle will much contribute. If we can make it do the whole that is required for the present, this will be
by far the best. The subject will have of course to be discussed in the Cabinet:
I think a division of the rate with the landlords a very probable upshot. My judgment is very hostile to taxing the Exchequer for local purposes. Even Sir R. Peel
went too far in that direction.
[PS.] about St Martins I am very forgiving.[3]

18. M.

Ch. 8½ AM. Up at 2.15 to answer Mr Hammond by Telegram.[4] Wrote
to Dean of Windsor—Ld Clarendon—Mr Hubbard—Sir A. Spearman—Mr Foster—Mr Cardwell—Ld Spencer—Ld R. Cavendish—
Mr Goschen—Sir R. Phillimore—Dr Cather[5]—Mr Childers (2)—&
minutes. Conferences with Dr Cather through Willy. Saw Jane Waters
to arrange their affairs. Saw Lord Granville (who came in afternoon)
—and Sir John Acton.

To LORD CLARENDON, foreign secretary,   Clarendon MSS, c. 497.
18 January 1869.

1. I entirely agree that the instructions from the Departments about protection
of British subjects abroad are fit matter for the Cabinet, and I have no doubt we
shall concur, when we talk it over. Perhaps a preliminary *Caucus* might be useful?

---

[1] See 9 Nov. 62; see 10 Jan. 69.
[2] Of 15 January, Add MS 44161, f. 150, supporting granting Lopes' demand for a commission on local taxation, and mentioning 'a plan' for local taxation.
[3] Goschen had rejected a petition for return to autonomy by St. Martin in the Fields
parish; ibid.
[4] Untraced.
[5] John Cather, 1814-88, archdeacon of Tuam from 1856, sent paper on Irish disendowment on 20 Jan.; Add MS 44418, f. 182.

2. In Flamburiani's letter the point which I wished to catch your eye was that he, a Greek of station & experience, & by extraction a Cretan, does not recommend the annexation of Crete.

3. As to the local autonomy under Suzerainty & tribute, my opinion has long been that this is by much the best arrangement *in itself* for Turkey & for the parties. But if the concession of it is only to be made a pretext or a standing ground for disturbing the Porte, it is impossible to expect or ask the Sultan to agree to it & matters must take their course otherwise.

4. I think we could best get at the D[aily] N[ews] through Glyn. In the little article I referred² to there was nothing hostile. But perhaps they want early intelligences, & take this way of shewing it.

5. I sent up a Telegram to Hammond, in the middle of the night: with many inward groans.

19. Tu.

Ch. 8½ AM. Wrote to Mr Fortescue—Mr Hammond—Mr Otway—Mr Cardwell—Mr Harvey—J. Watson & S[mith]—Dr Ward—Mr Chamberlain—Mr Whitehouse³—and minutes. Worked on Homer. One hour on Homer with Sir J. Acton. Some three with Lord G. and the Att.Gen. for I[reland] on the Irish Church. Whist in evening.

20. Wed.

Ch. 8½ AM. Wrote to Archdn Stopford—Rev Dr Russell—Mr West—Ld Clarendon—Mr [T. W.] Perry—Dean Ramsay—Mr Childers—Mr Weld Blundell—and minutes. Further & long conversations on the Irish Ch. question and its various branches with Granville—the Att[orney] General—and in the evg with Dean Howson.⁴ Also with Sir J. Acton. Walk with him & the Att[orney] Gen[eral].

To LORD CLARENDON, foreign secretary,   Clarendon MSS, c. 497.
20 January 1869.

It was obviously impossible to press at so late a period the alteration of the word *patriotism*. But the French⁵ did not take the nature of the objection which had occurred to me & which I ought to have explained. It was that to recognise the sympathy of a Greek of Greece with a Greek of Crete as patriotism

¹ See 11 Jan. 69.
² *Daily News* of 13 January 1869, brought to Clarendon's attention on 14 January; Clarendon MSS, c. 497.
³ Perhaps H. Whitehouse of the Chapel Royal.
⁴ Of Chester; see 8 Mar. 50.
⁵ During the conference; see 11 Jan. 69n. Clarendon had accepted the French view of the definition of 'patriotism' and had told Lyons not to insist on the British amendment; Clarendon to Gladstone, 19 January 1869, Add MS 44133, f. 183.

was by implication to give a sanction to the Panhellenic principle. It was in short a Philo-Turkish objection.

Unfortunately my F.O. key is in London: but it matters not for in point of hours it is nearly the same here & there though the free hours feel much more free which is a great thing.

Granville & the Irish A.G. are here, and we have had many hours of discussion on the working shape of the Irish Church Bill, which it is urgent to press forward. I am not without hope of having the main points of detail ready for the Cabinet next week: those of principle, strictly so called, are already nearly settled for us. Lambert, who distinguished himself so much in the Reform Bills, is at work in Ireland collecting evidence which will bear on the question as to the employment of the residue.

Granville has seen all your inclosures of yesterday & today. He goes tomorrow. We come up on Friday.

21. Th.

Ch. 8½ A.M. Wrote to Sir T. Biddulph—A. Kinnaird—Robn G. (2) —Watson & S.—The Queen—T.T. [sc. D.] Hornby—H.A. Bruce —A. Macmillan—Bp of Oxford—Mrs Bennett—and minutes. Wrote a brief abstract of the intended Bill. Conversation with Granville & Sullivan who went off. Woodcutting with Willy. Revising Irish Ch. papers. Worked on Homer. Attempted to re-establish order with a view to departure.

To H. A. BRUCE, home secretary, 21 January 1869.   Add MS 44536, f. 104.

Granville & the Irish A.G., also Spencer & others have been here, & after various conversations, I have drawn, & the two first named have seen and approved the inclosed sketch of the sort of reply that might be written to the Irish Prelates. I send it to you for greater facility of communication between us before the Cabinet on Tuesday, which will settle the matter.[1] I expect to be in London, Sat forenoon, & from Monday afternoon.

To S. WILBERFORCE, bishop of Oxford,   Wilberforce MSS d. 37.
21 January 1869. 'Private'.

I shall read with interest what Lyttelton may send me. It will be pleasant to me to know that you individually have adopted & urge the opinions which you describe.[2] But these opinions (forgive me if I speak plainly) are perfectly nugatory as regards any utility to the Church, unless & until they are denoted by some public action. Trench seems to be a dreamer of dreams: and talks of

[1] *Bruce showed the proposed reply to the abp. of Armagh; Add MS 44086, f. 19.
[2] Wilberforce's acceptance of Irish disestablishment in the form of a letter to Lyttelton was in proof, but after reading it Gladstone advised Wilberforce, 30 January 1869, Wilberforce MSS d. 37, not to publish 'and decide the matter by single combat', but to develop 'joint action'.

negotiating at a time when all negotiation will have gone by. I must look, & the Government must look, to justify our measure in the eyes of those by whom it is supported; & who, if they keep together, are *amply sufficient* to carry it. Therefore my duty is to the best of my power to keep them together. Therefore the Bill must be framed with reference to those who support it, and not to those who oppose it. Now for every practical purpose all those who have opposed it are opponents still, until they signify, as emphatically as they spoke or acted before, that with the change of the scales their opinion as to the right mode of action has changed. Those who *act* like Archdeacon Stopford become our practical supporters, & have a right to be considered if they are of sensible number and weight, in that capacity. But those of whom the world knows nothing, except that to the utmost of their power they opposed us last year, count with the world for opponents still, & the private changes in their opinions *cannot* weigh with us in the formation of the Bill. *De non apparentibus, et non existentibus, eadem est ratio.*[1] And now is the time. Less than five weeks may show, by irrefragable & final proof, how true are these words that I am writing. I have gone as far as my duty would allow in representing, in various quarters, the true state of the case: and I think I have now pretty well washed my hands of responsibility. Yes even the small change is an immense relief about the Bp. of S[alisbury]. God be thanked.

22. Fr. [London]

Ch. 8½ AM. Wrote to Mrs L. Gladstone—Ld Kinnaird—Mr J. Blackie —Mr Cardwell—and minutes. Packing—paying Bills—bidding farewells—& off at 3.20 for Q[ueen's] F[erry,] Chester and London at 10¼. Saw Mr Jacob Bright.[2] Saw S.E.G[ladstone] in London. Worked a little on my Homer. Read Baxter on Taxation.[3]

23. Sat. [Osborne House]

Wrote to Mr Childers—Mr Devereux[4]—Ld Spencer—Mr Twisleton—Ld Granville—Mr Fortescue—and minutes. Saw Mr Glyn— Mr Thornton Hunt—General Grey—Duke of Argyll—Mr Alg. West —Ld A. Paget. 12.40-5¼. Journey to Osborne. Read Trench on Ireland.[5] Saw the Queen on the Irish Church especially & gave H.M. my papers with explanation which appeared to be well taken.[6] She was

[1] 'what is not apparent must be considered non-existent'.
[2] Jacob *Bright, br. of John,* 1821-99; liberal M.P. Manchester 1867-74, 1876-95.
[3] R. D. *Baxter, *The Taxation of the United Kingdom* (1869).
[4] Richard Joseph Devereux, b. 1829; liberal M.P. for Wexford 1865-Jan. 1869 (unseated), Feb. 1869-72; had sent wild-fowl; Add MS 44536, f. 104.
[5] T. R. F. C. Trench, *Reconstruction of the Church in Ireland* (1869).
[6] In fact, *Victoria could only follow the arguments after *Martin had written a *précis*; see *LQV*, 2nd series, i. 577.

altogether at ease. We dined with H.M. afterwards. Then went to the Household Drawingroom.

To C. S. P. FORTESCUE, Irish secretary,   Carlingford MSS CP1/22.
23 January 1869.

It may be convenient to you to know that I do not think we can get to the Irish Church question on Tuesday: but I suppose we may then fix a day for a Cabinet upon it.

We must however send an answer to the Irish Bishops about their Memorial praying for a Convocation: and one is drafted and in circulation but it may not reach you before Tuesday. The case is one hardly admitting of doubt now that we know the attitude of the general body of the Bps & therefore of the Church to be one of decided hostility. Such is the sense of the draft: with an intimation that in any case we could not have looked to the Irish Convocation as being with reference to the present crisis what the Memorial seems to assume that it is, namely an adequate representative body for the *Church* of Ireland though the laity are excluded from it. This little sketch will enable you so far as the matters within my reach are concerned to judge whether you should come for Tuesday.

[P.S.] I write also to the Ld. Lieut.: & wait for further information respecting Fenians.

To EARL SPENCER, Irish lord lieutenant,   Add MS 44306, f. 51.
23 January 1869.

I have just found & read your letter & its enclosures, in your description of which I entirely agree.[1]

The Archbishop [of Armagh] is right in saying that I 'have shown a determination to press the measure without regard to' what he deems 'the just rights of the Church': & he may be quite assured that so far as depends upon us the determination will not be in the slightest degree relaxed by the impolitic opposition which he has unhappily decided upon offering. The only difference will be that without doubt we shall be less in a condition than we might otherwise have been, to pay attention to the feelings & prepossessions of the Church——, this he will be able probably to read in the Bill when it appears; though we shall I dare say ask in it for all that we can fairly expect our supporters on the two sides of the water to agree to.

The archbishop says he is in the dark. He knows however that he has had every encouragement which with propriety I could give to seek for light by friendly communication with us.

A House of Commons has fought and decided——a nation has done the same, & a Ministry has run away, but the Archbishop (how militant he is) waits for 'the field of battle'!

Roundell sustained the argument right well all through: the Archbishop deserves credit for his temper. All we can do is to give any legitimate encouragement in our power to a cross or national movement in the sense of the Bishop of

---

[1] Spencer had sent (on 22 January 1869, Add MS 44306, f. 38) a record of a talk between C. S. Roundell and the abp. of Armagh 'after dinner on the 21 Jan, 1869', 'so valuable' that he sent it immediately.

Peterborough, of course without shewing, for indeed we need not feel any fever-
ish anxiety for it.

May I keep a copy of this Mem.? I should like to shew it to Granville & one
or two.

24. Septa S.

Whippingham Ch. mg & aft. Wrote to Ld Clarendon—Rev. Mr Wil-
liams. Saw Prince Leopold—Princess Beatrice[1]—Gen. Grey—Mr
Duckworth—and H.M. who spoke very kindly about Lord Claren-
don—Mr Bright—Mr Lowe—the Spanish Crown—Prince Leopold[2]
—Bps Lonsdale & Gilbert[3]—Mr Mozley—& so forth: but not a word
on the Irish Church. We dined again with H.M.—C. sitting by the
Queen. Read Alford No VII[4]—Williams's Introduction & (began)
Corresp. on Eastern Church.[5]

25. M. Conv.St P. [London]

Off at 9.45 to London: arr. 2.45. Wrote to Bishop of Down—Dr
Monsell—Chancr of Exr—Ld Lurgan—Bp of Oxford[6]—Ld Lyttel-
ton—Sir J. Coleridge—Mr Fortescue (2), & minutes. Wrote Mem.
on Glebes.[7] Dined with De Tabley. Saw Ld Granville—Mr Childers
—Ld De Tabley—Mr Ouvry. Saw 3[R]. Read Q.R. on W.E.G.[8]—
Realities of Irish Life.[9]

26. Tu.

Wrote to The Queen (2)—Lady Llanover—Mr Hughes—Sir E. Colebrooke—Mr Towse—Mr H.A. Bruce—and minutes. Dined at Lord
Granville's. Cabinet 2.30-5¾. Read Trench on Ireland[10]—Ld Russells

[1] Beatrice Mary Victoria Feodore, Victoria's fifth da., b. 1857; m. 1885 Prince Henry of
Battenberg.
[2] Probably her son (see 7 Apr. 53); whose tutor was Robinson Duckworth, 1834-1911;
the Spanish crown was offered later in the year to Leopold of Hohenzollern.
[3] J. *Lonsdale, d. 1867 (see 16 Feb. 27) and A. T. *Gilbert of Chichester (see 22 Jan.
32).
[4] H. *Alford, Quebec Chapel sermons preached in 1854-57, 7 v. (1854-57).
[5] G. Williams, The Orthodox Church of the East in the eighteenth century (1868).
[6] Advising *Wilberforce to send his (never published) 'Answer of the constituencies',
accepting Irish disestablishment as inevitable, to *Magee, which he did; Add MS 44536,
f. 105; Wilberforce, iii. 283.
[7] Circulated to the cabinet on 3 February; Add MS 44757, f. 106.
[8] [W. R. *Greg's] hostile review of 'A chapter of autobiography'; Quarterly Review,
cxxvi. 121 (January 1869).
[9] W. R. Trench, Realities of Irish Life (1868).   [10] See 23 Jan. 69.

Third Letter. Eheu.[1] Saw Gray & another[R]. Saw Dr Maziere Brady—Mr Macmillan—Ld de Grey—Mr G. Glyn—Mr Cardwell —Mr Bright—Lord Edw. Clinton—Mr Bruce.

Notes for Cabinet Jan 26. 69[2]
√ 1. Navy Estimates 880m[ille] red[uctio]n
√ 2 Reply to Irish Bishops. Summary[3]
   3. Time for a Cabinet on Irish Church[4]
√ 4. Grammar Schools Bill.[5]
   5. ⟨Scotch Education Bill.⟩ Arming of Native Troops in India.
√ 6. Turco-Greek Conference: contingency of Greek Refusal. To be still, & recommend others [to do likewise].
√ 7. U[nited] S[tates] communications, recital.
√ 8. Army. Number of men fixed. 11m[ille] reduced.

Notes for Cabinet Jan. 26.
Answer to memorial of Irish Bishops.
Queen to open Parliament, or not.
Day for Cabinet on Irish Church.

27. Wed.

Wrote to Bp of Chester—Att.Gen.Irel.—The Queen—Mr Fortescue—Sir F. Doyle—Lord Spencer (2)—Mr T.B. Potter—Mr Hamilton—Mr Miall—and minutes. At Christie's with C. Saw Sir W. Farquhar—Mr Monsell—Mr G. Glyn—Sir A. Spearman—Mr Bruce —Mr Helps—Ld Granville—Sir R. Phillimore—Mr Millais. Saw Two[R]. Read Memoir of Faraday[6]—Trench's Realities.[7] Arranged papers & books a little.

28. Th.

Wrote to Ld Granville—Bishop Hinds—Ld Spencer—Mr Childers —The Queen—Mrs Thistlethwayte—Ld Clarendon—Mrs Gringer —and minutes. Worked a little on Homer. Saw Mrs Flaesch X. Saw Mr Baxter—Mr Goschen—Bp of Oxford *cum* Bp of Chester—Bp

---

[1] Earl Russell, 'A third letter to . . . Chichester Fortescue on the state of Ireland' (1869); Gladstone hoped to take up its points verbally; Add MS 44536, f. 106.
[2] Add MS 44637, f. 15.
[3] *Bruce's reply of 29 January, refusing permission for an Irish convocation, in *The Times*, 3 February 1869, 5b.
[4] See 1 Feb. 69.
[5] *Forster had circulated a printed cabinet paper of 21 January 1869 on the Endowed Schools Bill; Add MS 44609, f. 8.
[6] Probably J. *Tyndall, *Faraday as a discoverer* (1868).   [7] See 25 Jan. 69.

of Chester (in evg)—Mr Liddon—Mrs Matthews.[1] Read Trench's
Ireland—Murphy on Irish Church.[2] Arranging papers.

29. Fr.

Wrote to Ld Clarendon—L. Rumpff[R]—Att.Gen. for Ireland—
Mr Moncreiff (Ld Adv.)—Rev Dr Russell—A. Gordon[3]—and
minutes. Saw Ld Granville—Do cum Mr Bruce—Sir John Gray—
Mr Glyn. Saw Mrs Gringer: & another[R]. Read Trench on Irish Life
—Macmillan's Mag. Worked on Homer. Arranging papers &c.

30. Sat. [Pembroke Lodge, Richmond]

Wrote to Bp of Oxford—Ld Clarendon—Mr Lambert—Chancr of
Exchr—Watsons—Sir A. Maitland[4]—Mr Fortescue (2)—Mr Lyon
—and minutes. Read Doyle's Lectures[5]—Trench on Ireland. Saw
Sir C. Pressly—Mr Homersham Cox—Mr G. Glyn—Bp of St David's
—Ld Stanley [of] Alderley—Mrs Gringer: gave £10[R]. At 4.30
we went to Pembroke Lodge. We found Lord Russell well: and I had
several hours of conversation with him on public affairs.

To LORD CLARENDON, foreign secretary,   Clarendon MSS, c. 497.
30 January 1869.

It is melancholy to read these interesting letters,[6] which show so plainly that
there is dirt in the sky, though it may be long before it comes down. A war between France and Germany would be sad but the compulsory or fraudulent
extinction by annexation of the Free State of Belgium would be worse. I cannot
however believe that this can be effected by force, and I hope we may assume
that the public opinion of Belgium will remain true to itself. For this purpose
the two things that I suppose to be most essential are a mild policy in regard to
religion so as to obviate feuds on that score, and the wise financial administration and economy in public expenditure which will give every Belgian a subject
of daily & standing satisfaction when he compares the condition of his own
country with the increasing burdens & extravagance of France.

It is really bad finance that renders Greece unable to play a part in the East.
If that little state could and would pay her way, she would count for much in
Eastern affairs. But she is above these vulgar ideas, and such an epoch is indefi-
nitely distant.

[1] Not further identified.
[2] J. J. Murphy, 'An Irish churchman's view of Irish politics', Contemporary Review,
x. 53 (January 1869).
[3] In T.A.P.S., new series li part 4, 49.
[4] Sir Alexander Charles Ramsay-Gibson-Maitland, 1820-76; 3rd bart. 1848; liberal M.P.
Midlothian 1868-74; asking him to move the Address (he refused): Add MS 44536, f. 108.
[5] Sir F. H. C. *Doyle, Lectures delivered before the university of Oxford 1868 (1869).
[6] Unclear which; no letter from Clarendon to Gladstone between 19 January and 11
February in Add MS 44133.

Sexa S. Jan 31.

Petersham Ch 11 A.M.—St Matthias 3.30. Saw H. Taylor—Jane Wortley—and others. Much conversation with Lord R. on the Irish Ch. & other matters. Revised a little of 'The Olympian system'.[1] Read Eastern Ch. papers—Equities of Transition[2]—Howson on St Paul's Metaphors.[3] Walk with Ld R. in the grounds.

Feb.One 1869. [*London*]

Wrote to Archbishop Leahy—Lord Clarendon—Ld Granville— Duke of Argyll—Chancr of Exr—Mr Mundella[4]—Ld Harrowby— Watsons—The Queen (2) & minutes. Revised some Homer. Saw Ld Granville—Mr Hammond—Mr Newman Hall—Ld Clarendon—Mr Childers—Ld Lansdowne—Mr A. Kinnaird—Sir F. Doyle—The Wortleys. After another *Sederunt* with Ld Russell,[5] and after seeing the school, we returned to London. Fifteen to dinner.

2. *Tu. Purification.*

Wrote to Mr Childers—Ld Chancellor—Sir W. Jenner—Mr T.C. Anstey—Mr Fortescue—Mr Delane—Mr H. Cowper[6]—The Queen —and minutes. Cabinet 2½-5½. Saw Mr E. Hamilton—Mr Glyn— Mr Delane—Chancr of Exr—E. Cardwell. Dined with De Grey: the Sheriff's dinner. Saw Cooper: & another[R].

Notes for C[abinet]. F. 2. 69.[7]
√ 1. As to an inquiry into Freedom of Voting.[8] Postponed.
√ 2. Fenian amnesty[9]
√ 3. Admiralty reductions.
√ 4. F[oreign] O[ffice]:— Russian Telegraph to Greece
                    Thornton's letter resp[ecting] Claims Convention:
                    Senate unlikely to ratify.

[1] For *Juventus Mundi.*
[2] Possibly A. *Clissold, *Transition; or the passing away of ages or dispensations* (1868).
[3] J. S. *Howson, *The metaphors of St Paul* (1868).
[4] Asking him to second the Address; Add MS 44536, f. 108.
[5] Gladstone told Clarendon this day, Clarendon MSS, c. 497: 'by and large I bring a very favourable report. No unpleasantness; no sign of soreness . . .'.
[6] Henry Frederick Cowper, 1836-87, s. of 6th Earl Cowper; liberal M.P. Hertfordshire 1865-85; asking him to move the Address: Add MS 44536.
[7] Add MS 44637, f. 17. On a separate but adjacent sheet, undated, are listed: 'Irish Church—Irish Railways—Rate Paying Clauses—Education? (B & F.)—Universities (C) —Resignation of Bishops?—Commission on Ritual Bill?—Bankruptcy—Trade Unions— Succession to Realty in case of Intestacy—' and another, smudged, phrase. Ibid., f. 18.
[8] i.e. the ballot; see 6 Mar. 69.
[9] Start of Gladstone's persistent attempts at releasing Fenian prisoners; see 27 Jan., 4 Aug. 69.

√ 5. Purchase of the Telegraphs. Monopoly? Decided to ask for it.[1]
  6. Cabinet Sat[urday] 1. PM. [6 February 1869.]

3. Wed.

Wrote to M. Bousquet[2]—Mr Macmillan—The Queen (2)[3]—Att.Gen.
for Irel.—Mr Bruce—Mr Morley MP.—Mr Delane—Mr Bright—
& minutes. Dined at Ld Dartrey's. Saw Sir W. Jenner—Lord Granville—Mr Gurdon—Mr Delane—Mr Glyn—Ld Clarendon—Duke
of Argyll—Gordon X. Read Prof. Sedgwick.[4] Worked on Homer.

To J. BRIGHT, president of the board of trade,   Add MS 43385, f. 24.
3 February 1869.

You cannot be more anxious than I am to forward Childers in his work.[5]
I think it quite clear that he must be supported. But on the other hand I think
the process has been somewhat sharp in some of its incidents: & it is because I
wish to offer not only a sincere but a successful resistance to the Clubs that I am
as anxious we should shew *both* that we have stood by the public interests &
that we have applied every practicable mitigation.

The onward movement of the Irish Church measure at this moment is chiefly
in Dublin where the drafting is going on. On Saturday or Sat & Mon., I hope the
Cabinet will decide on the substance of the main proposals. The heaviest part of
the whole job will be sitting in *caucus* on the draft to sift it line by line. This
must come in the week after next. I have circulated an interesting paper on
Glebehouses.

No doubt Mr. Hadfield represents a great breadth of opinion.

I rather think Mrs. Bright is not in town? My wife, in the same belief, has not
called on her: if she is here, I hope she will come to dine tomorrow when you
give us the favour of your company.

To J. T. DELANE, 3 February 1869.   Add MS 44536, f. 109.

This is the paper[6] which I could not find yesterday. It has now come back to
me. It may not be published as you see: but it helps, though in form out of date,
to complete the view of the situation. Please send it back in an envelope.

---

[1] See 20 Mar. 69.
[2] G. de Bousquet, had written about Gladstone's publications: Add MS 44536, f. 109.
[3] She had declined to open Parliament personally; Gladstone told *Bruce this day (Add
MS 44536, f. 109) 'to convey to the Queen the purport of the reports you have had fr. the
Police'. See Guedalla, i. 156.
[4] A. *Sedgwick, *A memorial by the trustees of Cowgill Chapel* (1868).
[5] Bright to Gladstone, 3 February 1869, Add MS 44112, f. 77: 'I think Mr. Childers was
rather discouraged yesterday—he felt a little "bowled over" by what was said. . . .'
[6] Not found.

4. Th.

Kept my bed till 3½ to help off a cold. Wrote to Bp of Peterborough
—Professor Sedgwick—The Queen—Mr Delane—& minutes. A
letter from H.M. today showed much disturbance: wh I tried to
soothe.[1] Saw Rev. Dr Vaughan—Lord Granville—Sir R. Phillimore.
Fifteen to dinner: Cabinet & wives. Read Sedgwick's charming book
on Cowgill Chapel: and Doyle's Lectures.[2] Saddened by young J.
Wortley's appearance.

To J. T. DELANE, 4 February 1869.   Add MS 44536, f. 110

I do not know what more to do in the way of trying the archbp. of Dublin, but
I should be glad if you would instruct me.
    Unaware what time suits you best, I will merely say I shall be at home to-
morrow until 3, & free, I think, except fr. 11.30 to 12.30.
    There is another subject on which I should like to say a word.

5. Fr.

Wrote to Bp of Oxford—Ld Clarendon—Mr Bruce—Sir W. Jenner
—Robn G.—A.B. Cochrane—Att.Gen.Irel.—Mr Fortescue—&
minutes. Dined at Political Economy Club: debate on Seignorage.[3]
Saw Mr Lambert 2 hours[4]—Mr Thornton Hunt—Mr Walker of
D[aily] N[ews][5]—Mr Levy—Mr Glyn—Mr M'Coll—Scotts. Read
Trench. Worked a little on Homer.

6. Sat.

Wrote to C. Villiers—Bp of Lichfield—Att.General—Duchess of
Roxburgh—Mr Dodson—Mr Breakenridge—Ld Spencer—Rev Mr
Rawson—The Queen—& minutes. Dined at Ld De Grey's. Saw
Irish Presb[yteria]n Deputation 12-1¼.[6]—Mr Glyn—Mr Childers—
Mr Brodrick—Ld De Grey—Ld Clarendon. Read Stanley on Irish
Churches.[7]

---

[1] Guedalla, i. 157 and Add MS 44419, f. 19.   [2] See 30 Jan. 69.
[3] Discussion led by *Bagehot; *Political Economy Club*, ii. 55 (1872).
[4] On his report; see Gladstone to Goschen, 8 February 1869, Add MS 44536, f. 112.
[5] Thomas Walker, 1822-98, ed. *Daily News* 1858-69, *London Gazette* 1869-88; prominent Congregationalist; perhaps seen on next d's. leader on the Queen.
[6] See *The Times*, 8 February 1869, 7f. and Add MS 44418, f. 241.
[7] A. P. *Stanley, 'The three Irish Churches; an historical address' (1869).

To EARL SPENCER, Irish lord lieutenant,   Add MS 44536, f. 111.
6 February 1869.

I thank you for your interesting letter & its enclosure.[1] It is a great pity that
the rational line has not been taken by some Prelate of greater weight. The Irish
bishops have spurned a great responsibility at a time when a man like the Archb.
of Canterbury advised moderation, & when three or four English Bishops of
weight were quite ready to declare in the sense of Archn. Stopford. I think they
overestimate their resources. We shall see.

7. *Quinqua S.*

Chapel Royal mg. St James evg. Saw Mr Fortescue on Irish Church
—Mr E. Hamilton—Ld De Tabley. Read Romanoff[2]—Coleridge's
Keble[3]—Worked on Hom. Ethics.

8. *M.*

Wrote to Ld Chancellor—Mr Bruce (Kenmet)[4]—Mr Gilpin—Mr
Hammond—Mrs Thistlethwayte[5]—Mr Weld Blundell—Archdn
Stopford—& minutes. Wrote Mem. on Irish Ch. for Cabinet. Saw Mr
Westell—Att.Gen.—Mr Glyn—Sir R. Palmer—Count Maffei[6]—
Bp of Peterborough—Ld Granville *cum* Mr Fortescue—Cabinet $2\frac{1}{2}$-
$5\frac{1}{2}$ on the Heads of Irish Ch. Bill. Saw Sir T. Freemantle—M. Musurus
cum Count Bernstorff. Dined at Mr Moffatt's: for a stiff talk of 2
hours on Bankruptcy. Read Doyle's Lectures.

(1) Cabinet Feb[ruary] 8. 69[7]
   Irish Church Bill. Cons[idere]d.
Began by reading Mem[orandum] wh[ich] was printed in Ev[enin]g. No. III.
Worked by No II. Heads 1-15 agreed to.—Mem[orandum] printed.[8]

9. *Tu.*

Wrote to Sir T. Biddulph—Mr Wingfield Baker[9]—Mr Bright—Ld
Clarendon—Mr Greg—Mr G. Burnett—Mrs Jeune—Mr Chadwick

---

   [1] Spencer to Gladstone, 5 February 1869, Add MS 44306, f. 63, reporting bp. of Down's
satisfactory attitude (see 27 Feb. 69), and enclosing record of Irish bps.' meeting.
   [2] See 20 Sept. 68.   [3] Sir J. T. *Coleridge, A memoir of . . . Keble* (1869).
   [4] Unclear.   [5] Unusually, copied by the secretary: Add MS 44536, f. 112.
   [6] Count Carlo Alberto Ferdinando Maffei di Boglio, 1834-97; first secretary at the
Italian embassy.
   [7] Add MS 44637, f. 19.
   [8] Add MS 44757, f. 120, marked 'No III. General View. *Secret*' in Gladstone's hand;
dated 8 February 1869.
   [9] Richard Baker Wingfield Baker, 1801-80; liberal M.P. S. Essex 1857-9, 1868-74.

—Chr of Exr—The Queen—& minutes. Cabinet 2½-6¼: we completed the heads of the Irish Ch measure to my great satisfaction. Read Trench on Ireland. Saw Mr Glyn—Duke of Argyll. Six to dinner. Worked on Irish Ch. official papers. Worked on revising MS.

(2) Continued Feb[ruary] 9.[1]
Remaining heads: passed.
Arr[angement] of Caucus: circulate Draft Bill throughout the Cabinet.
⟨Grammar⟩ or Endowed Schools Bill—Scotch Education Bill—Bankruptcy—Weekly tenants' Bill—County Financial Boards—Irish Church.

10. Ash Wed.

Ch 11 A.M. Wrote to Bishop of Lichfield—Bp of London—Mrs Clifford—Bp of St Asaph—Mr Bright—Duke of Cambridge—and minutes. Saw Ld Granville—do cum Mr Goschen—Mr Glyn—Mr A. Kinnaird. Worked on Homer revision. Worked on Queen's Speech.

11. Th.

Wrote to Ld Clarendon—Mr G.A. Hamilton—Mr [W.] O. Stanley and minutes. Saw Scotts. Saw Mr Lambert—Mr Glyn—Baron Rothschild—Mr A. Peel. At six, admitted a Member of the Guild of Fishmongers: the dinner followed. Spoke 20 m? in the sense of 'keep the majority together'. Granville spoke very well. Bright made a strange mess. Lowe halfway between. Only got away at 11.45.[2] Finished Trench. Read Bagehot on Univ. Money.[3]

To LORD CLARENDON, foreign secretary,   Clarendon MSS, c. 497.
11 February 1869.

I like this outline[4] very much & think it wants only grammatical conversion: but on the paragraph about the US. I wish to know if you have deliberately considered whether you are obliged to be so succinct. After the declarations of Reverdy [Johnson], & even those of Stanley, there will be a disappointment to find all was still in the air. Nevertheless I suppose you cannot safely make special reference to anything but what is absolutely secured? Pray do not understand

[1] Add MS 44637, f. 20.
[2] *Bright's speech was self-admittedly 'fragmentary': *The Times*, 12 February 1869, 5.
[3] W. *Bagehot, *A practical plan for assimilating the English and American money, as a step towards a universal money* (1869).
[4] Clarendon to Gladstone, 11 February 1869, Add MS 44133, f. 186, considered 'the propriety of more *bunkum* for the US. and something more solid for home consumption', but decided on as short a dispatch as possible.

me as expressing an adverse opinion: I am only anxious to be sure we know our ground.

P.S. You will perhaps return your sketch which I send lest you should have no copy.

12. Fr.

Wrote to Duke of Argyll—Att. General—The Speaker—Ed. Lpool Merc.[1]—Robn G.—The Queen (2)—Sir T.G.—Ld De Tabley—and minutes. Put in order for the Cabinet the *disjecta membra* of the [Queen's] Speech. Saw Mr Mundella—Mr Glyn—Ld Granville— Dean Stanley—Sir H. Holland and others. Local Taxn Deputn 2-2¾.[2] Cabinet 2¾-6¼. Settled the Speech. Dined at Sir H. Holland's: & evg party. Worked on Homer MS.

Cabinet Feb[ruary] 12. [1869][3]
1. Queen's Speech read amended and adopted.
2. Resolved to have a measure for the relief of certain Occupiers.[4]
3. Copies of the Speech to
   Lord Granville—Lord Malmesbury—⟨Lord Russell⟩ Lord Salisbury—Mr Disraeli
4. Army estimates: approved Reduction about 1050 m[ille].
5. Argyll. Shall we send [blank]

13. Sat.

Wrote to The Queen—Ld Hartington—Sir J. Acton—Mr A. Billson—and minutes. Dined at Count Bernstorff's—Lady De Grey's afterwards. Saw Mr. G.A. Hamilton—Mr Homersham Cox—Mr Glyn—Mr H. Cowper cum Mr Mundella—Ld Granville (2)— C[ount] Bernstorff—B[aro]n Brunnow—Ld De Grey—S.E.G. Saw Mrs Harvey. Revision of MS. Hom.

14. 1 S.Lent

Chapel Royal mg & evg. Bp of Peterb. preached. Wrote to Ld Chancellor—Mr Fortescue—Mr Headlam—Ld Clarendon (2)—Ld Granville—Gen. Grey (Tel.)—& minutes. Saw Sir R. Palmer (Ir.Ch.)[5]

---

[1] On use of charitable funds in Lancashire: Add MS 44536, f. 115.
[2] No account found.   [3] Add MS 44637, f. 27.
[4] The 1867 Reform Act rating clauses proved administratively chaotic; the Queen's Speech included a rating relief proposal.
[5] *Palmer, attempting to mediate between Gladstone and abp. Trench, sent a mem. on 11 February, see Selborne, II i. 116.

—Ld de Grey—Mr West. An indifferent Sunday. Read Armstrong's Sermon[1]—Bp of Argyll's Charge[2]—Irish Ch. Tracts—Barnes's Sermon.[3]

15. M.

Off at 8.40 to Osborne—Back at 6. Dinner of 39: read the Queen's Speech. Large evening party followed. Saw H.M. at Osborne: very satisfactory: & attended Council. Saw General Grey—The little Theodore—Ld Sydney—Ld De Grey—Ld Lyttelton—Ld Granville—Ld Clarendon—D. of Cambridge—Prince Latour d'Auv.— The Speaker—and others. Revised MS of Arès and Hephaistos in the Rail.[4] Wrote to Ld Clarendon—Ld Granville—Sir Thos G.—Mr C. Villiers—Ld Spencer—Mr Bright.

Notes for Osborne. Feb. 15/69.[5]
1. The Irish Church. Delay. Seeing Abp. of C.—his offer. Hartington's letter.
2. The Speech. 3. The Answer to the Address, to be recd. in person?
Anglesea—Ld Lieutenancy. Rev. A.O. Medd for Peel district of Amble Warkworth.[6] Mr Childers withdraws his proposal as to the V. Admiralship.

To J. BRIGHT, president of the board of trade,   Add MS 43385, f. 28.
15 February 1869. 'Private.'

I think that for once Mr Miall,[7] for whom I have the greatest respect, reckons according to your account of him, without his host. The Presbyterians are determined to have the governing body made a party to the receipt of the commutation money by the clergymen by themselves & have no objection to it whatever as far as the Church is concerned. They would resent extremely a change such as is suggested, and of course if applied to the Church it must be applied to them also.

The one point in which we have gone very far in liberality to the Church is that of the Glebe houses. I mean in principle: practically the amount is very small. The Presbyterians will also have some concessions beyond strict right, such as reorganising the Assistant Successors, & paying for the Belfast Buildings. All the parts of a complicated scheme of this kind have to be considered in relation to one another, & no doubt as you suggest cannot be sifted too much.

All went well at Osborne today—to my great satisfaction.

[1] N. Armstrong, perhaps from *Sermons on various subjects* (1854).
[2] A. *Ewing, 'On materialism in Christianity' (1867).
[3] R. W. Barnes, perhaps 'The repentance of Judas' (1865).
[4] For *Juventus Mundi.*   [5] Add MS 44757, f. 3.
[6] Arthur Octavius Medd, rector of Amble 1869.
[7] See Bright to Gladstone, 14 February 1869, Add MS 44385, f. 83, on a talk with Miall, H. Richard, and Presbyterians; Miall sent suggestions on disestablishment on 23 January, Add MS 44418, f. 198.

16. Tu.

Wrote to Ld Granville—Ld Stanley Ald.—Mr Glyn—Capt. Galton —Ld Ebury—Mrs Tennyson—Mr Delane—Mr Salisbury—& minutes. Revised Artemis MS. Read Fowler on Land.[1] Saw The Speaker (3)—Mr Ayrton—Mr Glyn (2)—Ld Granville—Scotts— Bp. of Oxford. H of C. 4½-8½. Spoke on Address.[2] Saw ... who has fought hard[R]

To Capt. D. S. GALTON, 16 February 1869. Add MS 44536, f. 116.
'Private.'

I am very much obliged by your letter[3] and I can conceive it very possible that a plan such as your sketch might be worked into shape. Before despairing however in the matter of the argument for immediate purchase, I wish to know whether the short leases are so entirely out of the question in Ireland where the relations of Railways are of little complexity as in England where they are highly complicated & become more so every day? In Ireland I imagine the country could be divided without much difficulty or even one company might possibly lease the whole.

17. Wed.

Wrote to Sir H. Moncreiff[4]—Chancr of Exchr—The Queen—Bp of Argyll—Ld Brougham—Ld Sydney—minutes. Caucus on Irish Ch. Bill from two to seven.[5] Saw Ld Lyttelton—Mr Grogan—Mr Glyn —Ld Granville—Mr A. Peel—Sir W. James. Dined at Sir W. James's. Revised a little MS.

18. Th.

Wrote to Abp of Canterb.—Ld Clarendon—Capt Galton—Mr Fortescue—Ld Russell—Mr Disraeli[6]—The Speaker—Mr Childers— Mr Delane, & minutes. Saw Mr Macevoy—Mr Glyn—Ld O. Fitzgerald (2)—Ld Granville—Mr Adam—Chancr of Exr—Sir E. May. Saw Gerald X. Read The Templar.[7] Conclave on Irish Church Bill

---

[1] W. Fowler, *Thoughts on 'Free trade in Land'* (1869).
[2] *H* cxciv. 74. [3] Untraced, as is Galton's reply.
[4] 'Your university [Edinburgh] has probably acted with wisdom in refusing to have me for their Chancellor: but I much regret now to be without any function which would afford me excuse & cause for visiting my friends in Edinburgh'; Add MS 44536, f. 116.
[5] i.e. cabinet cttee.; membership list at Add MS 44537, f. 21; notes for it, ibid., ff. 21-6.
[6] Informing him of Victoria's return to London, and of proposed address of the whole House; Add MS 44419, f. 89.
[7] *The Gladstone Government*, by A Templar (1869), semi-hostile.

2-7¼:[1] with ¾ hour interval at H. of C. to arrange about the reception of the Address.

To LORD CLARENDON, foreign secretary,   Clarendon MSS, c. 497.
18 February 1869.

Many thanks.[2] I will tell you when we have an opportunity my transaction about Monte Cassino.[3]

Annexation of Belgium is a terrible spectre. And the present wrath of France seems so absurd if it be considered with reference to the immediate occasion of the Railway that it naturally awakens suspicion.

I suppose it is desirable in the first instance to be positively assured, upon the best evidence, of what I for one believe, but do not know, that the true public opinion of Belgium is possessed with a sense of nationality, & is resolved to struggle for its maintenance. That is the only possible standing point I apprehend for permanent resistance.

To have France well girt about with strong neighbours is the needful security against this demon of ambition and aggression which seems still to linger within her, though not with a sway as undisputed as in former times. It must be long I fear before Spain can be stout. But Italy would be strong the moment she could 'make both ends meet'. The only way for strength for Italy as an European Power is through sound finance and to this she cannot come without cutting down her expenditure and especially her military expenditure. Reduction of army & navy is I believe her only road to true force in arms, and to a capability of curbing i.e. helping to curb France in case of need. But I did not mean to run on so far in speculation. I thought your draft about this Railway business very judicious.

To Capt. D. S. GALTON, 18 February 1869.   Add MS 44537, f. 117.

I had hoped that in Ireland the comparative backwardness and slowness of the Railway movement would have greatly diminished the difficulty attending the question of auxiliary works and have left it capable of being settled by fair arrangements as between Landlord and Tenant. The working of Railways by Government in this country (I mean the U.K.) staggers me very much. I would exhaust all alternatives before resorting to that. Ireland wants unity of management and I suppose lower fares. Could a money offer be made on the double condition of amalgamation among the companies and reduction of fares? Could the State also render these companies so amalgamated more nimble and workable by lightening their load of Capital in becoming proprietor of the permanent works, or would this be best done by acquiring the reversion of the whole? I always think these enormously heavy masses of investment are singularly ill-adapted to trading concerns which should always keep down their proportion of immovable capital.

---

[1] On position of curates; notes in Add MS 44757, f. 33.
[2] Clarendon's letter untraced.   [3] See above, v. lxxi.

19. Fr.

Wrote to Mr Childers—Ld O. Fitzgerald—Ld Sydney—Mrs L. Bell(?)[1]—The Queen—and minutes. Saw Mr Glyn—Ld Granville —Lord O. Fitzgerald—The Speaker—Ld Lyttelton—Ly Lyttelton in evg. Revised some Homer MS. Read The Templar. At Lambeth 12-1½ explaining to the Archbishop. Irish Ch. Conclave 2-7 with interruptions. H. of C. 4½-5.[2]

20. Sat.

Wrote to Att.Gen. Ireland (2)—Lord Chancellor—Mr Thring[3]— Archdn Stopford—Mr O. Stanley—The 'Templar'[4]—Mr Bright —Ld Gainsborough—The Queen—Mr Macmillan—& minutes. Cabinet 2-6¼. All well: but critical at one moment on I.C. Saw Mr Glyn—Hon Mrs Grey—Sir R. Phillimore—Mr Brand. Dined at Mr Goschen's, & had much interesting conversation with Mr Deutsch on Phoenicia.[5] Also with Mrs G. whom I liked much.[6] Revised a little MS: this is at a snail's pace in little morsels of time. Read the Templar.

For Cabinet Feb 20. 69.[7]
(1) Irish Church measure. Report

Progress
{ Ejectment Clause to be abandoned
Susp. Clauses.
Moiety of Commutation No.
Churches to be given upon Decl[aratio]n

(6) Mr Childers respecting Mr Corry's Memorandum[8] & motion for its production. Not to be given as unopposed return.
(8) Lopez motion for a Commission.[9]
⟨( ) Lowe on Clerkships.⟩
(2) Business in the Lords: Ld Granville. Resolved to recommend a second Committee—Lord Kimberley to be Consulted on the introduction of Bills
(3) Clarendon. To repeal the Aberdeen Act.[10]
(4) Argyll. Bill on India Council
(5) Mil. & Nav. Estimates Reduction 2050 m.

[1] Unidentified; possibly the courtesan.
[2] Answered question on 1867 Reform Act and rating: *H* cxciv. 127.
[3] Drafting the Irish Church Bill.
[4] Anon. author [W. C. M. Kent] (see 18 Feb. 69): Add MS 44536, f. 118.
[5] Emanuel Oscar Menahem *Deutsch, 1829-73; epigraphist and assistant librarian of British Museum.
[6] Lucy, *née* Dalley, m. 1857 G. J. *Goschen and d. 1898.
[7] Add MS 44637, f. 28.
[8] H. T. L. *Corry, *Disraeli's first lord, had left *Childers a mem. on navy reform, which he publicized on 8 March: *H* cxciv. 900.
[9] Sir L. M. *Lopes withdrew on 23 February his motion for a royal commission on local taxation after promise of govt. action: *H* cxciv. 223.
[10] *Aberdeen's Brazilian Slave Trade Act; repeal begun 2 March: *H* cxciv. 471.

(9) De Grey Cattle Plague
(7) Whether to amend the Pensions Act. Mem. drawn for the purpose

21. 2 S.Lent.

Whitehall mg (Dr Mansell) and All Saints aft. Wrote to Mr Fortescue
—Helen G. Wrote on I. Church. Saw Ld Dufferin. Saw Gerald X—
mixed[R]. Read Gatty's Sermon[1]—Wordsworth's Sermon[2]—Moncreiff on Creeds.[3]

22. M.

Wrote to C. Fortescue (2)—Bp of Peterborough—Ld Spencer—Bp
of Oxford—Mr Childers—Ld Dufferin—The Queen—and minutes.
H. of C. $4\frac{1}{4}$-$5\frac{1}{2}$: at work.[4] Read The Templar. Saw Duke of Argyll—
Mr Glyn—Ld Granville—Mr Childers. Conclave on Irish Ch. 2-$4\frac{1}{4}$
and $5\frac{1}{2}$-$7\frac{3}{4}$. After 20 hours work we finished the Bill—for this stage.[5]
Revised some MS.

To C. S. P. FORTESCUE, Irish secretary,   Carlingford MSS CP1/36.
22 February 1869.

1. I think your plan about Loans[6] is good: but I would make the term during
which the Act should operate a short one.
2. I prefer my plan about the Glebe Houses to yours, chiefly as much more safe
in respect to raising parallel claims. It does not recognise the Glebe Houses as
saleable property when severed from the land, a severance which we owe to your
suggestion & which seems to me very wise.
3. I think you might reserve a power of future legislation in respect to the Church
grave-yards, if you limit it: 'with a view to securing the free exercise of all the
rights now enjoyed by law in the same'—or in some such manner.
4. The Maynooth Clauses only represent the first idea now wholly altered &
much improved.
What do you say to this. Take the whole money now given 1. To Presb[y-
teria]n Widows' Fund 2. To Gen. Assembly's Colleges 3. To the non-orthodox
Presb[yterian] Professors 4. To Maynooth, and throw them in with the Pres-
b[yteria]n Ministers' Compensation money. This might all be put in one Clause:
& the Ministers' Compensation Money would then determine the number of
years' purchase. I think it would be not less than *14*.[7]

[1] A. Gatty, 'Church and state. A sermon' (1869).
[2] C. *Wordsworth, probably *The history of the Church of Ireland, in eight sermons*
(1869).
[3] Sir H. W. *Moncreiff, *Creeds and churches in Scotland* (1869).
[4] Questions, spoke on political pensions: *H* cxciv. 165.
[5] Printed version, with MS alterations, in Add MS 44609, f. 53.
[6] Add MS 44121, f. 118.
[7] Reply untraced.

23. Tu.

Wrote to Mr Angerstein—Ald. Salomons—Mr J.B. Smith—Mr Bill-son—Mr Salisbury—Mr Fortescue—Att.Gen.Irel.—and minutes. Worked on Irish Ch.Mema. H of C. 4½-11.[1] Work. Saw Mr Lambert (I.Ch.)—Mr Goschen—Mr Glyn—Att. General—Att.Gen. Ireland *cum* Mr Fortescue—C. Lyttelton. Saw Ld Hastings's Pictures. Revised a morsel of MS.

24. Wed.

Wrote to Bp of Durham—Mr Salisbury—Mr Goschen—Att Gen. Engl.—Earl of Devon—Att.Gen.Irel. (2)—Mr Lambert—Kg of Belgians—The Queen (2)—Archbp of York—Ld Clarendon. Revised a little Homer. Saw Archdn Stopford—Mr Homersham Cox—Mr Glyn —Ld Granville—Mr West—Ld Clarendon—Dr Vaughan—Bp of Oxford—Also Lady Palmerston—Prince La Tour—Ld De Tabley —Dined at Lady Herbert's—Read Tracts on Irish Church.

25. Th.

Wrote to Abp of Canterby—Mr Cardwell—Bp of Peterboro.—Ld Granville—Mr Macmillan—and minutes. H. of C. 4½-6½.[2] Revision of MS. Read Adair on I. Church.[3] Saw Baron Beaulieu[4]—Att.Gen. Irel. *cum* Mr Fortescue—Ld Devon *cum* Mr Baxter—Prince Latour d'Auvergne—Mr Lambert—Mr Glyn—Bp of Peterboro.—Bp of Oxford—The Speaker *cum* Sir G. Grey. Eight to dinner.

26. Fr.

Wrote to Ld Clarendon—The Lord Mayor—The Queen (2)—and minutes. 11-4. Worked with Mr Sullivan Mr Thring & Mr Law[5] through the text of the Irish Church Bill.[6] Worked on Irish Church papers. Saw Duke of Argyll—Chancr of Exr—Mr Currie *cum* Mr Glyn—Mr Russell (Star)[7]—Mr Fortescue—Mr Sullivan. Read the 'Gladstone Adminn'.

[1] Opposed Vacating of Seats Bill: *H* cxciv. 221.

[2] *Goschen's Assessed Rates Bill: *H* cxciv. 315.

[3] R. A. S. Adair, Baron Waveney, *The Established Church of Ireland, past and future*, 2 v. (1869).

[4] Baron Alcindor de Beaulieu, Belgian ambassador 1869-72.

[5] Hugh *Law, 1818-83; legal adviser to lord lieutenant 1868; Irish solicitor general 1872, attorney general 1873, 1880-1; liberal M.P. Londonderry 1874-81; Irish lord chancellor 1881-5.

[6] Working copy in Add MS 44757, f. 43.   [7] Unidentified.

27. Sat.

Wrote to Bp of London—Mr Fortescue (2)—Att.Gen. Ireland—Ld Spencer—The Viceroy—Mr Delane—The Queen—Bp of Chester —& minutes. Cabinet 1½-5½. Saw Mr Fortescue—Mr Neilson Hancock[1]—Mr Glyn—The Brazilian Minister—The Prussian Ambassr. Worked on Ir.Ch. papers. Attended the Speaker's party before dinner: then went off, and dined with C. & A[gnes] at the French Ambassador's. Lady de Grey's afterwards. On a sad account of the Bp of S[alisbury] went to Grosvenor St. Read Gladstone Cabinet.

Cabinet Sat Feb. 27.[2]
√ 1. Levée & Drawingroom Arrangements.
√ 2. Irish Church. Commut[atio]n—Curates.
√ 3. Col. Wetherall.[3]
√ 4. British Officers for Shah of Persia.
√ 5. Consult[atio]n on Election procedure. Thursday?
√ (6) Clarendon's report F.O. Telegram
√ (7) Important Bills to be circulated in Cabinet.
√ 8 Week's notices.
√ 9. Lord President to be on the Governing body of Eton, asked by the College. Decline civilly.
√10. Lord Redesdale's motion.[4]

To J. T. DELANE, 27 February 1869.   Add MS 44419, f. 132.

As I find you are out of town I put a few words on paper.
1. A person whose name is immaterial said to one of my colleagues today 'I know the Govt. plan: disestablishment, disendowment, compensation for vested interests, & application of the surplus to secular purposes.['] This is true in a certain sense, yet has the same relation I think to the truth as the skeleton to the man.
2. The English bishops have behaved extremely well in Convocation under the guidance apparently of my Lords of Peterborough & Oxford. You gave them credit a few days ago—they have now finished the business & overcome the lower House, & they deserve another slice.
3. The 'thorough' Church party in Ireland are not at one among themselves & are building upon the hope of our divisions & the splitting off of sections, or the excitement of religious prejudices. I think we shall give no fair ground for such a revival: but our friends will do well to be warned.
4. Unless I am much mistaken the great fight of the opponents will be upon the demand of the whole Post-Reformation Endowments, as contra-distinguished

---

[1] William Neilson Hancock, 1820-88; Irish statistician and economist; many mema. by him in 1869 on Irish glebes etc. in Add MS 44610.
[2] Add MS 44637, f. 29v.
[3] Appt. of Sir Edward Robert *Wetherall, 1815-May 1869, soldier, as *Spencer's undersec. in Ireland, led to a storm; see 5 Mar. 69.
[4] *Granville successfully opposed *Redesdale's motion on precedents for appropriation of property: *H* cxciv. 689.

from the concession we made with regard to private gifts really given to the present Irish Church. This ground will not be bad for us.

To EARL SPENCER, Irish lord lieutenant,   Add MS 44536, f. 120.
27 February 1869.

In answer to your interesting letter[1] I have only time to say a few words. Nothing in my opinion could be more judicious than your conversation with the Archbp. of Dublin. Though we have not obtained from the Irish Bench all we could desire, & they have probably made a mistake in leaving it to the Bishop of Down alone to take the bold & rational part yet on the whole the communications with the Church authorities have done much good. You will I hope be pleased, as I have been, with the proceedings of the English Bishops, mainly guided by my Lords of Oxford & Peterborough in their convocation. The work on the measure is now at the last moment extremely severe but all goes *well* in all quarters. I am to begin please God at $4\frac{1}{2}$ or 5 on Monday but when I shall *end*, I really do not know. Probably before Christmas.

28. 3 S.Lent.

Whitehall Chapel mg (Dr Barry) & St James's Evg. Dined with the Lothians. Wrote to Ld Clarendon—Lady Johnstone—Mr Glyn—Archdeacon Stopford—Att.Gen. Ireland. Saw Lady M. Farquhar. Read Todd on Irish Ch;[2] Reid;[3] thoughts on Questns of the Day;[4] &c. Worked on Irish Ch.

Mond. Mch One 1869.

Wrote to Scotts—Mr Bruce—Att.Gen. for I. (2)—Mr Hammond—and minutes. Saw Dr N. Hancock—Att. General for Ireland—Mr Glyn. Worked on Irish Ch papers & speech. H. of C. $4\frac{1}{2}$-$8\frac{3}{4}$. Explained the Irish Ch measure in a long speech 4.50-8.10. Thank God it was well received by the House: however unequal the speech to the subject.[5] Dined with the Jameses: a short walk afterwards. Read Gladstone Cabinet.

2. Tu.

Wrote to Ld Lansdowne—Ld Spencer—E. Ellice—The Queen (2) —Mr Thring—Scotts—and minutes. Woolwich Deputn 3-4.[6] H of

---

[1] Of 26 February 1869, Add MS 44306, f. 75, relating a talk with Trench, in which Spencer urged him to speak out moderately.
[2] C. H. Todd, *The Irish Church: its disestablishment and disendowment* (1869).
[3] Perhaps J. Reid, *Voices of the soul answered in God* (1866).
[4] Perhaps C. *Girdlestone, *The questions of the day by the creature of an hour* (1859).
[5] Irish Church Bill 1°R: *H* cxciv. 412.
[6] Against dockyard closure; *Kentish Mercury*, 6 March 1869.

C. 4½-8.[1] Saw Duke of Argyll—D. of Newcastle *cum* Mr Ouvry & Mr Richards—Bp of London (Incr[ease] of Sees)—Mr Lambert—Mr Glyn. Finished Gladstone Cabinet. Read Morgan on Health in Towns.[2]

3. Wed.

Wrote to Mr Thomas—Mr Cardwell—Mr Newman Hall—D of Newcastle—Sir T. Biddulph—Lord Spencer—Col. Foley—Mr Fortescue—Mr Childers—Lord Lyttelton—Ld Devon—Bp of Chester—Ld Clarendon—Gen. Grey—Ld Kinnaird—and minutes. The Queen's Court at 3. Twenty to dinner: & evening party afterwards. Saw Mr Glyn.

To Sir W. HEATHCOTE, 3 March 1869.   Add MS 44536, f. 121

I have desired that a copy of the Irish Church Bill may be sent to you. Do not notice it unless you see occasion. There must be in it, though it is the fruit of much labour, points open to consideration. One of my great anxieties was so to start it as to avoid exciting jealousy & suspicion at the outset on the part of those favourably inclined. This I think has been accomplished: & it will enable us with all the greater advantage to consider on their merits suggestions of detail touching the parties interested. I always think of you on the way to & from Osborne, as well as at other times.

Pray do not scruple to write to me about Clergymen whom you may consider eminently good: describing their politics *quoad* the present crisis so far as you are able or think right.

If you come to town I trust we shall hear of you.

To EARL SPENCER, Irish lord lieutenant,   Add MS 44306, f. 89.
3 March 1869.

If Stopford has played fair with us (which I must presume, though many churchmen seem to denounce him as a jobber) his main cause of complaint is that we have not adopted his *half & half* Clause for absolute Commutation.

We have done what is *far better* for him. We have got our Bill in without awakening the jealousy or suspicion either of Presbyterians, Dissenters or R-Catholics. This being so we are in a condition to consider without prejudice amendments of detail. I told Stopford I should not wonder if his Clause were adopted, or something of the kind, in the course of the discussions. But the Cabinet after a great deal of consideration thought it a dangerous clause to start with.

My opinion is that the aspect of the measure will probably improve in the view of the Church as it is further considered. I only hope that with this improvement there may not be any opposite change in our own side.

[1] Question on Ireland, misc. business: *H* cxciv. 482.
[2] J. E. Morgan, 'Town life among the poorest' (1869).

Meantime I am glad to say that so far as I yet know it is not unfavourably viewed by some church people here as we could fairly look to. I have *seen* some, & you will be amused when I say that those whom I have heard of are Mrs. Tait, Lyttelton, & the Bp of Oxford—not however a bad typical selection. We are all much pleased: which I hope will raise your pulse.

How well the secret was kept—a copy of the Bill goes to you by post. P.S. The Dean of Westminster [A. P. Stanley] I am told is very wrath.[1]

4. *Th.*

Wrote to Sir John Hanmer—Mr A. Russell—Archbp of York—Dean Ramsay—Lord Petre—M. de Bousquet—Mr Henry Ley[2]—Sir C. O'Loghlen—Bp of St David's—Mr W. Rathbone—& minutes. 1-2. Audience of the Queen.[3] $2\frac{1}{2}$-4. Deputation from Cheshire on Cattle Plague Rate. Deputation on Beerhouses.[4] Saw Bp of Chester —Duke of Argyll—Mr Glyn—M. Bratiano—Mr Maguire—Ld Chancr Ireland—Mr Monsell—Mr Rathbone—Mr Baines. Read Miss Lott's Nile Journey.[5] Saw Gerald X. H of C. $4\frac{1}{2}$-$8\frac{3}{4}$.[6]

Buckm. Palace. Mch. 4. 69. Conversation with H.M.[7]
Navy Estimates & policy. Army d[itt]o. D[itt]o Staff. D. of Cambridge—Honorary Colonelcy—Prince [*sic*] Louise, Allowance?—Prince of Wales's Income, his journey to Constantinople, his constant & excessive expences, Jewellery—Ld Clarendon—the Belgian Railway—Ld Lieutenancy of Essex, Queen approves Ld Petre—Prince Arthur to have a Patrick—Constitution of Admiralty.

5. *Fr.*

Wrote to Chancr of Exr (2)—Dr Sterndale Bennett[8]—The Queen (3) —Duke of Argyll—Mr Whitmore—Mr A. Kinnaird—Ld Clarendon —Mr [R.] Green Price[9]—Rev. Dr Russell—and minutes. Saw Mr Cardwell—Do *cum* Ld Granville—Mr Glyn—Ld Lyttelton—Mr Bouverie—Chancr of Exr—Mr Fortescue—Rev. Dr Irons. H of C. $4\frac{1}{2}$-$8\frac{1}{2}$ and $9\frac{1}{2}$-$11\frac{1}{2}$.[10] Revised a little 'copy'. Read Emmeline Lott.

[1] Spencer had sent further accounts of talks with Irish bps.; 1 and 2 March 1869, Add MS 44306, ff. 81, 85.
[2] A retiring House of Commons clerk.
[3] On Prince of Wales' debts, see Magnus, *Edward VII*, 100.
[4] See *The Times*, 6 March 1869, 12b.
[5] E. Lott, *The Grand Pacha's cruise on the Nile*, 2v. (1869).
[6] Spoke not opposing select cttee. on elections but recalling that the ballot was traditionally 'an open question' (Gladstone remained opposed to it): *H* cxciv. 660.
[7] Add MS 44757, f. 6.
[8] (Sir) William Sterndale *Bennett, 1816-75; principal of Royal Academy of Music 1866; kt. 1871; requesting govt. financial help: Add MS 44536, f. 121.
[9] Thanking R. Green Price (see 12 Jan. 66) for resigning to let Hartington get a seat; he was cr. bart. 1874. See Add MS 44536, f. 124.
[10] Defended *Wetherall's appt. (see 27 Feb. 69): *H* cxciv. 756.

6. Sat.

Wrote to The Queen (2)—Chancr of Exr—Lord A. Paget—and minutes. Revised some MS. Cabinet 2.30–5.45. Saw Gen. Grey—Mr Glyn—Mr Bright—Sir J. Gray. Dined at Baron L. Rothschild's. Saw Dowager Duchess of Somerset after Cabinet: a friend some 36 years ago. Read [blank]

Notes for Cabinet. Mc. 6. 69.[1]
3. √ As to Committee on Abyssinian Expedition—Not to object.[2]
2. √ Committee on Election Procedure.[3]
    √ Numbers 19 ⅛[4]
    √ Chairman. Ld Hartington—ask Glyn
    √ Course of inquiry discussed
1. √ Belgian Railway Affair. Draft Dispatch to Ld Lyons read, & approved.[5]
4.   Mr Leatham's motion to refer to the Committee on Election Procedure the question of methods of secret voting.—Not to object if the last words are left out.[6]
√ 5. Chanc[ello]r of Exch[eque]r on the new Law Courts.[7] Statement.—To decide next time.
√ 6. Dispatch to Belgium recommending to accept a proper reference.
√ 7. Cardwell obtained sanction for certain prospective statements respecting Militia.
√ 8. The weekly list—Harcourt's [Voter Registration] Committee[:] Grant[8] —To throw out Ld R. Montague's Bill, if politic[9]

7. 4 S.Lent.

Windmill St Ch mg with H.C.—St And. Wells St aft. Saw Mrs Thistlethwayte. Wrote to Ld Clarendon—Ld Lyttelton. Read Bp of Ossory's pamphlet[10]—Ingle on H. Scripture[11]—Spinoza's Letter[12]—Joyce on Court of Appeal[13]—Romanoff on Greek Church.[14] Corrected some Proof.

---

[1] Add MS 44637, f. 30.   [2] Report in *PP* 1868-9 lxiii. 713.
[3] Hartington's Cttee. of 21 nominated on 16 March, two added on 19 March: *H* cxciv. 663. Reported in *PP* 1868-9 viii, 1870 vi, eventually recommending the ballot.
[4] i.e. 11 liberals, 8 tories; notes on ratio of govt.: opposition representation on select cttees. since 1833 in Add MS 44637, f. 31.
[5] Lyons' report of interview in PRO FO 27/1750.
[6] Leatham's motion for Instruction to the cttee. on elections to consider forms of the ballot, discussed 16 March and withdrawn: *H* cxciv. 1470.
[7] A perennial topic since the early 1860s; see 9 Mar. 69.
[8] See 9 Mar. 69n.   [9] On cattle plague: *H* cxciv. 996.
[10] J. T. *O'Brien, 'The disestablishment and disendowment of the Irish branch of the United Church considered' (1869).
[11] See 19 Nov. 65.
[12] B. de Spinoza, 'A letter expostulatory to a convert [A. Burgh] from Protestant Christianity' (1869).
[13] See 1 May 53.   [14] See 7 Feb. 69.

8. M.

Wrote to Mr Macmillan—Robn G.—Sir K. Johnstone—Dean of
Chichester—Mr Fortescue—Ld Granville—U.S. Cons. Genl—
Scotts—Dean of Lichfield—Sir F. Currie[1]—Ld Clarendon—Ld
Russell—Solr General—The Queen—and minutes. Saw Duke of
Argyll—Mr Ayrton—Mr Glyn—Ld Granville—The Speaker—
Mr Cardwell—A. Kinnaird—Educn Commee P.C. 2-3$\frac{3}{4}$. H of C. 4$\frac{1}{2}$-
9 and 9$\frac{3}{4}$-12$\frac{3}{4}$.[2] Read Doyle's Lectures. Revised proofs.

To W. F. HOOK, dean of Chichester, 8 March 1869.   Add MS 44536, f. 125.

It was with great pleasure that I learn you think favourably[3] of our plan for
dealing with the Irish Church—and that you are willing to give us the advantage
of your name & authority as well as your approval.

There is no doubt that every adhesion of the class & character of yours im-
proves our position as to the power of dealing equitably & favourably with the
Church.

I send some papers the material of which may be used, though no reference
should be made to them in public: and any inquiries you may make shall be
answered to the best of our ability.

9. Tu.

Wrote to Duke of Argyll 2—Pres. Maynooth—Ld Clarendon—Bp
of Gloucester—Chancr of Exr—Ld Clarendon—The Queen—Ld
Chancr of I[reland]—Dean of Ferns—and minutes. Wrote Mem. on
Law Courts.[4] Saw Mr Glyn—Mr Ayrton—Lord Granville—Mr
Goschen—Mr Fortescue. Irish Railway Deputation 3 PM.[5] Licensing
Deputation 4$\frac{1}{4}$ PM.[6] H of C. 4$\frac{1}{2}$-8$\frac{1}{2}$.[7] Revised proof. Read Doyle's
Lectures—Carrias on Gibraltar[8]—Indian RR. papers.[9]

To LORD CLARENDON, foreign secretary,   Clarendon MSS, c. 497.
9 March 1869.

Gen. Grey is himself inclined to be valiant on the subject of fighting even alone
for Belgium but I do not see how it is safe to go beyond making it known that
the day when this Nation seriously suspects France of meaning ill to Belgian independence will be the last day of friendship with that country, and that then a future will open for which no man can answer. But from the present complexion

---

[1] Sir Frederick *Currie, 1799-1875; in India; cr. bart. 1847; on council of India from
1858.
[2] Questions, navy estimates: *H* cxciv. 863.   [3] Hook's letter untraced.
[4] Add MS 44536, f. 126.   [5] No report found.
[6] See Harrison, *Drink and the Victorians*, 260.
[7] W. V. *Harcourt's motion for select cttee. on registration passed: *H* cxciv. 984.
[8] V. Carrias, *Gibraltar to Bourbonless Spain* (1869).   [9] *PP* 1868-9 xlvii.

of the affair it seems as though the present moment did not require the use of this kind of language.

I have read with grief Mr. Elliot's No 99 & inclosure describing the proceedings of Turkish authorities in the Sporades. I am not a little surprised that he transmits the paper without comment which it seems to me, perhaps owing to my ignorance, eminently to require.

10. Wed.

Wrote to Archdn of Meath—Dean of Elphin—Mr Ouvry—Bp of Lichfield—Sec. Rescue Soc. and minutes. At Christie's. Saw Mr Ouvry—Mr Glyn—Sol. Genl—General Grey—Sir R. Palmer. Dined with the Colonial Society, and returned thanks for Ministers. Cartier striking.[1] The Speaker's Levée afterwards. C. had a dinner-party wh I then joined. I was much touched with Ronald [Leveson-Gower]. It is a widowhood. H of C. $3\frac{1}{4}$-$5\frac{3}{4}$. Revised proof. Read Rescue Soc.s pamphlet.[3]

11. Th.

Wrote to Ld Ronald L. Gower—Lord Chancellor—Mr Baines—Count Strzelecki—Mr Fortescue—Ld Lansdowne[4]—Mr Glyn—Ld Granville (2)—D. of Argyll—The Queen—& minutes. H of C. $4\frac{1}{2}$-8 & 1-$1\frac{3}{4}$.[5] Audience of H.M. Saw Col. Greville Nugent—Mr Bouverie, Mr Locke, & conclave.—Mr Glyn—Ld Granville—Sir E. May—Sir J. Gray and others. Dined at Dowager Duchess of Somerset's.

Buckm. Palace Mch 11. 69. 1 pm.[6]
Mem. to ask: Mr Bruce, the Lord High C[ommissioner] for Scotland. Conversation on Reverdy [Johnson] & certain speeches—Belgian Differences with France—Bills in Parlt.—Constitn. of the Lords—Prospects of Ir. Ch. Bill—Irish Land Question—Ld Waterford & Mr. Vivian.

---

[1] *The Times*, 11 March 1860, 12. Sir George Etienne Cartier, 1814-73; Canadian defence minister; cr. bart. 1868.

[2] Montagu's Contagious Diseases (Animals) Bill successfully opposed: *H* cxciv. 996.

[3] Probably sent by *Strzelecki whose mem. on emigration of rescued prostitutes to Australasia Gladstone forwarded to Granville and Russell; Gladstone sent him £100 and made him K.C.M.G. See Add MS 44536, f. 132 and Ramm I, i. 18n.

[4] Dissuading from resignation Henry Charles Keith *Petty-Fitzmaurice, 1824-1927; 5th marquis of Lansdowne 1866; junior treasury lord 1868; under-sec. for war 1872-4, for India 1880 (resigned); governed Canada 1883-8; viceroy 1888-94; unionist; later war and foreign secretary. See Add MS 44536, f. 128.

[5] Army estimates: *H* cxciv. 1111.

[6] Add MS 44757, f. 9.

To G. G. GLYN, chief whip, 11 March 1869.   Add MS 44536, f. 128.

I think the enclosed will do as the basis of a communication from you to Noel.[1]

Inclosure—That we cannot agree in the justice of the claims that the Opposition shall on all Committees which are named by Conference between the two sides be represented by a number only one less than the number chosen from the side of the Govt. That to prevent debate & expedite business we are willing to acquiesce in this method of proceeding on the present occasion though we cannot think it just or equal as among the members of the House. That we reserve an entire freedom for the future & must be free to state our opinions & the circumstances which have occurred on any occasion when discussion may arise.

With these reserves we [blank] to name a Committee of 21 in 11 & 10.

Perhaps they will not object to name on their side one gentleman not committed & open to consider the matter respecting the Ballot.

12. Frid.

Wrote to Ld Advocate—Mrs A. Harvey—Mr Maguire—Sir C. Trevelyan—The Queen—and minutes. H of C. $4\frac{1}{2}$-$8\frac{1}{4}$ and 9-$2\frac{1}{4}$.[2] Saw Mr Glyn—Mr Ayrton—Chancr of Exr. Saw Ormond—hopeful[R]. Saw Scotts. Read Barnes on my Chapter[3]—Romilly on Ballot.[4] Attended meeting of Trustees of N. Portr. Gallery.

13. Sat.

Wrote to Christie's—Ld Clarendon—The Queen—Cardinal Cullen[5] —and minutes. Cabinet $2\frac{1}{2}$-6. Dined at Ld Clarendon's. Saw Sir R. Murchison—Mr Maclaren—Mr Glyn—Sir R. Phillimore—Dr Russell & Maynooth Professors—Ld Lansdowne—Ld Stratford de Redcliffe. Lady de Grey's in evg. Read [blank] on Ecce Homo.

Cabinet Mch 13. 69.[6]

√ 1. Franco-Belgian question. To prepare draft for Paris.[7]

√ 2. Joint Committee[8]

√ 3. Account of proceedings in H[ouse] of C[ommons]:
  Locke King's [Real Estate Intestacy] Bill
  Stapylton's [Representative Peers (Scotland and Ireland) Bill] d[itt]o.[9]

[1] Gerald James Noel, tory whip.
[2] Spoke on mail steamer contracts: *H* cxciv. 1307.
[3] R. Barnes, *Thoughts on Mr. Gladstone's Chapter of Autobiography, in its legal aspect* (1869).
[4] H. Romilly, *Public responsibility and vote by ballot* (1867).
[5] On cathedrals and glebes; Add MS 44419, f. 198, 209.
[6] Add MS 44637, f. 34.
[7] Gladstone's softening comments on Clarendon's draft, in Add MS 44536, f. 129; see Guedalla, *Q*, i. 167.
[8] Joint cttee. of both houses to expedite business; see Ramm I, i. 16n.
[9] *H* cxciv. 956, 984.

√ 4. Business of next week
>   Lords—Ld Russell's notice—Scotch Education Bill: encouragement to
>   higher branches. D[uke] of Argyll. agreed to
>   Commons. Leatham's Ballot motion—Party Processions Act—Rev.
>   Officers Bill.

√ 5. Argyll on India Council Bill & power of Sec[retary of] State as to secret
>   Dispatches

√ 6. Childers Greenwich Hosp[ital] Bill.

14. 5 S.Lent.

Chap. Royal mg: Bp of Lichfield. Whitehall aft. Bp of Peterborough.
The former was the greater. Wrote to Ld Clarendon. Dined with the
Lothians. Saw Lady Lyttelton—Ld St Germans. Read Coleridge's
Keble[1]—Romanoff on Gk Church[2]—Mant's Hist Ch. of Ireland[3]—
Leighton's Sermons.[4]

15. M.

Wrote to Ld Clarendon—Ld Spencer—Mr Fortescue—Mr W.R.
Greg—Sir H. Holland—Rev. Mr Rawson—Dr Pusey—The Queen
and minutes. Eleven to dinner. Saw Mr Ouvry—Mr Kirk *cum* Mr
Machin—Mr Glyn—Scotts. H of C. 4½-8 and 9½-1¼.[5] Read Doyle.[6]
Corr. proofsheets [of *Juventus Mundi*].

To C. S. P. FORTESCUE, Irish secretary,   Carlingford MSS CP1/39.
15 March 1869.

>   I inclose a note from Clarendon with a letter he has sent me, for your perusal.
>   Upon reflection I think that Disraeli's practice of systematically speaking into
> the small hours when he makes a motion against a Government absolves us from
> putting up a Minister to answer him there & then: and I believe it would do per-
> fectly well if you like to close for us on Thursday evening, speaking say at ten,
> when there will probably be an abundant but quiet House, and let [W. H.]
> Gregory follow Disraeli as G. would probably consider it a compliment. So pray
> choose & let me know in the House.

16. Tu.

Wrote to Adm. Hamilton—Duke of Argyll—Earl Russell—Dean
Ramsay—The Queen—Mrs Thistlethwayte—Ld Grosvenor—&

[1] See 7 Feb. 69.   [2] See 7 Feb. 69.   [3] See 29 Apr. 40.
[4] R. *Leighton, Sermons* (1692).
[5] Questioned on Irish church property; Endowed Schools Bill 2°R: *H* cxciv. 1352.
[6] See 30 Jan. 69.

minutes. Depn agt Sunday openings at 2.30: some 300. Deputation for do at 3.15: some 150.[1] Saw Ld de Grey—Mr Lowe *cum* Mr Layard—Mr Glyn. H of C. 4½-9 and 9¾-2¼.[2] Read E. Lott's Nile Voyage.

To EARL RUSSELL, 16 March 1869.   Add MS 44537, f. 130

I am very glad that there are to be movements in the House of Lords in different branches of the subject which I would call Reform of that House, except that the name might perhaps raise associations of political controversy which would be both disagreeable and mischievous. You take the question of Life Peers, and Lord Grey as I understand proposes to deal with the Representative system of the Irish and Scottish Peerage.[3] I cannot but hope that the question of Proxies will receive further consideration; though it would not appear on a Bill. There is yet another head which, not in an official capacity, I should like to present to you for consideration. Would it shock you very much to do these two things: 1. To allow any Peer of age under 25 to be elected to the House of Commons renouncing his option to take his peerage during that Parliament for which he was chosen. 2. To allow any Heir apparent or Heir presumptive to a Peerage, upon being elected to the House of Commons, to declare by option that he would sit for the Parliament and so lose the power to take up his Peerage. This declaration to be at the time of the election. I have heard some persons question whether one or both of these could not be done under the present law. If you encourage these ideas, or any like them, I will mention them to Ld Granville.

It gives me particular pleasure to see you and Ld Grey move in this business, because it is above all things desirable to keep it out of the vortex of Party and I do not see why rational men of all sides should not come to an agreement. With this view it appears almost indispensable that it should also be kept, at the outset, out of the hands of the government of the day.

17. Wed.

Wrote to Mr Rawson—Ld Clarendon—Mr Ouvry—and minutes. Dined at Baron A. Rothschild's. Br Museum Eln Meeting 6 P.M. Saw Mr Williams—Att.Gen. with Chancr of Exr—Ld Granville—Baron Beaulieu. H of C. 1½-6: spoke on Mr Monk's [Revenue Officers] Bill.[4] Corr. Irish Ch. Speech. Corr. Homer MS. Proofs. Evening party at home.

18. Th.

Wrote to Ld Shaftesbury—The Queen—and minutes. Finished revision of Speech on Irish Church Bill. Saw Ld Granville—Mr Glyn—

[1] On Sunday opening of museums; he was noncommital; *The Times*, 17 March 1869, 12f.
[2] Oppose Leatham's motion (see 6, 13 Mar. 69): *H* cxciv. 1518.
[3] Respective bills introduced 9 April: *H* cxcv. 452, 473.
[4] Successfully opposing it: *H* cxciv. 1592.

Ld Hartington. Dined at Sir E. Buller's. H of C. 4½-8 and 9½-1: Irish Church Debate.[1] Read Henry VIII.

19. Fr.

Wrote to Sir J. Lawrence—Abp of Canterb.—The Queen (2)— Chancr of Exchr—Mr Clode[2]—Count Strzelecki—Scotts—Sir H. Holland—Mr Clode—Padre Tosti—& minutes. H of C. 4½-8¼ and 9¼-1. Admirable speeches from Bright and Sullivan.[3] Saw Mr Burnett—Mr Glyn—Mr Dent. Dined with the Wests. Corrected proof. Saw Broughton[R]. Read Henry VIII.

20. Sat. [Latimer]

Wrote to Sir J. Ramsden[4]—Archdn Stopford—Mr Glyn (2)—W. Darbishire—The Queen—Mrs Maguire[5]—Bp of Down—and minutes. Off to Latimer[6] at 4/40. Cabinet 1½-4. Saw Mr Glyn— Mr West—Duke of Argyll. Corrected proof. Read divers pamphlets.

Cabinet Mch 20. 69.[7]
√ 1. Clarendon—Franco-Belgian [railway] question.
√ 2. Abyssinian Crown. to go to Kensington.
√ 3. American Mail Contracts—
    Meaning of 'one month'—
    Day of adjournment in the event of an adverse report from the Committee to be altered.
      Govt. to support Committee.[8]
√ 4. Whether Govt is to ask a monopoly of Telegraphs. Yes.[9]
√ 5. Course of inquiry in El[ection] Procedure Committee considered.
√ 6. Good Friday Ernest Jones meeting in Trafalgar Square.[10]
√ 7. Next Cabinet.

---

[1] *H* cxciv. 1662.
[2] C. M. Clode had sent his *Military forces of the Crown*, 2 v. (1869); Add MS 44536, f. 132. See 6 Feb. 49.
[3] *H* cxciv. 1876.
[4] Denouncing his attending a constituency banquet on the night of the Irish Church division; Add MS 44419, f. 244.
[5] Wife of J. F. *Maguire, who had requested a post for him: Add MS 44536, f. 132.
[6] Chesham's place in Buckinghamshire.
[7] Add MS 44637, f. 36.
[8] Select cttee. on mail contracts reported on 23 March 1869: *PP* 1868-9 vi. 265.
[9] Implementation of the 1868 Telegraph Act was contingent on funds to be voted in 1869; see J. L. Kieve, *Electric Telegraph* (1973), ch. viii.
[10] Feeble demonstration in memory of *Jones, whose post-Chartist legal career Gladstone had aided; *The Times*, 27 March 1869, 9d.

21. *Palm Sund.*

Latimer Ch mg & aft. Conversation with D. of Argyll on his 'Primitive Man' all of which I read.[1] Read Keble's Coleridge.[2] Walk with Mr Arnold.[3]

22. *M.* [*London*]

Wrote to Earl Cowper—Ld Clarendon (2)—Mr Lowe—Mr Bouverie —Mr Bruce—The Queen—Sir Thos G.—and minutes. Dined with Sir W. James. H of C. 4½-8¼ and 9½-12½.[4] Saw Mr Murphy[5]—Mr Kinnaird—Mr Glyn—Ld Hartington—Mr Dent. Corrected proofs.

To LORD CLARENDON, foreign secretary,   Clarendon MSS, c. 497
22 March 1869.

   Ought not Argyll, and perhaps Bright, to see Thornton's letter,[6] in order that they may be on their guard against Sumner whom with you I conceive to be our arch-enemy.[7]
   If Mr. Motley comes here as Minister I hope he will be good enough to explain his having in substance declared me a liar some years ago in a published document, I think a letter.[8]
   I should be much obliged if you would let Mr. Thornton know this.
   [P.S.] If the Americans *claim* for all the sufferings of their marine, we may quite as well or much better claim for the *Lancashire Famine.*

23. *Tu.*

Wrote to Ld Bessborough—Ld Stanhope—Mr Maguire—The Queen —& minutes. Corrected proofs. Dined with the Jameses. Saw Mr Lambert—Mr Glyn—Ld Hartington—Mr Seeley—and in the Division Lobby Conclave on Packet Contracts. Worked papers on Irish Ch. H of C. 4½-8¼ and 9-3¾. Spoke 1¼ hour after Mr Hardy rising at 1¼ AM, and voted in 368:250, a notable & historic Division.[9]

[1] G. D. *Campbell, duke of Argyll, *Primeval Man* (1869).
[2] *Sic*; see 14 Mar. 69.   [3] See 30 Mar. 69.
[4] Questioned on Greece; Irish Church Bill: *H* cxciv. 1896.
[5] Nicholas Daniel Murphy, b. 1811; liberal M.P. Cork 1865-80.
[6] Probably Thornton's analysis of Grant's new cabinet and Sumner, 8 March, PRO FO 5/1159, f. 69.
[7] In another note, Gladstone told Clarendon he did not mean 'that part of it which relates to the rejected suggestion'.
[8] See 1 Apr. 69.
[9] Irish Church Bill 2°R: *H* cxciv. 2106 and Bassett, *Speeches*, 380. Annotated division list in Add MS 44609, f. 249.

24. Wed.

Wrote to Robn G.—Ld Granville—Att.Gen.Irel.—Mrs Bennett—
& minutes. Dined with the Lothians. All Saints Ch. in aft.—late.
Saw Duke of Argyll—Mr Davidson[1]—Dean of Carlisle—Ld Clarendon—Ld Granville—Mr G. Richmond—Mr Glyn. Saw Bp of Salisbury. He looked much better. He was more moved than could I fear
be good for him. Worked on MS. correction. Read Denison's Concio[2]
—Sir N. Campbell's Journal.[3]

25. Thurs. Annunciation [Wilton]

Church 7 P.M. (at Wilton). Wrote to Lord Lyttelton—Mr Hamilton
—Mr Cadogan—Lord Kildare—Sir Thos G.—Mr Glyn—Dr Guthrie—& minutes. Off at 11¼ for Wilton. Arrived at 3. Walk with
Strzelecki. All my family here except Stephy. The Herbert younger
generation very pleasant and satisfactory. Music in evg. Read Lady D.
Beauclerc's Tour in Norway:[4] and looked at a very strange and evil
volume wh I have seen before.[5]

26. Good Friday.

Church 10½ A.M. & 7 P.M. Domestic Prayers 10 P.M.: as good &
hearty as ever. Wrote to Ld Clarendon—& minutes. Walk with Strzelecki & A. Herbert & Mr Doyle. Social conversation with A.H: who is
I fear *out of gear* in great matters.[6] Read Coleridge's Keble—Cobbett's Hist. Reformation!![7]—Contemp.Rev. on the Two Religions:[8]
both writer & Editor I think much to be condemned—Thomas
A'Kempis—Greenwich Ch. Union Sermon.

27. Sat. Easter Eve.

Church 10½ A.M. Walk with Count S. & others. Wrote to Mr C.
Fortescue—Mr W. Johnson—Mr Layard—and minutes. Worked on

[1] Probably John Robert Davison, 1826-71; liberal M.P. Durham 1868-71; judge advocate general 1870.
[2] G. A. *Denison, *Concio Archidiaconi de Taunton in sistendo prolocutore Cantuarensi habita* (1869).
[3] Sir N. *Campbell, *Napoleon at Fontainebleau and Elba* (1869).
[4] Lady D. de Vere Beauclerk, *A summer and winter in Norway* (1868).
[5] i.e. pornography in the Wilton library.
[6] Auberon Edward William Molyneux *Herbert, 1838-1906, s. of 3rd earl of Carnarvon; fellow of St. John's, Oxford 1855-69; *Northcote's sec. 1866-8; liberal M.P. Nottingham 1870-4. Prominent republican in early 1870s.
[7] W. *Cobbett, *A history of the Protestant 'Reformation' in England and Ireland* (1824).
[8] *Contemporary Review*, x. 321 (March 1869).

Homeric MS. Read Lady D. Beauclerk—Studies on Homer[1]—Palgrave's H. of Commons.[2]

28. Easter Day.

Wilton Ch. 10½ A.M. and H.C.—Salisbury Cathedral at 3. P.M. Wilton H. Prayers at 10 P.M. Wrote to Ld Lieut. of Ireland—Ld Clarendon—D. of Argyll—Chancr of Exr—Gen. Grey—& minutes. Read Coleridge's Keble—Swinny's Sermons[3]—and [blank]. Walk with Clem. Hamilton[4]—Saw Mrs H.

To General C. GREY, 28 March 1869.   Add MS 44536, f. 134.

I have this day received your letter, & sent it to the Lord Lieut. He is obviously the proper person to give an opinion with authority. He has with him his Law Officers & he will doubtless consult the U. Sec. & the Chief of the Constabulary. I cannot be surprised at the Queen's anxiety, we must not of course raise any phantoms, but nothing that rational & well informed persons would deem a risk ought to be run. I am rather sanguine in the matter but in Ireland they are better judges. I have not seen the article in the Pall Mall Gazette to which you refer, nor should I attach much authority to the opinion of that journal, & I own I do not infer that the purpose of the release of the prisoners has failed on account of improper or seditious language among them since their release. For our purpose & duty is to endeavour to draw a line between the Fenians & the people of Ireland, & to make the people of Ireland indisposed to cross it. But as to the general connexion of those who are Fenians already I do not expect much—when they have once committed themselves, their self love & pride become enlisted & the mere sense that their chances of proselytism are diminishing (if so it were) might increase their wrath.

To EARL SPENCER, Irish lord lieutenant,   Add MS 44536, f. 135.
28 March 1869.

Will you kindly consult with the proper persons on the subject of the enclosed letter from Genl. Grey.[5] The Queen's uneasiness cannot be wondered at; but I can hardly suppose there is any personal danger to the young Prince in the projected journey—you however & those about you will be far better judges in this matter than I am. The Pall Mall Gazette may be right but very little weight is to be attached to its authority, & I cannot agree with Genl. Grey that there is any proof of failure in the conciliatory effect hoped for. *That* effect is an effect made less on Fenians *in spe* than on Fenians *in posse*—our object is to stop the

---

[1] i.e. his own book.
[2] Sir R. F. D. *Palgrave, 'The House of Commons' (1868).
[3] Probably H. H. Swinny, *Sermons on several occasions* (1865).
[4] Clement Edward, s. of bp. W. K. *Hamilton.
[5] On prince Arthur's visit to Ireland; Spencer's reply, 30 March 1869, Add MS 44306, f. 95, did not recommend postponement. Spencer thought 'some thing from the Pope would have a good effect'.

manufacture of Fenians which has so flourished of late years; & it is even conceivable that rage at some commencement of success in this purpose might exasperate the Fenians that are & might make them more outrageous. In or about the year 1844 Sir R. Peel procured a declaration or exhortation from the Pope to the Irish Clergy & people in the sense of law & order. I have been talking over with Clarendon the notion of such a thing now, I have little doubt we could get it if it be desirable. How does it strike you? Many thanks for your congratulations which I reecho. The Parliamentary prospects are up to this time very good; almost too good to last.

29. M.

Wilton Ch. 10½ AM. Music in evg. Worked on Homer MS. Read Cent Nouv. Nouvv.[1]—Gallwey's Pamphlet[2]—Ld Carnarvon on Greece.[3] Wrote to Mr Fortescue—Ld Granville—Ld Halifax—Ld E. Clinton —Watsons—Baron Beaulieu[4]—Ld Lyttelton—Marion Watson— G. Burnett—Sir H. Moncreiff—and minutes.

To C. S. P. FORTESCUE, Irish secretary,   Carlingford MSS CP1/41.
29 March 1869.

It occurs to me that the question most awkward *for us* in the Committee on the Irish Church Bill may after all prove to be the 14 years for Maynooth. And this seems so far likely that I should be glad to know whether we could not take in hand the framing of a measure with regard to Trinity College as a defensive movement.

I am not well enough acquainted with the subject matter to know whether this is practicable, but I think it deserves consideration.

The defensive effect of the introduction of such a Bill, I apprehend, would be that it might prevent the opposition from falling in *en masse* with the Aytoun faction.

I conclude we should neutralise the University & secure on its behalf a large part of the endowments, leaving to the College as a denominational institution a portion of them for its own purposes.

I may be supposing a danger that is not real, but 'forewarned is forearmed'. [P.S.] We can speak about this matter on Thursday.

To LORD HALIFAX, 29 March 1869.   Add MS 44536, f. 136.

Accept my best thanks for your kind congratulations.[5]

The most notable feature of the situation was, I think this; that Disraeli manifested an unequivocal desire to carry the whole affair speedily to issue, & so to get rid of it. He is utterly at odds with the men on his own side: & his high doctrine of Supremacy & State Church has not taken.

[1] See 13 July 48.   [2] See 16 Jan. 69.
[3] H. J. G. *Herbert, Lord Carnarvon, *Reminiscences of Athens and the Morea* (1869).
[4] Had sent tracts on Belgian railways: Add MS 44536, f. 136.
[5] Of 26 March, Add MS 44184, f. 251.

In general, matters look well for the Comm[on]s. No serious flaw has yet been detected in the Bill, though some few minor contingencies are unprovided for. I expect however, that attempts will be made to give us trouble about Maynooth.

I hope we shall have other opportunity of talking over this matter when you come to town.

[PS.] The accts. of Pembroke have certainly improved.

30. Wed. [sc. Tuesday]

Ch. 10½ AM. Wrote to Ld Clarendon—Mr Kingsley—Mr M. Arnold —Mr [W. T.] M. Torrens—The Viceroy—Cav. Braila—Ld Russell —Dowager Ly Lothian—Ld Sligo—& minutes. Walk with Strzelecki & accounts of his singular work and experience.[1] Also some examination of his MS. Book. Attended the Wilton Church Soc.s Concert 9-10½: and spoke briefly.[2] Read Shaw Abuses of the Irish Church[3]—Froude's Lect. at St Andrew's[4]—Arnold Preface to Culture and Anarchy. Worked a little on Homer.

To MATTHEW ARNOLD, 30 March 1869.   Add MS 44536, f. 137.

I thank you very much for your kindness in sending me your book.[5] If the body of it is as interesting as the Preface, I shall read it with much avidity. The questions which you handle in the Preface are of a constantly growing importance. But I am one of those who think that when we pass away from the present Church Establishments, they will be succeeded not by a new fashion of the like species, but by what is termed the voluntary system. I can contemplate this result without great uneasiness, not because I think it absolutely good, but because it may be the best & safest of the alternatives before us, as the most likely to keep in a state of freshness the heart & conscience of man. Of the narrowness which you ascribe to Nonconformity, I find the root not the absence of State influence, but in what I may call renunciation of the Past, or incapacity, from whatever source, to claim & appropriate our full share of our heritage.

I have always thought it one of the great blanks of my life not to have known Dr. Arnold. He was very kind about it, but my work like his, was hard, & I little anticipated how soon the door was to be closed against me.

Pray remember the breakfasts.

---

[1] In Australia; see Add MS 44536, f. 137 and 10 Mar. 69n.
[2] See The Times, 7 April 1869, 9e.
[3] Sir C. Shaw, The abuses of the Irish Church (1866).
[4] J. A. *Froude, 'Inaugural address' (1869).
[5] *Arnold had sent Culture and Anarchy (1869), discussed at Latimer (see 21 Mar. 69), 'for the sake of a passage about Presbyterianism on the Church of England'; Add MS 44419, f. 281.

To LORD CLARENDON, foreign secretary,   Add MS 44536, f. 137.
30 March 1869.

Johnson[1] has in my opinion taken a great & indeed an outrageous liberty in making 'officially' a proposal which his Govt. has not authorized, & that after all his previous failures. It looks as if he was fishing for the means of making a character with his own ctry. by presuming on our weakness, & taking his chance of being enabled to say 'see what I have done.'

It is really the false position in which we are placed by an indefensible frontier in Brit. N. America, & the consciousness of weakness thence resulting which has made poor J. Bull content to exhibit to the Americans a submissiveness such as he has never to my knowledge shewn to any other people upon earth. He will still have to keep his temper, & be very quiet: but there are limits to all things.

I retain Bowring's statement which we can talk about, I did not know there was *fortune* to warrant a Baronetcy.

31. Wed.

Wilton H. Prayers at 9. Wrote to Sir R. Anstruther—Mr Nosotti—Mr Bruce—Ld Clarendon—Ld Lyttelton—Rev Mr Buchanan—and minutes. Worked on Homer MS. Drove C: and walked with Count S. In evening, table turning and music. In the former, I proved to be rather obstructive. Read Palgrave on H of C.

Thurs Ap.One. 1869. [London]

Wrote to Duke of Argyll—Ld Clarendon—The Queen—Ld Spencer—H.N.G.—Mr M. More[2]—Mr Leatham—C.G. and minutes. Wilton H. Chapel Prayers at 9. Off at 10¾ to London with a large party. Saw Mr Glyn—Solr General—Saw Gerald X. Dined with the Wests. H of C. 4½-6½. Sheridan gave me warning.[3] Read Hom. Studies to wind up my MS.

To the DUKE OF ARGYLL, Indian secretary,   Add MS 44536, f. 138.
1 April 1869.

All that you say[4] about my being misunderstood is most just. A man who has a particular view all to himself lays himself out for this & must expect it. Moreover a man who commits an error as I did in declaring when I was Minister an

---

[1] See *Clarendon to Gladstone, 29 March 1869, Add MS 44133, f. 202: 'Reverdy Johnson's answer to my inquiry . . . shows that he had no special authority to make the proposal to us.'   [2] Unidentified.

[3] Of his motion of 6 April to reduce fire insurance duty: *H* cxcv. 305.

[4] Long letter from Argyll, 31 March 1869, Add MS 44101, f. 37, urging diarist to come to terms with John Lothrop Motley (1814–77, historian and American ambassador in London 1869–70); Gladstone complained that Motley had accused him of falsehood in a despatch on the Newcastle speech (see 7 Oct. 62); Granville successfully mediated where Argyll and Clarendon failed; see Ramm I, i. 24ff.

opinion which (whether for their ultimate good or not) the Northern Americans had a right to resent should be considerate towards others. This I desire to be: and nothing but the gross & unmannerly imputation of falsehood would not have been noticed by me, nor have I troubled Mr. Motley or anyone about this until circumstances arose when as I understood Mr. Sumner recommends & the U.S. Govt. intends to place him in a situation of rather close relations with me as well as with Clarendon. Even now it is not for any satisfaction to my personal feelings that I am desirous this should come before Mr. Motley (and perhaps all the better if before Mr. Sumner also) but simply because I have a public capacity to sustain which ought not to be dragged through the mire. The strange conduct pursued by the U.S. Govt makes me not less but more desirous to make as little of the thing as may be, & my complaint is limited to the publication. Every man has a right to his opinion, however enviable or unenviable it may be.

PS. Were it possible that I should exercise the smallest influence on Mr. Motley's appt. one way or the other, I should utterly shrink from the responsibility; nor do I in my own mind allow any prejudice against him beyond the simple matter of fact. Thanks for your news of A. T[histlethwayte?].

2. Fr.

Wrote to Lady Trevelyan—Mr Richmond—Chancr of Exr—Mr Pim MP[1]—Ld Chancellor—The Queen—Mr Latouche[2]—Attorney General—C.G.—and minutes. H of C. 4½-8¼ and 9½-1½.[3] Finished Homeric MS. Saw Miss Kelly (Cameo)[4]—Mr G. Glyn—Scotts— Chancr of Exchr. Saw Mr Dickinsons Portrait of Cobden.[5] Read Foreign Relations[6]—Glamorgan Inquiry.[7]

3. Sat.

Wrote to Mr Macmillan—Ld Clarendon—Lady Herbert—Chancr of Exr—C.G.—Ld Spencer—Mr Crawford. Attended the Levee. Saw Mr Homersham Cox—Greek Minister[8]—Ld Clarendon—Persian Minister[9]—Mr Glyn—Bp of Kingston—D. of Argyll—Chancr of Exchr—1½ hour: he will have an admirable Budget—Sir R. Gerard —Mr Monsell—Prince Latour. Saw Marshall X. Missed Ld Russell. Dined at Dowager Duchess of Somerset's. Sent off the last of my MS. to Macmillan. Read Glamorgan Inquiry. Attended the French &c. Exhibition.

[1] Jonathan Pim, 1806-85; merchant and liberal M.P. Dublin 1865-74.
[2] Declining his invitation to visit Ireland at Whit: Add MS 44536, f. 139.
[3] Spoke on civil service and navy estimates: *H* cxcv. 40, 80.
[4] Not traced; by Dickinson?   [5] Now in National Portrait Gallery.
[6] *Our foreign relations and how they should be conducted* (1869).
[7] Possibly the 1837 commission on Glamorgan charities.
[8] Pierre B. Armeni.
[9] Hadji Mohsin Khan was Persian chargé d'affaires.

4. 1 S.E.

Chapel Royal mg with H.C. Whitehall aft. Dined with Mr G. Glyn.
Saw Bp of Salisbury (again he was much affected)—Mr Liddon—
Lord Sligo—Mrs Glyn: still an invalid. Saw Broughton[R]. Read
Binney's Sermons[1]—Liddon's Assize Sermon[2]—Wilson's Pleas[3]—
Coleridge's Keble. Wrote to Dr Binney—Ld Bessborough—C.G.—
Chancr of Exr—Ld Lyttn.[4]

5. M.

Wrote to Ld Lyttelton—Archdn Stopford—The Queen, and minutes.
Worked on proofs & references. H of C. $4\frac{1}{2}$-$8\frac{1}{4}$ and 9-$12\frac{1}{4}$.[5] Read
Glamorgan—Palgrave. Sat to Mr Lucy.[6] Saw Mr Glyn—Mr Ayrton
—Mr Macmillan.

6. Tu.

Wrote to Mr Cardwell—Lord Advocate—The Queen—Archdn
Robinson[7]—Dr Irons—Ld Carysfort—& minutes. Cabinet 1-$4\frac{1}{4}$.
Saw Mr Glyn—Mr Lowe—and others. H of C. $4\frac{1}{2}$-$11\frac{1}{2}$: various slip-
pery questions: the House behaved well on all.[8] Read [blank]

Cabinet Ap 6. 69.[9]
√ 1. Irish Church Comm[issio]n.[10] Mr Disraeli's question. Not to comply.
    W.E.G. mentioned Ld Monck—Mr G. Hamilton (vice Anderson)—Judge
    Lawson.
    (Stands over to next Cabinet.)
    There was mentioned Kirkman Hodgson—impossible?[11]
√ 2. Mr R[everdy] Johnsons proposal to allow *all* claims to be referred,[12]
    ans[we]r. to decline entertaining any new proposal in present circ[um-
    stance]s.
√ 3. Budget stated & accepted.[13]
√ 4. Motions of the day considered.

[1] By T. *Binney (1869); sent by the author; Gladstone replied that 'individually' he
would change civil but not ecclesiastical law to allow marriage with a deceased wife's sister;
Add MS 44420, f. 9. See 17 Apr. 69.
[2] H. P. *Liddon, 'Christ and human law; a sermon' (1869).
[3] E. Wilson, *The Pleas of the Church. Five essays addressed to . . . Gladstone* (1869).
[4] Who corrected proofs of *Juventus Mundi.*
[5] Estimates: *H* cxcv. 181.
[6] Charles Lucy, 1814-73, portrait in Victoria and Albert Museum; too poor to be worth
reproducing.
[7] See 9 Apr. 45.
[8] Spoke on Commons arrangements, fire insurance: *H* cxcv. 301.
[9] Add MS 44637, f. 37.   [10] See 7 May 69n.
[11] See 8 Apr. 69.   [12] See *LQV* 2nd series, i. 588.
[13] Diarist's jottings on it at Add MS 44637, f. 38.

√ 5. Release of Lynch: refer to Canada[1]
√ 6. Beerhouse Bill. Govt. to promise a comprehensive com[missio]n with Report of [18]54 for starting-point.[2]

7. Wed.

Wrote to D. of Argyll—Sir T. Tancred—Ld Clarendon—Mr Macmillan—Mr H. Cole—Rev. W. Denton—Mr Cardwell—and minutes. [Added at foot of MS, p. 21:—] Add. Wrote to Sig. Costa[3]—Lady Llanover—Sir R. Palmer—Dean Atkins—Ld Spencer. [Text resumes:—] H of C. $2\frac{1}{2}$-$4\frac{1}{2}$.[4] Saw Ld Granville—Mr F. Leveson—Count Maffei—Mr Glyn—Mr Grant Duff—Ld Clarendon. Dined with the Queen: as did C. & Agnes, at B. Palace. She was low: I had learned why.[5] Sir W. James's afterwards. Saw Gerald X. Read Putnam's Art. on W.E.G.[6]

8. Th.

Wrote to Mr Macmillan—Chancr of Exr—Mr Hamilton—The Queen—and minutes. Saw Mr W. Richmond—Sir H. Moncreiff—Mr Innes—Lord Kinnaird—Mr Glyn—Mr G. Hamilton—Ld de Grey—Duke of Argyll. Presbn Deputn 3-3$\frac{3}{4}$[7]—Owens's Coll. do $3\frac{3}{4}$-$4\frac{1}{2}$.[8] H of C. $4\frac{1}{2}$-9. The Budget was very successful. Not being very well, I was let off early.[9] Ten to breakfast. Worked on MS of Homer. Read Dr Brady on Irish Parl. Records.[10]

9. Fr.

Wrote to The Queen (2)—Ld Dufferin—Rev. Mr Daly[11]—Ld de Grey—Sir A. Spearman—Ld Clarendon—Mr Fortescue—Mr Brookfield—Mr Liddon—and minutes. H of C. $4\frac{1}{2}$-8 and 9-1$\frac{1}{2}$:

---

[1] A Fenian.
[2] Bruce supported 2°R of Ibbetson's bill, promised inquiry (commission unmentioned) and govt. bill next year; *H* cxcv. 1762.
[3] Offering a knighthood to (Sir) Michael Andrew Agnus *Costa, 1810-84, conductor; Add MS 44536, f. 141.
[4] Irish poor law: *H* cxcv. 309.
[5] Probably Prince Leopold's continued illness; Guedalla, *Q*, i. 168.
[6] G. M. Towle, 'W. E. Gladstone', *Putnam's (Monthly) Magazine*, xv. 287 (March 1869).
[7] On the Irish Church; notes in Add MS 44757, f. 136.
[8] Requesting govt. financial assistance; Gladstone promised cabinet discussion, but without optimism: *The Times*, 9 April 1869, 10d; see 24 Apr. 69.
[9] After questions on Maynooth, and Asia: *H* cxcv. 361.
[10] W. M. *Brady, 'Vice-regal speeches and episcopal votes in the Irish parliament', Chap. V. of *Essays on the English State Church in Ireland* (1869).
[11] William Daly, vicar of Kilbride, Wicklow; see Add MS 44536, f. 142 and 44420, f. 21.

working on various matters.[1] Saw Dean of Lichfield—Dean of Windsor—Mr Macmillan—Lord de Grey—Conclave on Amendments to Irish Church Bill 2½-4¼—Chancellor of Exchequer—Mr Layard—Sir J. Coleridge—Mr Glyn. Worked on Homeric MS. Read Palgrave on H. of C.

Apr. 9 69.[2]
1. Att Gen. to write to Judge Lawson. 2. To postpone Clause 3. 3. Salary of Commissioners to stand over. 4. 20 Congregations not having fulfilled the 3 years. admit. 5. Amnt. as to old ministers. 6. Admit vested interests *created* before the passing of the act. 7. Widows fund—whole receipt to be at 14 years. 8. Capitalise the Profession fund at 14 years.

10. Sat.

Ill with bowel complaint in the night: & up late. Wrote to Lord Sydney—The Queen—Mr Macmillan—and minutes. Finished revision of my recovered Chapter of Juventus Mundi. At 11½ went to H.M. at B. Palace: much conversation on her occupations & ways of life which gave me opportunities.[3] Saw Mr Liddon—Sir A. Spearman—Ld Granville, Ld Clarendon, & Ld Sydney, together, on the Mordaunt business[4]—Mr Maclaren & Edinb. Depn[5]—Mr Goschen *cum* Mr Bright—Mr Glyn—Ld Hatherley—Abp of Canterbury. Read Ch of Rome & Prot. Govts.[6] Dined at Ld Hatherley's. Afternoon visit at Baron L. Rothschild's & discussion on the Budget. Cabinet 2½-5¼.

Cabinet Ap 10. 69.[7]
√ 1. Airy's[8] Message from Gibraltar—as to illumination at Gibraltar on the 50th Anniversary of his ordination: Permit to do as they please
2. Owen's College [Manchester][9]
√ 3. Hadfield's Burials Bill—to be put off if possible.
√ 4. Life Peerages Bill—to be entertained.[10]

[1] Spoke on appointments: *H* cxcv. 494.
[2] Notes for conclave; Add MS 44757, f. 139.
[3] Her persistant reclusiveness.
[4] Sir Charles Mordaunt, 1836-97, 10th bart., tory M.P. S. Warwick 1859-68, threatened to cite the Prince of Wales as co-respondent in divorcing Harriet Sarah, *née* Moncrieffe. Gladstone consulted Sir A. W. White, *Victoria's solicitor, who advised against direct contact with Mordaunt, who, in January 1870, did not cite *Wales, but called him as a witness; see 12 Apr. 69, Add MS 44420, ff. 90, 139, 212 and Magnus, *Edward VII*, 107.
[5] MacLaren, a United Presbyterian, opposed a board giving grants to denominational schools; see D. J. Withrington, 'Towards a national system, 1867-72', *Scottish Educational Studies* (1972), 114.
[6] *The Church of Rome under Protestant governments* (1866).
[7] Add MS 44637, f. 40.
[8] Sir R. Airey, see 15 Mar. 65, but never ordained.
[9] See 8 Apr. 69.
[10] Russell's Bill (see 16 Mar. 69) 1°R on 9 April, eventually abandoned.

√ 5. Clarendon—Reported on Belgian question and Thornton's answer respecting Mr R[everdy] Johnson's late proposal. Answer to preclude his inference.
√ 6. Mr Goschen's Assessed Rates Bill.[1]
√ 7. Duke of Argyll. Pay[men]t of annuities of Council to be raised? No.— Facilitate retirement of present mem[bers] on pensions.
√ 8. Clarendon respecting paying the expenses homewards of distressed British lunatics.
√ 9. D. of Argyll on Scotch Education Bill as to denominational Schools. Duke of A. will argue for Bill as it stands.[2]
√10. Fortescue on Motion respecting Irish Society. To decide when on the [front] bench.
√11. County Financial Boards.
√12. Howard's Motion.[3] Discourage: but express opinion ag[ains]t the practice for so long a period.
√13. Notice to be given with a view to a Bill for taking the Telegraphs with a monopoly.

11. 2 S.Easter.

Chapel Royal mg: St James's evg. Wrote to Duke of Argyll—Ld Granville(2)—Dr Binney—Rev. Dr Russell—Mr Lingen—Dean of Windsor—Abp Manning. Saw Williams X. Saw Ld Granville—Missed Mr Arnold White.[4] Tea with the Lothians. Read Coleridge's Keble— De Pressensès on Ch & State[5]—Binney's Sermons.

12. M.

Wrote to Ld Clarendon—Mr Stopford Brooke—Ld Sydney— Chancr of Exr—Mr Macfie—Dean of Elphin—The Queen—Dean of Cashel—Lord Ardmillan—& minutes.[6] Conclave on Irish Ch. Bill Amts 1-3. Saw Ld Granville—Do *cum* Duke of Argyll—Mr Arnold White (respecting Prince of Wales)[7]—Mr Hope Scott—Mr Lowe— Mr Glyn—Mr Bruce—The Lord Advocate. Eleven to dinner. H of C. 4½-8¼ and 9½-12¼.[8] Read Brady on Irish Records—Shirley on Homer.[9]

To R. LOWE, chancellor of the exchequer,   Add MS 44536, f. 142.
12 April 1869.

Glyn tells me that Disraeli is to fire off a strong financial speech tonight. If

---

[1] Requiring modification: see *H* cxcv. 842.
[2] Argyll's bill, already in difficulties (see *H* cxcv. 569), eventually withdrawn.
[3] See 13 Apr. 69.   [4] See next day.
[5] E. de Pressensé, *The Church and the French Revolution*, tr. J. Stroyan (1869).
[6] On police handling of the many threatening letters he was receiving; Add MS 44420, ff. 54-62.   [7] See 10 Apr. 69.
[8] Spoke on retiring bps., ways and means: *H* cxcv. 581, 600.
[9] J. *Shirley, *Evenings with Homer* (1869).

you are in Downing St. between half past two and three, I will look in upon you. I should like to know whether you contemplate any measures either to restore the equality of public receipt & payment or compensate for its partial disturbance. The *main* question of course is whether it will be permanently convenient to the community to pay Income, Land & Assessed taxes in one & the same quarter. If you are clear on this probably some measure can be devised to prevent the inconveniences of two high spring tides in the Exchequer.

I imagine it would be open to you, if it prove to be politic, to postpone altogether the anticipation of Income Tax, & its reduction to 5d.[1]

To W. WARBURTON, dean of Elphin, 12 April 1869.   Add MS 44536, f. 143.

I have read your letter[2] with much interest but I am concerned to find, in your encl[osure]s from the evening conference, another proof of the unreasoning spirit which seems for the moment to prevail among Churchmen in Ireland. I am not aware what can be gained by it to anyone: certainly nothing is lost to us. But it prevents the advantages, which might have grown out of friendly counsel. The day cannot be far from distant when it will be generally recognised in Ireland that at this great crisis the more moderate counsel were the wiser ones.

13. Tu.

Wrote to Mr Fortescue—Archdn of Meath—Sir M.S. Stewart[3]—D. of Cambridge—Th. Turner—Dowager Duchess of Somerset—The Queen(2)—Duke of Sutherland—and minutes. Saw Mr Homersham Cox—D. of Argyll—Mr Glyn—Mr Burnett—Mr Helps—D. of Sutherland—Ld Granville—D. of St Albans. Rode—for the first time. H. of C. $4\frac{1}{2}$-8 and 9-12$\frac{1}{2}$.[4] Read O'Connell on Ireland[5]—Palgrave on H. of C. At Christie's.

14. Wed.

Wrote to Dean of Windsor—Ld Clarendon(3)—Gen. Grey—Mr Hamilton—Mr Acland—Mr Machin[6]—Chancr of Exr—Dr Cavendish—Ld Sydney—Abp Manning—Mr White—& minutes. Saw Mr Glyn—Ld Clarendon—Mr Twisleton—Bp of Salisbury: appy better. Dined at Ly Waldegrave's—Lady Granville's party after. Read divers pamphlets and Q.R. on Party Govt.[7]

---

[1] No reply in Add MS 44301.

[2] Untraced; letter of 8 March with reply is in Add MS 44419, f. 184.

[3] Sir Michael Robert Shaw-Stewart, 1826-1903, lord-lieut. Renfrewshire 1869; prominent mason.

[4] Spoke on Howard's motion on Cumberland and Westmorland lord lieutenancy: *H* cxcv. 748.

[5] D. *O'Connell, probably *Letters to the reformers of England* (1832).

[6] Unidentified.   [7] *Quarterly Review*, cxxvi. 394 (April 1869).

15. Th.

Wrote to Mr Dowse MP[1]—Lord J. Hay—Dean of Windsor—Mr Fawcett—The Queen—and minutes. Nine to breakfast. Saw Mr Glyn—Mr Liddon—C. Strzelecki—Mr West—Mr Goschen. H of C. $4\frac{1}{2}$-$12\frac{3}{4}$. Spoke, winding up the Debate on I.C: & voted in 355: 229.[2] Read Q.R. on Irish Ch.[3]—Palgrave on H. of C. (finished). Rode with Agnes. Made a final review of Revises, first & second batch.[4]

To LORD CLARENDON, foreign secretary,   Add MS 44536, f. 145.
15 April 1869.

Whenever there is an Odo [Russell] in the box satisfaction instantly preponderates.[5] I think he has the true idea of the Roman Court, viz. that from the necessity of its position (until some great man arises to change it) every civil, human & social interest is absolutely evanescent in its view, & the Church in the very narrowest sense of that word offers the only interest to be cared for. I think it will be a great *coup* if the Empress goes to India for one I should be delighted. I hope this is right.

16. Fr.

Wrote to Ld Bessborough—Ld Clarendon—Rev Mr Spurgeon[6]— Mr Redgrave—Sir T. Biddulph—Rev Mr Williams—The Queen (2) —R.Adm. Hamilton—and minutes. H of C. $4\frac{1}{2}$-8 and 8.35-1. Spoke on Clause 2 & voted in 344:221.[7] Rode with Mary. Saw the Lord Mayor—Mr Glyn—Mr Rathbone—Edinb.Univ. Deputation on Scots Educn Bill.[8] Read de Pressensè—Memoir of C. Maclaren.[9]

17. Sat.

Wrote to Ld Clarendon—Rev Mr Henderson—Ld Powis—Bp of Chester—Ld de Grey—Rev. Mr Withers[10]—The Queen—Lord Granville—Mr P. Earle[11]—Ld Monck—Gen. Grey—Mr Stephens

[1] Richard Dowse, 1824-90; liberal M.P. Londonderry 1868-72; Irish solicitor general 1870, attorney general 1872; baron of exchequer 1872.
[2] In cttee.: *H* cxcv. 924; annotated division list in Add MS 44610, f. 24.
[3] *Quarterly Review*, cxxvi. 559 (April 1869).
[4] Revised proofs of *Juventus Mundi.*
[5] Russell to Clarendon, 30 March 1869, PRO FO 43/103B.
[6] On Maynooth, Add MS 44536, f. 145.   [7] *H* cxcv. 1044.
[8] Probably school masters in London for the Scottish Bill; see *The Scotsman*, 16 April 1869, 5.
[9] C. *Maclaren, Select writings*, ed. R. Cox and J. Nicol, 2v. (1869).
[10] Lovelace B. Wither had sent his tr. of the Odyssey; Add MS 44536, f. 146.
[11] *sc.* Erle; see 18 June 53.

—& minutes. Cabinet 2½-5. Saw Mr Hamilton—Mr Glyn—D. of Argyll—and others. Visited Water Colour Exhibn. Off at 7.15 to dinner & Chapel before it at Lambeth Palace. Conversation with Ld Lawrence on India—with Mrs Tait on Ch of Ireland—Abp of York on Bill for Church Building—Bp of Oxford on Episcopal resignations. Read.

Cabinet Ap. 17. 1869[1]

1. Lord Mayor's dinner—Wednesdays open in June 16th & 30th.   *30th*
2. Letter of the Archbishop of Canterbury respecting retirement of Bishops.[2]
   a. Not to pay. To speak to Abp. Three points. 1. resignation—2. coadj[utores] cum jure succ[essionis ad sedem]—3. Provision for mental incapacity.
3. Irish Church Bill—Names of Comm[ission]. a. see Mr. Hamilton
4.   ditto   —Value of Clerical Lives—Rescind.
5. Clarendon. Frere Orban.[3] Satisfactory assurances from France: and
6. Read R[everdy] Johnson's answer to his note respecting Mr. J[ohnson]'s last proposal. Congratulations to [President] Grant. Question whether to lay papers on Clarkes Conventions? To stand over till next Saturday.
7. Gregory's Motion on Law Courts.[4] Cabinet sanction Mr. Lowe's arguing for his own plan.
8. Treasury letter respecting penknives pencils India Rubber [and] paperknives. Recalled.
9. Granville. Production of the O'Farrell papers.[5]—Passage respecting P. of Wales to be omitted.
10. [Marriage with a Deceased] Wife's Sister Bill.[6] Mr. Bright wishes to support it for Civil Marriages. Chancellor objects. Nothing to be done by the Govt.
11. Annuity Tax Repeal Bill. Govt. to support.
12. India Council Re-Elections. Discretion of Sec[retar]y [of State] with limit of five years & for reasons.
13. Chanc[ellor]: respecting Scots peers: will Govt. issue proclam[atio]n on report of a vacancy? Wait report of Committee.[7]
14. Ld Clanricarde's [Tenure (Ireland)] bill—on Tuesday [20 April]. Not to oppose: but it does not settle the question.
[Note passed in Cabinet] Did you ever do anything about obtaining a rescript from the Vatican in the cause of law and order?
   I spoke strongly to Manning but didn't venture to apply to the Vatican. The Pope wd. have been pleased with such an appeal as an ackt. of his authority & he wd. have told Cullen to do as he pleased. [Clarendon].[8]

---

[1] Add MS 44637, f. 41.
[2] *Tait's bill, to enable bps. to retire, passed this session.
[3] President of Belgian council; see Clarendon to Lumley, 6 March 1869, Clarendon MSS, c. 475, f. 62.
[4] Favouring the Thames Embankment site: *H* cxcv. 1202.
[5] Deathbed statement by the Fenian O'Farrell, already printed in Australia; govt. publication in U.K. successfully resisted: see 27 Apr. 69.
[6] *Bright spoke for the bill on the 21 Apr.: *H* cxcv. 1312.
[7] On rights of sundry peers to vote for representative peers; *Lords' Sessional Papers*, 1868-9 xxvi.
[8] Note dated 'Ap. 17'; Add MS 44637, f. 43.

To LORD CLARENDON, foreign secretary,   Clarendon MSS, c. 497.
17 April 1869.

Many thanks. I think your letter will do good.[1] The Queen is essentially fair: her prejudices I think are never original, always imbibed: & her good sense & equity enable her to overcome them. It did not occur to me until after I had written to you yesterday, but I ought perhaps to have expressed what I felt, namely a perfect willingness to be trotted out in your rear in support of your doctrine that menace is a bad basis for a system of international communications upon the arrival of difficulty. But there was little need, & there would have been little use.[2]

18. 3 S.E.

Whitehall Chapel mg: Ch. Royal aftn. Wrote to Ld Granville. Dined with the Lothians. He is much interested in matters of religion, as well as Lady L. Saw Ld Monck. Read Coleridge's Keble—Goalen's Gideon[3]—La Bible dans L'Inde[4]—Ward's Reply to Ffoulkes.[5]

To LORD CLARENDON, foreign secretary,   Clarendon MSS, c. 497.
18 April 1869.

I have no doubt that good has been done by the correspondence of which I return the last letter: but there is no doubt considerable sensitiveness, wrought upon by others & requiring to be much spared in the forms of language.

Since we have been in office I have not I believe said to anyone a single word about the Suez Canal; and at no period that I am aware of have I authorised anyone to speak of any opinion of mine about it. The neutralization of it I have always supposed to be most desirable and I remember *years ago* trying to move Lord Russell in that direction. It is quite another question whether now, in the hour of success, we ought to start such a proposition or to seem anxious about its success.

19. M.

Wrote to Dr Purvis—Mr A. Delmar[6]—Mr W. Grogan—Sir W. Knollys—Sir Thos G.—Dowager Duchess of Somerset—The Queen—and minutes. Dinner (25 m) with the Jameses. Saw Mr Samuelson MP.—Archbishop of Canterbury—Lord Monck—Mr Glyn—Mr F.

[1] Not found.   [2] Part in Millman, 139.
[3] W. Goalen, *Gideon, a poem* (1868).
[4] L. Jacolliot, *La Bible dans l'Inde* (1869).
[5] W. G. *W[ard], *Strictures on Mr. F's Letter to Archbishop Manning* (1869).
[6] Accepting the invitation of Alexander Del Mar, secretary of the American Free Trade League, to be a corresponding member, but declining 'to seem forward in any burden of advice to your countrymen'; Add MS 44420, f. 153.

Knollys—Sir R. Palmer. H. of C. 4½-8½ and 9-12¾: working Irish Ch. Bill in Committee. Good progress.[1] Read MacLaren.

20. Tu.

Wrote to Sir A. Spearman—Att.Gen.I. (2)—Sir Jas Lawson—Ld Clarendon—Rev W.R. James[2]—The Queen—and minutes. Saw Mr Hamilton—Mr Glyn—Mr Sullivan—Mr Torrens—Mr Forster—Mr Acland. H of C. 4½-7¾ and 9-1¾.[3] Rode with A. & M. Read MacLaren: M'Culloch.[4]

21. Wed.

Wrote to Mr Hammond—Mr J. Howard MP.[5]—Mr Bass MP.—and minutes. Annuity Tax Deputn at 2.[6] Saw Mrs Hamilton, who again hopes, building upon prayer. Saw Rev Mr Williams—Mr A.W. Pugin —Mr Glyn—Ld Clarendon—Gen Grey—Mr Forster—Mr Creary[7] —Dr Guthrie. Dined at the Duke of Argyll's. Read MacLaren.

22. Th.

Wrote to Rev. Mr Harris—Dean of Westmr—Ld Sidmouth—Ld Clanricarde—The Queen—Lord Devon—and minutes. Twelve to breakfast. Saw one[R]. H of C. 4½-8½ and 9-12¾, on Irish Church Bill.[8] Saw Earl of Devon—Mr Palgrave—Mr Glyn—Ld Granville—Mr Rathbone—Ld Halifax. Visit in Chesham Street.[9] 11 A.M.-12¼. St Paul's Kn. The marriage of Mr Wood to Lady A. Courtenay with H.C. for them.[10] We attended the breakfast afterwards.

23. Fr.

Wrote to Ld Clarendon—Mr Macmillan—Gen. Grey—Bp of Argyll —Mr Hamilton—Ld Listowell—Ld Bessborough—Mr G.H. Moore

---

[1] *H* cxcv. 1152.
[2] William Richard James, on quotations: Add MS 44536, f. 149.
[3] Questions on Irish church, spoke on new law courts: *H* cxcv. 1268.
[4] J. R. *MacCulloch, probably *A Dictionary of Commerce* (new ed. 1869-71).
[5] James Howard, 1821-89; liberal M.P. Bedford 1868-74, Bedfordshire 1880-5; on cattle plague: Add MS 44536, f. 149.
[6] Edinburgh Annuity Tax Bill 2°R on 30 June 69.
[7] Name scrawled; perhaps William Creasy, London merchant and Councillor.
[8] *H* cxcv. 1392.
[9] Obscure; perhaps C. H. A'Court Repington at n. 15.
[10] C. L. *Wood, 2nd Viscount Halifax, m. Agnes Elizabeth, da. of 10th earl of Devon; she d. 1919.

—Bp of Argyll—Ld Spencer—The Queen (2)—and minutes. Saw Mr Street—Ld Granville—Mr Glyn (2)—Mr Forster. At Christie's. Rode with Helen. H of C. 4½-12½: working Irish Ch. Bill in Committee.[1]

24. Sat.

Wrote to Ld Clarendon—Mr Hamilton (2)—Chancr of Exr—Sir T. Western—The Queen (2)—Abp of Canterbury[2]—Mr Merritt—Mr Thring—& minutes. Dined at the Turkish Embassy. Saw Gerald X: obtained a kind of promise for the niece. Saw Mr Glyn—Duke of Argyll—Mr Brand—Mr Homersham Cox—Mr Freshfield *cum* Rev. Mr Denton.[3] Cabinet 2½-5½. Visited Nat. Gallery to see the rehanging;[4] & Water Colour Exhibition. Read [blank]. Lady de Grey's in evening.

Cabinet Ap. 24.[5]
√ 1. Owen's College. No.[6]
√ 2. D[uke] of Leinster, Irish R[ail] R[oads].
√ 3. A[rch]b[isho]p of Canterbury, Episcopal Resignation. To communicate further
√ 4. Irish Church Comm[issio]n[ers] Q[uer]y to be P[rivy] C[ouncillor]s?
√ 5. Clarendon: read [despatches] on Belgian Railway—Cuba—Ocean Postage with U.S.—Return of Criminal Lunatics.
√ 6. Childers. Explosive bullets. Agree to Russian proposal.[7]
√ 7. Bruce. Cabinet Comm[ittee] on Extradition.[8]
√ 8. Mauritius Dinner. Not to interfer[e]
√ 9. De Grey: allow alternative body to erect Cattle Market.
√ 10. Life Peerages. Object to Categories.
√ 11. Contagious Diseases Act Extension: paper to be circulated by Mr Bruce.[9]
√ 12. Telegraphs. Conversation.
√ 13. Question on Irish Railways. A colourless answer to be given by ⟨Mr Fortescue⟩ W.E.G.[10]
√ 14. Dover House: Mr Cardwell to answer it has not been purchased but Govt. are considering of consolidating W[ar] D[epartment]
       Cabinet Committee appointed[11]—Granville—Kimberley—Chanc[ello]r of [the] Ex[cheque]r—Childers—Cardwell—Layard.
√ 15. Irish Outrages discussed.

[1] *H* cxcv. 1514.
[2] Arranging *Thring's help in drafting the bps. retirement bill; see Add MS 44536, f. 150 and 17 Apr. 69.
[3] See 13 June 51.   [4] Completing the Gallery's reorganization.
[5] Add MS 44637, f. 44.   [6] See 10 Apr. 69.
[7] Not found. In general, see E. M. Spiers, 'The use of the Dum-Dum Bullet', *Journal of Imp. and Commonwealth Hist.*, 1975.   [8] Jottings for names in the margin.
[9] Not found; perhaps to use Sir J. Simon's arguments of 3 Apr. 69, PRO HO 45/9322/17273, f. 236, against the Lords' cttees.' request for extension; Bruce on 19 Apr. had declined to let the H.O. administer the Acts.
[10] *H* cxcv. 1577.   [11] See 9 Aug. 69.

25. 4 SE.

Chapel R. mg: St James evg. (St Mark). Dined with the Lothians. Saw Bp of Salisbury. Read Coleridge's Keble—Lecky on Moral Opinion.[1]

26.M.

Wrote to Mr Hamilton—Ld Monck—Judge Lawson—The Queen —Att.Gen.Eng.—Robn G.—Sir P. Braila—& minutes. Saw Mr Glyn—Ld Stanhope—Lord Halifax. Visited Foster's Room. Rode with H. H of C. $4\frac{1}{2}$-$12\frac{3}{4}$: minus 30 m. for dinner.[2] Read Dr M. Brady on I.C. Bill.[3]

27. Tu.

Wrote to Ld Dalhousie—Mr J. Roche[4]—Mr Ouvry—Lord Grey— Meer Ali Murad[5]—and minutes. Saw Mr Merritt—Mr Glyn—Mr Dodson—Mr Walpole—Ld Granville—Sir R. Gerard.[6] Rode with Helen. H of C. $4\frac{1}{2}$-$9\frac{3}{4}$ and $10\frac{3}{4}$-$12\frac{1}{2}$.[7] Read 'La Bible dans L'Inde'— Goethe's Egmont, Intr &c.[8]—Armstrong's Poems.[9]

To EARL GREY, 27 April 1869.   Add MS 44536, f. 151.

You are reported in the Times to have stated last night that 'The Irish Church question was brought forward last year by those who admitted that their eyes had been opened to the urgency of the evil by the Fenian Conspiracy.' I cannot be wrong in supposing that I am at least included in this statement, supposing it for the moment to have been correctly given: & I therefore write to acquaint you that I have never said anything of the kind. If upon enquiry you find yourself wrong I have no doubt you will be more anxious than I can be that you should set yourself right.[10]

[1] W. E. H. *Lecky, *History of European morals from Augustus to Charlemagne,* 2v. (1869).

[2] Irish Church Bill: *H* cxcv. 1585.

[3] W. M. *Brady, *Some remarks on the Irish Church Bill* (1869).

[4] A grocer; had sent some tea; Add MS 44536, f. 153.

[5] Meer Ali Murad Khan of Khyrpoor had sent congratulations on the formation of the govt.: Add MS 44536, f. 151.

[6] Sir Robert Tolver Gerard, 1808-87; *Victoria's A.D.C. from 1867; cr. Baron 1876.

[7] O'Farrell's papers; not to be printed: *H* cxcv. 1741; see 17 Apr. 69.

[8] J. W. von Goethe, *Egmont,* perhaps the ed. by C. A. Buchheim (1869).

[9] See 28 Dec. 65.

[10] Grey replied on the same day that his comment referred mainly to *Granville; Add MS 44420, f. 182. See 28 Apr. 69.

28. Wed.

Wrote to Ld Clarendon—Lord Bessborough—Sir T.E. May—Lord Athlumney[1]—The Viceroy[2]—Lord Talbot de M.—T.N. Roberts[3] —Mr T.B. Potter MP.—Ch. of Exr—The Queen—and minutes. Visited the Lothians to cons. *their house* arrangements. Saw Mr Glyn —W.H.G.—Ld Carew[4]—Bavn Min.[5] Saw Marshall X—Mrs Mildmay? At Christie's. Read La Bible dans L'Inde. Dined at Ld Camperdown's. Admiralty party afterwards. And then C.s Ball.

To LORD CLARENDON, foreign secretary,   Clarendon MSS, c. 497.
28 April 1869.

1. I think you are quite right about the instructions with reference to Spanish vessels and I propose to summon the Cabinet for Friday at *two.*[6]
2. I think that all threats in the *future pluperfect potential* are to be condemned. They are too commonly the resort of cowards: & the great difficulty of complimenting Belgium on her conduct is that (I apprehend) we are not in full possession of the facts. To compliment her on the result is quite another thing, and the other matter might perhaps stand over till you are more fully informed.
3. On the other hand the claim of La Guerronière for relations of preference is a piece of brazen faced impudence which perhaps would be most strongly condemned by treating it as incredible. If he really held such language as is imputed to him, the Belgian Secretary deserves some credit (if adequately supplied with physical force) for not knocking him down.
   But as regards France, the present evidence from the facts, of course only presumptive, is that what you have done has been most useful, and that you have done enough. I do not know the ground for the censure on Lord Lyons.
4. Your report from Windsor is very acceptable.[7] I have no doubt the Dean himself one of my oldest friends has cooperated in producing what he describes.

To EARL GREY, 28 April 1869.   Add MS 44536, f. 152.

Thank you for your letter,[8] & as I am not directly or partly concerned by any particular words of mine in the passage I referred to, I will not trouble you further.
   Undoubtedly I admit with Granville that the Fenian outrages, & especially their overflow into England, have had a very important influence on the question

[1] Sir William Meredyth *Somerville, 1802-73; 1st Baron Athlumney 1863; supported the Irish church and land bills.
[2] i.e. Spencer.
[3] Thomas Nicholls Roberts, secretary to the Liberal Registration Association.
[4] Robert Shapland Carew, 1818-81; 2nd Baron Carew 1856; a liberal.
[5] Count Ferdinand de Hompesch.
[6] Clarendon to Gladstone, 27 April 1869, Add MS 44133, f. 212: 'We must send out instructions to the Naval Officers on the W. India Station where things are beginning to look ugly....'
[7] 'The Dean of Windsor [Wellesley] told a friend of mine that you had found the way of completely managing the Queen & that you wd. never have any difficulty.' Ibid.
[8] See 27 Apr. 69.

of the time for moving upon great questions of policy for Ireland: for (in my opinion) they wholly altered the attitude of the general mind both in England & in Scotland, & I further suppose that Ld Derby's Govt. must in substance have shared this impression, when, before we as a party had proposed anything, they thought it their duty to propound a policy for Ireland including in it the questions of Church Land & Education.

To EARL SPENCER, Irish lord lieutenant,   Add MS 44536, f. 153.
28 April 1869.

One St. Patrick is offered to Ld. Carysfort the other meditated to Ld. Gosford. Both Lds Kildare & Sligo have declined. Talking to Granville yesterday, I suggested that it might be worthwhile to compare the assassinations of the present moment, or rather period, with those of former periods within the last 20 years or so when the same terrible infection has gone abroad. It is I think very sanguine indeed to assume that any land bill we could produce at this moment would have a soothing effect—a compound controversy is like a compound fracture; & the Church is enough for today. Moreover if we are right in our Church policy, the framing of our Bill will of itself soothe the general sentiment of Ireland. I still hope to get the report before Whitsuntide.

29. Th.

Wrote to C. Fortescue—Lord Vernon[1]—Ld Spencer—The Queen—Mr Thring—and minutes. Saw Mr Glyn—Robn G.—Ld de Tabley—D. of Argyll—Sir F. Crossley—Ld Halifax—Mr Cardwell—The Speaker—Sir S. Northcote—Mr [R. B.] W. Baker MP.—Seven to breakfast. Rode with Helen. Irish Church Comm. 2-3¾. H of C. 4½-12¾, working Irish Church Bill.[2] Read Mant's Irish Church[3]—Lockhart's Valerius.[4]

30. Fr.

Wrote to Mr R. Denman—Mr Robinson—Mr Pugin—Bp of Oxford—The Queen—The Viceroy—and minutes. Cabinet 2-4½. 10½-12 At the Private view, Royal Academy: very good. Saw General Grey—Mr Glyn—and others. H of C. 4½-8½ and 9¼-1½: spoke on Irish Land, trying to cover Bright.[5]

[1] Augustus Henry Vernon, 1829-83; 6th Baron Vernon 1866; had sent his fa's tr. of Dante: Add MS 44536, f. 154.
[2] H cxcv. 1856.   [3] See 14 Mar. 69.
[4] [J. G. *Lockhart], Valerius, a Roman story (1821).
[5] Taunted by the tories, Bright strongly reaffirmed his belief in the need for a major Irish land bill; Gladstone did not wholly disavow him, but refused to commit the govt. to specific action: H cxcv. 2024 and Steele, Irish Land, 87.

Cabinet Ap. 30. 69.[1]
1. Clarendon. Instructions respecting proceedings of Spanish Ships in W[est] I[ndian] waters. Instructions to go, modified.[2]
2. Irish Outrages. Discussion on changing the Law by making the District compensate for lives lost.
3. Mayor of Cork.[3] Q[uestion] between an indictment & a penal Act. The former was preferred. Mention inquiry to be made about the facts.

Sat. May One SS.Ph. & James.

Breakfast at Grillion's. Wrote to Mr Sullivan—Sir R. Palmer—Mr Watts—The Queen (2)—and minutes. Cabinet 12–2$\frac{1}{2}$. Royal Academy 3$\frac{1}{4}$–5$\frac{1}{2}$ with much delight. I have never seen so much poetry in the Landscapes. Academy Dinner 6–10$\frac{1}{2}$: returned thanks for Ministers. But the *noise* was Tory. A most extraordinary speech from Reverdy Johnson.[4] Saw Ld Chancellor—Sir R. Peel—Mr Reverdy Johnson—Abp of Canterbury—Lord Granville. Read Valerius.

Cabinet May 1: 69. 12 noon.[5]
1. Mayor of Cork. Decision of yesterday confirmed—A[ttorney] G[eneral] to proceed by criminal informn.
2. Discussion on the local suspension of the Habeas Corpus in Ireland. G[ranville] for.—B[right] L[owe] WEG. Ch[ancello]r ag[ains]t.
3. Bill to be drawn for cons[ideratio]n imposing a fine on districts in certain cases where a murder takes place.
4. Clarendon's ⟨Spanish⟩ Instructions for the case of the Dulce Proclamation

2. 5 S Easter.

Chapel Royal mg and H.C: St James's evg. Wrote to Ld Clarendon— Mr Fortescue. Saw Lady Lyttelton—Mr Thistlethwayte. Saw Gerald X. Read Coleridge's Keble—Douglas on Missions in China[6]—Union Review on Women[7]—La Bible dans L'Inde. Dined with the Lothians: and farewell.

3. M.

Wrote to Mr F. Knollys—Sir C. O'Loghlen—Mr Ouvry—Lord Bessborough—G.G. Glyn—Lord Athlumney—Lord Conyngham[8]—The

---

[1] Add MS 44637, f. 47.   [2] See 28 Apr. 69.
[3] Daniel O'Sullivan, mayor of Cork, was forced out by the govt. for expressing Fenian sympathies; a bill was introduced, prosecution proving too lengthy; see 4 May 69 and *LQV*, 2nd series, i. 595.
[4] Johnson ridiculed C. Sumner's pro-Fenian stance; *The Times*, 3 May 1869, 7d.
[5] Add MS 44637, f. 49.   [6] Untraced.   [7] *Union Review*, 193 (1869).
[8] Francis Nathaniel Conyngham, 1797–1876; 2nd marquis Conyngham 1832; offering him lord-lieutenancy of Meath: Add MS 44536, f. 155.

Queen—Rev. Dr Vaughan—and minutes. Saw The Duke of Argyll
—Mr Sullivan—Mr Glyn—Mr Maguire. Arranged papers pamphlets,
and books. H of C. 4½-8½ and 9¼-12¼.[1] Dined with the Wests.

4. Tu.

Wrote to Mr J.A. Blake—Ld Listowell[2]—Lord E. Bruce—Mrs
Thistl.—The Queen—and minutes. Saw Mr Farrer—D. of Argyll—
Mr Glyn—Mr Fortescue—H of C. 2¼-7 (Ir.Ch.) and 9¼-1 (Light
Dues).[3] Read Valerius. Saw Clayton.

Cabinet May 4. 69. 12 o'c.[4]
1. Mayor of Cork. Comm[unicatio]n from Ireland. Bill? By whom? Att[orney]
   Gen[era]l[5]
2. Abyssinia. ⟨confidential dispatch to be written to Lord Mayor⟩ Govt. not to
   discourage Committee: but to hope it will not be made to assume a polemical character.[6]
3. The Holidays—to Thurs. 27.
4. The Ameer of Affghanistan. Confidential dispatch to be written to Ld Mayo.[7]
5: Announcement from U.S: Clarendon's answer approved.

5. Wed.

Wrote to Charity Commn—Lord Spencer—The Queen—and
minutes. Read A. Wilson Case.[8] Saw Bp of Lincoln—Ld Advocate
—Mr Glyn. H of C. 12-4. Spoke on the O'Sullivan case.[9] Twenty to
dinner: evening party afterwards. Saw U.S. Minister—Mr J.G. Hubbard.

6. Ascension Day.

Chapel Royal (with H.C.) at noon. Wrote to The Queen—D. of Ar-
gyll—and minutes. Saw Duke of Argyll—Lord Advocate *cum* Mr
Baxter—Lord Granville—Mr Glyn. H of C. 4½-1½: working Irish
Church Bill. Spoke largely on Maynooth. The final division on the

---

[1] Irish Church Bill cttee.: *H* cxcvi. 22.
[2] William Hare, 1833-1924; 3rd earl of Listowel 1856; cr. Baron Hare Dec. 1869.
[3] *H* cxcvi. 110.
[4] Add MS 44637, f. 51; specially summoned for the Cork mayoralty issue, ibid. f. 50.
[5] Details of time-table for the Bill, ibid., f. 52.
[6] A select cttee. on the Abyssinian war was elected on 8 June 1869: *H* cxcvi. 1439.
[7] See 8 May 69.
[8] Perhaps A. Wilson, *Arbitration between the University of Cambridge and Andrew Wilson. Mr. Wilson's case* (1806).
[9] *H* cxcvi. 185; see 30 Apr. 69n.

pricking point with a majority of 107 was the most creditable (I think) that I have ever known.[1] Seven to breakfast.

7. Fr.

Wrote to Sir R. Palmer—The Queen—Abp of Canterb.—Bp of Peterb.—Archdn of Meath—Dean of Cashel—and minutes. H of C. 2-7. Irish Church Bill came out of Committee.[2] Rode—alone. Saw Granville—D. of Argyll—Mr Glyn—Ld Lyveden—Mr Bouverie—Saw Gerald: but alone[R]. Dined at Mr Thistlethwayte's: conversation on Irish Church.

8. Sat.

Wrote to Lord Gosford[3]—Mr V. Darbishire—The Queen—Lord Spencer—and minutes. Cabinet $2\frac{1}{2}$-$5\frac{1}{2}$. Saw Gerald: who promised [R]. Saw Mr E. Hamilton—Mr C. Robinson (Scotts)—The Rothschilds—Duke of Devonshire—Rev W.M. Goalen—Rev W. Rogers —Mr Glyn. Dined at Lady M. Alford's. Lady Waterford there: still young: both delightful. Saw Macready X.

Cabinet May 8. 69.[4]
1. Argyll's letter to Mayo read & approved.[5]
2. De Grey. Govt. draftsman not to draw Clauses for the Bishops' Eccl[esiastical] Courts Bill.
3. Kimberley. As to Scotch & Irish Peerage Bill.
            Minority vote: entertained.
            Q[uer]y stop creation of Irish Peers.
4. Life Peerage Bill.
5. Irish Church Bill—Palmer's Clause. Objected to: but a principle of compensation admitted, & a proposal to be made if necessary.[6]
6. Arrangement of Bills: Mayor of Cork. to be prosecuted without Adjournment.
7. Court of Chancery Funds Bill discussed.[7] to go forward with a Clause for interest in deposits if chosen.
7. [*sic*] Permissive Bill. To oppose on grounds of impending Legislation.[8]

---

[1] Maynooth lost its grant but gained some £400,000 in compensation: *H* cxcvi. 348; see E. R. Norman, *The Catholic Church and Ireland* (1965), 368ff.
[2] Lord *Monck, J. A. *Lawson and G. A. *Hamilton announced as Irish Church Commissioners: *H* cxcvi. 421.
[3] Archibald Brabazon Sparrow Acheson, 1841-1922; 4th earl of Gosford 1864.
[4] Add MS 44637, f. 54.
[5] Not found.
[6] On forfeiture of annuities; see *H* cxcvi. 760. Gladstone believed *Palmer's proposal to be 'most injurious to . . . the disestablished Church'; Add MS 44536, f. 156.
[7] See 31 July 69.
[8] Diarist's note at Add MS 44637, f. 55: 'Here is my Permissive Bill: As you're a drunken dog, / Permit me to prevent you / From buying a glass of grog.'

8. Clarendon recited state of Belgian-Spanish(Cuba)-United States questions. Conversation on views of U.S.—& Canada.[1]
9. Next Cabinet.

9. S.aft Asc.

Chapel Royal mg: St George's H.Squ. aft. Saw Ld Granville—do *cum* Ld Clarendon—Duke of Argyll—Ld Sydney—Mr O Donoghue —Att.Gen. for Ireland—Mr Glyn (2)—Cabinet 6-7 on Mayor of Cork's case. Wrote to Ld Bessborough—Mr O Donoghue—The Queen—Mr Fortescue—Att.Gen.Irel. Stephy here. Read Romanoff[2] —Five Years in Sisterhood &c.[3]—Coleridge's Keble.

Cabinet May 9 / 69.[4] *6. P.M.-11 C[arlton] H[ouse] T[errace].*
1. Read Abp. of Canterbury's & Bp. of Peterborough's letters:[5] and discussed the course to be taken with reference to Palmer's Clause.
2. Mayor of Cork. If he resigns Bill to be postponed: and dropped when a successor has been chosen. But no bargain.[6]

10. M.

Wrote to J. M. Gaskell—Dean of Windsor—Mr Triqueti[7]—Bp of Fredericton—Miss Wyse[8]—Lady M. Alford—Ld de Grey—Mrs Campbell[9]—Mr Hubbard—Rev Mr Musgrave—J. Davidson—Hon & Rev L. Neville—Ld Kinnaird—Lord A. Hervey—Mr Kirk MP— Mr S. Morley MP.—The Queen—and minutes. Sat on the Banda & Kirwee Notes case at the Treasury 11-2.[10] Saw Mr Hamilton—Lord Clarendon—Mr Forster—Ld Bessborough—Mr Childers. H of C. $4\frac{1}{2}$-$7\frac{3}{4}$ and 9-$1\frac{1}{2}$.[11]

[1] Printed mem. for cabinet, by E. B. Pennell, 6 May 1869, on Jervois' report on Canadian fortifications 1864, in Add MS 44410, f. 35.
[2] See 7 Feb. 69.
[3] *Five years in a Protestant sisterhood and ten years in a Catholic convent. An autobiography* (1869).
[4] Add MS 44637, f. 57: called in response to this day's note: 'The Mayor of Cork having placed his resignation in the hands of Mr Maguire and The O'Donoghue, the Cabinet are requested to meet here at 6 pm precisely. W.E.G.'; ibid., f. 56.
[5] Gladstone had sent *Tait and *Magee copies of *Palmer's clause, adding 'there is no evidence that the [Irish] Clergy desire a defence of this kind'; Add MS 44536, f. 156.
[6] O'Sullivan resigned; see 11 May 69.
[7] Baron di Trequeti, about J. C. *Robinson, Add MS 44536, f. 157.
[8] Winifrede Mary Wyse (see 18 Dec. 58), had sent her *An excursion in the Peloponnesus* (1865).
[9] Miss Arabella Georgina Campbell, had sent her *Life of . . . Sarpi* (1869); Add MS 44536, f. 156.
[10] First sitting of treasury lords as a judicial court since *Liverpool's day, on booty captured at Banda and Kirwee during the Mutiny; see *The Times*, 24 May 1869, 11a; notes in Add MS 44757, f. 142.
[11] Pauperism: *H* cxcvi. 491.

11. Tu.

Wrote to Ld Clarendon—Mr Fortescue—The Queen—D. of Argyll
—Robn G.—and minutes. Saw Princess M[ary] of Teck[1]—Miss
Wyse—Mr Glyn—Sir Thos G.—Mr Baillie Cochrane. Saw Macready:
with hope X. Audience of H.M. 12-1 nearly. H of C. $2\frac{1}{4}$-$3\frac{1}{2}$ (Mayor
of Cork) and $9\frac{1}{2}$-$1\frac{1}{2}$.[2] C.s Ball afterwards. Dined with the Wests.[3]

12. Wed.

Wrote to Ld Clarendon—D. of Argyll—Mr S. Kay[4]—Att.Gen.Irel.
—Ld de Grey—Sir H. Verney—Mr Hughes—Bp of Down—Gen.
Grey—Sir T. Biddulph—Duc d'Aumale—The Queen—& minutes.
Saw Mr E. Hamilton—Lord Kinnaird—Mr Glyn—W.H.G (on Ch.
apptts)—Lord Clarendon—Dean of Windsor—Count Bernstorff.
Saw Macready: il y a de la veritable noblesse dans ce caractère là
[R].[5] Dined at Mr Milbank's. Royal Concert afterwards. Saw P. of
Wales, Pss of Wales, Mr Disraeli, Lady Beaconsfield, Duke of Cam-
bridge (on Ireland). Read Sumner's Speech.[6]

13. Th.

Wrote to Chancr of Exr—Mr Vesey Fitzgerald—Scotts—The Queen
—& minutes. Conclave at 4 P.M. on Irish Ch. Palmer's Clause.[7] Saw
Mr Childers—Mr Cyrus Field—Mr Glyn—Ld Granville—Ld de
Grey—Count Strzelecki—Mr Greg—Ld Granville—Dr Ball.[8] H. of
C. $4\frac{1}{2}$-$9\frac{1}{4}$ and $10\frac{1}{4}$-1. Irish Church, Report: all went well.[9] Read
Valerius. Rode.

14. Fr. [*Hawarden*]

Wrote to Miss Hampden[10]—Duke of Argyll—The Queen—Princess
Mary—Ld Spencer—Mr Childers—& minutes. Cabinet 12-$2\frac{1}{4}$. Saw

---

[1] On her income; see Gladstone to Princess Mary, 14 May 1869, Add MS 44420, f. 264.
[2] Withdrawing the bill on O'Sullivan's resignation: *H* cxcvi. 584.
[3] (Sir) A. E. *West, Gladstone's secretary, m. 1858 Mary Barrington.
[4] Unidentified.   [5] 'There is true nobility in that character.'
[6] C. Sumner, 'Our claims on England. Speech delivered . . . April 13 1869' (1869); violent attack on Britain, suggesting huge indirect claims.
[7] See 9 May 69.
[8] John Thomas *Ball, 1815-98; L.L.D.; tory M.P. Dublin university 1868-74; Irish lord
chancellor 1875-80.
[9] *Palmer withdrew his clause; *H* cxcvi. 766.
[10] Henrietta Hampden, da. of bp. R.D.*; had written on diarist's letters to her fa.; Add
MS 44536, f. 159.

Ld Clarendon—Mr Gibson—Mr Glyn. After a busy day off at 5 PM to Hn. Arrived before 11. Read Derbishire's Ballads.[1]

Cabinet May 14. 69.[2]
1. Childers's Memorandum respecting sending the Floating Dock for Bermuda read & approved.[3]
2. Mr Bright raised the question of Mr Thornton's fitness. Discussed [;] and Spain not to be filled up till after Mr Motley's arrival.[4]
3. Successor to Gen. Wetherell—Mr Burke generally approved.[5]
4. Guarantee for the Fortifications of Montreal.[6]
   Information to be prepared a. on the state of covenant b. on the military authority for a plan of defending Canada.
5. Next Cabinet tomorrow fortnight.

15. Sat.

Ch. 8½ AM. Wrote to Lord Lyttelton—Ld Granville—Mr West—Mr Grant Duff—Mrs Baring—Sir H. Bulwer—Mr Macmillan—Lord Spencer (Telegram)—and minutes. Arranging books & papers. Worked on MS of Homer. Saw Mr Austin—Mr Roberts. Read the Comedy of Convocation: acute yet tedious, & mischievous[7]—Also Julius Caesar. Walk with Harry to the really wonderful sea of hyacinths (say 30 acres) in the Booberry.[8]

16. Whits.

Church 11 A.M. with H.C. and 6.30 evg. Read Coleridge's Keble (finished)[9]—Crompton on Comprehension[10]—Five years in Sisterhood (finished)[11]—Plumptre's Sermon[12]—Nat. Review on Irish Church.

[1] Possibly G. Derbyshire, *Dunstable: a poem; and Graves of the poor; a poem* (1830).
[2] Add MS 44637, f. 58.
[3] *Childers missed the cabinet; see Add MS 44537, f. 160; note on the dock at Add MS 44637, f. 59.
[4] (Sir) Edward *Thornton, 1817-1906; minister in Washington 1867-81, in Russia 1881-4, in Turkey 1884-6. 'I do not doubt that the substitution of Odo Russell for Thornton . . . would be a very useful one for the public: but it seems to me quite clear that this should be done in a moment of lull such as is not unlikely to follow Motley's arrival'; to Clarendon, 17 May 1869, Add MS 44536, f. 161. *Layard was sent to Madrid in October 1869.
[5] Sir E. R. *Wetherall (see 27 Feb. 69) was replaced by Thomas Henry *Burke, 1829-82, Irish under-secretary 1869-82; murdered in Phoenix Park.
[6] See 15 Oct. 72 and *PP* 1870 i. 189 (Canada Defences Loan Bill).
[7] Archdeacon Chasuble [i.e. A. F. Marshall], *The comedy of convocation in the English Church* (1867).
[8] Bilberry wood, at the edge of the Park.   [9] See 7 Feb. 69.
[10] J. W. Crompton, 'Comprehension of dissenters. A letter' (1868).   [11] See 9 May 69.
[12] E. H. *Plumptre, 'Calmness in times of trouble. A sermon [on Luke xxi. 19]' (1868).

17. Whitm.

Ch. 11 A.M. Wrote to Lord Clarendon—Mr Palgrave—Mr Glyn—
Lord Spencer—Mr West—Major Beare[1]—Scotts—Lord Chancellor
—Mr Hornby—Mr Ouvry—Mr Caird—Mr Holden[2]—Robn G.—
and minutes. Read 'Chronique Concernant Le Prochain Concile'[3]—
Fraser (of Jan.) on the Ministry[4]—Juvenal Sat XV—Noble!—Cu-
vier's Theory of the Earth[5]—Cassell's Biography of W.E.G.[6] Worked
on proofsheets.

18. Whit Tu.

Ch. 8½ A.M. Wrote to Bp of Gloucester—Dss of Argyll[7]—A.E. West
—Rev Dr Russell—Mr Esmonde[8]—Rev. R. Seymour—Sir A. Paget
—Canon Mozley—Watsons—Mr Macmillan—and minutes. Worked
on proofsheets. Read Seymour's Ch.Ch. Dublin[9]—M'Gilchrist's
Biogr. of WEG. Moved Stephen to suggest to Shaw a *crypt* under my
Library.[10]

19. Wed.

Ch. 8½ A.M. Wrote to Duke of Argyll—Ld Clarendon—Robn G.—
Att.Gen. Ireland—Helen J.G.—Lord Granville—A. Gordon[11]—C.
Nosotti—Mr Glyn—and minutes. Rain, rain, rain: exercise stinted:
but a good day for my proof sheets. Read Seymour on Christ Church
Dublin.

To LORD CLARENDON, foreign secretary,   Clarendon MSS, c. 497.
19 May 1869.

I return Thornton's very interesting letter.[12] There were two points in the
American matter on which I had intended to write or speak to you. 1. One of

---

[1] Declining an invitation to join the Reform Club; after consultation with *Glyn, the
chief whip, this letter was not sent, and on 20 May he joined, resigning after the 1874 election; Add MS 44536, ff. 161, 164.
[2] James Holden had written claiming kinship; Add MS 44536, f. 161.
[3] Not found.   [4] *Fraser's Magazine*, lxxix. 113 (January 1869).
[5] See 8 Aug. 50.
[6] J. McGilchrist, *The Life of William Ewart Gladstone* (1868) in *Cassell's Representative
Biographies*.
[7] On the Motley affair (see 1 Apr. 69), and on Sumner; Add MS 44420, f. 281.
[8] Sir John Esmonde, 1826-76; liberal M.P. Waterford from 1852; 10th bart. 1868; Add
MS 44536, f. 161.
[9] Perhaps an article by Michael Hobart Seymour who wrote much on Irish ecclesiastical
affairs.   [10] i.e. under the 'Temple of Peace'; never built.
[11] In *T.A.P.S.* new series li, part 4, 50.
[12] Apparently Thornton to Clarendon N. 19, *ca.* 16 April 1869, missing in Clarendon MS
c. 480.

them he mentions (page 11) as having been opened by Mr. Fish. Early in the war, I felt a great anxiety that we should propose to the U.S. to set about laying down rules which might *in the future* govern all Alabama cases and the like: and I was assured that something of this kind had been done, without effect. It appears to me well worth consideration whether this might not now be done by us with advantage. Either a great good would be achieved for the future, or the Americans, if they refused, would be placed yet more palpably in a false position than through Sumner's egregrious kindness to his country they now are.

2. The other point is this: whether the time has come when the Government might with advantage employ the very best man they can find to state, independently and unofficially, the history of the whole case to the world: treating separately the recognition of belligerency, the case of the Trent which cost us a million & more, the Alabama escape—her subsequent reception in British i.e. Colonial Ports—our proceedings in other cases, especially the cruisers[?], & the heavy sums we paid to avoid giving umbrage to America, our refusal of arbitration (most unhappy as it was) followed by its acceptance, our proceedings, & theirs, in the consequent negotiations, and all this history illustrated (1) very fully by an account of the rules heretofore observed by the Americans themselves in like cases theretofore (2) lightly, by reference to the more marked Southern sympathies of other countries & our refusal to join in any plan for Recognition of the Southern States. Pray think of this.

The thing if done should be done by some eminently temperate & judicial man: such a man perhaps as Herman Merivale?

3. The unofficial proposal supposed to be confided to Motley seems to be a good one.

4. I hope that Thornton's answer to the Southerners at the dinner was rather more decisive than he reports it to have been. It would surely be a serious offence in an Envoy to tolerate or entertain discourse about making common cause with discontented subjects.

(5) I have no strong opinion about consulting Knollys; & I meant no more than this that reference might be made to the passage in Elliot's letter & willingness expressed to learn any facts in explanation of it.

(6) I inclose a communication from Baxter worth reading. What utterance of mine is referred to, I cannot conceive.

To G. G. GLYN, chief whip, 19 May 1869.   Add MS 44536, f. 163.

I have been reading such an able article in the Echo today on the future of the I.C. that it reminds me of my suggestion to you; which if the promoters of the paper are efficient & trustworthy still seems to me worthy of consideration. Now I am going to hazard what they may think too like shop. I imagine that as dependent on large sale it must go to press very early & therefore be little efficient as an evening paper. If it had countenance from us why should it not publish a late 2d Edition, perhaps on thicker paper at 1d? which may now be taken as a rather aristocratic price. This needs no immediate answer.[1] I should now like advice about the enclosed card. Perhaps if Irish debate is over I might go.

---

[1] None found.

20. Th.

Ch. 8¼ A.M. Wrote to Duchess of Argyll—Major Beare—Mr Glyn—
Viceroy of Irel.[1]—Ld Bury—Ld Granville—Ld Gort[2]—Ld De Tabley—Mr Parker—Rev A.J. Dowling[3]—Mr Fawcett—Professors of
Maynooth—The Queen—and minutes. Messenger with New Zealand papers in evening: sent them off, with minute.[4] Saw Mr Burnett.
Read Comte de Paris' Book—And Fuller on Crystal Palace.[5] Worked
on proof sheets. We felled four oaks.

21. Fr.

Ch. 8½ A.M. Wrote to Earl of Clarendon—Earl Granville—D. of Argyll—Mr Fortescue—Ld Lyttelton—Lord Sydney—and minutes.
Finished proofsheets. Conversation with Mr Shaw on Library accommodation at Castle. Read C. de Paris—Seymour on Ch.Ch. We felled
two oaks.

To LORD CLARENDON, foreign secretary,   Add MS 44536, f. 165.
21 May 1869.

1. Many thanks for your very interesting letter about the United States.[6] I am
sure Sumner has unwittingly done us a great service. It is for his countrymen to
consider what he has done them.
2. I return Lord Howden's letter,[7] I am personally a stranger to him: but it certainly gives a most favourable and winning idea of his character.
3. About the Oecumenical Council[8] I should like much to converse with you.
My ideas briefly indicated are these
      (a) not to discourage a combined action of the Governments, for it might im-
mensely strengthen the hands of the more moderate & right minded Bishops.
      (b) To plead for ourselves that on account of our want of direct relations
both to the Pope & to the Roman Catholic Churches in H.M.'s dominions we
naturally fall into the rear though without *renouncing* absolutely.
      (c) To suggest for consideration whether one or more of the R.C. Powers
might not submit to the Court of Rome that they should submit to the respective Governments of Christendom, some time before the Council meets, a

[1] i.e. *Spencer.
[2] Standish Prendergast Vereker, 1819-1900; sheriff of Galway 1844; 4th Viscount Gort
1865.
[3] Declining to sell him the copyright of *The State in its Relations with the Church*; Add
MS 44536, f. 164.
[4] Supporting *Granville's removal of last British troops; see Ramm I, i. 22n. and C. C.
Eldridge, *England's Mission* (1973), 58ff.
[5] F. Fuller, 'Shall we spend £100,000 on a winter garden for London' (1851).
[6] Clarendon to Gladstone, 20 May 1869, Add MS 44133, f. 226, giving his son George's
impressions of a Washington visit: 'Surprise is felt or pretended at the importance we have
given to Sumner's speech.'
[7] Clarendon had earlier promised him the Madrid embassy, and forwarded his 'unselfish
letter'; ibid.
[8] See Matthew, 'Vaticanism', p. 429.

statement of such of the subjects intended to be brought before it as bear *upon civil rights* or upon the *relations of Church and State.*

It seems to me that such a representation would be reasonable; might act as a salutary check; & is such as even we, in case of need, might join in or support. I say this much in the act of returning your draft to Lord A. Loftus as that will be (I believe) your *first* utterance respecting the Council. I entirely agree in thinking it most desirable, especially for other countries, that the press and people should a little bestir themselves: while I am not so sure about the need or utility of saying now anything which would have the effect of precluding the action, and even the concerted action, of Governments. The Syllabus was a great outrage: there may be an opportunity of helping to do what the Reformation in many things did—to save the Pope and the Roman Church from themselves.

I hope it is not true that there is a petition against Hyde: or at any rate a real one.

[P.S.] The only circs. in which I should the least fear the reproach of nepotism for O. R[ussell] would be if way were made for his appointment by a rough & untimely removal of Thornton whose faults I do not see so clearly as J. B[right] does.

22. Sat.

Ch. 8½ AM. Wrote to Ld Clarendon—Ald. Salomons—Mr West— Rev W. Rawson—Robn G.—Mr Bright—and minutes. Read as yesterday. Survey of operations at C. We felled two oaks.

To J. BRIGHT, president of the board of trade,   Add MS 43385, f. 30.
22 May 1869.

The letter you inclose to me is curious and interesting.[1] But it inspires in my mind some doubt, upon the question how the State after buying out the Landlord by a tempting price, is to get back its money? For the complaint of Mr. Brown is that in the Landed Estates' Court the people will have to buy Lord Waterford's Farms at their market value. Now the State, if I understand your proposal, is to buy land somewhat over the market value, because it is to *bring* sellers into the field. How then is it to give contentment by a remunerative sale, which must also be rather over the market value as hitherto understood, to men who make the necessity of paying the market value a subject of complaint?

My fear is, that Mr Brown's letter does not tell the whole case, and that viewing the subject from the peculiar position incidental to the custom of tenant right he is not a trustworthy guide for general purposes.

I have this advantage for learning the Irish Land question, that I do not set out with the belief that I know it already; and certainly no effort that I can make to acquire the mastery of it will be wanting.

As to a native and a small proprietary, I have not a doubt that the substitution for absentees of it would be attended with great social and political advantages, and would be a very Conservative measure; (of course I mean, as you do, the substitution by regular and proper means). My doubts are, *first,* how far such

[1] Bright to Gladstone, 21 May 1869, Add MS 44112, f. 87. 'I send you a letter [untraced] from "Derry" on the Irish Land question.'

a substitution can be effected by the Government, taking upon itself, or upon a State organ, a very large operation of land-jobbing, i.e. buying land to sell again: secondly whether economical laws would not powerfully tend to undo the process of distribution, and cause the property in land gradually to return into fewer hands, however the occupation might be subdivided. Again, I must own that Mr Brown leads me to distrust his judgment, when he says that the Land Bills up to this date have not been worth the paper they were written on. And this for two reasons. First, the principle of compensation for tenants' improvements, whether sufficient or not, is surely one of vast importance: and it shows a certain levity, therefore, to treat it as of none. But secondly, your plan, if adopted in full, could only extend to a small proportion of the two or three hundred millions worth of land in Ireland: and I do not well see how the unprotected tenants of the land in general would take essential benefit from the purchase & owning of land by a few of their fortunate brethren.

There is no doubt of three things in my mind. First, we must all take this question to heart as our Number One, the moment that we see our way out of the question of the Irish Church. Secondly, we must approach it in the spirit in which we approached that first question. Thirdly we must anticipate both more difficulty and less support; and we shall have nothing to set against this expectation except our own hope of continuing together in the formation of our measure the qualities of circumspection and resolution. If we succeed with the Church, & fail with the land, we shall have done less than half our work.

This letter is rather critical in tone: but I am sure you will agree with me in thinking that the raising of doubts & difficulties, soberly conceived, is one of the greatest advantages of early friendly & confidential communication on subjects of great public interest.

23. Trin.S.

Ch 11 AM & H.C. and evg. 6.30. Wrote to Nawab Nazim.[1] Read Mr Dale's Tract[2]—Miss Marsh's new Book[3]—Milton Par. Lost—Essay on Convocations[4]—Clark on Open Churches: a fearful account from Liverpool.[5]

24. M.

Ch. 8$\frac{1}{2}$ AM. Wrote to Ld Stratford de Redcliffe—Lord Granville—A.E. West—Ld Clarendon—Robn G.—Ld Lyttelton—Ld Sydney—Mr Maguire—Mr Childers—and minutes. We felled two Oaks: and then had tea at Crackie's. Read Comte de Paris[6]—Haviland on Distribution of Disease.[7]

[1] The Nawab of Bengal; see 27 June 71.
[2] R. W. *Dale, 'Christ and the controversies of Christendom' (1869).
[3] C. M. Marsh, Shining light (1869).
[4] Perhaps J. Bandinel, Organic reform of Convocation. An essay (1868).
[5] Perhaps J. Clark, The Church as established in its relations to dissent (1866).
[6] Had sent his Les Associations ouvrières en Angleterre (1869); Gladstone shared his 'cheerful view of the question of Trades Unions'; Add MS 44536, f. 168.
[7] A. Haviland, Abstracts of two papers [on geographical distribution of heart disease and cancer] (1869).

25.

Ch. 8½ A.M. Wrote to Earl of Clarendon—The Viceroy—Mr Fortes-
cue—Miss Marsh—Mr Mackinnon—Mrs Munro—Att.Gen. Ireland
—and minutes. 2¼-8. To Chester to meet Robn about Seaforth
House. Saw also The Bishop and The Dean. A Clergy dinner. Read
Irish before Conquest[1]—Les Associations Ouvrières—Le Concile
Ecuménique et les Droits de l'Etat.[2]

To LORD CLARENDON, foreign secretary,   Clarendon MSS, c. 497.
25 May 1869.

I incline to think it would be best that you should introduce the subject of
the Viceroy to the Queen. I presume he[3] would not be treated as a Sovereign?
Would the country be called upon to pay the expense of entertaining him? If it
would, we could not proceed without the Chancellor of the Exchequer. Nor is it,
in my opinion, a very safe experiment to repeat often that we should go to the
House of Commons to supply the means of hospitality to distinguished person-
ages from abroad.

This was done in the case of the Sultan and with very queer effect. The sum
then was a large one.

The retirement of the Queen and the consequent reduction of her expenses[4]
does not make a good ground for a charge of this kind.

I send you for perusal rather a remarkable article from a halfpenny journal
called the Echo[5] which bears upon this subject and which perhaps has a latent
allusion to other topics than those which it expressly mentions.

I send on the letters of this morning's post to the Queen; but I am afraid they
may tend rather unduly to exalt Lumley at the expense of Lyons.

26. Wed.

Ch. 8½ AM. Wrote to Ld Clarendon—Ld Lyttelton—Mr Lynch[6]—
Mr Macmillan—Lady F. Cavendish—Mr Ratzinger, and minutes.
Read Juvenal—Savile's Letter to Bennett[7]—Dadobhed Naurozi's
Reply to Crawfurd[8]—Ratzinger, Armenpflege[9]—Associations

[1] Not found.
[2] Probably an anonymous French translation; see n. 6, 8 June 69.
[3] i.e. the Viceroy of Egypt; Clarendon replied, 26 May 1869, Add MS 44133, f. 233:
'we shd. gain more unpopularity by letting him pay his own bills than by asking the H. of C.
to do so for him'.
[4] Clarendon disagreed: 'she spends all her money on journeys and Mausoleums'; ibid.
[5] 'Obligations of Royalty', *The Echo*, 24 May 1869.
[6] T. T. Lynch; see Add MS 44536, f. 167.
[7] B. W. *Savile, 'A letter to W. J. E. Bennett . . . in reply to his "Plea for toleration . . ." '
(1868).
[8] D. Naurozji, *The European and the Asiatic races. Observations on the paper read by
John Crawfurd* (1866).
[9] G. Ratzinger, *Geschichte der kirchlichen Armenpflege* (1868).

Ouvrières—Julius Caesar—Bp of Argyll's Appeal.[1] Worked on Papers respecting my own affairs. Preparations for departure.

27. Th. [London]

Off at 8.15. Reached C.H.T. before 3. Saw The Speaker—Mr Cardwell—Mr Glyn—Mr Fowler—Chancr of Exr—Col. Wilson Patten —Mr Bright: much conversation in the train from Chester.[2] Finished Associations Ouvrières. Wrote to Earl Granville—Mr Cardwell— Rev. Dr Russell. H of C. $4\frac{1}{4}$-$11\frac{3}{4}$. Worked Civil Pensions' Bill.[3]

28. Fr.

Wrote to Ld Clarendon—Capt. Vivian MP.—The Queen (2)—and minutes. H of C. $4\frac{1}{2}$-8 and $9\frac{1}{2}$-12.[4] Saw Sir J. Lacaita—Mr Macmillan—Mr Glyn—Mr A. Kinnaird—Mr Stansfeld. Saw Bp of Salisbury. Saw Mr Manson. Saw Gerald: respecting niece[R]. Dined with the Wests. At Christie's.

29. Sat.

Wrote to Ld Granville—The Viceroy—Ld Sydney—Archdn Hale —Watsons—Ld Brougham—Sir S. Baker[5]—Comte de Paris—The Queen—and minutes. Saw Bp [Ewing] of Argyll—Mr C. Robinson —Mr Homersham Cox—Mr Glyn—Ld Clarendon—Ld Granville *cum* Chancr. Cabinet $2\frac{1}{2}$-$5\frac{1}{4}$. Saw Mr Layard & Mr Street with the New Plan.[6] Saw Macready: with good promise[R]. Dined with the Rothschilds: Lady Halifax's afr. Read Fraser on Dante.[7]

Cabinet May 29. 69.[8]
(1.Who to speak in the Debate on Monday
   3d R[eading] Irish Church. Spoke to E. C[ardwell] & F[ortescue].)[9]
(2.Course to be taken in relation to the disputed seat in the Scotch Representative Peerage[10] [Spoke to] Chanc[ello]r & Granville)

[1] A. *Ewing, *A plea for the Highland and Non-Juring Congregations of 1688–1745 of Scotland* (1869).
[2] On Irish land; see Ramm I, i. 24.   [3] *H* cxcvi. 863.
[4] Irish education: *H* cxcvi. 885.
[5] Sir Samuel White *Baker, 1821–93, explorer; leaving for the Sudan as pacha: 'In the threefold interest of peace, commerce, & freedom, I sincerely wish well to yr. expedition . . .'; Add MS 44536, f. 169.
[6] For the new law courts.   [7] *Fraser's Magazine*, lxxix. 651 (May 1869).
[8] Add MS 44637, f. 61.
[9] *Cardwell, *Monsell and Gladstone spoke for the govt.; see 31 May 69.
[10] A tie in the election; Lord Kellie got the seat; see Ramm I, i. 14n.

√ 3. Removal of regiment from New Zealand—sanctioned *ex post facto*.[1]
√ 4. Reception of the Viceroy of Egypt. W.E.G. to write to the Queen[2]
√ 5. Murphy's proposed Lectures at Sandbach.[3] To require a statement of danger to the peace from a meeting of Magistrates.
√ 6. Questions of the week.

30. 1 S. Trin.

Chapel Royal mg & aft.—Mr Woodford preached nobly. Saw Mrs Cracroft: sick calls: and at Gerald's where there seems a trick[R]. Wrote to Ld Clarendon. Saw Ld Granville—Mr West. Read N. Hall's Art on U.S. Relig.[4]—Account of B.N.A. Canon[5]—Chambers on the Cairns Judgment[6]—Romanoff on Gr Russ Church.[7]

31. M.

Wrote to Mrs Bennett—Mr Westall—Mr Macfice MP—Att. General —Gen. Grey—Mr G. Murphy—The Queen—and minutes. Rode— alone. Saw the Lord Mayor[8]—Att.Gen. for Ireland—Ld Granville —Mr Glyn—Mr Manson. Read G. Gladstone on Irish Ch.[9]—Dined with the Wests. H of C. $4\frac{1}{2}$-$8\frac{1}{4}$ and $9\frac{1}{4}$-1. Spoke on 3d R. I.C. Bill, & voted in 361:247.[10]

Tues. June One. 1869.

Wrote to Mr G. Hamilton—The Queen (2) & draft—Ld Brougham —Gen. Grey—& minutes. Attended the Levee. Saw Mr Locke King —Mr Glyn—Ld Clarendon *cum* Ld Granville—Ld Clarendon respecting Motley.[11] H of C. $4\frac{1}{2}$-8 and 9-$1\frac{3}{4}$.[12]

2. Wed.

Wrote to D. of Norfolk—Ld Devon—Duchess of Argyll—and minutes. Went to Mrs Malcolm's music. Saw Macready: who D.G.

---

[1] See 20 May 69.   [2] Guedalla, *Q*, i. 174.
[3] The Orangeman and agitator.
[4] C. N. *Hall, 'Churches of America' reprinted in *From Liverpool to St Louis* (1870).
[5] Untraced.
[6] J. D. Chambers, *Strictures on the Judgment of the Court of Appeal in the case of Martin v. Mackonochie* (1869).   [7] See 20 Sept. 68.
[8] Gladstone was trying to arrange *Victoria's appearance at a brief ceremony in the City; Add MS 44536, f. 169.
[9] George Gladstone (unrelated), *The Irish Church Bill: considered in a series of letters* (1869).
[10] *H* cxcvi. 1060; annotated division list in Add MS 44410, f. 57.
[11] See 1 Apr. 69.   [12] Spoke on British Colombia: *H* cxcvi. 1124.

goes home[R]. Saw D. & Dss of Argyll—Mr Westell—Mr Glyn—
Lord Granville; again on the Motley business.—Mr Young—Count
Bismarck[1]—Mr Delane. Birthday dinner in evg: followed by C.s
evening party. Read Street's Report[2]—Mill on Women[3]—Simon on
Cont. Diseases Act.[4]

3. Th.

Willy's birthday: God bless him. Wrote to Lord Granville (2)—Abp
Manning—Dean of Lichfield—Mr Crum Ewing—Ld Mayor—Abp
of Canterb.—Gen Grey—Ld Clarendon—The Queen—Mr Layard
—and minutes. At Christie's. At Chelsea, for inquiries. Saw Mr Bage-
hot—Mr Glyn (2)—Mr Cardwell—Sir T. May—Mr Kinnaird—
Baron Rothschild—Mr Ayrton—Mr Hamilton—Mr Layard—Ld
Granville. 3-4. Deputn on the Episcopate.[5] H of C. $4\frac{1}{4}$-8 and 9-12$\frac{3}{4}$.[6]
Read Blyden on Negro Race[7]—Archdn Hale's Tract.[8]

To J. S. MILL, 3 June 1869.   Add MS 44536, f. 170.

I thank you greatly for your book[9] which I am reading with much interest
and with a full conviction from experience, that whether I am able or not to
adopt your broad proposition I shall derive great profit from the perusal, &
everywhere find thickly scattered what will claim my sympathy.

Are you ever to be had now for dinner or breakfast? The slightest glimpse of
an affirmative answer will lead me to try my chance. I keep until I see you the
expression of your regrets for your not being among us.[10]

To A. C. TAIT, archbishop of Canterbury, 3 June 1869   Tait MSS, 87, f. 120
'Private and Confidential.'

In reply to Your Grace's letter[11] I have to say that any communication from
you, and especially one made with the direct sanction or authority of Her
Majesty, commands my most respectful attention.

I feel a difficulty in saying anything about amendments in the Irish Church
Bill with the particular view of acting, or enabling others to act, on the decision

[1] (Nikolaus Heinrich Ferdinand) Herbert, 1849-1904, and Wilhelm, 1852-1901, Bismarck's sons, on holiday in Britain; see *The Times*, 9 June 1869, 8a.
[2] Report by G. E. *Street, on progress of the Law Courts.
[3] J. S. *Mill, *The subjection of women* (1869).
[4] Section V of Simon's Annual Report: *PP* 1868-9 xxxii. 11.
[5] See *The Times*, 4 June 1869, 5e.   [6] Bankruptcy Bill: *H* cxcvi. 1211.
[7] E. Blyden of Liberia had sent his pamphlet, 'The Negro in Ancient History'; Add MS
44420, f. 255.
[8] W. *Hale, *The doctrine and government of the Anglican Church* (1869).
[9] See previous day.
[10] *Mill wrote from Avignon promising to breakfast on his return; Add MS 44421, f. 39.
[11] Of this day, Add MS 44330, f. 83. See Davidson, *Tait*, ii. 20, with a version of this
letter.

of the House of Lords on the Second Reading of the Irish Church Bill. Not only with reference to party interests, but with reference to the interests of conclusive settlement, a rejection of the Bill on the second reading is not the worst of the alternatives that may be before us. It is eminently desirable, indeed, that the Bill should be read a second time. But if I compare two methods both inexpedient, one that of rejection on the second reading, the other that of a second reading followed by amendments inconsistent with the principle, I know no argument in favour of the latter, except what relates to the very important question of the position and true interest of the House of Lords itself. As far as I know the mind of the House of Commons, on the subject of the Bill there is not that distinction between the questions of disestablishment and disendowment which exists in Your Grace's mind. A distinction there may be, but it does not I think amount to more than this; that, whereas disestablishment is absolute and uniform, the rule of disendowment admits of certain exceptions upon very marked & special grounds, such as those recognised in the provisions respecting Church Private Endowments, and (to a very large extent) glebehouses; perhaps as in the very wide construction which has been given to the doctrine or sympathy [sic] rather than doctrine of vested interests in the cases of the Curates permanent & non-permanent. For the grounds of such exceptions we have sought with care: that not one has escaped our notice I will not venture to affirm: but my opinion is that the House of Commons will not recognise changes in the Bill except they can be brought within the character which I have given.

To ARCHBISHOP H. E. MANNING, 3 June 1869.   Add MS 44536, f. 170.

I thank you greatly for your kind note.[1] The utmost acknowledgement I can claim is that of not having run away from professions & principles in very arduous, but also very encouraging circumstances. The House has moved like an army, & an army where every private is his own general.

Such a house will be well calculated to face the Land question, for which we must lay our first parallel the moment we are out of the Church. I hope we may get through it without stirring dangerous topics.

4. Fr.

Wrote to Ld Granville—Mr G. Burnett—Robn G.—Ld Clarendon —J.S. Mill[2]—and minutes. H. of C. 4½-8. Saw Mr Goschen—Saw Sir R. Anstruther—Mr Stansfeld—Mr Ouvry—Ld Granville—Mr Glyn—Bp of Salisbury—Scotts. At St J. Wood for inquiries. Read Coriolanus—J. Mill on Woman.

5. Sat.

Wrote to The Lord Mayor—Sir F. Rogers—Mr Layard (2)—Mr Blundell—The Queen (2)—Chancr of Exr—Mr Johnson MP.—

[1] Congratulations on the bill and 'a steadfastness I had not thought possible'; Add MS 44249, f. 76.
[2] Sent the previous day.

Lord Sydney—and minutes. Cabinet 2½-5: various reports from St James's Square.[1] Saw The Lord Mayor—Mr MacColl—Mr Glyn—Mr Kinnaird—Sir R. Phillimore—Dowager Duchess of Somerset—Ld Carnarvon—C. Apponyi—Sir R. Knightley. Dined with the Apponyis—Lady Carnarvon's afterwards.

Cabinet. June 5. 69.[2]
√ 1. Clarendon. French Elections: unfavourable.[3]
   Language of Lavalette to Dix: to be acknowledged.
   Exequatur to Mr Haggerty (Fenian)[4] as Consul at Glasgow. Cannot be given.
   The Young Rajah of Sarawak. To keep out of any recognition.
   Lopez & his outrages.[5]
   (see 6. Childers. The Dockyard Emigrants.)
√ 2. Layards Letters.[6] Natural History Museum. Entertained.
   8. Fortescue. Main provisions of the Loan Bill. Pledges to be examined: & Bill further considered.[7]
√ 3. New War Office & Admiralty [buildings] Cabinet Committee reported orally. Minute to be drawn for H.M. showing difficulties.
√ 4. Mr Bright. Plan of a common Library for the Offices. R. Meade's paper to be circulated.
√ 5. D[uke] of Argyll. Indian Railways: to circulate papers.
√ 6. Childers & his Emigrants.[9] Those who pay to be preferred.
√ 7. Committee on Competition Examinations & Division of Labour [in the civil service].[10] Ld Clarendon—Chanc[ello]r of Exch[eque]r—Mr Bright—Mr Goschen—Ld Kimberley—Ld De Grey—Mr Childers.[11]
   9. Scotch Educ[atio]n. D[uke of] A[rgyll] to say he can only promise Chairman & Sec[retary] shall be paid.
   10. Week's business reviewed.

6. 2 S.Trin.

Whitehall mg and H.C.—St A. Wells St aft. Heavy head-cold & headach. Read Church Restoration[12]—Bp Abraham's Sermon[13]—

[1] Perhaps of Derby's views, who lived there; his last speech was on 17 June 1869.
[2] Add MS 44637, f. 63.
[3] The second ballot took place on 6 and 7 June. Lavalette had rejoined the ministry as foreign minister; Dix was the American ambassador in Paris.
[4] The U.S. consul.
[5] Lopes' well-known hostility, voiced 7 June, to government's London poor law bill: *H* cxcvi. 1361.
[6] Of 3 and 4 June 1869, on placing natural history collections on the Embankment; Add MS 44421, f. 9ff; cabinet agreed, 44536, f. 171.
[7] See 26 June 69.   [8] See Guedalla, *Q*, i. 179.
[9] To Canada; see *H* cxcvi. 1298.   [10] See 31 July 69.
[11] Note from *Childers requesting to be put on the cttee. at Add MS 44637, f. 64.
[12] [W. J. Blew], *Church restoration; its principles and methods* (1869).
[13] C. J. *Abraham, 'The divine principles of Christian missions to the heathen. A sermon' (1869).

Pressensè on Ch. & French Rev.[1]—Romanoff, Russian Ch.[2]—Sadler on the Bible—Seebohm, Oxford Reformers.[3]

7. M.

Tried bed to subdue my cold. Half success. Wrote to Lord Lichfield —Gen. Grey—Abp of Canterb. H of C. $4\frac{1}{2}$-$8\frac{1}{2}$. Then home to bed. Read Julius Caesar—Mill on Woman (finished). Corrected proof sheets.

To LORD LICHFIELD, 7 June 1869.   Add MS 44536, f. 171.

If you would allow me I should prefer not to receive a deputation respecting the appointment of a Commission on Friendly & Burial Societies upon the ground that the question requires a close and minute attention which I am not able to give to its details, & probably could only be prosecuted with Departmental aid such as the Home Office or possibly the Board of Trade could give, but which I do not possess. I know enough of it to be aware that the appointment of a Commission by the Govt. on the subject of these voluntary institutions would be a serious (I am far from saying an improper) step, & I should not like to raise expectations by a proceeding which so far as I am concerned must terminate in & with itself as only a careful inquiry into documents & figures could enable me to form any trustworthy judgement. I shall be happy if you like to see you on any morning with reference to the intermediate subject.[4]

8. Tu.

Wrote to The Queen—Mr Cardwell—Bp of Ely—Dean of Chichester—and minutes. Saw Ld Granville. Corrected proof sheets: the last. Read Hook's Introduction & Lecture[5]—Nardi, Concilio Ecumenico.[6] Saw Ld Granville. Kept my bed all day.

To W. F. HOOK, dean of Chichester, 8 June 1869.   Add MS 44536, f. 172.

I am in one sense fortunate in being laid up today for it will give me a better & quieter opportunity of reading you than I should otherwise have enjoyed.

In the meantime pray accept my best thanks for your letter & your preface.[7] I have always thought we were most fortunate in the character of that minority among the Clergy who approve our measure: & especially I rejoice that it should be headed by him who has this for one only among many distinctions to have been by the voice of all men the first parish priest of his generation.

[1] See 11 Apr. 69.   [2] See 7 Feb. 69.
[3] See 15 Mar. 68 and 18 Apr. 67.   [4] See 9 June 69.
[5] W. F. *Hook, 'The disestablished Church in the Republic of the United States of America' (1869).
[6] F. Nardi, Il Concilio ecumenico e i diritti dello stato (1869).
[7] Hook had sent his pamphlet supporting the Irish Church Bill; Add MS 44213, f. 146.

9. Wed.

Wrote to Mr Fortescue—Lord de Grey—the Queen—General Grey —and minutes. Read Nardi's answer—finished—Fauriel on Dante[1] —Redesdale on Coronation Oath[2]—Macivor on Irish Education[3]— Economy of Navy estimates. Revised & dispatched Preface.[4] Saw Lord Granville—Lord Lichfield[5]—Mr Glyn—Sir R. Phillimore. Dinner & evening party here: which I did not attend. Drove out for half an hour.

10. Th.

Wrote to Ld Clarendon (2)—Gen. Grey—Mr T.B. Potter—Mr Ouvry —Sir C. Ricketts—Abp Manning—and minutes. H. of C. $4\frac{1}{2}$-$7\frac{3}{4}$.[6] Read Dr Brady's new work on Irish Church.[7] Breakfast party: also Dinner party of 15. Mrs Weldon. Saw Bishop of Oxford—Mr N. Hall —Mr Deutsch—Mr Kinnaird—Mr Glyn—Mr Hom[ersha]m Cox— Ld Carnarvon.

11. Fr.

Wrote to Mr Hamilton—The Queen—Mr Bruce—Bp of Ossory— and minutes. H of C. at 2-4-$5\frac{3}{4}$: and $9\frac{1}{4}$-$11\frac{3}{4}$.[8] Saw Sir W. Jenner[9] 11-12—Sir H. Bulwer—Sir G. Grey *cum* Mr Whitbread—Ld Granville (& Conclave on possible amendts in Irish Church Bill $2\frac{1}{4}$-4)[10] —Bp of Salisbury—Bp of Down. Read Dr Brady on Irish Ch. Saw Williams, & two others, incl. Peterborough case[R]. Dined with the Wests.

---

[1] C. C. Fauriel, *Dante et les origines de la langue et de la littérature italienne*, 2v. (1854).
[2] J. T. F. *Mitford, Earl of Redesdale, *Lord Macaulay on the Coronation Oath* (1869).
[3] J. MacIvor, *Some papers on intermediate education in Ireland* (1869).
[4] Of *Juventus Mundi.*
[5] 'I called on Gladstone . . . and he declined to receive the deputation [of Rev. J. Y. Strattan's cttee. for improving friendly societies] or to look at the memorial but said he would not object to Bruce recg. it & would speak to him. G. said he knew nothing of Govt. Annuities Bill now before the House'; mem. by Lichfield; Staffordshire R.O. D 615/P(P) 4/3/1. See 12 June 69.
[6] Motion for select cttee. on pauperism withdrawn: *H* cxcvi. 538.
[7] W. M. *Brady, *Essays on the English State Church in Ireland* (1869).
[8] Withdrew O'Sullivan's Disability Bill: *H* cxcvi. 577.
[9] An interview arranged with *Jenner, the Queen's doctor, who was excusing, on grounds of ill-health, her refusal to make public appearances: 'fanciful ideas of a woman about her own health, encouraged by a feeble minded doctor, become realities . . .' (to Grey, 10 June 1869, Guedalla, *Q*, i. 183).
[10] 1°R in the Lords on 1 June, 2°R began 14 June.

To H. A. BRUCE, home secretary, 11 June 1869.   Add MS 44536, f. 172.

I am of opinion that this question of a Welsh University or an extension of Lampeter or neither is too big for us to make progress in it without wider counsel: which might be had either by reference to the Cabinet, or by conferring with Granville & Lowe both concerned with London University. The question of a Welsh University seems to me a very difficult one; but I incline to think that if we were in that direction the extension of Lampeter *alone* would not do.[1]

12. Sat. [*Dufferin Lodge, Highgate*]

Wrote to Ld Lyttelton—Mr Dixon MP—The Queen (2)—Mr Boothroyd[2]—Mr Ouvry—Ld Foley—Bishop of Oxford—and minutes. Saw Messrs . . . —Ld de Grey—Mr Roundell—Mr Glyn—Ld Spencer—Ld Granville. Cabinet $2\frac{1}{2}$-$4\frac{1}{2}$. Calls. Dined at Ld Morley's. Off to Mr Glyn's afterwards (Dufferin Lodge). Read Dr M. Brady.

Cabinet. June 12. 69.[3]
O 1. Lord Lichfield's request.[4] Saw Mr Bruce
O 2. Mr Bradlaugh's letter.[5] Saw Ld Granville
√ 3. Civil Pensions. To include whom? *As* now.
√ 4. Ld Lyons & Irish Church division—C[larendon] to write he shd. come over [from Paris to vote].
√ 5. Ld Clarendon read acc[oun]t of interview with Motley.[6]
√ 6. Business of H[ouse of commons].
      Monday:[7] Endowed Sch[ools bill]—Cattle Bill pro formâ.—Civil Offices Pensions—Endowed Hosp[itals] Scotland. *Thursday*: Finish Army Estimates—Assessed Rates Bill. *Mond[ay]* 21:—Misc[ellaneous] Estimates
   7. Lanc[ashire] Magistrates. Cabinet favourable to Ld D[ufferin]'s plan[8]

To S. WILBERFORCE, bishop of Oxford,   Wilberforce MSS d. 37.
12 June 1869.

When I was a youth sitting behind Sir R. Peel there was a famous old Whig landlady at the inn at Fushie Bridge on the road to Edinburgh who had known me from a child & who though on the other side, used to say to me 'Now, mind I always see your face in the Divisions'. That is what I earnestly say to you, by

[1] Bruce had forwarded a proposal from St. David's College, Lampeter, for its extension; Add MS 44086, f. 38. See 14 Apr. 71.
[2] Of Bradford; had sent a resolution of support. Add MS 44536, f. 173. Gladstone's letter published together with *Bright's on Irish land; see *H* cxcvii. 121, and *The Times*, 15 June 1869, 9b.
[3] Add MS 44637, f. 65.   [4] See 9 June 69n.
[5] *Bradlaugh was being prosecuted as publisher of the *National Reformer*; see his letters to the Inland Revenue in *The Times*, 26 April 1869, 11c and H. B. Bradlaugh, *Charles Bradlaugh* (1894), i, ch. xxviii.
[6] See 1 June 69n.
[7] These details on a separate sheet.
[8] Tories were trying to wrest appt. of Lancs. J.P.s from chancellor of the duchy; Dufferin resisted; Add MS 44151, f. 52.

no means thinking only of the mere unit in reckoning the numbers. I need not therefore say, I am greatly pleased with the letter of Mr. Woodford, independently of his much too good opinion of me. As to the vote on the 2d reading and what it *must* mean there is no doubt. It does not happen to have occurred on this Bill, but I well remember that on the Reform Bill of Ld Grey Mr. C. Wynne in the Commons & Ld Harrowby & Ld Wharncliffe in the Lords (1832) accepted the 2d reading but only with the avowed intention to vote against the 3d reading unless it were amended.

But acceptance rather than approval is the thing meant: & that with the limitations I describe.

I cannot help feeling a similar anxiety about Salisbury for his own sake, but this it would be impertinent in me to say to him.

Things seem to look like our losing by a very small number: of all results the worst for the Derbyizers.

13. 3 S. Trin.

Highgate Church mg. Cholmeley School Chapel aftn. Read Pressensè[1]—Seebohm Oxf. Reformers[2]—Cordner on Protestantism.[3] A quiet day. Mr Glyn better but far from strong.

14. M. [London]

Wrote to Dowager Duchess Somerset—Mr Bazley MP.—Mr Tite MP. —Ld Clarendon—Mr White MP—Mr Palgrave—The Queen (2)— Ld Dufferin—Mrs Barber—and minutes. Saw Ld Granville—Mr Macmillan—Mr Glyn—Scotts. Returned from H[igh]gate 10.40. H of C. & H. of L. $4\frac{1}{2}$-$8\frac{1}{4}$ and 10-2.40.[4] Saw Sir J. Mitchell.[5] Dined with the Wests.

15. Tu.

Wrote to Ld Granville—Mrs Barber—Mr Wright—Mr Bruce—The Queen—and minutes. Saw Stuart X Ramsay X. Saw Mr Newmarch[6] —Ld Granville—Lord Russell—Mr Rathbone—Mr Glyn—Ld De Tabley—Att. General—Sol. General—Chancr of Exchr—Mr Ayrton. H. of C. and H. of L. $3\frac{3}{4}$-7.[7] Dined at Lady Herbert's. Saw Abp Manning. Then the Brunnow Ball: saw P. of Wales—Lady L. Egerton.

[1] See 16 Apr. 69.　　　　　　　　　　　　　　　[2] See 6 June 69.
[3] Perhaps J. Cordner, *Unitarianism* (1846).
[4] Irish Church Bill in the Lords, Endowed Schools in the Commons: *H* cxcvi. 1637, 1744.
[5] Probably Sir James William Mitchell, 1836–98, soldier and bart., though he did not use his title.
[6] See 19 Mar. 55.　　　　　　　　　　　　　　　[7] Irish Church: *H* cxcvi. 1794.

16. Wed.

Wrote to Lord Mayor—Mr W.H. Smith—Mr C. Neate—Ld Lyttel-
ton—Ld de Grey—Ld Granville—and minutes. H of C. 2¼-4½ and
5-6.[1] Saw Mr Forster—Mons. Chevalier—Mr Glyn—Mr E. Talbot
—Sir J. Simeon—Ld Granville—Mr West—Ld Spencer—Mr
Bright—Mr Fortescue—and others. Dined with the Sydneys. Saw
Mr Motley:[2] then to the F.O. party. Read Dr Mazier Brady. Saw
Ramsay X.

17. Th.

Wrote to Lady Brownlow—Mr Macmillan—The Queen (3)—Ld
Granville (2)—Col. Sykes—Sir J. Lacaita—Mr Heron—and minutes.
H of C. & H. of L. 4½-8 and 9-1.[3] Saw Ld de Grey—Ld Granville—
M. Wolowski—Rev Mr Williams—Mr Ouvry—Mr Burlingame—Dr
N. Hancock—Mr Glyn—Mr Bright—Mr Hamilton *cum* Mr Stans-
feld. U.P. Deputation on Irish Church & kindred matters.[4] Banda &
Kerwee Prize Money Deputation.[5] Read Dr Brady.

18. Fr.

Wrote to Bp of Lincoln—Mrs Thistlethwayte—Dr M. Brady—The
Queen—Pss Mary of Teck—Ld Clarendon—and minutes. Saw
Depn of Scotch Establ.Ch.[6] Read Borghetti on Eccles. Policy[7]—
Coriolanus. Saw the Lord Mayor—Ld de Grey—Ld Clarendon—
Ld Sydney—Mr Morley—Dr N. Macleod—Ld Granville. Went to
Windsor for the Council. Audience of H.M. H. of C. 3½-5¾. H of C.
& H of L. 9-1.[8]

Windsor June 1869.[9]
1. Ld Mayor. Bridge alone—any time in Octr? Failing whom. P. of Wales? Ld
Mayor to entertain the Viceroy? 2. Mr. Tite—to be knighted. 3. Act for Suffragan Bishops.

19. Sat. [*Dufferin Lodge, Highgate*][10]

Wrote to The Queen (2) . . . and minutes. Cabinet 2.45-6. Dined at
Devonshire House: then went down to Geo. Glyn. Saw The Lord

---

[1] Misc. business: *H* cxcvi. 1947.   [2] See 1 June 69n.
[3] Questioned on *Bright's public letter on Irish land: *H* cxcvii. 121.
[4] Annotated copy of United Presbyterian's 'Memorial' for the dpn. in Add MS 44610,
f. 59.   [5] See 10 May 69.
[6] On the education bill.   [7] Untraced, perhaps by G. Borghetti.
[8] Russell criticized aspects of the Irish Church Bill: *H* cxcvii. 162.
[9] Add MS 44757, f. 10.
[10] In Lords, Irish Church Bill 2°R carried by 33, *Thirlwall the only supporting bp.:
H cxcvii. 304.

Mayor—Mr Weld Blundell—Mr Glyn—Bp of Oxford—Lord Grey
—Abp of Canterbury—Baron Rothschild—Mr Delane. Read Dr M.
Brady.

Cabinet. June 19.[1]
√ Western Australia Pledge.[2] Send out families of convicts: & allow a further
case to be made.
O New Law Courts.
√ Communication of Money Clauses in Bills to Treasury before introduction: or
to Chanc[ello]r of Ex[cheque]r in Cabinet. Minute to be framed.[3]
√ Accomm[odatio]n for Foreign Princes.
√ Scotch Church Deput[atio]n—Recited.
Arr[angement] of business for the week
√ Thom's applic[atio]n for public aid in prosecuting Gurney.[4] Declined.
√ Mr Burlingame. Conversation reported.
√ F.O. Instructions to China approved.[5]
√ Clarendon reported state of feeling in U.S. improved.
√ Haggerty case.[6] Ask U.S. to show he is not *the* Haggerty.
√ Irish Church Amendments. Not to *offer* until *they* open commun[ication]s
√ Bright. Tunnel to France—Chevalier—Nicaraguan Paramount mentioned
√ Irish Peers. Allow to die?[7] Not to be proposed
√ Bill to enable Home Sec[retary] to make regulations respecting cabs
√ County financial Boards: to be postponed till later.
√ New Law Courts. Move for a Select Committee
√ Cardwell. Fortifications Bill.

20. 4 S.Trin.

All Saints mg. Penitentiary Chapel Evg. Conversation after dinner on
Future Punishment. Read Pressensé—Manning's Past[oral] Letter[8]
—Valerius[9]—The Invitation.[10]

21. M. [London]

G.G[lyn] drove me in at 10.45. Wrote to The Queen (2)—Ld Claren-
don—Ld Ebury—Ld Granville—Ld Halifax—Chancr of Exr—Mr
Fraser—Mr Cardwell—Mr Hamilton—Sir W. Stewart[11]—Gen.
Grey—and minutes. Saw A. Kinnaird—Ld Granville. H of C. $4\frac{1}{2}$-$8\frac{1}{2}$

[1] Add MS 44637, f. 67.
[2] Question answered by *Monsell on 5 July: *H* cxcvii. 1166.
[3] See 26 June 69.
[4] Govt. refused financial help in prosecuting Overend and Gurney for losses in the crash
of May 1866: *H* cxcvii. 987.
[5] Renegotiation of treaty of Tien-tsin; F.O.C.P. 1791.
[6] See 5 June 69.
[7] See 8 May 69.
[8] See 22 Feb. 68.
[9] See 29 Apr. 69.
[10] [T. Maude], *The Invitation; or urbanity, a poem* (1791).
[11] Sir William George Drummond-Stewart, 1795-1871; 7th bart. 1838; had sent a book.

and $9\frac{1}{4}$-$12\frac{3}{4}$.[1] Saw Williams[R]. Saw Ld Granville—Mr Childers—
Mr Kinnaird. Read Dr Brady—Pressensé on French Rev.

To LORD CLARENDON, foreign secretary,   Clarendon MSS, c. 497.
21 June 1869.

1. I hope that when Mr. M. Bernard speaks of the Acts of *Foreign* Governments,
he means especially those of the United States and that you would give to these
a distinct and sufficient place.
2. I agree with you[2] in misliking the easy way in which H.M. always seems ready
to contemplate rupture with France.
    As however these communications seem not to *March*, I hope you will con-
tinue to be sure that the door will remain open for proposing in the last resort
reference to a Third Power, before any startling result is arrived at.

22. Tu.

Wrote to Duchess of Argyll—Ld Chancellor—Ld Lifford[3]—C.
Wykeham Martin—Ld Lurgan—Mrs Malcolm—Ld Granville—Ld
Taunton—Mr Clay—Mr Stephenson—Sir C. O'Loghlen—The
Queen—and minutes. H of C. $2\frac{1}{4}$-$7\frac{1}{4}$ and 9-2.[4] Saw The Lord Chan-
cellor—Mr Crum Ewing—Chancr of Exr—Mr Glyn—Mr Forster
—Ld Granville—do *cum* Ld Salisbury (on I.C. amendments)[5]—Mr
Kinnaird—Mr G. Duff—Att.Gen. for Ireland.

23. Wed.

Wrote to Mr Tallents—Lord Rollo—Mr Crum Ewing—Mr Ouvry—
Sir R. Phillimore—Sir C. O'Loghlen—and minutes. Visited some
Art shops. Dined at Ld Zetland's. Read Dr M. Brady. Saw Lord Lif-
ford—Ld Ebury *cum* Mr Kingscote—Ld Halifax—Mr Glyn—D. of
Argyll—Mrs Thistlethwayte—Ld Granville *cum* Mr Cardwell. Con-
clave on Cape Question D St $2\frac{1}{2}$-$3\frac{1}{2}$.[6]

24. Th.

Fifteen to breakfast. Wrote to Mr Fortescue—Mr Sullivan—Rev C.J.
Glyn—Miss Wyse—The Queen—Equerry of D. of Cambridge—
and minutes. H of C. $4\frac{1}{2}$-$10\frac{1}{2}$ and $11\frac{1}{2}$-$1\frac{3}{4}$.[7] Saw Mr M. Bernard—

---

[1] Assessed Rates Bill: *H* cxcvii. 360.   [2] Clarendon's letter untraced.
[3] Arranging to see him on Irish Church amendments; Add MS 44536, f. 177; see 31 Oct.
30 and next day.
[4] Moved for select cttee. on new law courts: *H* cxcvii. 458.
[5] *Salisbury had voted for the 2°R.   [6] No notes found.
[7] Spoke on pensions: *H* cxcvii. 539.

Lord Rollo—Mr Goschen—Mr Panizzi—Mr Glyn—Ld Granville—
and others. Read Coriolanus. Sat to Mr Mayall, Photographer: without end.

25. Fr.

Wrote to Dr L. Playfair—The Queen—and minutes. Dined at Marlb.
House. Saw Ital. Minister[1]—Sir R. Temple—Gen. Grey—Mrs Hope
—Mr Glyn—Mr H. Cox—Ld Granville—Mr Cardwell. Privy Coun-
cil at 3. Visit from the Viceroy of Egypt at 4.[2] House afterwards: &
11-2. Conversation with D. of Cambridge respecting the Queen.
Read Sol. General's Speeches.[3] Saw E. Sweeting[R].

26. Sat. [Windsor]

Wrote to The Queen—Rev Mr Brameld—Mr Glyn—Archdn Stopford—Mr Nosotti—and minutes. Off to Windsor at 4.30. Read
Phineas Finn. Private Meeting on Irish Ch. 11-12¼. Cabinet 12¼-3.
Saw Mr Glyn—Rev. Mr Church (in evening)—Mrs Stoner, on her
affairs. Dinnerparty at the Deanery:[4] where burns ever brightly the
old fire of hospitality & friendship.

Cabinet June 26. 69.[5]
1. Cabinet Minute on communication with Treasury before introducing or announcing public charge, exemption, or the like.[6]
2. Amendments admissible in the Irish Church Bill.
   a. rectification of Commutation Money.
   b. commute 'Private Endowments' for 500m[ille].
   c. No Curate to be 'Permanent' unless charge for Curate has already been
      allowed.
   d. Glebe house charges. If remitted, limit the grant to cases where comm[is-
      sioner]s are satisfied
   e. Expenses of Church Body. Only to be granted as *articulus cadentis.*
   f. Seats of present Bishops in H. of Lords—to be resisted, without pledge of
      any kind
   Discussion on concurrent Endowment. Govt. do not entertain it.
3. Fortescue's [Irish Railways] Loan Bill—to be postponed till after I[rish]
   C[hurch] Bill.[7]

---

[1] Count Carlo Cadorna, 1809-91, Italian ambassador in London 1869-75.

[2] In Britain on an unofficial visit; see 25 May 69.

[3] J. D. *Coleridge, Baron Coleridge, 'Speeches delivered in the Court of Queen's Bench,
in the case of Saurin v. Starr and another' (1869).

[4] G. V. *Wellesley; Gladstone arranged for him to act as intermediary with abp. *Tait,
and also, by implication, between *Victoria and the Lords.

[5] Add MS 44637, f. 74.

[6] 'Draft minute of Cabinet' to this effect, at Add MS 44637, f. 72.

[7] See 3 July 69.

4. De Grey. Cheshire Cattle Loan. More information to be had.
5. Bills abandoned: Prop[erty] Valuation for the Country—Financial Boards.
6. Weeks business: Support Annuity Tax Bill.
   Moore: Prev[ious] question on 1. (pub.)—Negative 2.[1]
7. Clarendon: read Thornton's letter, interview with Mr Fish.[2]

27. 5 S. Trin.

Castle Chapel at 12 where Mr Church preached admirably: St George's
at 4.30. Read Pressensè—Thos a Kempis—Coleridge's Speeches.
Saw Ld Spencer—Ld Sydney—Dean of Windsor (respecting HM)—
do *cum* Gen. Grey—Sir Thomas Biddulph. Saw Queen's Library.
Prince & Princess Christian dined.

28. M. [*London*]

Wrote to Mr Spedding[3]—Lord Chancellor—Sir W. James—Sir C.
O'Loghlen—H.J.G.—Rev Dr Vaughan—The Queen—Treasurer of
I. Temple[4]—and minutes. C[arlton] H[ouse] T[errace] at 11¾. Saw
Wolsey's Chapel. Saw Archdn Stopford—Attorney General—Mr
Glyn—Lord Chancellor—Bishop of Oxford—Mr R. Meade. Sir
George Grey & conclave on Dublin Bill. Att Gen.I. & Mr Fortescue
on Irish Church Bill. H. of C. 4½-7¾ and 11-1.[5] Dined at Stafford
House: to meet the Viceroy.

29. St Peter.

Wrote to Mr Maclaren—Mr Robinson—D. of Argyll—The Queen
—and minutes. H of C. 3-7 and 9¼-2¾.[6] Dined with the F. Cavendishes. Saw Duke of Argyll—Archdeacon Stopford—Mr Glyn—Mr
Thring—Archbishop of Canterbury—Ld De Tabley. Read Goldwin
Smith's Address[7]—Mr Plunkett on Commutation.[8]

---

[1] G. H. Moore's resolutions on Fenian prisoners: *H* cxcvii. 798.
[2] Thornton to Clarendon, 14 June 1869, Clarendon MSS c. 480; Fish proposed the cession of Canada to the U.S.A. as an indemnity.
[3] See 16 Dec. 31; offering him the regius history chair at Cambridge; he declined; Add
MS 44536, f. 179.
[4] Charles Shapland Whitmore, 1806-77; on the vacant mastership; Add MS 44536,
f. 179.
[5] Spoke on public accounts audit: *H* cxcvii. 631.
[6] Spoke on University Tests Bill: *H* cxcvii. 796.
[7] G. *Smith, *The relations between America and England* (1869).
[8] W. C. *Plunket, 'Commutation considered specially with a view to compensation for
diminished security' (1869).

30. Wed.

Wrote to Chancr of Exr—Mr Spedding—Ld Clarendon—Ld Spencer—Ld Shaftesbury—Mr Fortescue—Sir W. Dunbar—Mr Bruce—Mr H. Stokes—Master of Rolls—Mr [H. E.] C. Ewing—Treas. In. Temple—and minutes. Read Dr M. Brady.[1] H of C. 4–6.[2] Saw Mr Ouvry—Archdeacon Stopford—Ld Granville—Mr Glyn—D of Argyll—Mr Hammond. Abp of Canterb. with Ld Chancellor & Mr Thring on Episc.Resign. Bill 3–4.[3] Ld Mayor's dinner 6¼–11½. Returned thanks for Ministers in what was meant to be a measured speech: one colleague only, de Grey, of those present, was frightened.[4]

To H. A. BRUCE, home secretary, 30 June 1869.   Aberdare MSS.

I send you a note from Argyll. I have seen him since & he appears to approve of the idea of a Committee. It might enquire 'Whether the appt. of a new Parliamentary officer to assist in conducting Scottish business through the House could be made conducive to the contraction or abolition of any of the administrative Boards or Establishments now maintained in Scotland & if so in what manner & to what extent'.

Will you communicate with Moncrieff upon this mode of dealing with the revolutionary movement which has arisen.[5]

Thurs. July One. 1869.

Wrote to Lord Lyttelton—Dr N. Hancock—Dr Rigg—The Queen—& minutes. Fifteen to breakfast. Saw Mr Homersham Cox—Mr A. Gordon—Dr Pusey—Duke of Argyll—Mr Glyn (2)—Dr N. Hancock. Dined at Mr West's 1 h. Radcliffe Trust 2–4¼.[6] H of C. 4½–8 and 9¼–1¾: spoke on Gurney Prosecution principally. One of my least bad.[7] Read Coriolanus.

2. Fr.

Wrote to Mr Stephenson—Mr E. Hamilton—Bp of St David's[8]—Ld Clarendon—Archdn Hincks[9]—Mr Lowe—Sir A. Grant[10]—and

[1] See 10 June 69.
[2] *McLaren's Edinburgh Annuity Tax Bill 2°R: H cxcvii. 838.
[3] 1°R in the Lords on 5 July 69.
[4] On the Irish church and the Lords; The Times (1 July 1869, 8c, 9d) found his speech 'eminently discreet'.
[5] No reply from Bruce found in Add MS 44086.
[6] See 25 May 55.   [7] H cxcvii. 987; see 19 June 69.
[8] Asking *Thirlwall for advice on filling the Cambridge history chair: Add MS 44537, f. 2.
[9] Thomas Hincks, 1796–1882; archdeacon of Connor from 1865.
[10] Sir Alexander *Grant, 1826–84; 8th bart. 1856; principal of Edinburgh university from 1868.

minutes. H of C. 2½-7.[1] Saw Duke of Argyll—Sir W.C. James—Mr Glyn—Sir J. Simpson—Mr Spedding—Dr N. Hancock—Att.Gen. Ireland—Mr Tollemache—A. Kinnaird—Sir C. O'Loghlen. Dined with the Thistlethwaytes. She promised some personal history.[2] Saw Ramsay X.

3. Sat. [Dufferin Lodge, Highgate]

Wrote to Col. Salem[3]—The Queen (2)—Archbp of Canterb.—Ld Dufferin—Earl of Devon—Mr Chambers—& minutes. Cabinet 2½-5. Saw The Lord Advocate—Do cum Mr Stansfeld—Mr S. cum Mr Hamilton—Mr Maguire—Lord Granville—Mr Glyn—Scotts—A. Panizzi. Dined at the Trinity House and returned thanks for Ministers.[4] Much pleasant conversation with Ld Hamilton by whom I sat. Drove to D. Lodge at midnight. Read De Pressensé.

Cabinet July 3. 1869.[5]

√ 1. Episcopal Resignations. WEG to write to Abp that he may proceed.[6]
  2. Trades Unions[7]
√ 3. Scots Parliamentary Officer. An Inquiry.[8]
√ 4. Irish B[isho]ps in H[ouse] of Lords. Ld G[ranville] to consider whether there should be a vote taken in H. of L.
√ 5. Ld Clarendon: Belgian railway question: stands well.
   Motley: U.S: Naturalization. Urges legislation.—Answer read amended & approved.
√ 6. Mr Bright. Treaty with Spain & Portugal. Paper to be circulated.
√ 7. Ld Granville: to substitute the 7 per Cent for Carnarvon's Clause—to be [blank:] it can be done.[9]
  8. Argyll cum Clarendon in the Muscat affair against the Indian Govt. Wish not to force Zanzibar to pay subsidy to Muscat.
  9. Childers. Maritime tour of inspection: including New York. Seward objecting, the visit to Bermuda & Halifax waived.
 10. Chanc[ello]r of Ex[cheque]r on (Cattle Plague) Cheshire Clause.
 11. Eccl[esiastical] Judge (De Grey) not to be paid by public.
 12. Fortescue. Irish Railway Temporary Loans. Six months renewal.
 13. Trades Union Bill.[10] To assent [?] to 2 R[eading] with unions.
   Macevoy's question on Eccl[esiastical] Titles. Legislate next year.[11]

[1] University Tests: *H* cxcvii. 1099. [2] See introduction above, v. lxii.
[3] Offering K.C.B. to (Sir) Edward *Sabine, 1788-1883, general and geographer.
[4] *The Times*, 5 July 1869, 5d.
[5] Held in *Granville's house in Bruton Street; Add MS 44537, f. 77.
[6] Introduced by Tait in Lords, 5 July. [7] See item 13.
[8] See Gladstone to Bruce, 30 June 69.
[9] For commutation for bps. and priests; see D. H. Akenson, *The Church of Ireland* (1971), 270.
[10] This day's decision in *Farrar* v. *Close* forced govt. to allow formal 2°R for Hughes-Mundella Trades Unions Bill on 7 July, on condition, agreed at meeting between Bruce and the Junta, that the bill be withdrawn pending govt. legislation in 1870, with a holding bill on union funds (see 10 July 69): *H* cxcvii. 1386 and G. Howell, *Labour legislation and labour movements* (1902). [11] Answered on 5 July: *H* cxcvii. 1169.

4. 6 S. Trin.

Miss Coutts's Ch. mg & Parish evg. Wrote two letters to the Queen: one for remaining longer at Windsor.[1] Also to the Dean. Read de Pressensé—Shipley's Book on Invoc. of Saints.[2]

5. M. [London]

Back to C.H.T. at 11. Wrote to Mr Tollemache—Gen. Grey—Mr Morrison[3]—Mr Cogan—Mr Macmillan—Mr Bright—M. Jules Duval[4]—Mr Leeman—Rev Mr Joyce—Mr De Vere—Ld Clarendon —The Queen—Dean of Windsor—and minutes. H of C. $4\frac{1}{2}$-$8\frac{3}{4}$ and $9\frac{1}{2}$-2 A.M.[5] Saw The Lord Mayor—Duke of Argyll—Mr Lambert —Mr Glyn—Ld De Tabley—Ld Otho Fitzgerald—Att.Gen. for Ireland—Dr N. Hancock.

To W. MORRISON, M.P., 5 July 1869.   Add MS 44537, f. 5.

I have read your letter[6] with much interest, & I thank you for the very friendly course you have pursued in pointing out the dangers of the proceeding which you apprehend.

I think Mr. Bruce must have been so anxious to avoid raising false expectations that perhaps he conveyed a less favourable impression than the case would have warranted. The Govt will support the second reading of the [Hughes-Mundella] Bill, with special reserve however as to one of the Clauses & with the belief that the measure is not now to be pressed further. To some extent I can comprehend the jealousies entertained by the workmen of the Manchester School, although that school conferred on them (in the cause of justice) the greatest benefit they have ever received. I do not apprehend the predominance of any extreme, or any sectional ideas on these subjects among my colleagues. For my own part I hope I am free from them. Nothing that I have read in relation to the great question of the unions has pleased me more than the book of the Comte de Paris.[7] But others who know more may find gaps in it which are not visible to me.

6. Tu.

Wrote to Ld Granville—Ld Chancellor—Scotts—Dr N. Hancock— Mr Burnett—Bp of Chichester—The Queen—and minutes. Sixteen

---

[1] Requesting her not to go to Osborne during the crisis over the Lords' amendments to the Irish Church Bill: Guedalla, *Q*, i. 185.

[2] O. *Shipley, ed., *Invocation of saints and angels* (1869).

[3] Walter Morrison, 1836-1921; liberal (unionist) M.P. Plymouth 1861-80, Skipton 1886-92, 1895-1900; friend of G. Howell.

[4] Jules Duval, 1813-70; French writer on colonial, and particularly Algerian, affairs.

[5] Misc. business: *H* cxcvii. 1214.

[6] Untraced.

[7] See 25 May 69.

to dinner in the interval from 7 to 9. H of C. 3-7 and $9\frac{1}{4}$-$2\frac{1}{4}$.[1] Saw
Lord Spencer—Att.Gen. for Ireland (3)—Archdeacon Stopford—
Dr N. Hancock—Mr Glyn—Ld Granville. Sad work in the Lords.[2]
Read Timon of Athens.

7. Wed.

Wrote to Ld Granville (2)—Sir R. Palmer—Mr Childers—Dss of
Argyll—Gen. Grey—Mr C. Robinson[3]—Lt Col Tenison[4]—Bp of
St David's—Lord Mayor—Sir H. Bulwer—Ld Clarendon—Mr
Max Müller—and minutes. Saw Mr Macmillan—Mr Lambert—Mr
Glyn—Ld Chancellor—D of Argyll—Mr Angerstein—Mr West—
Mr Baines MP.—Lord Granville (2 hours)—and made various calls.
Dined at Ld Foley's.

8. Th.

Nine to breakfast. Wrote to Chancr of Exr—Ld Granville—Dr Hancock—Mr Burnett—Ld Devon—Mr E.H. Scott—The Queen—and
minutes. H of C. $4\frac{1}{2}$-$8\frac{1}{2}$ and $9\frac{3}{4}$-$1\frac{1}{4}$.[5] Saw Att.Gen. for Ireland on the
strange amendments in the Irish Ch. Bill. Saw The Lord Mayor—Sir
J. Esmonde—The Speaker—Mr Bouverie—Mr Layard—Ld Granville—Mr Glyn—D. of Argyll—Christies.

9. Fr.

Wrote to Dean of Windsor—Messrs Robarts—The Queen (2)—and
minutes. Saw Dr A. Clarke [sic]—Mr West. Went to Forest Hill to
inquire respecting L. Sinclair: ascertained the negative only[R]. Saw
Mr Glyn—Lord Granville (2)—Abp of Canterb. (Episc.Resign.)[6]
Abp of York (Ch B. Bill & Dr. V.)[7]—Bp of Chester—Ld Dunraven
—Ld Chancellor of Ireland—Mr Hadfield—Mr Mundella—Mr For-
ster—& others. H of C. 4-7 and $9\frac{1}{2}$-$1\frac{1}{2}$.[8] Dined with the Heywoods.

---

[1] Welsh elections: *H* cxcvii. 1323.
[2] Who this day completed their amndts. to the Irish Church Bill: *H* cxcvii. 1268.
[3] Possibly J. C. Robinson; letter not recorded.
[4] Declining request for a peerage from Edward King Tenison, 1805-78, lord lieut. of
Roscommon from 1856; Add MS 44537, f. 6.
[5] Made observations on American negotiations: *H* cxcvii. 1425.
[6] See 3 July 69.
[7] Perhaps the Benefices Bill introduced by Wilberforce in 1870.
[8] Misc. business: *H* cxcvii. 1591.

10. Sat.

Wrote to Sir T.E. May—Lord Chancellor—The Queen—and minutes. Cabinet 2-5½. Glyn drove me out to dinner: I returned in evg. Went to inspect Mr Whitworth's notable objects 12-1¼.[1] Saw Mr Glyn. Read Mansfield Park[2]—and [blank]

Cabinet July 10. 1869[3]
√ 1. Scotch Education Board—and provision for Denominational Schools. Lord Advocate present. His proposals approved.[4]
√ 2. Nine principal points of the Irish Church Bill as p[er] Mem[orandum] within.
√ 3. Clarendon read U.S. communications. Mr Fish respecting Motley—Cuba. Decline interference.
√ 4. Bruce. To bring in Bill to *protect* Funds of Trades' Unions.[5] Agreed.
√ 5. Bankruptcy Bill. Chancellor's language to be held on compensation agreed on; & as to Chief Comm[issione]r Salary to adhere.[6]
√ 6. Cheshire Cattle. Give nothing.[7]
√ 7. Telegraphs Bill. Oppose Hunt's plan of limiting monopoly to 7 years.[8]
√ 8. Locke King's Bill. WEG to write to Lord Chancellor.[9]
√ 9. Land purchase Bill. Discussion postponed.[10]

To LORD HATHERLEY, lord chancellor, 10 July 1869.   Add MS 44537, f. 8.

After you left the Cabinet we discussed the 2d reading of Mr. Locke King's Bill. We concluded that our best course was to support the 2d reading but to leave ourselves as much elbow room as possible with respect to future legislation[11] and also not to argue the measure high. It was agreed that I should write to ask you to be so good as to see the Law Officers upon Wednesday & the Ch. of the E. who will be happy to attend you for the purpose of advising on the form of the argument, which we think it may perhaps be most prudent to leave a good deal in the hands of the Law Officers.

11. 7 S. Trin.

Chap. Royal mg & Savoy in evg. Read Christie's Five Lectures[12]— Vere on Revisers[13]—De Pressensé. Agnes who was declared on Friday

[1] Probably Joseph *Whitworth, see 9 Sept. 69.
[2] By Jane *Austen (1814).   [3] Add MS 44637, f. 78.
[4] Accepting modifications, see D. J. Withrington, 'Towards a national system, 1867-72', *Scottish Educational Studies* (1972), 117.
[5] Consequent upon decision of 3 July in *Farrar v. Close* and pending introduction of full scale bill: *H* cxcvii. 1753 and Webb, *Trade Unionism*, 258-9.
[6] i.e. *Hatherley's speech on 2°R in the Lords, *H* cxcvii. 1403.
[7] In reply to *Grosvenor on 13 July: *H* cxcvii. 1807; diarist note of this day at Add MS 44637, f. 79.
[8] This limitation, a remnant from the Tory bill of 1868, was struck out on 26 July 1869: *H* cxcviii. 766.   [9] Real Estate Intestacy Bill: *H* cxcvii. 1820.
[10] Not taken up again in cabinet until 30 Oct. 69.   [11] See 9 Dec. 69.
[12] A. J. Christie, 'Union with Rome. Five afternoon lectures' (1869).
[13] Untraced pamphlet by A. T. de Vere.

mg to have the scarlet fever has (thank God) been doing all along as well as possible. The children however are all scattered: C. & I downstairs. Further search of traces of L. Sinclair[R]. Saw Bp of Salisbury. Formidable accounts from & through Windsor.

12. M.

Wrote to Archbp Manning—Mr Cardwell—The Queen (2)—& minutes. Saw Ld Granville—Mr Delane—Dr Hancock—Ld Bessborough—Mr Glyn—and minutes. Cabinet Comm. on Irish Church Amts 2-4½. House 4½-8½ and 9¼-2.[1] Read Timon of Athens. The time grows more & more anxious.

To ARCHBISHOP H. E. MANNING, 12 July 1869.   Add MS 44537, f. 8.

I return Cardinal Cullen's letter.[2] The situation is at present in course of becoming very grave: but happen what may the acceptance of the Lords amendments in their spirit & substance, by the Govt. is absolutely impossible. As far as disendowment is concerned they convert the Bill into an imposture. I make a note of the various particulars of your letter.

13. Tu.

Wrote to Archbp Manning—Mr Cowen jun.—The Queen (2)—Ld Lyttelton—Mr Kirk MP.—Mrs H. Gladstone—The Lord Mayor— Ld Granville—and minutes. H of C. 5½-7 and 9-2½. Saw Mr G.H. Cavendish—Mr Glyn *cum* Mr Brand—Mr Walker (D. News)[3]—Lord Stair—Abp of Canterb.—D. of Argyll. Dined with the F. Cavendishes. Called at Mr Haurot's to inquire respecting L.S[inclair] [R].

To ARCHBISHOP H. E. MANNING, 13 July 1869.   Add MS 44249, f. 81.

The unexpected vote of the Lords last night on concurrent endowment has further complicated the position of the Irish Church Bill and of that House as connected with it. You will probably have observed that this vote is quite different from that proposed by the Duke of Cleveland. The Duke's proposal referred to Houses only. It was matter for argument whether, inasmuch as the Glebe Houses were to be surrendered to the Established Church on very favourable terms, some *corresponding* concession was not required by the principle of equality which was to form the winding up arrangements. But the vote of last night, which gave to three denominations (leaving 100,000 Methodists however

[1] Spoke on supply: *H* cxcviii. 1698.
[2] Not found; Cullen to Manning, 13 July 1869, Add MS 44249, f. 90, strongly deplored concurrent endowment.
[3] Gladstone approved of its article this day on *Granville; see Ramm, I i. 34.

in the cold) Glebes as well as houses is or rather would be a flat violation of all our pledges to the country.

In your late note[1] you have expressed so strongly and clearly your idea of the basis on which the late remarkable cooperation of the Liberal majority has been founded, that I see you think like me it is the only profitable basis. The question whether any other basis would be abstractedly better is a question, at this moment, for Debating Societies.

On Thursday at a quarter past five I shall move, please God, to restore to the Preamble the words of our solemn compact with the people. I have no doubt of the thorough soundness of the body of your co-religionaries. As far as numbers are concerned, we shall, on this particular question, have enough and to spare. But I think you will share my hope that with a view to unbroken moral force there shall be no defections. I therefore mention as rumour, for which I cannot be personally responsible, and yet not as idle rumour, three men, *very* different one from the other who on this occasion would I believe be the better for a little confirmation, in case you should have any discreet opportunity of conveying it. Moore, Blake, and Blennerhassett.[2] After dealing with concurrent endowment by the Preamble we shall proceed I trust to knock down the rest of the House of Cards.

14. Wed.

Wrote to Ld Lyttelton—Rev Mr Spurgeon—The Queen—Rev S.R. Hall[3]—Dean of Windsor—Mr [W.] Hepworth Dixon. H of C. 2¼-6.[4] Went again over the Amts with Att.Gen. for Ireland. Saw Lord C. Paget—Mr Baines *cum* Ald. Carter—Mr Glyn (2)—Mr Brand—Sir C. O'Loghlen. Dined at Lady Lyttelton's. Read Timon of Athens.

The first motion to be made tomorrow on the Irish Church Bill will be on the amendments to the Preamble. The Lords have struck out a passage which contains 1. the negative Declaration that the property is not to be applied to any Church &c. 2. the positive Declaration that it is to be applied for the relief of suffering.

The Cabinet will perhaps leave a discretion to be exercised on the [Front] Bench acc. to circs. But what I understand at present is that 1. I am to move the re-instatement of the Preamble *Talis qualis* 2. I am to move the whole in one motion. Am I right? W.E.G. Jul 14. 69.[5]

Glyn and Sullivan agree [W.E.G.]. I understood the decision of the Cabinet to be in the sense of what you propose. I entirely agree. G[ranville]. I concur. But if you find it, at the least, better to reinstate the two paragraphs separately, such a course wd. come I presume within the 'discretion' resolved. H. C. E. C[hilders].

[1] Probably that of 2 June 1869 (see 3 June 69n), rather than Manning to Gladstone, 11 July 1869, Add MS 44249, f. 79, which urged 'that the Bill should be restored to its original outline'.

[2] Manning this day reported on conversations with Blennerhassett and Moore, and intended to write to Blake; Add MS 44249, f. 84.

[3] Samuel Romilly Hall, 1812-76; president of the Wesleyan conference; had sent a Resolution; Add MS 44421, f. 114.

[4] Locke *King's Real Estate Intestacy Bill: *H* cxcvii. 1820.

[5] Circulated to the cabinet; replies follow; Add MS 44637, f. 81.

I agree with Mr. Childers de G[rey] 14/7/69. I agree J. B[right]. H[artington]. This was what I understood to be settled. A[rgyll]. I agree with Mr Gladstone's view. H[atherley]. I agree with Mr Gladstone. C[larendon]. I agree H. A. B[ruce]. I agree K[imberley]. I agree E. C[ardwell]. I agree C. P. F[ortescue].

15. Th.

Wrote to Mr Fortescue—Ld Granard[1]—Cardinal Cullen—Mr Lewis MP.—The Queen—and minutes. H. of C. 4¼-2, except 24 min. away for dinner.[2] Worked on Irish Church. 11 to breakf. Saw Miss Marsh—Bp Butler of Limerick—Mr Spedding—Mr Glyn—Scotts —Col. Ffrench and Irish Deputation[3]—Mr Baines & collection of Deputations with Irish Church Memorials.[4] Saw Dr N. Hancock. This day I received from the R.C. Bishop Butler[5] the assurance that he offered mass & that many prayed for me: and from Mr Spurgeon (as often from others) an assurance of the prayers of the Nonconformists. I think that in these and other prayers lies the secret of the strength of body which has been given me in unusual measure during this very trying year. Finished Timon.

To CARDINAL CULLEN, 15 July 1869.   Add MS 44537, f. 11.

I have had the honour to receive your letter of yesterday.[6] Beyond my best thanks, it hardly requires from me an answer. Nothing could induce the Govt. to acquiesce in the amendments of the Lords & any alterations of the Bill which they may either propose or acquiesce in will be such as are in their best judgement agreeable, & not, like the Lords amendments, opposed to the principles & main provisions of the Bill.

I think it highly honourable to the Heads & Clergy of the R.C. Church that they continue to pursue unswervingly their independent course.

16. Fr.

Wrote to Ld Granville—Sir C. O'Loghlen—Ld Belper—Lord Kinnaird—Lord Devon—The Queen—and minutes. Worked on Irish Ch. Bill. H. of C. 4¼-1¼ on do.[7] Saw Mr Glyn—Mr Lefroy—Ld Granville. A very laborious & exhausting day.

[1] George Arthur Hastings Forbes, 1833–89; 7th earl of Granard 1837; a liberal. See 19 Feb. 70.
[2] Spoke on Lords' amendments to the Irish Church Bill: *H* cxcvii. 1891.
[3] Fitzstephen French, 1801–73; liberal M.P. Roscommon from 1832.
[4] Printed mema. from them in Add MS 44421, f. 152.
[5] George Butler, 1815–86, bp. of Limerick from 1864.
[6] The Bill useless for Ireland in its amended form; Add MS 44421, f. 150.
[7] *H* cxcviii. 51.

17. Sat.

Wrote to Mr O'Dowd[1]—Lord Devon—Ld de Grey—Mr Glyn—&
minutes. Saw Mr Herbert—Mr Glyn. Cabinet 12-2¾. Went to Windsor by special train and saw the Queen. Then I had a supplemental
interview with the Dean of Windsor, on whom she leans increasingly.
With him I left a short memorandum. Back to town at 6.10. & drove
to Highgate for a restful evening which did me good.

On the 16th of July the Amendments made by the Lords in the Irish
Church Bill had been completely disposed of by the House of Commons. The last division, taken on the disposal of the residue, had,
chiefly through mere lazy absences, reduced the majority for the
Government to 72. This *relative* weakness offered a temptation to
the Opposition to make play upon the point.

The Cabinet met the next forenoon. We felt on the one hand that
it might be difficult to stake the Bill on the Clause for the disposal of
the Residue, supposing that to be the single remaining point of difference: but that the postponement of this question would be a great
moral and political evil, and that any concession made by us had far
better be one which would be of some value to the disestablished
Church.

We thought the Archbishop of Canterbury would probably enter
into this view: and that without committing the Queen to any particular recommendation, She might be disposed again to move him in
the sense of peace.

By desire of the Cabinet I went to Windsor in the afternoon, and
represented to H.M. what it was in our power to do: namely, although
we had done all we could do upon the merits, yet, for the sake of
peace & of the House of Lords a. to make some one further pecuniary
concession to the Church of sensible though not very large amount
b. To make a further concession as to Curates, slight in itself c. To
amend the Residue Clause so as to give to Parliament the future controul, and to be content with simply declaring the principle on which
the property should be distributed.

The Queen while considering that She could not be a party to this
or that particular scheme, agreed that it might be proper to make a
representation to the Archbishop to the general effect that the views
of the Govt. at this crisis of the measure were such as deserved to be
weighed, and to promote confidential communication between us:
She intimated her intention to employ the Dean of Windsor as a
medium of communication between Herself and the Archbishop, and

---

[1] Offering deputy judge advocate generalship to James Klyne O'Dowd, 1802–79, solicitor, which he declined.

wished me to explain particulars fully to him. I went to the Deanery and not finding the Dean had written as much as here follows on a scrap of paper, when he came in.

The desire of the Archbishop and Bishops generally is supposed to be to secure the greatest amount of property to the Church.

While this was hoped for by means of concurrent endowment, & concurrent endowment by means of the postponement of the Surplus, the postponement was an object to the Archbp, the Episcopal Bench, and many like minded lay Peers. The Clause for Concurrent endowment was condemned in the H. of Commons *without a division*, & the H. of C. has reinstated in the Preamble, and will unquestionably maintain them at whatever hazard the words which exclude any appropriation of the Surplus to religious uses. It does not therefore appear what interest the Bishops & other Peers above named can now feel in the postponement. The Govt. are still in a position in which it might be possible to make some small further concession in point of Temporalities to the Church: but if the postponement of the Surplus be insisted on by the Lords, this would be wholly out of the question.

The object of this paper was to induce the Archbishop to discountenance any plan for pressing the postponement of the provisions respecting the residue, and to deal with us in preference respecting any practicable concession to the Church.

When the Dean came in I explained this further, recited the purport of my interview with the Queen, and on his asking me confidentially for his own information let him know that the further pecuniary concession we were prepared to recommend would be some £170,000 or £180,000, and that this if applied to an average commutation would be of much more value to the Church than the same amount given in another way.

He proposed to see the Archbishop early on Monday.[1]

Cabinet Jul 17. 69. Noon.[2]
1. Clarendon. Greek Constitution.[3]

   Bill for acquiring extended Site.
   Bills to be dropped.
√ Irish Ch[urch] Amendments—possible course of Lords.
√ Fortescue's Loan Bill. To consider a simple form.[4]

Jul 17. Irish Church Amendments. Principal Points.[5]
1. Date.[6] Disagree—without (intention of yielding) persevering.

[1] Record of the crisis, 17–22 July, initialled and dated 14 August 1869, Add MS 44757. Extracts in Morley, ii. 273.
[2] Add MS 44637, f. 88.
[3] His talk with Valaoriti on its reform; Clarendon to Erskine, 22 July 1869, Clarendon MSS. c. 475.
[4] Glebe Loans (Ireland) Bill, delayed till next session: *H* cciii. 956.
[5] Add MS 44637, f. 83. More, undated, jottings follow.
[6] The Lords had amended the effective date of the bill from 1 January to 1 May 1871.

2. Tax on Livings & Visitation Fees. Disagree.
3. Seats in the House of Lords. Disagree: with intention of yielding
(4. Palmer Clause: *amend*).[1]
5. Charges on Glebe Houses. Disagree.
6. Carnarvon Clause. Disagree: insert 7 per Cent.[2] Reserve three more
7. Private Endowments and Ulster Glebes: assent to P.E. dissent from U.G.
8. Suspension of disposal of the property: Amend. Order in Council to *lie* on the Table.[3]
9. Salaries of Curates. Amend.

18. 8 S. Trin.

Chapel Royal mg & evg. Mr Melvill preached. He is still like a grand old warhorse.[4] Saw Granville respecting the overture from Disraeli. Wrote to Granville. Read Cazenove on Reformn[5]—De Pressensé, Fr. Rev.—B. North, Yes or No.[6] Saw Ld Wenlock.

In the afternoon Lord Granville called on me and brought to me a confidential memorandum, containing an overture, which Mr Disraeli had placed in the hands of Lord Bessborough for communication to us. He had represented the terms as those which he had with much difficulty induced Lord Cairns to consent to. This was the Memorandum. B.[7] While the contention as to the Residue was here abandoned, and pecuniary concessions alone were sought, the demand amounted, according to our computation, to between £900,000 and £1,000,000.

We discussed the matter at much length. The Amendments of the Lords had originally according to our computation given nearly £2,800,000 in money to the Church besides some £1,100,000 as its share of the concurrent endowment. In the Commons we had conceded £780,000. The new demand raised this (say) to £1,750,000 or nearly $\frac{2}{3}$ of the matter in dispute. This it was evident was utterly inadmissible. I saw no possibility of approach to it: & considered that a further quarter of a million or thereabouts was all which the House of Commons could be expected or asked further to concede. On the same afternoon Lord Granville, falling in with Mr Goschen, asked him what he thought the very most that could be had—would it be £500,000? Goschen answered £300,000 and with this Glyn agreed.

Mr Disraeli desired an answer before 3 on Monday.

[1] Clause 20 based on Palmer's proposal; accepted with modification on 15 July: *H* cxcvii. 1964.   [2] See 3 July 69.
[3] Clause 68; Gladstone announced on 16 July appropriation of surplus property by Order in Council: *H* cxcviii. 53.   [4] See 30 June 33.
[5] J. G. *Cazenove, 'Some aspects of the Reformation' (1869).
[6] B. *North, *'Yes! or No!' Genesis xxiv. 1–58* (1867).   [7] Lost, see Ramm I, i. 52.

19. M.

Wrote to A. Kinnaird—E. Cardwell—Mr Delane—Mr Hamilton—Chr of Exr—Ld Clarendon—Mr Delane—The Queen (2)—& minutes. Saw Dr A. Clarke—Ld Clarendon—Mr Glyn—Ld Granville—Mr Delane—Duke of Argyll—Mr Leeman—Archbishop of Canterbury—Dean of Windsor (2)—Mr Cardwell—Mr Parker. Conclave on Irish Ch. $2\frac{1}{2}$-$3\frac{1}{2}$. Sent ansr to the Disraeli overture: the prospects appeared to improve in the aftn. H of C. $4\frac{1}{4}$-$8\frac{1}{4}$ and $9\frac{1}{4}$-$1\frac{3}{4}$.[1] Read Br.Quart. on G. & the House of Lords.[2]

Those members of the Government who had acted as a sort of Committee in the Irish Church question met in the afternoon.[3]

We were all agreed in opinion that the Disraeli overture must be rejected though without closing the door: and a reply was prepared in this sense which Lord Granville undertook to send: as follows

The Govt. have already (in their own judgment) now strained every point in favour of the Church as far as the merits are concerned.

All that remains is to say to the majority of the H. of Commons *such and such a sum* is not worth the quarrel & the postponement.

This sum must be moderate.

The sum asked is according to estimate of the Govt. between £900,000 and a million.

No such sum nor any sum approaching it, could be asked of the majority.[4]

Meantime the Archbishop had arrived in Downing Street, in pursuance of the arrangements of Saturday: and a paper was either now drawn, or sanctioned by my colleagues, I do not remember which, in order to form the basis of my communication to the Archbishop. I here append it:

Points not yet settled[5]

1. 'Postponement' (absolute). This if urged puts out of the question all the rest. If not urged, let us go on.
2. Date. May be freely yielded *if House of Lords desire it.*
3. Commutation Clause. Lords' Clause cannot work: is a dead letter. Ours is preferred by the Church.
4. Glebe-Houses. Concession on this is now become impossible, from the close & palpable relation into which the subject has now come with 'concurrent endowment'.
5. 'Tax'. An amt. most impolitic for the Church as it will enable every congregation to throw on the *Central Fund* the expenses of its own worship.

---

[1] Supply: *H* cxcviii. 162.   [2] *British Quarterly Review*, l. 175 (July 1869).

[3] 'The Archbishop of Canterbury had previously come to me from Lord Cairns with a Memorandum in which he proposed as the basis of a settlement'; this sentence deleted; see 20 July 69.

[4] This section in secretary's hand; holograph at Add MS 44757, f. 152.

[5] This mem. dated 19 July 1869, Add MS 44756, f. 30; secretary's copy added to the mem. on the crisis.

6. Ulster Glebes. Any one may judge for himself whether any charmer cd. charm the H. of C. on this subject? Also the joint claim of the Presb[yteria]ns has been admitted by some on the Conservative side.
7. Deduction of Curates' stipends. On this if it stood alone, a further concession might be possible *simply as an act of deference to the H. of Lords: e.g. half-deduction.*

But supposing the discussions to have reached this point the question plainly arises whether, presuming a certain further amount of money is to be given this particular *mode* of giving it is the best.

On this point, if solitary, there would be difficulty[1] in arriving at an understanding.

I returned from my interview with the Archbishop, and reported, as I afterwards did to the Dean of Windsor, that his tone was friendly, and that he appeared well disposed to the sort of arrangement I had sketched.

To E. CARDWELL, war secretary, 19 July 1869.   Add MS 44537, f. 12.

It occurs to me that we have now reached a point in the Irish Church affair at which Palmer might be of much use if he is so inclined in averting a conflict of Houses through Salisbury or through the Bishops, with whom he has certainly been at a former time in communication.

Setting aside the question of the 'Postponement', the fundamental fact of our present position is as I take it this. We have now made *every* concession for which we can discover even the rag of a reason. Anything more that we recommend must be recommended at the risk of our own credit simply to meet the view of the H. of Lords. The House is not disposed to go very far on that line: & will not be better disposed, after the Lords shall have rejected Coleridge's Bill tonight. *We* are all willing I think to do what we can—but from the nature of the case our power is limited.

You are the natural channel of communication with Sir R.P. Pray consider whether you can make anything of the matter. If you see him it should not be later than 4 today, so that he might see Salisbury before the H. of Lords.

The 'Date' can of course be given up.

To J. T. DELANE, 19 July 1869.   Add MS 44537, f. 12.

If you can again find yourself in my little room at the H. of Commons this afternoon at 5, I shall be glad again to exchange a few words with you on the present aspect of the 'situation'.

20. Tu.

Wrote to Ld Granville—Abp of Canterbury—Ld de Grey—The Queen—& minutes. H of C. & H. of L. 3½-8¼ and 9½-1¾.[2] Saw

---

[1] Secretary's copy reads: 'no difficulty'.
[2] The Lords again voted down the Commons' Preamble: *H* cxcviii. 323.

Archbp of Canterb. (2)—Mr Levy—Ld Granville (3)—Mr Glyn—
Dr N. Hancock—Mr Henderson—Lord Mayor of Dublin & others
—Mr Saintsbury. Conclave of Colleagues, on Irish Ch. proceedings.
An anxious day: a sad evening.[1] Dined at Ld F. Cavendish's.

The Archbishop, who had communicated with Lord Cairns in the
interval came to me early today and brought a Memorandum as a
basis of agreement, which, to my surprise, demanded higher terms
than those of Mr Disraeli.

1. The Lords Amendment as to Curates to be adopted . . . . . . .380m[ille].
2. The Ulster Glebes　　　　　　　　　　　. . . . . . .465m.
3. The Glebehouses to be free　　　　　　　. . . . . . .150m
　　　　　　　　　　　　　　　　　　　　　995m.
Or, the Bishop of Peterborough's Amendment as to the Tax upon livings in lieu
of No 3 would carry a heavier charge by　　　. . . . . . .124m.
　　　　　　　　　　　　　　　Making　　　1119m.

I told the Archbishop the terms in which we had already expressed
ourselves to Mr Disraeli. The Archbishop saw me again in the afternoon, but had no more to say than that he did not mean to ask for
more than Mr Disraeli had asked. I told the Archbishop—whether
today or yesterday I am not sure, but today if not yesterday, the
nature and value of the pecuniary concession we were prepared to
make, placing it at near £300,000. This however was for himself
alone in strict confidence.

Meantime an answer had come from Mr D. stating that he could
do no more. Then followed the meeting of the Opposition Peers at
the Duke of Marlborough's. On the meeting of the Houses, a few of
us considered what course was to be taken if the Lords should again
cast out of the Preamble the words which precluded concurrent endowment: and it was agreed to stay the proceedings for the time, and
consider among ourselves what further to do. Lord Granville made
this announcement accordingly after the Lords had upon a hot
debate and by a large majority again excluded our words from the
Preamble. This had been after a speech from Lord Cairns, in which
he announced his intention of moving other amendments which he
detailed and which were in general conformable to the proposals
already made to us.

The first disposition of several of us this evening myself included
was was [sic] to regard the proceeding of the Opposition as now
complete: since the whole had been announced, the first stroke
struck, and the Command shown of a force of Peers amply sufficient

[1] Extracts from here to 25 July 69 in Morley, ii. 279.

to do the rest. The reports also were that this was expected and desired by the House of Commons. And I for one had no doubt that
the issue thus joined before the country would be intelligible and
that we should completely succeed. The idea did not however include
an absolute abandonment of the Bill but only the suspension of our
responsibility for it, leaving the Opposition to work their own will,
and with the intention, when this had been done of considering the
matter further.

Here I insert a passage from Lord Granville. 'On the return of the
amendments to the House of Lords, in answer to my question "I presume you have nothing to say to me?" Lord Cairns said "No".'

21. Wed.

Wrote to Mr Kingsley—Abp of Canterbury—The Queen, Telegram
—The Queen (2)—Mr Fortescue—Lord Chichester. Ten to dinner:
for Panizzi & Hudson. Cabinet 11-2¼. Stiff: but good. Saw Dean of
Windsor—Sir R. Phillimore—Mr Glyn (2)—Ld Granville—Mr West
—Ld Bessborough—Mr Delane—Dean Stanley. Saw Jeffreys X.
Read [blank]

The Cabinet met at 11: and I went to it in the mind of last night. We
discussed however at great length all possible methods of proceeding
which occurred to us. The result was stated in a letter of mine to the
Queen of which I annex a copy.[1] Most of the Cabinet were desirous
to go on longer: others, myself included, objected to proceeding to
the end of the Bill (Plan) or undertaking to remit the Bill again to the
House of Commons as of our own motion. It occurred to me however that we might proceed as far as to the end of the many amendments, about the middle of the Bill: and this appeared to meet the
views of all, even of those who would have preferred doing more, or
less.

Cabinet July 21. 69. 11¼-2¼. Irish Ch[urch] Bill.[2]
See Letter to HM[3]

1. Pet. [*sic*]
2. Returning the Bill to the H. of C. will weaken the position of that House—if
   it reject the whole amendments.
   a. Suppose we could—
   b. it wd centr[e][4]
   Nothing new to tender.[5]

[1] In Morley, ii. 645.   [2] Add MS 44637, f. 90.   [3] Morley, ii. 645.
[4] Word scrawled.   [5] Added on an adjacent sheet.

To A. C. TAIT, archbishop of Canterbury,   Tait MSS, 87, f. 169.
21 July 1869.

I thank your Grace for the note I have received this morning.[1]

Your Grace will remember the purport of the last conversation between us
when departing for a moment from the character of Internuncio you asked me
for your own information & as Archbishop of Canterbury what was in my
opinion the sort of boon [?] that the Govt could undertake to recommend to
the House of Commons: in reply I mentioned what occurred to me both as to
amount and form, adding that I spoke for as well as to Your Grace alone, and
that, in my conviction the word spoken was the last word.

All this I have made known to the Cabinet today.

I need but say that I have nothing further to communicate or propose. The
matter now lies with the majority in the House of Lords: which unless I much
mistook the character of your Grace's conversation contains within itself very
different elements. May *its* deliberations be wise and prosperous.

I must not omit to say that the present feeling of the House of Commons
shows me that it will not be easy, though it may be possible, to include Commutation Clauses in a future Bill.

22. Th.

Wrote to Att.Gen. for I.—The Queen; letter & Telegram—Abp of
Canterbury—Ld Granville—Ld de Grey—Mrs Monsell—and
minutes. Eight to breakfast. I asked Mr Street about a W. window for
Ch.Ch. Dublin.

I was obliged to take to my sofa & spent the day so, in continual
interviews with Granville—Glyn—West—Sullivan—especially the
first, on the detailed particulars of the negotiation respecting the
Irish Church Bill. The favourable issue left me almost unmanned, in
the reaction from a sharp and stern tension of mind. Saw also Bp of
Oxford and Sir R. Phillimore. Read Hirell.[2]

I was laid up today and the transactions were carried on by Lord
Granville, in communication with me from time to time at my house.

First he brought me a note he had received from Lord Cairns.

Private & Confidential   5 Cromwell Houses, 22 July 1869.
My dear Ld Granville, I have no right and no desire to ask for any information as
to the course which you propose to take tonight: but if the statements as to the
intention of the Govt. to proceed with the consideration of the amendments be
correct, & if you think that any advantage can result from it, you will find me
ready, as you know I have throughout been, to confer upon a mode—& I think
a mode can be suggested—by which without sacrifice of principle or dignity
upon either side the remaining points of difference might be arranged.

I leave this on my way to the Bankruptcy Committee. H. of L. I cld. see you if
you wish it either at the Col Off. or your own house. Yrs very truly (signed) Cairns.

[1] Offering further mediation; Davidson, *Tait*, ii. 41.
[2] J. *Saunders, *Hirell. A novel*, 3v. (1869).

He then saw Lord Cairns and obtained his terms. They were somewhat but not very greatly improved. The Ulster Glebes however were gone. He now demanded 1. The acceptance of the Amendment respecting Curates: 380,000. 2. Five per cent to be added to the 7 per cent on Commutations: 300,000. 3. The Glebe Houses to be given to the Church at 10 years purchase of the sites: in truth a slight modification of the Amendment of Lord Salisbury—say 140,000. I think these three heads were stated in a memorandum of Lord C's. I attach to each of these the money value we put upon them: and it appears that even in the mid hours of this final day Lord Cairns asked above £800,000.

We held our ground and declared we could on special grounds accede to the second amendment if that were accepted as sufficient: but not to the first nor the third. We offered however to reduce the 68th Clause to a simple legislative declaration, which in truth was from the first in our view the essence of it, but it had been inflamed and magnified by their suspicions. And we offered to meet an objection rightly taken by Lord Cairns on a point of detail with respect to the proof of the 'permanent' character of a curate, when our provision was not sufficient for its end.

In a second interview with Lord Granville, Lord Cairns gave up the proposal relating to Glebe Houses.

In a third, at which the Attorney General for Ireland was present, the substance of the demand as to Curates was given up: and it was agreed on our part that the Curate should be charged on the Incumbent not when a deduction for Salary had been allowed during the one year specified, but during a term of five years.

It was now 4.30 when Lord Cairns with much courage undertook to propose to his party acquiescence in these terms.

There was another change pressed by and conceded to him, which I have not yet mentioned. The $(7 + 5 =)$ 12 per cent were to be added to the Commutation mainly when $\frac{3}{4}$ instead of $\frac{2}{3}$ of the Annuitants had expressed their readiness to commute. This change tends to diminish the number of *commutants*, and thus positively to diminish, probably or possibly by some 30 or 35m. the pecuniary value of the concession we had tendered.

The news was brought to me on my sofa and between 5 and 6 I was enabled to Telegraph to the Queen. My Telegram was followed up by a letter at 7 P.M. which announced how the arrangement had been accepted by the House of Lords, and that a general satisfaction prevailed.

To LORD CLARENDON, foreign secretary,   Clarendon MSS, c. 497.
22 July 1869.

I am sorry to see there is increased tension in France.[1]

My own idea would be to exclude the ships of war belonging to belligerent countries from the Suez Canal in time of war only. But this question I shall be most happy to discuss after I.C.

The prospects of today are better and the communications look hopeful in Granville's skilful hands. Keep a little place in your mind for that matter of the pension. I trust you are better.

23. Fr.

Wrote to [blank] and the Queen. Read Hirell. My attack did not lessen. Dr Clarke came in the morning & made me up for the House whither I went 2-5 P.M. to propose concurrence in the Lords Amendments. Up to the moment I felt very weak but this all vanished when I spoke, & while the debate lasted. Then I went back to bed. Saw Mr Glyn—Att.Gen.Irel.—Ld Castlerosse—& others.

24. Sat. [Chislehurst, Kent]

Wrote to Ld Granville—Prince Latour—and by dictation to Abp of Canterbury—Chr of Exr—Abp of Dublin—Mr Acland—Abp Manning—Mr Mitchell—Ld Chancellor—Ld Clarendon—Mr Greenwell —and minutes. Saw Dr Clarke, who was almost constantly here— Ld Granville—Mr Gurdon—Mr Glyn—Mr West—Sir R. Phillimore. Better in aft & went off to Ld R. Cavendish's.[2] Read Hirell.

Cabinet July 24. 69.[3]
WEG absent. Granville's memorandum.[4]
Metropolitan Loan Bill. Lowe agrees to drop the clause. Mr Bright with the concurrence of the Cabinet hopes that you will make an appeal to the House to put off the motions on going into Supply—or in your absence that Bruce should do so. The Basses [Ceylon] Light House Bill. Go on. No serious opposition intended. Introduce the guarantee on Hudson's Bay Loan, to be carried.
Introduce the guarantee on the Canada Fortifications, with the hope of being able to abandon it, after its introduction.
Sacrificed [Bills]—None—all (excepting those hereafter described) supposed to be unlikely to meet any real opposition.
    (Must go on).
Fortification Bill (Cardwell).

[1] Clarendon to Gladstone, 21 July 1869, Add MS 44133, f. 248: 'I send the letters that I found here on coming from the Cabinet.'
[2] Thus missing the Cabinet, of which *Granville sent notes; Add MS 44637, f. 93.
[3] Add MS 44637, f. 93.
[4] This line in diarist's hand, the rest by Granville.

Scotch Education Bill. With much reluctance Lowe agrees to 3 paid Commissioners on the Board—which will satisfy the Scotch M.P.s
Telegraph Bill—Hartington suggested that supply should be stopped at *10* on Monday in order that it may be proceeded with.

To ARCHBISHOP H. E. MANNING, 24 July 1869.   Add MS 44537, f. 13.

Your last note[1] was of much value & showed me at once with what an accurate eye you had measured the situation. But I cannot thank for it alone; I am much indebted to you on behalf of the Govt. for the firm, constant, & discriminating support which you have afforded to our Bill during the arduous conflict now happily concluded. Some day when we meet, I may perhaps be able to go back upon some of the circumstances.

Should you happen to write to Card. Cullen, pray be kind enough to ask him to accept a similar tribute of acknowledgement from me.

25. 10 S.Trin. St James.

T.s birthday: our wedding day. How little worthy. Weak still, I presumed over much in walking a little, and fell back at night to my lowest point. Saw The Mostyns—Sir R. Phillimore—& my ever kind host. Read de Pressensé—Cazenove on Reformn—and [blank]

26. M.

By midday I was fairly mending again. Dr Clarke came down. Saw Sir R. Phillimore. Read Hirell wh I find unexpectedly striking.

27. Tu.

Wrote to Dean of Windsor—Lord Russell—The Queen—Lord Halifax—Mr C. Villiers—C. di Cesare—Sir C. Lyell—J. Watson & Smith —and minutes. Saw Mr West—Mr Glyn—WHG. Read Hirell—Barnes on Engl. Tongue.[2]

28. Wed.

Much improved thank God. Saw Dr Clarke—Dr Alfrey.[3] Saw Mr West—Mr Glyn—Lord Granville—Lord R.C. Wrote minutes: & dictation. Read Hirell, finished—Barnes on Engl. Tongue. Began Mansfield Park.[4]

[1] Sending congratulations; Add MS 44249, f. 97.
[2] W. *Barnes, *Tiw; or a view of the roots and stems of the English as a Teutonic tongue* (1862).
[3] C. H. Allfrey, physician in Chislehurst.   [4] But see 10 July 69.

29. Th.

Downstairs again. Wrote to Earl of Dalhousie—The Queen—Mr Lake—and minutes. Saw both the Doctors—Mr West—Mr Glyn —Rev Mr Murray—Read Barnes (finished)—De Pressensé (finished) —Mansfield Park.

30. Fr. [London]

Wrote to D. of Sutherland—Mrs Monsell—Ld Granville—Mr Villiers—Mr Fortescue—Chancr of Exr—Dean of Windsor—Mrs Thistlethwayte. Left Chislehurst at 2.30 for London after seeing Dr Alfrey. A quiet evening. Finished Mansfield Park. Read Burke on French Revol.[1]—Simpson's Hospitalism.[2] Saw Mr Glyn—Mr West.

To R. LOWE, chancellor of the exchequer,   Add MS 44537, f. 16.
30 July 1869.

Many thanks for your letter. I conclude the subject of a Treaty affecting the Wine Duty may be revived tomorrow.[3] Honest as Bright is, his mind may be & probably is somewhat warped, in this matter, by a general desire to lower or get rid of indirect duties. I think you may depend on receiving fair & firm support in whatever can be shewn to be needful for the defence of the Rev[enue]. All that I have hitherto learned or thought is adverse to tampering with any fiscal interests for the purpose of making commercial treaties.

31. Sat.

Wrote to The Queen (2)—Mr Bright—and minutes. Rose before luncheon. Cabinet 3-5¾. Saw Ld Clarendon—Ld Chancr—Mr Glyn —Ld Granville—Dr. Clark—Sir R. Phillimore—Sir S. Northcote —Ld R. Cavendish.

Cabinet Jul 31. 69.[4] *11 C[arlton] H[ouse] T[errace]*
√ Council & Speech. See Mem[orandum].[5]
√ Bright's suggestion: mission respecting land abroad. Fortescue to inquire.[6]

[1] E. *Burke, *Reflections on the revolution in France* (1790).
[2] Sir J. Y. Simpson, *Hospitalism; its effects on the results of surgical operations* (1869).
[3] At the previous cabinet Bright 'without any previous communication' proposed a cttee. on wine duties prior to a commercial treaty with Spain; Lowe had protested against commercial treaties, and wrote to Gladstone, 26 July 1869, Add MS 44301, f. 58: 'I submit that it is very necessary to reconsider the propriety of having a commercial treaty department at the Board of Trade. If they exist they must do something to justify their existence. . . .'
[4] Held in Gladstone's house; Add MS 44637, f. 97.
[5] Not found.
[6] See Steele, *Irish Land*, 102.

√ Scotch Education Bill:[1] Concede if necessary 1. The £10 heritors Clause. 2.
Clause retaining the liability of the heritors Ministers as now—if material. To
be settled without scandal. Bruce afterwards reported favourably from H of
C.—Meeting to be held on Monday.
√ Chancery Funds Bill. To be made the best of.[2]
√ W[ar] O[ffice] & Adm[iralty] Buildings. Circulate Minute before next Cabi-
net.
√ Law Courts site. Lowe related the state of the case. Wait for the autumn.
√ Committee or Joint Committees for both Houses. (Ld Granville) in matters of
Private Business.[3] Cabinet approve.
√ Minute of Cabinet Comm[ittee] on Civil Service.[4] (Provisionally approved. A
scheme to be prepared upon it: including Cons[ideratio]n of measures to
keep excellent [?] list alive). Discussion arose: minute to be again circulated.
√ Marriage Law. Ld Chancellor. Say No.[5]
√ Treasury arrangements. Committee to meet.

To J. BRIGHT, president of the board of trade,   Add MS 43385, f. 35.
31 July 1869.

Many thanks for your note,[6] to which, after the Cabinet, I am compelled to
reply in haste.

Thank God I am much better & only lack a little strength. I wish you may be
able to settle with your enemy after as short a tussle.

I mentioned to Fortescue your wish about a mission to Germany to get information respecting land. On this matter I am sure there will be *no* difficulty: but
we thought it best in the first instance to accept Fortescue's offer, as he has
kindly offered before the next Cabinet (Friday Aug. 6) to learn exactly for your
& our information what information is already accessible. Do you think you
shall be with us then?

The prospects of the Scotch Education Bill improve.

On Friday will also be considered the question of admission into the Civil Service by competition.

I do not wonder that after Herculean efforts you should feel disposed at the
end of the Session to look forward to that period of rest which I think every
man of sense should desire to be the close of a busy life if God in his goodness
permit. My own feelings are thoroughly in sympathy with yours. But the programme you transmit also leaves room and hope for a good deal more of friendly
cheerful & cordial cooperation before this Government has fulfilled its task.

I hope to write in a day or two about the U.S. correspondence.

[1] Last minute concessions on Argyll's Parochial Schools (Scotland) Bill failed to save it.
[2] i.e. Bankruptcy Bill, in difficulties with Lords amndts. but received royal assent 9
August.
[3] Lords appt. a cttee. 17 February 1870: *H* cciii. index.
[4] No record found; see to Lowe, 8 Dec. 69.
[5] Reading uncertain; could be 'Say Lowe'; Bruce declined to commit govt. to legislation
next session on Marriage Law Commissioners; *H* cciii. 1406.
[6] Of 30 July 1869, Add MS 44112, f. 91, suggesting a mission to study Prussian land.

10.S.Trin. Aug One 69.

Chapel Royal mg with HC. All Saints aft. Wrote to Dean of Windsor
—Bp of Chester (letter & telegr.)—Ld Chancellor—Lady Blantyre
—Edw. Hamilton. Saw Count Strzelecki—Ld Granville—Ld R.
Cavendish. Read the *In Memoriam* of S.H. Lear.[1] Apart from the
'spots on the sun' as respects matter of controversy, it is a truly won-
derful & most fascinating picture. Also Read Ker's Sermon[2]—Ball's
Vindication.[3]

2. M.

Wrote to Ld. O. Fitzgerald—Dean of Windsor—Ld Chancellor—
A. Kinnaird—Rev Mr Lake—Ld Granville—The Queen (2)—Edw.
Hamilton—and minutes. H of C. 4-7¾ and 9½-1¾.[4] 3-4: Meeting in
D.St. on Treasury arrangements.[5] Saw Sir Edw. Dering—Mr Ouvry
—Mr Glyn—D. of Argyll—Dr Clarke—Ld Devon *cum* Mr Parkes
—Mr Layard—Mr Maguire—Mr Childers—Solr General—T. Ac-
land—A. Kinnaird—The Speaker—and Mr Fortescue.

To LORD O. FITZGERALD, M.P., 2 August 1869.   Add MS 44537, f. 17.

Cross examining Glyn upon the cause of the hair breadth scapes & even worse
of last week, to which I have been myself a reluctant but large contributor, I
find that they are due in a considerable degree to the thin attendance of official
persons. That formidable little record, which is sent round weekly to act as a
conscience to us of the official tribe will serve to exhibit to you the amount &
proportions of the fact; & you will not I am sure be well satisfied with your own
place upon the division list. Forgive me for representing to you not only that the
attendance of members in office, requisite at all times, is more than ever necessary at this time of the year & session, but that as the duties of hard worked men
in their Depts. make their absolute uniform attendance very difficult indeed, the
Govt. is obliged to look especially to those who are less likely to be kept away
from the House by any call of public [?] duty.[6]

3. Tu.

Wrote to Mr Fortescue—Bp of St Andrews[7]—Dr Moberly—Bp of
Chester—Chr of Exr—Abp of Canterb.—Ld Advocate—The Queen

[1] Possibly Mrs H. L. Lear, 'Willie's grave' in *Tales of Kirkbeck*, 3rd ed. 2v. (1869).
[2] J. *Ker, probably from *Sermons* (1869).
[3] T. H. Ball, 'A vindication of the Established Church of England and Ireland' (1868).
[4] Spoke on Bishops' Resignation Bill: *H* cxcviii. 1125.
[5] Decided not to change the relationship between the Financial and Political Secretaries;
see Gladstone to Ayrton, 13 August 1869, Add MS 44537, f. 27.
[6] Fitzgerald replied, Add MS 44421, f. 232: 'I confess I have deserved the reprimand.
But the very late hours have been rather too much for me.'
[7] Charles *Wordsworth.

—and minutes. H of C. 2-5 and $6\frac{1}{4}$-7.[1] Conclave at H. $2\frac{1}{2}$-5 on Honours to be granted.[2] Saw Mr Glyn: Dr Clarke. Called on Lady Palmerston. Dined with Jane Wortley. He alas is a wreck. Read Mr Burke. Saw S.E.G. on his and the boys' tour.[3]

To C. S. P. FORTESCUE, Irish secretary,   Carlingford MSS CP1/57.
3 August 1869.

I think the time has come for giving some honours, & after consideration & consultation, I am inclined to recommend Col. Greville Nugent & Ld. Listowel for the H. of Lords, & James O'Connell for the Baronetage. At the same time two English R.C's, Edw. Howard, & J. Acton for the Peerage. The case of O'Hagan for the Peerage might be considered specially before the next Session.

Do you see anything wrong in this, & will you kindly call on me, if you find occasion. Also please to ask the Lord Lieutenant.[4]

4. Wed.

Wrote to Mr Fortescue—Earl Russell—Chancr of Exr—Mr Bright (2)—Dean of Windsor—The Queen—Mr Hamilton—Ld Aylesbury —Mr D. Robertson—Mr Wykeham Meade—E. Cardwell. Read Mr Burke. Saw Duke of Argyll—Dr Clarke—Mr Bruce—Mr Glyn— Mr West—Lady Dinorben (with her nephew)[5]—Lord Powis—Mr Gurdon—Baron L. de Rothschild—Ld Granville *cum* Ld Chancellor. Dined at Argyll Lodge.[6]

To J. BRIGHT, president of the board of trade,   Add MS 43385, f. 38.
4 August 1869.

1. I should suggest that it is for you to communicate with Col Sabine as an essential part of the case which Mr. Cooke wishes you to make;[7] or perhaps he might do it. I rather think it would on my part have an invidious appearance as regards Wheatstone.

2. Do you know any representative man who might go into the House of Lords on behalf partly of trade & manufactures but especially of Nonconformity? I have thought much & called in aid but hitherto without effect. I thought of Sir F. Crossley but others held him cheap. Of course it should be a man who will not only be safe against any reasonable criticism of the world but likewise be accepted by the Nonconformists as a good type of their class so far as it is one.[8]

---

[1] East India accounts: *H* cxcviii. 1169.   [2] See 9 Aug. 69.
[3] Of the Highlands; see 11 Sept. 69.
[4] Fortescue agreed, Add MS 44121, f. 147.
[5] Gertrude, *née* Smyth, widow of W. L. Hughes, 1st Baron Dinorben; she d. 1871; the nephew, untraced. Discredited at Court, she was attempting rehabilitation; Add MS 44537, f. 19.
[6] *Argyll's house in Kensington.   [7] See 1 Sept. 69.
[8] No recommendation found.

To C. S. P. FORTESCUE, Irish secretary,   Carlingford MSS CP1/58.
4 August 1869.

The enclosed letter from Maguire raises the question of some partial release of
Fenians, on which of course I in no way committed myself but I thought it quite
worth while that he should put his point in his own way.[1]

5. Th.

Wrote to Ld Clarendon—Agnes G.—and minutes: also Queen. Read
Mr Burke. Small breakfast: of 7. Saw Abp of Canterbury—Sir J.
Lacaita—Mr Lambert—Col. French—Mr Glyn—Mr Cardwell—Ld
Granville. House of C. 4–8¼: worked Bishops Resignation Bill through
Committee.[2] Then went at Mary's special desire to Box and Cox.[3]
This day I fell back. But I lay in bed late preparing draft of the
Queen's Speech for the Prorogation.

6. Fr.

Wrote to Abp of Canterbury—Mr [J.] Carvell Williams—Ld Lyttel-
ton—Mrs Hamilton—Mr Fawcett—Ld Clarendon—The Queen—
Ld Granville—and minutes. Cabinet 2½–5½. Saw Ld Devon *cum* Mr
Parkes—Mr M'Millan—Dr Clark—Mr Candlish—Mr Glyn—Ld
Clarendon—Mr Bright—Mr Fortescue. Revised Speech for Prorogn.
Arranged my letters. Read Burke. A day of advance.

Cabinet Aug 6. 69[4]
√ 1. Maclaren's notice respecting Ch[urch] of Scotland Parl[iamentary] Grants.
     Ans. cons[idere]d[5]
  2. Law Courts Site. Report of Comm[ittee] as to the positive part cannot be
     acted on.
  3. Measures for next year.
√ 4. As to proceeding with the Scotch Education Bill. Cabinet here [in Down-
     ing Street] leaned adversely: decision [later taken] in H[ouse] of C[om-
     mons] *for* proceeding.[6]
√ 5. Queen's Speech. Alternative Paragraph.
  6. Ayrton's representation as to the Metropol[itan] L[oans] Bill.[7] Ld
     C[larendon] will see him.

---

[1] Fortescue and Sullivan opposed further release, 6 August 1869, Add MS 44121, f. 151.
[2] See *PP* 1868–9 i. 285.   [3] *Sullivan and *Burnand's operetta.
[4] Add MS 44637, f. 98.
[5] *Maclaren proposed to end govt. grant to the Church of Scotland; Add MS 44611,
f. 42.
[6] Killed in Lords despite concessions; see D. J. Withrington, 'Towards a national system',
Scottish Educational Studies (1972), 107.
[7] The Lords squeezed it through between 6 and 10 August.

√ 7. Episcopal Patents. No more to be issued in Colonies with representative
Governments.
8. Prorogation: to the latest day.

7. Sat.

Wrote to Ld Clarendon—Dr Miller—Col. French—D. of Argyll—
S.R.G.—Miss Marsh—C.G.—Sec. N. British R.R. Co.[1]—Ld Granville—Admiral Glasse—Mr Bright—and minutes. Read Burke's Reflections—Pride & Prejudice.[2] Saw Dr Clarke (3)—Mr MacLaren—
Mr Glyn—Mr West. Stephy dined & staid evg.

8. 11 S.Trin.

Kept my bed. Morning Prayer alone. Read Liddon's noble Sermon on
Resurrection[3]—Stopford Brook's Sermons[4]—Cazenove's Essays
(finished)—Report of Convn on Discipline[5]—Sutton Episc.Fette.
Laity.[6] Wrote to Bp of Chester—Ld Clarendon—A. Gordon—Dr
Moberly—Watsons—V. Darbishire.

9. M.

Wrote to Ld Granville—Rev. C. Merivale[7]—Bp of Lincoln—Mrs
Thistlethwayte—Mr Bright—Dean of Windsor—The Queen (2) &
minutes. Finished Burke on Fr. Rev. Saw Dr Clarke (2)—Mr West
(2)—Mr Glyn (2)—A. Gordon—Mr Cardwell—Mr Fortescue—
Mr Bright—Ld Granville—Do *cum* Ld Clarendon & Mr Lowe—
Scotts—Mr Sanders (Dentist). Mending all day.

Cabinet 11 C[arlton] H[ouse] T[errace]. Aug 9. 69.[8]
1. WEG introduced Peerages. Mr Phillips recommended.[9] Consult Glyn.
2. Comm[issione]rs of Education for Scotland
Not to be named to P[arliamen]t as Queen's pleasure has not been taken.
3. Buildings Adm[iralty] & War Office.[10]
Postponed to Nov[embe]r.
4. Civil Service Admissions. Heads of Dept. to consider the case each for his own
Dept.

[1] Probably arranging his sons' expedition.   [2] Jane Austen; 29 Nov. 53.
[3] H. P. *Liddon, 'The power of Christ's resurrection' (1869).
[4] S. A. *Brooke, *Sermons preached in St James's Chapel, York Street* (1869).
[5] Report of a cttee. of convocation; see *The Guardian*, 30 June 1869, 735.
[6] Untraced.
[7] Offering him the vacant Cambridge history chair (see 2 Sept. 69), which he declined;
Add MS 44537, f. 23.   [8] Add MS 44637, f. 100.
[9] Unidentified; a Bright nominee, see 4 Aug. 69?
[10] Report of cabinet cttee. (see 24 Apr. 69) in Add MS 44611, f. 45.

10. Tu. [Walmer Castle, Kent]

Wrote to Ld Granville—Ld Lyttelton—Mr Ellice—Ld Sydney—
Dean Ramsay—S. Watson Taylor[1]—The Queen—and minutes.
Arrangements for departure and puttings away. Saw Mr Glyn—Mr
West—Lord Advocate—Mr Bruce—Ld Granville—Dr Clarke. Off
at 2. Reached Walmer Castle 5½.[2] We prowled about. Read Memoirs
of Catherine II[3]—Pride and Prejudice—Began Iliad: for Thesaurus.

11. Wed.

Wrote to Mr Stansfeld—The Queen (Peers & Baronets)—and minutes.
The James party came over. Read Pride & Prejudice—Memoirs of
Catherine—Campbell on Irish Land.[4]

12. Th.

Wrote to Dean of Windsor—Rev. C. Kingsley—Mr G. Glyn—The
Speaker—Robn G.—Miss Doyle—& minutes. Granville came:
much conversation on politics & other. Read Pride & Prejudice—
Fraser on Irish Ch. & Govt.[5] Long walk with C. to Deal & about it.
Also with G[ranville].

To J. E. DENISON, the Speaker, 12 August 1869.   Add MS 44537, f. 25.

I am very glad the Speech[6] pleased you. The materials of it were better than
usual: for the singular earnestness & straightforwardness of the House enabled us
to turn out a good deal of work.

It is I suppose matter of speculation how much of the credit which the household suffrage Parlt. has earned should be set down to its own qualities in their
average state, & how much to the definite character of the chief work it has been
engaged upon, & the thorough comprehension of that work by the country. It
will become difficult for the majority to hold together on the question of the
Irish land but I hope we may frame a measure which will satisfy reasonable men.
As far as I know Bright's opinions they are really moderate more so perhaps than
the Irish public may suppose.

I wrote a few days ago to your Chaplain to offer him the Chair of Modern
History at Cambridge.[7] Probably he is enquiring about the particulars of duty.

[1] Simon Watson Taylor, 1843–1902, of Erlestoke, Wiltshire, had unsuccessfully requested
a peerage; Add MS 44421, f. 249.
[2] Official seat of *Granville, as warden of the cinque ports.
[3] Memoirs of the Empress Catherine II, ed. A. Herzen (1859).
[4] G. *Campbell, The Irish Land (1869), an important influence on Gladstone's views;
see Steele, Irish Land, 104ff.
[5] Fraser's Magazine, lxxx. 257 (August 1869).
[6] The prorogation speech; see Denison to Gladstone, 11 August 1869, Add MS 44261,
f. 284.
[7] C. Merivale.

I will not ask you to write about yourself but I shall rest until undeceived in the comfortable belief that a little rest will do for you its proper work. This place we find very delightful except that the neighbourhood seems given to the vice of calling. I am thankful to say that I can report myself substantially well.

13. Fr.

Wrote to Mr O Donoghue—G. Burnett—Sir C. Trevelyan—Mr Ayrton—Chancr of Exr—Ld Clarendon—Mr G.H. Vernon—Mr Anderson—Mr Stansfeld—Mr West—& minutes. Much further conversation with Granville on all matters: the most delightful of colleagues. He went off at 2.15. Sir W. James dined: we had much conversation on Church matters. Read Mem. of Catherine II—Pride & Prejudice (finished)—Fennell on Greek Writing.[1]

To Sir C. E. TREVELYAN, 13 August 1869.   Add MS 44537, f. 27.

I have read with much attention and interest Mr Campbell's very able paper of which you were so good as to send me a copy. Its effect is on the whole disheartening but nothing can be more desirable than to know the worst of every question and I believe a vein of truth runs through the pages of this pamphlet. Pray send if you can a copy to Ld. Gr[anville].[2]

14. Sat.

Wrote to Ld Lyttelton—Mr M. O'Connell[3]—Ld Leigh—Bp of St Andrew's—Mr Burnett—Watson & Smith—& minutes. Walk to Deal & shopping. Read Seeley on Roman Hist.—On Milton[4]—Memoirs of Catherine II. Wrote Mem. with history of the days from July 17 to 22. Backgammon: a lesson to Herbert.

15. 11 S.Trin.

Walmer Ch. mg. Kingdown aft. Wrote to The Queen (Mem)—Archbishop of Canterb.—Ld Lyttelton—Scotts—Rev. Mr Carter—and minutes. Read Fremantle on Lay Power[5]—Wrote Mem. on it—

---

[1] Untraced.

[2] This day Gladstone encouraged Lowe 'in favour of an endeavour to recall Trevelyan to the service', of which nothing seems to have come; Add MS 44537, f. 26.

[3] Morgan O'Connell, 1804-85; Irish assistant registrar 1840; given civil pension October 1869.

[4] J. R. *Seeley, 'Milton's poetry' and 'Roman imperialism', *Macmillan's Magazine*, xix. 407, xx. 281 (March-August 1869).

[5] W. H. *Fremantle, *Lay power in parishes, the most needed Church reform* (1869).

Memoirs of Mad. Louise—Whitfield's Life—Haddan on Apostol. Succession.[1]

Memorandum. Private.[2]
1. I admire Mr Fremantle's able pamphlet and sympathise with most of its main propositions. 2. I subjoin points of dissent or hesitation. 3. I am doubtful as to the great enlargement of the sphere of the Bishop's authority and activity. 4. I am disinclined to plans which extend, at this time of day, the sense of the 'nationality' of the Church, for I think them likely a) to excite fierce controversy b) to produce sharp reaction c) not improbably to end in destroying the Nationality altogether. The idea conveyed by the word is not in these times robust enough to bear the additional strain proposed to be laid upon it. 5. Knowing that a fair number of clergy really desire to see lay Power put into action, I do not understand why no one has yet *tried out*, or even made in any definite manner, (so far as I know,) the experiment of what can be done under the present law in the way of an assisting and controuling lay organisation. And although I incline to think the only kind of it which will work or live is congregational, those who think that the whole parochial population would supply the proper organ can of course try their method as well as any others. 6. As far as *legal* change is concerned, in the sense of this pamphlet, it seems to me at this moment less opportune, than at former epochs, because of the great crisis of the Irish Church, which is likely to supply us with valuable lights of experience. 7. In the last sentence I do not mean to include any wise measure which might be suggested to supply congregations with defensive arms against arbitrary innovations.

16. M.

Wrote to Lord Granville—Messrs Williams—Mr Burnett—Ld Bessborough—Robn G.—The Queen—G.G. Glyn—and minutes. Worked on Homer. Saw Rev. Harrison.[3] Read Mem. of Catherine II. Stephy came.

17. Tu.

Wrote to Dean of Windsor—Duke of Argyll—Hon W. Eden[4]— Archdn Jones—Mr E. Arnold—Bp Moriarty—and minutes. Worked Homer, Thesaurus. Saw Dr Davey.[5] Walk to St Margaret at Cliffe, the S. Foreland Lighthouse, and St Marg. Bay. charming: back under the

---

[1] [H. L. Farrer], *The Life of Madame Louise de France* (1869); probably D. A. Harsha, *Life of the Rev. George Whitefield* (1866); A. W. *Haddan, *Apostolic Succession in the Church of England* (1869).
[2] Initialled and dated 15 August 1869; Add MS 44139, f. 283.
[3] John Branfill Harrison, vicar of Walmer 1854.
[4] William George Eden, 1829–90, 4th Baron Auckland 1870.
[5] R. S. Davey, physician at Walmer.

cliffs. 11 miles. Read Knox on Irish Ch. question[1]—finished Memoirs of Catherine.

To E. ARNOLD, 17 August 1869.   Add MS 44537, f. 30.

I was naturally much pleased with the article in the Daily Tel.[2] when I saw it, but it acquires an additional value in my eyes from learning that you were the writer & that my book has the honour of your favourable opinion. Thank you very much for your book:[3] & if I may judge from the recollection of former compositions known or reported to me as yours, I shall read it with very great pleasure & advantage. I hope you will kindly give me an opportunity hereafter of improving our acquaintance by breakfasting with me on any Thursday after Easter at 10.

18. Wed.

Wrote to Ld Granville—Mr Angerstein—Mr Glyn—Lord Sydney— Watson & S.—Mr G. Coode—and minutes. Read Capefigue Louis XIV.[4] Walk to Sandown Castle: vanishing.[5] Bp of Oxford came— also Archdn [B.] Harrison. Much conversation with both. Worked on Homer Thesau.

19. Th.

Wrote to C.P. Villiers—Sec.Eccles. Commissioners—The Queen (Mem)—and minutes. Worked on Homer. The Archdeacon went. Walk again to St Margaret's Bay. Much conversation with the Bp of Oxford: on men and things. Whist in evg: he joined. Read Capefigue —A. de Musset's Poems.[6]

20. Fr.

Wrote to Dean of Windsor—Mr Mackinnon—The Speaker—Mr T.S. Gladstone—Mr Acland—Rev. Mr Lucey[7]—and minutes. Walk with the Bishop. Read Capefigue—A. de Musset. Worked on Homer.

21. Sat.

Wrote to Rev. W. Rawson—Dean Ramsay—Robn G.—Mr Head- lam—Hon W. Eden—and minutes. Drive to Dover Castle & walk

[1] R. B. *Knox, The Irish Church (1867).   [2] Review of Juventus Mundi.
[3] The poets of Greece (1869) sent on 16 Aug.; Add MS 44421, f. 283.
[4] J. B. H. R. Capefigue, Louis XIV, son gouvernement et ses relations diplomatiques avec l'Europe, 6v. (1837, 38).
[5] Ruined blockhouse near Deal.
[6] L. C. A. de Musset, Poésies nouvelles . . . 1836-52 (1860).
[7] Ebenezer Curling Lucey, vicar of St. Margaret's, Dover.

back. Noble view & fine fabric. Unhappily I did not enter. Read Brock on W.E.G.[1]—Ch. of Exrs Speech on Coinage[2]—Carpenter's Address[3]—Capefigue's Louis XIV. Round game in evg. The Bp went.

22. 13 S.Trin.

Walmer Ch mg—St Andrew's Deal evg. Wrote to Mrs Glyn—Dr Pusey—and minutes. Read Haddan on Succession—Life of Soeur Thérèse de S. Aug.—Catholic Thoughts—Kirkman on Church Cursing.[4]

23. M.

Wrote to Dean of Windsor—Mr T.B. Potter—Mr V. Darbishire—and minutes. Worked on Homer. Read Capefigue. Went to see Deal Regatta. Commerce in evg. A little fray with Stephy.

24. Tu.

Wrote to Dean Ramsay—Bp of Chester—Ld Granville—Ld Clarendon—Mr Childers—Chr of Exchr—Mr Lambert—Mr Barnes[5]—Pro Sec.Eccl. Commn—and minutes. Worked on Homer. Read Capefigue—Vol II—Knocker on Cinque Ports.[6] Cricket round the hat with my four sons. Summer heat returned.

To LORD CLARENDON, foreign secretary,　　　　　　Clarendon MSS, c. 498.
24 August 1869.

Your interesting letters[7] have brought up a number of subjects. That of Layard[8] I postpone for today until I can learn a little more.
1. *America*. Besides the two men mentioned there is a third, namely [T. Milner] Gibson whom I think well worth considering. Bright could not be absent from the discussion of the Land question for Ireland and to this all the early part of the

---

[1] W. Brock, *Mr Gladstone the betrayer of the religion and liberties of the country* (1869).

[2] R. *Lowe, speech of 6 August 1869, on currency.

[3] M. *Carpenter, 'An address read at the conference on ragged schools held at Birmingham' (1861).

[4] [F. Myers], *Catholic thoughts on the Church of Christ and the Church of England* (1834-41); T. P. Kirkman, *Church cursing and atheism* (1869).

[5] James Bathe Barnes, liberal agent in Lambourne, Berks., had written requesting a non-Puseyite for the Oxford see; Add MS 44537, f. 36 and 44421, f. 295.

[6] E. Knocker, *An account of the Grand Court of Shepway* (1862).

[7] Of 17 and 20 August, from Wiesbaden, where he was treating his gout; reporting talks with Grasselini on the Council: 'at heart liberal but as timid as a mouse'; Add MS 44133, ff. 257, 263.

[8] Clarendon opposed Layard's appointment to Madrid; ibid.

next Session is dedicated or doomed. There is no shrewder man than Gibson nor any that keeps closer to his work. He would be thoroughly faithful to instructions, has a large fund of natural circumspection, & was thoroughly Northern throughout the War. He would also have Bright's best backing: and he would get on very well I think with Thornton or any one else unless very hard indeed to please.

As regards the terms of reference the more I think of them the more I incline to see advantage in making them wide. If our conduct outside the Alabama & cruisers question is let in to shew *animus* & otherwise, may it not let in the conduct of the U.S. themselves in analogous international questions, and may not this be of great advantage to us? In these remarks I am assuming that the question has been opened anew and if so that it has been opened by them.

If we agree to a wide reference, it may help them to dispense with the demand of a preliminary confession, which besides being untrue to our conviction and dishonouring before the world, would deprive a part of a very solemn proceeding of authority, and therefore of utility.

2. *Egypt.* On your draft respecting the financial charges against the Viceroy[1] I have put a pencil memorandum as follows: 'Query notice in this dispatch as possible pleas for the Viceroy 1. The costly aid we gave to the Porte in Candia. 2. The charge we must (I suppose) have incurred for the Suez Canal. It would be very interesting to have information on these two points in particular. A telegram from F.O. to Mr. Stanley of Aug. 19 was sent me. It records your sorrowful conviction that the Viceroy of Egypt has gone beyond his powers: which I can readily believe. I hope however, and indeed I make little doubt, that you are acting in unison with France on this point which has been before, and might be again, such a sore one.[']

3. *Rome.* I think you understate the value of your conversation with Cardinal Grasselini. His report bears out the worst surmises that have been entertained with respect to the Council. The whole affair is a pure piece of ultra-Sacerdotalism. The pretence for the exclusion of the lay element is a piece of effrontery: there never was a Council which dealt so much with matter *mixed* as between religious and temporal interests. I do not dispute the *risks* of interference by remonstrance even on the part of R.C. Powers: and our position reduces alike our responsibility and our means: but I for one am so convinced of the mischiefs both political and religious of these extravagant proceedings that I shall be very sorry if hereafter the Pope & Ecclesiastics are able to say with truth that they never received a friendly warning. I am very glad of what you were able to say to Grassellini & cannot help wishing Odo Russell were empowered to say some of it to Antonelli.

4. *Greece.* I cannot doubt that you are right in declining to countenance anything that savours of a *Coup d'Etat* even if covered by an appeal to the people such as that which was made by L. N[apoleon] after he had possessed himself of power. If it is a sham appeal, an appeal for an Aye or No carefully hedged, we can have nothing to do with it; if it is a real appeal, why is it not made under existing institutions? So far as I know we have never been informed, except in vague and general terms of what is really intended to be done: and 'void because of uncertainty' might be returned as an answer. I hope they will really inform you of *what* it is that they ask your approval.

Another important point is this: 'Non cuivis homini contingit adire Corinthum', it is not every man who by an act of *prepotenza* can attain his end.[2] What is there

---

[1] A. S. Green's mem. of 21 Aug. 1869, F.O.C.P. 1678.   [2] Horace, *Ep.* 1. 17. 36.

in this King or in the people about him which should lead us to believe that they have the kind of gift which L.N. showed himself to possess in so extraordinary a degree? We do not even know the nature of the existing evils. Is population, is trade, is shipping, is Education declining? Throughout the reign of Otho there was a boast I believe not untrue that the contrary was the case with each & all. I wonder what are the relations of Mr. Erskine with Genl. Church & Mr. Finlay. Their opinions, I mean C. & F. as well as E., would weigh much with me were I in your place. Finlay is a man of great talent: both have long experience, are sincere lovers of Greece in which they have acquired it, and at the same time I presume would regard the matter with the feelings of Englishmen.

5. *St Petersburg.* It is quite a mistake—unless my recollection wholly deceives me—to suppose that I spoke in the House of Commons of Russia as unwilling to define the Neutral Zone in Central Asia. I merely said the thing was not without difficulty, & had not been accomplished; but I believe I stated expressly the willingness and desire of both parties to attain the end. But it is true that you should be relieved from the rush of my douche bath. I need add but little except to thank you first for your good wishes as to my health of which I really can report everything desirable: & secondly to say with how much pleasure I learned that having ventured on the daring & doubtful experiment of opening my book you had thought favourably of it. I had hoped that no *colleague* would have heard of it: and I have now some fear lest it should be responsible for your quickened feelings of gout. Be this as it may, I hope you may soon be relieved, and you will not by any untoward cause be obliged to stint what is called your holiday.

[P.S.] Lord Russell's letter is a very kind one. He is right about Moncreiff's strange mistake. I never knew of the thing till it was done. I have replied to Dean Warburton.[1]

To J. LAMBERT, 24 August 1869.   Add MS 44537, f. 36.

I hope that on your tour you will look as much as you can at the question of Irish Land,[2] & I recommend your reading the enclosed[3] which seems to open up many of the sources of difficulty. I fear I must ask you to return it as it has some references of mine upon it, but I daresay that if you like it Mr. West could get you a copy through Sir C. Trevelyan who sent it to me.

25. Wed.

Wrote to Ld Clarendon—Dean of Windsor—Mr Glyn—Lady Blantyre—Mr Otway—Dr [W.] Haig Brown[4]—A. Kinnaird—Mrs Thistlethwayte—Mr Fortescue—and minutes. Worked on Homer. Read Capefigue—Noel's Poems.[5] Cricket round the hat as yesterday. Planned to go to St Margaret's tomorrow: but in the night I had a return of my complaint, caused I fear by a high wing of grouse yesterday.

[1] See Clarendon MSS c. 510.
[2] Long report by Lambert on 27 September, Add MS 44235, f. 44.
[3] Campbell's pamphlet, see 11 Aug. 69.
[4] On the Phoenicians; copy in Add MS 44421, f. 311.
[5] R. B. W. *Noel, Beatrice and other poems (1868).

26. Th.

Kept my bed. Wrote to Ld Granville—The Queen (Memm)—Mr
Fortescue—and the rest (almost all) by dictated minutes. Read Capefigue—Romola.[1] Improving all day. Played commerce with the children in evg.

27. Fr.

A good night DG. Wrote to Ld Clarendon—Robn G.—Ld Granville
—Mr Glyn—Ld Normanby—Mr Maurice—Chancr of Exchr—The
Queen (Mem). Discussing plans for our several journeys. Improved
greatly. The Archbp [of Canterbury] came in evg. Much conversation with him. Read Capefigue—Romola.

28. Sat.

Wrote to Abp of Canterbury—Mr West—Mr Fremantle—Mr Acland—Mr R. Barker—and minutes. Robertson came: also Mrs
Wortley. Worked on Homer. Read Capefigue—Romola. Commerce
in evg.

To T. D. ACLAND, M.P., 28 August 1869. 'Most private.'   Add MS 44537, f. 40.

Very many thanks.[2] If you can properly send me Dr Temple's letter pray do.
I have made up my mind to act, on a fitting opportunity. But the choice of it
will require care. It does not seem to be your opinion, but it is mine, that when
the hour comes there will be a great outcry. Indeed I have had some indication
of it this very morning. I should have thought that outcry no where likely to be
greater than in the Diocese of Exeter. Is your judgement otherwise? Now what
would be the *first thought* of your father? Of Ld. Devon? Two good representative men. Apart from *outcry* I should have thought the proper diocese for Dr.
Temple would have been a diocese where there is a great & robust work urgently
needed for the Church, such as a Welsh diocese if the language did not make too
great a difficulty, or the black country or a diocese of the Yorkshire or Lancashire latitudes. The next time however is a Cambridge one by rights.

29. 14 S. Trin.

M. Prayers at home. Walmer Ch. in aft. Wrote to Lady C.N. Grenville
—Lady Herbert—Mr Lowe—and minutes. Read Mad. Louise
(finished): a picture to raise *mixed* feelings[3]—Tischendorf on the

---

[1] By George *Eliot (1863).
[2] Acland's letter not in Add MS 44092. Temple's appt. as bp., see 22 Sept. 69n.
[3] See 15 Aug. 69.

Gospels—Genesis critically examined—Jacob's Sermon.[1] Conversation with Willy on his autumn plans: Stephy, on the tour: Harry, on his profession.

30. M.

Wrote to Duke of Argyll—Chancr of Exr—the Viceroy—Bp of St Davids—and minutes. Kept my bed, on account of physic, till the aftn. Robn—all the boys—& Mrs Wortley, went. Glyn came— much conversation on preferments and political arrangements. Read Capefigue—Romola.

To the DUKE OF ARGYLL, Indian secretary,   Add MS 44537, f. 42.
30 August 1869.

I think your papers[2] on the Punjaub Tenancy Act presuppose a more close knowledge of the subject than I possess. My impression would have been that the Prinsep[3] process was radically questionable, unless an express title for the readjustment of all rights had been reserved: & that if this had been reserved, it must have been very rashly exercised to make it right then to go back upon it. But as far as I can judge from the papers I should think the conclusion of your draft despatch the right one.

My perusal of them has been delayed as last week I was partially upset again, & have had new proof of the need of much care. I am not sure whether I have read the good words to which you refer but I am sorry to find from 1 or 2 nos. which I have lately seen that polemics are not excluded from it. We go on Sat. & on Sat. week I expect to be at Balmoral.

31. Tu.

Wrote to Sir G. Grey—Chancr of Exr—Mr Henderson—Lord Advocate—J.C. Robertson—and minutes. Much conversation on Church preferments especially, and walk to St Margaret's, & back by the sea. Read Capefigue—Romola.

Wed. Sept One. 1869.

Wrote to M. Michel Chevalier—Hon A. Kinnaird—A. Gurdon— Hon. F. Lawley—Mr M.F. Sadler[4]—Col. Ffrench—Lord Granville

[1] L. F. C. Tischendorf, 'Are our Gospels genuine or not?' (1869); E. V. Neale, *Genesis critically analysed* (1869); G. A. Jacob, probably from *The presence of Christ* (1858).
[2] Bundle sent on 23 August; Add MS 44101, f. 55.
[3] Henry Thoby Prinsep, 1793-1878; director of council of India 1858-74.
[4] Michael Ferrebee *Sadler, 1819-95; vicar of St. Paul's, Bedford 1854; declined bpric. of Montreal 1869; rector of Honiton from 1869.

—Mr Bright—Robn G.—Watsons—and minutes. Worked on Homer. G.G. G[lyn?] went off. Read Capefigue—Romola. Walk to Upper Deal, &c.

To J. BRIGHT, president of the board of trade,   Add MS 43385, f. 43.
1 September 1869.

I have directed a reply to Mr. Leone Levi in the sense you suggest,[1] & I will send for Mr. Fitzgibbon's pamphlet. The literature of the subject is large, & will be larger; much of it is trashy, and it is well to have indications of the best. I have seen lately a very interesting tract, which I have sent to Mr. Lambert to read, as he is going to Ireland; it is, I think, by a man named Campbell, and it compares Irish with Indian tenure.

Of late years the practice has been for the Cabinet to meet in November: but this year the two large subjects of Irish Land and Education in England might, I think, make an October meeting desirable to start our preparations. Pray let me know how this strikes you; we might then separate for a short time after the Ld. Mayor's day.

I am now about to start for the North in a few days and I think I will ask you to let me see the article on the Alabama question next month.

You could not be spared from Irish Land: but if it is found expedient to send a special Envoy to the United States, [Milner-] Gibson seems to me to have many qualities that would admirably fit him for the purpose.

Many thanks for your kind reference to my health. Since I have been here, there was a slight relapse owing to the accident, we think, of eating part of a tainted grouse. But, thank God, I am very well generally, & I expect much from the Deeside Climate, which always suits me admirably. I hope you have contrived altogether to banish your ailment.

I will see that Mr. Fothergill Cooke[2] is informed of his knighthood. There is often a delay in this particular matter, when the honour is personally conferred. My day for Balmoral is the 11th.

To M. CHEVALIER, 1 September 1869.   Add MS 44537, f. 43.

I find on inquiry that the F.O. does not seem to have received any copy of the Report of 67 for *me*. I make this reply in answer to your kind inquiry.[3] But I hope you will take no undue trouble in the matter. All is going well I hope with the recent changes, & the condition of the public mind in France.

Should you have occasion to write, pray tell me what you consider the work of highest authority on the small Landholders or Peasant Proprietary of France?

2. Th.

Wrote to Ld Clarendon (2)—T.D. Acland—W.B. Gurdon—Sir John Gray—Mr Seeley[4]—Mr Hammond—Mr Horsfall—Sir A. Spearman

---

[1] Bright's letter untraced.
[2] Sir William Fothergill *Cooke, 1806-79; inventor of telegraph.
[3] Untraced; sent report on French land on 3 Sept.; Add MS 44127, f. 24.
[4] Offering him the Cambridge regius history chair; he accepted; Add MS 44422, f. 33.

—Mr Barker—Mrs Thistlethwayte—and minutes. A long & heavy post: some 40 letters to dispose of: done by 4.15, i.e. 7 hours. Read Romola—W. Lyttelton on Laughter[1]—Capefigue.

To Sir J. GRAY, M.P., 2 September 1869.   Add MS 44537, f. 45.

I thank you very much for your letter, which removes an important misunderstanding.[2] I shall truly regret it, if, after our free & cordial cooperation in regard to the Ch. question, which you did so much to help forward, we should stand reciprocally to one another in a less happy position, with respect to the subject of Land Tenure in Ireland.

At present my duty is only by inquiry to try to understand the various methods of proceeding, which have been or may be proposed. It would be very kind, if either in MS. or in print, you would help me on a point in regard to which I am not yet clear. In what form, or by what provision, could the Ulster tenant right Custom be put into the form of law? I do not mean that this cannot be done: nor do I now refer to Bills & Clauses: but what would be the leading propositions, to which a legal shape would be given, & which would be made capable of enforcement in the courts? I am much grieved at the outrages in Mayo.

3. Fr.

Wrote to Lord Granville—The Queen (& M.)—Ld T. Clinton—Mr J.P. Heywood—Scotts—Mr M'Millan—Williams & Co.—Mr A. Day[3]—and minutes. Examined some prints in J[uventus] M[undi] and worked on Homer. Read Capefigue (finished IV)—Romola. Accounts & preparations.

4. Sat. [*London*]

Wrote to Duchess of Cleveland—Bp of Orleans[4]—Mr Burnett—Sir A. Panizzi—Mr Cornish—The Queen (& Mem)[5]—Ly Herbert— Sir T. Biddulph—Mr Bruce—Duke of Argyll—Mr Hammond—Mr Hugessen—and minutes. Off at 10.30 after an active morning. CHT. at 2.15. Saw Chancr of Exchequer—Ld Aylesbury—Ld Granville— Mr Gurdon—Mr Helps—Mr Glyn. Shopping. Read Romola—Fortn. & Contemp. on Homer.[6] Dined at Ld Granville's. Saw two X.

[1] Unpublished work by W. H. Lyttelton.
[2] Gray to Gladstone, 31 August 1869, Add MS 44421, f. 331, on *The Times'* misrepresentation of Gray's Irish land proposals as fixity of tenure and every third acre to the landlord.
[3] Alfred Day, had written on Homer; Add MS 44537, f. 51.
[4] Félix Antoine Philibert Dupanloup, 1802-78; bp. of Orléans 1849-78; led the inopportunists at the Vatican council.
[5] Probably that arguing for more peers sitting in the Lords; Add MS 44758, f. 156.
[6] G. W. Cox on Gladstone and Homer, *Fortnightly Review*, xii. 241 (September 1869); *Contemporary Review*, xii. 50 (September 1869).

5. 15 S.Trin.

St Peter's W. St mg with H.C. & Chapel Royal aftn. Luncheon with the Jameses. Saw Mr Glyn & dined at Highgate: a brighter day. Saw Mr Garden—Mr Gurdon. Failed in inquiry after L.R. Wrote to Station Mr Kings Cross—Lady Herbert—Agnes G.—Rev. Albany Christie.[1] Read Fortn.Rev. (68) on Homer.[2]

6. M. [Raby Castle, Co. Durham]

Wrote to Dean of Durham—Mr Cashel Hoey—W.H.G.—Ld Granville (2)—and minutes. Read Romola: Fauriel. Off at 8.30. Reached Raby[3] soon after five. Its first aspect is strikingly noble. Most kindly received. Saw W. at York: who took on his mother & Mary to Whitby. Walk with the D. of Cleveland before dusk.

7. Tu.

Went over this fine old castle in the forenoon: & drove to Barnard Castle in the afternoon. Wrote to Ld Clarendon—Mr Hammond—C.G.—Mr Glyn—and minutes. Read Romola—Baring Gould on Myths.[4]

To LORD CLARENDON, foreign secretary,   Clarendon MSS, c. 498.
7 September 1869.

Many thanks for your interesting letter of the 4th.[5] The case against any remonstrance or interference about the Council was well stated in a dispatch giving the French view. Yet I cannot help desiring that the European States were disposed to let the Pope know that in the absence of a frank declaration that the province of civil rights would be carefully saved, and viewing the character of the document termed the Syllabus, they could not but view the affair with regret and misgiving and could anticipate no good results from it, especially on account of the secrecy maintained as to its intentions.

The Irish Land question appears to me to be assuming formidable proportions & to have altered its aspect a good deal since you left England. The Times, & its Correspondent, if I gather the purport aright of articles which I have read but incompletely have I think changed their tone. Bright who in a conversation had

[1] Albany James Christie, 1818?-91; jesuit; had sent his *Union with Rome* (1869); Add MS 44537, f. 51.
[2] See 4 Sept. 69.
[3] Seat near Barnard Castle of the duke of Cleveland (see 6 Feb. 49), a liberal, and stepfa. of 5th earl of *Rosebery.
[4] S. B. Gould, *Curious myths of the Middle Ages* (1866).
[5] Add MS 44133, f. 1, from Wiesbaden, on Russian anger at the Council, and on Irish press on the land question: 'the people read nothing else & there is no antidote to the poison. The Priests inculcate the truths of the newspapers much more than those of the Gospel . . .'.

satisfied Bessborough of the thorough moderation of his views, is now afraid lest the subject should have outgrown them: and I am told that the Dublin Conservative Daily Press, except the Mail, recommends large measures, such as giving the force of law to the custom of tenant right and making it universal. You will probably have seen that this is directly recommended by Ld. Granard.

I certainly had thought two months ago that the elements were shaping themselves in such a way as to present the subject hopefully. I do not at present feel by any means so sure. Sir John Gray has written to assure me he is only 'going for' the tenant right custom. In my reply, without committing myself, I have asked him in what method, & form, he proposes to give to that custom the force of law? a question to which I await his reply with curiosity.

I think that viewing the gravity of this subject it would be well for the Cabinet to meet and at least to put it in hand a little earlier than the epoch of the Lord Mayor's day which has recently been fashionable, and I am inclined to propose the 25th or 26th Oct? What say you to this? Granville approves.

I came here [Raby Castle] yesterday, & go northwards to Balmoral on Friday. This is a most remarkable & interesting house, of vast extent, with more of actual antiquity in it than any I ever saw. I hope much good from the bracing air of Balmoral for though I am ostensibly well, there is a weakness of the organs not yet overcome.
[P.S.] The Bulwer letter is somewhat astounding.

8. Wed.

Wrote to Ld Granville—M. Chevalier—Watson & S.—Lady Herbert —Mr Burnett—Archbp of York—and minutes. Read Romola (finished)—Memoirs of Mad. Dubarrie 1775[1]—'State' of England 1732, 3, 4, 5.[2] Walk with the Duke & expl. to him about 'Concurrent Endowment'.

9. Th.

Wrote to Mr J. O'Connell—Mr Whitworth[3]—Mr Bazley—Ald. Salomons—Mr T. Salt—Maj.Gen. Seymour—W.H.G.—Mr Fairbairn[4] —Mr Crawford—Mr Hammond—Ld R. Cavendish—Archdeacon of Northern Ireld—and minutes. Read Memoirs of Mad. Dubarri. Ride with the Duchess & Ld Grey. Conversation with Lady M. Alford.

10. Fr. [Balmoral]

Wrote to Mr Hammond—Sir S. Scott & Co—Mr Glyn—and minutes. Up late from more cold. Read Mem. of Mad. Dubarri—Pemberton's

[1] Probably *Anecdotes sur M. la Comtesse Du Barri* [by M. F. P. de Mairobert] (1775).
[2] Probably A. *Boyer, *The political state of Great Britain*, published monthly 1711-40.
[3] Offering a baronetcy to (Sir) James O'Connell, 1786-1872, and (Sir) Joseph *Whitworth, 1803-87, arms manufacturer.
[4] Offering a baronetcy to (Sir) William Fairbairn, 1789-1874, engineer.

Monaco.[1] Departure with regret at 2—to Winston—Darlington—
Edinb.—Aberdeen—& Balmoral. Travelled all night. Parted from C.
& the girls at 11½ (Perth).

11. Sat.

Wrote to Mrs Wm G.—Mrs Thistlethwayte—Sec.Metrop. Districts
Co.—Sec. North British Co.—and minutes. Arrived at 6. Breakfast
—work—and bed 7½ to 9. S. and his brothers came at 12.30. I was
with them till six. We walked 14 m. together: then I had 4½ home.
Met the Queen out: & dined with her. Read Fauriel.[2]

12. 16 S. Trin.

Crathie [Presbyterian] Ch with H.M. at 12. Evening prayers in
Camerâ. A plan for meeting S. & the boys to have service in the
wood half way to Braemar was stopped by ceaseless rain. Saw Sir
T. Biddulph—Rev Dr Taylor[3]—and had an hour's conversation with
H.M. Read T.A. Kempis—Gasparin on Free Christianity—Maclear's
St Boniface.[4] Wrote to Abp of Canterbury—Bp of Oxford[5]—Abp
of York—Mr Gurdon—Mr Childers—Mr Helps—and minutes.

13. M.

Wrote to Mr Hammond—Dean of Windsor—Mr Gurdon—Sir T.
Biddulph—Ld Granville—Ald. Salomons—Mr Glyn—Mons. M.
Chevalier—Mr Maguire—C.G.—W.H.G.—and minutes. Wrote Mem.
on Irish Railways.[6] Read Fitzgibbon: truly a notable sign.[7] And the
very curious papers from Japan.[8] Much conversation in evg with
Prince Christian: who pleased me.

To M. CHEVALIER, 13 September 1869.　　　　　　Add MS 44537, f. 57.

I am very much indebted to you for your letter, & for the promised books.[9]
How to turn them to account I must consider well. The subject deserves a much

[1] H. Pemberton, *The history of Monaco, past and present* (1867).
[2] See 9 June 69.
[3] James *Taylor, 1813–92; minister and Scottish historian.
[4] G. F. Maclear, 'St. Boniface', from *Apostles of medieval Europe* (1869).
[5] Asking him if he might recommend him for Winchester: Add MS 44537, f. 56.
[6] Not found.
[7] G. *Fitzgibbon, *The land difficulty of Ireland, with an effort to solve it* (1869).
[8] Perhaps the accounts of consuls' journeys in *PP* 1868-9 lxiv. 297.
[9] Chevalier had sent 20v. of the Enquête Agricole; Add MS 44127, f. 33.

more thorough investigation than amidst the incessant pressure of official duties, I can give it.

At the present moment in particular it bears not only upon the Irish Land question, which will be the turning point of the Session of 70, but upon another question of great interest, the proposal to modify our present law of succession to land in the case of intestates.

In one way or another, I shall try to turn your goodness to account.

14. Tu.

Wrote to Ld Chancellor—Earl Nelson—Ld Westbury—Ld Granville (2)—Bp of Rochester—Mr Hammond—Mr Bazley—Mr Weld Blundell—Sir T. Biddulph—Ld Clarendon—C.G.—Mr Hammond & Tel.—and minutes. Wrote Mem. on the Creation of new Peerages.[1] Read Dix Hutton[2]—saw Hampton. Walk, amid showers. More conversation with Pce Christian. He seems to have an upright, penetrating, liberal mind.

To E. HAMMOND, 14 September 1869.   PRO FO 391/24.

The Queen is not very well today but I think she gave me sufficient authority to approve of your sending a complimentary message of acknowledgement to the Mikado of Japan. The terms may deserve some consideration. This opening of the door to friendly intercourse is an event of some importance. I do not in general like to encourage the resort of Foreign Sovereigns or their agents for light cause, since the mode of treating them is an embarrassing subject. But it would be a very good thing to have some intelligent Japanese here, & to use them liberally on the part of the country.[3]

15. Wed.

Wrote to Mr Fortescue—Sir S. Scott & Co—Duke of Argyll—Sir F. Rogers—Prince of Wales—Archbishop of Canterbury (2)—The Queen (& copy)—Ld Clarendon—Mr Cardwell—and minutes. Wrote a Mem. on Irish Land. Read Dix Hutton—Fauriel's Dante.[4] Royalties dined with *us* the 3d day running. Conversation on public Schools.

---

[1] In Ramm, I i. 55.
[2] H. Dix Hutton, *Proposals for the gradual creation of a farmer-proprietary in Ireland* (1868).
[3] Duke of Edinburgh's visit to Japan in August 1869; Japanese mission to Britain, August 1872.
[4] See 9 June 69.

To C. S. P. FORTESCUE, Irish secretary,   Carlingford MSS CP1/60.
15 September 1869. 'Private.'

I see from your letter and inclosures[1] that your mind has been going through a process which I too have to some extent undergone: and I heartily wish it were possible that you, Sullivan, & I could have some of those preliminary conversations on land, which were certainly of great use in the first stages of the Irish Church Bill. As this is difficult, let us try to compare notes as well as we can in writing.

Since our measure will involve difficulties of a kind that we had not to encounter in the case of the Irish Church Bill, and since it ought to be introduced on the very earliest day, I propose to call the Cabinet together not later than the 23rd or 25th October, or thereabouts, and then to appoint a Committee, of which the formation must be well considered, for the preparation of it. I anticipate that many members of the Cabinet will find it hard to extend their views to what the exigencies of the time, soberly considered, now require: but patience, prudence, and good feeling, will, I hope, surmount all obstacles.

I have been at work upon the subject for a short time, & I give you briefly what occurs to me on reading your letter.

1. Like you, I am unwilling to force a peasant proprietary into existence.

2. Yet I doubt whether in the Church Bill we might not properly have preferred the occupying tenant to the immediate lessee as a purchaser of Church lands.

3. I do not like to bring the Government into the Land Market as a buyer.

4. To get lands out of Mortmain would be very desirable, if there are any means short of compulsion by which we can promote it. A corporation is *almost* under a natural incapacity for the full discharge of the duties of a Landlord.

5. I can see much reason for introducing into Ireland the customary law of England. But, (a) if you enact that the Ulster Tenant Right shall become a legal custom, will this work, I mean as a practical rule in the Courts, and how? (b) the very recognition of the custom where it prevails will be *adverse* to its extension throughout Ireland?

6. The first point in this legislation, viz: that the presumption of law should give improvements to the tenant, is now, I suppose, very widely admitted, but no longer suffices to settle the question.

7. I read with pleasure your No 13. which is that the presumption of law shall be for a term not of twelve months, as now, but of (seven) years. But what are the difficulties attending this, to which you advert?

8. Could you send me the form in which the principle of compensation for improvements already made was adopted by the Aberdeen Government? The fact of such adoption is most important, and will weigh with several members of the Cabinet.

9. Now as to your 'compensation for disturbance'. This is indeed a question full of difficulty. It is very desirable to prevent using augmentation of rent as a method of eviction. I shall be most curious to see the means and provisions you may devise, without at present being too sanguine.

10. The part as to limited owners is perhaps the simplest portion of the whole.

11. Liberal Poor Law Relief to Tenants Evicted (otherwise than for non-payment of rent) seems to be a salutary provision.

12. You do not mention the Fitzgibbon pamphlet, which I have regarded as a very important sign of the times. I have arrived at no positive conclusion on his

---

[1] Fortescue's mem. of 13 September; Add MS 44121, f. 153.

plan; yet I lean to think it well worthy of consideration. Macarthy Downing's modification of it is, I think, outrageous as against the landlord: but, perhaps, a certain increment of 10 p.c., from the very beginning of the term of 31 years, might be fair. I dread binding men to pay something three years hence, as Fitz-gibbon suggests, & giving them fixed tenure in the meantime.

I will write in a day or two on the subject of Irish Railways, which will also be one hard to manage.

16. Th.

Wrote to Lord Mayor of L[ondon]—Abp Manning—Mr Acland—Chancr of Exr—Archdn Hale—Dean of Windsor—Mr Rawson—Bp of Chester—Mr Helps—The Queen, and copy: & Memm.—D. of Argyll—Ld Granville—Abp of Canterb.—W.B. Gurdon—Bp [Staley] of Honolulu—Mr Hammond—Ld Clarendon—C.G.—and minutes. Read Fauriel—Wendell Holmes, Autocrat of the breakfast Table[1]—Burton's Hist. of Scotland.[2] Walk with Col. & Mrs Ponsonby.

17. Fr.

Wrote to Mr Fortescue—Bp of Oxford—Abp of Canterb.—Miss Sellon—Sir Jas Clark[3]—The Lord Provost of Aberdeen[4]—Mr Dyce Nicoll[5]—and minutes. Read Ld A. Hervey's Charge of 1866—O'Brien on Irish Land[6]—Burton's Hist. of Scotland. Wrote on Irish Landlords. Dined with H.M. She was very gracious. Omnibus games on the billiard table afr. Walked to the Garrawalt.

Land Tenures in Ireland[7]	*Land Tenures in England*
1. Tradition & marks of conquest, & of forfeiture still subsist	1. They do not subsist.
2. Landlord does not find capital for improvement	2. Landlord finds capital for improvement
3. Landlord frequently absentee	3. Landlord rarely absentee
4. Landlords extensively object to leases	4. Landlords rarely object to leases.
5. In the parts of Ireland not under Tenant-right, the law which gives tenants improvements to landlord is rigidly construed & applied.	6. [*sc.* 5] The law which gives the tenants improvements to landlord is mitigated, and even in some cases reversed, by local custom.

[1] By O. Wendell *Holmes (1858).   [2] By J. H. *Burton, 7v. (1867-70).
[3] Sir James *Clark, 1788-1870, court physician.
[4] William Leslie, 1802-79; Aberdonian builder; provost 1869-73.
[5] James Dyce Nicol, 1805-72; liberal M.P. Kincardineshire from 1865; his d. involved diarist in the constituency, see 20 Nov. 72.
[6] Lord A. C. *Hervey, 'A charge delivered . . . in April 1866' (1866). J. T. *O'Brien, *The case of the established Church in Ireland* (1867).
[7] Initialled and dated in pencil, 17 September 1869, Add MS 44661, f. 50.

6. Landlord commonly (in the said parts of Ireland) differs from tenant in religion and politics.
7. Administration of justice, & local discharge of other public duties, not extensively entrusted to landlords, & not conducive to good relation with tenants.
8. Ireland occupier (yearly) holds by custom.

6. Landlord commonly agrees with tenant in religion & politics.
7. Administration of justice & local discharge of other public duties, generally entrusted to landlords, and highly conducive to good relations with tenants.
9. [*sc.* 8] England. By contract

To C. S. P. FORTESCUE, Irish secretary, 17 September 1869. 'Private.' Carlingford MSS CP1/69.

I send you herewith a paper, roughly drawn, which is intended to test, or make an approximation to testing the question, whether the Government can do more in the matter of Irish Railways.

Let us look for a moment at the 'situation'.

1. A number of Irish Peers, and members of Parliament, wholly without *controul*, over the Railway Companies, propose to us to buy them up.

2. The late Government, beginning, I fear, at the wrong end of the subject, appointed a Commission, which, without giving any opinion on the policy and principle, adjusted the details of a plan, and thus strengthened the hands of the irresponsible promoters of the scheme, without in the slightest degree strengthening the hands of the Government, either towards overcoming preliminary objections, or towards dealing with the vendors.

3. These vendors meantime astutely enough remain on the defensive, express no desire to deal with the Government, (except by asking for favours which bring no requital) & thus keep themselves in the very best position for exacting large terms.

4. To make matters better, some important members of the Cabinet—and I know not how many—objecting strongly to the purchase of the Railways in Ireland by the State, with a view to leasing them, have not shewn any inclination to ease the matter by a tertium quid.

5. It would be idle to act at all in the matter except to secure to Ireland the benefit of a *great* reduction of fares and rates. This will entail a large & certain loss, perhaps for a lengthened period. We can hardly ask England and Scotland to make a pure gift of the money. The movers, mentioned in No 1, offer an Irish Guarantee of a contingent character. When this contingent guarantee became actual, it would be held a grievance, and would become the subject of a new agitation and the clear prevision of this result would entirely prevent England and Scotland from accepting the Guarantee, or anything that was not in hand. Therefore without something in hand, against the expected loss, we cannot stir. If the loss is thought by Ireland not to be certain, we might provide that in the (highly improbable) event of its not accruing, a given annual payment shall be made from the Exchequer in aid of local rates in Ireland.

The 'consideration' proposed in my paper would, I apprehend, be a great administrative improvement. It is most important that Ireland should have an interest, & a sensible one in keeping down the charge of the Constabulary. My general conclusions then are, that the Government cannot take the initiative in the ordinary sense without getting into a false position; but that it might make a reasonable offer to Ireland: that means might be devised through which Ireland might signify its rejection or its assent: and that as a plan of the nature of that inclosed leaves the Railways independent, and free though subject to certain fixed conditions, it would not be unfair to ask the Cabinet to take it into consideration.

I did not in my last echo your words of friendly regret about Lady Palmerston, but I fully enter into them. The Queen has, I think, written to Lady Jocelyn.

18. Sat.

Wrote to the Queen (1)—with Mem. (2)[1] and copy—Abp of Canterb.—C.G.—Bp of Oxford—Ld Lyttelton—Mr Fothergill Cooke[2] —Mrs Thistlethwayte—Lady Derwentwater[3]—Mr E. Bowring—Dr A. Clarke—Bp of Winchester—S.E.G.—Rev. Mr Humble—S.R.G. —Ld Granville—Sir T.G.—Chancr of Exr—Ld Kintore—and minutes. Saw Sir T. Biddulph. Walk to the Garrawalt. Read 'Church Association' Report[4]—Burton's History of Scotland—And Sir James Clark's Memoirs of Dr Conolly.[5]—Mrs Th.s further supply of MS.[6]

19. 17 S. Trin.

Crathie Ch. mg. A singular sermon from Dr Wallace:[7] wh afforded much matter for conversation with Mr Duckworth & others. Afternoon prayers alone. Walk with a party to aftn tea at Lady Biddulph's. Saw Dr Wallace: a resolved Liberal, of rather wide scope! Wrote to Lord Clarendon—Rev Mr Hopwood[8]—Mr Bruce—Rev Mr Kinsman[9]—Sir J. Gray—Rev Dr Kynaston—Mr Fortescue—& minutes. Read Burton's Hist (Ch) of Scotland—Sumner's Consecration Sermon[10]—Thos a Kempis. Saw the Queen: & settled divers matters— Mr Liddon's Canonry (if open)—Ald. Salomon's Remainder—Palace Repairs Inquiry—Ayrton & Layard appointments.[11] She was exceed-

[1] On peers; see 14 Sept. 69.
[2] Offering knighthood to (Sir) William Fothergill *Cooke, 1806-79, for developing the telegraph.
[3] Amelia Matilda Mary Tudor Radcliffe, d. 1880, a Roman catholic, had asked Gladstone to further her claim to title of Countess of Derwentwater; he passed her on, see Add MS 44537, f. 65.
[4] Probably tracts from Ebury's Church Reform Association, for Prayer Book reform.
[5] Sir J. *Clark, A memoir of John Conolly (1869).   [6] See 2 July 69.
[7] Robert *Wallace, 1831-99, minister of Greyfriars, Edinburgh, 1868-76; ed. The Scotsman 1876-80; liberal M.P. E. Edinburgh from 1886.
[8] Probably Frank George Hopwood, rector of Winwick from 1855.
[9] Richard Byrn Kinsman, vicar of Tintagel 1851.
[10] G. H. Sumner, 'Peace. Christ's legacy to his Church' (1869).
[11] A. S. *Ayrton became first commissioner of works; *Layard, ambassador in Madrid; both contentious appts.

ingly easy and gracious. Dined with the Queen. NB. Prince Christian always comes to us afterwards.

20. M.

Wrote to Ld Clarendon—Chancr of Exr—Mr Maguire—Sir S. Scott & Co—Superior of Abn Sisterhood[1]—Dean of Windsor—Mr Austin —Ald. Salomons—Mr [W.] Jackson—Mr Hardman Earle[2]—Sir J. Ogilvy—Mr Cardwell—Abp of Canterb.—Mr Glyn—Mr B. Cochrane—C.G.—Rev Mr Hunt—& minutes. 14 mile walk to the Garrawalt & back by Geldie. 3¼ h.—To the falls 1 h. 14 m. Went round, as there was deerstalking. Read Burton's Hist. Scotland. Billiard table games in evg.

To J. F. MAGUIRE, M.P., 20 September 1869.   Add MS 44422, f. 54.
'Private.'

I have read the whole of the report[3] you kindly sent me, but I own it does not seem to me that your precept has yet been fully realised: 'the demand of the farmers while just & wise should be clear and distinct'.

I find the end in view described by different appellations, which, perhaps for want of knowledge, I am not well able to bring into harmony. Sometimes it is security: sometimes it is perpetuity: sometimes it is the Ulster tenant-right. Now I do not understand the Ulster tenant right to be perpetuity: nor can it well be, since it is apparently dependent on the will of the Landlord.

There is a question which I put to Sir John Gray some weeks ago: how—by what practical provisions—is the Ulster tenant-right, *talis qualis*, to be legalised: how is an adjustment, which I understand to depend upon the separate wills of three independent persons, to be put into such a shape as to be capable of being legally enforced? Is the outgoing tenant to have the right of saying to the landlord, I will not quit until your intending or incoming tenant pays to me such a sum as I think proper in respect of goodwill? If so, what is to prevent his demanding under the name of goodwill what in a free and open market would be paid to the Landlord as rent? Or is he to be restrained from doing so by resort to a tribunal, which is to determine how much is rent, and how much is goodwill? What rule is such a tribunal to adopt for defining goodwill—a thing totally separate from the value of tenants' improvements, which (I am now supposing) are admitted by all parties to belong in practice to the tenant. I find it difficult to obtain in my own mind a clear idea or sufficient test of this 'goodwill'. Understand, I beg you, that I am not now denying its existence, but I want a guide and a rule for appraising it. Good-will commonly arises from something in the nature of a legal or customary monopoly. I can comprehend that the pressure of demand for land in Ireland has created something of the kind. If so, then the

---

[1] Probably of St Margaret's [episcopalian] convent, Aberdeen.
[2] Offering a baronetcy to (Sir) Hardman Earle, 1792-1879, Liverpool merchant.
[3] Extracts from the Cork *Examiner* of 17 September 1869, reporting a tenant farmers' meeting in Cork; Add MS 44422, f. 40.

argument might work itself into a form something like this: that the disturbance of an occupier, depriving him of his immediate means of livelihood, and leaving him to the delays and chances of the wide world before he can find, and settle himself upon another holding, is a hardship upon him, even if he receives the value of his improvements. The mere interruption of the application of his labour, which is his chief capital, to the soil, it might be urged, requires compensation: that, in short, he has a title to something more than the value of his improvements. But I have never seen this defined to be the essence of the Ulster tenant-right. And, if it should be found on inquiry a thing fit to be recognised at all, would it not be better to attach to it some definite & certain, though only approximate measure in point of value, than to leave it to be determined by persons who would go to work with a bandage on their eyes, I mean with no uniform practical standard, & with no legislative light or aid?

To say that the Landlord's rent shall vary hereafter only according to the prices of produce as determined by a public authority, is not only to alter but, perhaps to destroy the relation between *landlord* and *tenant*, & to declare by law that the continuance of that relation is incompatible with justice, & with security to the tenant. Now such a principle, if sound, is no less applicable to England & Scotland, than it is to Ireland. It is therefore a principle essentially imperial: & the position of Ireland might not be very strong in the face of the world, if her agricultural population should commit itself to demanding the adoption of any rule which would fundamentally change the structure of society throughout the rural districts of the three countries, by placing the landlord substantially in the position of the proprietor of tithe commutation. Would not the case against the absentee, too, then become a very weak one indeed?

I think it possible that Sir John Gray (who has not answered me) may have taken my question about the Ulster custom as a merely controversial challenge. It was not so meant. In it, & in the whole of this letter, I am stating difficulties 'without prejudice', & without giving utterance to any final or binding opinion whatever: in order to see of what solutions, total or partial, these difficulties may admit.

I can suppose this argument to be made: that all the circumstances determining the relation of Landlord & tenant in Ireland, including even the law in its practical application, have been so different from those of the sister island, & that evils, acknowledged to exist by public authority, have been treated for a quarter of a century with such obstinate neglect, that Extraordinary measures must now be adopted for the remedy of an inveterate mischief. This is a broad proposition. But supposing it to be admitted; supposing, therefore, it were found necessary in Ireland to introduce into the law some provisions more restrictive of *liberty of contract* than are in force on this side of the channel, or than are in themselves desirable, still would there not remain strong arguments in favour of stopping short of any permanent & fundamental change in the landlord's position; perhaps even of inquiring whether a temporary character could be imparted to such of the remedial enactments as could fairly be called exceptional?

You will, I hope, take this letter simply as indicative first of my confidence and regard, secondly of my earnest desire to be informed; and in conclusion I think you are right in saying that the Govt. ought not to deprive itself of the advantage which the discussions of this recess, especially in Ireland, may afford them.[1]

---

[1] Maguire's lengthy reply gave rather 'the *impressions* of my own mind in reference to the topics you suggest, than formally dealt with them'; Add MS 44422, f. 137.

21. Tu.

Wrote to Ld Clarendon (2)—Abp Manning—T.D. Acland—Ld Fortescue—Sir S. Adair[1]—Mr Hamilton—Ld Spencer (2)—Mr Cardwell
—Bp Hinds—S.E.G.—C.G.—and minutes. Read Law of Patronage
in Scotland[2]—Burton's History. Went out shooting. Billiard table
Games in evg.

To E. CARDWELL, war secretary,   PRO 30/48/6, ff. 103, 127.
21 September 1869.

I forgot last night[3] to notice your reference to me on Irish Land.

I am too much given to the note of superlative and you never err in it. Nevertheless in the balancing of words I would not at this moment say 'the strictest
regard' to rights of property. Were I choosing for myself I think I should say 'a
careful regard to the security of property and of the just rights belonging to it'
or something of that kind.

I wish though I can hardly think you may be able to follow closely what is
going on in Ireland at this moment.[4] There is a wild agitation for laws which as
I understand them would destroy the relation of landlord and tenant. There is an
opinion among a more sober class of old land law reformers that you cannot
now restore confidence & get rid of the question by compensation for improvements, and that in a country like Ireland that does not really cover the loss and
hardship attending on eviction. There is an extensive desire for extending the
Ulster tenant right & giving it the force of law which does not seem to have
developed itself into any perfectly distinct meaning. Lastly there are singular
manifestations of Concession from among the landlord & Conservative class. By
all means read Fitzgibbon's pamphlet on the Land Question in Ireland.[5]

22. Wed.

Wrote to Ld Chancellor—Ld Chichester—Bp of Oxford (2)—Ld
Clarendon—Dr Playfair—Ld Granville—W.H. Lyttelton—Mr
Ellice—G.G. Glyn—Sir Thos G.—C.G.—The Queen (and draft)—
and minutes many. But one hour for walking. Dined with the Queen.
Conversation on Irish Land with Col. P[onsonby] & Dr Robertson.[6]
Called on Dr Taylor. Read Burton's Hist.—M'Combie on Irish Land.[7]

[1] Sir Robert Alexander Shafto Adair, 1811–86; 2nd bart. 1869; cr. Baron Waveney
1873; wrote on Ireland. Had requested a peerage, Add MS 44422, f. 38.

[2] By 'a member of the Established Church' (1869).

[3] PRO 30/48/6, f. 101 on treasury appointments.

[4] Cardwell was due to speak at Oxford at the end of the month; see Steele, *Irish Land*,
130.

[5] See 13 Sept. 69.

[6] Possibly William Robertson, physician.

[7] W. McCombie, 'The Irish land question . . . in a letter to . . . Gladstone' (1869); copy
in NLS.

Sent in my recommns for the 3 Bprics wh have been my daily & nightly thought.[1]

23. Th.

Wrote to Ld Clarendon—Col. Greville Nugent—Ld Spencer—Dean of Windsor—C.G.—W.B. Gurdon—Lord Mayor—and minutes. Pr. Xtn brought his boy[2] to pay me a visit. A beautiful mountain walk with Mr Duckworth. Closing audience of the Queen, very gracious & kind. Much conversation with Pr. Christian. Read Burton's Hist Scotl. —Sir W. Jenner's Lectures.[3] Read Burns. Sat to Taylor Photogr.

To A. W. F. GREVILLE-NUGENT, M.P.,   Add MS 44537, f. 70.
23 September 1869. 'Private.'

I shall send to [the] Lord Lieutenant [the] letter[4] I have just received from you, but [the] question of F[enian] P[risoners] is assuming such an aspect that it will probably be necessary to have [the] judgment of Cabinet upon it.[5]

Without denying that there is weight in your reasoning, I would observe: 1. That the revival of agrarian crime is practically though not logically a bar so far as it goes in the way of leniency. 2. That I have tried to obtain from some who recommend the release their own individual belief as to the future good conduct of those now imprisoned, but with a very limited measure of success. 3. That [the] case of soldier prisoners appears to involve a special difficulty.

24. Fr.

Wrote to Ld Clarendon—The Queen (and copy)—Rev. Dr Esdaile[6] —Sir J. Gray—Ld Spencer—Mr Childers—Rev. Mr Scott—Mr Gurdon—Sir R. Murchison—Mr Glyn—Bp of Lincoln—C.G.— E. Hammond—Lady Camperdown:[7] & minutes. Sixty two letters to dispose of this day! Drive to Linn of Quoich. Dined with the Biddulphs. Read pamphlets.

---

[1] S. *Wilberforce to Winchester; J: F. *Mackarness to Oxford; Lord A. C. *Hervey to Bath and Wells; F. *Temple to Exeter; the last caused a storm, Temple having contributed to *Essays and Reviews* (1860).

[2] Christian Victor, b. 1867.

[3] Sir W. *Jenner, probably *The practical medicine of today; two addresses* (1869).

[4] Resolutions from Longford, to which Gladstone also sent a formal acknowledgement; Add MS 44537, f. 70.

[5] See 5 Nov. 69.

[6] Probably David Esdaile, Biblical geographer.

[7] Juliana Cavendish, *née* Philips, widow of 2nd earl of Camperdown; she d. 1898. See 27 Sept. 69.

25. Sat. [Fasque]

Wrote to Chancr of Exr—Mayor of Waterford[1]—Lady Churchill—
The Queen—Ld Clarendon—Mr Glyn—E. Hammond—Mr Hil-
yard[2]—Lady Herbert—and many minutes. Read H. Jones Perfect
Man[3]—Lambert on Irish Land[4]—Steward's Memoirs.[5] Left Balmoral
at 10. Walked over the Cairnmount from Banchory Station.

To Bridge of Feuch	55 m[inutes]
To Bridge of Dye	..... 68 m
To the top	..... 65 m
To Clattering Brig.	...... 27 m
15 miles	.... 215 m

Then I most unexpectedly met the two L[ouisa]s who had kindly
come in the carriage. A family party, very good & homelike, at Fasque.
Also a great Post!

To LORD CLARENDON, foreign secretary,   Clarendon MSS, c. 498.
25 September 1869.

The *number* of 47 Candidates for the Gazette may not be remarkable but the
quality is. I take it there are few among them whom it would not be creditable
to appoint. Glyn has taken the sifting in hand.[6]
You will be amused by the inclosed from Sir J. Gray. It is rather impudent.
The Ulster tenant right is doubtless very imperfect. Yet probably the best
thing would be to legalise and extend it, if only this were possible. I have puzzled
& puzzled over it & cannot for the life of me see how it is to be legalized without being essentially changed. It is like trying in Algebra to solve a problem of
two unknown quantities with only one equation. The problem before us is more
difficult than that of last year which was pretty well too [sic] for that.
Before you receive this you will have had a reply from Mr West. But I own I
think that to promise to make no loan *abroad* would be a pure evasion. The
Porte ought to be satisfied with your suggestion about new & augmented Taxes
& I think it will be difficult for the French to go further because they have committed themselves as to the interpretation of the Firman of 67?

26. 18 S.Trin.

Wrote to Dean of Windsor—The Viceroy—and minutes. Saw Mr
Foxton—Lady H. Forbes—Ld Clinton. Chapel mg & aftn very

---

[1] Henry Francis Slattery; business untraced.
[2] Perhaps Temple Hillyard, canon of Chester.
[3] H. Jones, *The perfect man, or Jesus as an example of godly life* (1869).
[4] J. Lambert, *Agricultural suggestions to the proprietors and peasantry of Ireland*
(1845), or his report, see Steele, *Irish Land*, 137.
[5] *Memoir of G. S[teward]* (1868).
[6] Clarendon had written on honours and criticising extending tenant right southwards;
Add MS 44134, f. 35.

satisfactory. Walk with Tom: also with him & L[ouisa]. Read Steward's Life—In Memoriam Sermons.[1]

27. M. [*Camperdown House, Forfarshire*]

Wrote to Lord Advocate—Ld Clarendon—Ld Granville—Sir C. Locock—Mr Humble[2]—Mr Fortescue—Mr Gurdon—Mr Duckworth—C.G.—Mr Cardwell—Rev Dr Carr[3]—and minutes. Conversation, & walk with L: observing the improvements: also examined with much admiration Mary's works as a painter. Missed Lady Harriet [Forbes]. Read Fauriel.[4] Left Laurencekirk at 4.15. Reached Camperdown[5] at 8.30. Most kindly received. Conversations with Mr Jowett[6]—and Lord C.

28. Tu.

Wrote to Bp of Oxford (2)—Dean of Windsor—Dr Temple—Lord A. Hervey—Mr Glyn—Mr Mackarness—Mr Gurdon—Mr Macmillan—Mr Towneley[7]—Rev Mr Walters,[8] and minutes. Walk about the place, in pouring rain, with Ld C. & Mr Eason.[9] Also surveyed the house, wh has some very beautiful objects, like all great houses (nearly) in this country. Conversation with Lord C. about H. of Lords: with Mr Jowett about Oxford. Read Fauriel—Mrs Graham's Mystifications.[10]

29. St Michael. [*Carlisle*]

Attended service at St Ninian's in Perth & heard Provost Fortescue,[11] a remarkable preacher. Left Camperdown at 8½ AM. Awaited C. at Perth until 7 P.M. Then at 7.30 with C & the girls to Carlisle at 1.15. Of all the people in the stations those of Perth were the most enthusiastic. Wrote to Sol. Gen Scotland—Mr Fortescue—H. Glynne—Ld Clarendon—Mr Hammond—Col. Ponsonby—Mr Lambert—

[1] Probably of bp. H. *Phillpotts who d. September 1869.
[2] Henry Humble, canon of St. Ninian's, Perth.
[3] Probably Edward Carr, Ll.D., curate in St. Helen's.   [4] See 9 June 69.
[5] Seat near Dundee of 3rd earl of Camperdown (see 14 Dec. 65), an important whig influence in E. Scotland.
[6] On Ireland; see E. Abbott and L. Campbell, *Life of Jowett* (1897), i. 406.
[7] Charles Watson Townley, 1824-93, unsuccessfully offering him a post; Add MS 44537, f. 76; see 9 Dec. 73.
[8] Probably Henry Littlejohn Master Walters, 1819?-98; then unbeneficed; curate of Monkswood 1877; author.
[9] David Easson, Camperdown's factor.
[10] C. S. *Graham, *Mystifications* (4th ed. 1869).
[11] See 16 Jan. 53. He was now provost of St. Ninian's, Perth.

and minutes. Walked out to Scone Palace and saw the place. Finished 'Mystifications'. Read Fauriel.

30. Thurs. [*Hawarden*]

Up at 7½. Off at 8.45. Saw Wilson Patten, on Irish Land Question, at Warrington: where we had luncheon with him. We reached Hawarden at 3 P.M. Went to work on my letters. Wrote to Lord A. Hervey—Mr Gurdon—Bp of Oxford—and minutes. Read Fauriel. Thistlethwayte MS.[1]

Friday Oct One. 1869.

Chapel 8½ A.M. Wrote to Mr Macmillan—Mr Fortescue—Ld Granville—Chancr of Exr—Ld Halifax—Ld Aylesbury—The Queen—Lord Advocate—Mr Rawson—Lady Gladstone—Ld Russell—M. Chevalier—Mrs Thistlethwayte—and minutes. Saw Mr Burnett. Read Fauriel. Began the slow patient process of reducing letters papers &c. into order.

To C. S. P. FORTESCUE, Irish secretary,   Add MS 44121, f. 184.
1 October 1869.

I have read with much interest your letter of the 28th.[2]

My letters from London do not lead me at all to reduce my estimate of the difficulties which inhere in this subject.

Your extract from Mr Hancock seems in one part of it (not quite consistent, as I read it with what precedes) to throw some new light upon the question. He proposes to employ arbitration; not upon rent, but upon the compensation due to the outgoing tenants at the old rent, where he & the landlord cannot agree. You say it should be at a fair rent. I suppose the meaning of both probably to be at the old rent with a reservation of the right of the landlord to show that, apart from tenants' improvements, the land had been underlet. I hope this will be well turned about & sifted to see whether it will hold water. If it will, we shall have made some way. What I say next assumes it to be done.

The case we have to provide for is, I suppose, that of a tenant at will or for a short term, either under a notice to quit not grounded on non-payment of rent, or required to pay an increase of rent, which he is not willing to undertake under his actual tenure.

Now, for argument's sake, how would such a proposal as this answer: to give to such a tenant the following *options* a. to proceed by the Ulster Custom, as stated above, in the extract from Mr Hancock. This could only be available where that custom prevails? b. to require to have his improvements valued, and to receive the amount *together with* 20?/15? per cent thereupon for disturbance. c. to claim a lease of 31 years upon undertaking to pay his old rent together with

[1] See 2 July 69.
[2] Add MS 44121, f. 178; Steele, *Irish Land*, 146.

[five or ten] per cent in addition. Possibly with one repetition at the close of the lease, on a further & similar covenant of increase in rent. I do not enter upon details: but I would observe

1. It is a great matter to avoid multiplying the occasions for arbitration, & to maintain definiteness & simplicity of procedure.

2. Such a proposal embodies your principle of compensation for disturbance, and gives it an absolutely definite form without raising any new question in the particular case.

3. It does nothing for the *unimproving* tenant, except to offer him by (c) the opportunity of becoming an *improving* tenant.

4. It adopts the principle of Fitzgibbon: but gets rid of all the complication of specifying & registering improvements beforehand, & of inspecting to see whether they are properly executed. Surely the increased rent is the sufficient & proper test.

If, however, (c) were adopted, it would be necessary to have a provision for the landlord to prove that his land is actually in its present state underlet: & to prevent scourging or neglecting the farm towards the end of the lease.

Now supposing a tenant did not choose to adopt any covenant for the future, & had no improvements to be valued, should we be bound to do more for him than doubly invert the presumption of the law, by enacting that in the absence of contract, improvements should be deemed to belong to the landlord, & that the tenancy should be presumed to be for (four) years.

There are a number of points passed by: but the suggestion I have put goes to the heart of the problem.

2. Sat.

Ch. 8½ A.M. Wrote to Princess Christian—Telegram to Mr Gurdon—Ld Granville—Dr Temple—Ld A. Hervey—Mr Gurdon—Mr Mackarness—Mr Vivian—Bp of Oxford—Lady Llanover—Mr A.R. Clark[1]—Mr S.B. Lamb[2]—Ld Clarendon—Ld de Grey—Archdn Jacob[3]—Mr Acland—Archbp of Canterbury—W.H.G.—Solr General—Bp of Oxford—The Queen (& Memorandum)—and minutes. Also to Princess Christian—Sir T. Fremantle—Telegram to Ld Grosvenor. Saw Mr Austin—Stephen returned. Read Fauriel—Pope's Eloisa &c.[4]

To EARL DE GREY, lord president, 2 October 1869.　　　Add MS 43513, f. 272.

It would, I suppose, be very desirable that we should avail ourselves of some *early* occasion on our gathering in London to lay the foundation stone of our

[1] Andrew Rutherford Clark, 1828–99; advocate; Scottish solicitor general October 1869–74.

[2] Samuel Blackman Lamb, London solicitor, sent his views on land tenure; Add MS 44422, f. 91.

[3] Philip Jacob, 1803–84; archdeacon of Winchester from 1860.

[4] See 30 July 55.

Education measure in England. It might, I presume, immediately follow Bruce's return from Balmoral, & I hope that Forster will then be on the ground.[1]
  I trust we shall not unduly restrict your holiday by the coming Cabinets.

3. 19 S. Trin.

Ch. 11 AM with H.C. and [blank] In consequence of the death of the Bp of Carlisle, a perturbed Sunday.[2] Telegram to Mr Gurdon—Tel. to Lord A. Hervey—Wrote to Bp of Chester—Bp of Oxford—Abp of York—Mrs Goalen—Bp of Gloucester—Rev. Mr Harman—The Queen—Lord A. Hervey & minutes. Copied out Verses of 1838 for Lady Blantyre after reading them & giving them to C. to read. Read Spranger Acct of Election of Bishops[3]—Ramsgate Tracts[4]—Divers Sermons.

4. M.

Chapel 8½ AM. Wrote to Ld Chancellor (Telegr.)—Lady Blantyre—Ld Granville—Abp of Canterb.—Louey G.—Queen (Mem.)—Mr Melly MP.—Mr Onslow MP.—Mr Gurdon (2)—Rev. D. Robertson—Sir T. Biddulph—Lady Ailesbury—Ld Kinnaird—The Queen (and copy)—Postmaster of Chester—and minutes. Walk with Stephen: inspection of the Old Castle. Read Fauriel—Pope's Poems. Worked in evg on papers & accts a little. Agnes returned: a great joy after 3 mo. of separation.

5. Tu.

Ch. 8½ AM. Wrote to The Lord Chancellor—Ld Granville (3)—Mr Gurdon—Mr Hamilton—Mr Glyn—Mr W. Cowper—Dr Mayo—Mrs Thistlethwayte—The Queen (and copy)—Ld Clarendon—Mr Young—Sir J. Simpson—and minutes. Read Fauriel—Pope: Imitations &c. Mess[enge]r from London on New Zealand affairs.[5] A fresh supply of Mrs T.s MS: XI-XIII. The tale is told with great modesty, & its aspect is truthful though not quite coherent.

6. Wed.

Ch. 8½ AM. Wrote to Princess Christian—Dean of Windsor—Dean Ramsay—Bp of Oxford—Ld Clarendon—Mr Kinnaird—Ld

[1] See 5 Nov. 69.   [2] H. *Goodwin succeeded him.
[3] R. J. Spranger, 'Report on the Catholic mode of electing bishops' (1869).
[4] By Thomas *Scott, freethinker; see 15 May 55.
[5] Draft dispatch confirming withdrawal of British troops; see Ramm I, i. 58, 65.

Dufferin—Mr Mackarness—Mr Delane—Ld Lyttelton—Bp of Moray—Sir T. Fremantle—Mr Brand—and minutes. Saw Mr Burnett on private affairs—& on Irish Land. Read Pope—Fauriel— Tracts on Canadian Indepce. Saw the Waterses. Jane W. lived a pure life and died a holy death.

To LORD CLARENDON, foreign secretary,   Clarendon MSS, c. 498.
6 October 1869.

I do not like putting on paper, sometimes, words which could be spoken with perfect freedom; for they look ugly, on paper, when they partake even gently of objurgation. But as you ask it, you shall have *all* that I can say against your speech about Irish Land.[1] It does not come to much. I think that between 'wild spoliation' & 'felonious', your *gros mots*, so to call them were not unfairly balanced. But it also seems to me that though justified probably in the abstract, each goes rather beyond strict justice, regard being had to the history of the Land question in Ireland. And further, though with no dogmatic assertion, my feeling is that the circumstances are extremely delicate. That it is impossible to say at this moment whether our difficulties will arise most on the landlord side (where thus far they have lain) or on the other side—and that in these circumstances the safety of the Government lies in a great reserve, and, when an occasion arises which forces or requires speech of some kind, in the use of mild & general phrases. I am not a believer in the doctrine that it is easy to put down the course of feelings widely & energetically entertained by declarations beforehand from the Executive as to matters of legislation, between which & matters of law & public peace I distinguish broadly. My rule of silence would hold in full force, until we knew our own mind as a Government, & could *tune* our language to it with precision.

And now I think I have discharged all my venom. I am pleased by your asking me to do it. It is a sign of the relations which always have prevailed and if it be not *my* fault always will prevail, between us. And now I must end with two admissions. First that I think my objection to *gros mots* arises from my having sometimes sinned in employing them. 'He best can paint them who has *used* them most', and secondly that I do not think any real harm has been done. Finally I stipulate that you shall believe what is the truth, viz. that I have made a clean breast of it.

I thought Elliot seemed now to have got the affair of the Khedive on its right footing.

You are so kind as to ask us to the Grove. My wife will not be with us on my first visit to London. But if you will let me run down with you I shall gladly do it.

Our first Cabinet I think should be given to you—as you will have to recite the progress, or history at least, of several interesting questions.

The appointment of Dr. Temple I expect will make a little noise; but it is right. Rutherford Clark will be Sol. Gen. for Scotland.

---

[1] *Clarendon to Gladstone, 5 October 1869, Add MS 44134, f. 50, on his speech: 'I have a sort of notion, tho I can't say why, that you disapprove of what I said—pray tell me frankly if I am right or wrong by instinct.' Clarendon had denounced tenant right legislation by letter on 28 September; ibid., f. 39.

To J. T. DELANE, 6 October 1869.   Add MS 44537, f. 84.

Perhaps you would kindly as an act of justice to the Bp. of Oxford insert the enclosed paragraph or something like it in the Times.[1] He moves certainly not for lucre, but more from pluck & for power. The Cabinet will probably meet on the 26th & when I come up for it I should much like to see you on Irish Land Laws. Any error committed by the Govt. on that subject would in all likelihood be irremediable.

7. Th.

Ch. 8½ AM. Wrote to Bp of Sodor & Man—Sir W. Tite MP.—Mr West—Chancr of Exchr—Robn G.—Lord Advocate—J. Watson—Mr Hammond—S.E.G.—Mrs Thistlethwayte—and minutes. Replaced (after the alterations) some 500 to 600 Volumes. Called on Mr Barnes & paid a cottage visit. Walk with C. Read Fauriel—Remarks on Butt.[2]

8. Fr.

Ch. 8½ AM. Wrote to The Viceroy of Ireland—Ld Clarendon—Mr West—Ld Granville—S.E.G.—Ld Dalhousie—Mr Cornish—and minutes. Wrote Mem. on Irish Land. Read Fauriel—Pope.

To LORD CLARENDON, foreign secretary,   Add MS 44537, f. 88.
8 October 1869.

1. I do not see how in *reason* the case between Sultan & Khedive could stand better than it stands after the recent discovery. The status quo, coupled with the declaration on both sides of adherence to the Firmans, the promise of the Viceroy as to arms & Ironclads and the disclaimer of the Sultan about Egyptian Finance[3] appears to afford a most sound basis for a present accommodation, & it is to be hoped that both parties will have had a lesson. If you have reason to believe in any underhand intentions at Paris, that is a serious fact.
2. I send on West's letter to H.M.
3. I am desirous to prepare a draft reply about the Fenians, and I should be very glad if you could get me quickly the reply to the question whether the amnestied French had in any case been committed for overt acts of force against the supreme authority—so far as a reply can be had at all.[4]

---

[1] Para. on Wilberforce's salary, *The Times*, 8 October 1869, 7a.
[2] Not found.
[3] Clarendon to Gladstone, 5 October 1869, Add MS 44134, f. 50: 'The Sultan however has given up his claim to overhaul the Budget or interfere with the financial administn. of Egypt.'
[4] Clarendon sent a reply from the French minister on 15 October; Add MS 44134, f. 64.

9. Sat.

Ch. 8½ A.M. Wrote to Att.Gen. for Ireland—Sir T. Tancred—Dr Pusey—Mr Fortescue—Mr Gurdon—Chancr of Exchr—Mr Kirk MP.—Mr V. Fitzgerald—Ld A. Hervey—Col. Kingscote—Mr G. Moore[1]—Bp of Oxford—Dr Allon—Ld Clarendon (2)—The Queen —Bp of Oxford—and minutes. Worked further on Irish Land. Walk with Abp of York: & much conversation on Eccl. Legislation. Saw Mr Glyn on Irish Land—Mr A. Kinnaird on Irish & also on Church affairs. Read Fauriel—'Vorwort' to Der Papst und das Concil: a mighty document.[2] Thank God for it.

To C. S. P. FORTESCUE, Irish secretary,   Add MS 44537, f. 88.
9 October 1869.

1. As regards Fenians you will find that a letter of mine to the Viceroy[3] has crossed yours.
2. As regards land, I have been working upon your thoughts & my own & upon all I can collect from various quarters: & I think the question seems to open by degrees. I am disposed to lay before you for consideration the following three propositions which are in memo 1. within. In memo 2. will be found a series of proposed provisions as a kind of rough first outline to serve at any rate to draw the matter to a head.
3. I keep the Police report you have sent me for the present: the other inclosure is returned. I think it may be assumed that Irish business need not be taken on the 26th.

10. 20 S.Trin.

Ch. 11 A.M. and 6½ P.M. Wrote to Dean [Goodwin] of Ely (offering Carlisle)—Mr [E.] Austin (offering Honiton)—Dr Döllinger (on the book)—Ld Clarendon—Dr Pusey—Archdn Philpotts—Mrs Lane[4] —Rev. Mr Galton—Mr West—Mr S. Lawley—The Queen (Mem.) —& minutes. Conversation with A. Kinnaird. Read Der Papst &c.— Ramsgate Tracts.[5]

To J. J. I. von DÖLLINGER, 10 October 1869.   Add MS 44140, f. 270.[6]

I read last night the preface to 'Der Papst und das Concil, von Janus'. I have almost by default lost the right to address you at all: and my exercise of it is

---

[1] George *Moore, 1806-76; lace manufacturer and philanthropist.
[2] *Der Papst und das Concil. Von Janus* [i.e. J. J. I. von Döllinger, assisted by J. Friedrich and J. N. Huber] (1869), supposed by many at first to be by Acton.
[3] Add MS 44306, f. 154, requesting details of arguments on Fenians' release.
[4] Had described virtues of Ven. J. Sandford; Add MS 44537, f. 90.
[5] See 3 Oct. 69.
[6] Typed copy, apparently from the holograph; secretary's copy in Add MS 44537, f. 91.

further questionable when I am about to assume that you are the author of that preface. If you are not, then I am happy to think that there must be two men in Germany who could have written one of the weightiest & most noteworthy documents that has met my eye for many a day.

You will, I am sure, believe that I do not write this in the meanness of a sectarian spirit. Who can wish otherwise than well to the Church in which so many Christians live & die? If we lament, protest, or disapprove, our desire must be to see lessened or removed that which we may think gives just cause for such words or feelings. With all that tends to bring her nearer or to keep her near, to what is best in her, I profoundly sympathise. Against all that tends to curtail & disfigure within her borders the common inheritance of the Christian faith, I claim to feel not a speculative nor a random but a deep & sorrowful indignation. From a ground such as this I offer to you heartfelt thanks; & earnestly desire you may have strength given you for what is a noble & gallant, & what need not be because it seems to us an unequal effort.

The week I passed chiefly in your society in Munich, 24 years ago,[1] still lives in my grateful memory. And no public cares will prevent me from watching with an intense eagerness all that may now befall you, as far as I can learn it from the journals, from casual sources or from our friend Sir J. Acton.

Not insensible of the weight of the reasons urged in the last paragraph of the preface, I nevertheless plead guilty to entertaining the fear that the forceful[2] statements which the book may contain will fail to *gain* adequate attention so long as they remain anonymous. But if you shortly find there is 'a more excellent way' you are not I presume debarred from pursuing it.

May the *Curia Romana* prove to be other than Dante thought it, & other than what now for many years it has been trying to be with consequences so disastrous to the hopes of those who desire that knowledge & liberty should ever abide in holy unison with Reason[3] & Faith.

To E. B. PUSEY, 10 October 1869.   Add MS 44537, f. 90.

Since I wrote yesterday I have seen a very well informed person[4] who entirely confirms me with respect to Dr. Temple & says 1. There was no formal Editorship of Essays & Reviews.
2. Parker (J.W.) the publisher got up the book.
3. If assisted he was probably assisted by Jowett.
4. Dr. Temple simply sent an essay which he had previously *preached* in nearly the same form at Oxford without attracting notice. This you will be glad if as it appears to be it is the truth. I hope you have got Döllinger's reputed work 'Der Papst und das Concil'. I am profoundly struck by the preface the only part I have yet read. May the arrow reach the mark.

11. M.

Ch. 8½ A.M. Wrote to Mrs Thistlethwayte——D. of Argyll——Mr Gurdon——Ld Granville——Dr Hitchman——Mr Samuelson——Sir R. Murchison——& minutes. Conversation with Kinnaird, on Church & other

---

[1] See 30 Sept. 45.   [2] Typed copy in Add MS 44140, f. 271 reads 'powerful'.
[3] Typed copy reads 'Reverence'.   [4] Probably A. Kinnaird.

matters—With Glyn—Walk with do. Dinner party in evg. Read Der Papst. Worked on arranging books.

To the DUKE OF ARGYLL, Indian secretary,   Add MS 44537, f. 92.
11 October 1869.

I am so sorry you could not come here, but I hope you left Lady Percy going on well. I quite agree with you about Dufferin:[1] & before the close of the Session I proposed to Granville the question whether we might not associate with us both him & Bessborough in the question of Irish Land. I think I may write & ask him whether he can be in London at the end of this month. In the affirmative part therefore of your letter I agree: but without any disparagement to C. F[ortescue] whose views on Irish questions I have generally found thoroughly intelligent, liberal & *mild*? Sorry you are out at elbows in India. There is a good deal of noise about Temple. I am glad you like the batch.

12. Tu.

Ch. 8½ A.M. Glyn, who goes each morning, said to me 'this is thoroughly good for mind & body'. Wrote to Chancr of Exchr (2)—Ld Clarendon—Mr C. Howard—Mr Cardwell—The Queen—Mr Tomlinson[2]—Mr West—Mr Darbishire—Ld Granville—Mr Griffiths—Rev Mr Harvey—Sir Thos Bateson—and minutes. Willy & I cut our first tree for the season. Political conversations with Glyn. Dinner party. Read Der Papst. Examined the Parker Photographs.[3]

13. Wed.

Ch. 8½ A.M. Wrote to Lord Clarendon (3)—Lord Russell—Mr Ayrton[4]—Lord Dufferin—Mr Bright—Mr Hamilton—Mr West—Mr R.A. Ogilvie—Dr Temple—Ld Shaftesbury—Mr Locke King—Mr Kinnaird—Dr Pusey—Mr W. Cowper—Mr Hamilton (Telegr.)—and minutes. Tree cutting in aftn. Preparing answer respecting the Fenians: upon a draft from Ireland.[5] Whist in evg. Read Der Papst.

[1] Argyll wrote on 10 October, Add MS 44101, f. 71: 'I am very anxious you should take Dufferin (as much as you can) into council about Irish Land . . . he is sensitive about his position (not in the Cabinet) . . . and I look upon him as a far superior animal to Ch: Fortescue.'

[2] George Dodgson Tomlinson of Huddersfield; on a portrait of chancellors of the exchequer; Add MS 44537, f. 93.

[3] Of Roman antiquities, by J. H. *Parker, privately circulated; see *The Guardian*, 24 Nov. 1869, 1318.

[4] Offering him the Office of Works to resolve his incompatibility in the Treasury with *Lowe; Add MS 44422, f. 168.

[5] See 18 Oct. 69; draft by *Fortescue, in Add MS 44611, f. 81, by Gladstone in Add MS 44422, f. 216.

To J. BRIGHT, president of the board of trade,   Add MS 43385, f. 46.
13 October 1869.

1. The time has come when an answer must be made to the applications from Ireland for the release of the Fenian Prisoners. I had wished to bring the matter before the Cabinet but it is desirable to act soon and as far as I can learn the feeling of our Colleagues is without exception against the release. I have looked with anxiety for grounds sufficient to warrant it. The strongest ground in its favour is one put to me by my son who has just come back from Ireland & who urges that it would soften the popular feeling and facilitate the passing of a moderate Land Bill. But I cannot resist the sense of the Irish Executive, composed as you know of liberally minded & upright men: their objection is strong & they are answerable for the peace of the country & the working of the law. If I hear that you dissent and would desire to have the judgment of the Cabinet I shall postpone any step until we meet. In that case only I would beg you to telegraph to me tomorrow or Friday at the *Grosvenor Hotel Chester*, 'Suspend reply.'
2. I have worked a great deal on Irish Land and am gradually licking my ideas of a Bill into shape as is Fortescue. I find however that daily consideration suggests daily fillings in: but as soon as I can get something at all fit for your eye I shall send it.
3. It seems to me also most desirable to frame some rational basis of a policy upon Irish Railways. Politically it would be most difficult to stand upon the ample & absolute *non possumus*. On the other hand I know much objection is taken to State purchase. It seems to me possible to frame a plan which shall either do great good to Ireland or at the very worst silence objectors and acquit us of responsibility. I am sure you will give to any such plan a fair hearing.[1]

To LORD DUFFERIN, 13 October 1869.   Add MS 44537, f. 96.

There will be a Cabinet on the 26th & I expect to remain in London till the 10th of Nov. Are you likely to be there at that period?[2] I am naturally desirous to confer with you about Irish Land. This individually I might have attempted sooner; but I wish also if it can be managed to make your knowledge & experience more fully available than they could be through me for the benefit of the whole Government with reference to the great & difficult question of Irish Land. With united kind regards to Lady Dufferin. [PS] Anything from you in the interval will not fail to have my best attention.

14. Th. [Chester]

Ch. 8½ AM. Wrote to The Queen (& Mem.)—Mr Fortescue—Mr Maguire—Mr K. Digby MP.—Mr West—Sir E. Watkin—Bp of Man —Mr Hamilton—and minutes. Worked a little on Homer. Read Der Papst. Reached Chester at 5 PM. for the reception of the Prince of Wales with whom I had a good deal of conversation. We met him at the station. A great dinner at the Grosvenor [Hotel].[3] Saw Sir Watkin respecting Welsh Bishops. Saw the Bishop.

[1] See 16 Oct. 69.   [2] Dufferin agreed to come to London; Add MS 44151, f. 62.
[3] *The Times*, 15 October 1869, 9f.

To C. S. P. FORTESCUE, Irish secretary,　　　　　Add MS 44537, f. 97.
14 October 1869.

1. The amendment I wish to make in my paper is to meet the case of undevpt. lands in the hands of present tenants: & I should put in that in these cases no right to a lease for present tenant should accrue except at the full rent. Also that the landlord might at his option place his land under Ulster Tenant right, as defined by the Act.
2. I think some *months* have elapsed since I asked for a summary account of the Chief provisions of Irish Land Bills, but I have not received it. Will you kindly have it looked to. They must raise a variety of points requiring consideration. I enclose a letter from Maguire about the Fenian prisoners. Your notes of conversation are most interesting: will you kindly let me have a copy.

My son brings back from Ireland a hopeful view of the Land question.

15. Fr.

Wrote to Mrs Thistlethwayte—Ld Clarendon (2)—Dr Temple— Lady Herbert—Mr Parker—Ld Granville—Bp of Ely—Mr Roberts —Mr West—Scotts—& minutes. After a great breakfast the Addresses: opening of Town hall which I went over: visit to the Cathedral. Then the dejeuner: followed by a drive to Eaton. Another great dinner: & lastly the Ball.[1] Saw Sir Sydney Cotton[2]—Lord Ebury—& others. Read N.Brit.Rev. on Irish Land—and on Juventus Mundi.[3]

To LORD CLARENDON, foreign secretary,　　　　Add MS 44537, f. 98.
15 October 1869.

1. I will cause search to be made for the Lambert letter; *personally* I have not had it back.
2. I have had this morning & have read Nubar Pasha's explanatory note of October 1. To propose formally to the Porte the *status quo* would be in terms hardly compatible with its dignity, but in substance I do not see how Nubar's paper can be answered. The conflict of assertions between Sultan & Khedive does not admit I suppose of a trenchant solution even against the latter.
3. Dean Hoare states truly that I have been unable to recognise Irish disestablishment as a reason for an Hibernian invasion of English preferment. But further, the selection of an individual would probably gratify him & vex a score of rivals.
　　There are two Irish Clergymen whose claims on the Govt. stand out—Brady, as a Pioneer: Stopford, as a perfect master of the subject, with whom we had the great advantage of testing all our points as we went along.
4. I should judge that Motley will not remain long in England.[4] His own Government are in the act of giving him a slap in the face by withdrawing from him the Alabama question which he came to settle. It will be difficult for him to bear this without real disparagement.

[1] *The Times*, 16 October 1869, 9d.
[2] Sir Sydney John *Cotton, 1792-1874, soldier.　　　　[3] See next day.
[4] Clarendon this day sent a report of an interview with J. L. Motley, already partly disavowed by the U.S. government; Add MS 44134, f. 64.

5. I shall much lament Latour especially if followed by Drougin.

6. We are in the midst of the Prince of Wales Festivities, & I am preparing the negative answer about the Fenians. I wish that the Land legislation may prosper enough to allow us to let the vagabonds go before another 12 month is over.

16. Sat. [Hawarden]

Wrote to Lord Amberley[1]—Bp of Oxford—Mrs Malcolm—Mr Fortescue—Ld Nelson—The Qu. (& Mem)—Dr Pusey—Chancr of Exr —Ld Russell—Mr Mackarness—Mr Bright—Mr Wetherell—Mr Burnett—and minutes. Saw the Dean of Ely—Mr Roberts (R. Dee Co.). Further conversation with the Prince of W. & saw him off. Read Dublin Rev. on Irish Land[2] &c. Returned to Hawarden at 1. Mr E. Ashley came. Again considered, corrected, & sent off, my reply in the Fenian case.

To J. BRIGHT, president of the board of trade,   Add MS 43385, f. 49.
16 October 1869.

I told the P. of W. this morning at Chester the purport of your views about the Fenians,[3] and I have also written it to the Queen. I like so much the mode of expression that I must try to crib some of it for my reply now on the anvil.

Caird's views seem just but I look for his practical proposals, and particularly for what as at present advised I find the hardest part of the subject namely the mode of dealing with the Ulster Tenant right. I hope you may not think Fortescue, or me (when I am in a condition to send you anything) too revolutionary. The subject gives me much employment daily.

To C. S. P. FORTESCUE, Irish secretary,   Carlingford MSS CP 1/64.
16 October 1869.

I send you herewith my letter signed. As you would not be satisfied without a rap at the Fenians I inserted a passage of that kind: but I feel afraid to mention 'the constitution' as I suppose that the word has but a cold & hollow sound in the ears of the Irish people.

I send this letter that you may be enabled to dispatch it at once if you see fit: or may return it for further correction should you find cause.[4]

I have put in a new passage principally taken from a letter of Bright's heartily

[1] Gladstone and *Glyn planned (fruitlessly) to fill *Layard's vacant seat at Southwark with Lord Amberley; Gladstone to *Russell, 14 October 1869, Add MS 44537, f. 94. A split liberal vote lost the seat to the tories on 17 February 1870.

[2] [J. C. Hoey], Dublin Review, xiii. 443 (October 1869).

[3] In Bright to Gladstone, 15 October 1869, Add MS 44112, f. 95: 'In a reply to the memorials, the language should be soothing but firm . . . to release the prisoners immediately after the meetings and menaces in Ireland would be to prostrate the Govt. at the feet of the movement.'

[4] Fortescue criticized the draft as 'too general' and too concessionary; Add MS 44121, f. 204.

adopting the refusal. He is very moderate indeed about land: shocked at Fitz-gibbon.

The Chester festivities were brilliant & the visit most successful.

We shall I believe have no Commissionship of Customs to give.

Abp. of Canterbury, Bps. of London, Oxford, Ely, Worcester have written warm & kind letters to Dr Temple: also the son of the late Bishop.

[P.S.] I send a mem. of my son's after a recent visit to Ireland—please to return it.[1]

To T. F. WETHERELL, 16 October 1869.   Add MS 44537, f. 101.

I thank you very much for your number[2] & I hope it may have a prosperous career. The Irish land article seems to me mild & useful but perhaps not quite equal to the occasion: the one on my book judicial & kind.[3] As respects Land you will have another opportunity. May it be *only* one other! If we can we shall introduce our Bill by the middle of Feby. I hope tonight to make myself more largely acquainted with the Number.

17. 21 S. Trin.

Ch 11 AM. and H.C.—Prudentially kept the House afterwards as I had a threatening last night. Wrote to Mr A. Kinnaird—Mr Fortescue —Ld Mayor—Bp of Ely—& minutes. Read the Six first of Dr Temple's Sermons, with edification.[4] Bp Hare's Letter on the Study of H. Scripture,[5] and Der Papst u. das Concil. Conversation with Mr Ashley on the Hunter case in Ireland.[6]

18. M. St Luke.

Agnes's birthday: also Lady H. Forbes's: and (as I learn today) Mrs Th—so God bless them all. Rose at one. Wrote to Archbp of York —Mr Fortescue—Mr M. O'Connell—The Speaker—Dr Temple— Mr Layard—Mrs Thistlethwayte—Ld Granville—Corp. Dublin[7] —and minutes. Also once more corrected, and dispatched direct, my letter respecting the Fenian prisoners.[8] Read Q.R. on Irish Ch—On

[1] Not found.

[2] Of the *North British Review*, li (October 1869), Add MS 44422, f. 186; Thomas Frederick Wetherell, 1830-1908, a liberal catholic, its ed. 1869-71.

[3] G. Sigerson on land, G. A. Simcox on *Juventus Mundi.*

[4] See 6 Oct. 61.

[5] F. *Hare, 'The difficulties and discouragements which attend the study of the Scriptures' (1714).

[6] Murder of James Hunter, landowner; first agrarian murder in Mayo 'in living memory'; *The Times*, 31 September 1869 etc.

[7] Letter on Irish legislation in *Daily Telegraph*, 22 October 1869.

[8] Declining to release the Fenian leaders, recalling the Irish Church Act, and suggesting further Irish legislation; in *The Times*, 23 October 1869, 5d.

Convocation Policy.[1] Saw Mrs Stroud[2] on her affairs—Mr Burnett
on the Dundas property—Mr Webb.

To LORD CLARENDON, foreign secretary,   Add MS 44537, f. 102.
18 October 1869.

1. Layard wrote me a very kind letter nearly in the same sense.[3] He is certainly
a very strong as well as a very accomplished man, tho there is a screw loose in
him for House of Commons operations.
2. Your goodness has not been without fruit: for Ayrton (beyond my expectation) is in raptures; & Lowe I make no doubt will jump, as they say, out of his
skin.[4]
3. I have read today the very curious paper called Fuad's Testament.[5] The pec-
cant part of it is, *me judice*, his view of his Greek fellow-subjects. I am glad to
see there was a sentiment stirred up in Greece upon the first inkling of the
meditated stroke.
   As to Turkey, would not a federal system, or rather a quasi-federal one, be
more practicable & hopeful than the one of purely unitarian centralisation?
4. I am afraid Derby's day must at last be come—if so, Peace be with him.
[P.S.] Bright wrote me an excellent letter about the Fenians, my answer, negative of course, goes today.

To C. S. P. FORTESCUE, Irish secretary,   Carlingford MSS CP1/65.
18 October 1869.

1. Criticism cannot be too lively and wakeful in a case like that of the Fenian
letter.[6] I have struck out 'reluctant' and taken the substance I think of all your
remarks. The letter goes tonight direct: & I shall through London answer at once
the Address of the Dublin Corporation, and shall send them a copy of this letter.
I am glad you humanely suggested a mitigation of the sonorous anti-Fenian
sentence.
2. Thinking further over the Irish Land it occurs to me that to avoid needless
disturbances we might throw the larger occupants at once upon the future law,
and restrict the exceptional provisions in regard to present occupants to tenancies
under (£100?) per ann., or whatever best marks the line at which landlords who
find capital, and tenants who have really been able to hold their own, may be
considered to come in.
3. I have not the Irish Church Act by me: but the Quarterly says that in Clause
2 we speak of the said 'Irish Church'. If so, this is a curious slip of the pen,
which you may remember we took some pains to avoid.
4. Will Friday 29th suit you for an Irish Cabinet?

[1] *Quarterly Review*, cxxvii. 493 (October 1869).
[2] Unidentified; in the household? See 12 Feb. 70.
[3] Accepting Madrid; Add MS 44422, f. 158.
[4] *Clarendon had asked Gladstone to approve a letter to the treasury on expenditure;
Add MS 44134, f. 69. See 21 Oct. 69. Ayrton moved to the Office of Works, see 13 Oct. 69n.
[5] Fuad Mahomet Pasha, 1814–69, Turkish statesman, left vast palace and curious memoirs.
[6] Fortescue criticised the draft as 'too general'; Add MS 44121, f. 204.

19. Tu.

Ch. 8½ A.M. The letter of yesterday from Mrs Th. caused me to ruminate in a maze. But I believe all is right with her. Wrote to Mr Fortescue—Chancr of Exr—Ld Granville—Ld Clarendon Three letters[1] —Mr Bruce—Sir W. Knollys—Ld Grosvenor—Mr Hugessen—The Queen—Lady Gladstone—Sir W. Tite—Mr E. Ellice—Mr Cardwell (Tel)—and minutes. Read Q.R. on Water Supply—Janus (Eng. Transl.)[2]—Bennett & Froude on Ch. & St.[3] Cut down a tree, with W. The Murrays came.

To H. A. BRUCE, home secretary, 19 October 1869.   Aberdare MSS.

I have received your letter,[4] & I return the inclosure. My official letter refusing the release of the Fenians (I had heard your opinion through Glyn) went to Limerick last night & it will probably be known in Dublin tomorrow morning. The knowledge of our decision may alter the attitude of those who have projected the meeting for Sunday & the course you have to take.

As matters now stand, I can only say I quite agree in your view: to provide for public order, & to let the excitement (which *may* be even less than now) spend itself at once. Should the Police report to you a probability of disturbance, of course the matter will wear a different aspect.

20. Wed.

Ch. 8½ A.M. Wrote to Mr Fortescue—Ld Mayor—Bp of London— Ld Granville—Mr Acland—Mr Cardwell—Ld Bury—Solr General —Mr D. Jones—Mrs Thistlethwayte—and minutes. A letter from Mrs T. much wounded disturbed me. I have a horror of giving inner pain to a woman. Conversation with Sir C. Murray—with Agnes respecting Stephy—with Sir G. Prevôt respecting Dr Temple. Read M'Knight on Ulster Tenant Right[5]—Divorce for Desertion.[6] Treecutting with Willy.

To DANIEL JONES, 20 October 1869.   Add MS 44537, f. 106.

I thank you for your good wishes in respect to my present & future happiness: & I regret to find that the interruption of your employment thro' an

---

[1] On consuls, Antonelli, and *Hammond's salary; Add MS 44537, f. 104.
[2] See 9 Oct. 69.
[3] R. H. *Froude, ed. W. J. E. Bennett, *State interference in matters spiritual* (1869).
[4] Bruce to Gladstone, 17 October 1869, Add MS 44086, f. 42: the Fenians 'have no immediate object beyond preparation for any emergency they might deem favourable— a foreign war, or any strong domestic discontents, would probably bring them into mischievous activity'; Bruce's letter summarised police reports.
[5] J. MacKnight, 'The Ulster Tenant's claim of right . . . In a letter to Lord John Russell' (1848).
[6] Untraced.

accident has apparently placed you in difficulties.[1] The only means which have been placed in my power of 'raising the wages of colliers' has been by endeavouring to beat down all those restrictions upon trade which tend to reduce the price to be obtained for the product of their labour, & to lower as much as may be the taxes on the commodities which they may require for use or for consumption. Beyond this I look to the forethought not yet so widely diffused in this country as in Scotland & in some foreign lands; & I need not remind you that in order to facilitate its exercise the Govt. have been empowered by Legislation to become through the Dept. of the P.O. the receivers & guardians of savings. Should you wish to lay before me any more particular statement, perhaps you could kindly accompany with a reference. You are at liberty to make as much use of this letter as you may think fit.

21. Th.

Ch. 8½ AM. Wrote to Mrs Thistlethwayte (but with no power of sending)—Ld Clarendon (2)—Mr Childers—Mr Fortescue—Ld Fermoy—Chancr of Exr—Mr Bruce—Sir W. Farquhar—Sir T. Bazley—Mr Hildyard—and minutes. The Dean [Wellesley] of Windsor came. Conversation with him. Also with his charming & admirable wife. Also with Sir C. Murray. Woodcutting. Read M'Knight on Ulster Tenant R. Worked on corrections of Homer for 2d Edn.[2] Music in evg.

To LORD CLARENDON, foreign secretary,   Clarendon MSS, c. 498.
21 October 1869.

The dispatch from Fish to Motley[3] appears to me in its general strain a most offensive document. Its operative portions in the last two paragraphs happily do not correspond and seem to give you with regard to the course of proceeding they suggest a position of great advantage in reply. It is idle I imagine to make the general statements of the dispatch the subject of a diplomatic correspondence, if indeed it be written to serve any other purpose than as a tub to the whale for Motley and Sumner. They only show how necessary it is to have the case brought before some third person for trial. But on the whole I suppose the two paragraphs are really the dispatch and the rest the *bunkum*.

To C. S. P. FORTESCUE, Irish secretary,   Add MS 44537, f. 109.
21 October 1869.

1. I will do all in my power to promote your wishes about Irish business. But I do not think you can safely reckon on obtaining the definitive approbation of the Cabinet for any land tenures plan at its Oct. sitting. The distance between cup & lip is in this case considerable. The first part of the operation will in this

---

[1] Letter of 18 October from Jones, of Newcastle-under-Lyme, reporting his plight, in Hawn P.
[2] Of *Juventus Mundi* (25 January 1870).
[3] Of 25 September 1869; see Cook, *The Alabama Claims*, 119.

case be by no means the least delicate. I may reckon on seeing you in London I hope the day before the Cabinet. Shall it be Friday or Thursday? The Cabinet will I daresay be in a condition to give its opinion on Lowe's plan. 2. Perhaps you may like to see the enclosed letter from Mr. Glyn Senr. 3. I also send one from Ld. Fermoy. You will I daresay give what despatch you can to any meditated changes in the treatment of political prisoners as such.

To R. LOWE, chancellor of the exchequer,   Add MS 44301, f. 98.
21 October 1869.

There has come to me from the F.O. an unfinished correspondence with the Treasury, which I am sure we should all wish to prevent from growing into a departmental controversy. I send the papers herewith, including a proposed draft from the F.O. to know whether you see any difficulty in acquiescing in it. It seems to me that the Treasury would go beyond its proper province if it were to require Ld. Clarendon to state his reasons. It is a matter of enquiring: *primâ facie* there is nothing unreasonable or unprecedented, but the reverse. The amount is small & the arrangement does not appear otherwise than economical, & the For. Min. having deliberately considered the matter, I think may fairly ask compliance without a re-trial on the merits.[1]

22. Fr.

Ch. 8½ A.M. Wrote again to Mrs Thistlethwayte, from whom came touching, but bewildering, letters. Wrote also to Mr Fortescue—Mr Macmillan—Mr Ashley—Mast. of Balliol—The Queen (Mem.)— and minutes. Also Telegr. to Priv. Secretary. Tree cutting. Read M'Knight on Ulster Tenant Right. Worked on Juv. Mundi—Saw Sir G. Prevost respecting Dr T[emple]—Dean of Windsor—Sir C. Murray.

23. Sat.

Ch. 8½ AM. Wrote to Mrs Thistlethwayte—Sir T. Biddulph—Bp of Ely—Ld Stratford de R.—Mr Butt[2]—Ld Clarendon—Mr Glyn— Mr Morrison MP.—Rev D. Moore—Mr Acland and minutes. Walk with the Dean of Windsor. Finished M'Knight. Read Shee on Irish Land.[3] Conversation and arr. with Mr Burnett about the Dundas

---

[1] Lowe was objecting to secretaries of state pre-empting expenditure by announcements, 'in vague language which conveys no information', of proposed expenditure which the treasury could not then challenge; Lowe to Gladstone, 27 October 1869, Add MS 44301, f. 100. See 18 Oct. 69.

[2] Declining to release Fenians; Add MS 44537, f. 112, printed in *The Times*, 27 October 1869, 8.

[3] Sir W. Shee, *Papers, letters and speeches in the House of Commons on the Irish land question* (1863).

property for which I have been bold enough to offer £57000. If I have an ambition, it is to make an Estate for my children.[1]

To LORD CLARENDON, foreign secretary,   Clarendon MSS, c. 498.
23 October 1869.

I am pleased to find my impressions[2] of the American paper confirmed by your more acute perceptions.[3] The tone is *Sumnerian*: it is impossible to say any thing worse about it. Still, reflection makes me take a hopeful view of it. I do think all that rhetoric may be meant to shield the Govt., and pay off Motley with moonshine. I will even go further, & state for your judgment what occurred to me. It is idle, as you say, to reargue with that dispatch. But they ask for a proposal. Now we cannot with honour, I conceive, make a proposal, & I imagine you will be obliged in some shape to say this. But, in saying it, might you not (so as to save them from the difficulty of owning themselves wrong) glance at a method of proceeding and as it were put words into their mouth, which they might then take up Viz. such a method as this: that the two countries should set about the consideration of a good prospective system, & should thereafter, in the light of principles thus elucidated, reconsider the manner of arbitration, or any other mode of proceeding in the Alabama case. Might not something be hammered out of this?

I am not very suspicious in general: but query was Motley the *author* of the Fish dispatch, and has this privilege of a free pen been granted as a solace for being ousted from the real duties of his office?

24. 22 S.Trin.

Ch. 11 A.M. and 6½ P.M. Wrote to Abp of Canterbury—Mr Fortescue (2)—Ld Granville—Sir W. Knollys—Mr Bruce—Ld Stanley—Mr Gurdon—Prince of Wales—and minutes. A Lyttelton walk. Read Temple's Sermons—Ffoulkes's Second Letter: weak enough[4]—Abp Manning's Pastoral Letter.[5] Conversation with Sir G. Prevost.

25. M.

Ch. 8½ AM. Wrote to Mrs Thistlethwayte. Narrative and letters taken together I am indeed astonished, though interested, & bound in honour to do the best I can for her if she really needs it. Wrote also to Ld Clarendon—Mr M'Millan—Mr Cardwell—Mr Fortescue—Mr E. Ashley—Abp Manning—Mr M'Clure[6]—Ld Chancellor—Lord

---

[1] The Aston Hall estate, bought for £57,000 from Charles A. W. D. Dundas, November 1869. See above, introduction, section X.   [2] See 21 Oct. 69.

[3] Clarendon to Gladstone, 23 October, Add MS 44134, f. 80, reporting impressions of Russell, W. V. Harcourt, M. Bernard, on the dispatch: 'each answered in the same tone of indignation'.   [4] E. S. Ffoulkes, 'The Roman Index . . . a second letter to Manning' (1869).

[5] See 25 Oct. 69.

[6] (Sir) Thomas McClure, 1806-93; liberal M.P. Belfast 1868-74, Londonderry 1878-85.

Clinton—Lord Houghton—Mr West—Mr Morris—Ld Devon—
and minutes. Finished corrections for 2d Ed. *Juventus Mundi.*[1] Read
Manning's Pastoral Letter. Conversation with the Dean of Windsor on
Church and Clergy.

To LORD CLARENDON, foreign secretary,   Clarendon MSS, c. 498.
25 October 1869.

In this interesting letter of Thornton's (Oct. 12)[2] I cannot help reading Fish's
account of his dispatch to Motley as confirmatory of my rather sanguine view
of it. Thornton was no doubt right in giving a very limited answer off his own
hook, when Fish asked him whether we could express our regret. But I suppose
we must all admit that, even if we come out as I hope we may legally irresponsible, the neglect on the spot & the general miscarriage, in the case of the Alabama, must form for us matter of serious & enduring regret. Indeed for our own
sake we have to regret having been simply made fools of by the device of the
trial trip.

Enough until tomorrow when you will have your budget for us. My notion is
that some four or five Cabinets dispersed over the next fortnight will suffice for
the present & we may resume in Decr.

To ARCHBISHOP H. E. MANNING,   Add MS 44537, f. 114.
25 October 1869.

Expect me Wednesday at 4 in York Place.[3] I have to thank you for your pastoral
letter which came yesterday & which I am reading. Would to God that the personal feelings which will I trust ever subsist between us, were not accompanied
at least on my side, by a painful apprehension of an increasing divergence, & an
approach of the state of things in which what is to the mind of one the salvation
of Faith & Church is to the mind of the other their destruction. I seek relief in
writing myself ever affecty. yours.

I have been obliged to write a second letter about the Fenians on account of
an *argumentum ad hominem* about the Neapolitan Prisoners.

26. Tu. [*London*]

Off at 8¼. Wrote to Hon & Rev. E. Bligh[4]—Ld Strafford—Canon
Dale—Bp of Ely—Ld Devon—The Queen—Mr Morris—Euston at
2.30. Went to Scotts. D. St at 3. Saw Granville. Cabinet 3¼-5¾. Dined
at Mr Glyn's: with him & Granville talked over many subjects. Not

[1] See 21 Oct. 69.
[2] Clarendon MSS c. 480; Fish desired 'no recrimination' for his 'strong statement' in his
despatch to Motley.
[3] Meeting at Manning's request; Add MS 44249, f. 103.
[4] Edward Veysey Bligh, 1829-1924; br. of 6th earl of Darnley; vicar of Birling; on the
*Temple appt. row; in *The Guardian*, 3 Nov. 1869, 1215.

least, Willy's possible appointment.[1] Read Levy on Irish Land[2]—
... on do. Saw Hamilton X. Saw S.E.G. on Dr Temple & W.E.G.

Cabinet 26 Oct. 69.[3]
1. Foreign Office. a. Egypt & Turkey. French interprn. commun[icate]d & discussed. Fleet to go to the opening of the [Suez] Canal.
   b. U.S. & England. Heads of answer to Motley read: Abbot's
   Mem. to be printed for C.[4]
   c. U.S. & Spain. Recital.
2. Canada. Letter from Sir J. Young respecting apprehended Fenian raid.
2. Increase of the Episcopacy. Invite the Abp. to a Conference.[5]
3. Legislation for 1870.
4. Appointment of Scotch Judges. Lowe to inquire.
5. Question of proceeding against the Irishman for instigation to murder. Wait
for Irish Govt. to move us: Cabinet not disposed to initiative.[6]
4. [*sic*] Series of Cabinets. sketched.
5. Who will attend the Lord Mayor's feast? Agreed on.

27. Wed.

Wrote to Ld Clarendon (2)—Ld de Grey—Mr Fortescue—W.H.G.
—Mr Cardwell—Ld Lyttelton—Sir T. Biddulph—Mr Aldis—Mr
Childers (2)—Mrs Thistlethwayte—Mr Kinnaird—Ld Russell—Bp
of Oxford—Mr Delane—Sir F. Doyle—and minutes. Saw Conclave
on Conveyance of Royal Family Charges—Ld Granville & Mr Bright
(on Irish Land)—Ld Dufferin—Mr Glyn—Chancr of Exr—Mr
Nash—Sir T. Bazley—Mr West—Mrs J. Tyler—Mr Gurdon—Abp
Manning (in York Pl.).[7] Dined with the Wests. Worked late.

To LORD CLARENDON, foreign secretary,   Add MS 44537, f. 117.
27 October 1869.

I have your letter of today[8] with the French dispatch, on the question of the
Khedive, and surveying the language of it as a whole I have also had an opportunity of showing it to Granville, and to Bright, and we all agree that in the
language in which it is couched it may be supported: Bright adding a strong
reservation of his general principles, with much good humour.

---

[1] Gazetted as a junior lord of the treasury on 2 November 1869.
[2] Perhaps an untraced article by L. *Levi.
[3] Add MS 44637, f. 102. On Hawarden Castle notepaper.
[4] C. S. A. Abbott's mem. of 23 Oct. 1869 on Fish's 'rhetorical' despatch to Motley, 25
Sept. 1869; F.O.C.P. 1712.
[5] See 3 Nov. 69.
[6] The Hunter case? See 17 Oct. 69.
[7] See 25 Oct. 69.
[8] Add MS 44134, f. 83.

To EARL DE GREY, lord president,   Add MS 43513, f. 279.
27 October 1869.

Archbishop Manning, desirous to speak to you on the subject of Education, has asked me for an introduction which I readily give through the medium of this note. He requires no photographing. You will probably hear from him.

Very many thanks for your kind gift from the proceeds of the Harris forest.

To C. S. P. FORTESCUE, Irish secretary,   Add MS 44537, f. 117.
27 October 1869.

Do you think you can bring Sullivan with you to England to our meeting here on Friday (quite confidential) to stay over Saturday & come to the Cabinet. I hope he may be able to do it, & I understood he could. Of course the object is Irish Land on which we are now about to break ground. Say 2.30 pm.

I write in haste & postpone yours of yesterday.[1] I send a note of Portsmouth's to Granville which is well worth reading.

28. Th. St Simon & St Jude.

Today the first Bishop recommended by me is consecrated. May the richness of all holy gifts be given him.

Wrote to Mrs Thistlethwayte: in great gravity of spirit. Duty and evil temptation are there before me, on the right & left. But I firmly believe in her words 'holy' and 'pure', & in her cleaving to God.

Wrote to Abp of Canterbury—Abp Manning—Messrs G. & Co—Ld Clarendon—Robn G.—Rev. Dr Temple—The Queen: minutes as usual: and Mrs Thistlethwayte. C.G. came. We dined at Mr Glyn's. Mary also came, to see Dr Gull.[2] Saw Mr Fowler (C.E.)—Capt Helbert—Mr Bright—Mr Hom. Cox—Mr Glyn—Mr Childers—Mr E. Watkins—Mr Ouvry. Read M'Millan on Juv. Mundi.

To LORD CLARENDON, foreign secretary,   Add MS 44537, f. 120.
28 October 1869.

Having read Mr. Abbott's able paper I now answer you on Mr. Hammond's draft. In respect to details please see my notes in pencil on the margin. They are very few. On greater matters First, are we to reply to Fish or not? I shall cheerfully abide by the decision of the majority. The slight inclination of my mind is to reply, but to separate the retrospective from the prospective part, and to deal with it slightly later & in a separate form. If it is not to be dealt with, I have no comments to make upon all that part of the draft. But I still hold to the view I imperfectly tried to express on Tuesday. We want to make it easy not difficult for Fish to answer us on the practical part. By saying you throw the initiative on us, we throw it back upon you, we make it very difficult indeed. Why not expand

[1] On filling the Irish Rolls, Add MS 44121, f. 229.
[2] (Sir) William Withey *Gull, 1816-90; royal physician; cr. bart. 1872 for role in curing Prince of Wales 1871.

some such thought as this. True you throw upon us the initiative which we cannot honourably assume, but if it be true that you told Mr. Thornton as in the telegram, your words contain the outline of a basis on which we think it might be possible to proceed. There may be objections to this but I do not perceive them. In this way, if Fish desires to proceed, we can do it easily without dispute. If he does not, he cannot tell his people that we threw difficulties in his way.

29. Fr.

Wrote to Dean of Lichfield—Mr Macmillan—Sir Sydney Cotton—Mr J. Pittock[1]—Mr D. Lange—Rev Mr [R.] Burgess—Mr Cardwell—Rev Mr Moncreiff—Chancr of Exr—Ld Granville—W.H.G.—Ld Spencer[2]—The Queen—Dean Atkins—Sir Thos G.—and minutes. Saw Mr Childers—Mr Glyn—Ld Granville. $2\frac{1}{2}$-$4\frac{3}{4}$. Conclave on Irish Land: Ld G. Mr Bright & Mr Fortescue. Dined with Mr Glyn. Read Caird on Irish Land.[3]

30. Sat.

Wrote to Mr Burnett—Mr J. Watson—Ld Clarendon—Ld Bessborough—Sir C. Murray—Mr Kinnaird—The Queen (2)—Abp of Canterb.—Bp of Oxford—Mr B. Primrose—Ld Chancellor—Ld Shaftesbury—and minutes. Saw Mr Glyn—Att. General for Ireland—Ld Clarendon—Mr Brand—Ld Chancellor—Ld de Grey. Cabinet 2-$5\frac{1}{2}$. Dined with the de Greys. We broke ground very satisfactorily on the question of Irish Land.

Cabinet. Oct. 30. 69.[4]
1. Answer to Memorial of Church Association respecting Dr. Temple.[5]
2. Irish Land. Att. Gen. for Ireland explained his views fully & they were discussed.[6]
3. Episcopal conference Thurs.[7] 3 P.M.: Ld. Granville—Ld. Chancellor—Mr. Cardwell & W.E.G.

---

[1] Of Deal; had sent a gift; Add MS 44537, f. 121.
[2] Urging *Spencer that *Sullivan should not be appt. a judge: 'To carry a Land Bill without a lawyer who knows his subject, & commands the House is such an aggravation of difficulty, as I am loath to face'; Add MS 44537, f. 122.
[3] Sir J. *Caird, *The Irish land question* (1869).
[4] Add MS 44637, f. 104.
[5] Protests against *Temple's election as bp. of Exeter are in Add MS 44422, f. 271 ff.
[6] See Steele, *Irish Land*, 202.
[7] In fact 3 Nov. 69.

31. 23 S. Trin.

Chapel Royal mg and All Saints Evg. Dined at Mr Glyn's. Read Langdon on Ch. movement in Italy:[1] Cobb's Separation not Schism.[2] Saw Mr Glyn—Lord R. Cavendish—Dowager Duchess of Somerset —Dr A. Clark. Wrote to the Lord Chancellor. A pleasant conversation with Harry on his future profession.[3]

Mond. N.1. 69. All Saints.

$10\frac{1}{2}$–$12\frac{3}{4}$ All Saints Ch. where Mr Body preached: very notable.[4] Wrote to Mrs Thistlethwayte—Archbp of York—W.H.G.—Mr Estcourt—Mr Cardwell—and minutes. Saw Mr Fortescue—Mr Sullivan—Mr Delane—Mr Glyn (2)—Mr Cardwell. Party in evg to see School at the P. of Wales's Theatre.[5] Read Irish Land Tracts.

2. Tu.

Wrote to Mr Cardwell—Mr Ouvry—Mr Bruce—The Queen—and minutes. Conclave on Irish Railways Mr Bright Mr C. & Mr F. $2\frac{1}{2}$–$4\frac{1}{2}$. Saw Mr Hunt *cum* Mr Fowler—Mr Thompson (Irish Land)—Sir J. Lacaita—Mr Glyn—Duke of Argyll—Mr Knollys—Mrs Curtis. Dined at Mr West's: an active evening there with Granville and Glyn. Saw Gordon. Read Dufferin on Irish Land.

3. Wed.

Wrote to Mr Fortescue—Archbishop of Canterbury—Mrs Thistlethwayte—Mr Talbot—Ld Dufferin—Dr Kirby—The Queen (2) —Mr Ayrton—and minutes. Dined at Mr Glyn's: more business with him and Granville. Cabinet $2\frac{3}{4}$–$6\frac{1}{4}$. Chiefly on Irish Land: and stiff. Episcopal Conference 12–$1\frac{1}{4}$. Saw Bp of Oxford—Ld Granville *cum* Mr Fortescue—Mr Glyn. Read Brown's Laws affecting R. Catholics.[6]

---

[1] W. C. Langdon, *Some account of the Catholic Reform movement in the Italian Church* (1868).
[2] G. F. *Cobb, ' "Separation" not "Schism". A plea for the position of Anglican reunionists' (1869).
[3] As a merchant.
[4] Probably Elihu Edmund Body, vicar of Wonersh.
[5] 'School' by T. W. Robertson.
[6] By J. B. Brown (1813).

Cabinet Nov. 3.69.[1]

1. Reported result of Episcopal Conference. Cabinet authorised First Lord to acquaint the Archbishop that they will not decline to proceed upon the Act of Henry VIII.[2]
2. Clarendon's answer to Mr. Fish's dispatch to Motley. Revised & sanctioned.
3. Lavradio's inquiry about Portugal. Decline any answer to hypothetical question.
4. Discussion on the Irish Land Tenures. Five questions as to tenancies at will.[3]
5. Determined not to distribute any more Russian guns.

To LORD DUFFERIN, 3 November 1869.   Add MS 44537, f. 125.

I have read your paper on Irish Land Tenures, & am very glad to find a great community of view between you & most of those with whom I have exchanged ideas on that most difficult subject, though the apparent differences, & the real differences of form may be considerable. You have not quite drawn your plan in such a way as to enable me to judge to what extent you would seek to alter a memorandum which Fortescue has drawn. In form his is an *extension* of Tenant right (though fully admitting of accompanying arrangements for its extinction) but the main aim is to give effect to principles which seem to me to correspond with yours.

Those who walk as far in company as you & Fortescue are not I think likely to part for the rest of the road.

4. Th.

Wrote to Mrs Thistlethwayte—Ld Granville (2)—Ld Spencer—Sir R. Palmer—Ld Russell—Ld Clarendon—J. Watson—Ld de Grey —Mr S. Storey[4]—and minutes. Dined at Mr Glyn's. Read . . . on Telegraphs. Saw Ld A. Hervey—Mr Fortescue—Sir D. Salomons —Mr Glyn—Mr Goschen—Mr Foster. Saw Campbell[R].

To LORD CLARENDON, foreign secretary,   Clarendon MSS, c. 498.
4 November 1869.

I have received two drafts on the Egyptian difficulty this evening. 1. That to Mr. Elliot seems to me excellent but in the very last sentence it is stated that the *status quo* requires that the assent of the Porte should in some form or other be *obtained* for any Loan contracted by the Viceroy: whereas the admission described in the last sentence of the other draft as having been made by France is 'that of obligation in some form or other to *ask permission* of the Sultan to contract a Foreign Loan'. I rather suppose that the latter is the more correct description. Of course the meaning is some *becoming* form, which word might perhaps be inserted. 2. with respect however, to the concluding Paragraph of the

---

[1] Add MS 44637, f. 106.

[2] Conference on suffragan bps.; Tait's legislative proposals were rejected, but the govt. agreed to use the Bps. Act 1539, 31 Henr. VIII c. 9.

[3] See Steele, *Irish Land*, 203.

[4] Samuel Storey, 1840-1925; liberal M.P. Sunderland 1881-95, 1910.

despatch to Mr. West, I think it bears a rougher aspect than perhaps you would suppose. There are so many things which may be said in conversation & which assume another character when stereotyped in writing: and one passage surely involves a direct censure on the dispatch of the French, with whom we are co-operating. 'In the despatch he had just read to me much regard was shewn for the feelings of the Khedive and *little for those of the Sultan*: that'. Might not this be left out? And might you not say further on 'difficult to obtain' instead of 'useless to recommend'?[1]

I admit that I am influenced in this matter by the conviction that, if there is a row in the East about this affair of the Loans, which is of no significance whatever for four years to come, though the world may censure both parties (& will), the main weight of blame will fall upon the Sultan. And further by this; that while the Viceroy may have as much to lose as the Sultan personally, Egypt cannot go to pieces but the Ottoman Empire can and there is a great interest of Turkey as well as of peace in settling the matter on the easiest terms.

To EARL DE GREY, lord president,   Add MS 43513, f. 282.
4 November 1869.

I have read Forster's able paper & I follow it very generally.

On one point I cannot very well follow it: the proposal to found the Rate schools on the system of the British & Foreign Society would I think hardly do. Why not adopt frankly the principle that the State or the local community should provide the secular teaching, & either leave the option to the Ratepayer to go beyond this *sine quâ non*, if they think fit, within the limits of the conscience clause, or else simply leave the parties themselves to find Bible & other religious education from voluntary sources.[2]

I suppose you have got exact information as to the mode in which (so we are told) religious education is reconciled with nationality & universality in Prussia?

If you & Forster like to come here at 12 tomorrow I shall be most happy to see you.

To EARL RUSSELL, 4 November 1869.   Add MS 44537, f. 126.
'Private.'

The Govt. as a whole & many of its members individually, are weighing the Irish Land question with much patience & care; & I am sure there need be no fear of their adopting any precipitate resolution.[3] Further I see no disposition to adopt what is commonly understood by fixity of tenure, or any of the plans which strike vitally at the relation of Landlord & tenant. That which does appear to be recognised by the great body of writers & enquirers at the present junction is, that the question at issue overpasses the limits of simple compensation for improvements to tenants at will. Mr. Thompson (late MP) who, exceptionally, seems disposed to confine legislative remedies to such compensation, admits that the evicted occupier has under the circumstances of Ireland, a grievance, at

---

[1] Clarendon adopted the changes; Add MS 44134, f. 89.
[2] De Grey expected talks with Forster would produce 'a modified arrangement less liable to objection'; Add MS 44286, f. 74.
[3] Russell had expressed moderate alarm for the landlord, 2 November 1869, Add MS 44294, f. 203.

least an injury which they do not cover. The problem before us is, I do not say wholly but in great part, this, how to make equitable provision for a security against the suffering *now* consequent upon eviction, without subverting the foundations of the relation between Landlord & tenant. *Some* propose to do this in one way & some in another. If we can find a method on the whole advisable I think we shall have no fundamental difficulties to encounter in the other parts of the question. Some time ago I had to call for information bearing on the question of a monument to Brougham. I am afraid that no old precedent at all covers it, & the creation of new ones is difficult in such a case. May all happiness attend your journey out & home.

To EARL SPENCER, Irish lord lieutenant,   Add MS 44537, f. 125.
4 November 1869.

Granville has sent me your notes on the Irish Land question[1] & I think the Cabinet would wish before proceeding to any decision to be in possession of your views. I see there are shades of difference between you & Fortescue about the Ulster Tenant right, & the expediency of building on it for the rest of Ireland. The period is happily too early for anyone to bind himself absolutely to this or that particular method, & it is therefore highly favourable for the expression & free discussion without prejudice of first views.

Setting aside many important but easier parts of the subject the knot of it evidently lies in the tenancies at will. And the knot of that knot, at the stage which mens minds have now reached seems to be this. Shall we recognise on behalf of the tenant at will whose tenancy is disturbed by the landlord any claim beyond that of compensation for improvements (forwards & backwards) which appears now to be universally allowed.

I conceive that there is such an ulterior claim & this opinion seems to me to prevail more & more. If so there comes the question as to the force of the recognition. Shall the claim be compensated in time as by a lease, or by a fixed rule of money payment, or by what the goodwill will fetch, or upon a computation of anticipated profits, or in what other way.

With good dispositions on all hands I trust that all dangerous conflict may be avoided in this critical affair. Thanks for your letter about Sullivan[2] to which Fortescue will reply.

5. *Fr.*

Wrote to Mrs Thistlethwayte—Ld Clarendon—The Queen—Mr Miall MP.—Sir H. Verney—W.H.G. (Tel.)—Bishop of Oxford—W.H.G. (L.)—and minutes. Saw Mr Goschen—Mr Fortescue—Ld de Grey & Mr Forster (on Education in England)[3]—Rev. Divie Robertson—Sir R. Phillimore—Ld Clarendon. Cabinet 2½–6¼. Dined with the Lytteltons.

[1] Spencer replied (5 November 1869, Add MS 44306, f. 184): 'My notes to Granville were very hurriedly drawn up . . . first views are very likely to be modified.'
[2] Of 30 October 1869, Add MS 44306, f. 176.
[3] Forster found the meeting 'very satisfactory'; see Reid, *F*, i. 472.

Nov. 5. 69. Cabinet.[1]

√ 1. ⟨Whitby Meeting⟩ Treatment of Fenian prisoners—to be removed to Weedon—To be further cons[idere]d
√ 2. Amnesty letter—Minute approved.[2]
    3. Legislative &c. business for 1870.[3]
√   Proceedings in the City tomorrow. Who shall attend?
√   Ld Clarendon's Mem[orandum] in reply to Fish considered amended & approved.[4]
√   Review of many principal subjects of business.

Local Taxation Plan for 1870.[5]
1. Act to determine what subjects shall be rated.
2. Resolution on past-rating owners.
3. County Financial Boards.
4. Committee on present Grants from the Consolidated Fund.
5. Redistribution of charge as between the Exchequer.
      on (1) Committee of Cabinet: Chancr. of Exchr.—Mr Goschen—Ld Kimberley—Mr Bruce—Ld de Grey—appointed.

Election Procedure
Ld Hartington—Mr Bright—Attorney General—Childers—will undertake to consider of the provisions of a Bill.

To LORD CLARENDON, foreign secretary,   Clarendon MSS, c. 498.
5 November 1869.

    Many thanks for your kind note. I entirely adopt your view of Egyptian independence[6] and you have a delicate part to play which will require all your skill. It is a fresh complication, if the fact really be that the Viceroy can, with a particular firm, go on at once, should he think fit, to make a new Loan. It had occurred to me last night that if there were a real breathing space of four years or even less, it might afford an honourable way out of the dispute, after some such fashion as this. Let the *status quo* be declared in the terms on which you & the French appear to be agreed. And let the Sultan by some formal imperial act, announce that he will, at such period as he shall choose, define further the manner in which he will require the Khedive to approach him in order to obtain authority to contract a foreign loan. A declaration of this kind would be a weapon of great power for it would strike at the *credit* of the Khedive in any such negotiation: while it would seem to be a step within the Sultan's own com-

---

[1] Add MS 44637, f. 108.
[2] Declining to meet a depn. from the Amnesty Cttee., in *The Times*, 17 November 1869, 10e.
[3] Undated holograph list, placed at Add MS 44637, f. 124, reads: 'Irish Land—Irish Railways—Election Procedure—Education—University Tests—Licensing System—Local Taxation—Ecclesiastical Titles—Land Intestacy etc. Bill'.
[4] See 26 Oct. 69; F.O.C.P. 1713.
[5] Undated notes on adjacent sheet, apparently referring to item 3; Add MS 44637, f. 110.
[6] 'The French will encourage him [the Khedive] . . . to *go in* for independence wh. wd. make Egypt even more of a French province than it now is. The Sultan must resist this to the death . . .'; Add MS 44134, f. 89; see 4 Nov. 69.

petency. I do not say he would be *wise* in doing even this; but it would be less dangerous to him than touching the Firman, which will get him into a scrape.

6. Sat. [Grove Park, Watford]

Wrote to Mr Cardwell—Ld Clarendon—Mr Glyn—Ld De Tabley —Ld Spencer—Bp of Argyll—Ld Southesk—W.H.G.—Bp of Lincoln—Col Greville Nugent[1]—Sir J. Acton—Mr [W. P.] Beaumont —Mr Fitzpatrick—Mr Robartes—Ld E. Howard—& minutes. Saw Ld Dufferin—Ld Granville—Mr Goschen—Mr Odo Russell—Mr Glyn. Off at 4 to Ld Clarendons: a delightful hospitality. Walked with Mr Layard from the Station. Read Westminster Review on Prostitution.[2]

To EARL SPENCER, Irish lord lieutenant,   Add MS 44537, 129.
6 November 1869.

There is no *great* hurry about preparing your paper on Irish Land[3] but I think it should be printed here at the F.O. for circulation among the members of the Cabinet by Dec. 1. Mr. Samuelson [sic] in the Daily News of Nov. 1. (or about that day) is long but well worth reading.[4]

7. 24 S.Trin.

St Andrew's Watford mg & aft. Then to Cassiobury for tea.[5] Wrote to W.H.G. Saw Mr Odo Russell respecting the [Vatican] Council. Saw Ld Clarendon. Read Macleod's Closing Address—Langdon's Catholic movement—Union Review—Westmr Review (Theology).[6]

8. M. [London]

Wrote to Ld Listowell—The Queen—Lord E. Howard—Mr Grote —Mr H. Thompson—Lord Mayor—Mr Glyn—Mr Samuelson— Hon. Mr Elliot—D. of Argyll—Mr Delane—Mr Bright—D. of Leinster—Chr of Exchr—and minutes. Conversation with Mr Bright on U.S. and Canada. Saw Mr Kinnaird—Sir John Coleridge

[1] This day he offered U.K. peerages to Nugent, Acton, Southesk, Howard, Agar Robartes, Fitzpatrick; Add MS 44537, f. 130.
[2] *Westminster Review*, xxxvi. 179 (July 1869), 556 (October 1869); see also 8 July 50.
[3] Spencer apologised for delay; Add MS 44306, f. 182.
[4] Letter from H. D. Henderson on Tenant Right in *Daily News*, 29 October 1869, 2.
[5] Lord Ebury's; see 12 Aug. 71.
[6] N. *Macleod, 'The concluding Address to the General Assembly of the Church of Scotland, May 1869' (1869); see 31 Oct. 69; *Union Review* (1869); *Westminster Review*, xxxvi. 415 (October 1869).

—Sir A. Spearman—Sir Curtis Lambson.[1] 5-7. Interview with Mrs Thistlethwayte. Dined with the Wortleys: Jim *looked* so much better. Read Pamphlets on Ireland.

To the DUKE OF LEINSTER, 8 November 1869.   Add MS 44537, f. 133.

I take the liberty of proposing to Your Grace that you should accept the first of the two Garters now disposable through the deaths of Ld. Derby & Ld. Westminster. I will not speak of the pleasure it gives me to convey this offer to one, who apart from the high station he holds, is the object of universal respect & regard: but it will be gratifying to Your Grace to know that the Queen was pleased to express a special satisfaction in approving the recommendation touching Your Grace, which I had submitted. At this period in particular, I feel that the tender & acceptance of this offer will be regarded, should you allow it to take effect, as highly appropriate.[2]

9. Tu.

Wrote to Ld Clarendon—Mr Childers—Mr Sturges—D. Dss Somerset—Mr Ouvry—Ld Granville—Mr J. Ripley[3]—Ly Lyttelton—Gen. Sabine—Mrs Wortley—Mr Fordyce.[4] Saw Ld Lyttelton—Rev Mr Burgess—Mr Glyn—Ld Hartington—Sir J. Gray—Ld De Tabley—Mr Reed MP—Sir C. Lambson—Mr Ouvry—Chancr of Exchr— & minutes. With De Tabley, *inter alia* I talked over Mrs Th. I had some signs of my old malady but slight. Off at 6.20 to Guildhall: where I spoke thanks for the Government.[5] The combination of physical effort with measured words is difficult. Read Wales & its people[6]—Campbell on Ir. Land.[7]

To W. FORDYCE, M.P., 9 November 1869.   Add MS 44537, f. 134.

Though I am quite sure Lord Kintore would receive kindly any representation made to him by me if it involved no impropriety, I am unwilling to seem to intrude upon his office by making any representation about Mr. McCombie.[8] Yet in writing to you, & assuming that Mr. McC[ombie] is possessed of the proper qualifications for a D[eputy] L[ieutenant] I would shew these three things—first that it is very desirable, especially at the present day to recognize as worthy of respect and as capable of wielding influence, the position of the tenant-farmer. Secondly that it is also very politic to give to those, who have

---

[1] Sir Curtis Miranda Lampson, 1806-85; fur merchant; cr. bart. 1866.
[2] Leinster declined it, Stratford de Redcliffe and Ripon later accepting.
[3] John Ripley of Whitby (where Willy faced a by-election) had written about bp. *Temple's appt.; Add MS 44537, f. 134.
[4] William Dingwall Fordyce, 1836-75; advocate and liberal M.P. Aberdeenshire 1866-8, E. Aberdeenshire from 1868.
[5] *The Times*, 10 November 1869, 5d.   [6] [K. K.], *Wales and its people* (1869).
[7] See 11 Aug. 69.   [8] Fordyce's appeal untraced.

been chosen M.P.s such reasonable social distinctions as their Station admits of. Thirdly that Mr. McCombie so far as I have seen, is one who stands forward as preeminent for a shrewd intelligence even among the tenant farmers of his country; & I know of no objection to him unless it be his rich Aberdeenshire brogue which for one I delight in.

I have been told that Mr. Reid M.P. being a tenant farmer was made a D.L.

10. Wed.

Wrote to Mr Roundell—Col Grev. Nugent—Ld Granville—Mr G. Burnett—Mr Grote—Ld Clarendon—Gen. Grey—Ld Bessborough —Mr Fowler—Sir C. Lambson—Mr Childers—Mr Fitzpatrick— Dean of Windsor—The Queen (2)—and Telegr. Saw Ld De Tabley —Ld Kinnaird—A. Kinnaird—Mr Ouvry—Mr Glyn (2)—Mr Fitzpatrick—Mr Childers—Chancr of Exr—Ld Clarendon—Ld Granville. Cabinet 2-4¾. Saw Mrs Th. 5¼-7¼. Dined with the Phillimores. Read P. Kennedy on Ireland.[1]

Cabinet Nov 10/69[2]
√ 1. Next Cabinet. When will Estimates be ready? ⟨Dec 4 (Sat)? or⟩ Dec. 6 (Mond.)?[3]
√ 2. Peabody's remains.[4] Send to Am[eric]a in Ship of War?
√ 3. Invitation to ⟨express opinions on Ir⟩ offer *suggestions* or *queries* on Irish Land Say by Nov 25?
√ 4. Civil Service Exam[inatio]n—Next Cabinet
√ 5. Education. De Grey & Forster's Mem[orandu]m[5]
√ 6. Release of Fenian prisoners in Canada: Leave to Young the entire responsibility.
√ 7. Fenwick & Schneider. Cannot be supported.[6]
   8. Granville's Church dispatch for Jamaica. Approved.

To LORD CLARENDON, foreign secretary,   Clarendon MSS, c. 498.
10 November 1869.

I have answered you by anticipation about Elliot. The matter of form rests with Cardwell & the W.O.[7]

I hope you will not disapprove of what I said of U.S. last night.

You do not say expressly whether you are to be in town today. If you are I should like to mention to you *before* the Cabinet the subject of Mr Peabody's remains to America in a Ship of War. I have looked into the matter & am disposed to recommend it.

[1] P. Kennedy, *Legendary fictions of the Irish Celts* (1866).
[2] Add MS 44637, f. 113.
[3] Changed to '7', a Tuesday.   [4] See 12 Nov. 69.
[5] On the framing of the bill; in G. Sutherland, *Policy Making in Elementary Education* (1973), 119ff.; see also Reid, *F*, i. 463ff.
[6] Obscure.
[7] Able to wear his ribbon at the Suez canal opening; Add MS 44134, f. 98.

On Irish land I send you a letter of Ld Portsmouth to Granville, with its inclosure: worth reading.[1]

I consider that none of us are held for Feb. & March to tentative opinions spoken in October & November, so we may speak fearlessly.

My present impressions are 1. that the *strongest* thing we are likely to do is to extend *backwards* compensation for improvements. 2. That the most vital question for consideration now before us is, shall we in our legislation on the tenant's behalf go, in principle, *beyond* compensation for improvements (whether forwards or backwards). 3. Upon affirming this proposition we have then a great practical question as to the best *form* in which to convey this boon to the tenant. 4. Therefore it is most desirable we should have before us the various forms that may be proposed. At present *Fortescue* is the only man who has presented his suggestions in a shape to be *fired into*. A judgment cannot be passed, while this is the case.

Is not this 'so far so good'? Don't reply.

To C. S. ROUNDELL, M.P., 10 November 1869.   Add MS 44423, f. 75.

I agree with you in thinking that the University Tests Bill has suffered by delays at the commencement of the Session, that it is very desirable the measure should pass, & also very desirable that it should be in the hands of the Govt.[2] But *one* thing, vital for all contests, the Govt. have not to give, & that is *time*. I think that the Bill in its old form would probably not require time, the argument being exhausted. But this opinion does not apply to the bill in an altered shape. I cannot help hoping that, as it is, the House of Lords might be induced to accept it: as several of the men who would have most to say to it are men who would look at the question with singleness of mind & eye. Further, I apprehend that the Bill if altered at all in the sense of extension ought to be altered not in one particular alone, but in several. It would not be wise to open the ground of one fresh & stiff battle now with the prospect of its being very soon succeeded by another. With respect to the altered Bill, in any case, no pledge as to support could be given by the Govt., until we had seen it in its new form. I have seen Sir J. Coleridge on the subject of the Bill, & I presume you will be in communication with him next week. He will, I think, be able to state what I take to be the present position of the Govt. in respect to the measure: which I have generally indicated in this letter.

11. *Th.*

Wrote to Mr Merivale—Mr Ellice MP.—Gen Grey—Ld Stratford de R.—Mr Merivale—Dean of Windsor—Mr Herbert—Sir W. Knollys —Mr Burgess—Abp Manning—The Queen—Ld Granville—Mr Childers—Mr W. Williams—& minutes. Saw Ld Clarendon—Ld Granville—Mr Ayrton—Sir C. Lambson [*sic*]—Mr Bruce—Mr Fitzpatrick—Ld de Grey—Mrs Thistlethwayte—Dowager Duchess of Somerset—Mr Gurdon (Pensions & RB)—Mr Barker—Do *cum* Mr

[1] See Ramm I, i. 66.
[2] Roundell to Gladstone, 9 November 1869, Add MS 44423, f. 69.

Burnett, on the Aston Purchase—Ld Kimberley—Lord E. Howard.
11.45. Went off to the Council at Windsor where I had a very satisfactory audience. Dined with the Thistlethwaytes. Saw Henderson
48. X.

Mem. Windsor Nov. 11. 69.[1]
Deanery of Ely—Garter 1. Bessborough, 2. Stratford de R[edcliffe], 3. Ports-
mouth[2]—Peerages, *report*, Mr. *Ellice*—M. F. Tupper, Pension?[3]—Mrs Thurston
Tennyson, d[itt]o?

To ARCHBISHOP H. E. MANNING,   Add MS 44249, f. 112.
11 November 1869.

One line with reference to the latter part of your note.[4] Whatever the differences between us, in matters too of high import, it is wholly impossible that
under any circumstances I would imagine you to be guilty of an intrigue against
Dr. Newman. Indeed I have no recollection of so construing Mr. Ffoulkes pamphlet. But had this been my interpretation I should without in the least impugn-
ing his veracity have set him down as mistaken.

12. Fr.

Wrote to Sir C. Lambson [*sic*]—C.G. (Telegr.)—Sir E. Dering—Mr
Forster—The Queen (Mem)—W.H.G.—Ld A. Hervey—Mr Burgess
—& minutes. Attended the funeral of Mr Peabody:[5] a touching and
solemn spectacle. Mrs Thistlethwayte called here & looked at the
family pictures. Saw Ld Clarendon—Mr Motley—Mr Barker—
[Chaplain] Gen. Gleig (Russ)—Mr Glyn. 5–7. With Mrs Th. to whom
I read Helen's notable paper on Ambition. Dined with the Lytteltons.
Read Pitt Kennedy—Layard's & Dufferin's papers.[6]

13. Sat. [Windsor]

Wrote to Ld Clarendon—Ld St Germans—Lady Llanover—Mr
Bruce—Mr Childers—Mr West—Ld Dufferin—Mrs Th (2)—
Chancr of Exr—Mr Neate—Helen G.—and minutes. Saw Mr
Wetherell—Mr Glyn—Mr Lambert—Mr Childers *cum* do—Mr
Primrose—Scotts. Off at 5.15 to Windsor. I made a few verses, by
way of translation, for Mrs Th. Dined with the Queen as did C. At

---

[1] Add MS 44757, f. 11.   [2] 'St. German's' here added later.
[3] Delayed till 1873; Hudson, *Tupper*, 260. See 7 Feb. 70.
[4] Holograph, dated 8 November 1869, from Paris, Add MS 44249, f. 110, stating his
office prevented full explanation of the affair, for which see *Newman*, xxiv. 366ff.
[5] George Peabody, American financier and philanthropist, d. 4 November 1869; after
a funeral in Westminster Abbey his remains were taken to the U.S.A. in H.M.S. *Monarch*.
[6] On Irish land.

night I had to write & copy out a letter respecting the Yacht and the Admiralty.[1] Read Tracts.

To LORD DUFFERIN, 13 November 1869.   Add MS 44537, f. 140.

So far from complaining of your second memorandum[2] am I, that I hope you will go further. It is really not possible to compare your suggestion with Fortescue's until you have reduced it to a state of equal definiteness. I was in hopes you might be able to do this by taking his paper as a basis & making corrections upon it. But your blank maximum, & the rules by which the Court is to range between it & a minimum are points so essential that I do not see how you can be put into the scales against the other jockey till you have supplied them. If you could do it in an independent paper containing simply (like his) the essential propositions, it could not but be very useful.

Your presentation of alternatives affecting you personally is as handsome & disinterested as, from you, all would expect, but I am sure we need not entertain these as practical questions. On one point of political economy, no part of a land creed, I am unable to follow you. I cannot admit there has been any serious or appreciable diminution of the value of gold.

I have no authority to circulate Cabinet ministers generally: but your wish can quite well be made known to the Cabinet when it meets.

[14.] 25 S. Trin.

St George's mg & aft. Audience of the Queen. Visited Dr Hornby.[3] Walk with the Dean & C. Saw General Grey. Wrote to Mrs Th. Read Arnold on St Paul[4]—Bp Ewing & Law on Atonement[5]—Church's Sermon[6]—Honesty of Interpreters of HS.[7] Music in evg: excellent.

15. M. [London]

Wrote to Ld Clarendon—Mr Childers—Ld Portsmouth—Mr Cardwell—Mr Mundella—Chancr of Exr—and minutes. Visited Christie's. Saw Mrs Thistlethwayte (at 11½). Conversation with Mr Rowsell. Dined at Mr Glyn's. Mrs Thistlethwayte's afterwards. Saw Mr Glyn—Robn G. and his party. Returned from Windsor at 1. Read Pitt Kennedy—Mr Ferguson on Irish Law.[8]

---

[1] Expenses of the royal yacht; Add MS 44537, f. 141.
[2] Sent 12 November, Add MS 44151, f. 64.
[3] James John *Hornby, 1826–1909; headmaster of Eton 1868–84.
[4] M. *Arnold, St Paul and protestantism (1870).
[5] A. *Ewing, intr. to W. Law, 'The atonement' in Present Day Papers (1870).
[6] R. W. Church, 'The two-fold debt of the clergy' (1869).   [7] Untraced.
[8] W. D. Ferguson, The Common Law Procedure Amendment Acts (Ireland) (1857).

16. Tu. [Windsor]

Wrote to Mr Hammond——Abp Manning——Ld Chancr——Ld Spencer ——& minutes. Drew queries on Irish Land & sent them to I[reland]. Visited Christie's. Saw Mr Glyn——Ld Monck——Mr Goschen——The Queen——Mr Cardwell——Mrs Thistlethwayte on the way to G.W.R. Off to Windsor at 5. We dined with H.M. a party of 13. Long conversation with the King of the Belgians in evg. Also saw P. of Wales who expressed a particular desire to see me at M[arlborough] House for the purpose of conversing on Irish questions. Read Trevelyan's Verses[1]——Ferguson & Vance's Report.[2]

To ARCHBISHOP H. E. MANNING,   Add MS 44249, f. 116.
16 November 1869.

[3]I have no difficulty in answering you: the state of my speculative mind, so to speak, is not the portion of me that I have most difficulty in exhibiting; and I do it in the familiarity of ancient and unextinguished friendship.

When I said that there had always been in me a turn towards rationalising, I did not mean to use the term in its technical sense, but only meant it had always been my habit and desire to give to religious doctrine a home in my understanding, so that the whole mind might embrace it, and not merely the emotional part of it. It was in the year 1830, I think, that I began to be powerfully acted upon by the writings of Bishop Butler (one of my four great teachers), and I then wrote a paper on his chapter concerning Mediation,[4] the matter of which I still view with interest in no way abated. The tendency to rationalise in this sense has continued, and I wish to encourage it, believing it to be truly Evangelical, Apostolical, and Catholic.

My first recollection of difference from you was in 1835 or 1836 about a question at 67 Lincoln's Inn Fields, where I had been (with Lord *Cholmondeley*) to support the bishops, and you to vote against them.[5] My second went deeper, and left a strong mark in my memory. You sent me (I think) a proof sheet of a Sermon about the working of the Holy Spirit in the Church, and the Infallibility of the Church. I thought it by much too absolute, and argued this, more or less, in reply. You kept to your text, and it was what I should call further exaggeration of that already over-absolute proposition, which you embodied in a paper as your immediate vindication for joining the Church of Rome. I saw that paper in 1851, but never had a copy. It seemed to me that in it, you broke altogether away from the teaching of history and experience, respecting the methods of God in dealing with his Church. But I am becoming aggressive.

I remember well, though not so accurately as you, the scenes at the time of the Gorham Judgment.[6] Suddenly plunged into a vortex of complicated controversies

---

[1] G. O. *Trevelyan, *The ladies in parliament* (1869).
[2] W. D. Ferguson and A. Vance, *The tenure and improvement of land in Ireland, considered with reference to the relation of landlord and tenant, and tenant-right* (1851).
[3] Mostly printed in Purcell, ii. 406; Manning especially drew Purcell's attention to this letter, ibid. Manning's letter of 13 November, from Nice, accused Gladstone of rationalism, Add MS 44294, f. 113.   [4] See 9 July 30.
[5] See, perhaps, 22 Apr., 28, 31 May 36.   [6] See 8–16 Mar. 50.

on the relations of Church and State, I was a good deal tossed about: and in 1850 family cares and sorrows wrought me (for I was a kind of spoilt child of Providence) into an unusual susceptibility. But to sum up all in a few words: (1) I view the judgment itself as I did then. (2) I hold firmly by the doctrine of the Supremacy of the Crown, as I then worked it out for myself. (3) I over-estimated the *scope* of the judgment: the Bishop of St. David's is right when he says, such a judgment *could* not rule anything except the case it decided and, through the Courts, any case in precise correspondence with it. (4) Soon after that judgment the Church of England recovered its corporate capacity, and its voice; a great change which you, or I, had never anticipated. Then and before, she lost the most brilliant of her children, that she might have cause to know the meaning of the words, 'Not by might, nor by power, but by My Spirit.' All her gloss was rubbed away. Those who have adhered to her, have done it without illusions.

In the Edinburgh Discourse[1] to which you refer, I said something about the necessity, and difficulty, and value of a philosophy of religion. And the master-hope, the master-passion of my soul is to be permitted, when my present work (which cannot last very long) is done, to gather up from off the battlefield of politics all that may remain of my being, and to be permitted by the Divine mercy to dedicate any residue of life to some morsels of that work. I profoundly believe in a reconciliation between Christianity and the conditions of modern thought, modern life, and modern society. While I see that in the common idea and tradition of the time, even in this country, and yet more on the Continent, they are farther than ever from being reconciled.

In 1839, Lord Macaulay covered me with not ill-natured, yet unqualified and glittering ridicule, because in my imperfect way I had professed my loyal allegiance to two principles which in religion, at least, he appeared to regard as incompatible: freedom and authority. After thirty more years of the blasts of life, I remain rooted, as much as before, in regard for authority, and even more than before in the value I set upon freedom. It has pleased God, at a heavy cost, to give it the place of a foundation-stone in the being of Man, the most wonderful of His known works. The difficulty of training and rearing it aright, I feel; but under no inducement whatever could I, without treason to duty, consent, whether in religion or secular affairs, to its being trodden under foot. And hence, while my creed is what it was, and perhaps even more sacramental, I regard with misgivings, which approach to horror, what may be called sacerdotalism. In this sacerdotalism I recognise a double danger: first, that many elect and tender souls may forego one of the great prerogatives and duties of their nature; secondly, that the just reaction from their excess, co-operating with other causes less legitimate, may yet more estrange the general mass of humanity from God, and from religion.

Lastly, I did not recommend Dr. Temple as a bishop because the Church of England retained him, any more than you would choose Mr. Ffoulkes on a similar ground: but because of his combinations of mind and life for the Office, together with the futility or insufficiency of any charge which was (to my knowledge) advanced against him.

And now my dear friend, what a flood of egotism you have unwittingly brought down on your devoted head! I must recognise the terms of your letter as most kind and considerate; I do not feel equally certain about my reply. Pardon it, as you have pardoned much before.

---

[1] His last Edinburgh rectorial, see 3 Nov. 65.

P.S. My speech about Ireland was (whether mistakenly or not) advisedly low-toned: but it did not indicate, or proceed from, any access of discouragement.

17. Wed. [London]

At Castle Chapel Prayers. Saw the King once more & left at 10.20. Wrote to Dowager Dss of Somerset—Ld Chancellor—Bp of Lichfield—Helen G.—Sir J. Hanmer—Mr Milbanke—Mr G. Glyn—F.O. (Mem.)—Mr Milbanke [sic]—Mr Whitlock—Ld Spencer—The Speaker—Sig. P. Villari—Mr Wetherell—Mr Cardwell—Lord Clarendon—Abp of Cefalonia[1]—and minutes. Saw Ld Clarendon and [blank]. Dined at the Grosvenor Hotel with the Metaphysical Society, though I only listened to the discussion raised by Professor Huxley, it fatigued my poor brain sadly.[2] I slept like a top for 7 hours. Went at 10 to see Mrs Th. I was lionised over her pretty room.

To E. CARDWELL, war secretary, 17 November 1869.   PRO 30/48/6, f. 138.

I meant to call on you at the War Office but I find you are out of town for a day or two.

The only scruple that occurred to me on reading your paper[3] was whether it will not produce an effect on the position of the Horse Guards beyond what it avows, & whether if so the effect will arise through any distinct change that ought to be more clearly stated. You mention that the General Commanding will attend your Council, & you mention on the other hand the extension of his power. I do not mean to imply an opinion, but rather to ask an explanation which you I do not doubt could give.

The other question in my mind is whether you should ask an audience. No-one (unless the C. of E.) is more succinct than you but in your paper you have much to say, & the Queen is I think loath to face any lengthened statement, therefore likely to take an opinion on it second hand. Possibly you might prepare her mind in conversation. This again is only a point for your consideration & decision. Please to look at page 5.

I must close: I am going to have a discussion, initiated by Huxley, on the immortality of the Soul!

To LORD CLARENDON, foreign secretary,   Add MS 44537, f. 144.
17 November 1869.

You are more likely to know than I,[4] but I do not see that we have the means of showing that the French have acted with bad faith in this Egyptian business.

[1] Encouraging Orthodox Church bps. to protest against papal infallibility: Add MS 44537, f. 143.
[2] Discussion raised by *Huxley on 'The views of Hume, Kant, and Whately upon the logical basis of the doctrine of the immortality of the soul', Metaphysical Society Papers, n. 5.
[3] War office reform; see T. F. Gallagher, 'Cardwellian Mysteries', Historical Journal, xviii. 339 (1975).
[4] *Clarendon's comments apparently made verbally.

I am afraid there has been a visible want of concert between the two Ambassadors at Constantinople, but I am also not without the fear that Mr. Elliot in his interviews after making demands in your name allows the Turk to see that they will not be pressed by him, & assumes as his basis of argument what the Turkish Government are willing to concede, doing little more than trying to amend the form & particulars. It seems to me the kindest advice to the Sultan is to drive home the demand about not raising the taxes. If the Viceroy [of Egypt] refuses this the Sultan will have some chance of being supported by European opinion which I cannot help thinking will be adverse if he quarrels on the loans *simpliciter*. If a firman comes I trust it will be one not leading to action. It may be that the Porte has been more honest than the Viceroy in this business, but it seems to me that its stupidity has been extreme, & I am afraid of its being overwhelmed with ridicule if it publicly claims the censorship[?] for the correction of Egyptian Extravagance.

Mr. Elliot's of Nov. 7. certainly narrows the point of difference: if the Viceroy has not been tried on this precise footing might we not with the French try him?

18. Th.

Wrote to Bp of London—Ld Devon—Mr Trevelyan—Dr Vaughan —Sir C. Murray—Ld A. Hervey—Ld Clarendon—Helen G. (2)— and minutes. Arranging my accounts. Saw Mr Westell—Mr Th. Hunt —Mr Glyn—Mrs Thistlethwayte 4½-6: we talked of deep matters. Read Ferguson & Vance's Report—Döllinger on the Council.[1] Went to drive with SEG and to the Mission service at his Church in Lambeth which pleased me much.

To LORD DEVON, 18 November 1869.   Add MS 44537, f. 145.

I thank you very much for Mr. Ferguson's pamphlet[2] of which having marked your copy, I send you back another. I am more struck with the general argument than with *some* of the practical recommendations so I cannot help being curious to know the points on which you reserve your judgment. His chap. III[3] is what I like the least.

19. Fr. [Hawarden]

Slight attack of the bowel complaint. Wrote to Lord Eversley—Sir S. Scott & Co.—Bp of Oxford—Mrs Thistlethwayte (2)—and minutes. Read Ferguson & Vance on Irish Land. Arranging prints &c. Saw Mrs Stumme (her affairs)—Sir W. Heathcote—Mr Glyn—Dr A. Clark, who allowed me to go off. Off at 4½. Reached Hawarden 10.50. Found Stephen, & Helen. Unpacked: & up late.

[1] See 9 Oct. 69.   [2] See 16 Nov. 69.   [3] On leases.

20. Sat.

Kept my bed till 11.30. Wrote to Bp of Oxford—Ld Clarendon—
Mr Gurdon—Mrs Thistlethwayte—Mr Forrest—Mr Greener[1]—and
minutes. Moved my clothes &c. into my new (old age) dressing room
on the first floor. Worked a little on my books. Cut down a stump.
Read F. Hill on Land Laws[2]—Segur's Les Femmes[3]—G. Lewis on
Irish Disturbances.[4]

To LORD CLARENDON, foreign secretary,   Clarendon MSS, c. 498.
20 November 1869.

The welcome news of a concession from the Viceroy has trodden on my heels
as I came down last night. It will I hope be the means of settling a question on
one side frivolous & on the other full of danger. I conclude that with the concurrence of the French you will support a settlement on this basis: & I write not as
announcing an absolute opinion but to save your time if you agree. Supposing
however we with the French recommend this, I think the time has come for
recommending strongly and fairly washing our hands of the affair in case of non-
acceptance.

21. Preadvent S.

Hawarden Ch. 11 AM (& H.C.) Wrote to The Queen—& Mem.—Mr
Cardwell—Ld de Grey—Ld Granville—D. of Argyll—Bishop of
Lichfield—Mr Hamilton—and minutes. Read Pryce on Early
Church[5]—Union Rev. on Eastern Ch.[6]—Janus;[7] and Dr Temple's
Essay.[8] On re-perusal it seems to me crude and unbalanced, but
neither heretical nor sceptical.

22. M.

Ch. 8½ A.M. Wrote to Mr [W.] Digby Seymour—Mr Glyn—Mr Fortescue—Ld Clarendon—Mr Hayward—& minutes. Saw Mr Burnett
—Worked 6 hours on my books arranging and rearranging: the best
brain rest I have had (I think) since Decr last. Cut down an alder.
Read Segur's Les Femmes—Lewis on Irish Disturbances.

[1] Untraced.
[2] F. H. Hill, 'Ireland', from *Questions for a reformed Parliament* (1867).
[3] A. J. P. de Ségur, *Les femmes, leur condition et leur influence dans l'ordre social*, 3v.
(1803).
[4] See 25 Aug. 45.
[5] J. Pryce, *A history of the early Church. A manual* (1869).
[6] *Union Review*, 323, 432 (1869).   [7] See 9 Oct. 69.
[8] The cause of the controversy; in *Essays and Reviews*; see 10 May 60n.

To C. S. P. FORTESCUE, Irish secretary,   Add MS 44122, f. 9.
22 November 1869. 'Private.'

1. It is a great misfortune that Hancock cannot produce his papers in moderation as to length, and I really hope you will give him a lesson about it. During
the Irish Church debates, we reached a point at which I viewed with horror his
name on an envelope; and now his account of Irish Land Bills is about six times
as long as I had hoped it would be. In fact the bills themselves, with breviates
would be much more available than a document of such length. I speak of its
length only, for I do not know how to commence the study of it. This is really
a serious matter.
2. I cannot say that I think the memoranda as yet printed have done much to
advance our consideration of the Land question. But all agree in this, that we
must go beyond compensation for improvements. What do you think of tenant
right with an option to the landlord to bar it by a 31 yrs lease at the present rent
(or value) and with compensation for permanent improvements at the end?
3. I am obliged to trouble you with the inclosed from Digby Seymour. I reply
thanking him in general terms, & promising to consider, but with a doubt whether I can answer him before the Cabinet meets.
4. It will be of great importance that the *Irish Govt* should if possible report
with one voice on the question of the Land.[1]

23. Tu.

Ch. 8½ A.M. Wrote to Mr Douglas Gordon—Ld Clarendon—Dr J.
Brown—Mr Cartwright—The Queen—Duke of Argyll—Chr of
Exchr—Mrs Hampton—Mr Goschen—Sir R. Levinge[2]—Mr Glyn
—Mr Ayrton—Mr West (Tel)—Mrs Thistlethwayte—and minutes.
Four hours on my books & papers. Read Dilke's Greater Britain.[3]

To W. C. CARTWRIGHT, M.P., 23 November 1869.   Add MS 44537, f. 150.

I thank you very much for your interesting letter,[4] which I take the liberty
of sending to Ld. Clarendon for his perusal. Your view of the alteration of temper & expectation at Rome is strikingly in harmony with our latest accounts
from Vienna dated Nov. 17.

But Pius IX & the Jesuits are hardened offenders & like you I shall not believe in their having sense enough to steer clear of the rocks ahead until they
show it in act. It is something however to be allowed to hope.

It is very pleasant to me to reflect that if the plan of proclaiming infallibility
is even tacitly abandoned this will be a great blow to the doctrine in its practical
effect. You will never I hope think information from you can require apology.
Pray remember us to Mrs. Cartwright.

[1] Fortescue sent replies, adding 'I was rather surprised that you did not impose upon me
directly'; 22 November 1869, Add MS 44122, f. 10. For Seymour, see 26 Nov., 7 Dec. 69.
[2] Sir Richard George Augustus Levinge, 1811-84; 7th bart. 1848; soldier, liberal M.P.
Westmeath 1857-65; wanted a peerage, see Add MS 44537, f. 150.
[3] See 11 Nov. 68 and above, v. xxiv.
[4] Untraced. See 30 Sept., 27 Dec. 66.

To LORD CLARENDON, foreign secretary,   Clarendon MSS, c. 498.
23 November 1869.

In treating the Viceroy's concession as substantial,[1] I was partly guided by
Elliot's opinion and description of it. It is in itself by no means conclusive. Still
I think there is matter in it. A Loan for the Canadian war would clearly not be
one for internal administration: or one for Sir S. Baker's Expedition—if it were
to require one. But the great virtue of it I thought was this that as a shifting of
ground and a concession on the part of the Viceroy it made matters easier for
the Porte, by enabling it to postpone the definitive solution. The act which the
Sultan is now going to perform seems to me one of great and gratuitous folly,
tending to shew the inability of the Turk to enter into European ideas. I really
believe he does not like a quarrel and yet he is going to invite one on a matter
which by his own avowal has no practical character for four years to come. But
' "wilfu" man maun hae his way' and, you having done your best with both
parties, I am now chiefly anxious that we should stand clear of responsibility in
the business.

I send you an interesting letter from Cartwright about the Council.[2] He is
usually judicious, & very well-informed.

Buchanan's observation to Kaufmann[3] was very just. What are the 'extraordinary rights' exercised over the daughters-in-law?

To R. LOWE, chancellor of the exchequer,   Add MS 44537, f. 149.
23 November 1869.

1. I think it very likely that your proposed method of proceeding with regard to
the Civil service will prove to be the right one,[4] but I have several remarks to
make, rather in furtherance than otherwise. (1) I hope you will call the Com-
[mitt]ee of Cabinet together. The plan would leave Clarendon & Bright so insu-
lated that their ground would be untenable. Perhaps they might in conversation
come to terms. (2) I think it would be prudent as well as courteous to allow the
head of the Govt. staff in each Dept. to be *heard*, before we actually decide.
(3) & to keep intact the right of retracting or modifying in particular cases, or
particular features of the place. For some classes of office, perhaps the Police
plan might be the best. Sometimes I have thought that a portion of places might
be usefully given to old soldiers in such a manner as to raise the quality of the

---

[1] On the Egyptian loan; Clarendon replied, 24 November 1869, Add MS 44134, f. 102:
'I suppose the Porte will issue an explanatory Firman with wh. we shall have nothing to do
& the opportunity will be a good one for washing our hands & taking leave of the business.'

[2] See this day's letter.

[3] General Konstantin Petrovich Kaufmann, Russian expansionist, governed Turkestan
1867-83.

[4] Lowe wrote to Gladstone, 10 November 1869, Add MS 44301, f. 104: 'As *I* have so
often tried in vain, will you bring the question of the Civil Service before the Cabinet today
—something must be decided—we cannot keep matters in this discreditable state of abeyance. If the Cabinet will not entertain the idea of open competition might we not at any
rate require a larger number of competitors for each vacancy? . . . Perhaps the 1st Class
might be thrown open and the 2nd restricted to a large but limited Competition.' See 8 Dec.
69. Lowe to Gladstone, 22 November 1869, Add MS 44301, f. 106, proposed to 'put all the
departments we can control, the Treasury, Board of Works, Audit Office, National Debt,
Paymaster General, Inland Revenue, Customs and Post Office on open competition at once
. . . we might leave Clarendon, Bright and my other obstacles alone'.

army. I only name these points as good to the extent of keeping the hands of the Govt. free. (4) Promises may have been given to individuals to such an extent, with reference to coming vacancies, as to make it desirable to allow a vacancy or so to pass before the application of the new system. This would have to be remembered in framing the order.
2. I readily accept your judgment in respect to the organization of the commission for I can well believe you right in thinking the new system would require two paid Commissioners.
3. Do you think any compliment ought to be paid to Twistleton?[1]
4. Pray mention Dunbar's case to the Cabinet.

24. Wed.

Ch. 8½ A.M. Wrote to Mrs Thistlethwayte—Mr Fortescue—Ld Monck—D. of Argyll—The Queen—The Viceroy of I.—Mr Buxton—Mr Fitzpatrick—and minutes. Finished arranging my books and pamphlets. Saw Sir W. James—Lord Halifax—Conversation with C.G. on Rev. Mr Austin's case. Read Sir G. Lewis.

25. Th.

Ch. 8½ AM. Wrote to Mr Macmillan—Lord Granville—Clarendon—Churchill—Mr Goschen—Chr of Exr—Ld Belper—Mr Fortescue—Miss Doyle—The Queen—Mr Bright—and minutes. Walk with Ld Halifax. Saw Mr Barker. The ball came in evg: & went off with great *éclat*. I was sent to dine with a party of six at the Glynne Arms. Read . . . on Popery—Lewis on Irish Disturbances.

To J. BRIGHT, president of the board of trade,   Add MS 43385, f. 51.
25 November 1869.

The importance I attach to the Railway question[2] grows *chiefly* out of its relation to the Land question to which it may render an effectual assistance.
I now send you my Memorandum[3] which I think will hold water tolerably. I look upon such a change as I propose with respect to the Constabulary with great desire. The present arrangement is as mischievous as that by which we have heretofore allowed our Colonies to make war at our expense, or that by which before 1861 the power of the American Union was made available to support slavery in the Southern States. I should endeavour to throw upon the companies themselves the responsibility of settling the relative values of their interests for amalgamation. Please to take care of the paper as I have no other copy and I shall soon wish to consult the Ch. of the Exchequer upon it. I agree very much

[1] Edward Turner Boyd Twistleton, 1809–74; civil service commissioner 1862–70; apparently got no honour.
[2] Bright, on 24 November 1869, sent extracts from a letter by J. W. Murland on govt. aid to Irish railways; Add MS 44112, f. 101.
[3] Not found.

with you about Caird.[1] But Lowe will have a great deal to say to the question
who shall succeed Mr. Hamilton. Your information from Murland is interesting
& to the point. But were I an Irish Landlord I think I should lean to tenant right
with a maximum, especially if I had the option of giving a lease. If the great fish
(Railways) eat up the small, that may be the best form of amalgamation.

To LORD CLARENDON, foreign secretary,   Clarendon MSS, c. 498.
25 November 1869.

I should think Hammond[2] is right up to the point at any rate of recommending a policy of indifference, meaning by the term that we are readily & frankly
to welcome any American movement, but not to shew a fussy solicitude to bring
one about. Time is I think on our side. Surely the Yankees cannot suppose we
are bound by the stipulations of the arrangement they rejected & it can hardly
be *necessary* to say anything on the subject.

If, as I daresay, Musurus is right about the Khedive's Loans,[3] what ineffable
folly in the Sultan to stir the question, & not to be content with the *status quo*
backed as it must in that case be by such irrefragable testimony.

Lyons takes I think a very just view of the Treaty question. If the French
Govt. persist in dividing the two branches, they ought not simply to re-ensure
—but to enlarge & extend the first. I send the letters on to the Queen.

To C. S. P. FORTESCUE, Irish secretary,   Add MS 44538, f. 3.
25 November 1869.

This return, carried through Ireland, will be very valuable. I am not sure
whether it came to me from you or the Viceroy. Of course it may happen that
you & he do not get exactly the same point of view for the Land question—
but if you two & the Attorney Genl. fortunately agree it will be a circumstance
of weight for the Cabinet. Hartington I believe has come to the Tenant right
view. Kimberley told me he had been dissatisfied with his own printed paper.
Monck is very strongly for very strong tenant right.

Ferguson & Vance in their report write that it prevails more or less in (I
think) 28 counties of Ireland.[4] I cannot understand why from the Landlords
point of view it should be more formidable if covered by a maximum & especially if balanced by the power of tendering a lease than 'a hard & fast' enactment
for carving out of the Estate through all time a compensation for disturbance. If
you then of the Irish Government are not quite of one mind now, I would take
a little time before coming to the expression of any discordant opinion.

26. Fr.

Ch. 8½ AM. Wrote to Mr Fortescue—Mrs Thistlethwayte—Professor
Blackie—and minutes. Much conversation on Irish Land with Ld

[1] Bright to Gladstone, 22 November 1869, Add MS 44112, f. 99, recommended Caird to
succeed Hamilton at the Treasury.
[2] See Add MS 44134, f. 102.
[3] *Clarendon reported Musurus' comments; see 23 Nov. 69n.
[4] Ferguson and Vance, op. cit., p. 302.

Halifax[1] (on each of these days) & with Mr B. Johnstone.[2] Wrote Mem. on ditto. Read Sir G. Lewis—Malet's Olive Leaf[3]—Walpole's Hist. Doubts.[4] A minor ball in evg.

To C. S. P. FORTESCUE, Irish secretary,   Add MS 44122, f. 23.
26 November 1869.

I entirely agree with you about Digby Seymour:[5] perhaps it will be proper to give it the honour of burial in the *Cabinet*.

With regard to the suspension of the Habeas Corpus for the suppression of agrarian crime I hope we have not descended quite so low as that. But our first duty is I suppose to supply the agricultural population of Ireland with conditions of life under the Land Laws, not as they now are grossly unjust. After we have done that only can we expect to rally the sentiment of the population round us for the suppression of Habeas Corpus, if it shall then prove to be our deplorable & disgraceful necessity which God forbid, or for anything else.

Cannot the following statement be made good, & if so is it not very curious & instructive.

For a century (in round numbers) we have been gradually removing the penal & ascendancy laws in Ireland.

For a century (1761) Irish disturbances have prevailed. Simultaneously with the *extension* of the first process has been the extension of the second.

Whiteboyism was originally for the removal of a particular grievance. It was extended (apparently very much by the agency of the Landlords) to Tithe.

After emancipation, in 1831-2, the disturbances were carried on (see Lewis)[6] with a view to wider objects. Abolition of tithe was now primary—abolition of taxes (he supposes this to mean county cess) also, & menaces about rents. Still we went on without touching the laws that immediately affect the condition of the agricultural masses, except to aggravate the mischief at its sorest point by the Landed Estates Act, & the sale of the Tenants improvements over his head.

Now therefore came the last & extremest development of the political disease in the shape of the monster we term Fenianism—which represents the 'irreconciliables' of France. While thus political legislation has become more liberal (without yet touching the vital point) and agitation more hostile & extreme, a third process has been going on: the agitation has become less savage—personal torture & wanton cruelties are not heard of. Victims are despatched in the most summary manner by agrarian crime, while Fenianism aims at giving to resistance the noble form of public war.

Is this a true aperçu?

[1] See Steele, *Irish Land*, 226.
[2] Henry Alexander Munro-Butler-Johnstone, 1837-1902; liberal-conservative M.P. Canterbury 1862-78.
[3] See 26 July 68.
[4] H. *Walpole, *Historic doubts on the life and reign of King Richard the III* (1770).
[5] Fortescue deplored Seymour's proposal for a petition on release of Fenians; Add MS 44122, f. 17; see 7 Dec. 69.
[6] See 25 Aug. 45.

27. Sat.

Ch. 8½ AM. Wrote to Mr Fortescue—D. of Argyll—Ld Clarendon
—Mr G. Pringle—Archd. M'Kenzie—Bp of Ely—Rev Mr Burgess
—Mr Bruce—Bp of Lincoln—and minutes. Saw Mr Barker—Ld
Halifax. Ir. Land &c. Worked on letters & papers: also Catalogue.
Large party in evg. Read Sir G. Lewis—Mr Campbell (on Irish
Land).[1]

28. Adv.S.

Ch. 11 AM & 6½ PM. Wrote to Mrs Thistlethwayte—Ld Clarendon
—Sir J. Gray—Rev Mr Holland—The Queen—Mr Fortescue—Mr
Goschen—Mr Kinnaird—Chr of Exchr—and minutes. Some skir-
mishes with Lady Herbert. Read Manning's Pastoral (finished)[2]—
Mozley's fine Sermon[3]—Harcourt's What is Truth[4]—Dupanloup's
Letter to his people: wind![5]

To Sir J. GRAY, M.P., 28 November 1869.   Add MS 44423, f. 233.

You will readily believe that I am blown upon by many blasts from many
quarters but desirous not to be carried away by any of them.

I know not why any hopes ever entertained respecting the Land Measure of
the Government should now be either dissipated or depressed. That we could
not purpose to convert the land lords into stipendiaries has all along been reasonably assumed; so at least I suppose. I know of none who can have spoken for the
Govt. in such a way as to lower any expectations within the bounds of reason.
From my own mouth, though I have never been authorised or disposed to make
announcements, I am confident that nothing has been gathered from me[6] beyond
these two propositions, first that the distinctions between the Irish and the
British cases are broad and deep, secondly, that the land question of Ireland cannot now be settled by any measure limited to compensation for improvement.

I am no whit despondent, although I know that unless great efforts be made
on all hands to moderate expectations and desires, no less than jealousies and
idle fears, we shall certainly fail. But the Phoenix that rises from our ashes will
be a formidable portent.

29. M.

Ch 8½ AM. Wrote to M. Michel Chevalier—Ld Clarendon—Ld de
Grey—Duke of Argyll—Ld R. Gower—The Speaker—Ld Lyttelton

---

[1] A re-issue, with new preface and second report; see 11 Aug. 69.

[2] H. E. *Manning, *The Oecumenical Council* (1869); see Purcell, ii. 425.

[3] J. B. *Mozley, 'The Roman Council' (1869).

[4] W. V. *Harcourt, *'What is Truth?'* *A poetical dialogue on the philosophy of natural
and revealed religion* (1869).

[5] F. A. P. Dupanloup, 'Lettre . . . au clergé de son diocèse relativement à la définition de
l'infaillibilité au prochain concile' (1869).

[6] 'from me' added in pencil by diarist on the secretary's copy.

—Mr Mozley—and minutes. Cut alders with W.H.G. Conversation with Archd. Durnford.[1] Dinner party. Worked on Irish Land Clauses and papers. Read Lewis on Irish Dist.

To the DUKE OF ARGYLL, Indian secretary,   Add MS 44538, f. 6.
29 November 1869.

I have just been thanking that kind Ronald [Leveson Gower] who thought me worthy of a note about his Sister's death. What a mercy he was there.

Give to Irish Land all the thought that India will let you. I go with Ld. Spencer, if he accords to your argument on the Tenant Right, all the praise of clearness, vigor, & decision. But forgive me if I say that it does not & cannot *conclude* the questions, because it does not grapple with the main allegations on which the advocates for Tenant Right found themselves. For the last two months, I have worked daily, I think, upon the question, & so I shall continue to do. The literature of it is large, larger than I can master: but I feel the benefit of continual reading upon it. We have before us a crisis, & a great crisis, for us all, to put it on no higher ground: & a great honour, or a great disgrace. As I do not mean to fail through want of perseverance, so neither will I wilfully err through precipitancy, or through want of care & desire at least to meet all apprehensions, & all expectations, which are warranted by even the show of reason. My strong belief is that the main question must be whether we are prepared to go beyond compensation for improvements, & that *if* we are, there ought to be no vital difference lying beyond yr. point.

I send you two letters, which have just passed between Sir J. Gray & me.[2] I will look to the Torrington letter. I cannot feeling [*sic*] rather pleased with Fish.

To M. CHEVALIER, 29 November 1869.   Add MS 44538, f. 6.

I thank you very much for your letter & inclosure.[3] With respect to the latter I shall include it with the other matter relating to French agriculture, which I earnestly desire to see sifted & set forth for the better information of the people of this country. As regards the controversy now arising in France (& more or less in this country) respecting Free Trade, your letter is most reassuring. Were you to recede from the provisions of the Treaty, imperfect as they are it would be something like reviving the forms of writ, which run in our law by the name of 'De haeretico comburendo'.[4] I feel the utmost confidence in the views of the Emperor, who fixed his mind on the true point of the case for a Sovereign, namely the operation of Free Trade on the welfare of the *people*. And I need

[1] Staying with his family; see 9 Jan. 68.
[2] Argyll replied next day, Add MS 44101, f. 96: Gray's line 'is simply this—"Unless you give Fixity of tenure, with Government Rents, all Ireland will be Fenian". Well, if this be so, it must be faced. But I do not think we ought to be responsible for proposing to Parlt. a measure which is unjust in principle and which in its economical effects will certainly be disastrous. There is no argument for it—except Gray's—which is simply fear. . . .'
[3] Précis of the Enquête Agricole (see 13 Sept. 69); Add MS 44127, f. 48.
[4] Act of 1401 against Lollardy; R. Phillimore, *Ecclesiastical Law* (1895 ed.), ii. 842.

not add that we all attach the greatest value to your intelligent & determined championship. You will, I trust, have many & stout supporters.

30. Tu. St Andrew.

Ch. at 11 A.M. Wrote to Dr Lyon Playfair—Rev Mr Austin—Sir T.G.—Rev Mr Rawson—Mr Goschen—Ld Clarendon—Mr Bright —Mr Fortescue—Mr Hamilton—Ld R. Cavendish—Ld Monck— Sir T. Biddulph—and minutes. We cut down a large Elm. Dinner party. Conversation with Mr Tollemache[1] on Irish Land. Read Lewis on I.D. (finished)—Bp Thirlwall's Charge (began).[2]

To J. BRIGHT, president of the board of trade,   Add MS 43385, f. 53.
30 November 1869.

1. I thank you for your very kind & considerate letter and for your judicious advice about the Edinburgh banquet.[3] There are three reasons against it which together if not separately are conclusive: two are those you mention, the necessity of sparing strength, and the inopportuneness of the present juncture for crowing. The third is that the hard & heavy work of every day really does not admit of it without injury to that study of the Irish Land question which I am pursuing *daily* with all the patience I can. Will you then be so very kind as to explain to Mr. McLaren, with my best thanks for his kindness. Let us but settle the Irish land & then please God we will feast a little, if the health is still in our bodies.
2. Of course my Railway paper is open to review, & I am thankful for the conditional favour with which you regard it.
3. With respect to that department of the Land Laws on which you touch, I apprehend the English & the Irish case, perhaps also the Scotch?, are in substantial correspondence. If so they must be dealt with together, and not in the Irish Land Bill, which indeed will have plenty of material without this addition. But we are under some kind of pledge either to consider favourably Locke King's Bill or to take it up and enlarge its field. This is one of the subjects which I should be inclined to view as 'urgent' for the coming session: & I should be glad if a Committee of Cabinet were appointed to consider it together with the Law Officers. This I hope will be agreeable to your views.

Wed. Dec. One 1869.

Ch. 8½ AM. Wrote to Ld Clarendon—Ld Granville (2)—D. of Argyll—Mr Childers—D. of Windsor—Mr Fortescue—Mr Burnett— Mr O. Russell (Telegr.)—Lord Acton—and minutes. Worked on

---

[1] J. Tollemache (see 10 June 53) staying at the Castle with his nephew Henry James Tollemache, 1846-1906, tory M.P. Cheshire 1881-1906.

[2] C. *Thirlwall, 'A charge . . .' (1869).

[3] Bright advised refusal of D. *McLaren's invitation to an Edinburgh banquet; Add MS 44112, f. 103.

the tree of yesterday. Read Campbell on Irish Land——Finished Bp of St Davids.

To LORD ACTON, 1 December 1869.   Add MS 44093, f. 96.

I thank you for your most interesting letter.[1] It is a very sad one. I feel as deep and real an interest in the affairs of other Christian communions as in my own, and most of all in the case of the most famous of them all, and the one within which the largest number of Christian souls find their spiritual food.

I habitually attach very great weight to information received from you. On this account I cannot wholly put aside, though I cannot fully accept, your belief that my opinion may be cited and turned to account in Rome. Therefore, from the great interest attaching to the subject, I have at once requested Lord Clarendon to telegraph to Mr. Odo Russell in cipher tomorrow as follows: 'Please tell Lord Acton he may use the strongest language he thinks fit respecting my opinion on the subject about which he desires it should be known. I will write by the earliest opportunity.' That subject I take to be the effect in this country of 'Ultramontane' doctrines and proceedings upon legislation, policy, and feeling, with respect to Ireland, and to the Roman Catholic subjects of the Crown generally.

That effect is, in my opinion, most unfavourable. Comparing this moment with thirty or forty years back, the number of Roman Catholics in England is increased, persons of extraordinary talent and piety have joined the Latin Church; but the bulk of thinking, conscientious, and religious people are, so far as I can judge, much farther removed from, or at any rate very much more actively and sharply adverse to, the Church of Rome than they were at the former period.

There is one question of first-rate national importance coming on, with respect to which I regret that this effect of Ultramontanism will be conspicuously exhibited: it is the question of popular education in the three countries. Indeed, we have already had a taste of it in the powerful opposition which was raised against the very moderate measure of justice which we attempted to carry in 1866 with respect to the Irish colleges and the Roman Catholic University, and the storm will rise again when we come back, as we must before long, to the subject of the higher education in Ireland. The specific form of the influence will be this——it will promote the advancement of secularism. Ultramontanism and secularism are enemies in theory and intention, but the result of the former will be to increase the force and better the chances of the latter. Notwithstanding my general faith in any anticipation of yours, I cannot think it possible that Archbishop Manning will represent my opinions at Rome in any light different from this: and for the simple reason that he is a man of honour. He is, from our old friendship, thoroughly aware of my general leanings on these matters; and he has had particular reason to know them with reference to the present function. For, recently he wrote to me about an interview, and in replying (it was to be just before his departure) I used expressions which I would cite textually if I had them at hand. But the purport was this: 'How sad it is for us both, considering our personal relations, that we should now be in this predicament, that the things which the one looks to as the salvation of Faith and Church, the other regards as their destruction!'

[1] Of 24 November, from Rome on the Janus letters; Add MS 44093, f. 92, copy in Clarendon MSS, c. 498.

There has since been a very amicable correspondence between us, in which this idea has been canvassed and developed, but not in any measure qualified. Of course the terms used would have admitted of qualifications, had I not been desirous that my words should be strong and definite with respect to the present crisis, and plain speaking is our invariable rule. I shall send this letter to the Foreign Office, to go by the earliest safe opportunity for Rome. And much as I should like to have you here, I am glad you are there. It is also a great pleasure to me to address you by your new title, not as a mere decoration, which you would want less than any other man, but because I trust it opens to you a sphere of influence and action. We are in the thickest of the difficulties of Irish land tenures.[1]

[P.S.] Dec. 2. This morning I have seen what you say to Lord Granville, of course what I have said may be used by Mr Odo Russell if it is thought proper.

To LORD CLARENDON, foreign secretary,   Clarendon MSS, c. 498.
1 December 1869.

I have a most interesting letter from Lord Acton, of which I send you a copy withholding only a paragraph which is purely private & personal. I think it quite worth your sending on to the Queen. Though I am surprised at the importance which he seems to attach to what Manning will say of *me*, yet I think all that comes from him is weighty & I should therefore be glad if you would kindly telegraph to Odo Russell (who I presume has arrived at Rome) as within.[2] I have been warned not to write to him by post but I will send a letter to him to go by the first opportunity from F.O.

Mr Cox[3] *is* to have the offer of the Church of Upper Chelsea which I am very glad of.

I send on Elliot's interesting letter.

2. Th.

Ch. 8½ A.M. Wrote to Mrs Thistlethwayte—Ld Chichester—Mr Bruce—Ld Clarendon—Mr Goschen—Mr Fortescue—Ld Halifax —Ld Granville—and minutes. Worked on my Irish Land papers. Louisa (Lady G) came over. Cutting alders in aft. Read Japanese Debates.[4] Finished Mr Campbell on Ireland.

To H. A. BRUCE, home secretary, 2 December 1869.   Aberdare MSS.

Our first duty of course is to support the Irish Govt. with material means of preserving the public peace; & that is an easy one.[5] The next is to confide in them with regard to any prosecutions they may institute, & the third to give

---

[1] Mostly in Lathbury, ii. 49.

[2] 'Please tell Lord Acton he may use the strongest language he thinks fit respecting my opinion on the subject about which he desires it should be known. I will write by the earliest opportunity'; copy in Clarendon MSS, c. 498.

[3] Frederic Cox, curate in Upper Chelsea from 1869.   [4] Untraced.

[5] Bruce sent Irish press reports, Add MS 44086, f. 58.

great weight to their judgment, should they ask us to obtain for them further powers. I am not, however, as yet aware that life & property are on the whole to any serious extent less secure in Ireland now than in many former or even ordinary years. This point of course can be elucidated by facts.

As to Fenianism I think there is much in a letter which Mr. Bright has sent me, & which I pass on to you begging you to return it to him. For myself I incline to believe that it is like Satan in the Apocalypse who is described as very furious because it is his last time. However painful & shameful the Lowth Exhibition must be allowed to be, it is in my view good as a *symptom* rather than bad. The outpourings of the Fenian papers are loathsome, & they are fresh signs of the inveterate character of Irish evils. But as to the amount of fresh mischief caused by them, I do not feel so certain & wait to be convinced. Perhaps this may seem cold & stoical. I am only however describing impressions which may be modified & altered by further evidence & the judgments of others. Generally I think offences not carried into overt acts, nor directly intended to produce them, are less mischievous where tolerated than where assailed: but there are exceptions without doubt.

I hope Coleridge will report to us on the state of facts respecting his Bill.[1]

To C. S. P. FORTESCUE, Irish secretary,   Carlingford MSS CP1/72.
2 December 1869.

I am much pleased to find a great substantial concurrence in these papers: 1. Mr Dodd's which I now return, 2. A minute of de Grey's which I have sent to F.O. to be printed, 3. A paper from *Halifax* which I send you herewith.

With all three I *think* both you & I sympathize in the main—I have nearly shaped out my idea of applying your principle. The weak point in Halifax's paper I take to be that it assumes too largely the practice of tenant right *payments*. But it seems to me right to go upon the custom wherever we can: and the proper supplement to it seems to be that where the actual *facts* of customary payment are not proximate enough, the evidences of solvent persons as to what they are willing & able to pay may be taken.

I should try to conciliate the opponent of your idea by allowing the landlord the alternative of leases? An alternative which seems to me capable of being put into shape. Please to send Halifax's paper to Argyll marked *Early* & beg him to return it to Granville. We might do well to print it privately?

[P.S.] I am much struck with Campbell's argument pp. 68–71: & I think one of the great advantages of your idea is that in a vast number of cases the *two* claims would be merged in one, more easy to deal with than either separately. Only when they passed the *maximum* would it be needful to separate them.

To LORD HALIFAX, 2 December 1869.   Add MS 44183, f. 286.

I am much pleased with & very thankful for your paper.[2] Its weakest point seems to me that though the idea of tenant right is really universal or nearly so in Ireland, yet the facts of it, & especially the facts of it as recognised by the Landlord, are not so, though they too may be very widely spread. It seems to

---

[1] University Tests; Bruce sent report of Cambridge demand for complete abolition; ibid.
[2] On tenant right, arguing for flexibility; sent, with Fortescue's comments, 1 December, Add MS 44184, f. 275.

me, as at present advised, that this might be met in two ways, conjointly. 1. By taking the evidence of solvent persons, as to what they would be willing & able to give for the right of occupation, in illustration of, & by way of supplement to any evidence of tenant right not previously belonging to the holding or its immediate neighbourhood. 2. By allowing the landlord perhaps to bar tenant right by leases. You quite understand the scope of my paper. The assumptions I think will be made good up to this point, that the *material* form of the disease of Ireland is *the under cultivation of the soil by want of confidence.* Now that confidence has been given by tenant right in Ulster. The occasional extravagance of the amount would have to be checked by a maximum.

It is a great pleasure to me to feel instinctively that we are not likely to be very far apart in our views of this vital question.[1]

3. Fr.

Ch. 8½ A.M. Wrote to Ed. Chester Chronicle[2]—Mr Fortescue—Bp of Down—Mr W. Harcourt—A.E. West—Rev. N. Hall—Rev W. Rawson—and minutes for (in all I think) 28 letters. Mr Lambert[3] came in afternoon: & we had much conversation & work on my Queries & Mema (partly prepared in the forenoon) during the evening. He is admirably [*sic*]. Read Lewis (Appx)—Dilke Greater Britain.

Heads of further enactments requisite.[4]
1. Issues from the Exchequer. 2. County cess to be charged like the poor rates. 3. Powers of limited owners. 4. Possible improvements in the law on behalf of the landlord, as for example to prevent deterioration of farm in the closing years of a lease. 5. Loans to persons desirous to purchase waste lands where landlord is willing to sell; and to occupier to purchase lands in cultivation, and for the payment of improvement and occupation values on the joint application of landlord with consent of occupier. In all cases to be a first charge on landlord's estate. 6. Cases in which sub-letting or sub-dividing may be allowed, as for example (quarter acre?) allotment to labourers required for the service of a farm. 7. If any new judges are appointed under the Act they should be paid from the Consolidated Fund for ten years with a personal guarantee of salary to them and pensions, except when appointed to some other suitable office? 8. Stamps upon leases should be so regulated that the expense of holding from year to year should be fully equal to that of holding a lease. 9. Every notice to quit shall carry a stamp duty of (1s.?)

To C. S. P. FORTESCUE, Irish secretary,   Carlingford MSS CP1/73.
3 December 1869. 'Secret.'

You will receive by the next post a paper intended to be strongly in favour of your general view, as I understand it, with respect to the land question: very

[1] Halifax replied, 7 December, ibid., f. 288: 'The question between us is not as to the payment, but as to the mode of fixing the amount.'
[2] Probably inspiring its denial on 4 December that he was profiting from public appts.
[3] J. Lambert of the poor law board, superintending land inquiries at Dublin Castle.
[4] Printed (for the Cabinet) together with mem. at 14 Dec. 69, Add MS 44612, f. 1; secretary's draft, with Gladstone's additions, at Add MS 44758, f. 80.

inferior to yours in its development as regards machinery; but meant (1) to embody certain conclusions, (2) to raise the question in what may be (as matters now stand) a more favourable form, I think, for attracting assent.

I am also preparing, after the very proper example of some others, a paper by way of argument on the question.

The sky is at present very far from clear: but we must 'bate no jot of heart, or hope'.

My first named paper is gone to London to be copied. It is the material one. But I shall wish to have your judgment on the general arguments used in the other, before I think of circulating it.

Meantime, I inclose a short memorandum showing the points of deviation. Will the option of giving leases, as is proposed by me, repel the farmers? I hope not: but this point is very grave.

[P.S.] If you chance to have lost Lowe's paper pray ask another (by telegraph) from him to replace it, that you may let me have it.[1]

Memorandum

1. The Court can in no case presume a rent less than the actual rent. 2. The procedure will not be divided as under custom, or under act, but will in all cases be prima facie under custom. 3. Tenant right quoad [?] the element of good will, may be barred by a lease, unless when it can be shown that lease & tenant right have heretofore existed. This is of great weight. 4. All arrears of rent may be deducted from compensation monies. No tenant right is *created* by the act in holdings above a certain value.

4. Sat.

Ch. 8½ AM. Wrote to Mr Fortescue—D. of Argyll—The Queen—Mrs Bennett—Mr Bright—Chancr of Exr—The Viceroy—and minutes. Then work with Mr Lambert who fully possessed himself of my meaning & went on to Ireland to do the work there. Worked on letters (arranging). Read Sir J. Davies on Ireland:[2] Newman's letters to Mrs Helbert.[3]

To the DUKE OF ARGYLL, Indian secretary,   Add MS 44538, f. 10.
4 December 1869.

There would be no good purpose served by my returning to my observation on the *scope* of your ten arguments,[4] but as everything is useful which narrows differences I will observe that my paper is simply an exhibition of what follows

---

[1] Fortescue's reply urged rent as the real problem with tenant right; Add MS 44122, f. 43.

[2] Sir J. *Davies, A Discouerie of the True Causes why Ireland was never entirely subdued* (1612).

[3] Wife of Mrs Gladstone's rescue home assistant (see 27 Sept. 66); on her proposed conversion to Rome (which she effected 1874) and the Council; see *Newman*, xxiv. 323, 328 etc.

[4] Add MS 44101, ff. 90–104.

upon certain assumptions, & neither concludes nor proposes to conclude any-thing. Am I right in gathering from the latter point of your letter that you are prepared to take the property of the landlord in part improvements & give it to the tenant within whatever limits, but that prospectively, & outside the range of the Ulster custom, you are not prepared to offer to the occupiers of the Irish soil above £10 per an. anything beyond compensation for improvements?

With regard to those below £10 the question arises what will be the best prac-tical rule for ascertaining the amount of eviction damages? Can you find a better than this. That the Court should ascertain what has been heretofore given by incoming to outgoing tenants for like holdings, & two where the former cannot be sufficiently learned what would be given within a limit by a solvent man for the holding itself? I do propose this polemically for you have said nothing against it. But what I would most *earnestly* entreat of you is not to rely too much on Highland experience, but to acquaint yourself by careful reading with the rather extensive facts & history of the Irish Land question. My own studies in it are very imperfect though pursued to the best of my ability: but it has re-vealed to me many matters of fact which have seriously modified my views most of them connected with & branching out of the very wide extension of the idea & even the practice of tenant right mostly perhaps *unrecognised* beyond the limits of the Ulster Custom.

To J. BRIGHT, president of the board of trade,   Add MS 43385, f. 56.
4 December 1869. 'Secret.'

I can by no means obey your request to keep your able paper[1] until we meet in London: for I want to ask you to alter it a little.

It is not the courageous part of your paper to which I now object; though I doubt the policy of the reference to feebleness & timidity as men in a Cabinet do not like what may *seem* to imply that they are cowards.

It is your argument (a very overstrained one in my opinion) against Fortes-cue's propositions, and your proposal (so it reads) to put them back in order of discussion to the second place, *now*, when the mind of the Cabinet has been upon them for six weeks.

You do not require to be told that the effect of such a statement, as is in pp 5, 6, is most feebly counteracted by your adding 'all this may be necessary'.

Had the Cabinet adopted at this moment a good and sufficient scheme for dealing with the Irish tenants as tenants, I should care little how much you de-preciated such a scheme in comparison with one for converting them into owners.

But the state of things is most critical. This is not a time at which those who in substance agree can afford to throw away strength by the *relative* deprecia-tion of those parts of a plan of relief to which they do not themselves give the first place in importance. It is most dangerous to discredit *propositions which you mean to adopt* in the face of any who (as yet) do not mean to adopt them, and who may consistently and honourably use all your statements against them, nay who would really be bound to do so.

No part of what I have said is an argument against your propositions. To the bulk of them I am not indisposed in principle. The three first are for the U.K.

[1] Of 1 December 1869, in Cobden MSS, West Sussex R.O.; see Steele, *Irish Land*, 215, 339.

The sixth is done in principle, & I am told we have gone as far as the existing rights of Lessees will permit. The fourth is I consider unquestionable. The fifth I shall be glad to find practicable. And in the sense of the 7th I shall be glad to act if possible, hoping that some other *mode* than State Land jobbing may be discovered. But thus much I say that you may understand that my anxiety is to be in the direction of what you heavily damage, and not of what you recommend.

My general opinion is, however, that it is desirable to act upon the land laws generally, at the present time: but that if your seven propositions were law today, you would have made but a very small progress towards settling the land question of Ireland. I promise you, nevertheless, that I will not put an argument to this effect into a minute for the Cabinet.

For all this very plain speech, you will I am sure forgive me.

5. 2 S.Adv.

Ch 11 AM with H.C., and [blank space]. Wrote to Mrs Thistlethwayte—After receiving & reading her number XXVIII. Also wrote to Ld Clarendon—Mr Fortescue—W.H.G.—Baron Banneto(?)[1]—Mr Buxton. Conversation with Mrs Helbert on the Roman Controversy. Read N. Hall on Peabody[2]—Bp of Ely's Charge[3]—Dean Milman's History[4]—Bp of Rochester's Charge[5]—Nicene Canons.

To LORD CLARENDON, foreign secretary,   Clarendon MSS, c. 498.
5 December 1869.

Individually I should be for 'unrestricted arbitration' in the sense defined by Thornton, no less than for 'kind words'; if the concession have value in the eyes of the Americans.
[P.S.] I am afraid it is not that I am charitable about motives, but only stupid.[6]

To C. S. P. FORTESCUE, Irish secretary,   Carlingford MSS CP1/75.
5 December 1869. 'Private.'

I am a good deal staggered at the idea of any interference with present rents.[7] But I shall not speak on this subject to others. It will be difficult enough to carry the substance of the plan you proposed without any enlargement of it. I hope to see you again before the question comes on in the Cabinet.

On Sat. Sun. & Mon. Dec. 11-13 I am to be out of town—I hope.

Bright is very full of wastelands & generally of his own plan, considerably (at present) to the detriment of yours. He wants the Govt. to buy waste lands, &

---

[1] Or Baretto; unidentified; had requested a baronetcy; Add MS 44538, f. 12.
[2] On Peabody's d. in November 1869.   [3] E. H. *Browne, 'A charge' (1869).
[4] See 27 Aug. 54.   [5] J. C. Wigram, 'A charge' (1864).
[6] Clarendon's letter of 4 Dec., Add MS 44134, f. 109, admitted he had been oversceptical about Fish.
[7] Fortescue's letter of 4 December 1869, Add MS 44122, f. 43, suggested 'indirect' interference with rents.

says this is not against political economy but yours is. (I think he will come right).[1]

It appears to me we might in the case of waste lands lend money (on proper conditions) to *any buyer* (in the case of other lands we are only to lend to occupiers). What do you think of this? No hurry for reply. I go tomorrow.

6. M. [London]

Church 8½ A.M. Wrote to Ld Granville—Rev Mr Rawson—Bp of Ely—Mr Wetherell—Mr West—Mr Burnett—and minutes. Finished Sir John Davies's very valuable volume. Worked on papers & preparations for departure. Off at 3.30. London at 10. Went to see Mrs Th: & so home.

7. Tu.

Wrote to Master of St John's [Cambridge][2]—Ld Dufferin—Ld Spencer—Mr Digby Seymour—the Queen—Watson & Smith—Mr Walker—C.G.—& minutes. Saw Ld Camperdown—Ld Granville—Mr Glyn—Sir J. Lacaita—Ld Clarendon—Mr Childers—Chr of Exchr—Mr Cardwell—Mr Goschen—Ld Dalhousie. Cabinet 2½-5½. Dined at Dowager Duchess of Somerset's. Saw Harris X. Read Prendergast's Cromwellian Settlement.[3]

Cabinet Dec. 7/69.[4]
√ 1. Ld Lieut[enant of Ireland]—Ld Dufferin:[5] Copies of Cabinet Minutes.
√ 2. Digby Seymour's proposal.[6]
○ 3. Khelat. Proposed Declaration.[7]
√ 4. State of Ireland[8]
   5. Next Cabinets. 9. 10. 14. 16. 17.
   6. Chanc. of Exr. Civil Service Appts. Circular to ask the views of the heads of Depts.
√ 7. Land Intestacy & Bill.
√ 8. Terms discussed for a dispatch on the Alabama question.
√ 9. Khedive. Sultan to be advised not to require answer.

[1] See Add MS 43385, f. 56.
[2] On arrangements for the depn. on 15 December; Add MS 44538, f. 12.
[3] J. P. Prendergast, *The Cromwellian settlement of Ireland* (1865).
[4] Add MS 44637, f. 115.
[5] *Dufferin and Spencer were permitted to see cabinet minutes on Irish land; Add MS 44538, f. 13.   [6] See 26 Nov. 69.
[7] *Argyll requested, in an undated printed cabinet paper, a declaration to Persia of British paramountcy in Khelat; Add MS 44637, f. 119.
[8] Sheet following this agenda reads: 'Committee on such questions connected with the descent and disposition of Land as are not confined to Ireland. Dec. 7' Add MS 44637, f. 116.

√ 10. Musurus. asks 20 m̃ cartridges. Letter has been sent giving 5m̃. To be re-
    called as liable to misconstruction.
√ 11. Childers—may sell a wooden ship to Prussia.
√ 12. C. of E.: Minton[?] and Sir W. Dunbar's absences.[1] 5 mo. & 3½ mo.
    leave this year.

To C. S. P. FORTESCUE, Irish secretary,   Carlingford MSS CP1/77.
7 December 1869. 'Secret.'

The paper I sent you goes into many details, which it is not urgent to settle
at this moment, though I went through them for the purpose of raising the
points.[2] But one thing is of pressing urgency, & that is that there should be clear
mutual comprehension and concurrence among some of us as a *nucleus* around
which the deliberations of the Cabinet may group themselves in practical forms.
It would not be possible, *now*, that you & I should make progress by correspondence in detail. Therefore I enclose a very brief memorandum which contains
those principal matters that seem to me suitable for submission to the Cabinet.[3]
I think we should now keep to this strictly documentary manner of proceeding,
& perhaps (without prejudice to the paper you announce) you would kindly
note down on paper what you approve or, where you differ from the developments or additions which I have made to your original basis, what you would
substitute. If you are not to be here till next Monday I think it will then be too
late to set about *forming* the basis of a plan. But unless we are now *agreed* on
the main propositions, your coming over at once is absolutely necessary. From
Saturday to Monday I do not know where the Cabinet will be, & it must therefore be on *Thursday* & *Friday* next that I must definitely endeavour to ascertain
opinions, if the regular discussion is to stand over till Tuesday.
    The grounds of all I have said I will beg you to take for granted, as far as they
are not apparent, until we meet.[4]

To EARL SPENCER, Irish lord lieutenant,   Add MS 44538, f. 12.
7 December 1869.

1. I have read to the Cabinet today your statement dated yesterday of the views
of the Irish executive Government with reference to the present juncture.[5] Any
demands you may make with regard to force will be cheerfully & promptly met.
We await the reports you may make as to the policy or impolicy of prosecuting
anyone as for instance the priest who held forth upon 'trembling'. But we see
no reason to question in any way the propriety of your present intentions. The
recent excitement about the Irish situation has not I think disturbed the equilibrium of our minds any more than of yours.

    [1] T. J. Minton, engraver to the Mint.
    [2] Fortescue's of 6 Dec. denied tenant right was widespread enough to base a bill on it;
    [3] Gladstone apparently sent him draft of mem. at 14 Dec. 69.
    [4] Fortescue replied with a mem. on 8 Dec.; ibid., f. 66.
    [5] Add MS 44306, f. 193: 'At present we do not think that an outbreak is planned or
imminent. . . . We hope that the Show of troops in disaffected places, & the knowledge that
we are ready for the worst will stifle the rising excitement.'

2. I mentioned to the Cabinet your desire to have copies of any minutes printed by the Cabinet for its members individually on the question of Irish Land. You are well aware 1. that these documents are of the most secret character, 2. that they for the most part express not the positive or final, but the partial & provisional views of those who write them. With this explanation, the Cabinet are most willing that you should have copies of the minutes which its members will send to you accordingly. I may probably myself add one to the number.

8. Wed.

Wrote to Chancr of Exr—Baroness M. de Rothschild—M. Gladstone —Mr Fortescue—Sir R.S. Adair—Ld Fermoy—Mr Stephenson— Sir W. Dunbar—Sir W. Farquhar—Ld Devon—Ld Halifax—Sir T. Brinckman[1]—C.G.—and minutes. Saw Mr Thornton Hunt—D. of Argyll—Mr Glyn—Chancr of Exr *cum* Mr Lowe—Conclave on new appointments—Ld Bessborough—Mr Ouvry—Mrs Rothesy— Cambr.Univ. Deputation on Tests[2]—Saw Mrs Thistlethwayte. Dined at Mr Glyn's: & sat 10¼–11¾ with D. of Devonshire on Irish Land. Read Froude's Hist.[3]—Maclagan on Irish Land.[4]

To C. S. P. FORTESCUE, Irish secretary,   Add MS 44538, f. 14.
8 December 1869.

I shall not form a conclusive opinion until tomorrow morning, & shall then telegraph to you if I find it necessary in conformity with the views expressed in my letter of yesterday. Your letter opens a very wide field of discussion, which may perhaps be narrowed by my brief mem: but it is absolutely necessary that something short & summary containing heads of a plan should be ready *before* we come to the day of the Cabinet for discussing it; & I do not think the Cabinet will on any terms consent to meddle with rents now paid. My mem. of yesterday was an effort to bring the matter to a head, for at present as far as preparation for discussion is concerned, we are behind the point where we stood 6 weeks ago. I think you are in objecting to the form of *veto* on improvements. I had forgotten the provision of 66.

To R. LOWE, chancellor of the exchequer,   Add MS 44538, f. 13.
8 December 1869.

Perhaps you will kindly communicate with Frem[antle] & Steph[enso]n to give the opportunity of stating their views on the question of throwing open first appointments in the C.S.[5]

There is another person whose position is more delicate, I mean Glyn, as the change would affect more or less the basis of his office, his *quid pro quo*. Of

[1] Sir Theodore Henry Lavington Brinckman, 1798–1880; cr. bart. 1831; unsuccessfully requested a peerage; Add MS 44538, f. 14.

[2] See *The Guardian*, 15 Dec. 1869, 1396.   [3] See 23 May 56.

[4] P. Maclagan, *Land culture and land tenure in Ireland* (1869).

[5] See 23 Nov. 69.

course the Cabinet will decide nothing on what touches his functions without hearing him, unless indeed he is satisfied to say what he has to say to you & me. For this purpose I shall be very glad to see him with you if you think proper. I shall probably see him this morning & will tell him what I have written to you.

9. Th.

Wrote to Mr Fortescue—Watson & Smith—The Queen—Earl Russell—C.G.—Att.Gen. Ireland—D of Argyll—Miss K. Gladstone—and minutes. Worked on Irish Land. Saw Mr Thornton Hunt—Sir R. Phillimore—Mr Kinnaird—Ld Chancellor (Irish Land)—Ld Hartington (do). Cabinet 2½-5½. Dined at Sir R. P[hillimore']s. Read Maclagan—Dupanloup's First Letter.[1]

Cabinet Dec. 9. 69[2]
1. Clarendon: Khedive submits—Expectations of the French in Rome—U.S. dispatch. What private letter to be written to Thornton on claims[3]—Dispp. about French Treaty—proceedings in France.
2. State of Ireland—Reports.
3. Ecclesiastical Titles Bill. To be repealed with a Declaration in the Preamble.[4]
4. Mr Bruce gave an outline of a Licensing Bill with a power to inhabitants to check increase. To be prepared.[5]
5. Bill on the basis of Locke King's measure is being prepared.[6] Committee of Cabinet reported to this effect.

Query[7]
The leanings of the Cabinet are to kind words.
    to unrestricted arbitration as limited in scope by Mr Thornton—to examining maritime law in regard to the duties of neutrals with a view to greater precision & the avoidance of causes of dispute De.9.

To the DUKE OF ARGYLL, Indian secretary,   Add MS 44538, f. 16.
9 December 1869.

I exceedingly regret your disappearance from among us, & yet more its cause.[8] Your note conveyed the idea of a great anxiety. God grant that on your arrival

[1] See 28 Nov. 69.
[2] Add MS 44637, f. 120. Note passed to Fortescue (Add MS 44637, f. 123) reads: 'May I see you on Irish Railways after Cabinet—for a few minutes only. [In diarist's hand.] Yes [Fortescue].'
[3] Notes for it at Add MS 44637, f. 122.
[4] The attempt at repeal failed 1870, succeeded 1871.
[5] Bruce announced on 3 May 1870 inability of govt. to produce a bill that session: *H* cci. 84.
[6] Real Estate Succession Bill introduced and dropped 1870; see 13 Mar., 10 July 69.
[7] Add MS 44637, f. 122.
[8] Duchess' severe, prolonged illness at Inverary; Argyll hinted at but did not offer resignation to be with her; Add MS 44101, f. 129.

today you may find it wholly removed. The Duchess has indeed had a heavy strain upon her for some time, & I cannot wonder at her feeling the effects severely. Fortescue will not be here till Monday. No Irish Land till Tuesday. I fear we must take it then. I think I understood you yesterday to be inclined to give *whatever it may be right to give in the form and on the basis* of recognising customs wherever this can be done. I lean strongly in that direction. Halifax sent me a paper in that sense which ought to have reached you before this time. I had two interesting & satisfactory conversations yesterday with Ld. Bessborough & the Duke of Devonshire.

[P.S.] I send you a short mem. which I think comprises the knottiest part of the [question.]

To C. S. P. FORTESCUE, Irish secretary,   Carlingford MSS CP1/79.
9 December 1869. 'Private.'

Three material points on which we do not yet seem to be at one, are 1. Whether present rents shall be subject to interference. I will not argue this. My impression is that you will find too many or rather all ready to argue it against you. 2. Whether it is expedient to adopt *wherever* it can be made available the custom of the country as the basis for compensation on eviction & the like. I cannot make out from your papers whether you wholly dissent from this. From your reception of Halifax's paper (which I hope you sent on but I have heard nothing of it) I hoped you had agreed on it. I have acquired a strong conviction upon it; of which I have written out the grounds; but I shall not circulate the paper till I understand your views more fully. When the evidence from past transactions fails I think the solvent tenant subject to a limiting scale better than a scale alone—but this may be of less consequence.

3. My proposal is that by leasing the Landlord may cut off the tenant right. You incline to substitute what would come to this, that Landlord & tenant may by a lease 'contract themselves' out of the Act *quoad* tenant right. I should like to converse fully on this with you. And as you intimate that the Attorney General can come with you I hope you will bring him.

On Monday till evening I shall be out of town & I have a duty dinner to attend but if you & he will come here at 10 (or I will drive to your house) we can talk over these points & either then or on Tuesday morning we can I think get matters sufficiently into shape. I therefore do not telegraph to you.

[P.S.] I thought & think it a great merit in your first paper that it tended so greatly to merge all claims in one. If *convenient* please to send back the detailed paper you received on Sunday by return of post. I have only a very rough draft.

10. Fr.

Wrote to Mr Fortescue—D. of Newcastle—Mr Western—Lord Clarendon—C.G.—Ld Chancellor—The Queen—The Viceroy of I. —Mr Helps—Mr Knollys—Mr Lingen—and minutes. Saw Ld Granville & Ld Bessborough (on Irish Land, 11-12½)—Mr Glyn (2) —Mr Stephenson—Conclave on appointments—Mr Lingen. Dined at Ld Lyttelton's. Saw Mrs Th. after—Read Maclagan on Irish Land (finished).

Cabinet D. 10/69.[1]
√ 1. Day for the meeting of Parlt.—Feb. 8. subject to recon[sideratio]n if required.
√ 2. Clarendon's letter to Thornton.
√ 3. Bills to be prepared: a. Merchant Shipping b. Mutiny Bill—recast. c. Matrim[onial] Jurisdiction (Ireland) d. Naturalisation Bill
     Committee of Cabinet. For the Lords: e. Courts of Appeal—Union of Courts of Justice
√ 4. Mr Childers stated the outline of the Navy Estimates—which was approved.
√ 5. Mr Cardwell. Army Estimates not ready: reduction will be somewhere about £700,000.
     Stated the Colonial arrangements with reference to Colonial Policy: & Ld Granville stated his general view.

To LORD HATHERLEY, lord chancellor,   Add MS 44538, f. 17.
10 December 1869.

The enclosed very rude sketch[2] contains an outline of very short propositions embracing the knottiest points of the Irish Land Bill. Substantially what I call 'subject to a maximum & minimum' would I think correspond with your scale of 'damages for eviction'. But I am wellnigh convinced that there would be very great practical advantage in taking our stand upon the custom of the country so far as it can any where be ascertained, subjecting it to any needful limitations, & applying secondary or auxiliary means of judgment where direct evidence of custom is not forthcoming.

To EARL SPENCER, Irish lord lieutenant,   Add MS 44538, f. 17.
10 December 1869.

I have received your paper[3] & will desire that it be circulated forthwith. No one can fail to appreciate its just & liberal spirit & it will form a liberal contribution to our stock of materials for dealing with this very difficult but not unhopeful question. My expression of a wish that you & Fortescue might be near one another, has ended I think in leaving you a little nearer to him than to me— I mean as to the form, as to spirit & substance I do not think there is much difference among us. I am greatly pleased with Bessborough's views. I had much wished to pay my respects to Lady Spencer, but it has really been beyond my power to call.

11. Sat. [*Boveridge, Dorset*]

Wrote to Ld Normanby—Chancr of Exr—D. of Argyll—Ld Granville—G.G. Glyn—Rev Mr Sadler—Ld de Grey—C.G.—and minutes. Off at 10.30 with A. K[innaird] to join Mrs Th. and her party at Waterloo. We reached Boveridge[4] in heavy rain between 2

---

[1] Add MS 44637, f. 127.   [2] Not found, but see 14 Dec. 69.
[3] Papers on tenant right; see Add MS 44306, f. 198.
[4] Boveridge House, A. F. Thistlethwayte's house near Cranborne.

& 3. Saw the fine *stud*. And walked a little about the place. Much conversation with Mr Carnegie[1] the Vicar who dined. Also with Miss Kennedy. Saw Mrs Th. several times. Read Miss Barnard Smith's Poems[2]—Sir W. Petty on Ireland[3]—Les Emprunts Publics.[4] Read aloud Longfellow's Building of the Ship.[5]

To R. LOWE, chancellor of the exchequer,   Add MS 44538, f. 18.
11 December 1869.

I enclose my rough papers on Irish Railways a sort of wing to the Irish Land measure. I rather think you will find Cardwell not unfavourably disposed in principle to this sort of plan which I have detailed to him in general terms. Mr. Lingen at once accepted. It remains rather private until de Grey has been informed.

12. 3 S.Adv.

Cranborne Ch mg no service aftn. Mr T. read a Sermon of over an hour. Wrote to C.G. Read Dr Prothero Smiths notable papers[6]— Sterne's Sermons[7]—Baring Gould's Religious belief[8]—Tischendorff's (most interesting) 'When were the Gospels written?'.[9] Mrs Th. came to my rooms aft. & at night. Walk with her. Miss Fawcett[10] let down her hair: it is a robe. So Godiva
                    'the rippled ringlets to the knee'.[11]

13 M. [*London*]

Wrote to Ld Granville—Mrs C. Rumpff[R]—Miss Harris—and minutes. Dined at Mr Glyn's: 3 hours with Fortescue & Sullivan on Irish Land. Read Hist. Dorsetshire[12]—Irish Tracts. Went with Mrs Th. who drove to the 'meet' at Mr Churchills,[13] when I made acquaintance with Ld Ranelagh[14] & others. Rode back with her. Also she came with us to Fordingbridge station. How very far I was at first

---

[1] John Hemery Carnegie, vicar of Cranborne from 1842.
[2] C. Barnard Smith, *Poems* (1869).
[3] See 23 July 47.   [4] Untraced.
[5] H. W. Longfellow, 'The building of the ship' from *Poems of Longfellow*, 2v. (1880).
[6] P. Smith, probably *Scriptural authority for the mitigation of the pains of labour* (1848).
[7] *The sermons of Wm. Yorick [L. *Sterne]*, 7v. (1760-69).
[8] S. B. Gould, *The origin and development of religious belief*, 2v. (1869-70).
[9] See 29 Aug. 69.   [10] Unfortunately unidentified.
[11] Tennyson, *Godiva*, 47.
[12] Probably J. Hutchins, *The history and antiquities of the County of Dorset*, 3rd ed., 4v. (1861-73).
[13] George Churchill, J.P., of Alderholt Park.
[14] Thomas Heron Jones, 1812-85; soldier; 7th Viscount Ranelagh 1820.

from understanding her history and also her character. Came up with
A. Kinnaird. Arrived at 7¼. C.G. here.

14. Tu.

Wrote to Sir H. Elliot—Mr Bouverie—Mr Pringle—Sir H. Elliot—
The Queen (3)—Sir J. Simpson—Mr Cogan MP.—Duke of Argyll
—C.G.—Mrs Thistlethwayte—and minutes. Cabinet (Irish Land
&c.) 2½-6. Dined at Sir A. Panizzi's. Saw Mr Cardwell—Robn G.—
Ld de Grey—Mr Glyn. Read Raleigh's Life[1]—Sargant on Ireland.[2]

Cabinet Dec 14/69.[3]
1. ⟨Fix day for meeting of Parliament.⟩
   Home Sec[retary] read Viceroy [of Ireland]'s letter.[4] Further communication
2. Irish Land Bill. Leading provisions considered for 3 hours. Agreed to 1. 2. 3.
   and the doctrine of limit *generally* received preponderating approbation[5]
                                                                          WEG

Mem[orand]a for Cabinet of Dec. 15 [sc. 14, 1869].[6]
1. Opening of Parliament
2. Date for the adjournment *Feb. 6*
3. Clarendon—caution as to speech[7]
3. [*sic*] Crown Preferments in Ireland. Mem[orandum] drawn.

Irish Land[8]
General Propositions adopted Dec. 14. 69.
1. To recognize custom commonly known as the Ulster custom of tenant right.
2. As between tenant and landlord, to reverse the presumption of law as to property in improvements.
3. To recognize the general customs of the country as to payments to outgoing
   tenants, whether by incoming tenant or by landlord, if paid in respect of
   occupation value, so far as they can be ascertained, but subject to limitations.
4. Where evidence of the facts of custom is deficient, court (or arbiter) to award
   damages for eviction according to a scale.
5. Landlord desiring to bar title of outgoing tenant to any payment, may (except in Ulster) so do by giving in lieu of it leases for not less than 31 or more
   years.

[1] Probably E. *Edwards, *The life of Sir Walter Raleigh* (1868).
[2] W. L. Sargant, 'Ireland and the tenure of land', in *Essays of a Birmingham manufacturer*, i (1869).
[3] Add MS 44637, f. 130.   [4] On Irish agrarian crime.
[5] For these, see Steele, *Irish Land*, 252, 277 ff.
[6] Add MS 44637, f. 129. On Windsor Castle notepaper.
[7] Not found reported.
[8] Add MS 44612, f. 1; mem. printed (for the Cabinet) from a holograph at Add MS
44758, f. 123; the holograph is correctly dated as above; in transcribing it for the printer the
secretary changed the date to 1 December 1869.

Proposed Limitations of Proposition 1. a. When the tenant right is shown to have been bought up by the landlord, the Ulster custom cannot be pleaded. b. The custom to be recognized is that of the estate when there is an estate custom; when there is not, that of the district, or neighbourhood or county. c. When the landlord removes a tenant, ought he to pay him the price paid on entering to the tenancy, or the price of the day? The latter. d. Arrears of rent to be deducted from the tenant-right money as under the present custom.

Limitations of Proposition 2. 1. Not to affect any existing lease or existing written contract when there are covenants to a contrary effect. 2. Nor any improvement proved to have been made by landlord. 3. Nor any made by tenant under covenant with landlord for valuable consideration. 4. Nor any specific improvement barred by covenant with landlord as inconsistent with the general advantage of his estate. 5. Nor to any executed previous to the occupancy of the present tenant, and of those from whom he has purchased or derived. 6. Nor in the case of future leases of 31 years and over, to any improvement except in—*a.* buildings. *b.* reclamation of land. 7. Nor to include any improvements but such as are suitable to the holding and increase its value. Present value to an incoming tenant to be the test. 8. Nor in the cases of past improvements, to any which are not shown to have been executed (unless they be buildings or reclamation of land) within (20) years before the passing of the Act. 9. Nor to any exhausted improvement. 10. Nor to any improvement which the landlord has himself covenanted to make, until after the lapse of a reasonable time without fulfilment of the covenant.

Proposed Limitations of Proposition 3.
Provisions of the measure respecting customary payments to outgoing occupiers, outside the range of Ulster custom, to be limited as follows: 1. To apply only when the occupier is disturbed by act of the landlord. 2. Should not labourers upon a farm holding a portion of land not greater than ($\frac{1}{4}$) acre by way of garden be allowed to contract themselves out of the Act? (Disposed of by being remitted to Mr. Fortescue, in Ireland). 3. Nor to future leases of (31) years and upwards. 4. Nor to any holding which shall hereafter be sub-let or sub-divided without the written consent of the landlord. 5. Nor to any case of eviction on account of non-payment of rent. 6. Arrears of rent and damages to the farm to be chargeable against any sum awarded in respect of occupation value. 7. And the maximum to be (7) years rent, liable to increase at the discretion of court, if said maximum shall not fairly cover tenants improvements in respect of buildings and reclamation.

15. *Wed.*

Wrote to Ld Granville—Mr Bouverie—Mr Pringle—Sir H. Elliot—Mr Bruce—and minutes. And wrote to Watson's—Scotts—Mr Twisleton—Mr Goschen—Robn G. Broke perforce my engagement to dinner. Dissenting Depn on University Tests 2½-3½.—Cambr. & Oxf. Deputations (united) on do 4½-5¼.[1] Saw Ld Napier—Ld Normanby—Mr M'Coll—Mr Gilpin *cum* Mr Read—and [blank]. Read Tennyson, new vol. Went to bed at 7 fairly shut up by a light cough.

[1] Cambridge mem. in Add MS 44612, f. 3.

16. Th.

Wrote to Mrs Thistlethwayte—Ld Granville—Ld Russell—The Queen (Tel. & Mem.)—and minutes. Saw Ld Bessborough—Mr West —Dr Clark (bis). In bed all day:[1] & coming round. Read all Tennyson to the end. Much beauty but a downward movement. Read also on Ireland and worked on MS. of the Irish Land question.

To EARL RUSSELL, 16 December 1869.   PRO 30/22/16F, f. 129.

In my last I meant to assure you that the Viceroy had been placed under no inhibition or restraint by the Cabinet either in relation to press prosecutions or otherwise.[2] Since I wrote it we have had further communications from him which render it quite possible that before Parliament meets he may make specific proposals. It is agrarian crime which at present offers a more menacing aspect than Fenianism. The noise, the bluster, the interruption of Land law meetings, the insult to law & decency in the election of Rossa, and the tone of the Fenian Press, do not look like an intention of immediate or very early outbreak: they may even show that such an idea is receding into the distance. Still they are active both in Ireland & England: & they are most closely watched by the Govt. One of their worst papers, the People, is we are told about to die immediately, & the Irishman is stated to have declined greatly in circulation. So far so good.

I am not sure whether I am to understand that you think that we ought to propose for the three kingdoms whatever we propose for Ireland in regard to Land Tenures. I suppose we should 'think twice' before doing this. Neither am I quite sure in what sense I am to understand the improvement of Ireland since 1829, as regards the mass of the people. All the accounts I ever heard of their feelings from the formation of the Government of 1859 onwards were to the effect that disaffection was deeper and more determined than ever. But you probably refer to material improvement, and to the great and favourable change in all above the mass: in regard to which I trust there is no doubt.

The state of the Duchess of Argyll is most sad: but I believe her case is not hopeless. The paralysis is of the left arm (like the Archbishop's) and this is said to be less perilous in immediate consequences than the right.

I will make use of your information about Amberley on any fitting occasion that may offer.

17. Fr.

Better D.G: rose at 1 for the Cabinet. Wrote to Lady Stanley (Ald[erley])—Bp of Gloucester—The Queen—Ld Hartington—D. of Argyll—C.P. Fortescue—Watsons—and minutes. Cabinet 1½-6 on Irish Land. Saw Chancellor[,] G. Glyn & Fortescue on Sullivan's case.[3] Saw Mr Glyn—Dr Clark—Mr West. Dined with the Phillimores. Saw Sir R.P.—conversation on *progress* of the Church in our

---

[1] Thus missing the cabinet.

[2] Russell wrote from Rome of the Irish press's treason; Add MS 44294, f. 211.

[3] *Sullivan wished to resign; see Ramm I, i. 78 and Add MS 44423, f. 312.

time. Read L. Stanley on Univ. Tests[1]—Irish Tenant Right—Sargant's Essays.[2]

Cabinet D. 17. 69[3]

√ 1. Abp of Canterbury asks for a suffragan Bp.
√ 2. Report on University Test Deputations[4]
√ 3. Army Estimates. Reduction of 10400 men. Saving 700 to 800m[ille]. Approved.
√ 4. Irish Land considered at great length. a Bill to be drawn. Mema. prepared for Mr Thring[5]

To C. S. P. FORTESCUE, Irish secretary,　　　　Carlingford MSS CP1/81.
17 December 1869.

I hope we shall not be under the necessity of retracing the steps which the Cabinet found itself able to make on Wednesday.

I understand you to be apprehensive lest the taking of evidence upon general customs of tenant right in Ireland should have the effect of barring any remedy for over-rented occupiers.

The Cabinet has not yet considered the question whether such a remedy should be given. But if they decide on giving it I cannot see how their intention as to tenant right customs need interfere with it.

Within the maximum there could be a discretion and words might if necessary be inserted to let in the point. But it is surely the tenant not the landlord who will produce evidence of their customs: and when the tenant thinks it for his interest rather to fall back upon the damages for eviction without reference to custom, he will do so.

I hope we shall today go over the limitations & conditions which must accompany the leading propositions of Tuesday. You will be ready I hope with your compensation-scale, as in the paper sent to me,[6] or as you may have considered it further. And pray also think of any other heads or particulars of the Bill to which a preliminary assent may be needful.

[P.S.] I hope to meet you at 1.30.

18 Sat.

Rose at 10.15. Wrote to Mrs Thistlethwayte—Lord Wrottesley[7]—Lord Devon—Lord Chancellor—Justice Mellor[8]—Ld Kimberley—C. Rumpff[R]—Mr Fortescue—Mr Lingen—and minutes. Dined at home with C., Willy, & Stephy. 11-2. Mr Thring with Mr Fortescue:

---

[1] E. L. *Stanley, *Oxford university reform* (1869).　　[2] See 14 Dec. 69.
[3] Add MS 44637, f. 133.　　　　[4] See 8, 15 Dec. 69.　　[5] See 14 Dec. 69.
[6] Fortescue's mem. of 9 December 1869, Add MS 44122, f. 74.
[7] Arthur Wrottesley, 1824-1910; 3rd Baron Wrottesley 1867; court office 1869-74, 1880-5.
[8] Sir John Mellor, 1809-87; justice of Queen's bench 1861-79; kt. 1862; had unsuccessfully requested pension for the widow of Sir George Hayes, late justice of Queen's bench; Add MS 44538, f. 22, 24.

instructions for draft of Irish Land Bill. Saw Ld Granville—Ld de Grey—Ld Dufferin—Mr Acland—Rev. Dr Barry. Read Sargant on Ireland—Raleigh's Life.[1]

19. 4 S.Adv.

Temple Ch. mg to hear Dr Vaughan: Chapel Royal aft. Wrote to The Queen—Robn G.—Jane Wortley (& copy). Much conversation with C. & some with Jane respecting Mrs Th. Read Newark Ch. meeting.[2] Luncheon with the Wortleys. Saw Kinnaird respecting Holy Trin. Oxford. Saw D. of Sutherland. Dined with Glyn. Much conversation with Goschen—& with Hartington.

20. M.

Wrote to Mrs J.S. Wortley—Mrs Thistlethwayte—Mr Justice Mellor —Scotts—Lady Hayes[3]—Mr Justice Keating[4]—Duke of Argyll— Mr M. Downing[5]—Mr Odo Russell—Mrs C. Rumpff. Saw Mr Childers—Mr Ouvry—Ld Chancellor—Rev M.T. Sadler—Mr Glyn (respecting Mrs Th.). Dined at Sir A. Panizzi's. Read Stirling on Unionism.[6]

To ODO RUSSELL, 20 December 1869.　　　　　　Add MS 44538, f. 25.

To rise higher still, I watch with an intense interest the proceedings of the Council. It is curious that Manning has so greatly changed his character. When he was Archdeacon with us, all his strength was thought [to] lie in a governing faculty, & in its wise moderation. Now he is ever quoted as the *Ultra* of Ultras, & he seems greatly to have overshot his mark. The odds seem to be that the child yet unborn will rue the calling of this Council. For if the best result arrive in the triumph of the Fallibilitarians, will not even this be a considerable shock to the credit & working efficiency of the Papal system. You must really be *all* eyes & ears, a very Argus in both organs, until the occasion has gone by.

21. Tu. [Hawarden]

Wrote to Ld Clarendon—The Queen (Mema)—Mr Thring—Mr Cornish—Sir Thos G.—Ld Spencer—& minutes. Packed books, arr.

---

[1] See 14 Dec. 69.　　　　　　　　　[2] Untraced; probably anti-Temple.
[3] On her proposed pension; see 18 Dec. 69n.
[4] Sir Henry Singer Keating, 1804–88; judge of common pleas 1859–75; kt. 1857.
[5] MacCarthy Downing, 1814–79, independent liberal M.P. Co. Cork from 1868, had sent his pamphlet on Irish land; Add MS 44538, f. 25.
[6] J. Stirling, *Unionism: with remarks on the report of the Commissioners on Trades' Unions* (1869).

letters, & prep. for departure. Saw Mr Glyn—Mr Ouvry *cum* Mr Hardwick—Mr West. Off at 2.45. Hawarden at 9. Read Vestina's Martyrdom[1]—Ireland under Engl. Rule (Hist.Mond.).[2] Unpacked books &c.

22. Wed.

Wrote to W.H.G.—Attorney Gen. for Ireland—Registrar of Chester Diocese—C.G.—& minutes. Saw Mr Lambert (from Dublin)[3]—Mr Burnett. Read Irel. under Engl. Rule[4]—Life of Th. Parker[5]—Greater Britain.[6] Kept bed & house for my residue of cough. Wrote a few Verses.

23. Th.

Wrote to Mr Fortescue (2)—Ld Clarendon—The Queen—Mrs Douglas—D. of Argyll—and minutes. Read Greater Britain— Theodore Parker's Life. Worked on Railway Mema. Again kept the House. C.G. returned.

To C. S. P. FORTESCUE, Irish secretary,   Add MS 44122, f. 116.
23 December 1869.

1. I had read Malone's letter some time back with much pain, & I thank you for the valuable comment. It might be worth *circulating*.
2. Though *apprehensive* about touching any present rents, I feel that there is much force in your arguments for it, & I shall be very glad if, without acting upon them directly, we can gain the end in view.
  I still incline to think we might adopt what I call the Hartington proposition *with* the counterpart to which you appear to incline. The direct effect is to put the tenant on the defensive ground: & your damages for eviction would not only give him more than the old 'solvent tenant' idea, but would be less likely perhaps to raise any of the difficulties *in limine* which we must all be so anxious to avoid.
  Of course he would claim by local custom, if he thought it for his advantage, & if the facts enabled him.
3. It seems to me you should consider whether the law of distress calls for any mitigation. It is, I apprehend, too strong both in England, & in Ireland: but unless there are practical grievances of a serious kind which we cannot get rid of except by now changing it, we shall do well to let it alone.
4. I saw Lambert 'en route' to London yesterday. His mission will bear fruit.
5. We are *not* yet through our difficulties, but I think we shall come through without dangerous jars.

[1] E. R. Pitman, *Vestina's martyrdom; a story of the catacombs* (1869).
[2] *Ireland under British rule* (1868).
[3] See 3, 4 Dec. 69.   [4] See 21 Dec. 69.
[5] Probably W. H. Channing, *Lessons from the life of Theodore Parker* (1860).
[6] Dilke; see 11 Nov. 68.

24. Fr.

Wrote to Duke of Argyll—Ld Granville—Mr Cardwell—Bp of Winchester—The Queen—Justice Mellor—The Viceroy—Mr Bruce—Mrs Thistlethwayte—Telegr. to Mr Hammond—and minutes. Read Greater Britain—Th. Parker's Life.

To LORD CLARENDON, foreign secretary,	Add MS 44538, f. 26.
24 December 1869.

1. I would only suggest for your consideration[1] a change in the first part of the proposed Telegram to mitigate any appearance of wrath. For example 'Doubtless U.S. Govt. must be aware that if the dispatch to M. is produced alone, this Govt. will be obliged to publish the answer at once by presentation to Parlt. if sitting, & if not in the Gazette.'
2. I suppose the dispatch of Nov. 6 is the short one. It is most extraordinary that Ld. R[ussell] should propose to refer to arbitration his *No. 6*, a question between the F.O. & the Treasury. At the proper time pray ascertain the facts as to this No 6. In a former edition of the same statement, Ld. R. gave to *me* what he now assigns to the Bd. of Treasury: but I had never heard a syllable on the subject. I should not wonder if there were some error of memory.
3. I am sorry to be too well prepared to concur in Odo Russell's anticipations only I think the papalists are not going *backward* to the Middle Ages. I wish they would go *forward* to the Middle Ages.

I thank you much for so kindly inquiring. My cough is much better, but I have not yet quite shaken it out of me. I hope you will have a goutless Xmas & New Year, & will smile upon smiling babies. I forward a letter from Argyll respecting Khelat & I concur in the proposed instruction.

To EARL SPENCER, Irish lord lieutenant,	Add MS 44538, f. 28.
24 December 1869.

I inclose a letter from Ld. R.[2] for your perusal and consideration. Relatively to the impression entertained, I am rather pleased with the comparative crime returns of 68 & 69.

Abercorn's speech[3] is a greater offence than many a crime for which his fellow countrymen have had to answer. But what can you expect from a dandy of 55 turning statesman?

It seems to be established by testimony that rents are even better paid than usual in Ireland this year, & I believe it to be quite possible that this fact belongs to the same group of causes as the increase of agrarian crime.

[1] Clarendon sent news this day, Add MS 44134, f. 119, that Fish had published 'their own insolent dispatch with our meek answer' and suppressed the accompanying British memorandum. Clarendon wished not to be seen 'truckling to the Americans'.
[2] Earl Russell had sent comments on the 1833 Act, see Add MS 44306, f. 202. Gladstone told Spencer, 28 December 1869, Add MS 44306, f. 206: 'I thought Lord Russell's letter . . . worth your seeing. But in estimating it as an authority we must bear in mind the likelihood that he may have changed his mind by this time, as he both writes and unwrites to a great degree off-hand.'
[3] Protestant demonstration against Gladstone, disestablishment and Maynooth endowment; *Belfast Morning News*, 10 December 1869.

25. Sat. Xmas Day.

Church 11 AM (H.C.) and 7 P.M. Pleased with the new (Seeland) Curate's[1] preaching. Wrote to Ld Clarendon—Sir D. Marjoribanks: and Verses, wh I sent to Lady Phillimore, on Sir R.P.s Farming.[2] Also minutes. Read Life of Parker—Pryce on the Early Church.[3] Cath. laid up: from over exertion.[4]

To LORD CLARENDON, foreign secretary,   Clarendon MSS, c. 498.
25 December 1869.

If you will turn the hose upon Sumner I will gladly bear a hand to work the engine. But my Fish I will not yet abandon: not until I see that he palpably fails to do the best he can, under unfavourable circumstances. But I cordially concurred in the proposal transmitted by Hammond, to publish here before *their* ink is dry.[5] Thanks for the account of Genl. Banks. A happy Xmas, & many of them. I hope Mr. Cock's [*sc.* Cox] appointment to Chelsea is going forward.

26. S aft Xmas.

Ch 11 AM 3 PM. Wrote to Ld Granville—The Queen—and Mem.— Rev. Sydney Linton[6]—A. Panizzi—and minutes. C. suffering from erysipelas, with signs of fever. Read Janus.[7] Sadlers Conference Paper[8]—Howson on Cathedrals.[9]

27. M. St John.

Ch. 11 A.M. C. still suffering. Determined to lie up, for or rather agt the remains of my cough. Read Greater Britain—Ireland under Engl. Rule. Wrote to Ld Granville—Bp of Chester—Rev. S. Linton—Ld Clarendon—Lady Herbert—Sir E. Watkin—Mr Bright (2)—Lady Portsmouth—& minutes.

[1] J. E. Tompson, see 16 Jan. 68.
[2] Verses opposing *Phillimore's farming activities; see Phillimore's diary, 7 January 1870, Phillimore MSS and Add MS 44758, f. 140.
[3] See 21 Nov. 69.
[4] Gladstone told *Argyll (31 December 1869, Add MS 44538, f. 34): 'My wife has had a poorish attack with erysipelas in the *head*, & it is thought only a good & strong constitution prevented it from becoming typhoid.'
[5] See 24 Dec. 69.
[6] Appointing him to Holy Trinity, Oxford; see 19 Dec. 69 and Add MS 44538, f. 29.
[7] See 9 Oct. 69.
[8] M. F. *Sadler, 'Address . . . Manifestation of the Incarnation in the birth, life and death of Christ' (1867).
[9] J. S. *Howson, 'Dean Milman and St Paul's', *Quarterly Review*, cxxvi. 218 (January 1869).

28. Tu. H.Innocents.

Kept my bed.——C. improving. Saw Dr Moffatt. Wrote to Mrs Thistle-thwayte——Mr Trevelyan——Mr Helps——Att.Gen.Irel.——The Viceroy——Dr Angus[1]——Mr Rawson——and minutes. Read Dilke Greater Britain——Ireland under Engl. Rule.

29. Wed.

My sixtieth birthday. Three score years! And two score of them at least have been full years. My retrospect brings one conclusion. 'Mercy Good Lord is all I seek', for the past: for the future grace to be Thine instrument if scarcely Thy child.

My review this year includes as a prominent object L[aura] T[histle-thwayte]: the extraordinary history, the confiding appeal, the singular avowal. It entails much upon me: and as I saw most clearly of all today, first to do what in me may lie towards building up a true domestic community of life and purpose there.

Saw Sir S.R.G. respecting the see of Manchester.[2] Wrote to Duchess of Sutherland——Mr Woodgate——The Viceroy——Mr Palgrave——The Queen——Ld Clarendon——Robn G.——Chancr of Exr——Mr Bellairs——Bp of Chester——Mr Gurdon——and minutes. Read Dilke——Ireland under Engl. Rule——Th. Parker's Life.

To LORD CLARENDON, foreign secretary,   Clarendon MSS, c. 498.
29 December 1869.

I understood Acton to be of just the same mind as Odo Russell about the issue of the Council.[3] He has always conveyed to me his opinion that the Pope would prevail, the only hope in my mind is that there may be a *real* minority & that it may speak plainly. A few bold men would easily insure to themselves a noble immortality. But will *any* have the courage?

The Italian Government have one and only one method in their hands of fighting the Pope: and that is to run against nomination from Rome the old and more popular method of choosing Bishops by clerical election, with the *approbation of the flock*. Unless they resort to this they can do nothing.

I will write to Bright.[4] An article in the D. News two days ago looked alarmingly like leakage.

Remember I only send your inclosures to the Queen when you desire it.

[1] The nonconformist; see 15 Jan. 40.
[2] Gladstone appointed J. *Fraser; see 16 Dec. 61.
[3] See 1 Dec. 69n.
[4] Clarendon suggested, 27 December 1869, Clarendon MSS, c. 501, 'the expediency of *coaching* Bright' for his Birmingham speech.

Gladstone's First Cabinet, by Lowes Dickinson. Seated, clockwise: Lowe, Bright, Argyll, Clarendon, Bruce, Hatherley, Ripon, Granville, Kimberley, Goschen, Gladstone. Standing, left to right: Hartington, Fortescue, Cardwell, Childers,

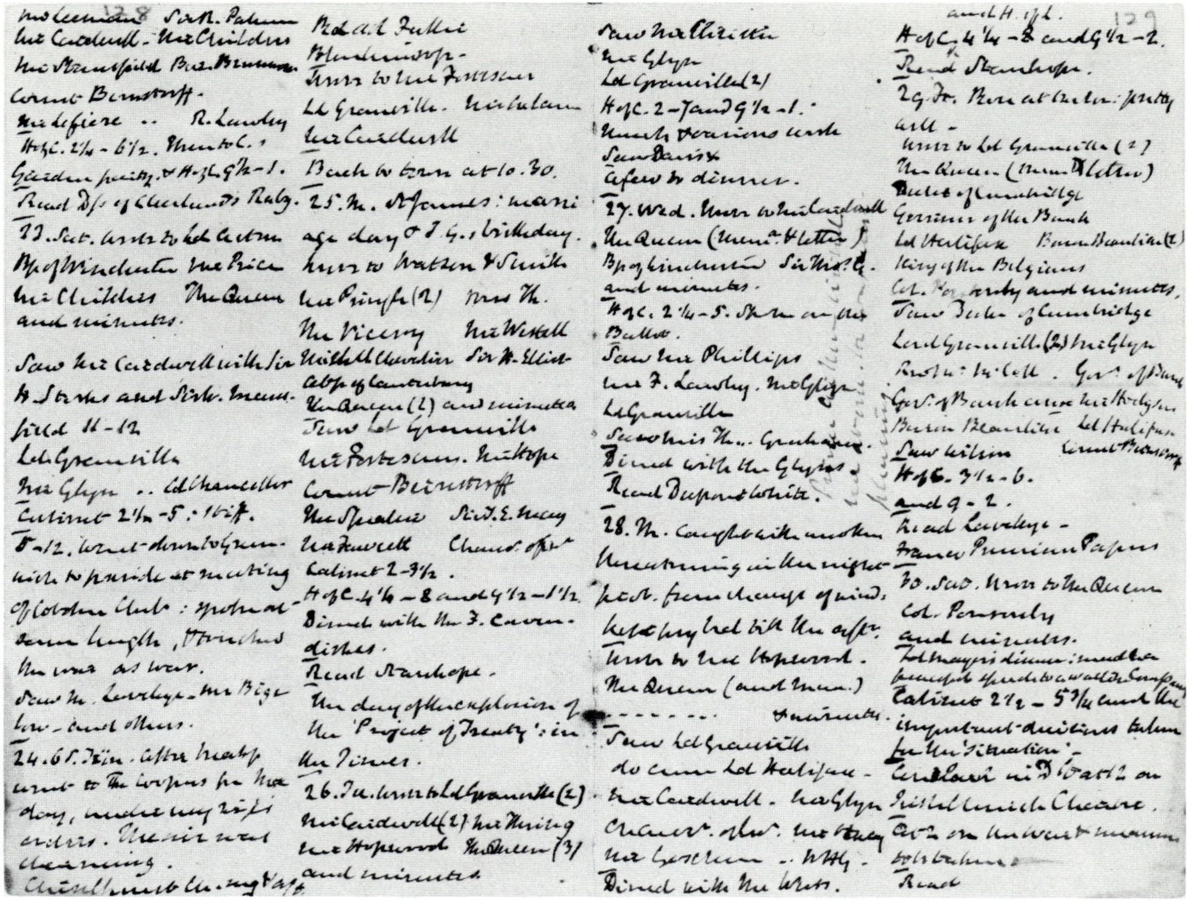

Facsimile of 22–30 July 1870, Lambeth MS 1441, ff. 128–9

Tenniel's cartoon 'Critics', captioned: 'MR. G–D–S–T–NE. "*Hm!—Flippant!*"
MR. D–S–R–LI. "*Ha!—Prosy!*" ', *Punch*, 14 May 1870

Photograph of Gladstone speaking at Blackheath, 28 October 1871

Speech at Blackheath, 28 January 1874, *Illustrated
London News*, 7 February 1874

30. Th.

Kept my room till the evening. Saw Dr M[offat] X——Dr Clark: C. thank God much better yesterday & today.

Wrote to Dean of Windsor——Mr W. Johnson——Mr Glyn——Lord Nelson——Mr Bright——Mr M'Millan——S.E.G.——Watsons——and minutes. Read Dilkes Greater Britain——Musae Etonenses (the New)[1] ——Bp of Exeter's Sermon[2]——Sedley Taylor on Clerical Subscription.[3] Saw Sir James Meek[4]——Dr Clark conversation on philosophy and Theology. Conversation with Harry on his future profession, and plans for work until London. Saw Mr Burnett.

To J. BRIGHT, president of the board of trade,   Add MS 44538, f. 33.
30 December 1869.

You cannot treat Birmingham as I am able to treat Greenwich, & you are I believe to address your constituents shortly.

Your utterances on Irish Land will of course be watched with the utmost avidity. Fortunately you have your own favourite department of the subject, & that is by much the least dangerous one. The part on which it is necessary to maintain the most absolute secrecy, & not to 'light' the path, or track *towards* our intentions, is that which concerns tenants as such. I do not see what any of us can safely say on this subject, except that while law & order are to be firmly maintained the cultivators of the soil have a great grievance for which we must find a remedy.[5] I should not have presumed to say so much, but for the unfortunate circumstance that our intentions have been more or less roughly divined: & that very lately, in an article of the Daily News some 2 days old.[6] I do not believe there has been any leakage from the Cabinet, but the effect is to put curiosity on a special scent that it may find something in the words of a Minister to interpret in the suggested sense. I hope the F.O. will send you the Report of Consul from Marseilles on the movement in favour of the Treaty.

31. Fr.

Down at noon: & walk with Dr Clark before luncheon. Wrote to Ld Clarendon——Sir Geo. Grey——Mr Fortescue——D. of Argyll——Sol.Gen. for Ireland——Ld Granville——Sir Thos G.——Mr Cope——and minutes. Read Greater Britain——Th. Parker's Life——Helps's Realmah.[7]

[1] See letter to R. Okes, 18 Jan. 1870; Add MS 44538, f. 55.
[2] On his enthronement the previous day.
[3] Gladstone told A. *Macmillan this day (Add MS 44538, f. 33): 'I have read with pain the pamphlet of Mr Sedley Taylor on Clerical Subscription which you have been so kind as to send me. He . . . has never had in his mind the true grounds on which alone (in my opinion) subscription can rightly be given or taken.'
[4] Sir James Meek, 1815-91; banker in York; kt. 1869.
[5] Bright replied on 1 January 1870, Add MS 44112, f. 118: 'I shall avoid dangerous questions——& I know nothing more dangerous than the Irish Land question.' See 13 Jan. 70.
[6] *Daily News*, 27 December 1869, second leader.
[7] By Sir A. *Helps (1868).

And at midnight listened to the bells which closed this for me notable year. Its private experience, in the case mentioned on Wed. has been scarcely less singular than its public. May both be ruled for good. Certainly my first 12 months as Minister have passed with circumstances of favour far beyond what I had dared to anticipate. Thanks be to God!

To LORD CLARENDON, foreign secretary,   Clarendon MSS, c. 498.
31 December 1869.

Having been myself for 20 years an advocate of open competition in first admissions to the Civil Service, I cannot be over well qualified to act as *amicus curiæ* in advising upon your Draft which relates to that subject. Desirous however to give full effect to the decision of the Cabinet that our several *autonomies* should be respected, I would suggest whether you would not best fortify your position by resting altogether on the speciality of the case of your Department. If you agree in this it will entail an omission from p. 4 to p. 6 of the draft: and were I in your place I would not appeal in p. 11 to the Treasury for its opinion on a matter when your own will suffice.

I trust Lowe will not put me down as a traitor for offering these well-meant suggestions.[1]

---

[1] See to Lowe, 23 Nov., 8 Dec. 69.

Hawarden
Saturday Jan. One 1870. The Circumcision.

Hawarden Ch. 11 A.M. Saw Marq. of Westminster—Mr Burnett. Wrote to Sec.Eccl. Commn (2)[1]—Mr Bruce—D. of Argyll—The Queen—& minutes. Read Realmah[2]—Greater Britain.[3] In afternoon cut down a birch.

To H. A. BRUCE, home secretary, 1 January 1870.   Aberdare MSS.

I am afraid I am not sufficiently abreast of the Metropolitan Government question to render you much assistance without further information.[4] I do not even well remember the points of difference between the Ayrton & the Buxton views respectively. I think however you must be pretty safe, if on your own deliberate judgment you promise support to a second reading with the condition of a Committee to follow. But if you have the slightest doubt, why not call in Goschen. There would be some advantage in consulting Ayrton, unless you are afraid of a clash, in which case it would not be worth while. Certainly if it were a matter of free choice to determine the legislation of each succeeding session, I for one would put municipal Govt. among the real if not indispensable *agenda* of 1871. It is therefore desirable in a high degree to take any step during the present year (as we must today call it) which may promise to bring the materials into readiness. Should you think it requisite pray supply me with some précis of the present state of the case which may enable me to arrive at a more definite opinion.

2. S.

Ch. 11 A.M. & H.C. No aft. service—evg forbidden. Read to C. in evg. Wrote to Mrs. Thistlethwayte—Mr Browning[5]—Mr. Bright—Sir J. Lacaita—Ld Brougham—Sir J. Coleridge—Mr Gurdon—Edith Gladstone—Ld Granville—& minutes. Read Seymour's Sermon—Johnes on Dissent in Wales[6]—Janus[7]—Union Review.[8]

3. M.

Wrote to Mrs. Thistlethwayte—Ld Clarendon—Mr Glyn—Mr Fortescue—The Queen—Ld Chancellor—Mr Roberts—Dean Ramsay

---

[1] St. Thomas, Seaforth, affairs; Add MS 44424, f. 1.
[2] See 31 Dec. 69.   [3] See 11 Nov. 68.
[4] Bruce's letter untraced; no London govt. Bill was introduced in 1870. See 3 Dec. 72.
[5] Thanking Robert *Browning, 1812-89, poet, for a testimonial; Add MS 44538, f. 36.
[6] A. J. Johnes, *Preface to a reprint of an essay on the causes of dissent in Wales* (1870).
[7] See 9 Oct. 69.
[8] *Union Review*, viii (January 1870).

—Mr Fraser—Lord Nelson—and minutes. Worked on private papers. Read Janus—Greater Britain—Irel. under Engl. Rule (finished)— Life of Th. Parker.[1] Cut trees in afternoon.

To LORD HATHERLEY, lord chancellor,   Add MS 44538, f. 37.
3 January 1870.

After my best salutations on the New Year, I wish to invite your consideration of the case as it stands between us as to Church patronage of the Parochial Class. I have never heard anybody commend the distribution of the Parochial Preferment either by First Lords, or by Lord Chancellors as such, & most assuredly, speaking of the present incumbents of the two offices, the last thing I should desire would be to draw patronage out of your net into mine. But what I do desire is to bring to their proper distribution, the proportion of public claims made upon us respectively. The number of applications made to me on really strong & purely public grounds both for stalls & for livings is such as to convince me that in regard to the latter especially it is impossible that you should have a stock of the *same quality* in *6 fold* or *7 fold* number which is what you ought to have. The truth as to benefices they simply throw me into despair. I do not speak of applications as such, but of applications which ought to be attended to. It seems contrary to the comity[?] believed to prevail among wild beasts (parcet [*sc.* parcit] cognatis maculis similis fera)[2] & politicians, that in declining them I should point out the numbers of Benefices set out in the Clergy List as appertaining to our respective offices. Were I to send you *ad Libitum* that portion of *good* applications with which I have no hope of dealing, I am afraid it would seem as if I am making a convenience of you, & adopting a plan likely to interfere with your free judgment. Yet I am [*sic*] your desire is to have the best cases before you, & to be free from all professional or other undue pressure. On the whole I incline to think that periodically, say at the end of 6 months, I might cause a selection of good parochial cases to be sent to you, & dealt with according to your discretion. You would see from the quality of these how the case really stood, & we might continue the practice or not accordingly. This does not require an immediate answer, but perhaps you will kindly think it over, & may if there be ground for doing anything suggest something better.[3]

I have another word to say on quite different grounds, with regard to Cathedral Preferments. You urged upon me the case of Dr. Hook: & there are few things I desire more than to offer him a Deanery (since he is over old for the Bench) less out of proportion to his immense merits. But I wish to lay before you a list of distinguished men, Authors, Divines, Scholars, Teachers, Preachers: of some one of whom I hope you might think upon occasion, when Cathedral Preferment, or anything Parochial which approximates to it, falls into your hand.
Mr Curtis Lichfield Coll.
Mr Lowe Hurstpierpoint
Mr Liddon
Prof. Rawlinson

---

[1] See 22 Dec. 69.
[2] Juvenal, Sat. 15. 159: in diarist's version: 'a wild beast *will* spare another of the same kind'.
[3] No reply found.

Mr Derwent Coleridge, late of St Mark's.
Mr. Elwin late (too Liberal) editor of Quarty. Review
Mr Perowne: who wrote on the Psalms.
Dr Barry Principal of King's Coll.
Dr Vaughan M. of Temple
Dr Scott M. of Balliol
Dr Irons of Brompton
Dr Hannah of Trin. Coll. Glenalmond
Dr Hessey Merch. Taylors
Dr Kynaston St. Paul's
Mr King Cuddesdon Coll.
also men among the Parochial clergy with somewhat special claims: Dr Miller of Greenwich—Rev. D. Moon of Paddington—Mr Fremantle of Claydon—Mr Woodford of Leeds—Mr Seymour of Kinwarton—Mr Tarver, Broadstairs, late Tutor to P. of Wales.
Pray understand I do not wish to transfer the weight of these men to your shoulders: but only to give them another chance. I think the first list generally so strong, that it could not be matched by such another from the whole mass of non-dignified clergymen of the Church of England.
(Private) I hope Mr. F[raser] of Upton will be Bp. of M[anchester] but I am told his benefice will go the same course that so many others have taken.

To DEAN E. B. RAMSAY, 3 January 1870.   Add MS 44538, f. 38.

I send you my rather shabby contribution of £10 to the Chalmers memorial. I wish it were more, but I am rather specially pressed at this time. And I think I refused Robt. Bruce altogether not long ago. I quite understand the feeling of the Scotch aristocracy, but I should have thought Lothian would have been apart from as well as above it. But the *number* of subscriptions is the main thing, & very many they ought to be if Scotland is Scotland still. He was one of nature's nobles. It is impossible even to dream that a base or unworthy thought ever found harbour for a moment in his mind.
Is it not extraordinary to see this rain of Bishoprics upon *my* head? Nor (I think) is it over. The next 12 months (wherever I may be at the end of it) will probably produce three more. Bp. Temple is a fine fellow, & I hope all will now go well. For Manchester (this is secret) I hope to have Mr. Fraser of Upton, a very notable man, in the first rank of knowledge & experience on the question of Education. Many pressed him for Salisbury. I can truly say that every Bishop who has been appointed has been chosen simply as the best man to be had. Ah! when will you spend that month here, which I shall never cease to long for.

4. Tu.

Wrote to Ld Granville—Sir R. Phillimore—Mr Bright—Lady Herbert—Mr Glyn—Mr Goschen—Mr Bruce—Watson & S.—Mr Lowe—Rev. Mr Austin. Walk to Buckley with S.E.G. Read Wells, Report on Revenue &c. of U.S.[1]—Cairnes (Fortn.R.) on Irish

---

[1] D. A. Wells, *Report ... on taxation, wages, high prices, monopolies, duties and special legislation* (1869); see next day.

Land[1]—Fraser on Dr Rob. Lee[2]—Greater Britain—Life of Th. Parker.

5. Wed.

Wrote to Bp of St David's—Mr D.A. Wells (U.S.)—Mr Bruce—Bp of Winchester—D. of Argyll—Mr Kinnaird—Rev Mr Kidd—Ld Clarendon—Gen Grey—Mr Gurdon—Scotts—Bp of Winchester—Ld R. Cavendish—& minutes. Cut alders in the afternoon. Read The Diplomatic Service[3]—Life of Th. Parker—Seebohm on Engl. Tenures[4]—Hayward on Irish Land[5]—Greater Britain (finished).

To the DUKE OF ARGYLL, Indian secretary,   Add MS 44538, f. 42.
5 January 1870.

I do not think I have ever 'founded' upon 'Irish ideas', as the warrant for our land measure.[6] I 'found' (not on hares & rabbit but) on Irish circumstances first of all, which are a different matter. Next on Irish history. And only in the third place on Irish ideas, & that simply insofar as they sprung out of Irish history: Irish history not the polemical, but the normal. I dare not say & shall never say in public what I think of the Irish evictions, & of some of them in particular. My desire is to make a strenuous effort for a quick settlement with 'stability' of tenure to the people, and the deliverance of the whole status of the Landlord from present paralysis, & future chaos.

I am thankful for your continuing good account of the Duchess. My wife thrives. The Archers are here with Miss Callander. Thring must, I think, have a spare copy: I will ask him to send it to you. Cabinet on Jan 21. St Asaph will be vacant almost immediately. My fear is Canterbury cannot hold long.[7] *Both* will be extremely difficult. I hope you have read Dilke's Greater Britain: or at least those parts of it, which refer to the treatment of the Nations in India by the English, I mean *personally*. I take it to be an important *political* question.

---

[1] *Bright had sent J. E. *Cairnes, 'Political economy and land', *Fortnightly Review*, xiii. 41 (January 1870). Gladstone commented this day to Bright (Add MS 44538, f. 39): 'I agree with yr. unfavourable view of his leading proposn. He is (however) I think right abt. prices as a criterion of fair rent in p. 57, & I much like the 2 last pages.'

[2] *Fraser's Magazine*, lxxxi. 86 (January 1870).

[3] *The diplomatic service of England. Its position and prospects* (1869).

[4] F. *Seebohm, 'The land question; feudal tenures in England', *Fortnightly Review*, xiii. 89 (January 1870).

[5] A. *Hayward, 'Ireland and the Irish land question', *Fraser's Magazine*, lxxxi. 121 (January 1870).

[6] Argyll wrote on 4 January, Add MS 44101, f. 177: 'Of course I am not denying that Traditional feelings of long descent have influenced and do influence "Irish ideas". But I do not think that they can with safety be made the basis of any argument by a Minister responsible for practical legislation.'

[7] Tait's illness.

To LORD CLARENDON, foreign secretary,   Clarendon MSS, c. 498.
5 January 1870.

The turn of affairs in the East is very ugly.[1] The Sultan in my opinion behaved ill to us, & to France about his Firman. But, apart from complaint, the meaning of his Act was 'leave *me* to look after my own vassal'. I hope therefore you may think we ought to be very slow to interfere *between* them. Not only however would I withold all countenance from the Viceroy in any act or non-act of bad faith, but I suppose we might as friends communicate with the French in this sense. It is too horrible if the corruption there is as you suppose. It is nearly as bad as what I read of myself a fortnight ago in an obscure Brighton journal.

Thanks for your suggestion about mustard leaves. We go on well here, & Argyll reports continued improvement. [P.S.] I think I would *not* consult the Queen on the point of waiting for the Committee on Diplomatic Reductions, but only if you make up your own mind *not* to wait.

To C. THIRLWALL, bishop of St. David's,   Add MS 44538, f. 41.
5 January 1870.

I have this day learnt that the Bp. of St. Asaph is about to resign: but for the present this must be considered as absolutely secret. It is material, however, that I should lose no time in availing myself of all the assistance I can obtain in the very difficult task of choosing a person to be recommended as his successor. In a letter some months back[2] (which is not now by me) your Lordship signified very briefly that your mind had dwelt upon the kind of person who ought under the present circumstances to be appointed to any vacant Welsh Sees. I am very desirous to be favoured with your full counsel upon this subject if you will be kind enough to give it. My own impression is that it is most important to find if possible some one who has the gift of preaching together with the free & popular use of the Welsh tongue, provided that besides being a man of zeal & piety & loyalty to the Church, he has the qualities necessary to make a just governor, & attractive administrator. The persons whose names have up to this time been principally before me (for, knowing the difficulty of the task, I have in some degree prepared for it by anticipation) are Archd. B. Jones, Mr [David] Howell, Cardiff, Mr Lewis, Dolgelley, Mr Phillips, Aberystwith, Mr [Hugh] Jones, canon of St Asaph. On persons, as well as in regard to general conditions of fitness, any suggestions from Your Lordship will have my respectful attention. With reference to the actual tone of the Clergy of the Diocese, I am of opinion that if what is called a Low Churchman be appointed it is essential that he should be a man of tact, and a conciliatory spirit.

I do not know how far Mr. [E. H.] Perowne comes within the category of Welshmen for the present purpose.[3]

[1] Clarendon reported, 4 January 1870, Add MS 44134, f. 127, that the Khedive would not surrender ships and arms due to the Sultan.
[2] Of 9 July 1869, Add MS 44421, f. 132.
[3] Similar letters went to Bruce and Kinnaird; Add MS 44538, f. 40-1. Thirlwall replied, 7 January 1870, Add MS 44424, f. 20, that 'a mere popular preacher, suited to the Welsh taste, would lower the Episcopate', but approved of Jones.

To D. A. WELLS,[1] 5 January 1870.   Add MS 44538, f. 43.

I beg to offer my best thanks for your kindness in sending me your interesting Report made as Special Commissioner of the Revenue of the U.S. I watch with the utmost interest the gigantic movement of the fiscal, as well as of the other interests, of your country. And I continue to cherish the hope that the good example you are setting with reference to the energetic action on the debt may be of use both to us, & to Continental States of Europe some of which appear likely to stand in great need of assistance. Of the American Tariff I will not speak. Having bought Free Trade at a great price, we are now dealers with the world, & any Tariff, of whatever country, which hits us at one point favours our interests at others by virtue of the very same restrictive provisions. We are not therefore to pretend a special interest in the matter: but I wish well to your arguments, in the interest of mankind at large.

6. Th. Epiph.

Ch. 11 A.M. C's birthday. Blessings on her. Wrote a letter to Mrs Th. which I reserve for further consideration.[2] Wrote also to Rev. A. Mildmay—Mr Acland M.P.—H.J.G.—Sec. Indian Pen.Railw.Co.— Mr Gurdon—Mr Bright—Ld Granville—Sir G. Grey—and minutes. Saw Miss Waters. Read Life of Th. Parker—Ed.Rev. on Irish Land.[3] Arranging papers &c. Cut down a Birch.

7. Fr.

Wrote to Abp of Canterbury—Abp of York—Mr Gurdon—Ld Chichester—Mr Rawson—Dean Ramsay—Mr Fraser—The Viceroy —Mr Glyn—Ld Chancellor—Mr Linton—Mr Cardwell—Ld Greville[4]—Miss Whately[5]—Mr Reeve—Mr Dasent—Mr Burnett—and minutes. Tree-felling in afternoon. Examn by Dr Moffatt, who reports some poverty of blood indicated by sound in the jugular vein. Read Th. Parker—Finlason on Tenures[6]—Blaint 'Espagne et Cuba'.[7]

To LORD GREVILLE, 7 January 1870.   Add MS 44538, f. 45.

I return Mr. Reynolds letter with many thanks. I regret that in one sense the victory in Longford[8] has been so dearly won. But all looks as tho' it were to be no less permanent in its effects than it is signal & gratifying in its political & moral character. Formidable as the land question is, my hopes outweigh my fears. Had we a Peel leading the opposition I should of course be much more sanguine. I think we shall be found not very far from what I take to be your mark.

---

[1] David Ames Wells, 1828–98; American free-trader; his post of special commissioner abolished as result of his anti-protectionist report of 1869.
[2] See 19 Jan. 70.   [3] *Edinburgh Review*, cxxxi. 256 (January 1870).
[4] Fulke Southwell Greville-Nugent, 1821–83; cr. Baron Greville 1869.
[5] E. J. Whately, the abp.'s da. and biographer.
[6] W. F. *Finlason, *The history of the law of tenures of land in England and Ireland: with particular reference to inheritable tenancy* (1870).   [7] Untraced.
[8] Liberals held the seat against a home-ruler in by-election on Greville's peerage.

8. Sat.

Wrote to Ld Granville—Sig. C. di Cesare[1]—Ld Acton—Watson & Smith—Ld Clarendon—Mrs Thistlethwayte—Mr Bruce—Mr Fortescue—and minutes. Stephy went. Party in evg. Saw Mr & Mrs Austin on their matters. Read Buchanan's Poems[2]—Th. Parker's Life —Prendergast, Cromwellian Settlement.[3]

To LORD ACTON, 8 January 1870.   Add MS 44093, f. 110.

I take the opportunity of a messenger from the Foreign Office to write a few lines.

My answer[4] to your appeal was written on the instant, and I stated that which first occurred to me namely the additional difficulties which the rampancy of Ultramontanism would put in the way of our passing measures of public Education which should be equitable and not otherwise than favourable to religion.

But in truth this was only a specimen. There is the Land Bill to be settled, and there are the wings of the Church Bill: one the measure relating to Loans for Building, the other having reference to the Ecclesiastical Titles Act. Even the first will be further poisoned, and either or both of the two last may become the subject of fierce and distracting controversy so as to impede our winding up the great chapter of account between the State and not the Roman Church or Priesthood but the people of Ireland.

The truth is that Ultramontanism is an anti-social power and never has it more undisguisedly assumed that character than in the Syllabus.

Of all the Prelates at Rome none have a finer opportunity, to none is a more crucial test now applied, than to those of the United States. For if there, where there is nothing of covenant, of restraint, or of equivalents between the Church and the State, the propositions of the Syllabus are still to have the countenance of the Episcopate, it becomes really a little difficult to maintain in argument the civil right of such persons to toleration, however conclusive is the argument of policy in favour of granting it.

I can hardly bring myself to speculate or care on what particular day the foregone conclusion is to be finally adopted. My grief is sincere and deep, but it is at the whole thing, so ruinous in its consequences as they concern Faith.

In my view the size of the minority, though important, is not nearly so important as the question whether there will be a minority at all. Whatever its numbers if formed of good men it will be a nucleus for the future, and will have an immense moral force even at the present moment, a moral force sufficient perhaps to avert much of the mischief which the acts of the majority would naturally entail. For this I shall watch with intense interest.[5]

---

[1] Carlo di Cesare, 1825–82, Italian political and economic writer, had sent a work; Add MS 44538, f. 47.

[2] R. W. *Buchanan, probably *London poems* (1866).

[3] See 11 July 67.

[4] See 1 Dec. 69 and Acton's letter of 1 January, urging action, in Figgis and Laurence, *Lord Acton's Correspondence*, 95.

[5] In Figgis and Laurence, 97 and Lathbury, ii. 51.

To the DUKE OF ARGYLL, Indian secretary,   Add MS 44101, f. 190.
8 January 1870.

I thank you for your absolving me[1] from the work of comment on particulars & I do not think there is anything in your scruples which ought to contribute a serious difficulty in the face of such a question as we have before us. Indeed I am persuaded many of them would melt of themselves could I get you to take that large dose of Irish History which I have sometime prescribed, & which I have partially drunk myself; not merely of Irish history 200 years back & over, but especially the Irish history of the last 100 years. I do not know on what authority you affirm that leases have been until lately the usual form of Irish tenure. I should have supposed the leases to *occupiers* to have been insignificantly few, until they became frequent for political purposes after 1793: and again they fell into disuse after the war & after 1829. You would I think find that the old Irish lease implied in the common understanding that absolute cessation of interest which we connect with the idea—the direct contrary is constantly asserted of the Ulster leases. When I agreed to the Bill of 1866, I had not studied the question, & I then supposed that that Bill was enough in the sense of satisfying the demands of justice. I now suppose it would have been 'enough' but in a different sense, that of settling the question as it was accepted by the Irish people a great proof of the moderation which has only now been compromised after what (to you) I must call the *mockeries* of the last 25 years of justice scandalously delayed. Justice seems to me to demand certainly no *less* than what will form the first draft of our Bill, I mean as to the main outlines. I quite agree with your remark that the argument for 'Prevention of Pauperism' can hardly be confined to agricultural holdings.

9. 1 S.Epiph.

Ch mg & evg. Wrote to the Queen (Mem.)—Rev Messrs. [L. W.] Owen—Church—Ross—Mr Bruce—Mr Gurdon—and minutes. Read Ramsgate Tracts[2]—Johnes on Welsh Dissent finished[3]—Janus, finished.

10.

Ch. 8½ A.M. To my great joy, I am at length permitted to resume: it does not affect the cough. Wrote to Mr Fortescue—Lady Herbert— Mr Thring—Ld Clarendon—Sir H. Holland—Ld Granville—Sir S. Scott & Co—Mr Johnston MP.—Rev. J. Fraser—Ed. Manchr Examiner (& Tel)[4]—Duke of Argyll—Mr Hammond (Telegr.)—and minutes. Read Th. Parker. The Abp of Syros came with his suite to dine & sleep.[5] The effort of talking German to him sorely tried my head.

[1] In Argyll's letter of 7 January, which enclosed his criticisms of the land proposals sent by Gladstone to Granville; Add MS 44101, f. 181.
[2] See 3 Oct. 69.   [3] See 2 Jan. 70.
[4] Sending news of Fraser's appt. as bp., *Manchester Examiner*, 11 Jan. 1870, 5.
[5] Alexandros Lykourgos, archbishop of Syros and Tenos; promotor of Orthodox-anglican conversations; a visit of oecumenical importance; see Matthew, 'Vaticanism'.

To C. S. P. FORTESCUE, Irish secretary,   Carlingford MSS CP1/86.
10 January 1870. 'Secret.'

The form of Thring's draft is so different from that of the Memorandum of Instructions from the Cabinet that I find it most difficult to judge how far it gives effect to them.

The mode in which he treats what were called rather loosely in the Memorandum of Dec. 18 'general customs' entirely overlooks the distinction between these & the Ulster Custom. Naturally enough therefore with his premiss vitiated he proposes to treat them together.

The vital distinction is between custom *which can be treated as covenant*, and custom (or practice, or usage) which cannot.

I apprehend we mean by the Ulster custom the former. The other analogous usages not being covenants, we propose to take into view only under limitations & conditions. Two ways of doing this suggested themselves

1. To enact that wherever evidence of usage could be found sufficient to guide the Court in measuring the real damage of eviction, it should be taken as a guide; leaving the conventional scale of damages to be pleaded by the tenant only where such evidence was not forthcoming.

2. To enact a conventional scale of damages, and to allow in some shape the parties or the Court to substitute an appeal to local custom.

The Cabinet have decided on the former for the purpose of drafting the Bill. But there is no difference (that I see) in principle between them. The *importance* of the decision for present purposes is because some do conceive themselves to see a difference.

I send you the 'Notes' to Thring's draft—but they ought never to have been printed. They are an argument on the whole principle of the measure so far as it goes beyond compensation for improvements. I advise your keeping these & Bill No 2 strictly to yourself unless you find occasion requiring you to act otherwise: I mean the *first six pages of the Notes*.

If progress is to be made at all, I see no other way but following the framework of the Memorandum. In various other points the Draft seems to me to vary from the Mem.: but the details may be considered hereafter one by one.

Please to send me back the copy of my letter to Thring: keeping another copy if you have occasion. You will I hope hear from him on Wednesday, and will be in a condition to judge how to proceed. Meantime there is plenty of matter in the Draft besides what I have written on.

P.S. I hope you keep Glyn constantly informed of all that touches Election matters.

11. Tu.

Ch. 8½ AM. But my overwork was telling and I was obliged to lie up afterwards. Wrote to Mrs Thistlethwayte—Ld Chichester—Mr Rawson—Chancr of Exchr—Mr Bruce—The Queen (Mem.)—and minutes. Abp of Syros went in afternoon. Read Neate on Entails[1]— Th. Parker's Life—Prendergast. Out a little. Conversation with Archd. Ff[oulkes].

---

[1] C. *Neate, The history and uses of the law of entail and settlement (1865).

12. Wed.

Ch 8½ AM. Wrote to Mr Thring (Telegr.)—Mr Fortescue—Mr Bruce—Abp of Canterb.—Mr J. Gordon[1]—Abp of York—D. of Argyll—Bp of St David's—Mr Bramston—Bp of Llandaff—Ld Clarendon—Ld Bessborough—Mr Fortescue (Telegr.)—and minutes. Treefelling. Quite set up again today. Read Th. Parker's Life—Prendergast.

To C. S. P. FORTESCUE, Irish secretary,   Add MS 44122, f. 129.
12 January 1870. 'Most Private.'

There can surely be no advantage in further argument between you & me at this stage[2]—especially after so many hours & pages of it—on the recognition of usage beyond the limit of Ulster Custom as a distinct head. You pressed your view repeatedly on the Cabinet, which did not adopt it. Till the Cabinet alters its mind we have no option except to use every effort to get the Bill drawn according to its instructions.

Forgive me if I say that I think you do not take sufficiently into view the state of things which became perfectly visible in the Cabinet, when your first paper—which I did everything in my power to support—was discussed.

What we have to do is to obtain the consent of the Cabinet to a bill, on the substance of which you & I are agreed: and this, it is my duty to say, will in my judgment be greatly endangered by any further prolongation of the subaltern controversy between us.

The point of danger you cannot fail to see, is the scale of damages for eviction. My object has been first to minimise this point of danger. If it hereafter appears that a Bill can pass as readily in the precise form to which you are so much attached, I shall not be the person to object to the prevailing sense of the Cabinet. I am sure it must have been the fault of my own modes of expression, which has prevented me from carrying into your mind a perception of the real motives by which I have been governed all along, and among which has of course been this, that I am the person who would be the most deeply responsible for an unnecessary shipwreck.

I have now written very explicitly, but I am sure you will take it in good part. I have not indeed even time or strength to prosecute it further.

P.S. (1) Pray deal with Dease as you propose, but working all along in concert with Glyn where elections are concerned. Perhaps you will tell D. I would have written to him but that the complications of the case are more easily dealt with *viva voce*. (2) Thanks for Trench's interesting paper. I have only two things to say on that part of the subject. (1) to have as *few* Government appointments as possible (2) to have as much as possible done by arbitrators *voluntarily* chosen by the parties.

(3) Thring offers to come down here & I accept. It seems Granville & the Chan-

---

[1] John Campbell *Gordon, 1847–1934; had declined a 'nominated' treasury clerkship (Add MS 44538, f. 50). He succ. his br. as 6th earl of Aberdeen 27 January 1870; lord lieut. of Ireland 1886, 1905–15; governed Canada 1893–8; cr. marquis of Aberdeen and Temair 1916. See Add MS 44090.

[2] Fortescue's reply to letter of 10 Jan. 70 untraced.

cellor have—as he thinks—given him opinions that he need not go over. I shall try to persuade him.[1]

To C. THIRLWALL, bishop of St. David's,   Add MS 44424, f. 88.
12 January 1870.

This most grave matter of nomination for a Welsh bishopric has now become practical as I have received from the Archbishop of Canterbury the letter in which the Bishop of St. Asaph expresses his desire to resign. Besides general considerations of weight[,] many which are special in connection with the position of the Welsh Church at this time weigh much upon my mind.

I think it beyond doubt most important, amidst this singularly susceptible population, once so much attached to the Church, to consider thoroughly whether any man can be found who being possessed in all other respects in a sufficient degree of the other important qualifications of a bishop is also not only a Native Welshman, but a practised efficient & impressive preacher in the Welsh tongue. This grave question I wish to sift to the bottom, & to treat it in the utmost possible degree as a question of fact apart from political or other predilection.

In this difficulty I naturally turn to the Welsh prelates especially those of South Wales where most of the noted Welsh preachers are to be found & with especial reference to your Lordship's diocese. I should be greatly obliged if you would take the matter into consideration & inform me whether you can confidently name any clergyman as corresponding with the description I have ventured to give.[2]

13. Th.

Ch. 8½ A.M. Wrote to Mrs Thistlethwayte—Lord E. Clinton—Mr West—Rev. J. Bramston—Mr Bright—Lord Cawdor—Scotts—Lord Clarendon—and minutes. Saw Mrs August & arranged her Income Tax application. H.G. respecting invest[men]t for Miss M.[3] Mr Thring came: & we had 2½ good hours on the Irish Land Bill. Tree felling with Willy. Read Keogh on Janus:[4] and made some references—MacCarthy Downing on Irish Land.[5]

To J. BRIGHT, president of the board of trade,   Add MS 43385, f. 73.
13 January 1870. 'Private.'

You seem to me to have succeeded admirably at Birmingham in your treatment of the Land question. You effectually kept it out of the region of commonplace

[1] Fortescue apologised for being 'overanxious in pointing out . . . the practical difficulties'; Add MS 44122, f. 131.

[2] *Thirlwall suggested firstly D. Howell, an evangelical; 14 January 1870, Add MS 44424, f. 97. The vacancy occasioned a vast correspondence from many correspondents. See 16 Jan. 70n.; *Letters of Lord Aberdare*, i. 294; Morgan, *Wales in British Politics*, 32.

[3] Probably his sister's companion.

[4] E. S. Keogh, *A few specimens of 'Scientific History' from Janus* (1870).

[5] MacCarthy Downing had sent his 'The Irish land question', *The Month*, l. 86 (January 1870): Add MS 44538, f. 51.

& maintained all the dignity & interest of its position yet shed no ray of light on particular intentions. I hope you will come up strong & well for the 21st. There or soon afterwards you may want all your manhood.

To LORD CLARENDON, foreign secretary,   Clarendon MSS, c. 498.
13 January 1870.

Though the enclosed letter from Acton, in its rags of envelope, is long, it is interesting and worth a careful perusal. He must know how difficult it is for England to take any ostensible initiative: but I have always regretted the back-wardness of France and the other Powers in a matter of such vast social as well as religious interest.[1]

It is marvellous that an Imperial Prince should play these pranks with regard to matters of political & civil right, as well as to those purely theological. Directly that the Episcopal minority wished for support *ab extra* it ought I think to have been given.

14. Frid.

Ch. 8½ AM. Wrote to Mr Fortescue—Rev J.L. Ross—Lady Herbert —Mr Goschen—Sir A. Panizzi—The Queen—Mr Stephenson— Mr M'Carthy Downing—Ld Eversley—Mr Thring—Mr C. Dickens[2] —Mr West—J. Watson & Smith—Mr Burnett—and minutes. Fare-well calls, & business: arranging books, & papers &c. for departure. Read Th. Parker (finished Vol. I.)—Rae on American Claims[3]— Case of St John's College Appeal.[4]

15. Sat. [Hagley]

Ch. 8½ A.M: a farewell service. Wrote to Ld Clarendon (2, & Tel.)— Ld Granville—Watsons—Ld Dufferin[5]—Scotts—Capt Egerton[6]— Sir C. Dilke[7]—Mr Glyn (2)—and minutes. Off at 11.20 to Hagley: arrived at 4½. Large and happy party: delightful family music. Read Campian on Ireland[8]—Pantaleoni on the Council.[9]

[1] See Matthew, 'Vaticanism', p. 432.
[2] Inviting the novelist to dinner on 26 January; an accident prevented his attendance; Add MS 44538, f. 51, 44424, f. 180.
[3] W. F. *Rae, 'American claims on England', *Westminster Review*, xxxvii. 211 (January 1870).
[4] *The appeal of five Fellows of St John's College to the Visitor* (1869); on open fellow-ships.
[5] Sending him cabinet papers on Land Bill preparation: Add MS 44538, f. 53.
[6] Asking Francis Egerton R.N. (1824–95, liberal M.P. Derbyshire 1868–86) to move the address; Add MS 44538, f. 54. Gladstone told Glyn his nephew C. Lyttelton should not be asked as he 'does not represent the element of *independent* support never more wanted'; ibid.
[7] Sir Charles Wentworth *Dilke, 1843–1911; 2nd bart. 1869; liberal M.P. Chelsea 1868–86, Forest of Dean from 1892; under-sec. at foreign office 1880–2, president local govt. board 1882–5; ruined by divorce scandal 1885. See Add MS 44149.
[8] E. *Campian, *A historie of Ireland* (1571).
[9] D. Pantaleoni, *Del Presente e dell' Avvenire del Cattolicismo a proposito del Concilio Ecumenico* (1870).

To Sir CHARLES W. DILKE, M.P., 15 January 1870.   Add MS 44538, f. 54.

I hope you will do my Colleagues & myself the favour of undertaking to second the address on the 8th February in answer to the Speech from the Throne. I write to Capt. Egerton begging him to move it, & I feel that the combination if I can effect it will be very satisfactory. If we fail to frame a satisfactory measure on the tenures of land in Ireland, it will not be from a due sense of the gravity of the issues, nor from want of conscientious pains. In the rear of this measure I hope may come Education, Election procedure, University Tests & other matters of great importance but I need not say that before the 8th & when the speech is framed, I shall be happy to afford you personally all information you may desire. One other word: only within the last 6 weeks have I been able to peruse your Greater Britain throughout. This I have done with much admiration & interest, & your able discussion of Colonial relations adds to the force of the desire which has prompted this letter. I feel that the circumstances of this juncture give a peculiar importance to the choice to be made.[1]

16. 2 S.Epiph.

Hagley Ch mg & Evg. Wrote to Ld Clarendon—Ld Granville (2)—Mr Cardwell—Archbp of Canterbury—Mr Bruce—Mr West—C.G.—Ld Penrhyn—and minutes. Read Th. Parker's Life—Pryce's Early Church[2]—Pantaleoni on Council. Conversation with G. respecting Welsh Bishopric.[3] Began to re-peruse L.T's MS.[4]

To LORD CLARENDON, foreign secretary,   Clarendon MSS, c. 498.
16 January 1870.

1. I do think with Lyons the Turk should justify his telegram about the Khedive, & if he cannot do it to be told he should be more reticent. We have other fish to fry.
2. The treaty with France is, it seems, *not* to be hanged first & tried afterwards, but I think the position & language of the French Govt. very unsatisfactory about it. The whole 'situation' in Paris seems cloudy.
3. I do not venture to say[5] that the Emperor was wrong in his decision about the Council last summer but he now has (through the negative power of force) great power & I am sorry he does not use it. The reform of the Monastic Orders is I think another trick. At present the Benedictines—the old nucleus of rational thought & action in the Roman Church—have no General & cannot have the strings pulled from Rome. The object seems to me to reduce them to the condition of the other orders. Odo Russell's letter on the Condemnation of Friars Bill seems to me very sagacious.

---

[1] Dilke agreed, observing: 'Your selection will perhaps be read as having some bearing on the colonial question & that will make my position an unusually delicate one'; Add MS 44149, f. 1.   [2] See 21 Nov. 69.
[3] Problematic vacancy at St. Asaph's (see 12 Jan. 70), eventually filled by Joshua Hughes, 1807–89, vicar of Llandingat.   [4] See 18 Sept. 69.
[5] Long letter on the Council from Clarendon this day; Add MS 44134, f. 134.

17. M.

Wrote to Mr T. Goalen—Ld Hartington—C.G.—Mrs Talbot—&
minutes. Conversation with Lady Lyttelton (Dowager) on the circle
here. Saw Mr Thring 2 h. on Irish Land Bill. Read Th. Parker's Life
—Campian on Irish History—The Commonwealth: and L.T.s Auto-
biographical MS.—some three hours. We (three) commenced the
cutting of a huge beech.

18. Tu.

The birthday of my brother John: deep & sweet be his rest. Wrote to
Mrs Thistlethwayte—Bp of Llandaff—Ld Granville—Bp of Chester
—Mr Cardwell—Rev Mr Bramston—C.G.—Provost [Okes] of
King's—Mr Mallet—Mr Stephenson—and minutes. Read Th. Par-
ker—and three more hours were spent on continuing the reperusal
of Mrs T.s really marvellous & most touching tale. We continued our
work on the great beech. But a good third remains to do. Saw Rev.
Mr Baldwin on the Church in Wales.

To R. OKES, provost of King's, Cambridge,   Add MS 44538, f. 55.
18 January 1870.

I find that I owe you the kindness of presenting me with a copy of the new
Musae Etonenses as well as the honour of finding a place among the authors. The
latter causes me a satisfaction not unmingled with tinges of conscience; the former I accept from you with unmixed pleasure & thankfulness. I have read through
your notices which form so important a part of the work, & I cordially congratulate you on the discrimination & fine tact as well as upon the scholarship, they
display. The attempt was bold & I think you have greatly done as you have
greatly dared.

Having said this it is perhaps a further compliment if I notice the instances in
which I had an intimate personal knowledge, & which I think would have borne
a somewhat heightened colouring. Bishop Denison was a man as it seemed to me
& to some better judges of notable discernment, & of comprehensive wisdom.
Arthur Hallam was within *my* sphere of knowledge at Eton & Oxford by *far* the
most remarkable person of his generation. The difficulty with me is to place anyone second to him, though I think in his gifts as they were in youth, I put James
Hope. My title to speak of A. Hallam is that I was extremely intimate with him
at Eton, but even then he, though younger, was too far above me. Afterwards at
Cambridge he seemed entirely out of my reach. There he more fortunately fell
upon Tennyson.

Allow me to say that while I feel the need of enlargement especially by way
of alternatives in our old system of Education, I heartily sympathise with you in
the desire that the ancient standard of culture among all really capable persons
may be maintained in its honour & preference, & I am one of those who if it is
lost cannot consent to accept anything else which may be gained as an adequate
compensation.

By capable persons (I ought to have said) I mean capable of that particular culture. Lyttelton is full of the praises of your prefatory notices.[1]

19. Wed.

Wrote to Ld Hartington—Dr Irons—Duke of Argyll—Mr Acland —The Queen—C.G.—Mr West—& minutes. At half past four the great Beech came down with a mighty crash. The woodmen allowed 27 hours, or 3 axes at nine hours. It was done in 26½, very close. Finished the L.T. MS. and reviewed my unsent letter of the 6th which expresses the firm desire of my better mind to build up her married life into greater fulness and firmness not withstanding the agonies out of which it came & in which it grew. Read Dean Alford on the Idylls of Tennyson[2]—and Th. Parker's Life.

Secret. 1. That Canada & every person in Canada shall have, as far as we are concerned, perfect liberty of thought & speech, in regard to her future political destiny.
2. That as a part of her political freedom, no less than in justice to the British people, we have sought and shall seek to carry over to her, with due regard to time and mode, the ordinary and primary charge of the great question of her own defence.
3. That with regard to defence the proper place and office of Great Britain is to assist Canada in defending herself.
4. That Great Britain must ever be the judge of the manner & measure of that assistance but that in our belief where this country was satisfied as to the cause whether Canada were[3] independent of us or not, such assistance would be freely accorded & would only be limited by our means.
5. That if and so long as Canada shall continue to desire as we believe she now does a political connection with this country upon the free and honourable footing which has been described, that connection should be upheld with the whole power of the Empire.[4]

---

[1] *Okes replied on 22 Jan.; Add MS 44424, f. 162. For diarist's piece for the *Musae*, see 3 Oct. 27.
[2] H. *Alford, 'The Idylls of the King', *Contemporary Review*, xiii. 104 (January 1870).
[3] 'politically' here added, then deleted.
[4] Holograph, dated 19 January 1870, Add MS 44759, f. 1, circulated to several cabinet members. Granville noted on it: 'I quite agree with 1, 2, and 3—I should think it safer to say in No 4 "That Great Britain must ever be the judge of the manner and measure of that assistance, but that H.M's Govt. fully admitted the reciprocal obligation of the Empire with all the resources at its command". These are the words you approved in my dispatch to Sir John Young withdrawing the troops. I see your object in promising the unlimited assistance of the Country, if Canada separate from us, but I am not sure of the prudence of pledging ourselves on such a contingency. No 5 appears to leave too much in the exclusive power of the Dominion, the question of reparation. May not circumstances arise, in which it would be politic of this country to say "you are now so rich and strong, that we must take the initiative and ask you to agree to a friendly reparation." '

20. Th. [London]

Rose early and wrote to Mrs Thistlethwayte a letter covering that of the 6th. Also wrote to Archdn Sandford—Dowager Lady Lyttelton —Mary G.—and minutes. Off at 10.15 to London: arr. at 3: much conversation with a Lady who proved to be a professional musician. Saw Mr Fortescue—Dined with Granville, as did Glyn, for conversation on business. Spent $3\frac{1}{2}$ h. in two visits at 15 G.S.[1] Read Spenser on Ireland.[2]

21. Fr.

Wrote to C. Lyttelton—Messrs Watson—The Queen (& Mem.)—Ly Shaftesbury—Ld Spencer—L. Sinclair—Mr Glyn—Prince of Wales[3] —C.G.—Ld Belper—and minutes. Saw Mr Cardwell—Duke of Argyll—Mr Glyn (2)[4]—Mr Chambers MP.—Chancr of Exr—Ld Clarendon—Mr Bruce—Mr Goschen—Mr Bright. Cabinet $2\frac{1}{2}$-5. Dined at Sir H. Holland's & went to Professor Tyndale's Lecture afterwards, Then saw Mrs Th. & bid farewell. Read Lord Russell.[5]

Cabinet. Jan 21. 70.[6]

√ 1. Clarendon read dispatch to Mr Thornton respecting Mr Fish's public[atio]n of the controversial U.S. dispatch on Alabama case without the Mem. in reply.[7]

√ 2. Also respecting the lapse of the San Juan convention. Passage at the close respecting international courtesy to be omitted.

√ 3. Cardwell proposed the Numbers for the Army Estimates and plans of Army Reform. Question as to Controller & his seat in Parliament postponed.

√ 4. Childers. Further reduction of 500 men. Dockyard Expenditure opens more & more ground for reduction.

√ 5. Gratuity to Mr Reed.[8] £5000 for his inventions.

√ 6. Order in Council for Navy Retirements to be passed before the Vote. No exception for official men.

√ 7. Take the land bill tomorrow.

[1] i.e. Mrs Thistlethwayte.
[2] i.e. the Elizabethan poet; see 13 June 45.
[3] Offering to explain the govt.'s Irish policy; Add MS 44538, f. 58.
[4] Circular sent out to liberal M.P.s summoning them to meeting of Parliament on 8 February, in *The Times*, 24 January 1870, 9e.
[5] *Selections from Speeches of Earl Russell 1817 to 1841, and from Despatches 1859 to 1865*, 2v. (1870).
[6] Add MS 44638, f. 2.
[7] PRO FO 115/500 f. 91 (misdated).
[8] [Sir] Edward James *Reed, 1830-1906; ship designer and chief constructor of the navy 1863–July 1870; liberal M.P. Pembroke boroughs 1874-80, Cardiff 1880-95, 1900-5; K.C.B. 1880.

To EARL SPENCER, Irish lord lieutenant,   Add MS 44538, f. 57.
21 January 1870.

I have received your letter & am examining the papers with much interest.[1]
From what you say in few words, I presume that Fortescue will state shortly
the views he & you may entertain in common, & I need not say the whole
matter will have careful consideration. As yet I do not feel that I have the whole
subject in my mind. Without expressing or having formed any opinion I would
suggest this point to you. You have before you a terrible picture of impunity &
intimidation in respect to crime. But the permanent evil of this impunity lies in
its tendency to make crime spread, & yet agrarian crime though it presents a
revival most lamentable has not spread to anything like the dimensions of some
former periods. In this there is some degree of consolation. Of how many former
periods however can it be said that they greatly exceed the year 1869 in agrarian
crime? The papers you have sent me are very interesting but more information
of the same kind will I think be desired by the Cabinet, & Fortescue is considering about it. Since I began to write I have spoken to Fortescue, & I find that the
matter is in hand & will come regularly before us. We go to Irish land tomorrow.
I found all well & all happy at Hagley. Lady L[yttelto]n senior has made an
admirable rally. She gave me an opportunity of speaking to her of you.

22. Sat.

Wrote to M.F. Tupper—Ly Shaftesbury—Mr Bruce—Count Caruso
—Mr Ayrton—Chancr of Exr—The Queen—Mr Hammond—&
minutes. Dined at Panizzi's: he was in great force. Saw Mr Stansfeld
—Mr Gurdon—Mr Knollys—Mr Ayrton—Mr Glyn (2)—Sir J.
Lacaita. Cabinet 2-5¼. Irish Land. C. came.

Cabinet Jan 22. 70.[2]
Clauses 1 & 2 of the Land Tenures Ireland Bill considered & revised.

23. 3 S.Epiph.

Vere St Chapel mg (Mr Ashley) & Ch. Royal aft. Wrote to Mr Fortes-
cue—Bp of St David's—Robn G.—Mr O. Russell—Ld Lyttelton
—Abp Manning. Saw Duke of Argyll—Mr Bruce—Dr A. Clark.
Read Parker's Life—Q.R. on The Council[3]—M. Shaw on Conscience
Clause[4] and divers Tracts.

To ARCHBISHOP H. E. MANNING,   Add MS 44249, f. 133.
23 January 1870.

I have lost no time in communicating with the Home Secretary on the main
subject of your letter.[5] Neither to him nor me does the proposal of a Committee

[1] Figures on agrarian crime; Add MS 44306, f. 209.   [2] Add MS 44638, f. 4.
[3] [E. S. *Ffoulkes], *Quarterly Review*, cxxviii. 162 (January 1870).
[4] M. Shaw, 'National education and the Conscience Clause' (1870).
[5] From Rome on priests' access to prisoners; Add MS 44249, f. 131.

seem free from objection though it may be necessary to fall back upon it. Even what is now going on at Rome enters I think into the elements of any question raised when an appeal of whatever kind to the Legislature is involved. It will be better to proceed if practicable to such a remedy in Executive Agency: & we will see what can be done in this safe way. We shall hope to deal with Ecclesiastical Titles this year but I am not sanguine as to effecting it at an early period of the session.

I think the present prospects about Irish land are as good as the extreme gravity & difficulty of the question would permit us to expect. It is however a good deal complicated by the unhappy outburst during 1869 of agrarian crime. It is a pleasure to me to think that upon this subject, I need not anticipate, though I know nothing of your views in *detail*, any grave difference of opinion between us. The same I trust may hold good with reference to the Irish Prelates of your Church.

Of the Council I will say nothing except to express my earnest desire that it may end well: the only thing it is in my power to say without the fear of giving you pain.

24. M.

Wrote to Duke of Argyll—Ld Hartington—Ld Halifax—Bp of Winchester—Ld Clarendon—Bp of Gloucester—Sir F. Rogers—Lord Chancellor—Mr Bruce—The Queen—& minutes. Saw Rev. Newman Hall—Rev Jas Fraser—Mr Cardwell. Worked on arranging books and papers. Evening at home. Read Q.R. on Byron—Q.R. on Irish Cauldron[1]—Teetgen's Poems.[2]

To H. A. BRUCE, home secretary, 24 January 1870.   Aberdare MSS.

The situation of the viceroy is a painful one, & he has every claim to our favourable predispositions. At the same time, the most important duty we can now perform is to sift the matter to the bottom so that in the event of our acting we may know beforehand something of the scope, & range of objections. I have raised some of the points in the inclosed short mem. Send it or a copy to Ireland, if you think fit.[3]

Memorandum.[4] In any project of exceptional legislation for Ireland, I apprehend it should be shown, as clearly as possible, 1. What is the present state of agrarian Crime, relatively to *ordinary* former years—to the years of highest crime without special legislation—& to the years of those degrees of crime which were formally deemed to require it, especially the lowest of them. (Part of this is done). 2. In what manner the proposed measure is to attain its end. I do not gather from Ld. Spencer's letter of the 20th that exceptional legislation as to the Press is contemplated. But I rather infer from it that the power of imprisonment would be exercised not merely with reference to suspicion of guilt in a particular case, but upon notorious connection with the Ribbon Societies. This is a some-

---

[1] *Quarterly Review*, cxxviii. 218, 251 (January 1870).
[2] See 31 Jan. 70n.   [3] No response by Bruce found.
[4] Initialled and dated 24 January 1870; Aberdare MSS.

what formidable aspect of a discretionary power of imprisonment. We fail, it is true, to discover the perpetrators of crime: but have we *tried* to discover the offence of belonging to a secret society? 3. The letter of the Inspector General presents very forcible considerations; but do they not come to this that it exposes the inconvenience of working by any law whatever, & therefore proposes (in given districts) wholly to dispense with it? 4. The provisions of any proposed measure should be carefully exhibited in comparison with those of former measures, as to severity: particularly those of 1833, 1846 (not passed), & 1848. 5. It is also desirable to know as far as possible not only the prevailing sentiment of the Irish public, but that of the Irish Representatives, of whom even a small number by a resolute opposition might cause very great mischief, if the case were short of a perfect one by which I mean such as that of 1866.

To LORD CLARENDON, foreign secretary,   Clarendon MSS, c. 498.
24 January 1870.

I have not lost my faith in Fish but I admit that Thornton's letter contains a rather astonishing communication.[1]

On several points there is much in what Fish says (I should like to know the truth about the outlet for Red River produce) but his title to say it and to ask the private!! communication of the views of the Government upon it is another matter. I think we shall still have to maintain our present composed temper.

To answer Fish's question would be inconsistent I apprehend not only with the dignity but with the decencies of self-respect.

We might I think refer him to public documents such as the instructions, from time to time, of Secretaries of State, which unequivocally describe the relations of the Colonies of B.N. America to the mother-country as a perfectly free relation. Were they under any restraint from us Mr Fish might naturally and legitimately ask of us in what way we proposed to use the power kept in our hands, but as we have no such reserved power there is no place for his question.

Might we not especially object to any private communication in a case where our respect for the free inhabitants of the Provinces absolutely requires that we should have no secrets from them, and any transactions with third parties behind their backs would amount to insult.

It is fair to own that there are great peculiarities in the case, and that Mr Reverdy Johnson held in London last year at a public dinner language much akin to what we now hear: but I wish we could with *civility* (which is difficult) ask Mr Fish how he would like any corresponding question to be put to him. You will have thought more & better on this matter: but the letter was too interesting to go back without comment. You will probably send it to Granville before the Cabinet? As he is out hunting, I write to Rogers to beg him to get together any *relevant* passages from the official correspondence with B.N.A.

25. Tu. Conv[ersion of] St Paul.

Dr Mackarness's Consecration.[2] C. much wished to go. Wrote to the Ld Justice Clerk—Ld Lyttelton—The Queen—Bp of Winchester—

[1] Thornton to Clarendon, 8 January 1870, Clarendon MSS, c. 481, reporting Fish's suggestion for union with the U.S.A. of British Columbia, and, possibly, the dominion of Canada also, sent by Clarendon on 23 January, Add MS 44134, f. 141: 'I can only say that if you still believe in the honesty of Fish you have faith enough to remove mountains.'

[2] As bp. of Oxford, in Westminster Abbey.

Mr M'Laren—Ld Dufferin. Saw Ld Granville—Mr Glyn—Ld Chancellor—D. of Argyll. Cabinet 2½-6¼. The *great* difficulties of the I.L. Bill *there* are now over—Thank God. Read Irish Land Papers—American Opinions.[1]

Cabinet Jan 25. 70.[2]
√ 1. Clarendon read Mr Thornton's Report of Mr Fish's language respecting Canada the British Possessions and the Questions between the two countries.[3] Draft to be prepared.
   2. Irish Land Bill. Clauses 3 & 4.

26. Wed.

Wrote to Mr Thring—Mrs Thistlethwayte—Lady Llanover—Sir S.R.G.—Mr P. Rylands—Robn G.—G. Hopwood—The Queen—Mr Dowse—& minutes. Wrote Mem. on Irish Land Bill & sent it to the Queen. Saw Lord Greville—Mr Kn. Hugessen—Mr Walker *cum* Mr Dicey—Mr Glyn (2)—Ld Granville—Mr Fortescue—Mr Thring. Cabinet 2½-6¼. Dinner party at home. Read Ld Russell.

Cabinet Jan 26. 70.[4]
Irish Land Bill, Clauses 5 and following.
Argyll's Clause adopted with amendments.[5]
Clauses respecting Court to be further matured for Friday.
Use of public money for land purposes in Ireland considered.

27. Th.

Wrote to Mrs Thistlethwayte—Watson & Smith—Mr Lambert—M. Chevalier—and minutes.[6] Read much on Ireland through the evg. Saw Duke of Argyll—Mr Bright—Mr Goschen—Mr Glyn. Saw Lady M. Farquhar. Saw Nicholls X.

To M. CHEVALIER, 27 January 1870.   Add MS 44538, f. 64.

It has gratified me much to see that you and other eminent friends to liberty of commerce in France have stood manfully to their colours in the contest now rising and I thank you for the direct assurances you have kindly given me and for the copy of your excellent Speech. We watch your proceedings with great interest but as far as possible I shall be silent about them: and if challenged in Parliament shall (as at present advised) endeavour to treat the question as more, as

---

[1] J. W. Dwinelle, *American opinions on the Alabama and other political questions* (1870).
[2] Add MS 44638, f. 6.   [3] See 24 Jan. 70.
[4] Add MS 44638, f. 7.   [5] Clause ten; see Steele, *Irish Land*, 289.
[6] Circulating correspondence on the vacant St. Asaph see; Add MS 44759, f. 5.

even more French than English—and this it is. French labour has if not a larger, certainly a larger *direct* influence in its maintenance. And our position in commerce is now of such a nature that our only true policy is to look for the *world* as our customer, and to any particular country's legislation and policy mainly with reference to its influence on the world. It was the vast and great influence which we knew the example of France would exercise in all countries, that constituted in my eyes *much* of the charm of the French treaty: but the main reason I think for modest and low-toned language here is that if we were to dwell much against our Protectionists upon the importance of maintaining the Treaty in the sense of British interests we should be playing into the hands of your adversaries. We are hard at work in preparing for the business of the Session and are well enough pleased with the progress and prospects.

28. Fr.

Wrote to D. of Argyll—Mr Lambert—Ld Egerton—The Queen—and minutes. Cabinet 2-6. Saw Mr Lambert—D. of Argyll—The Lord Chancellor. Read Dean on Irish Land[1]—FRGS on do.[2]—Thomas Hist.Dioc. St Asaph.[3]

Cabinet Jan 28. 70.[4]

To consider next Tuesday the *subjects* to be named in the Speech.

√ Clarendon's reply to Thornton considered, reduced, terms fixed. To be in a dispatch.[5]

√ Dispatches from O. Russell.[6] Pope to condemn Fenianism explicitly. Will be read from the altar throughout Ireland. Irish Bps. agreed: do not wish to be compromised by announcing it. To be read in U.S. also. Odo thinks the Definition will be favourable on the whole to the good of mankind. Spoke in the same sense: Clarendon—Bright—Argyll—Lowe. Contra WEG.

√ Granville asked whether we were as asked by N.Z. Commn to recede from the decision at once to withdraw all troops. *No*—Disturbances supposed to be nearly over.[7]

Irish Land Bill. Tenant right Clauses further consd. Court further consd. & rudiments of clauses adopted.

Mr Bright will prepare propositions touching the use of public money.[8]

Question of expropriating the London Companies.

---

[1] G. A. Dean, *A treatise on the land tenure of Ireland* (1869).

[2] Possibly W. Hughes, F.R.G.S., *The geography of Scotland and Ireland* (1852).

[3] Earlier version of D. R. Thomas, *Esgobaeth Llanelwy. A history of the diocese of St. Asaph* (1874).

[4] Add MS 44638, f. 10. Jotting at top of the page reads: 'Settle with Chancellor 1. Respecting applicns. for livings 2. Respecting St. Asaph.'

[5] See drafts of the dispatch in Add MS 44638, f. 11.

[6] O. Russell to Clarendon, 24 January 1870, Clarendon MSS, c. 487.

[7] Granville was under strong pressure to reverse his decision of October 1869, which followed previous tory policy, to withdraw all British troops from New Zealand: the last troops left in February 1870; see C. C. Eldridge, *England's Mission* (1973), 63.

[8] The 'Bright clauses' for land purchase; see Steele, *Irish Land*, 289.

29. Sat.

Wrote to Chancr of Exr—Bp of St Davids—The Queen—Serjeant Dowse—Gen. Grey—Mr W. Evans[1]—Sec.Eccl. Commn[2]—and minutes. Sederunt on Irish Land Bill with Fortescue Thring & Att. Gen. for Ireland 11-2¼. Saw Mr Fortescue—Mr Glyn—Mr Byng. Read Thompson on Ireland[3]—Fitzgerald on Bp Temple.[4]

30. 4 S.Epiph.

Chapel Royal mg and aft. Saw Lord Dufferin—M. Van de Weyer— Ld Camperdown—Ld Lyttelton—Mr Glyn—Sir R. Phillimore. Wrote to Bishop of Llandaff—Ld Penrhyn—The Queen (draft). Read Wesl.Meth. Magazine[5]—Hancock's Sermon[6]—Edwards's (remarkable) Letter on Welsh Bishops[7]—And Pro aris et focis,[8] not less noteworthy.

31. M.

Wrote to Ld Houghton—Mr Teetgen[9]—The Queen—Mrs Aikin-Corwright [*sic*]—Ld de Grey—Ld Granville—Sir J. Gray—Mrs Thistlethwayte—Mrs C. Rumpff (2)—Ld Clarendon—Mr Stephenson—Serj. Dowse—and minutes. Saw Ld Camperdown—Mr Cardwell—Mr Glyn. Made a search for L.R. but in vain. Saw Kennedy— & another[R]. Dined with the Phillimores. Read Jenkinson on State Emigrn[10]—Prendergast's Cromwellian Settlement.[11]

To Mrs FANNY AIKIN KORTRIGHT,   Add MS 44538, f. 66.
31 January 1870.

I beg you to accept my thanks for your eloquent work on 'women's rights', which I have read alike with interest & with sympathy.[12] Observing that it is

---

[1] Unidentified.   [2] J. J. *Chalk.

[3] H. S. Thompson, *Ireland in 1839 and 1869* (1870).

[4] J. F. G. P. Fitzgerald, 'A letter of earnest remonstrance to . . . Gladstone' (1870).

[5] *Wesleyan-Methodist Magazine*, xvi. (1870).

[6] T. Hancock, 'A bishop must have the good report of those who are without the Church' (1870); on *Temple.

[7] H. T. Edwards, 'The Church of the Cymry. A letter to . . . Gladstone' (1869).

[8] See 31 Jan. 70n.

[9] Alexander T. Teetgen had sent his poems, probably *Fruit from Devon. And other poems* (1870); Add MS 44538, f. 66.

[10] J. E. Jenkins, 'State emigration. An essay' (1869); see 3 Feb. 70n.

[11] See 11 July 67.

[12] Fanny Aikin Kortright, novelist and anti-feminist; had sent her *Pro Aris et Focis* (1869); Gladstone assisted its publication (1870) (Add MSS 44424, f. 273, 44425, f. 181) and sent it to the Queen; Guedalla, *Q*, i. 220.

privately printed, &, therefore, not accessible in the usual manner, I take the great liberty of saying how much I should wish to be possessed of one, or were it possible of two, other copies. They are intended for destinations, which I am sure you would consider worthy. Forgive me if I have made any mistake in your address.

Tues. Feb.One. 1870.

Wrote to Ld Clarendon—Ld Cawdor—Chancr of Exr—The Queen —and minutes. Saw The Lord Chancellor—Mr E.M. Barry—Mr Glyn—Mr E. Ashley—Mr Bright (on his plan).[1] Cabinet 2½–6. Read Baxter on Parties[2]—Bombay Civilian on Land.[3] Dined with the Farquhars.

Cabinet Feb. 1. 70.[4]
√ Irish Land Bill (a) Reserved points considered.
   Mr Thring
   Att[orney] Gen[eral for] I[reland] } attended.
O (b) Mr Bright's propositions.
O (c) who to bring in the Bill
√ Topics for the Queen's Speech. Agreed upon.
O√ State of Ireland.[5] Mock of mentioning it, & what is to be done. To be considered tomorrow.

2. Wed. Purification.

Wrote to Mr Lambert—Sir S.R.G.—Dean of Windsor—The Queen —Archdn Stopford—Ld Granville—& minutes. Cabinet 2½–6¼: on Irish Land Bill & State of Ireland. Saw Sir C. Dilke—Mr Glyn (2)— Ld Clarendon—Chancr of Exr—Mr Bruce. Read Sanderson on Irish Land.[6] Dined at Ld de Grey's, to frame the list of Sheriffs. Wrote some rudiments of the Queen's Speech.

Cabinet Feb. 2. 70.[7]
√ 1. Cardwell's plan. Vivian to become Under Sec. Storks to be capable of

---

[1] See 28 Jan. 70.

[2] R. Dudley *Baxter, *English parties and Conservatism* (1870); Gladstone told him (2 February 1870, Add MS 44538, f. 68): 'I cordially wish that the action of the Conservative party may be governed by the spirit which in yr. closing sentences you wisely recommend.'

[3] *The land question in Ireland, viewed from an Indian stand-point. By a Bombay civilian* (1870).

[4] Add MS 44638, f. 12; jottings, for Queen's speech, on next sheet read: 'Ireland: Land —Higher Education—Railways. England: Primary Education—County Boards—Local Taxation.'

[5] Fortescue had submitted a series of cabinet papers on Irish crime requesting wider powers to prohibit firearms and prohibition of processions for three years; Add MS 44613, f. 65.

[6] J. Sanderson, *The Irish land question* (1870).   [7] Add MS 44638, f. 14.

sitting. Approved. Lordship of Treasury to remain suspended for the present.[1]

√ 2. Proposal for exceptional legislation in Ireland. a. as to extending the punishment for sedition to seizure of [printers'] types—not adopted. b. as to suspending Habeas Corpus locally at the discretion of the Lord Lieutenant. Not adopted: but mode of stating the case of Ireland considered & stretched slightly for the speech.[2]

√ 3. Mr Bright's Clauses considered.[3]

3. Th.

Wrote to the Dean of Ch.Ch.—Mr Fortescue (2)—Master of St Johns—Dr Irons—Ld Chancellor—P. of Wales[4]—Dean of Elphin—and minutes. Dined at Duchess of Somerset's. Saw Deputn on Emigration[5]—Bp of Winchester—Mr Bouverie—Ld Granville—Mr Kinnaird—Saw Mrs Glyn—much better. Read Lavelle on Ireland—Kenward's Poems.

To LORD HATHERLEY, lord chancellor,   Add MS 44538, f. 69.
3 February 1870.

As I understand, the Speech, though read by Commissioners, should be in the first person *as if* delivered by the Sovereign?[6]

Thinking over parts of our conversation in Cabinet yesterday, I much wish we could have seen our way to the experiment of special inquiries more or less on the model of the Sheffield one.[7] It touches directly the real mischief, it has not been tried—it would tend somewhat to repress mischief, while it was being tried —it might encourage some of the timid to come forward. It is an act of respect to liberty—& if it failed & the mischief continued the failure would much improve the case for extra-constitutional remedies. I admit these are not reasons for doing anything false & unreal: but I should much like to have the matter *considered* by the Irish legal authorities, before the idea is finally abandoned.[8]

To H. G. LIDDELL, dean of Christ Church, Oxford,   Add MS 44538, f. 69.
3 February 1870.

I have received your letter[9] enclosing a draft bill on the subject of University Tests & I will bring it under the early consideration of my Colleagues. After this

---

[1] War Office reorganisation under 33 & 34 Vict. cap. 17; John Cranch Walker Vivian (1818–79) became the first financial sec. of the W.O. 1870, and Sir H. Storks surveyor-general.

[2] See 1 Feb. 70n.

[3] See 28 Jan. 70; Gladstone's notes at Add MS 44638, f. 5.

[4] Arranging the meeting on 7 Feb. 70; Add MS 44538, f. 69.

[5] From the National Emigration League; speeches in *The Times*, 4 February 1870, 8b, and first leader. Gladstone effectively declined govt. help.

[6] Hatherley replied it was in the third person; Add MS 44205, f. 33.

[7] Special commission on violence in Sheffield set up by 1867 R.C. on Trade Unions; *PP* 1867 xxxii. 397.

[8] Hatherley replied: 'I will think further on the possibility of "Inquiry" in Ireland before we meet tomorrow.'   [9] Add MS 44236, f. 315.

letter from you I regard it as having the joint assent of the two bodies of Promotion in Oxford & Cambridge respectively.

4. Fr.

Wrote to Rev Mr Liddon—Bp of London—The Queen—Archdn Davies—Mr Caird—Mr Fortescue—Mr Chalk—Mr Stephens—Mr Holland—and minutes. Saw Ld Chancellor—Lord E. Bruce—Mr Pringle—Sir R. Phillimore—Mr Glyn *cum* Mr Brand—Ld Granville —Mr Goschen. Cabinet 2½-6. The Speech agreed on. Dinner party at home. Read Murphy on Ireland.[1]

Cabinet Feb. 4. 70[2] [*Bruton Street*]
√ 1. Queen's Speech. Draft. Read in full. Then Par[agraph] by Par[agraph]. Arr[angement] of Irish Part altered. Speech considered & approved.
√ Days—Irish Land 14 or 15. Education 17th. N.Z. if possible the 21st. Army as soon as possible.
√ Committee on Diplomatic Salaries &c. To be taken up by Govt, in concert with Mr R[?][3]
Education Bill[4]
O O'Donovan Rossa.[5] A Resolution to be moved declaring the seat vacant.
√ Ld Hartington's plan for the reduction of postage on Newspapers & printed matter.[6]

5. Sat.

Wrote to Mr Fortescue—Mr Piddock[7]—the Queen (Mem)—Abp of Canterbury—Mrs Childers—Bp of Llandaff—Solr General—Lord Cawdor—and minutes. Dined with the Lothians. 8¾-6¼. Went to Osborne for the Speech Council. Audience of H.M. who agreed to retaining the passage about her non-appearance.[8] Saw Bp of Oxford— Ld Sydney—Ld de Grey—Dean of Westr—Mr Bruce. Read Lavelle on Ireland[9]—M'Coll's pamphlet.[10]

[1] J. N. Murphy, *Ireland industrial, political and social* (1870).
[2] Add MS 44638, f. 22; held in *Granville's house in Bruton Street.
[3] No minutes found.
[4] See de Grey to Forster this day (Reid, *F*, i. 477): 'The bill is through—compulsion and all. . . .'
[5] J. O'Donovan Rossa, d. 1915; Fenian, elected for Tipperary November 1869, declared ineligible, as a felon; see 10 Feb. 70.
[6] From 4 oz. for 1*d.* (1855) to 2 oz. for ½*d.* (7 October 1870).   [7] Untraced.
[8] The lords commissioners expressed *Victoria's regret 'that recent indisposition has prevented Her from meeting you in person, . . . at a period of remarkable public interest'; *H* cxcix. 3.
[9] P. Lavelle, *The Irish landlord since the Revolution* (1870).
[10] M. MacColl, *The Ober-Ammergau Passion Play* (1870).

Osborne F. 5. 70.[1]

Ask H.M. to give dispatch to any question of Promotion & retirement connected with the Navy Estimates—Dowse's Appt. Irish Solr.—Dale & Liddon, H.M. pleasure.

6. 5 S.Epiph.

Went to St Mary's [Lambeth] & heard Stephy preach a strong & high-toned Sermon. Chapel Royal in aft. Saw Fitzgerald. X. Saw Capt. Egerton—Mr Glyn. Wrote to Capt. Egerton—Abp of Canterbury—Mr Fortescue—Mrs Thistlethwayte—& minutes. Read Mackay's Sermons[2]—Basil Jones's do[3]—Parker's Life.

7. M.

Wrote to Bp of Chester—Canon Dale—M.F. Tupper[4]—Mr Helps—Ld Clarendon—Ld Granville—& minutes. Read Gibbs on Ireland.[5] Saw Sir C. Dilke[6]—Ld Bessborough—Mr Bright—Mr Gurdon—Mr Glyn. With the Prince of Wales $3\frac{1}{4}$-$4\frac{1}{4}$ explaining to him the Land Bill: & on other matters. He has certainly much natural intelligence. Sick calls. Speech dinner: & large evening party afterwards.

8. Tu.

Wrote to Bp of Llandaff—The Queen (2)—and minutes. Lay up a little. Saw Mr Cardwell—Mr Cardwell *cum* Mr Childers—Mr Motley—Mr Glyn—Duke of Argyll—Mr Thring—Mr Jacob Bright—Mr Fortescue. H. of C. $4\frac{1}{4}$-$8\frac{1}{2}$. Spoke on the Address.[7] All went off exceedingly well. Read Lavelle on Irish Land—Gibbs on do.—Morris, Death of Paris.[8]

9. Wed.

Wrote to The Queen (& Mem.)—Mr Fortescue—Mr Liddon[9]—Bp of Llandaff—Dr Hannah—Mr Delane[10]—Mrs Tait[11]—and minutes.

---

[1] Add MS 44757, f. 12.

[2] J. Mackay, *Molochology not Theology: Penang sermons* (1870).

[3] W. B. T. *Jones, *The peace of God* (1869).

[4] Sending him £400 from official funds, to recover from an accident; see D. Hudson, *Martin Tupper* (1949), 261, Add MS 44538, f. 71.

[5] F. W. Gibbs, *English law and Irish tenure* (1870).

[6] Seconding the address; see 15 Jan. 70.   [7] On Ireland; *H* cxcix. 92.

[8] W. *Morris, 'The death of Paris' from *The Earthly Paradise*, 4 pts. (1868–70).

[9] Offering him a canonry in St. Paul's; Add MS 44538, f. 72.

[10] Details of recent church appts.; ibid.

[11] Asking her to ask the bed-ridden abp. his recommendation for St. Asaph; Add MS 44424, f. 272.

Read Maccarthy on Ireland, Scriven on do.[1] Saw Duke of Argyll—
Ld Granville—Mr Glyn—Mr Brand. Dined with the Amn Minister.[2]
We were most kindly entertained. Lady Cork's afterwards.

10. Th.

Wrote to Ld Halifax—Mr Macmillan—Scotts—Murray Gladstone
—Mrs C. Rumpff—Mr Bruce—Sir R. Palmer—The Queen (2)—
Atty General—Mr F. Lawley—and minutes. 11-3. A stiff & useful
Session on the Irish Land Bill, in conclave. Saw The Lord Chancellor
—Solr General—Mr Woodgate—Bp of Exeter—Mr Cardwell. H. of
C. 4¼-7¾.[3] Dined at the Dean of Westminster's. Read M'Carthy on
Irish Land.

To LORD HALIFAX, 10 February 1870.   Add MS 44538, f. 73.

I should have been very happy, had circumstances permitted to tell you what
we are about in the Irish Land Bill, of which the provisions have now very nearly
fallen into shape. But this I may say, that while we have proceeded in the general
direction, which you and I spoke of at Hawarden, I think we have escaped some
of the difficulties which then seemed to press. Mr. Thompson's pamphlet is
notable, most of all I think as indicating the force of the case, which has completely driven him from the position he took on his return from Ireland viz. that
nothing should be granted to Tenants except compensation for improvements.[4]

To F. LAWLEY, 10 February 1870.   Add MS 44538, f. 73.

Your very interesting letter[5] has reached me today & I will not fail to communicate with Clarendon upon it. I hope we shall meet soon. In the mean time
I may say it is the fear of appearing meddlesome & not indifference to the great
operation now proceeding in France or to the Emperor's commanding part in it
that has made us seem reticent in the matter.

In truth the period since we came into office has been one of universal &
almost total silence in the H. of C. with regard to foreign affairs.

11. Fr.

Wrote to Mr Fortescue (2)—Dean of Chichester—Mrs Rumpff—Dr
Payne-Smith[6]—Mr Bruce—Mr Westell—Mrs Bright[7]—The Queen

[1] D. MacCarthy, ed., Dissertations chiefly on Irish Church history [by M. Kelly] (1864);
J. E. Scriven, An Irish farmer on the land difficulty (1870).
[2] J. L. Motley.   [3] Spoke on O'Donovan Rossa: H cxcix. 123.
[4] Halifax replied, 11 February, Add MS 44185, f. 7: 'I think Caird and Thompson both
wrong in their action of five years being required to recoup a tenant for outlay.'
[5] From Daily Telegraph office, on visit to Paris and Napoleon's sincere liberalism; Add
MS 44424, f. 264.
[6] Robert *Payne Smith, 1819-95; professor of divinity at Oxford 1865; dean of Canterbury January 1870.
[7] Conveying *Victoria's interest in *Bright's health; Add MS 44538, f. 73.

(Tel and letter)—Watsons—& minutes. Dined with the Wortleys. C[hief] J[ustice] Cockburns after to hear Joachim.[1] Went down to Brixton & saw Mrs C. Rumpff[R]. At Christie's. Saw Mr Glyn—Mr Kinnaird—Mr Goschen—Mr Cardwell—C. of E. (respecting $2\frac{1}{2}$%s). Read 'The Dean'.[2]

12. Sat.

Wrote to Sec. River Dee Co.—Provost of Oriel—T.B. Potter—Ld Chancellor—The Queen—Ld Clarendon—Mr Bruce. Cabinet $2\frac{1}{2}$-7. The week's business—Irish Land—& other matters. Saw Mr Ouvry —Principal of King's College—Mr Glyn—Ld Granville—Mr Fortescue. Dined at Marlborough House. Much conversation with Prince —Princess—D. of Cambridge—Lady Leinster—Mrs Stroud (whom I greatly like).[3]

Cabinet Feb. 12. 70.[4]

√ Shall India pay a share of the charge of taking up the purchase system *quoad* Ensigns &c.
√ Bpric of Kilmore.[5]
√ Convocation Address on Lectionary. answer agreed on: sent to Mr Bruce.
√ Numbers to be chosen for Select Committees from the two sides respectively. Offer terms as written.
√ Bishops in Lords. Bill
√ Mr Goschen—to put the inmaintenance of work-house upon the Common Fund. Agreed to as a fair compromise.[6]
√ County Local Boards: not to be introduced *because* Commn. shd. be appointed on the expediency of dividing Rates between Owners & Occupiers.[7]
√ Ballot Committee. Omit Bright: to stand at 19.
√ Fawcett's motion.[8] (C. of E. to see Solr. General). Inadmissible.

13. Septua S.

Whitehall Chapel mg to hear Bp of Exeter: a noble Sermon. Chapel Royal aftn. Read Parker's Life—Hook's Essay[9]—Orby Shipley on Liturgy.[10] Wrote to Mrs Thistlethwayte—Mrs C. Rumpff—A. Kinnaird—Mr Newdigate—and minutes. Saw Ld Bessborough, &

[1] Joseph Joachim, 1831–1907; violinist, played in London annually from 1862.
[2] B. Aikin [F. Aikin Kortright], *The Dean; or the popular preacher*, 3v. (1859).
[3] See 18 Oct. 69.   [4] Add MS 44638, f. 25.
[5] Vacant on dec. of H. Verschoyle; Thomas Carson (1805–74), his successor, was the last bp. appt. by the crown in Ireland.
[6] Achieved in Metropolitan Poor Law Amendment Act 1870.
[7] Eventually the *Goschen select cttee. on local taxation: *PP* 1870 viii.
[8] On opening Epping Forest for recreation: *H* cxcix. 186 (14 February 1870). See L. Stephen, *Life of Henry Fawcett* (1886), ch. vii.
[9] See 8 June 69.   [10] O. *Shipley, *The daily sacrifice and divine liturgy* (1868).

explained to him the [Irish Land] Bill as it stands. Saw Mr Glyn—
Lady Lothian.

Dear Herbert, very ill last night, could not be confirmed: but thank
God grows rapidly better.

14. M.

Wrote to Viceroy of Ireland—Mr Fortescue—Mr Maguire—Watson
& S.—Bp of St David's—The Queen—and minutes. H. of C. $4\frac{1}{2}$-$8\frac{1}{4}$.
Spoke on Epping Forest.[1] Saw Mr Fortescue—Sir John Gray—Mr
Glyn—Mr Parker—Sol. General. Worked up the papers on the Irish
Land question until a late hour.

15. Tu.

Wrote to Mr Fortescue—Sir H. Moncreiff—Mr Graham—Sir W.
Knollys—The Queen—Bp of Winchester—Abp Manning—&
minutes. Saw Mr Fortescue—Mr Glyn. Worked steadily on Irish Land
papers & notes for speech. H of C. $4\frac{1}{2}$-9. Introduced The I.L. Bill in
a speech of $3\frac{1}{4}$ hours.[2] Well received by the House at large: query the
Irish popular party? Read The Dean—'Military Adminn 54-70'.[3]

16. Wed.

Wrote to Chancr of Exchr (& Mem.)—Rev. J.L. Ross—Mr Glyn—
Mr Pringle—D. of Argyll—Ld Clarendon—Ld Dufferin—Abp
Manning—The Viceroy—Bp of Llandaff—Mr Gibson—Mrs Thistle-
thwayte—The Queen—Ld Granville—and minutes. Saw Mr Buck
—Mr Childers cum Mr Goschen—Mr Fortescue cum Mr Thring—
Mr Glyn—Mr Buck. Read Gibbs. Dined with the Beauchamps. Even-
ing party at home afterwards. Read Gibbs.

To the DUKE OF ARGYLL, Indian secretary,   Add MS 44538, f. 76.
16 February 1870.

You are quite right to shield from writing the precious treasure which has
been (as it were) restored to you. I will take care that nothing shall be done in
the Intestacy Bill at present.[4] Your absence I hope will not be very long, & there
is no great hurry about the Bill, while the subject deserves a mature consideration.

[1] Moderating *Fawcett's motion (see 12 Feb. 70): H cxcix. 263.
[2] H cxcix. 333, published as 'A correct report of the speech . . . on proposing the Irish
Land Bill' (1870).
[3] See, probably, 19 Mar. 69n.
[4] Argyll had written from Inveraray on 14 February, Add MS 44101, f. 216, that he
must stay another week, and asking no details of the Scottish Intestacy Bill be settled.

It is early to speak of the Irish Land Bill which has not yet seen the light for 24 hours. But thus far the reception of it has been so favourable as almost to make me tremble. The Irish popular party are disposed (at present) to accept it: our immediate friends decidedly approve: None I believe are better pleased than the Conservatives, their pleasure partaking largely of the character of relief. Granville writes to me that we must really get some Landlords to object violently.
Bright does well physically but is not up to brain work. Clarendon still an invalid.

To LORD CLARENDON, foreign secretary,   Clarendon MSS, c. 498.
16 February 1870.

I return the letters from Loftus, & the Telegram. A wet blanket is very much wanted for Bismarck: & I hope you may contrive or may have contrived to let him know how much you are disappointed at his answer to your overture.[1] Otherwise your very proper intention to dissuade the French Govt. from any general step may be misinterpreted by him as an approval of his course.

What pretext has he for interfering in Bavaria.

I am very glad you have suggested a form, which seems to me quite unexceptionable, for giving effect to Acton's wish about a suggestion to Count Beust.

The *reception* of the Irish Land Bill has, though I was rather sanguine, thus far surpassed all my expectations. The Conservatives are relieved, and pleased (I hear) as well as relieved. They seemed favourable while I spoke. So did our own more immediate friends behind us. And all I hear leads me to suppose that the popular Irish party mean to accept. God grant all this may come true. It is the fruit of the kindly & most patient labours of the Cabinet which have really surpassed all I ever knew.

You are I trust getting round & I shall communicate to H.M. that you are expected at F.O. today.

P.S. Thinking that the Speech of last night offered a fair opportunity, I, in conformity with your suggestion, said a few words of good will about the Emperor's constitutional experiment (not calling it by that name).

To ARCHBISHOP H. E. MANNING,   Add MS 44538, f. 77.
16 February 1870. 'Private.'

[2]By this post I send you two copies of our last print of the I.L. Bill. I cannot yet say whether it will be finally, or only approximately accurate, but the substance of it you may take for granted. You will at once see that here as oftentimes the circuitous road is really the only one practicable, & is to be much preferred to scaling & descending precipices. It would be most objectionable to call in public authority to determine every case of proposed eviction on the merits, & would tend to draw towards the Govt. more than ever the hatred of the people.

The policy of the Bill is this, to prevent the Landlord from using this terrible weapon of undue & unjust eviction by so framing the handle that it shall cut his hands with the sharp edge of pecuniary damages. The man evicted without any fault, & suffering the usual loss by it will receive whatever the custom of the

[1] See Clarendon to Loftus this day, Clarendon MSS, c. 474.
[2] In Hammond, 100; Manning answered that Irish bps. were initially favourable; ibid., 102.

country gives & when there is no custom according to a scale beginning with 7 years rent, under or up to £10 valuation, & ending with two yrs rent over £100: besides whatever we can claim for permanent bgs. or reclamation of land. Wanton eviction will, as I hope, be extinguished by provisions like these. And if they extinguish wanton eviction, they will also extinguish those demands for *unjust* augmentations of rent, which are only formidable to the occupier, because the power of wanton, or arbitrary, eviction is behind them. I give you here, for the information of your Irish brethren, what is in truth the pith of some 8 or 10 columns of the small print of the Times today: to which you & they will not have the time to pay attention. I am confident you will think we have honourably & thoroughly redeemed our pledge.

The reception *thus far* has been beyond my expectation good in all q[uarte]rs. Please give one copy to Cardinal Abp. Cullen.

17. Th.

Wrote to Ld Clarendon—Viceroy of Ireland—and minutes. Saw Mr Cartwright—Sir J. Lacaita—Ld Granville—Sir J. Gray—Mr Johnstone—Waterford Estate Deputation[1]—Mr Childers *cum* Mr Lowe—Mr Glyn—Scotts—Mr Forster—Mr Fortescue. H of C. $4\frac{1}{2}$-$8\frac{1}{4}$ and 9-$9\frac{3}{4}$.[2] Read the Dean—Gibbs on Ireland (finished).

To EARL SPENCER, Irish lord lieutenant,   Add MS 44538, f. 79.
17 February 1870.

I do not know whether it is possible that if the reception of the Land bill on your side the water be as good as here, the Fenians in aggravated fear of losing their gains & ground for good should be driven to make some mad attempt. At any rate you will be able to take this suggestion at what it may be worth.[3]

The Irish members have met today. They desire to amend but with support.

18. Fr.

Wrote to Mr Sharland[4]—Chancr of Exr—The Queen—B. Armitage[5]—Sir W. Hutt—Professor Sedgwick[6]—Mr J. Watson—Sol. General—Sir A. Grant—Mr [P.] Macmahon—Mr Bruce—Ld Clarendon—The Queen—the Viceroy—The Sol. Gen for Ireland. Saw Mrs C. Rumpf, and discussed fully her affairs[R]—Mr Glyn—Ld Granville

[1] Deputation led by R. P. Dawson 'to arrange for a loan on behalf of tenant farmers and to explain . . . the tenant right of Ulster'; *Londonderry Sentinel*, 22 February 1870.
[2] *Forster introduced the Education Bill: *H* cxcix. 438.
[3] 'With regard to the Fenians, I took your hint, & issued a notice for renewed precautions'; Spencer to Gladstone, 18 February 1870, Add MS 44306, f. 213.
[4] Engaged in the Rumpff affair; Add MS 44538, f. 80.
[5] Benjamin Armitage, 1823–99; Manchester cotton manufacturer; worked with *Cobden on 1860 treaty; liberal M.P. Salford 1880-5.
[6] Adam *Sedgwick, 1785-1873, Cambridge geologist.

—Mr Lambert jun—Solr. General—Mr Lefevre. Dined with the Jameses. Read The Dean—Jones Jones on the Welsh Language.[1]

To LORD CLARENDON, foreign secretary,   Clarendon MSS, c. 498.
18 February 1870.

I return Bismarck's confidential letter on disarmament.[2] As the matter appears to me, the best that can be said for this letter is that it contains matter which might be urged with more or less force in a conference on disarmament by way of abating the amount of relative call on Prussia: but as an argument against entertaining the subject is futile and he ought at any rate to be made to feel his responsibility which I daresay you will contrive while acknowledging his civility.

To Sir W. HUTT, M.P., 18 February 1870.   Add MS 44538, f. 80.

The subject of your letter[3] is by no means new to me; but I think the opinion prevailing among us is that while there is no urgent call for public interference in regard to Irish emigration, and while the difficulties attending much interference would evidently be great it would we think be unfortunate at this particular moment to associate in the minds of the Irish people this particular idea with the Land Bill.

19. Sat.

Wrote to Viceroy of Ireland—Mrs Douglas—Mr T. Goalen[4]—Mr Dalgleish—The Ld Advocate—The Queen—Mrs Bennett—Mrs O'Donovan Rossa—and minutes. Saw Mr Homersham Cox—Mr Glyn —Ld Chancellor (2)—Mr Delane—The Speaker—Mr Goschen— Mr Ayrton. Cabinet 2.30–6. Dined at the Speaker's. Lady de Grey's after. Read Greg's Essays[5]—The Dean.

Cabinet Feb. 19. 70[6]
1. Ld Granard.[7] Statement of case to be prepared. Cabinet if necessary.
⟨2. Lectionary.⟩
3. O'Donovan Rossa. Information to be prepared. I send intermediate answer.[8]
4. Week's business. Postpone reply to Scots about an Edn Bill. Birley [motion on] French Treaty: refuse Committee.

[1] Perhaps J. Jones, *A reply to the Rev. W. B. Knight's 'Remarks' on Welsh orthography* (1831).
[2] Sent this day by Clarendon, Add MS 44134, f. 151: 'It is courteous but as to disarming, no.'   [3] Untraced; not in Add MS 44424.
[4] One of Gladstone's Goalen relatives; lived in Tottenham; Hawn. P.
[5] W. R. *Greg, *Political problems for our age and country* (1870).
[6] Add MS 44638, f. 29.
[7] Perhaps his conversion to Roman catholicism 1869. An embarrassment later, see 19 July 72.
[8] Through the Fenian's wife, declining an interview, but promising 'full attention' to the case (see 4 Feb. 70): Add MS 44538, f. 82.

5. Tramways.[1] Lefevre desires (a) a Bill with general conditions: (b) & a Joint Committee (c). Hang up the particular Bills. a. Yes. b. no. c. yes.
6. Mr Cardwell. Military Offices Building. Estimate to be prepared for it on the Embankment with the intention on the part of the Cabinet that the Admiralty shall follow: places to be prepared accordingly.
7. Inclosure Commissioners. Bill to be prepared for consn. by a Committee.

20. Sexa S.

Vere St Chapel mg and St James's evg. Wrote to Archdeacon Grant —Rev H. Allon—Mr G. Moffatt—Rev Dr Russell—Mrs Thistle-thwayte—and minutes. Read The Dean—Sir T. Phillips on Welsh Church[2]—Gorman on Athn Creed.[3] Saw Ld Granville—Ld Lyttelton—Mr Glyn. Dined with the Lothians.

21. M.

Wrote to Bp of Winchester—Ld Shaftesbury—The Queen—Mr Smythe—The Viceroy—and minutes. Saw The Portuguese Minister —Sir S.R.G. on Welsh Bishopric—Mr Farrer—Mr Glyn—Mr Lefevre—Mr Broughton. H of C. $4\frac{1}{2}$-$7\frac{3}{4}$ and 9-$12\frac{1}{4}$.[4] Read Tighe Hamilton on Irish Land[5]—Rearranging my room with W.

22. Tu.

Wrote to Mr Ouvry (2)—The Viceroy—The Queen—Mr Bruce— Mr Wintle[6]—and minutes. H of C. $4\frac{1}{2}$-$7\frac{1}{4}$.[7] Saw Mr [A.] White (Prince's Solr)—Ld Kimberley—Ld de Grey—Bp of St David's— Mr Hugessen. $11\frac{3}{4}$-$3\frac{1}{2}$. To the Council at Windsor. Long audience of the Queen. Dined with the Jameses. Mrs Baring's music afr. Read Ld Russell's Introduction. Have lately seen the persons named White Graham & another. The two first in great part reclaimed; the third hesitating[R].

Windsor Feb. 22. 70. Audience[8]
Mr Duckworth—sees: St. Asaph, Chichester Dean Wellesley?, Canterbury—Mr Bright's health—Land Bill & Education Bill, Prospects—Ld Kildare, to go to

[1] Bill introduced 1 March 1870: *H* cxcix. 1080.
[2] Sir T. *Phillips, *Wales: the language, social condition, moral character and religious opinions of the people* (1849).
[3] T. M. Gorman, *The Athanasian Creed and modern thought* (1870).
[4] Spoke on local taxation: *H* cxcix. 657.
[5] W. T. Hamilton, 'The Irish land Bills of the late government' (1853).
[6] Thanking R. W. Wintle for details of d. of bp. of Chichester; Add MS 44538, f. 84.
[7] Spoke on revenue officers: *H* cxcix. 702.
[8] Add MS 44757, f. 15. Written in ink over pencil jottings.

the H. of Lords—Duke of Edinburgh: some person of influence to be near him if possible—P. of W[ales]: Mordaunt case: H.M. wishes me to speak to the P. seriously: has asked the Chancellor.

23. Wed.

Wrote to Bp of St David's—Mr Kinnaird—The Queen (2)—Ld Clarendon—Mr Bruce—Prince of Wales—& minutes. Council of King's Coll. 2-3. Visited Christie's. Saw Col. Stepney—Mr F. Lawley (2)—D. of Argyll—Mr Glyn. Arrangements at home for the reception. P. & Princess of Wales dined here with a large party: extremely gracious & kind. It is a critical time. We had music in the evening, after sharing the Italian juvile [*sic*] &c. Read 'The Dean'.

To LORD CLARENDON, foreign secretary,   Clarendon MSS, c. 498.
23 February 1870.

I return the letters & am glad the Emperor was pleased with my few words.[1] Though you have most properly disdained the notion of making any speech in Parliament *apropos* of your pacific effort, I hope we all remain free to denounce, when occasion offers, the system of huge armaments prevailing on the Continent: as Sir R. Peel did when the case was not half so strong.

The Irish interpretation of my speech about perpetuity of tenure is wholly Irish, i.e. was not attached to it by anyone on this side the water, & is due to some cause that I cannot understand. I am not *aware* of having used the words 'for the present' at all. But I can plainly see the sense in which, if used, they were meant to be taken. After holding a House, anxious for the Bill, during a long period, with a preliminary argument of that kind, some apology was due, & I might well observe that I had said enough, at any rate for the present, & until some new arguments were produced, to warrant me in at once announcing that the Govt. could not give any countenance to the plan of perpetuity of tenure. The words, if used, referred to a prolongation of the speech, & not to the conclusion. As far as I am concerned I am quite willing to have what I have now written published in Ireland if it be desired.

24. Th.

Wrote to Ld Clarendon—Editor of L'Illustration[2]—Bp of Ely—The Queen—and minutes. H. of C. 4½-7¼.[3] Read Ld Russell.[4] Saw Dean of Windsor—Bp of London—Mr Leeman—Sp. Minister[5]—Mr Glyn —Mr Howard *cum* Mr Clutton—Chancr of Exr. Lady Lyttelton's party in evg.

[1] See 16 Feb. 70.
[2] Its ed. of 19 Feb. 1870 had a profile of diarist by Henry Cozic.
[3] Spoke on consuls: *H* cxcix. 794.   [4] See 21 Jan. 70.
[5] Don Manuel Raucès y Villanueva; see 26 Feb. 70.

To LORD CLARENDON, foreign secretary,   Clarendon MSS, c. 498.
24 February 1870.

Many thanks for your letter.[1] In the Roman business I would suggest that you might inform the French of what you have so properly written to Berlin & Vienna. I will write to Acton when there is an opportunity from the F.O.

With regard to Gibraltar I should think the simplest & quickest answer was the best, as for example that we could not advise any attempt at an overture. Layard I doubt not knows all the things he might say on it from himself. Even were we ready for such a thing I apprehend the suspicions now entertained about abandonment of the Colonies would supply a conclusive reason against our giving the slightest encouragement. Looking however to the contingencies of the future, I think it may be a question whether you should not fortify yourself by mentioning the subject on Saturday in Cabinet.

Ld Russell's letter is genial but one is sorry to notice an apparent failure in the handwriting.
[P.S.] We may well be thankful about Prince Arthur. No attempt can be too desperate for the Fenians under present circumstances.

25. Fr.

Wrote to Mr Fortescue—The Queen—and minutes. Attended HM's Court at 3. Saw Mr Richard, on Welsh Bpric.[2] H of C. 4½-8¼ and again at 9.[3] Went to the Operetta &c. at Mr Freeks's.[4] Circuit to Brixton & Chelsea. Saw the two Herberts. Read M. de Beaumont on Ireland.[5]

26. Sat.

Wrote to Ld Chancellor—Dean of Windsor—Mr Bruce—Sol. General —The Queen—and minutes. Went to Brixton to see & advise Mrs C. Rumpff. Correcting proofs of Speech on Irish Land. Cabinet 2½-6. Saw Ld Granville—Dean of Westmr—Ld Dufferin—Ld Kimberley —Mr Glyn—Ld Chancellor—Mr James QC. Dined with the Lytteltons. Lady Waldegrave's afterwards. Saw Oates[R]. Read The Dean.

Cabinet Feb. 26. 70. 2.30 PM.[6]
√ O'Donovan Rossa: next Cabinet.
√ Land Transfer & Intestacy Bills. Mr Hardy's question. To be discussed by Cabinet next Saturday.

[1] Of 23 February, Add MS 44134, f. 152, on his letters urging Prussian and Austrian co-operation on the Council.
[2] i.e. Henry *Richard, on the St. Asaph vacancy.
[3] Opposing *Fawcett's motion, he promised govt. would 'announce the establishment of a system of open competition upon an extended scale': *H* cxcix. 814.
[4] (Sir) Charles James Freake, 1814-84; London property developer; stood as tory in Chelsea 1868; cr. bart. by diarist 1882.
[5] G. A. de la Bonninière de Beaumont, *L'Irlande sociale, politique et religieuse*, 2v. (1839).   [6] Add MS 44638, f. 31.

O (The sick Fenian mentioned by Maguire. WEG)
√ Patronage in Scotland. Not now.
√ Brogden. bribery. form a Committee.[1]
√ Arrangement for the Board of Trade business. Ld Kimberley to help Mr Lefevre in the absence of the [President of the] Board of Trade.
√ The Week's business.
√ Scotch Education Bill: ansr. to be made, dilatory.
√ Workmen's Exhibition: Fee on Patents: concession to be made.
√ Chanc. of Exr. Quarterly Payment of Dividends. postponed.[2]
√ Clarendon to decline civilly a [sc. to] entertain Spanish proposal for giving up Gibraltar.[3]

27. *Quinqua S.*

Chapel Royal mg: St John's Brixton aft. where dear Herbert was confirmed by the Bp of Winchester. Thence to Campden Hill where I saw Dss of Argyll: wonderfully recovered but not very strong I thought. Thence to 15 G.S.[4] That is a case with an extraordinary claim for sympathy arising from an unparalleled history: but it embarrasses. Saw Bp of St David's. Wrote to A. Kinnaird—Mrs Thistlethwayte—Sir R. Anstruther—A.W. Forster. Saw Bp of Winchester on the Kilmore vacancy. Read Parker's Life[5]—Hughes on the Welsh Colleges[6]—Williams Ch. of the Future[7]—Forster on Ch. of Ireland.[8]

28. *M.*

Wrote to Mr O. Russell—Ld Clarendon—Bp of Brechin—Dean of Windsor—Bp of Llandaff—The Queen—and minutes. H of C. 4½-7¾ & 10¾-1.[9] Dined at Panizzi's. Saw Mr Ayrton (2)—Mr Stansfeld (2)—Mr Glyn—New Zealand Delegates.[10] Read The Dean. Worked on proofs of Irish Land Speech.

To LORD CLARENDON, foreign secretary,   Clarendon MSS, c. 498.
28 February 1870. '*Most Private.*'

1. I follow with a sorrowful concurrence the two first papers of Odo Russell's letter.[11] In the third he agrees apparently with the majority of the Cabinet.[12]

---

[1] The Bridgwater election: *H* cxcix. 803, 880 (25, 28 February 1870).
[2] Plan for partial conversion, in which Gladstone found faults; see Add MSS 44301, f. 131 and 44538, ff. 75, 89.   [3] See 24 Feb. 70.
[4] i.e. Mrs Thistlethwayte.   [5] See 22 Dec. 69.
[6] Venias [i.e. Joshua Hughes], 'The university of Brecknock' (1853?).
[7] Probably untraced work by George Williams of King's.   [8] Untraced.
[9] Spoke on treaties of commerce: *H* cxcix. 882.
[10] Commissioners sent to re-establish 'cordial relations' between New Zealand and Britain; W. P. Morrell, *British colonial policy in the mid-Victorian age* (1969), 367.
[11] O. Russell to Clarendon, 22 February 1870, Clarendon MSS, c. 487; infallibility expected by Easter.
[12] 'a clearly defined position between the Papacy and the civilized world.'

On Saturday I talked that matter over with Dean Stanley & was glad to find him strongly in the same sense with myself.

2. With regard to the Spanish debt, under Ld Palmerston if I remember right it was concluded that we had better give it up formally by an Act of Parliament. Its present position is unsatisfactory. Either we should trust it seriously with Spain or we should hold our tongues about it.

3. As to hints from me to Lowe,[1] not a week passes without them. I must do him the justice to say that he receives them well: still they cannot be indefinitely multiplied. Again, I am persuaded that the occasions for them, which are frequent & lamentable, are not due to any want of honourable & just intention, but to a blank in his very extraordinary mental constitution. Unhappily the matter does not improve: he 'goes and does it again'.

Tues.Mch One 1870.

Wrote to Dean of Windsor——Gertrude Glynne——Abp Manning——The Queen——Ld Acton——and minutes. Rode with Agnes. Saw Oates: some hope[R]. Saw Archdeacon Grant——Mr Glyn——Ld Halifax——Ld Clarendon——Mr Fortescue. Attended the Levee. H of C. $4\frac{1}{2}$–8 and $8\frac{3}{4}$–12: spoke on Emigration.[2] The House had been uncertain, but voted well. Read 'The Dean'.

To LORD ACTON, 1 March 1870.   Cambridge University Library.

I have waited for an opportunity to answer by Messenger your letter of the 16th. Immediately on its arrival I sent it to Lord Clarendon. He has had every desire to forward your views though with little hope of effecting any considerable result. In truth I am myself sorrowfully conscious that it is in our power to do little or nothing with advantage beyond taking care that the principal Governments are aware of our general view, and our repugnance to the meditated proceedings, so that they may call on us for any aid we can give in case of need. However Ld Clarendon has gone beyond this and has conveyed to the German Courts the kind of intimation you wished. But Bismarck apprehends positive mischief from his taking a forward position, and the King of Bavaria is I suppose disabled by the overthrow of Hohenlohe. He (B.) points to the attitude of Austria as indecisive and I understand him to say the only thing to be done is to exhort the Austrian Bishops to work with their German brethren and that as far as Prussia is concerned they may rely upon being thoroughly supported by the Government on their return home. As respects France you know we have done the little that in us lay.

I never read a more extraordinary letter than that of Newman to Bishop Ullathorne which doubtless you have seen: admirable in its strength, strange in its weakness, incomparable in speculation, tame and emasculated in action.[3]

[1] Clarendon complained Lowe had behaved like a 'caballero completo' to the Spanish minister: 'a warning from you might *possibly* render Lowe more discreet'.

[2] Opposing resolution of (Sir) Robert Richard *Torrens (1814–84, in Australia, then liberal M.P. Cambridge 1868–74) for a state emigration system: *H* cxcix. 1064. See 18 Feb. 70.

[3] Sent privately by Newman to Ullathorne, published unofficially 6 April; *Newman*, xxv. xxi.

The Irish Land Bill is to be attacked, as it is said, on the second reading, from the extreme Irish quarter, by a motion to the effect that nothing short of carrying the Ulster custom through Ireland will meet the wants of the country. It does not follow that because they make this motion they will desire to poison the public mind in Ireland with respect to the Bill. But they are probably under pressure from knots of their constituents. Those probably who are more or less affected by Fenian sympathies. And to Fenians proper it is absolutely vital to distract & break up the remedial process. Hence probably the manifestations of violence at elections in Ireland. For this is a case where violence instead of being used for an end, is itself its own end. To disturb the country is the way to arrest the remedy. But the Irish members are at the best playing with edged tools: & I make no doubt the Prelates will do all in their power to discountenance any proceeding that could even by possibility serve the pernicious purposes of Fenianism.

Apprehending that fear will be the governing agent in determining the issue at Rome, I can only desire as I do from my heart that the fears of the majority may be more violent than those of the minority. A great courage I suppose may win, on that side. Nothing else can.[1]

To ARCHBISHOP H. E. MANNING, 1 March 1870.   Add MS 44538, f. 86.

It did not occur to me to send you the Education Bill.[2] There is a messenger today & I do it now, though in all probability you will have had it before this reaches you. You will I hope find it a carefully framed & well balanced measure. Opposition to it here—such as it may be, will arise mainly from the quarters of secularism. And so I fear it will be with the Irish Land Bill. Demands will be made by a portion of the Irish members which we cannot entertain. The Bill gives & with some reason [blank space] and defences to the Irish occupier which are unknown in England & in Scotland. It will be contended that this is not enough. Probably there will not be two M.P.s other than Irish to support them. Even of them I hope that they will not push their demands so far as to impair the prospects of the new law when adopted in Ireland itself. If you read the 'Times' of today you will see how we are resisting passively the pressure for strong measures of another kind. But an undoubted terrorism prevails & if our remedy is refused by those in whose interest it is offered, (which I trust it will not be,) & if through its refusal terrorism continues, on the one hand we shall be at the end of our tether as regards concession to justice, on the other we shall remain under one absolute obligation with regard to the maintenance of peace & order—These are grave subjects of reflection. All who have influence in Ireland must now be asking themselves where is all this to end? The beginning & ending of my idea in all these political controversies is to try to be in the right: & to trust to the intrinsic power of right to execute the work of peace. I am aware of the difficulties which may beset some of the Irish members, & am not much afraid of mischief from their acts if they keep in mind & *act according* to the desire which I believe they one & all entertain that the Bill shall not fail. I am greatly pleased with the report you send me of the disposition of your Irish Bishops. Personally they do me much greater kindness than I deserve: but I hope

[1] In Figgis and Laurence, *Lord Acton's correspondence*, 105.
[2] Manning had written from Rome, Add MS 44249, f. 139: 'I am anxiously waiting for a copy of Mr Forster's Bill. From the Report I have both hopes, & fears.'

much on this great occasion for their country, from their discernment patriotism & influence. In speaking of the Bill of course I do not mean the Bill *talis qualis* in all particulars but refer to its general sense & spirit.

2. Ash Wed.

St Martin's 11 AM. and Temple Ch. in evg. Wrote to Dean of Windsor —Bp of Chester—Sol. General—Mr Fortescue—A. Kinnaird—Mr Cardwell—Mr R.N. Grenville—The Primate—Bp of Winchester— & minutes. Saw F. Lawley—Mr Glyn—Ld Granville. Read The Dean. Saw Hampton: better but a wreck.[1] Saw Mrs Glyn. Saw Mrs Th.: matter for thought. Dined at Mr Glyn's. Worked on proof sheets of Land Speech.

To C. S. P. FORTESCUE, Irish secretary,   Carlingford MSS, CP1/104.
2 March 1870.

1. We ought to settle the O'Donovan Rossa case on Saturday. It is too plain I fear that circumstances do not allow us to comply with his wife's prayer. As to the impediments of the answer I believe you have already a memorandum of the acts of Rossa? and I should like also to know what marked or palpable signs there are of Fenian action in Ireland at this moment, which justify our regarding it as an obstacle to our efforts.
2. With reference to what you told me last night pray remember that before the Cabinet can come to any new resolution respecting a coercive measure (so to call it) for Ireland it will be necessary to have the whole case for such a measure set out clearly & fully, which has not yet been done.[2] I can hardly overstate the gravity of the case: the first effect of it would be—I feel satisfied—Bright's resignation, & you may readily judge of the aspect that would bear in Ireland.

I *think* Spencer is mistaken if he supposes that the introduction of the Land Bill was in the view of the Cabinet an epoch after which the subject would be reconsidered, independently of any change of circumstances. For that is virtually a mere act of the Executive & conveys no pledge or even indication on the part of Parliament.

3. Th.

Wrote to Ld Granville—Mr Maguire—Mr Bruce—Mr Fortescue— The Queen—and minutes. Dined at Winchr House. H of C. 4½-7¾ and 10-12½.[3] Saw Sir S.R. G[lynne] (Welsh Bpric)—Sir T. Bazley —Mr Richard—Mr Rathbone—Mr Glyn—Ld Granville—Mr Kirk —Mr Fortescue—Sol. General—Mr Forster—Scotts. Read Ulster Tenant Right.

[1] See 31 Oct. 70.
[2] Gladstone sent queries on 9 March; Add MS 44122, f. 141.
[3] Misc. business: *H* cxcix. 1111.

To H. A. BRUCE, home secretary, 3 March 1870.   Add MS 44538, f. 89.

The Viceroy's letter contains matter entitled to serious consideration, but the Cabinet has not yet had placed before it *that entire & careful statement of the case*, with reference alike to precedent & to policy, by which they would have to convince Parliament of the necessity of extra-constitutional legislation, & by which it is requisite that they should in the first instance convince themselves. The circumstances are unexampled: an active and organised body in Ireland, namely the Fenians, are now the promoters of violence & crime, not with a view to ulterior ends, but for the sake of violence & crime: to distract Ireland is their only effectual means of saving their trade from destruction.

But I own I do not understand the state of things in which the armed parties going out at night cannot be repressed, & in which when the magistrates of Westmeath ask for a hundred new constables only fifty can be sent them.

[P.S.] I think you might at once circulate the Viceroy's letter: and this note with it if you think fit.[1]

4. Fr.

Wrote to Dean of Windsor—Chancr of Exr—Card. Cullen—Ld Chancellor—Robn G.—Mr Stephenson—Mr Girdlestone—& minutes. H of C. $4\frac{1}{2}$-$8\frac{1}{2}$.[2] Saw Mr Monsell—Ld Castleton[3]—Mr Glyn—Rev M. M'Coll. Ld Dudley's concert in evg. and saw Mrs Th. The visit left matter for thought. Saw also the Ld Chancellor—Sol.Gen. Ireland —Mr Bouverie—Sol.Gen. England.

To R. LOWE, chancellor of the exchequer,   Add MS 44538, f. 89.
4 March 1870.

1. I think your proposal[4] about the Stocks is greatly improved by your retaining the present quarter days, & getting rid of all direct charges to the public in effecting the change you desire. Will you kindly cause to be put on paper a note of the actual figures by which it may be seen how your plan as it now stands would work as respect the three stocks.

2. It seems to me, though I say it with hesitation to you, that you have perhaps fallen into a fallacy in your reference to the 'fructifying' argument in connection with the liquidation of deb[enture?]s.[5] For when we pay off debs by the purchase of stock to whom does the money go, but to the people, who are the holders of stock, & with whom it is at once to fructify? Even during the period between raising it as tax, & disbursing it as price of stock, it is not withdrawn, because being by the supposition surplus revenue, it raises the balances at the Bank, & enlarges in proportion its powers of loan & discount.

[1] No response by Bruce found.
[2] *Cardwell's army reforms: *H* cxcix. 1158.
[3] John Wilson-Fitzpatrick, 1807–83, formerly liberal M.P. Queen's Co.; cr. Baron Castletown December 1869.
[4] Long mem. by Lowe, printed for the cabinet, Add MS 44613, f. 172, proposing consolidation of the three principal stocks, with payments of dividends quarterly instead of half-yearly.
[5] Lowe argued 'there is great force as a mere question of gain and loss, in the "fructifying in the pockets of the people" argument'.

3. Your argument for frequent payments is strong, but it is liable to a deduction. I am rather inclined to question whether the greater frequency of payments of Dividends is an advantage, or a disadvantage to Trustees. It is certainly in their case more mixed. What is the present relation between *single* accounts & joint (which are, I believe, chiefly trust) accounts at the Bank? Long ago, I think about 1853, I got the facts from the Bank: trust accounts were then a considerable proportion & were fast or steadily increasing. It would be interesting to know how this is now. But I do not say or know that in any view it could destroy the advantage of quarterly payments.

4. I could not accede to the doctrine that we are likely to be borrowers in the market, rather than buyers of stock: more especially if you base it in any degree upon the supposition that democracy is to cause us to borrow money in time of peace for the purpose of civil govt. *That* I hope at any rate will not happen in the residue of my time.

5. As regards the additional charge to be imposed upon the state as a buyer of stock, it occurs to me that there is a set off, which has not been mentioned in the discussion, & I am about to obtain some information about it.

6. Upon the whole, though I wish to get the question more fully into view before striking the balance, I am not as yet able to get over the disadvantages to the State which would I fear arise from the inaccessible impregnable position of the one great United stock. Mr. Goulburn's reduction represented a saving of *35 millions*. In 1852, a strong Govt. might probably have been able to effect something not much less considerable. Unless I am much mistaken, it is held, & may almost be taken as practically fixed, that *Consols* can only be paid off upon 12 months notice: & though I will not trust my memory absolutely, I think that this most awkward proposition does not hold in reference to both or one of the other Stocks. Perhaps you will kindly learn how this is: for I see your expectation of meeting a favourable[?] reason amounts only to this that a method might perhaps be devised. I remember well the pressure of the difficulties, & was never able to see how it could be overcome by any direct action of the State: & I have had reason to know from experience that a twelve months notice may prove a fatal impediment in the way of any operation for acting upon the debt as it affords time for a total revolution in the conditions of the money market.

7. Perhaps the request in (1) may drop, if I may assume that 'Reduced' should have read 'Reduced and new[?]' in which case the ⅛+ would but slightly overbalance the ⅛− on Consols.

8. With reference to a remark near the close of your paper, you may perhaps find that annuities for lives are more largely bought when the funds are low. I am not quite sure how this is.

5. Sat.

Wrote to Att. General—Dean of Peterb.—The Queen (2)—Ld Clarendon—The Viceroy—Mr Pringle—and minutes. Saw Mr Stephenson—Mr Fortescue—Ld Granville—Ld Dufferin—Ld Halifax—Dr Vaughan—Mr Glyn (2)—F.R. Lawley—Ld de Grey—Ly Herbert (respecting Emigration).[1] Cabinet $2\frac{3}{4}$-$6\frac{3}{4}$. Dined at Lady Herbert's: Lady Stanhope's afterwards.

[1] She encouraged state emigrationalists (see 1 Mar. 70): Add MS 44538 *passim*.

Cabinet Mch 5. 1870. 2½ PM[1]

    1. Question on Peninsular Govts. Debts to this country.[2]

√ 2. Transfer of Lands: to be introduced in H. of L. within the fortnight.

√ 3. Succession in cases of intestacy.[3] to be similarly introduced as to time:
√   but in H. of Commons. C. of E. will look to the am[endmen]t of the Draft
    Bill.

    4. Red River. Ld Granville stated what had been done.[4]

√ 5. Minority Vote—Hardcastle's Bill. Support.[5]

√ 6. Redesdale's Bill—to oppose.[6]

√ 7. Mr Cardwell—Sir R. Anstruther's Question as to Over Regulation Prices.
    Are they to be recognised on the occasion of the abolition of the rank of
    Ensign. *No.*

√ 8. Report of Sub Committee on changes in Irish Laws for security of Life
    and Property.[7]

To EARL SPENCER, Irish lord lieutenant,   Add MS 44538, f. 92.
5 March 1870. 'Secret.'

Granville showed me your letter to him today. On no account could I think
of prosecuting the idea of asking Ld Kimberley to go over to Dublin after you
had taken the view of such a proceeding which you had expressed in that letter.
Kimberley himself too had expressed some reluctance to undertake the duty.
That the mission was not intended as a slight I am sure you believe. And that it
was agreeable to precedent I could very easily show you by the case of a mission
of Lord Clarendon to Paris which was indeed a much stronger one. Pray do not
understand this explanation as meant controversially. We have today considered
largely the state of Ireland [and] asked Fortescue to prepare for us such information as will bring together the whole case that there may be to submit to Parliament. The general sentiment was in favour of acting immediately after the 2d
reading of the Land Bill. The modes of action discussed were chiefly 3: 1. Strengthening the ordinary law. 2. Suspension (or local suspension) of the Habeas Corpus
Act. 3. Exceptional power in a form approaching that of the Coercion Act of
1833.

The feeling of the Cabinet leaned to No 3 rather than No 2. but the Cabinet
will meet again probably about Thursday, to resume the subject, which I think is
one of the nicest & most difficult ever presented in Cabinet within my experience.

In concluding this very hasty account I may add that I am on Monday to
state that we will make known our intentions immediately after the 2d reading
of the Land Bill. The Primate has written to me about the Kilmore Bishopric &
I hope to write to you definitely in a day or two.[8]

   [1] Add MS 44638, f. 33.   [2] See 2 Apr. 70.
   [3] See *Thring's mem. of 16 December 1869 on an Inheritance Bill, with a draft of the
Bill; Add MS 44638, f. 36.
   [4] See Ramm I, i. 93; Gladstone suggested a plebiscite before Red River was returned to
Canada.
   [5] Gladstone had on 14 February not opposed Hardcastle's bill to repeal the minority
vote clauses of the 1867 Reform Act: *H* cxcix. 267. Three member constituencies remained
until 1884. See 15 June 70.
   [6] To amend the Irish Church Act: *H* cxcix. 991.
   [7] Printed for the Cabinet: Add MS 44614, f. 3.
   [8] Spencer replied, mollified: Add MS 44506, f. 231.

6. 1 S.Lent.

Chapel Royal mg with H.C.—St Geo[rge's] H[anover] S[quare]
aftn. Wrote to Archdn Stopford—Bp of St David's—The Viceroy
—Ld Granville—Archbp Cullen. Saw Lady H. Forbes—Duchess of
Argyll—Mrs Thistlethwayte. Read Stopford's Notes of Preparn[1]—
Th. Parker's Life—Clark's Dangers of Ch. of Engl.[2]

I[3] circulate a letter from archbishop Cullen to Mr Monsell and a copy of one
I have written.[4]
I ought to add that the Irish Bishops have sent through Abp. Manning an
application for the extension of the Ulster custom throughout Ireland.

7. M.

Wrote to Archbp of Syra—Mr H. Richard—Ld Granville—Mr Mac-
laren—Chancr of Exr—Robn G.—Ld Sydney—Ld Devon—The
Queen—and minutes. Saw Mr Lambert—Mr Cardwell—Mr Glyn—
Mr Gregory—Mr Goschen. H of C. $4\frac{1}{2}$-8 and $9\frac{1}{4}$-$12\frac{1}{2}$: Irish Land
Debate.[5] Read Ld Russell.

8. Tu.

Wrote to Ld Clarendon—Sir S. Adair—Mr Locke King—The Queen
(3)—Gen. Knollys—and minutes. Worked on Irish L. Bill and Crime.
Saw Ld De Tabley—Mr Childers—Mr Clay—D. of Argyll—Mr
Glyn (ill)—Ld Granville. H of C. $4\frac{1}{2}$-$8\frac{1}{4}$ and $9\frac{1}{4}$-$1\frac{1}{2}$ Irish Land Bill
&c.[6] Read Ld Russell.

9. Wed.

Wrote to Ld Primate—Watsons—Mr Adam MP[7]—Robn G.—Mr
Fortescue—The Queen—Mrs MacPhail[8]—Dr W. Smith—& minutes.
Saw Mr Childers—Mr Bruce—Mr Adam—Ld Shaftesbury—Mr
Forster—Mr Floyer[9]—Ld Normanby. Saw Hartmann X & Wilson—
also Turner. Dined at Sir E. Buller's: Lady Cork's party afterwards.

---

[1] E. A. Stopford, *Notes of preparation for the General Convention of the Church of Ireland* (1870); see Lathbury, i. 163.
[2] W. G. Clark, *The present dangers of the Church of England* (1870).
[3] Add MS 44638, f. 39; for cabinet.   [4] Draft in Add MS 44425, f. 192.
[5] 2°R: *H* cxcix. 1373.   [6] *H* cxcix. 1634.
[7] William Patrick *Adam, 1823–81; liberal M.P. Clackmannan 1859–80; as liberal whip 1874–80 organised Midlothian campaigns; governed Madras 1880. See Add MS 44095.
[8] Of Dingwall, on the d. of Mrs Chisholm (see 29 Aug. 53); Add MS 44538, f. 96.
[9] Untraced.

Read Winthrop's Address on Peabody.[1] Worked on Irish Land & Crime. Educn Deputations 3-5¼.[2]

10. Th.

Wrote to Ld Chancellor—V.Chanc.Oxf. *cum* Dean of Ch.Ch.—Mr Bruce—Att. General—The Queen—& minutes. Rode, with Helen. Worked on Irish Land Bill. Dined with West. Saw Mr Ouvry—Mr West—Ld Granville—Ld Halifax—Mr Forster—Mr Adam. H of C. 4½-8¼ & 9¼-12½.[3] Read Longfield.[4]

Circulate[5]

In the introduction of the Irish Land Bill, I argued against perpetuity of tenure.

My impression is that it would be right to follow this up in the present debate by an argument as decided against *valuation of rents* which I believe to be logically and practically, though not immediately, the same thing.

No doubt I think ought to remain in the Irish mind as to our intentions in a matter so vital.[6] WEG March 10. 70.

11. Fr.

Wrote to Watson & Smith—Mr Burnett—Ld Devon—Archdn Durnford[7]—Robn G.—Rev. Joshua Hughes—Mrs Wilson—The Queen —& minutes. Worked on private affairs. Saw Mr Adam—Chancr of Exchequer—Mr Forster—Educn (Union) Depn at 3.45.[8] Dined with the Wests. H of C. 4½-8¼ and 9¼-1½. Spoke (1½ h) on 2 R. Irish Land Bill.[9] Read Ld Stanhope.

To Rev. JOSHUA HUGHES, 11 March 1870.   Add MS 44426, f. 237.

I have to propose to you, with the sanction of H.M., that you should be nominated by the Dean & Chapter of St. Asaph as the successor to Bishop Short.

The selection of your name has been the result of a long and very laborious though interesting search in which I have been engaged for some two months

[1] R. C. Winthrop, 'Eulogy pronounced at the funeral of G. Peabody' (1870).

[2] Notes on a Welsh deputation and on that of the National Education League in Add MS 44759, f. 68. Joseph *Chamberlain, 1836-1914, was chief spokesman for the latter; see Garvin, i. 111-4.

[3] Irish Land Bill: *H* cxcix. 1634.

[4] M. *Longfield, *Tenure of land in Ireland* (1870).

[5] Add MS 44638, f. 40. Replies all agreed; ibid.

[6] Next day's speech disavowed govt. responsibility for what 'is sometimes called fair rents, and sometimes called valuation of rents': *H* cxcix. 1843.

[7] Offering him the see of Chichester; Add MS 44425, f. 235.

[8] Large deputation led by Cowper-Temple from the National Education Union; Gladstone replied 'in a very few words'; *The Times*, 14 March 1870, 6d. Notes in Add MS 44759, f. 75.

[9] *H* cxcix. 1828; the bill then 2°R in 442:11.

past. You owe my recommendation of you simply to the belief I entertain respecting the true necessities of the Church of Wales, & your capacity to meet them. I have been fully informed as to your sentiments on matters which divide the Church:[1] but I have also been assured that you are a person likely to govern a diocese in a spirit liberal and kindly towards those who differ from you. I venture to mention this circumstance because the Clergy, and I think the Laity, or the leading laity of St. Asaph though I think very free from extremes, would not be found to lean quite in the same direction, for the most part with yourself.

I hope it may be agreeable to you to accept the proposal I now make and I sincerely trust that if you do your accession to the Episcopal Bench may be followed by all the religious advantages which I am led to anticipate from that event.[2]

12. Sat.

Wrote to Sir S.R.G.—Mr Rathbone—& minutes. Cabinet 12–3½. Saw The Queen at B. Palace. Saw Mr Cardwell—Sir R. Phillimore. Went with Sir R.P. to the Gaiety Theatre: excellent entertainments 8–11¼.[3] Read.

Cabinet March 12. 70. 12 noon.[4]
√ Noise in Throne Room: notified.[5]
√ Letter from Abp. Manning & inclosure respecting Land Bill: notified.[6]
O Amendment in Clause 3.
√ Education Bill. Dixon's motion. mode of dealing with considered.[7]
√ Crichton's motion.[8] Capt. Coote.
√ Irish Crime. Character of intended Legislation.
  Communicate with Mr Bright? (Cabinet disapproved) or Mr Bright jun?
√ Childers Plan of retirement. Revise H. Lennox.
  Press Law in Ireland. C. of E. suggests power to Executive to seize [publications].
  Next Cabinet. Friday.
  Cardwell, Purchase.[9]

B. Palace. Mch. 12. 70.[10]
√ 1. Account of Cabinet. √ 2. Mr Leslie to be Bp of Kilmore. √ 3. Knights. Mr A.

---

[1] *Hughes was much influenced by C. *Thirlwall's supposed unorthodoxy.
[2] Hughes delayed before accepting; see Add MS 44425, f. 248, 252.
[3] 'Uncle Dick's Darling', and ballet.   [4] Add MS 44638, f. 42.
[5] Sydney had complained of noise there; Gladstone agreed; Add MS 44538, f. 95.
[6] See 6 March 70.
[7] G. *Dixon's amndt. to 2°R, that no permanent settlement of the education question was possible which left religious instruction in public funded schools in the hands of the local authorities; moved on 14 March: *H* cxcix. 1931. See letter to Platt on 14 Mar. 70.
[8] Motion by John Henry, Viscount Crichton (1839–1914, tory M.P. Enniskillen 1868–80, Fermanagh 1880–5, tory whip 1876–80, 4th Earl Erne 1885) deploring the dismissal of Capt. Coote from the shrievalty (for tampering with a jury) moved 14 March 1870: *H* cxcix. 1877. Gladstone arranged early discussion.
[9] Apparently first cab. discussion of purchase; unclear what Cardwell proposed.
[10] Add MS 44757, f. 15.

Brady & Mr Briggs, Admiralty, Mr Lange, Mr [blank]. √4. Mr Forster. Suggested
Ld de Grey to be invited with him.

13. 2 S.Lent.

Lambeth Ch. & Holy Comm. 11-2½: for the ordination.[1] Our dear
Son's demeanour was full of modest concentrated devotion. Whitehall Chapel (Bp of Salisbury) in the afternoon. Wrote to Ld Clarendon—The Viceroy—Mr Fortescue—Archbp Manning. Read Parker's
Life—Littledale's Chapter of Ch History[2]—and other Tracts. Dined
with the Wortleys. He is a model of patience in a crippled life.

To LORD CLARENDON, foreign secretary,   Clarendon MSS, c. 498.
13 March 1870.

I have read the account of Daru & Chigi.[3] My confession of faith respecting
France & the Council is this 1. The idea of danger to the Pope is moonshine.
2. Withdrawal of the troops is the only measure within the power of France to
take which the Pope & his myrmidons care about. 3. Now that Daru has made it
known authentically that he will in no case withdraw them, the mission of his
Ambassador becomes a secondary matter & probably Rome will take care that
long before he gets there the matter shall be settled. 4. It is by threats & threats
alone that the Court of Rome, as to its Roman & Church policy, is influenced:
its whole policy is based in the rejection of reason & any course of dealing not
conformable to this axiom will be turned upside down. After having vented myself of all this blasphemy on a Sunday it is now time to go to Church.
The Queen spoke most sympathetically about your health yesterday. She
complained much of London but looked better than I have seen her look for
some time.

14. M.

Wrote to Watson & Smith—Ld Granville—Mr Duckworth[4]—Archdn
of Meath—Mr Platt—Mrs Thistlethwayte—Mr Childers—The
Queen—and minutes. Dined with Sir W. James. Saw Mr [G. C. W.]
Forester—Mr Glyn—Chancr of Exr. Saw Maitland, & another: 12
hours work, £30 p.a. with some meals at Lad. Elise's. H of C. 4½-9¾
and 10¾-1¼.[5]

---

[1] Of his son Stephen, as priest.
[2] R. F. *Littledale, probably preface to *The Holy Eastern Church* (1870).
[3] The Daru initiative on infallibility; see Matthew, 'Vaticanism', 432.
[4] Robinson Duckworth, 1834–1911; Prince Leopold's tutor, 1866–70; Victoria's chaplain 1870–1901; on a living, Add MS 44538, f. 100; see Guedalla, *Q*, i. 222.
[5] Case of Capt. Coote (see 12 Mar. 70n.), then *Dixon's amndt. (see ibid.): *H* cxcix.
1877.

To J. PLATT, M.P., 14 March 1870.   Add MS 44538, f. 99.

The very hostile step proposed to be taken tonight by Mr Dixon (the Parly. character of which I am persuaded he has not perceived) tends as far as it goes to throw all proceedings on the Education Bill into confusion.

The question which he raises is one eminently open to future consideration, & ought not be peremptorily dealt with at this unusual stage. We should wish to consider carefully your view of the matter among others.

15. Tu.

Wrote to A. Kinnaird—Prof. Sedgwick—Scotts—C. Watkin Williams —The Queen—& minutes. Rode with Agnes. Saw Bp of Winchester —Mr Glyn—Mr Kinnaird—Ld Granville—Mr Forster. H of C. $4\frac{1}{2}$-$8\frac{1}{4}$ and 9–$12\frac{1}{2}$.[1] Worked on Land Speech.

16. Wed.

Wrote to Chancr of Exr—Mr Bright—Archdn Durnford—Sir P. Braila—Dean of Windsor—Watsons—Ld Fermoy—The Queen— Ld R. Cavendish—Mr Thring—and minutes. Saw Ld Bessborough —Do *cum* Irish Sol. General—Mr Geo. Campbell—Mr Glyn (2)— Mr Forster (2)—Ld Granville—Ld Cowper—Ld Chancellor—The ODonoghue. Cabinet $2\frac{3}{4}$-$7\frac{1}{4}$. Dinner party at home: & musical party after with Q. of Holland[2] & Prince & Princess of Teck.

Cabinet March 16. 70. 2.½ P.M.[3]
√ 1. As to Intestacy & Successions Bill. To be introduced by Att. Gen. on Friday.
√ Transfer of Land Bill—To be introduced by Chancr. on Friday
√ Irish Land Tenures Bill—amendments in. Adjusted.[4]
√ Peace Preservation Ireland Bill: form of draft.[5]
√ Ballot Bill. Approved.[6]
√ Juries—unanimity. Say nothing now.
√ Educn Bill. Modification. Approved, over.[7]
√ Fenian prisoners—Inquiry. Agree: reserving our discretion as to the compos[itio]n[8]
Red River.
a) Chancr. of Exr. Mr Pim's question on Lease stamps[9] b) Mr Fortescue. Mem. on Bill. Information to H.M. c) [Lord] Chancellor. Ld Shaftesbury's Bill[10]

[1] *Dixon's amndt. to the Education Bill: *H* cxcix. 1963.
[2] Sophia, wife of William III of Holland.   [3] Add MS 44638, f. 46.
[4] Notes on them in Add MS 44759, f. 77.
[5] Printed draft, with alterations and doodles, in Add MS 44614, f. 33.
[6] Leatham this night moved his private members Ballot Bill $2°$R; Hartington offered govt. support for the $2°$R, on condition Leatham then postponed the Bill, to allow govt. consideration of the select cttee's report: *H* cc. 33.
[7] See following note and 18 Mar. 70n.   [8] Announced next evening.
[9] Ibid.   [10] On Ecclesiastical Courts: *H* cc. 64.

Rate Schools and others.[1]
1. Public notice by Time Table of school instruction in (secular) subjects for wh.
Govt. grants are paid. 2. Also of the times of religious instruction. Attendance
voluntary. (No notice of withdrawal required). 3. In all rate-provided schools,
when School Board decides Master shall teach in religion, Building *must* be
opened to other denominations.

To J. BRIGHT, president of the board of trade,   Add MS 43385, f. 74.
16 March 1870.

It was a pleasure to see your handwriting again:[2] but that pleasure would be
marred if I did not feel persuaded that you will be content to wait patiently as
you are & not allow the idea of any change to enter your mind. It is yet but a
very short time since you commenced your temporary & enforced retirement.
There is but one wish predominant over every other, that you may soon come
back among us with all your wonted vigour: but next to this is the desire that
you will allow much time to elapse in order to give fair play to the forces of
nature, strained at the point where they are the most delicate of all.

You understand, I am sure, why we do not trouble you with letters. Nor will
I now overstep the line, & talk of business, except to give you these two general
assurances, first that we have made a special arrangement among ourselves for
the temporary care of the business of your Department, which will I think prevent for a good while yet any practical inconvenience: secondly that such decisions as we have had to adopt in Cabinet since your chair there has been vacant,
are without exception, I am firmly persuaded, such as would have had your full
& cheerful concurrence.

The Queen asks much about you & with warm sympathy: & further prospects
are I think good.

And now may the Almighty, in whose hands we stand, of His goodness speedily
enable you to render also in voice & act to your country the signal services, which
you are still rendering by name & fame, & through the grateful memory of your
countrymen. Whenever you feel yourself quite strong enough, news can be given
you of all we are about through whatever channel you may yourself prefer. Nor
is the earnest interest about you which prevails with the whole Govt. a merely
selfish one, for you have made all your colleagues hope & believe they may also
claim to be reckoned among your friends.

17. *Th.*

Wrote to Prince of Wales—Lord Mayor of Dublin[3]—Mr T.B. Potter
—Mr Chalk—Lady Milltown[4]—Mr Bruce—Lady Llanover—Wyllie & Co.—Mr Fortescue—Sir T.E. May—Ld Lyttelton—The Queen
—and minutes. Saw Ld Camperdown—Mr Pringle—Mr Monsell—

[1] Add MS 44638, f. 49. Marked at the bottom in diarist's hand: 'Mr. Forster. Mch.
16. 70.'
[2] *Bright had sent a brief note; Add MS 44112, f. 130. He did not reply to Gladstone's
letter.
[3] Regretting the Dublin Municipal Council's hostile reception of the Land Bill, but declining to amend it to include fixity of tenure or fair rents: Add MS 44538, f. 102.
[4] Barbara, widow of 4th earl of Milltown; she d. 1874.

Att. General—Mr Glyn (2)—Ulster T.R. Deputation[1]—Att.Gen. Irel. *cum* Mr Thring & Conclave. H of C. 4½-8½ and 10-12½.[2] Dined at Bp of Winchesters. Read [blank]'s Poems.

18. Fr.

Wrote to Ld Clarendon—The Queen (and Memm)—Rev Mr Woodard —P. of Wales—Rev Mr Tarver[3]—Ld Belper—Ld Lyttelton—Mrs O D. Rossa—Sir R. Phillimore—& minutes. Rode with Helen. Saw Mr Childers—Mr Forster—Mr Monsell—Mr Gurdon—Mr Glyn— The Speaker—Mr Knowlys [*sic*]. H of C. 4½-8¼ and 9-12¾. Spoke on Education.[4]

To Sir R. J. PHILLIMORE, 18 March 1870.   Phillimore MSS.

Will you be kind enough to look at the two letters herewith, signed by the V.C. of Oxford & the Dean of Ch. Ch. jointly; and to advise me upon the course it may be proper to pursue.

The only candidates of whom I know at present are Neate and Bryce—both men of merit, Neate well advanced in life though I believe still active in mind & body, Bryce young & rising. Neate is poor I am afraid. His services to an independent conscientious & not violent Liberalism in the University are worthy of remembrance.[5]

19. Sat.

Wrote to Ld C. Clinton—Rev Mr Hughes—Mr Lewis—The Viceroy—The Queen—Sir J.K. Shuttleworth—and minutes. Rode with Helen. Saw Sir R. Phillimore—Ld Granville—Mr Glyn—Mr Childers —Mr Cave—Adm. Robinson. Cabinet 2½-6. Dined at Ld Abercrombie's. Read Ld Stanhope.

Cabinet. D. St. Sat. M. 19; 2.30 PM.[6]
√ Ld Clarendon. Ecumenical Council: conversation on concurrence in possible French move. HM Govt to stand in 2d rank.[7]

[1] No report found.
[2] Questioned on Fenian prisoners by G. H. Moore; Peace Preservation (Ireland) Bill then brought in: *H* cc. 78, 116.
[3] Charles Feral Tarver, 1820-86, once prince of *Wales's tutor; vicar of St. Peter's, Thanet, 1863.
[4] Announcing govt. reconsideration of the Conscience Clause (see 16 Mar. 70). *Dixon then withdrew his amndt. and the bill received 2°R: *H* cc. 303.
[5] Phillimore sent mem. on duties of professor of civil law, but no view on candidates; Add MS 44278, f. 62; Bryce was appt., see 10 Apr. 70.
[6] Add MS 44638, f. 51.
[7] The Daru initiative proposing joint representations to the Vatican; see 13 Mar. 70.

Thornton's letter.
√ Ld Granville. Red River. Determined to send an agent to Ottawa to watch &
  if need be guide negotiations.[1]
√ Peabody Statue. To write to the Queen.[2]
√ Moore's question to WEG.[3] To ackn..the substance.
√ Easter holidays consd. Probably Ap. 11 or 12.
√ Burials Bill. r[efer] to Select Committee.
√ Col. Emigr. Committee. Discourage.
√ Mr Cardwell, Committee of Cabinet:[4] D. of A[rgyll], E. C[hilders], K[imber-
  ley], de G[rey], C. of E.

20. 3 S.Lent.

Chapel Royal mg (Bp of Oxford, very good) and aft. Saw J.S. Wortley
—Miss White. Wrote to Rev.Prof. Hoppus[5]—Mr Bruce—Dean of
Windsor—Mrs Thistlethwayte. Read Hoppus's Address—Judged by
His Words[6]—Bp of Winchr on O.T. Heroes[7]—and divers Tracts.

To H. A. BRUCE, home secretary, 20 March 1870.   Aberdare MSS.

I have read these curious papers respecting the condition of Unst,[8] & certainly a more impudent proceeding than that of the three partners, who represent the laity, & appear each with a different designation as to occupation in life,
never came under my knowledge. Probably they belong to different congregations, & each has made his pastor sign. The true case for this state of things is in
my opinion *exposure*. I do not know whether the Times would interfere; but I
think Levy of the D. Telegraph would very probably be willing to send down a
'Special' whose letters would be full of interest at this period, & would probably
lead to an entire reformation of the vicious & oppressive system. My son could
communicate with Levy for you if you like.[9]

21. M.

Wrote to Ld Granville—Mr Cardwell—Ld Howard—Mr A. Denison
—Watsons—Bp of Winchr—The Queen—Mrs Goddry (respecting
her daughter) and minutes. Dined with the Jameses. Worked on
proofs I.L. Speech. Saw Mr Glyn—Ld Granville—Att.Gen. for

[1] See Ramm, I, i. 97n.
[2] Clarendon suggested (f. 52) that secret service money be used, if Commons reluctant
to pay for it.
[3] Moore wanted clarification of Gladstone's answer (see 17 Mar. 70n.): *H* cc. 320.
[4] On distribution of military changes between Britain and India consequent on exchange
printed papers by *Cardwell and *Argyll, 10 March 1870, Add MS 44614, f. 7.
[5] John *Hoppus, 1789–1875; independent minister; professor of philosophy at London
1829–66; had sent his 'Recollections of student life' (1868).
[6] By [T. Gribble] (1870).   [7] S. *Wilberforce, *Heroes of Hebrew history* (1870).
[8] In Shetland.
[9] W. H. Gladstone had written on Ireland in the *Telegraph*; see 2 Aug. 66.

Ireland. H of C. $4\frac{1}{2}$-$8\frac{1}{4}$ and $9\frac{1}{4}$-$12\frac{1}{2}$.[1] Saw Mills, & wrote as above X.[2]
Read Stanhope's Vol.[3]

To S. WILBERFORCE, bishop of Winchester,   Wilberforce MSS, d. 38.
21 March 1870. 'Private.'

I feel I cannot advise as to the balance of expediency in regard to an Education meeting on behalf of the Govt. Bill beyond this that if you hold it you had
better not be too well pleased with the provisions.[4] Subject to that condition I
see no cause for restraint.

I think, flatly, that your letter put Mr. Winterbotham in the wrong box. Such
is evidently the opinion of the Times or they would have given him a larger type.[5]

22. Tu.

Wrote to Watson & Smith—Ld Granville—Ld Houghton—Mr Phillips—Mr Tallents—Ld Sydney—The Queen—and minutes. Read
Butt on the Amnesty.[6] Finished correcting proofs. Saw Mr Jackson,
who relieved my ear by syringing. Saw Mr Glyn—Lord E. Clinton.
Family dinner party, with Mr Dumaresq[7] the nephew to be who
seemed satisfactory. H of C. $4\frac{1}{2}$-8 and 9-$1\frac{1}{4}$. Spoke on Irish Crime
Bill.[8]

[*Holograph memorandum circulated to the cabinet*].[9]
Upon reflection, I think this motion, to be made by Mr. Johnson,[10] cannot be
resisted in argument. And I suppose it probable that it may be supported by the
Ulster Landlords.

We propose 1. to legalise the Ulster custom, as being a *covenant* 2. to protect
the Irish Occupier, on the ground of his need, by damages for eviction 3. but not
to cumulate the two, because the Ulster custom, besides being a covenant, commonly operates as a protection, & thus removes the need, which is the ground of
our proposal. 4. But if, as now appears, there are unquestionable cases, where
the Ulster Custom has been so ground down by a real counter-custom, that it
does not constitute a protection—e.g. When one year's rent covers all claims,

[1] Replied again to Moore: *H* cc. 321.   [2] i.e. to her mother, Mrs. Goddry.
[3] P. H. *Stanhope, Lord Stanhope, *The history of England . . . 1701-1713* (1870).
[4] Wilberforce asked, 21 March 1870, Add MS 44345, f. 146, if he should allow an anglican
meeting in support of the Education Bill.
[5] Dispute about dissenters between Wilberforce and H. S. P. Winterbotham, *The Times*,
18 and 19 March 1870.
[6] I. *Butt, probably *Land tenure in Ireland* (1870); or a press letter.
[7] William Alexander Dumaresq, who m. 27 October 1870 E. H. Gladstone, the diarist's
niece; see 20 May 50n.
[8] *H* cc. 491.   [9] Add MS 44638, f. 54.
[10] W. Johnston (1829-1902, liberal M.P. Belfast from 1868) intended to amend Clause 1
by inserting that the tenant of a holding, subject to the Ulster tenant right, shall be entitled,
on foregoing such right, to claim compensation under the other provisions of the Act. See
H cc. 1014 (31 March 1870); the amndt. was withdrawn, pending govt. proposals.

improvements excluded—the Ulster Tenant, in such cases, stands like any other Irish occupier, entitled to the protection afforded by the Bill.

It would be hard indeed, if the fact of his possessing a distinct & independent right as covenanted were to debar himself from the same shelter by eviction-damages as we give to the rest of Ireland, where it can be shown that he has the same title to it.

Bessborough takes this view strongly; and he tells me that Dufferin is equally decided. (A note from D. has just confirmed this.) WEG Mch. 22.70.

[*Holograph comments*:] So does O'Hagan—and Monsell G[ranville]. I agree see note[1] R. L[owe]. I assent Argyll. I agree H[atherle]y. I agree H. A. B[ruce]. I entirely agree. I don't see how, upon the principles of the Bill itself we can resist the proposal. The option might be subject to the consent of the Court CPF[ortescue]. I have no objection; but the change would, I think, render necessary a similar amendment in Cl. 2. de G[rey]. I agree, but I think the tenant should be compelled to make his option before he goes into court: and that the option should extend to Clause 2 K[imberley]. I concur in this view H C E C[hilders].

It appears to me that some check on this option will be necessary—supposing that a Landlord has bought up the Tenant right on a farm & paid all that can be claimed under it, will that Tenant be entitled then to claim compensation under the provisions of the Act? C[larendon].

Undoubtedly W.E.G.

I agree with Lord Clarendon E. C[ardwell].

I agree with Ld Clarendon that some check on this option will be necessary. I do not see why the tenant should have the right of making his claim under that Clause which he thinks will give him most, if the Landlord is not to be heard on the point. This was discussed in the Cabinet, not with reference to Clauses 1 & 3 but to Clause 2 & 3, & though the Bill finally omitted any reference to an option on either side, I think that it was agreed that if the tenant had an option the landlord should have it also, & the Court should decide between them. H[artington].

23. Wed.

Wrote to Sol. General—Mr Dumaresq—Mr Lewis MP[2]—Lord Ernest Bruce—Ld Clarendon—Mr Knowles (cancelled)[3]—Mr Pender—and minutes. Saw Mr Glyn—Ld Granville. Rode with Helen. Expn westward 3-7. Saw Fitzgerald X. Saw Duchess of Argyll. Dined with Lady Cowper.

24. Th.

Wrote to Dean of Ch.Ch.—Col. Wilson Patten—Mr Cardwell—Rev. N. Woodard—Earl Russell—Sir Thos. Bateson—Earl of Clarendon —Chancr of Exr—The Queen—Dr Döllinger (began)—Mrs Th.—

---

[1] Add MS 44638, f. 59.

[2] John Delaware Lewis, 1828–84; liberal M.P. Devonport 1868–74; had complained of govt. order of business; Add MS 44538, f. 106.

[3] (Sir) James Thomas *Knowles, 1831–1908; architect and publisher; ed. *Contemporary Review* 1870–7; founded *Nineteenth Century* 1877. See Add MSS 44231-2.

and minutes. Saw Sir Thos Gladstone—Mr Glyn—Ld Clarendon—
Prince of Wales—Sir S. Northcote—Ld Granville—Sol. General. C.
went off on another of her errands of love: to Lady Lyttelton, at
Hagley. H. of C. $4\frac{1}{2}$-$8\frac{1}{4}$ and $9\frac{1}{4}$-$1\frac{1}{4}$. Irish Crime Bill.[1] Read Stanhope.

To LORD CLARENDON, foreign secretary,   Clarendon MSS, c. 498.
24 March 1870.

I agree with you that Dr. Döllinger expects far too much from anything we
could say.[2] I cannot agree on the other hand with Lord Lyons, & what I may
call the Indifferentists. Non-Latin as well as Latin Powers are affected by these
insane proceedings, the United States perhaps (in my view) the only exception.
It is far from improbable that, some time hence, we may see one of their results
in a repetition of the fury of 1850-1, & that, much sooner, we may feel them in
augmented obstacles to political & social justice. I agree with Dr. Döllinger about
France. They have made a wretched mess of it: & the Pope has snubbed &
trampled upon that Govt. most relentlessly, as he was certain to do, the moment
he knew the troops would not be recalled. I think we have a very strong hold on
the Priesthood, quite independently of the question what language we hold
about the Council: still I cannot dispute the opinion that, if France will not
recall the troops, there is no other resource for the Episcopal minority *except*
their screwing themselves up to the point of an indomitable resolution to go
through and through with the part they have sought to play. Herewith are interesting letters from Acton.

To H. G. LIDDELL, dean of Christ Church, Oxford,   Add MS 44538, f. 107.
24 March 1870.

Many thanks for your note[3] & for the kind manner in which you convey the
intimation of state of feeling I must say alike disagreeable & causeless.
When the Government put into the speech from the Throne a paragraph
respecting the University Tests Bill, they gave not only an assurance, but the
most solemn assurance in their power of their intention to use every effort to
carry the measure. I know only of two suppositions that will warrant the feeling
you describe; one that the University Tests Bill ought to take precedence of the
Irish Land & the English Education Bill: the other that the Government or to
speak more plainly I myself am acting in bad faith. Perhaps I ought to add a
third: viz. that those to whom you refer are better judges of the very difficult
subject of the arrangement of business in the House of Commons than those
who have spent their lives in dealing with it. With any one of these three suppositions it is rather difficult for me to deal. In an extreme anxiety to meet many
wishes & attain many public objects we have undertaken an unusual amount of
engagements which it will require unremitting care & labour to redeem. As far
as I can at present judge we shall be free to prosecute the *practical* stages of the
Tests Bill as the first important measure of legislation after the Committee on
the English Education Bill. In the interest of the measure it would be a decided

---

[1] Spoke on its time-table: *H* cc. 632.
[2] Döllinger's letter of 15 March, calling for declaration in the Commons; copy in Clarendon MSS, c. 498.   [3] Untraced.

error to introduce it (in itself an easy matter) too long before we could see our way to an open field for the 2d reading & Committee. If as I hope the House will make some sacrifices to carry on the Land Bill, & if a reasonable spirit prevails in dealing with the English Education Bill, I shall have no fear about our bringing the Tests Bill to issue in ample time for every practical purpose. If you are likely to be in London, I should ask you to take the trouble of seeing me about the professorship of Civil Law & the possible Candidates for it.[1]

To LORD RUSSELL, 24 March 1870.   PRO 30/22/16F, f. 152.

It seems strange to have passed so long a time, I scarcely know how long it is, without writing to you. But on the one hand I have read you (in the interval between H. of C. and sleep) with much interest and pleasure, and on the other my work has been very very hard.

This Cabinet is the most laborious as a whole that I have ever seen. It is happy I think in this, that it contains so many men who though not young in experience are young in hard departmental work, and who therefore step out freely and freshly. I do not include myself as I am an old hack, & what is called groggy.

On the Land Bill I expect much labour but no other form of difficulty. The Crime Bill is an unhappy incident not only with reference to its cause but also with reference to time; it cuts more than one clear week out of an already overloaded Session. The University Tests Bill will follow the Education Bill. The Education Bill itself is the one critical measure.[2] It involves principles of vast sweep & much novelty, the questions of universality, compulsion, local rating, gratuitous teaching; and along with these of course comes up again our old friend the religious difficulty, with the rival claims of all the different modes of eluding or arranging it. A state of clear firm & well balanced opinion is the best help we can have in working through such a mass of complication, but such is not the actual state of opinion. Men are divided not between two courses or even three but four or five. Secularism, Bible reading, Bible reading with unsectarian teaching (to be limited and defined on appeal by a new sort of Pope in the Council Office) Bible reading with unlimited exposition—or lastly this plus Catechisms & formularies, each of these alternatives viewed more or less in the light of 'private interests and partial affections', & these complications recomplicated with the competition between local and central authority: all this shows a state of things in which it will be very difficult to maintain the equilibrium of the measure, and in which mere resolute resistance or even untoward help might be attended by very awkward results.

Still there are favouring circumstances. Forster's position is excellent. Great admissions are made. The Dissenters and the Church are both represented by many reasonable men. Lastly all except pure secularists or very bitter men seem to feel that great embarrassment would ensue upon the loss of the Bill for the year. Such is the map of the situation, not very legible.

For my own part I think the sum of my desires is that, with a measure on all the other points worked up to the point of real efficacy, we should have religion free & not discountenanced or disparaged, protect conscience effectually, & keep the State out of all responsibility for or concern in religious differences.

Home questions absorb all our time, & I do not touch upon foreign: especially because I have no doubt Clarendon continues to keep you more or less

---

[1] See Ward, *Victorian Oxford*, 259.

[2] Russell's letter to Forster of 21 March, supporting Dissenters, in *The Times*, 25 March 1870, 5c.

informed. All I will say is that I think he has been doing his work extremely well while he continues to be what he always was a delightful colleague and fights manfully, I trust he may fight long, against physical suffering & inconvenience.

We have had a most variable and fluctuating winter trying to health. I am glad you have not been exposed to its vicissitudes. Among others Disraeli has been suffering and only tells me he is mending slowly.

My wife is just gone to Hagley where I fear the Dowr. Lady Lyttelton is now rather fast approaching the turn of a singularly honoured life.

25. *Annunciation*

Wrote to Dr Döllinger (finished)—Mr G. Tallents—Mr Hubbard—Mr R. Roberts—The Queen—and minutes. H of C. 2-6½ and 9-1¼ on Irish Crime Bill.[1] Saw Ld de Grey *cum* Mr Stansfeld—Conversation with Harry respecting King's College & studies. Saw Mr Glyn. Read Stanhope.

To J. J. I. von DÖLLINGER, 25 March 1870. Add MS 44426, f. 15.
'*Private.*'

I had scarcely finished writing to you under the impression which the preface to 'Janus' left upon me (I have since perused the work) when I began to doubt whether I had been justified in such a personal appeal. Your letter which I received yesterday,[2] sets me at ease & convinces me that you could indulgently sympathise with the feeling which had prompted mine.

Such a letter as you have addressed to me, coming from you, could not but engage my deepest attention: not less so, indeed, than if I had been able to believe you were accurate in your estimate of my power, or of the power of the British Government, to exercise an influence on the course of ecclesiastical proceedings at Rome. Speaking generally I feel that a consciousness of a great Elevation would turn me giddy & throw me off my balance. But on this particular question I have a keen desire to concur with you if I could in the belief that we, or that I possessed any power which could be made available in arresting by lawful means the infatuated proceedings of the Roman Court. I am sorrowfully convinced, that we have no such power; through Lord Acton, it is well known at Rome by all who care to know it, that I regard those proceedings, quite apart from their other aspects, as most injurious to the prospects of any future legislation in this country which may have for its object the rendering of full justice, in matters of Education or otherwise, to the members of the Roman Communion.

In my opinion there are but two agencies that could avail to stay this light minded, & hot headed Pope, with his satellites, in their deplorable career. The one is the power of France to withdraw that military support, which she has most wrongfully given through a period of more than 20 years with an ever increasing responsibility. The other is a firm undauntable resolution on the part of the Bishops of the minority to adhere to their purpose and prosecute it at all hazards, and to all extremities. I know of no other help. The rest lies in the hands of the Almighty.

[1] *H* cc. 670.
[2] Of 15 March 1870, calling for a Commons declaration; see 24 Mar. 70.

I am sure it would not be wise to create by force, as it were, an occasion for a Parliamentary declaration on this matter. If the occasion came, it should not be avoided. But I should not be without the fear of a counter declaration which might come from any quarter, & might express a very wide spread feeling which prevails, in strong contrast with mine. It is the feeling which first identifies the whole Latin Church as a body with the Court of Rome & the Pope (and for this identification or solidarity present proceedings afford but too strong a plea) and then treating this body as a sort of Incarnation of an evil principle assumes that the worse it behaves the greater will be the reaction & recoil of mankind, which reaction & recoil they treat as so much of accession on the side of good and truth. The whole of this theory I need not say I regard as radically false, but it prevails, and widely.

I agree with you in deploring the weak, inconsequent, ill sustained action of the French Government with regard to this question: which it may, I fear be too late to retrieve.

No more singular phenomenon is exhibited I think in these strange & critical times than the mind of Dr Newman. Such an abundance of power, such an excess of beauty, hardly ever I suppose, have appeared in conjunction with some latent defect or peculiarity which seems to penetrate the effect of all his gifts, & to exhibit him in a position of impotence before the world at the cardinal moment which others have been showing him how to use.

All the years however which have passed since I had the well remembered pleasure of spending a week in your society at Munich[1] have disposed me more & more to feel how as a general rule in each section of Christendom there is enough to engross and absorb the thought of those who have the nearest interest in it, & to relieve them from the duty of overlooking their neighbours' affairs. But this occasion is special: It opens up the whole field of common interest for those who prize the principle of Belief, now exposed to a subtle & frightful danger through the agency of those who claim for themselves its paramount if not its exclusive championship.

P.S. I do not know if you have had time & means to notice the warm and indeed affectionate reception which has been given in this country to the Archbishop of Syra & Tenos by all classes especially our higher ecclesiastical authorities. It is rather a remarkable sign of the times.

The welcome has been reciprocated on his part in a manner perhaps yet more remarkable.[2]

26. Sat.

Wrote to Ld Sydney—Abp Manning—The Queen—Chev. Chatelain[3] —C.G.—Ld Harrowby—Mr Curzon—and minutes. Saw Mr Glyn —Gen. Knowles.[4] H of C. & Cabinet 1-5½. Dined at Ly Waldegrave's. Music (Mrs Sartori's) afterwards. Heard Mad. Neruda[5] so well: it was delightful. Read Morris's Pygmalion.[6] Saw Hurley X.

[1] See 30 Sept. 45.   [2] See V. Conzemius, *Döllinger Briefwechsel* (1965) ii. 270.
[3] Jean Baptiste François Ernest de Chatelain, 1801–81; French literary critic and translator.   [4] *sc.* Knollys?
[5] Wilma Norman-Neruda, 1839–1911; concert violinist; gave an annual series of London concerts from 1869; m. 1880 Sir Charles Hallé.
[6] W. *Morris, 'Pygmalion', from *The Earthly Paradise* (1868).

Cabinet. Mch 26. 70. 2.30 PM.[1]

√ Irish Land Bill. option for Ulster Tenant—agreed.[2] Other custom Tenant—open to discretion? Tenant Right.

√ Hypothek—a distinct answer at beginning on new Session. Notice now.[3]
Graves's motion on Postage.

√ Queen's birthday Sat 28th (May).[4]

√ order of Big Bills—Irish Land—Engl[ish] Education—Univ. Tests—
$$\left\{ \begin{array}{l} \text{Ballot} \\ \text{Licensing} \end{array} \right.$$

√ The week's business
Support Hughes: and bring in a Bill accordingly if the Address is carried.[5]

To ARCHBISHOP H. E. MANNING,   Add MS 44249, f. 148.
26 March 1870. 'Private.'

I am very hard driven in consequence of the Irish Crime Bill which has supervened upon a state of business already crowded to excess.

And there will be a time of nearly six weeks before we can get into committee on the English Education Bill. Nevertheless I think it right at once to tell you which way on that measure the pressure lies. It is all from the side of secularists or (what I may term) unsectarians. You will see a most ill timed letter of Ld Russell's in the Times. That exhibits the milder form of what there may be to meet. I am sorry to say I cannot hold out expectations on either of the points you mention.[6] I need not say that the R.C. position in relation to all such demands is much damaged by the impressions here of what is going on at Rome.

As to the year's interval, & the maintenance of the system of Privy Council grants, nothing has occurred to shake the intentions of the Govt. But to *hold* their ground on these points will probably require all their strength.

What would be easy for them would be to escape from present difficulty by throwing the subject over to another year. But this you would not recommend, & it is a thing far from our desires & views. Whatever demands are left *now* open from the quarter I have indicated, will run up with compound interest at a high rate.

27. 4 S.Lent.

Chapel Royal mg (Bp of Carlisle) and aftnn. Wrote to Mrs Thistlethwayte—Dr Newman—C.G. Saw Ld Granville—Mr West—Mr Glyn—W. Hampton: his journey is fast downhill—Lady Lothian.

[1] Add MS 44638, f. 53.
[2] See 22 Mar., 1 Apr. 70.
[3] i.e. rights of Scottish landlords; the Lord Advocate's statement was less 'distinct' than this suggests; *H* cc. 723.
[4] *Victoria's actual birthday was on 24 May.
[5] T. *Hughes' motion on public schools on 6 April; the deb. was adjourned; *H* cc. 1379.
[6] *Manning wrote from Rome on 20 March, Add MS 44249, f. 146, requesting more time to start Roman catholic schools, and deploring the proposed School Boards: 'The only hope of Justice for us is to be under the Privy Council.'

Read Macarthy's Tr. of Calderons[1] Two Lovers of Heaven—Newman's Ch. on Nat[ural] Religion.[2]

28. M.

Wrote to Ld Clarendon—Sol.Gen. Ireland—Ld Acton—Dean of Windsor—Mr Ronalds[3]—Mr Richard MP—The Queen—Bp of Manchester—Mr Poulett Scrope—& minutes. Rode with Helen. Saw Mr Gore—Mr Glyn—Mr Monsell. Read Morris's Pygmalion—Stanhope's Queen Anne. H of C. 4½-8½ and 9-12½ Irish Land Bill.[4]

To H. RICHARD, M.P., 28 March 1870.   Add MS 44538, f. 112.

The difficult & numerous questions connected with the Irish Land Bill must for some time chiefly engross my attention but I shall take care to turn it, not less anxiously to all contested points in the Education Bill, some time before that Bill goes into Committee. I have, however, read with much interest the Mem[oria]l you have sent me.[5] And I should be much obliged if, in the course of the next three or four weeks, you are able to give me an answer to the following question: whether in the view of the Mem[orialist]s generally, the unsectarian Education in the Rate Schools, for which they ask, would (setting aside the question of Paedo-Baptism) admit of a pretty complete religious instruction in those Schools, according to the use & within the limits of the ordinary teaching of the Non-Conformist Pulpits? I would also submit one other point of inquiry.

Supposing that in unsectarian Schools, such as are intended by the memorial, a Schoolmaster is charged with expounding the Holy Scriptures in the sense of the Sacramental doctrines of the Church Catechism: *who* is in this, & in any series of like questions, to have fixed authority to decide the case, & then to draw the line between sectarian & unsectarian education? This seems to be a matter of great difficulty but it lies at the root of the proposal? I am very thankful for the kind terms in which you write; & I sincerely trust that a spirit of intelligent equity towards all parties will enable us to dispose of the controverted matters in the Education Bill, which many appear to find so perplexing.[6]

29. Tu.

Wrote to Sir G. Grey (NZ)—Do by Telegram—Ld Granville—Sir H. Storks—The Queen (Mem)—D. of Grafton—Ld Carnarvon—Sol. General—Duchess of Roxburghe—The Queen (letter)—and

[1] D. F. *MacCarthy, *The two lovers of heaven . . . from the Spanish of Cálderon* (1870).

[2] J. H. *Newman, *An essay in aid of a Grammar of Assent* (1870); Gladstone's thanks for his copy and Newman's reply are in *Newman*, xxv. 72.

[3] (Sir) Francis *Ronalds, 1788-1873; telegraphist; offering him a knighthood; Add MS 44538, f. 112.   [4] *H* cc. 737.

[5] Memorial from the Calvinistic Methodists of North Wales on the Education Bill. Richard's answer to the queries is in Richard to Gladstone, 23 April 1870, Add MS 44426, f. 155.   [6] Some in Lathbury, ii. 139.

minutes. Saw Abp of Syra—Mr Forster—Mr Glyn—Sol. General—
Scotts—Mr C. Howard—F. Cavendish. H of C. $4\frac{1}{2}$-8 and $9\frac{1}{4}$-$1\frac{1}{4}$.[1]
Read A Mother's Appeal[2]—Dr Williams's Narrative.[3]

To Sir GEORGE GREY, 29 March 1870.   Add MS 44425, f. 317.

I have received a Telegram, which I understood to be yours, respecting the Newark Election, to which I think it safer to reply by post. I annex a copy of the
Telegram. I should be most happy to afford reparation in any case where there
was matter of just complaint, but I am aware of no such matter in the present
instance.[4]

If Mr Stanhope has gone down to advise Sir Henry Storks in matters pertain-
ing to the Newark Election, and has confined himself to that private and personal
duty, I am at a loss to know how you can deem yourself injured thereby. Your
general title to solicit the suffrages of a constituency I do not for a moment
question, and I think it an honour that you should in any manner give your adhesion to the existing Government; but as I understand the present case a gentleman who was until a few days ago serving under and I hope will be soon a
member of that Government was already a Candidate for Newark when you
appeared there. Truth compels me to add that the return of Sir Henry Storks is
of great consequence to the efficient prosecution of the reforming measures now
in progress in the administration of the Army. It has been with his efficient aid
that Mr Cardwell has been enabled since he took office in December 1869 [*sic*]
to reduce the Army Estimates by above two millions while he has strengthened
rather than weakened the defensive force of the country.

The adequate representation in the House of Commons of a Department engaged upon a work such as this is a matter of much public importance. In reply
then to the Telegram you compel me to say first that I earnestly desire the
return of Sir Henry Storks, secondly that I hope Newark in which I feel a natural
and lively interest will not be added to the list of places in which the Liberal
party has earned discredit by divisions too often referable to local or personal
causes and injurious to the public objects for the sake of which it exists.

I send a copy of this letter to Sir Henry Storks with liberty to make use of it.

30. Wed.

Wrote to Sir R. Palmer—Dean of Windsor—Mr M'Lure[5]—Bp of
London—Mr Claflin[6]—Mr O. Russell (Tel.)—Ld Clarendon—Mr

[1] Newdegate's select cttee. on convents and monasteries established against the govt.'s
wish: *H* cc. 906.
[2] *An appeal to the people of England on the recognition and superintendence of prostitution by governments. By an English mother* (1870).
[3] C. J. B. Williams, *Authentic narrative of the case of the late Earl St. Maur* (1870).
[4] Sir G. Grey had returned from New Zealand hostile to aspects of supposed liberal colonial policy; despite this letter he refused to withdraw, coming a bad third; Storks did withdraw, eventually winning at Ripon in Feb. 1871.
[5] (Sir) Thomas MacClure, 1806-93; liberal M.P. Belfast 1868-74, Londonderry 1878-
85; cr. bart. 1874; had written on tenant right; Add MS 44538, f. 114.
[6] W. Claflin, 1818-1905, governor of Massachusetts; on Peabody's statue; Add MS
44538, f. 114.

Hitchcock[1]—& minutes. Wrote Mem. on Irish Land Clauses.[2] Saw Mr MacColl—Lord Stanhope—Mr Glyn—Mr Newdigate—Mr Motley—Bp of Winchester—Mr Platt—Mr Cardwell—Ld Stratford. Read Newman on Contagious Diseases Bill[3]—Worth on do— & I.L. Tract.

31. Th.

Wrote to Ld Clarendon—Dean of Windsor—Ld Minto—Mr G. Tallents—Sir G. Grey MP.—Dep.Mast.Trin. House[4]—Mr Kirk MP— Mr Johnston MP. Saw Ld Granville—Capt. Lawley—Mr Glyn—Mr Fortescue—Mr Forster. Rode with Helen. H. of C. $4\frac{1}{2}$-$8\frac{1}{4}$ & 9-1: State of business, & Irish Land.[5] Read Tracts. Saw Hampton: farther downhill: hopeful of life but resigned.

Frid. April One. 1870.

Wrote to Bp of Winchester—Bp of Chester—The Queen—Ld Clarendon—Mr Bruce—and minutes. Dined with the Jameses. H of C. 2-$6\frac{3}{4}$ and 9-$1\frac{1}{2}$. Stiff both on Irish Land & on Fawcett's motion, which ended well.[6] Irish Land: Irish Educn. Made some of my repositories more tidy. Saw Mr Glyn—Ld de Tabley.

2. Sat.

Wrote to Dean of Lichfield—Mrs Cardwell—Ld Lorne—The Queen —Mr Tallents—and minutes. Saw The Dean of Christ Church— Chancr of Exchr (Budget)—Mr Glyn—Ld Granville—S.E.G. The Rothschilds (Tea). Dined with Lady Lothian. Went with C. to the French Picture Exhibition, & rather licentiously bought three.[7] Saw Duke of Norfolk & R.C. Deputation.[8] Cabinet $2\frac{3}{4}$-$5\frac{1}{4}$. Read Carpenter's Tract[9]—Stanhope's Hist.

---

[1] Also re Peabody.   [2] Untraced.

[3] F. W. *Newman, The cure of the great social evil (1869).

[4] Sir Frederick Arrow, 1818-75; deputy master from 1865.

[5] H cc. 992, 1006. Notes in Add MS 44759, f. 96.

[6] Diarist's amndt. to give equality to usages similar to Ulster tenant right (see 22, 26 Mar. 70) agreed to: H cc. 1051. For *Fawcett's motion (H cc. 1119), see letter to Russell on 3 April 1870.

[7] Not traced which.

[8] No report found; Norfolk wanted a commission rather than a select cttee., if an inquiry into convents was unavoidable; inquiry found the majority for a cttee. unreversable; Add MS 44426, ff. 84-8, 127.

[9] Probably A. *Carpenter, 'Some points in the physiological and medical aspect of sewage irrigation' (1870).

Cabinet. April 2 1870. 2.30 PM.[1]

√ Inquiry into conventual & monastic Institutions.[2] We shall expect 1. Impartial Committee 2. Inhibit compulsory summons & examn. of women.

○ State of business in the H. of Commons: morning sittings.[3]

√ Debts of Spain & Portugal. Chancr. of Exr. to use conciliatory language in his Budget Speech.

√ Mrs Gordon. Say No.[4]

√ I[rish] Land Clauses Amendments.[5] (a) Option to Landlord of allowing to sell interest (b) Limit for freedom of contract to be reduced to £50. *Liberty to act as may be fit* (c) Section curtailing freedom of contract shall be in operation for 20 years from Dec. 31. 70 and thereafter until Parliament shall otherwise direct. *Yes.* (d) enlargement of Clause 6 ($\frac{1}{2}$ circulated & agreed to): *described* (e) Cardwell's proposal as to assignment: he says Downe will prepare Clause.

√ Mr Taylor's motion for Bill for payment of members. *Oppose.*[6]

√ Election procedure report: shall Candidates pay necessary expenses? Hartington to consider.

√ Compulsory Sites Bill for Churches & Schools. Enlarge powers of limited owners & same as to Churches. S[chools] provided for by Education Bill.

√ Mr Cardwell to proceed with absorption of Ensigns' Commissions, in anticipation of the vote.[7]

3. 5 S.Lent.

Chapel Royal mg (Bp of Salisbury, admirable; H.C.): All Saints aftn. Wrote to D. of Norfolk—Mr Newdigate—Mr O. Russell—Marquis of Lorne[8]—Mr Childers—The Solr General—Warden of Trin.Coll. N.B.—Mrs Thistlethwayte—Mr O. Russell (Telegr.). Saw Mr Glyn —Bp of Salisbury—Ld De Tabley. Dined with De Tabley. Read Urlin on J. Wesley[9] and many Tracts & Sermons.

To ODO RUSSELL, 3 April 1870. 'Private.'   Add MS 44538, f. 117.

The sage advisers of Pope Pius the Great, if they care about the condition of their co-religionists here, may find some material of instruction, as to the effect of their present proceedings, in the Parliamentary 'situation'. We maturely considered in Cabinet yesterday whether we should try to reverse or alter the Vote

[1] Add MS 44638, f. 61.

[2] See 29 Mar. 70n., reported as *PP* 1870 vii. 1. See also letter on 3 Apr. 70.

[3] On 31 March Gladstone requested morning sittings on Tuesdays and Fridays until the recess but strong objections were raised: *H* cc. 994.

[4] Dilke was campaigning for a pension for the widow of G. W. Gordon of Jamaica, militarily executed: *H* cc. 1169.

[5] These points apparently written before Cabinet met. Words italicised were written during or after Cabinet, recording its decisions.

[6] See 5 Apr. 70n.   [7] Following his answer on 18 March; *H* cc. 208.

[8] Letter of warning to *Lorne who had voted against the Irish Land Bill, though not on the major division, on 1 April 1870; Add MS 44538, f. 116. *Argyll was annoyed with his son, but found him uncontrollable; Add MS 44101, f. 225.

[9] R. D. Urlin, *John Wesley's place in Church history* (1870).

on Conventual Institutions.[1] We decided that we could not attempt it. But we propose to inhibit the Committee from the compulsory examination of women, which the Roman Catholics regard with just horror. On Friday Mr. Fawcett proposed a motion respecting Trin. Coll. Dublin the real *effect* of which would have been to prevent any one educated in a Roman Catholic College from proceeding to any Irish University Degree. It was only by making this question a question of *confidence* outright (& the use of such a weapon must needs be very rare) that we were able to defeat it. Like influences will be found, probably, to be at work on the English Education Bill: possibly on the Irish Land Bill. And if complaint is made nothing will be easier than to retort the cool declaration of Antonelli, & to assure him glibly that the State will carefully confine itself to matters of civil right, which God entrusted to it, & will in no wise intrude on the sacred domain of religion. What a grievous mess the French have made of it. Please to show this to Ld. Acton. As I know not when it will reach you, I telegraph today.

4. M.

Wrote to Duke of Norfolk—The Queen (2)—Scotts—Sol.Gen. Ireland—and minutes. Rode with Agnes. Dined with the Wests. Saw Mr Thompson jun.—Mr Mundella—Mr Glyn—Mr Fortescue—Mrs Stume—The Speaker—Mr Newdigate. H. of C. 4½-8¼ and 9-12¾. Spoke on Disraeli's amendment. A majority of 76: but the navigation is at present extremely critical.[2] Read Stanhope's Hist.

5. Tu.

Wrote to Duke of Argyll—Lady Desart—Sir R. Palmer—Dean of Windsor—Mr R. Roberts—Mr G. Burnett—The Queen—and minutes. H of C. 2-6¾ on Irish Land and 9-12 Payt of members.[3] Saw Mr Glyn—Sol. General—Att. General—Mr Maguire—Sir R. Palmer—Mr Fortescue—Saw White. X. Read Judge Longfield on I.L.[4]

To LORD CLARENDON, foreign secretary,   Clarendon MSS, c. 498.
5 April 1870.

I have received your note[5] just before the House meets on the Land Bill & it is not possible for me to read through the note of Daru; I am however quite

---

[1] Telegram of 30 March announcing the vote, at Add MS 44426, f. 51.

[2] *H* cc. 1252; see Morley, ii. 295.

[3] He opposed payment of members: 'To see this House composed and constituted of men who have received a limited education and are in dependent circumstances would be a most calamitous thing': *H* cc. 1358.

[4] See 10 Mar. 70.

[5] Of this day, enclosing Daru's note, and suggesting instruction to O. Russell to give unofficial, verbal support; Add MS 44134, f. 174.

willing to agree to the few & safe words you propose to send to Odo, only I do not see any reason why they should be unofficial. It seems to me that they *wisely* forbear to affirm either the sufficiency or the insufficiency of the French proceedings but simply wish them well such as they are, & this I should think they might do without qualification expressed.

I do not see the necessity of a Cabinet because I think it was felt that we must give a modest support to France if she moved: but by all means let us have one if you are not satisfied on this head, as I am.

6. Wed.

Wrote to Mr Fortescue—Ld Athlumney—Mr Cardwell—and minutes. H. of C. 2½–6.[1] Read Bernard's Work.[2] Saw Mr Osborne Morgan—Sir Thos G.—Mrs Stume—Mr Bruce (2)—Mr Glyn—Mr Fortescue—Sol.Gen.I.—D. of Argyll—Sir R. Palmer—Mr Bowring. Worked on Irish Land. Consultation with Mr [M. W. P.] O'Reilly, Mr [W. H. F.] Cogan—Mr Murphy:[3] with a view to adjustment of amendments. The crisis is sharp. Dined with the Duchess of Argyll: she was wonderfully recovered, but the best of her bodily life has sunk. Saw Mrs Th. Late. Attended the Speaker's Levee.

To C. S. P. FORTESCUE, Irish secretary,   Carlingford MS, CP1/107.
6 April 1870. 'Immediate.'

I apprehend (though Glyn has not yet given me his estimate) that 'Seven years' may be considered as Danger point: & that if we can round it we can pretty well weather the storm.

I am very anxious to know whether the opinion is a sound & solid one that the very small tenant say under £20 *will very rarely indeed be able to make good a claim for improvements* except in reclamation of land (and Buildings?? very doubtful?)

If this is *not* so we have been inconsistent in not reducing the number of years for the small tenant.

But if this *is* so, then may it not be said that as to the small tenant the attempt to separate improvements from loss is futile, and that the basis of the old scale was better at the lower end?

In this view I have seen Glyn whose present impression is that some concession on the scale will be requisite.

I have framed the enclosed. Please to consider it. I am inclined to think it will keep our majority together. Will it offend the Irish? It reintroduces that principle of option on which you will remember that when first trying the amendment of the scale we wished to proceed.

I could explain the *operation* vivâ voce if you think it difficult. 'Provided that

[1] Misc. business: *H* cc. 1382.
[2] M. *Bernard, *A historical account of the neutrality of Great Britain during the American Civil War* (1870).
[3] Nicholas Daniel Murphy, 1811–?; liberal M.P. Cork 1865–80.

no tenant valued over £20 & claiming more than 4 years rent & no tenant who-soever claiming more than five years rent, under this scale shall be entitled to make a separate claim for improvements other than permanent buildings & reclamation of land.'[1]

To LORD HARTINGTON, postmaster general,   Add MS 44538, f. 120.
6 April 1870.

You were prevented by the course of the debate from speaking on the Second Reading of the Land Bill but I think there would be a good opportunity tomor-row on the scale, & I should be very glad if you would then take part in the debate.[2] I am working on the subject to see if we can make our proposal quite sound & right & should be happy to see you tomorrow at 11 or 11.30 if con-venient.

7. Th.

Wrote to Ld Clarendon—Sir R. Palmer—Watson & Smith—Bp of Bangor—Mr Oswald—Mr Fortescue—The Queen—and minutes. Rode with Mary. Saw Archdn Durnford—Ld Hartington—Mr Glyn —Mr Fortescue—Att. General. Dined with West. H of C. $4\frac{1}{2}$-8 and 9-$12\frac{1}{2}$. A most anxious day from end to end. Early in the evening I gave a review of the state of the Bill: and late, another menace of overturn if the motion of Mr Fowler, which Palmer had unfortunately (as is too common with him) brought into importance, should be carried. We had a majority of only 32.[3] Read Ld Stanhope.

8. Fr.

Wrote to Mr Cardwell (2)—Mr G. Burnett—Mr Acland—The Queen —Mr Macfie—Mrs Th.—and minutes. Dined with the Phillimores. A short drive with C. Saw Ld Granville—Mr Glyn—Sir R. Phillimore —Mr Melly. H of C. $2\frac{1}{4}$-7: very anxious: Irish Land Bill not yet out of danger. H of C. again $9\frac{1}{2}$-$10\frac{1}{4}$.[4] Visited Mrs Thistlethwayte afr. She is indeed an excepted person: & strangely corresponds with me in some of the strangest points. Read Bernard.[5]

To E. CARDWELL, war secretary, 8 April 1870.   PRO 30/48/7, f. 39.
'Private.'

I cannot but feel some doubt whether Palmer has considered 'the situation' which is a matter extrinsic to the Land Bill; & in which he is playing the principal

---

[1] No reply found.   [2] Hartington did not speak.
[3] Fowler's motion sought to deny compensation for disturbance to larger tenants; H cc. 1458. At least twelve liberals voted against the govt. See Steele, 303 ff.
[4] H cc. 1507.   [5] See 6 Apr. 70.

part. It is this fact of which I cannot but suspect that he is not fully conscious. Last night he brought us, after all our efforts to conciliate, which so much exasperated a man like M'Carthy Downing, within an inch of shipwreck. Did he, or did he not know that, if the Bill, the Parliament, & the Government succumbed, *he* before all other men, & much before Mr Disraeli (under the circumstances) would be the person to whom the country would have a right to look as responsible for the Government of Ireland?

If he knows it, I have not a word to say. But he ought to know it; for his operations, I fear, have not yet ceased.

9. Sat. [*Windsor Castle*]

Wrote to Ld Clarendon—Bp of Lincoln—Sir H. Verney—Mr Kirk —Sir W. Lawson—Mr P.A. Taylor—Ld St Germans—Miss Marsh —Mr Acland—The City Remembrancer—Sir R. Palmer—and minutes. Saw Mr Milner Gibson—Mr Ouvry. Cabinet 2-4½. Then off to Windsor Castle with C. & Agnes. We dined with the Queen. Conversation with the Dean—Col. Ponsonby. Read Longfellow's Poems[1] —Montagu Bernard—London Tess[ellated] Pavements.[2]

Cabinet D. St. Ap. 9. 70. 2 PM.[3]
√ Budget. Sanctioned
√ View of business in H. of C. Prospects of Education Bill. Land—14 years.[4] Palmer. retrospective clause. meeting of party? Not without Cabinet.[5]
√ Buildings on Embankment Land, a) of Metrop[olitan Water] Board b) of Crown. Chancr. of Exr. authorised to arrange with Mr Ayrton with a view to proposing to place the Natural History B[ritish] M[useum] Building at S. Kensington.
√ New Zealand Loan Guarantee for Emigr[atio]n. civilly decline
√ Capitation Grant. Cardwell indicates a Commission as probably necessary.[6]

To LORD CLARENDON, foreign secretary,   Clarendon MSS, c. 498.
9 April 1870.

I presume you have now only, in the matter of disarmament, to express your inability to recede from your opinions & your regret at the result of the correspondence. If inclined to touch the point you might with perfect justice say that while our naval responsibilities for overseas defence have no parallel or analogue in the world, we have taken not far short of 2 million off our estimates, & have not announced that the work of reduction is at an end; which whether satisfactory or not is enough to show that you do not preach wholly without practising.

[P.S.] I am much delighted with the masterly composition of Bernard's Book, in the early part which alone I have yet read.[7]

---

[1] See 18 Dec. 48.   [2] Untraced.   [3] Add MS 44638, f. 65.
[4] *Palmer proposed to reduce the 31 year lease limit to 14.
[5] No party meeting was held.
[6] Proposed increase in the capitation grant for the volunteers; no royal commission was appointed.   [7] Part in Millman, 158.

10. Palm S.

Castle Chapel 10 and 12 (Mr Moorhouse preached): St George's 4.30.
A noble anthem of Mendelsohn's. Walk all through Eton. Saw Mr
Parker & Dr Hornby.[1] Audience of H.M. at 3. Wrote to Viceroy of
Ireland—Dean of Chichester—Rev Mr Anson—Mr Glyn—Mr Bryce.
Read Rigg's Art. on Educn—Visit to the Waldenses—Place of Wes-
ley in Ch. History.[2] Dined again with the Queen: who is most kind.

1. Recital of Cabinet: Budget—Land Bill—Education Bill. 2. Ld. Lyons's letter.
3. Oxford C[ivil] L[aw] Professorship. 4. Ld Kildare to be called up. 5. Mr
[G. H. G.] Anson to be Archdn. of Manchr. 6. Mr. Bryce to be professor of Civil
Law at Oxford.[3]

11. M. [London]

Wrote to Lord Chancellor—Duke of Norfolk—Lord Kildare—Lord
Dufferin—Viceroy of Ireland—Sir R. Palmer—Mrs Hartmann—Mr
Wingfield Baker—Ld Devon—The Queen (L[etter] & M[emoran-
dum])—and minutes. Saw Dean of Windsor—Lord F. Cavendish—
Mr Glyn—Mr Acland—Mr Dent—Mr Newdigate—Mr Forster.
Rode with Helen. Returned from Windsor at 11. Dined at Mr Forsters.
H of C. 4½-8¼ and 10½-1¾.[4]

12. Tu. [Hawarden]

Wrote to Scotts—J. Watson & Smith—Ld Russell—Mrs Thistlethwayte—Mrs Hartmann—& minutes. Saw Mr Homersham Cox—
Mr MacColl—Mr Glyn. H of C. 2-4: spoke on the block of business.[5] Packed books & otherwise prepared for departure. Off by the
5 PM. reached Hawarden 11¼. Read Q.R. on Ch. in Wales—And on
Govt of Ireland.[6]

To LORD RUSSELL, 12 April 1870.   PRO 30/22/16F, f. 165.

I am in the hurry scurry of preparation for a run into the country this evening
but I must not omit to thank you for your very kind & welcome letter.[7]

[1] J. J. *Hornby, the headmaster.   [2] See 3 Apr. 70.
[3] Notes for the Audience, dated 10 April 1870: Add MS 44638, f. 66. James *Bryce,
1838-1922; author; regius professor of civil law at Oxford 1870-93; liberal M.P. Tower
Hamlets 1880-5, S. Aberdeen 1885-1906; chancellor of duchy 1892-5; cr. Viscount 1914.
This day's letter, offering him the chair, in Add MS 44538, f. 123.
[4] *Lowe's budget: H cc. 1607. He wrote to Lord Devon this day (Add MS 44538, f. 124):
'As being interested [as a shareholder] in the District [underground railway] Line, I do not
give any vote upon the Bill today. . . .'
[5] House adjourned until 25 April 1870: H cc. 1719.
[6] Quarterly Review, cxxviii. 386, 560 (April 1870).
[7] Probably that of 28 March 1870, from Rome, Add MS 44294, f. 217, mainly on education.

We have had a most anxious time in regard to the Irish Land Bill. Often do I think of a saying of yours more than 30 years back which struck me ineffaceably at the time. You said the true key to our Irish Debates was this, that it was not properly borne in mind that as England is inhabited by Englishmen, & Scotland by Scotchmen, so Ireland is inhabited by Irishmen. The fear that our Land Bill may cross the water, creates a sensitive state of mind among all Tories, many Whigs, & a few Radicals. Upon this state of things comes Palmer with his legal mind, legal point of view legal aptitude & *in*aptitude (vide Mr Burke), & stirs these susceptibilities to such a point that he is always near bringing us to grief. Even Grey more or less goes with him. We have made our Bill as moderate as we can, & have confronted (as was our duty) all the wild Irish ideas; but an insufficient Bill is worse than no Bill at all, & we cannot be parties to passing one. Thank God however there is now but one point of great danger remaining, the proposal to reduce the 31 years lease, which we put in the bill as the alternative to the scale of damages, & which is for the small Irish holder (all above £50 valuation will have free contract) the lowest term which signifies stable tenure. Palmer proposes to cut this down to 14 years! But I cannot help hoping he will recede.

I have not left myself time to write on Education. There we have great difficulties too from the very crude state of opinion and now *time* is threatening to be an obstacle too. I shall address this to the care of the British Embassy in Paris.

13. Wed.

Hawarden Church 11 AM: and 7 PM. Wrote minutes. Read Kenrick's Phoenicia[1]—Baring Gould's Development of Belief[2]—Merry Wives of Windsor—[blank]'s History of Wales.[3]

14.

Illness in the night kept me in bed until one. Wrote to Chancr of Exchequer—Ld Clarendon—Mr Hammond—Mr Crawford—Scotts —Mrs Thistlethwayte—Dean Hook—and minutes. Read Dean Hook on Educn[4]—Merry Wives (finished)—Two Gentn of Verona (began —some trash?)—Southey's Thalaba Books.[5]—Q.R. on Lanfrey's Napoleon.[6]

To LORD CLARENDON, foreign secretary,   Clarendon MSS, c. 498.
14 April 1870.

I am not informed as to the detail & interior history of the ministerial crisis in France. But *if* the Emperor is really stickling for the right to refer when he

---

[1] See 16 June 63.   [2] See 12 Dec. 69.
[3] Perhaps J. *Williams, *A history of Wales* (1869).
[4] See 9 July 46.   [5] R. *Southey, *Thalaba, the destroyer*, 2v. (1801).
[6] *Quarterly Review*, cxxviii. 342 (April 1870).

pleases to the people for an Aye or No upon a proposition which he is to frame, that in my opinion reduces constitutional Government to an absolute mockery, just as it would reduce to a shadow the power of a Legislative Assembly? Meanwhile the partial abeyance of the Executive at this moment is very unfortunate with reference to the transactions in Rome. The Pope & his satellites will not fail to use their opportunity.

[P.S.] Having been unwell in the night, I have been late today & have read yours too late to telegraph (7 miles off) in time for office hours. With Daru out of office I suppose the Note to be all but dead. I see nothing however to mend in your reply to Odo Russell & I write this to Hammond.

15. Good Friday.

Ch. 11 A.M. with H.C., and 7 P.M. Wrote to Vice Chancr of Oxford —Ld Bessborough—The Queen—Mr T.B. Potter—Mr West—Ld Lyttelton—Ld Fingall[1]—W.F. Larkins—Mr Ayrton—and minutes. Read Fornari, Vita di Cristo[2]—J. Wesley's Place in Ch. History[3]— Ackland (on Reverence),[4] Hebert, & other Tracts.[5]

To LORD SPENCER, Irish lord lieutenant,   Add MS 44306, f. 277.
15 April 1870.

I ought to be in possession of any information which may be available about Irish Farms on the morning of Thursday the 28th. That which you have collected in the printed papers is very valuable. It goes far to show that if pressed we may without much danger agree or submit to exclude yearly tenancies over £100 *now existing* from the operation of Clause 3.

1. But this position would be greatly strengthened if by the time I have named you could obtain even *approximative data* to show that a large portion of them are grazing farms.

2. There is a point of serious danger opened by Palmer our only formidable antagonist. He proposes to take down the 31 years lease, which is to take people out of Clause 3, to 14 years—while even Ball gives 21.

Now what I believe is that the term of 31 years has in Ireland the same relative place in the mind of the people as 21 and 19 on this side of the water: and that it is the shortest term which could be expected to satisfy reasonable expectation. Bessborough pressed us hard to make it 41 years.

(2) [*sc.* 3] I should then be very glad of any information which would analyse the character of the *21 years leases and under* in Ireland outside of Ulster. What proportion of them are for 14 years, or other terms less than 21 years? What proportion are grazing farms? What proportion are on those estates where the landlord makes the improvements? Are they often or ever given with a permission to sell the goodwill at the end of the term? Are they acceptable to the people? What view will the people take of them in comparison with yearly tenancies defended by the scale of damages for eviction?

---

[1] Arthur James Plunkett, 1819–81; 10th earl of Fingall 1869, a liberal.
[2] V. Fornari, *Della vita di Gesù Cristo*, 3v. (1869).   [3] See 3 Apr. 70.
[4] J. Ackland, *The spirit of reverence* (1870).
[5] C. Hebert, 'A reply to . . . W. G. Clark' (1870).

You will understand my object: and I am sure you will kindly get me as much as you can. I hope that when we get well over these points we shall be out of danger though not out of difficulty.

Strange to say I am beginning to believe that it was our resolute resistance to fixity of tenure and valuation of rents which made the Opposition think they might safely assail the bill as it stood, while they had before regarded it as a needful means of escape from greater evils. This is a pretty return for even-handed dealing.

Athlumney has declined the ribbon and I have written to Fingall by Bessborough's advice.[1]

16. Easter Eve.

Ch. 8½ AM and 7 P.M. Wrote to Archbishop Manning—Lord Clarendon—Mr West—Dr Dollinger—Robn G.—and minutes. We felled a considerable Oak. Read Renaud (on Educn Bill)—Bence Jones on Irish Land[2]—Montalembert's & Lacordaire's Testament[3]—Quarterly on non historic Times[4]—Beddoe on Bulk & Stature &c.[5]—Two Gentlemen of Verona.

To ARCHBISHOP H. E. MANNING, 16 April 1870.   Add MS 44249, f. 152.

Your letter of the 7th has only reached me today.[6] In answering it, I must draw a clear distinction between my personal opinions, and the action of the Government which represents and ought to represent something much weightier. *My* feelings and convictions are as you will know decidedly with your 'Opposition' which I believe to be contending for the religious and civil interests of mankind against influences highly disastrous and menacing to both. But the prevailing opinion is that it is better to let those influences take their course, and work out the damage which they will naturally and surely entail upon the See of Rome and upon what is bound to it. Consequently, there has been here a great indisposition to forward even that kind of interference which alone could have been dreamt of, namely a warning, in terms of due kindness and respect, as to the ulterior consequences likely to follow from the interference of the Pope and Council in the affairs of the civil sphere. If asked we cannot withhold, perhaps, the suppression of our conviction: but we have not been promoters; nor do I consider that any undue weight would be given even to the most reasonable warnings by the authorities at Rome.

But there is a more limited aspect of these affairs, in which I have spoken to you and to others, and that without the smallest idea of anything that can be called interference. From the announcement of the Council, I have feared the

[1] Mem. of answers in Add MS 44306, f. 279.

[2] Gladstone read Bence *Jones's untraced article at R. R. *Palmer's suggestion and commented (Add MS 44538, f. 132): 'he always seems to think his own horizon is the horizon of the Planet . . .'.

[3] *Le testament du P. Lacordaire . . . publié par le Comte de Montalembert* (1870).

[4] *Quarterly Review*, cxxviii. 432 (April 1870).

[5] J. *Beddoe, 'Address to the Anthropological Society, London. Delivered . . . 18 January 1870' (1870).

[6] Add MS 44294, f. 150, opposing any attempt to influence the Council on doctrinal matters.

consequences of (what we consider) extreme proceedings upon the progress of just legislation here. My anticipations have been, I regret to say, much more than realised. An attempt was made to force our hands on the subject of the higher Education in Ireland, and practically to bind the House of Commons to an absolute negation of the principles which we laid down in 1865 & 1866. This attempt, premature I think even from the point of view held by its friends, we were only able to defeat by staking our existence as a Government upon the issue. Then came Mr Newdigate's [sic] motion on Inspection of Religious Establishments. Not only was this carried entirely against our expectations, but the definitive reports since made to me of the state of feeling in the House are to the effect, that it cannot be reversed, even by the exercise of the whole influence of the Government. These facts are striking enough. But I seem to myself to trace the influence of the same utter aversion to the Roman policy in a matter to me at least of the most profound and absorbing interest, I mean the Irish Land Bill. Perhaps Bishop Furlong's extraordinary letter[1] and the manner in which it seems to exhibit his ideas of the mode of discriminating between things secular and things spiritual, have helped to establish in the minds of men an animation they might not otherwise have conceived. Be that as it may, the tone and atmosphere of Parliament about the Land Bill have changed: again, for the second time within a fortnight, I have been obliged to resort to something like menace: the strain thus far has been extreme: and I regret to say it is not yet over. I apprehend that these ill effects will be felt in other matters which impend, in two especially which are close at hand, Ecclesiastical Titles and National Education. What I have described is no matter of speculation: I know it by actual and daily touch. I am glad you have moved me to state it in some detail. It is to me matter of profound grief, especially as regards Land in Ireland. For I feel as if the happiness of some millions of God's creatures were immediately committed to us, so far as the things of this life (and their influences on the other) are concerned: and until it is disposed of, it seems to engross and swallow up my whole personal existence. *When* it is settled, I shall begin to detach my hopes and interests, if I may, from the political future.

Quite apart from what I have said, the question of National Education is passing I fear into great complications; and crude opinion of all kinds is working blindly about like hot & cold moist and dry in Ovid's Chaos.[2]

Pray do not think or speak of 'displeasure' in connection with me. For my displeasure if I had it would be at your convictions: but as they are sincere I do not conceive them to be proper objects of a feeling, which would imply my right to be your judge. Whatever you communicate to me, I take as a mark *pro tanto* of confidence. And the plainer it is the better. Besides if you apologise much more must I retaliate. Veniam petimusque damusque vicissim.[3]

17. Easter Day.

Church 11 AM with H.C: and 7 P.M. Wrote to The Viceroy of Ireland—Mr Forster—Mr Bruce—Lord de Grey—Lord Beauchamp

[1] Printed in *Pall Mall Gazette*, 29 March 1870; the Land Bill 'totally inadequate'; see V. Conzemius, *Döllinger Briefwechsel* (1965) ii. 276. Thomas Furlong, 1802-75, bp. of Ferns.　　　　　　　　　　　　　　　　　　　　　　　　[2] *Metamorphoses* I 19.

[3] ' "Painters and poets were always allowed to take any liberties they liked." I know, and seek this indulgence, and give it in my turn . . .'; Horace, *Ars Poetica*, 9-11. Letter forwarded to Döllinger for him and Acton; Add MS 44140, f. 277.

—and minutes. Read Miss Collet on the new Indian Theism[1]—
Keshen [blank]'s Lectures[2]—Lacordaire's Testament. At the Altar
this day it was the Irish Land question that I presented before God
more than aught else living or dead. Finished J. Wesley's place in Ch.
Hist.

To H. A. BRUCE, home secretary, 17 April 1870.   Add MS 44086, f. 143.[3]

Many thanks for the information about the Article on the Welsh Church.[4] I
did not think much of it.

It occurs to me that as the Cabinet have never had the Burials Bill before
them, it might be convenient if when you come to the stage of Draft Reports
you were then to mention the subject. It is not probably desirable to arrive at
that stage too hurriedly at least if extreme claims are to be pushed. The most
rational settlement I think would be, if parties were content with it.[5] [1. To relieve the clergyman from the obligation to perform the funeral service when he
& the parties agreed in that sense. 2.] To allow all parishioners to bury in the
Churchyard upon notice, without service.

The difficulties would be especially great in dealing with R.C. services in the
Churchyards—and also in determining *who* were ministers for the purpose of
performing Dissenting Services.

To EARL DE GREY, lord president,   Add MS 43514, f. 5.
17 April 1870.

I should be very glad some day after the recess to confer with you on the
question of a Charter for Keble College. I apprehend it may have a bearing on
the course to be taken in Ireland when we come to deliberate about the higher
Education there. If it can be done with propriety, I should lean to direct acts of
incorporation rather than relegating bodies not Commercial to the general category of Joint Stock.[6]

18. Easter M.

Ch 11 AM. Wrote to Govr of the Bank—Chancr of Exr—Mr West
—Ld Clarendon—Mr Moffatt—Bp of Winchester—Dr Hannah—
Mr Hubbard—Mr Chambers—and minutes. Long interview with Mr
W. Malcolmson & Mr Robinson.[7] Felled a tree 2f.8/2f.4 diam. It

[1] S. D. Collet, *Indian Theism, and its relation to Christianity* (1870).
[2] Reading obscure.
[3] Copy in Aberdare MSS transcribed by secretary, signed by diarist; holograph in Add MSS.
[4] Untraced; no relevant letter from Bruce in Add MS 44086. See 13 Apr. 70?
[5] Section in [ ] deleted in copy sent to Bruce.
[6] de Grey replied, Add MS 43514, f. 5, that he expected Keble's Royal Charter to be a
'very special case'. See 14, 21 May 70.
[7] Messrs. Malcolmson, Waterford cotton millers, in commercial difficulty, requested
govt. assistance; Gladstone this day told R. W. Crawford, director of the Bank of England

took me 1 h. 20 m. A walnut. Read Two Gent. Ver. (finished)—Titus Andronicus (began)—Swift's Poems &c.[1]—Ewing's Lecture on England.[2]

To LORD CLARENDON, foreign secretary,   Add MS 44538, f. 129.
18 April 1870.

I send you my reply to Manning's letter[3] of which you take, I think, a very just view. I dare say the 'support' of the respective Governments will be valuable to the Opposition Bishops (if they hold out) after their return home. In this view, the several states have some power in their hands. But this applies very little to us, among whom the Roman Church is organised on the voluntary principle. In the 6th page of the inclosed copy you will read what may at first sight seem to you like exaggeration, I mean my estimate of the subject of Irish Land. But I assure you it is literally a transcript of my deliberate conviction. I feel about it as a bee might feel if it knew that it would die upon its sting: except that I believe it has no sting, but tends (among other things) to open a mine of wealth for all. It will also strike you as odd that I should write this to our High Popish Archbishop: but the explanation is that, during much of my earlier life we were very intimate.

I send Thornton's No. 66[4] to the Q. & return the other. I hope rightly. I must say all I read of him raises him steadily in my opinion as a faithful, patient, dispassionate, & sagacious Minister.[5]

19. Tu.

Ch. 11 AM. Wrote to Mr Darbishire—Viceroy of Irel.—Sir Thos G. —Pres. of Maynooth—Mr West (Telegr.), & minutes. Kibbled the large Oak Tree. Read Boissard on Dante[6]—Mr Huntington on Church Unity[7]—Titus Andronicus (certainly Shakespeare's I think, & a very crude early effort?)—Pericles Prince of Tyre. Harry & Stephen returned from the funeral of the dear & good old Lady Lyttelton: but

(Add MS 44538, f. 192): 'I have acquainted Mr. Malcolmson and Mr [Joseph] Robinson . . . that the Govt. can assume no pecuniary responsibility whatever. . . . But I have told them I would call your attention to the statements. . . . I do not doubt that the Irish govt. must be right in believing that the origin of the difficulties . . . is connected with special circumstances of a political nature. While there can be no doubt that any cessation of the vast employment depending on the action of the House would even approach to the character of a public calamity.'

[1] *Poetical works* (1736).
[2] T. J. Ewing, 'The distribution of Parliamentary borough constituencies' (1867).
[3] See 16 Apr. 70.
[4] N. 66 of Thornton's private series to Clarendon, 5 April 1870, Clarendon MSS, c. 481 on Prince Arthur's visit.
[5] Clarendon replied, 21 April 1870, Clarendon MSS, c. 501, '. . . it will be of no use. Manning and his fellows have no other aim than to increase the power of their Church. . . .'
[6] F. Boissard, *Dante revolutionnaire et socialiste mais non hérétique* (1858).
[7] W. R. Huntington, *The Church-idea. An essay towards unity* (1870).

C. came not with them, having gone straight from Hagley with her usual bravery to Herbert at Penygroes near Dolgelly where he is reported to have one of his attacks.

20. Wed.

Ch. 8½ A.M. Wrote to Sir R. Palmer—Mr Ouvry—C.G.—Mr Caird —and minutes. 3-6. Went with Mr Burnett, S.R.G., & H.G., over much of the Aston property: greatly pleased. E. Talbot came: with good news of Herbert. Read Dublin Review on Ireland—& on Paolo Sarpi[1]—Boissard's Dante—Pericles Pr. of T. (finished). Conversation with E.T. on Education.

21. Th.

Ch. 8½ AM. Wrote to Sir R. Palmer[2]—M. Chevalier—Mrs Cardwell —Mr Fortescue—Ld Clarendon—Supt G.W.R. (Chester)—D. of Argyll—Ld Chancellor—Mr Hammond—Bp of Winchester—C.G. —and minutes. Saw Mr Robinson. Read Life of Father Paul[3]— Antony & Cleopatra—Boissard on Dante—Rejected Addresses.[4]

22. Fr.

Ch. 8½ AM. Wrote to Supt G.W.R. Chester—Ld Clarendon—Ld Meath—Rev Dr Monsell—C.G.—Mrs Thistlethwayte—Mr Ouvry —and minutes. C. brought Herbert home successfully. Two hours walk with Mr Burnett on the lower portion of the Aston property. Read Antony & Cleopatra—Boissard on Dante—Jesse's Memorials of London.[5]

To LORD CLARENDON, foreign secretary,   Clarendon MSS, c. 498.
22 April 1870.

I do not understand what Odo Russell means when he states that by giving our support to the French note (such as it is) we damage the minority by recognising the Ecumenicity of the Council. We recognise nothing, to my knowledge, except that the Council is a power; of course a moral power, *bien entendu* that in such matter moral includes immoral. However the Note is not worth much pen & ink.

With regard to the Land Bill I think if they will let it pass ('they' meaning

[1] *Dublin Review*, xiv. 451, 347 (April).
[2] Palmer had sent a memorandum on the Fowler amndt. to the Land Bill (see 7, 9 Apr. 70); he agreed to give way; see Selborne, II, i. 145 ff.
[3] See 10 May 69n.   [4] See 19 Nov. 41.
[5] J. H. Jesse, *London and its celebrities*, 2v. (1850).

R. Palmer & others on our side) it will succeed. But whether it succeeds or not it will radically change the relative positions of England & Ireland in point of right & wrong, & therefore, apart from success it is (I think) worth every effort, & every sacrifice. With regard to the menace[1] the case stood thus on the principal occasion that of Fawcett. First I learn from Glyn the state of the House & what is necessary in order to win. His language on that night was most explicit: defeat & disgrace on our side, escape on the other from both. There was time to consult the colleagues on the bench. Nothing could be more marked than their assent; & their cheers through which when I spoke they managed to speak too. On the second occasion that of Fawcett's motion, the necessity was reported to me in the same way but only at the last moment. And you will remember that in Cabinet we had carefully gone over the concessions to be made & had not included this. My language was more veiled than before: but the division could not have been saved without it. Do not however suppose I am insensible that this use of neck-or-nothing remedies is a great calamity. It is playing the last card. I hope we shall not again be placed in the position of 1866. If we are the result will be the same, the passing of a stronger measure, for which Disraeli *this time* has kept himself quite open.

I must not conclude without thanking you much.

23. Sat.

Ch. 8½ A.M. Wrote to Bishop of Brechin—Sir Thos G. (2)—Mr Glyn —Mr Burnett—and minutes. Read Dublin Rev. on Jurors—On Education Bill[2]—Antony & Cleopatra: the closing part is very wonderful—Jesse's London. We cut down a great ash. Saw Mr Burnett —Mr [T. T.] Griffith (of Wrexham).

24. 1 S.E.

Broughton Ch 10½ A.M. (& H.C.)—Mr Evans excellent. Hn Ch. evg. Wrote to M. Dormiel[3]—A.E. West—& minutes. Read Boissard (finished)—Testament de Lacordaire (finished)—Alford's Sermon on Suffragans[4]—and other Tracts.

25. M. St Mark [London].

Packed &c. Off at 8.10. Reached H.C. at 3. Wrote to Mr Robertson MP. —Mr Fortescue—The Queen—Mr Cardwell—C.G.—and minutes.

---

[1] Clarendon complained on 21 April 1870, Add MS 44134, f. 188, 'these quasi-menaces [to get the bill through] have done harm, i.e. they have been used in justification of an ill humour that pre-existed'.

[2] *Dublin Review*, xiv. 430 (April 1870).

[3] Possibly of Messrs. Dormeuil, London silk merchants.

[4] H. *Alford, 'The compacted body . . . with an appendix on . . . Suffragan bishops' (1870).

Saw Duke of Norfolk and R.C. Deputation[1]—Sir R. Palmer—Mr Glyn—Sol.Gen. Ireland—Mr Crawford—Mr Rathbone—Chancr of Ex.—Sir J. Hanmer. Dined with Mr West. H of C. $4\frac{1}{2}$-$8\frac{3}{4}$ and $9\frac{3}{4}$-$1\frac{1}{2}$.[2] Read Stanhope.[3]

26. Tu.

Wrote to Sir F. Grant—Ld Granville—Sol. General—Mr Johnstone MP.—Scotts—Mr J. Cowen jun.[4]—Mr Burnett—Mrs Thistlethwayte —The Queen—& minutes. Saw Mr Glyn—Scotts—Ld de Grey— Mr Lefevre—Sol. General—Sol.Gen. Ireld—Mr Fortescue—Dr Clark: at some length: to whom I mentioned the 'consciousness' in the left leg. Read Stanhope. H of C. $4\frac{1}{2}$-$8\frac{1}{4}$ and 9-$12\frac{1}{2}$. Spoke on Colonial Policy.[5]

27. Wed.

Wrote to The Viceroy—Mr R. Barker—Scotts—C.G.—The Queen —and minutes. H of C. 1-3. Spoke on Marriage (Wife's Sister) Bill.[6] Cabinet 3-$5\frac{1}{4}$. Saw Rev. Dr Irons—D. of Argyll—Mr Glyn—Ld Clarendon—Saw Hartmann, & others. Dined at Ld Ashburnham's.

Cabinet Ap 27. 70. 3 PM.[7]
√ 1. Greek Brigands—Telegrams approved.[8] See Report to H.M. Agreed that the amount of Greek responsibility is not yet clearly ascertained.
√ 2. Land Bill amendments. Approved—notice to be given.
√ 3. Public Schools. Hughes's motion. Sir J. Coleridge's letter & plan approved.[9]
√ 4. Eccl[esiastical] Titles. Lords? Yes. Ld Kimberley to introduce. Chancellor to consider words for a Preamble.
√ 5. Next Cabinet. not on Saturday.
√ 6. Newdigate's Motion.[10] state of the case reported.
√ 7. Burials Bill.

[1] Papers in Add MS 44426, f. 152.
[2] Misc. bills: *H* cc. 1781.   [3] See 21 Mar. 70.
[4] Joseph *Cowen, 1831-1900; radical M.P. Newcastle 1873-86; see 4 Dec. 71.
[5] Opposing R. Torrens' motion for a select cttee.: *H* cc. 1898.
[6] Supporting, for the first time, the dissenters' bill: *H* cc. 1922.
[7] Add MS 44638, f. 67.
[8] Lord and Lady Muncaster and a party of tourists were seized by brigands at Oropós (see 18 Dec. 58) on 11 April; Muncaster and the ladies were sent to treat for a ransom, the brigands killing several British hostages on 21 April. Gladstone believed 'the newspapers except D. News . . . most precipitate & unjustifiable abt. the Greek Govt.' (to Clarendon, 26 April 1870, Add MS 44538, f. 135). The Queen was much alarmed; Guedalla, *Q*, i. 226. See also Jenkins, *The Dilessi Murders*, ch. 3.
[9] *Hughes' motion allowed non-anglicans to be governors of leading public schools: *H* cci. 193, 1683.
[10] On convents, see 2 Apr., 2 May 70 and *H* cc. 2025.

28. Th.

Wrote to Mr Cowan—Ld Clarendon—Dr Clark—The Queen—and minutes. Seven to breakfast. Saw Provost of Oriel—Mr Childers—Mr Glyn—Mr Rathbone—Mr Forster—Prince of Wales. Rode in R[otten] R[ow]. Read Reports &c. on Irish Land. H of C. 4½-8 and 9-1.[1]

To LORD CLARENDON, foreign secretary,   Clarendon MSS, c. 498.
28 April 1870.

Though I did not expect or desire that you would refer to the Cabinet the question whether Odo Russell should give a written as well as a verbal support to the French Note at Rome,[2] reflection leads me to think myself right in the belief that it would not be desirable that he should *separate* from the others & exhibit an apparent schism, or what might be represented as such, in the face of the Roman Court. But on the other hand it occurs to me to suggest whether you might not instruct Odo Russell to take some opportunity of signifying that we did not enter directly or indirectly into the question of Ecumenicity, which is one far beyond us, but simply viewed the Assembly at Rome, under the Pope, as one having *de facto* power to exercise a great influence over a large portion of the Christian world.[3] I am afraid the French new constitution is in its root a sham, whether so meant or not.

29. Fr.

Wrote to Ld Clarendon—Mrs Th.—Ld Listowel—Mrs Bennett—Ld Granville—& minutes. H. of C. 4½-8½.[4] Saw Bp of Winchester—Mr Glyn—Ld Granville. Rode in R.R. Dined with Sir W. James. Saw Maurice. X. Read Stanhope—and Campbell on Irish Land.[5]

30. Sat.

Wrote to Mr Glyn—Sec. New Brunsw.Hist.Soc.[6]—Ld Granville—J. Watson—Lady Herbert—Mr Ayrton—Viceroy of Irel.—and minutes. Saw Dr A. Clark—Rev. Dr Monsell—Prince of Wales—Saw Vernon X. Went 2-5 to the Exhibition: enjoyed it much: the monkeys threw me into rapture: conversation & instruction of the artists, as ever, delightful.[7] At the dinner, which was followed by

[1] Irish land: *H* cc. 1969.
[2] Clarendon told Gladstone, 28 April 1870, Add MS 44134, f. 196: 'I am sorry you did not expect or desire that I should consult the Cabt. as to whether Odo Russell should give a written as well as a verbal support to the French note, but I really did not see that any other course was open to me....'
[3] This far docketed, 'Copy to Odo'.
[4] Spoke on progress of business and the Education Bill: *H* cc. 2096.
[5] See 11 Aug. 69.   [6] Letter untraced.
[7] *The Times*, 2 May 1870, 10e. He referred to monkeys in his speech to the Royal Academy.

delightful glees, from 6 to near 12—Returned thanks for Ministers.
Read Constitutio Dogmatica[1]—Webster on Time of H. of C.[2] Wrote
down an imagined *ultimatum* on the Education Bill.[3]

3 S.E. May One 1870.

Chapel Royal mg (with H.C.) and All Saints aftn. Saw Ld Hartington
—Sir J. Ogilvy—Mrs Th.—Ld Morley—Lady Lothian—The Pri-
mate—Mr West. Wrote to The Dean of Windsor—Ld Granville—
Mr Liddon—Mr Herbert RA. Read Perowne on the Psalms[4]—Hun-
tington's Church Idea[5]—Booth on Lord's Supper[6]—Job, Animal
Magnetism[7]—Greek Massacre Papers.[8]

2. M.

Wrote to Ld Clarendon—Sol.Gen.Engl.—Chancr of Exr—Bp of
Winchester—The Queen—& minutes. Read M. Bernard on Am[eri-
ca]n War.[9] Rode with Agnes. Saw Mr Glyn. Dined with the Wests.
H of C. 4½–8 and 9–2. Irish Land & Conventual Instns Inquiry.[10]

3. Tu.

Wrote to Chancr of Exr—The Queen (2)—Mr Bright—Mr Ouvry
—Robn G.—The P. of Wales—& minutes. Saw Dr Clark—Mr Glyn
—Mr R. Barker—Mr Ayrton—Mr Samuelson. Rode with Agnes. H.
of C. 4½–8 and 9¼–1.[11] Read Lythgoe on Metrop. RR.[12]—Montagu
Bernard.

4. Wed.

Wrote to Bp of Manchester—Mr Kinnaird—Mr Hammond—The
Queen (Mem.)—Mrs Thistlethwayte—Dean of Westminster—Mr
E.M. Barry—Mr Ayrton—and minutes. Dined at Grillion's. Levee
(P. of Wales). Saw Ld Clarendon—Mr Tupper—Mr Glyn—Count

---

[1] *Costituzione dommatica riguardante la Fede Cattolica*, published for third session of the Council, 24 April 1870.
[2] E. Webster, *The public and private business of the House of Commons* (1868).
[3] Not found.   [4] J. J. S. *Perowne, *The Book of Psalms*, trs. (1870 ed.).
[5] See 19 Apr. 70.   [6] J. Booth, *The Lord's Supper, a feast after sacrifice* (1870).
[7] M. J. Job, 'Can it cure? A treatise on animal magnetism, or electricity' (1867).
[8] *PP* 1870, lxx. 465.   [9] See 6 Apr. 70.
[10] Clause 3; *Palmer withdrew his opposition to the 31 year lease limit: *H* cci. 26; Gladstone secured modified terms of reference for the conventual select cttee.; ibid. 80.
[11] French treaty, select cttee. defeated: *H* cci. 176.
[12] J. P. Lythgoe, but report untraced.

Cadorna—Mr Gurdon. Made sick calls in aftn—also saw Vernon's friend[R]. Read Garibaldi's Clelia.[1]

5. Th.

Wrote to Dean of Windsor—Mr Kinnaird—Mr Cardwell—V.C. of Oxford—The Queen—Messrs Watson (also Telegram)—Count de Lomas[2]—Bp of Colombo—& minutes. Dined with West. H of C. $4\frac{1}{2}$-8 and 9-$1\frac{1}{4}$.[3] Saw Mr Fortescue—Mr MacColl—Mr Glyn—Mr Herbert—Mr S. Cooper[4]—Christie's—Ld Granville. Read Garibaldi's Clelia—Sir J. Hay's statement.[5]

6. Frid.

Kept my bed till 6 P.M. Wrote to Mr C. Villiers—G.G. Glyn—Robn G.—The Queen—& minutes. Saw Mr Gurdon—Mr Glyn. Went over to dine with Lucy and H of C. $8\frac{3}{4}$-1.[6] Read Garibaldi's Clelia—Stanhope's Hist.—Future Church of Scotland.[7]

7. Sat.

Rose at one. Saw Dr Clark. Wrote to Mrs Thistlethwayte—Sir J. Elphinstone—Mr Chalk—Mr Kinnaird—The Queen (2) and minutes. Saw Sir W. Mansfield—Mr Glyn (2). Read Dryden's Hind & Panther[8] —Garibaldi's Clelia. Cabinet $2\frac{1}{2}$-$6\frac{1}{4}$. Up to bed at $7\frac{1}{2}$: a dinner party and evening party were given of wh the whole burden fell on C. & Willy.

Cabinet D. St. May 7. 70. 2½ PM.[9]
√ Greek murders. 1. C[larendon]'s letter to Braila approved as amended—
  2. Instructions respecting aid for Mr Erskine—3. Palmer's motion—premature.[10]
O Red River Reports.
O Irish Land Bill progress
√ Lectionary. Bill in Lords. To be introduced forthwith.
√ Eccl. Titles Bill. Draft considered & agreed on.

---

[1] G. Garibaldi, *Clelia. Il Governo del Monaco. Roma nel secolo XIX* (1870).
[2] Untraced.   [3] Irish Land Bill clause 4: *H* cci. 290.
[4] (Thomas) Sidney *Cooper, 1803-1902, artist.
[5] Sir J. C. D. Hay, *Memorandum. Rear-Admiral . . . Hay's compulsory retirement from the British Navy* (1870).
[6] Misc. business: *H* cci. 330.   [7] Not found.
[8] See 11 Dec. 40.   [9] Add MS 44638, f. 68.
[10] R. R. *Palmer eventually only made 'Observations': *H* cci. 1123 (20 May 1870). The cabinet were under strong press pressure for a Palmerstonian reaction; see Jenkins, *The Dilessi murders*, 80 ff.

○ Revision of Authorised Version.

√ Woman's Franchise Bill. Support Bouverie: without making a Cabinet question.[1]

√ Election Procedure Bill considered.

Week's business

√ Paragraph from the Gaulois. C[larendon] will cause to be contradicted.[2]

√ Dr. Livingstone: a limited advance.[3]

√ New Zealand Guarantee. Cardwell Lowe Bruce reluctant or opposed. Approved or allowed, in principle.[4]

√ R.C. Chaplains in Workhouses

√ Ld Shaftesbury's Bill [on] Eccl. Courts. Not to go, he says, beyond 2 R[eading]. Eyed askance.[5]

8. 3 S.E.

Saw Dr Clark who bound me to House & bed. Read M. Prayers. Read Garden on Mr Hibbert's Bill[6]—Parker's Life—an awful and solemn close[7]—Dryden Religio Laici,[8] & finished Hind & Panther—Woodford Report. Saw Ld Granville. Up for 3 hours in the evg.

9. M.

Up at 10. Wrote to Mrs Thistlethwayte—Dean of Windsor—Scotts —Sir W. Jenner—Ld Granville—Mr Weld Blundell—Bp of Lincoln —Viceroy of I.—The Queen (2)—and minutes. Saw Mr Glyn—Mr Forster—Mr Cardwell—Sir R. Palmer. H of C. $4\frac{1}{2}$-$8\frac{1}{4}$ and $9\frac{1}{4}$-2.[9] Dined with the Wests. Read Clelia.

To C. WORDSWORTH, bishop of Lincoln,   Add MS 44538, f. 143.
9 May 1870.

    I am quite willing to bring under consideration of the Cabinet the question of empowering the ritual commission to deal with the subject of proper Psalms:[10] but I think my Colleagues would desire that the subject should be brought before them if not by the Convocation by some combination of the Bishops,

[1] E. P. Bouverie successfully moved the cttee. sit in six months: *H* cci. 607 (12 May 1870).   [2] Not found.

[3] *Livingstone had journied west from Ujiji; *Stanley began his 'rescue' from Zanzibar in January 1871.

[4] Britain tried to reduce New Zealand's guaranteed loan from £1 million to £500,000, but eventually guaranteed the whole; see Ramm I, i. 99n. 2.

[5] *Shaftesbury's bill's $2°$R had been postponed on 17 March; $2°$R on 21 July: *H* cciii. 614.

[6] F. *Garden, *Can an ordained man become a layman? Some remarks on Mr Hibbert's Bill* (1870).

[7] See 22 Dec. 69.   [8] See 11 Dec. 40.

[9] Parlt. Elections Bill $1°$R: *H* cci. 431.

[10] Wordsworth's request at Add MS 44346, f. 397.

presumably speaking for the whole body, before they should at this late period alter the scope of the Commissioners Inquiries.

It would I think be difficult further to postpone our proceeding upon the Lectionary report, not only on general grounds but because we are informed that the suspension of employment in printing Prayer books & Church Services has caused much distress.

10. Tu.

Wrote to Ld Sydney—Bp of London—Mr Bruce—Bp of Lincoln —Bp of Rochester—Archbp of Canterb.—The Queen—and minutes. Saw Prince of Wales—Mr Glyn—Ld Granville—Mr Monsell—Scots (Glasgow) Depn on Edn[1]—Bp of Saint Asaph.[2] Rode with Helen. H of C. 4½-8 and 9-12¾.[3] Read Clelia.

To C. WORDSWORTH, bishop of Lincoln,   Add MS 44538, f. 143.
10 May 1870. 'Private.'

Without prejudice to what was stated in my letter of yesterday, it occurs to me that if the Ritual Commission are able & disposed to move in the matter of the Psalter, & to move promptly it might be practicable to have a report from them in time to amend a Lectionary Bill on its passage through the Houses so as to bring it the psalms. But the Bishops advising it must make themselves responsible I suppose for adopting a change of that kind without giving the Clergy in Convocation an opportunity of utterance upon it.

11. Wed.

Wrote to Ld Clarendon—Mr Ouvry—The Queen (2)—and minutes. 12-1. At Opening of London Univ. Building by H.M.[4] Saw Sir W. Jenner—Mr Glyn—Conclave on I.L. Amendments—Welsh Clergy Deputn—National Soc. Depn[5]—Ld de Grey—Mrs Thistlethwayte. 10-1¼. Royal Concert at B. Palace. Read Clelia—Bernard on Amn War.

12. Th.

Wrote to Ld Clarendon—Dean of Windsor—Lord Stair[6]—Mr T.B.

---

[1] No account found.
[2] Joshua Hughes, the new bp.
[3] Misc. business: *H* cci. 480.
[4] *The Times*, 12 May 1870, 9d.
[5] See *The Times*, 12 May 1870, 9c: 'Mr Gladstone expressed no opinion on the view which the deputation impressed upon him.'
[6] John Hamilton Dalrymple, 1819-1903; liberal M.P. Wigtown 1841-56; 10th earl of Stair 1864.

Potter—D. of Argyll—Lord Granville—Mr Boxall[1]—The Queen—
and minutes. Eleven to breakfast. Read Clelia. 12–1¼. Meeting of R.
Commn at Marlborough House.[2] The O. Fitzgerald wedding breakfast afr.[3] Saw Ld Granville—Rev Mr Gurden[4]—Mr Glyn—Count
Jarnac—The Prince of Wales. Dined with Mr West. H of C. 4½–8¼
and 9¼–2. We threw out the Woman's Franchise Bill.[5]

13. Fr.

Wrote to Duchess of Sutherland—Ch.J. Whiteside—The Queen—
and minutes. Saw Mr Glyn—Att. General and others. Quakers'
Deputn on Edn—Architects' Depn on the case of Mr. Barry.[6] Read
Clelia—Papers on Greek murders. 11–1. Discussion with Ld de Grey
& Mr Forster on Edn Bill Amendments. Very grave.[7]

14. Sat.

Wrote to Lord Spencer—Ed. Daily News[8]—Mr Ayrton—Mr For-
tescue—Scotts—The Queen—& minutes. Read Lewis's letters.[9]
Rode with Helen. Cabinet 2¾–6¾. Saw Ld Lyttelton—Ld De Tabley
—Mr Glyn—Mr Leeman—Ld Dunraven—Baron Bernstorff—Ld
Bessborough—Count Apponyi. Dined at Mr Fortescue's. The Duchess
of Marlborough's afterwards.

Cabinet May 14 2.30 PM[10]
Order of business in H. of C.

Cabinet May 14. 2.30 PM.[11]
√ Sir R. Palmer as to enabling Corporate & Trust bodies to invest in mortgage.
   Referred to Ld. Chancellor.
√ Lord Mayor's dinner—what day in July. Sat 23.
√ Road through St James's Park. Mr Ayrton to report on modes of.[12]

[1] (Sir) William *Boxall, 1800–79; directed National Gallery 1865–74; kt. 1871.
[2] Of the 1851 commissioners, planning 1871 International Exhibition; *The Times*, 14
May 1870, 12c.
[3] Marriage of Lord O. Fitzgerald's step-da., Ursula Elizabeth Denison, to George Cockburn Dickinson, anglican priest.
[4] William Gurden, vicar of Westbury from 1817.
[5] He supported Bouverie's amndt. to put off the Bill for six months: *H* cci. 618. See
7 May 70.
[6] Not found.   [7] See 21 May 70.
[8] On an article on disestablishment. Add MSS 44538, f. 146, 44426, f. 214.
[9] Sir G. C. *Lewis, *Letters . . . to various friends*, ed. Sir G. F. Lewis (1870).
[10] Add MS 44638, f. 72.   [11] Ibid., f. 73.
[12] Gladstone asked Ayrton for information: 'The Cabinet were like me rather taken by
surprise'; Add MS 44538, f. 146. Queries in Add MS 44759, f. 98.

√ Sugar refiners—see over[1]
√ Greek murders. Ld Clarendon's draft, inviting the Powers to cooperate. Postponed
√ Complimentary mission of Corps Diplomatique to French Emperor. Reserves in assent to Telegram. To be made clearly known to French Govt. & Emperor.[2]
√ Naturalisation Treaty. Signature announced. Dispatch of Ld C[larendon] approved by Chancellor.
√ Ld de Grey. Keble College Charter.[3] (Chancr. reported parties willing to run the risk of coming under the Bill). inquiries to be made [by] Ld de G[rey] as to the footing of the Undertaking in relation to the University.
√ Univ. [Tests] Bill to be read 2° on 23d.
√ Motion on Tuesday respecting Emigration to the Colonies. Oppose.
√ New Zealand Loan Guarantee. Dispatch to Commissioners agreed on, taking notice of the terms as well as amount.[4]
√ Refiners to be relieved in respect of their stock of high duty Sugar.
√ Change made by Lords in War Office Bill to be acquiesced in.
√ Camperdown Report. No steps this year: will be weighed in the Autumn.[5]

15. 4 S.E.

Chapel Royal mg: the Abbey evg, where Mr Body[6] preached with much power but over strained his physical force. Wrote to Dean of Windsor—Sir Thos G.—Ld Clarendon—Mrs Thistlethwayte—Dean of Chichester—Ld Chancellor. Saw Sir W. James—Mr E. Talbot—Bp of London—Ld Lyttelton. Read Maude.[7]

To LORD CLARENDON, foreign secretary,   Clarendon MSS, c. 498.
15 May 1870.

I really am not ill pleased with the efforts of Mr. Fish to wriggle out of the Alabama (retrospective) controversy,[8] & I hope you will be able as Thornton recommends to avoid any further elucidation of the question of official or non-official. This may give us a little fund of strength & credit to spend upon the Red River question in encouraging them to be strict against Fenian Sympathisers.

---

[1] See third last item.
[2] Clarendon to Lyons, 14 May 1870, Clarendon MSS c. 474: 'The cabinet are greatly annoyed at the diplomatic congratulations to the Emperor on the Plebiscite', if the address is inevitable, see it 'contains nothing approving the *plebiscite power* as part of the Constitution. . . .' See 14 Apr. 70.
[3] Charter by incorporation, dated 6 June 1870; see 17 Apr. 70.
[4] See 7 May 70.
[5] On naval victualling yards: *PP* 1870 xlvi. 397.
[6] G. Body of Wolverhampton's sermon was 'marked by a singular disregard of pulpit conventions'; *The Guardian*, 18 May 1870, 568.
[7] See 14 July 59.
[8] Reported in Thornton to Clarendon, 3 May 1870, Clarendon MSS, c. 481, forwarded on 15 May, Add MS 44134, f. 201, also enclosing a letter from Lord Russell who 'sniffs mischief'.

In the Milmore-Peabody matter I think we must draw further upon Thornton's kindness for advice.[1]

No doubt you will require all your skill & tact in managing the Greek question with Russia: unless you like to hand it over to Lord Russell's 'boldness' to conduct.

16. M.

Wrote to Ld St Germans—Editor D. News[2]—Rev. Mr Dale[3]—Duke of Cambridge—Watsons—Lord de Grey—Mr Richard MP—The Queen—& minutes. Saw Mrs Welby Pugin[4]—Ld Granville—Mr Glyn —Sir Hamn Seymour[5]—Ld Granville—Sir R.M. Alcock—A. Kinnaird—Conclave at Treas. $3\frac{1}{2}$ on Competn & Office Organisn.[6] Dined with West. H of C. $4\frac{1}{2}$-9 and 10-$12\frac{1}{2}$.[7] Rode with Helen. Read Greek Papers—Clelia.

To EARL DE GREY, lord president, 16 May 1870.   Add MS 43514, f. 10.

When I saw you with Forster on Friday about the proposed Amendments to the Education Bill, I was not at all prepared, from anything that had previously happened, for the important provisions limiting and defining in certain respects the powers of the Local Boards as to religious instruction; and, in making upon them such remarks as occurred to me at the moment, I failed to take into view what I may call the previous question.

Without at all abating my sense of the gravity of the subject matter of these provisions, I am strongly of the opinion, in which I think you and Forster may be disposed to concur, that we ought not to tender any new proposal, going beyond those which we have promised, in the difficult point of placing restraints on religious instruction, without having much stronger reason to anticipate, than we now possess, that it will be accepted and therefore final.

The limited channel in which the debate ran on the second reading, and the silence (with very few exceptions) of the Conservative party up to this time, have very much narrowed our means of estimating the real state of opinion, and balance of forces, in the House of Commons.

The particular method of adjustment, which is proposed on the printed sheet, is one for which no one has asked. It is dangerous for a Government to propose an amendment, in the most difficult part of the Bill, which has neither been solicited nor announced. If the course of the debate on the Speaker's leaving the Chair, and the tenor of the information which may *then* be expected to flow in

[1] Disagreements about proposed statue of Peabody by M. Milmore, American sculptor; Thornton to Clarendon, 18 April 1870, Clarendon MSS, c. 481.

[2] See 14 May 70.

[3] Thomas Pelham Dale, 1821-92, ritualistic rector of St. Vedast 1847-81; on d. of his fa., T. *Dale (see 5 June 36); Add MS 44538, f. 147.

[4] Louisa, widow of A. W. N. *Pugin.

[5] Probably, though not knighted, George Hamilton Seymour, 1797-1880, retired diplomat.

[6] Arrangements for treasury minute of 25 May 1870, opening competition and reforming the office; M. Wright, *Treasury control of the civil service* (1969), 33-4.

[7] Spoke on Irish Land Bill; *H* cci. 759.

much more copiously, should point to this particular solution, the plan would then have acquired at all events increased title to consideration, by all those who were open to accept its principle: and few probably would doubt that spontaneous demand for it, or a state of things in which this would be thought generally obvious as the fairest meeting point for conflicting claims, could be a very weighty element in the case.

Whether our Bill, with the amendments indicated on the Second Reading, can be satisfactorily carried, may not be certain: but I see no reason at all to believe that in this altered form it would have any more certain prospects. But indeed I must go further, and say that I think the Government would expose itself to censure, and would greatly impair its own authority and moral weight, if, after having very deliberately announced certain amendments at the close of a long debate, it were without previous notice thus vitally to alter their effect: and indeed, as matter of personal honour and feeling, and as having been the person to declare the intention of the Government, I do not very well see how I could enter into this proceeding; though it is not any personal difficulty but the general bearings of this part of the case which I took pen in hand to present to your view.

Pray let Forster see this.[1]

17. Tu.

Wrote to Bp of Winchester—Dean of Windsor—Sol. General—Mr Fortescue—Duc d'Aumale—Sir R. Palmer—The Queen—Mrs Thistlethwayte—and minutes. Saw Wilson X. Saw Mr Glyn—Solicitor General—H of C. $4\frac{1}{4}$-$8\frac{1}{2}$.[2] Read Reply to Mrs Fawcett[3]—Lewis's Letters—Garibaldi's Clelia.

18. Wed.

Wrote to Ld Chancellor—Mast. St Joh.Camb.[4]—Ld Kimberley—Sir R. Palmer—& minutes. Evening party at home. Saw Sir Thos Bazley—Mr Gurdon—Mr Glyn—Ld Chancellor—Dr Ball—Mr Cardwell—Ld Derby—Mr Motley—D. of Argyll—Judge Lawson[5]—Ld Westbury. Audience of the Queen at Windsor: where I attended the Council. Middle Temple dinner $5\frac{3}{4}$-$10\frac{3}{4}$. Returned Thanks for the Ministers.[6] Read Clelia—A spice of Lothair[7]—Greek papers.

[1] De Grey replied, 19 May 1870, Add MS 44286, f. 88, denying the proposed amndt. to clauses 14, 17 and 22 were original or unexpected.

[2] India: H cci. 825.

[3] *The Grosvenor papers: female suffrage, an answer to Mrs H. Fawcett on the electoral disabilities of women* (1870).

[4] William Henry Bateson, 1812-81; master of St. John's, Cambridge, from 1857.

[5] James Anthony *Lawson, 1817-87; liberal; former Irish law officer; judge in Ireland 1868.

[6] No report found.

[7] By *Disraeli, published on 2 May; *Tenniel's famous cartoon of Gladstone reading *Lothair* and *Disraeli, *Juventus Mundi*, was published in *Punch* on 14 May 1870.

Windsor May 18. 70.[1]
Ecclesiastical Titles, Chancr. Mem.—Greek murder, Greek people—Mr Ayrton.

19. Th.

13 to breakfast. Wrote to Archbp of York—Ld Chancellor—Ld
Clarendon—The Queen—and minutes. Saw Rev. Mr Bellairs—Sir R.
Palmer—Mr Glyn—Bp of Chester—Mr Robinson—Sol. General—
Mr C. Forster. Dined at the Wests. Rode with H. H of C. $4\frac{1}{2}$-8 and
9-$12\frac{3}{4}$: Irish Land Bill.[2] Finished Clelia.

20. Fr.

Wrote to Duke of Devonshire—Dr Döllinger—Lord Mayor—The
Queen—and minutes. Saw Mr H. Farquhar—Rev. M. MacColl—Mr
Glyn. Saw Vernon. H. of C. $4\frac{1}{2}$-8 and $10\frac{1}{2}$-3. Spoke on the Greek
Murders: and on various subjects.[3] Dined with the Brownlows. She
retains all her charms of character as well as person.[4] Read Lothair:
Ld C.J's Letter to Ld Chancr on Judicature.[5]

21. Sat.

The King of the Belgians breakfasted: a party of 13 all included. He
was even over kind. Wrote to Rev. J. Lockhart Ross—Sir Th. Bazley
—Sir Thos G.—Bp of Rochester—Mr Holms MP.[6]—Mr Ayrton—
Sol. General—The Queen—& minutes. Saw Mr Glyn (2)—Ld
Clarendon—Mr Hammond—Sir P. Braila. Cabinet $2\frac{3}{4}$-$6\frac{1}{4}$. Dined
with the Morleys. Mad. Bernstorff's after. Read Lothair. Saw Mad.
Charles.[7]

Cabinet 10 D. St. May 21. 70. 2½ PM.[8]
√ Irish Land Bill. Report Thurs?
√ Education Bill Amendments. Print as to 1. Time Table Clause. 2. Election of
Boards.

[1] Add MS 44757, f. 16.   [2] *H* cci. 976.
[3] *H* cci. 1152, replying to Palmer's observations. Gladstone told *Clarendon (19 May
1870, Add MS 44538, f. 149): 'Palmer has been here today, & says Carnarvon is resolved
to go on [in the Lords]. This being so unless I hear from you to the contrary, I shall not ask
Palmer to put off again.'
[4] See 30 Oct. 63.
[5] Sir A. J. E. Cockburn, 'Our judicial system. A letter to the Lord High Chancellor'
(1870).
[6] John Holms, 1830-91; manufacturer and liberal M.P. Hackney 1868-85; minor office
1880-5.
[7] Rescue?   [8] Add MS 44638, f. 76.

√ Bishops in House of Lords. Oppose.
√ Contagious diseases. Commission in lieu of Mr Fowler's Bill.[1]
√ Budget Bills; next to Navy Estimates.
√ Game Bill. Wed[nesda]y. Oppose Mr Taylor. Thursday
√ Maclaren Scotch Church.
√ Irish Land Bill. Augment the Salaries in the Bill? Promise it next year.
√ Mr Ayrton's Road. WEG to write.[2]
√ Census inquiries.
√ Keble College Charter. To proceed.
√ Act of Uniformity & service in College Chapels. Question stands over.
√ Alabama. Was the Mem[orandu]m official? Clarendon's dispatch read & approved, passing by the question whether the Memn. was 'official'.[3]
√ Greek comm[unication]s. state of
√ Is the Suez Canal Route to be contemplated as available during Wars? Committee of Cabinet to inquire.[4] Clarendon—Granville—Childers—Cardwell—Kimberley.
√ Scottish Valuation Bill. Bruce will speak to the Lord Advocate.

Business. Before Whitsuntide[5]
1. Irish Land. Through. 2. Univ. Tests. 2d R[eading]. 3. Budget Bill. 4. Navy Estimates. Building Vote. HOPE to adjourn Thursday. it may be Friday.

22. 5 S.E.

Chapel Royal mg and St James's Evg. Wrote to Lord Chancellor—Mr Cardwell—Mr J. Ball—Mr Bellairs—Ld Clarendon. Read Phillips on Wales[6]—Bagdon on Angl. & Gk Churches[7]—Blenkinsopp on Development.[8] Finished Maude. Saw Mrs Th. Walk with C.

23. M.

Wrote to Sol. General—C. J. Whiteside—Bp of B. & W.—Robn G. —Lord Granville—D. of Argyll—Dean of Ferns—Ld Sydney— Dean of Windsor—D. of St Alban's—Dean of Wells—The Queen— and minutes. Rode with Mary. Saw Mr H. Farquhar—Mr Forster— Mr Glyn. H of C. $4\frac{1}{2}$-8 and $11\frac{1}{4}$-$1\frac{1}{4}$. Spoke on Univ. Tests Bill.[9] Dined at Marlborough House. Curious conversation with Mrs. Lowe. The

---

[1] W. N. Massey's royal commission on the acts reported in *PP* 1871 xix.
[2] See 14 May 70 and Add MS 44538, f. 150.
[3] Clarendon's 'Observations' of 6 November 1869, published in *PP* 1870 lxix. 453; their status questioned by Fish.
[4] See 28 May 70.
[5] This section is encircled; other undated lists of bills in progress are on Add MS 44638, f. 78. Committee's report not found.
[6] See 20 Feb. 70.
[7] J. O. Bagdon, *A brief comparison of the fundamental doctrines of the Anglican and Greek Churches* (1869).
[8] E. C. L. Blenkinsopp, *The doctrine of development* (1869).   [9] *H* cci. 1225.

Prince swims with the stream & wishes for institutions curtailed in Greece. Read Lothair.

To LORD CLARENDON, foreign secretary,   Clarendon MSS, c. 498.
23 May 1870.

I agree in thinking that a cautious answer should be given to the French Telegram respecting Greece.[1] For my own part I have not yet arrived at the belief that Brigandage in Greece has been owing to the free institutions of that country; & if we are driven to such a conclusion, I hope it will be upon very clear evidence; for we shall be smartly challenged for it in Parliament. But I suppose we may thank them, & promise to communicate as soon as the facts shall be so presented to us as to give us any clear connected view of causes & remedies.

24. Tu.

Wrote to Ld Chancellor—Mr Brand—The Queen—and minutes. H of C. $4\frac{1}{2}$-8 and $9\frac{1}{2}$-$11\frac{3}{4}$. Spoke on Welsh Church.[2] Saw Mr MacColl—Mr Glyn—Sir R. Palmer—Sol.Gen. Ireland—Sir W. Wynn—Lord Granville. Saw Vivian X. Read Lothair—Noted down queries on Education[3]—Twelve to dinner.

25. Wed.

Wrote to Dean Ramsay—Dean of Windsor—Ld de Grey—Lord Chancellor—Mrs Thistlethwayte—& minutes. The afternoon was occupied with five successive deputations on the Educn Bill.[4] Saw Mr MacColl—Rev. Mr Glyn—Count Bernstorff. Finished Lothair. Saw Isaac—Wilson X. Dined at Ld Lurgan's—Dev[onshire] House & Lady Salisbury's afterwards.

26. Th. Ascension Day.

Chapel Royal & H.C. mg. 12-$2\frac{1}{4}$. Wrote to Sir T. Biddulph—Bp of Winchester—The Speaker—Ld Houghton—The Queen—Ld de Grey—and minutes. Read Lewis's Letters.[5] Ten to breakfast. Saw Lord Salisbury—Mr Glyn. At Christie's. H of C. $4\frac{1}{2}$-9 and 10-$1\frac{1}{2}$.[6]

[1] Proposed changes in the Greek constitution; Add MS 44134, f. 208.
[2] Successfully opposing a resolution for its disestablishment: *H* cci. 1291.
[3] Untraced; see 25, 29 May 1870.
[4] From nonconformist M.P.s, Wesleyan ministers, public school headmasters, miscellaneous worthies; *The Times*, 26 May 1870, 5e.
[5] See 14 May 70.
[6] Cttee. stage of Irish Land Bill completed: *H* cci. 1442.

To J. E. DENISON, the Speaker, 26 May 1870.   Add MS 44538, f. 154.

I have received your note.[1] As the power of dismissing strangers is one of our 'ancient institutions,' I should like, if it is not too great a demand, to have a few days to think & talk over the matter, & mention it to the Cabinet (on Sat.) as to the mode of reform, which is to be applied to it. I am not quite clear whether a minority should be absolutely divested of this power; but I shall be teachable in the matter.

27. F.

Wrote to Bp of Winchester—Dean of Chester—Bp of Argyll—Mast. of Balliol—Ld Chancellor, & minutes. Saw Mr Forster—Mr Hope Scott—Mr Glyn—Mr Ayrton. Rode with Agnes. Read Lewis's Letters. Dined at M. Van de Weyers to meet K. of Belgians. H. of C. $4\frac{1}{2}$-8 and $10\frac{3}{4}$-$12\frac{1}{4}$.[2] Saw Isaac[R].

28. Sat.

Wrote to Sol. General—Sir R. Phillimore—Mr Forster—Ld Shaftesbury—Mr Ayrton—Mr Hope Scott—The Queen—and minutes. Saw Mr Glyn—Sir G. Grey—Mr O. Morgan *cum* Mr Richard[3]—The L. Rothschilds (tea)—D of Norfolk—Mr Ayrton—Mr Brand. Cabinet $2\frac{3}{4}$-$5\frac{3}{4}$. Birthday dinner to 29 & an enormous evening party wh K. of the Belgians attended. I went up quite exhausted a little before one. Read Lewis's Letters.

D. St. Cabinet May 28. 2½ PM. 1870.[4]
√ Case of Gen. Gordon.[5] D[uke] of A[rgyll] proposes to recall him. Agreed to.
√ Arr. of business after Whitsuntide. Univ. Tests Bill 13th. Educn. [Bill] 16th
√ Precedence of Bps.[6] There being no R[oman] C[atholic] Bps. in the O[rder] in C[ouncil] now, determined there is no necessity for interference.
√ [Irish] Land Bill. [To be] Read 2° [in] H. of L. on 14th June.
√ Granville reported from the Committee on Mauritius, so far as regards Suez Canal. Cabinet agreed that as between 1. Closing. 2. Open like the sea, with power to fight. 3. Open as harbour (3) was preferable.
√ Clarendon reported on state of the French Ministry: weak.
√ Read dispatch to Paris respecting French Overture on Greek Constitution.[7]
√ Mr Bruce may if he thinks fit agree to Committee on the Game Laws.
√ Order in C[ouncil] for competitive examn. in Civil Service agreed to.

[1] Not found; see 28 May 70.   [2] Misc. business: *H* cci. 1499.
[3] On Welsh university: see Morgan, *Wales in British Politics*, 46.
[4] Add MS 44638, f. 79.
[5] Archibald Gordon, 1812–86; inspector-general of hospitals 1867–1 July 1870.
[6] Draft for order in council on ecclesiastical precedence at Add MS 44638, f. 82 and Add MS 44759, f. 100.
[7] See 23 May 70.

√ Merchant Shipping Bill: Pakington asks [for] a Comm[ittee] on the Bill to take evidence. Offer a Committee on the Clauses; unless Mr Lefevre objects.[1]
√ Lords Report on the Kitchen. C. of E.——Kimberley——Lansdowne——Childers, to confer with Mr Ayrton
√ Kensington Road Consider
√ St James's Park Road
√ Exclusion of strangers from H. of C.[2] Let it alone: But if needful to take some step, appoint a Committee
√ Cardwell's letter fixing relative positions of Sec. of War & commr. of Forces. (to Ld de Grey) agreed to.[3]

29. S.aft Asc.

Chapel Royal mg & Whitehall aft. Wrote to Ld Shaftesbury——Mrs Biddescombe[4]——Mrs Thistlethwayte. Read M'Carthy's Calderon[5]—— An Engl.Cath. on Infallibility.[6] Wrote a Mem. on Education, the Religious difficulty. Saw Mr Glyn. We drove to the Lothians at Clapham Park to dine and spend the evening. Met the Frouds [*sic*].[7]

Rate Provided Schools[8]

Plan I—as in the Bill

The plan of the Bill for Education, as it stands, leaves the local communities, acting through the Boards, to regulate the provision for religious instruction in Rate-provided Schools, with no limitation except that of the timetable Conscience Clause. It is founded on free teaching, and free withdrawal. It however provides religious instruction for *some* at the expense of *all*.

If, by reason of the dissensions to which it may lead, this undeniable characteristic of the plan is to be taken as a conclusive objection to it, the obvious remedy would seem to be the acceptance of the proposition that, in a greatly divided community, public authority should not attempt, by its own direct action, to provide religious instruction, but should be content with giving freedom and facility to private persons, or to the religious bodies to which they belong.

Plan II.

This end would be gained completely, by enacting that no part of the Rate should be applied towards paying the Schoolmaster for religious instruction, or towards providing such instruction in any other manner.

[1] *Pakington withdrew his amndt. for a select cttee., after Gladstone declined a cttee. to take evidence: *H* cci. 2008 (13 June 1870).
[2] See 26 May 70. On Crawfurd's demand, strangers had been excluded from the Commons for the deb. on the Contagious Diseases Acts on 24 May: *H* cci. 1306.
[3] Not found.   [4] Unidentified.   [5] See 27 Mar. 70.
[6] W. Sweetman, *A few thoughts on the infallibility of the Pope* (1870).
[7] J. A. *Froude was then writing *The English in Ireland in the Eighteenth Century* (1872-4).
[8] Initialled and dated 28 May 1870, though apparently written this day; Add MS 44759, f. 104. Marked for circulation to Granville, Glyn, Sir G. Grey. For their comments see Ramm I, i. 100 and Add MS 44162, f. 320.

It would remain in the discretion of the Board to allow individuals or bodies to make arrangements, with the Schoolmaster or otherwise, for such instruction, subject of course to the conditions of the Time Table Conscience Clause.

It does not appear that any other legal limitation would be necessary; unless it were a provision that the Board, if it allowed such arrangements, should do it equitably as between different religious communions, regard being had to their respective numbers, to the capacity of the School buildings, and to convenience of hours; so that an opening might be afforded for the greatest amount of good to be done in the fairest manner. There are cases in which, without such a provision, religious prejudice might perhaps prevent full justice.

This plan would have some great advantages over the first. It meets the objection founded on the rules of religious liberty: for no man's money would be applied to teaching a religion he did not embrace. Even the use of the School Buildings for religious instruction, if allowed, might be charged for. It would preclude the Board, as such, from intermeddling with the controul of religious teaching, for the direct regulation of which it would be unfitted. Good sense would commonly secure non-interference: but in some cases the thing might be done, & might lead to inconvenience and heart-burning.

It appears, however, that some Churchmen and many Nonconformists are at present averse to this plan, as savouring too much of secularism, and think that the Rate may be applied to the use of the Holy Scriptures in the Schools, all creeds and formularies remaining excluded. This concord of opinion appears to be due to a great anxiety to maintain a direct connection between religion and popular education, a sentiment worthy of all honour: and to be effected by a double compromise, the Churchmen to surrender Creed and Catechism, and the Nonconformists giving up the principle that the money of all should not be applied by law to teaching the religion of some, or indeed, as most of them are understood to hold, that public money should not be applied at all to the teaching of religion; or in other words the famous voluntary principle.

This plan does not present the elements of what can properly be called a compromise in the immediate subject matter, that is, as to the nature of the religious instruction in rate-provided Schools: because the Church surrenders the Catechism, which is its legal and ordinary instrument for the religious teaching of the young, whereas the Non-conformists, properly so-called, (and not therefore including the Wesleyans,) have no such surrender to make, since they do not make use of any Catechism. But it has been said that this arrangement, favourable to Dissenters, should be made in the Rate-provided Schools, in consideration of their acquiescing in the continuance of the Privy Council grants, and in allowing Local Boards to give aid out of the Rates to denominational Schools.

This plan, for using the Holy Scriptures in the Schools exclusively of Creed or formulary, is susceptible of being put into many varying shapes.

First: the mere terms of it do not solve the question whether there is to be religious observance, prayer for example, in the schools. If there is to be prayer, it could hardly be proposed to require by law that the Schoolmaster should not make use of any formulary. Secondly; apart from this question of accompaniment, arises another: who is to superintend and control the Schoolmaster in the use of Holy Scripture? It could not be proposed to compel the Board itself to undertake this duty in detail. If the Board is allowed to devolve the duty on others, it will very naturally, and perhaps very properly, look to religious teachers of this or that denomination for the purpose; and such teachers could hardly be regarded as the most suitable guardians of the principle of generalised or unsectarian instruction, if that principle were to be adopted as the basis of the plan. Thirdly. As to the immediate matter of instruction, or the rule by which the use of the Holy Scriptures is to be regulated. Here three modes of proceeding have been suggested. a. That the Bible shall be read, without exposition. b. That the Bible shall be read and explained. c. That the Bible shall be read and explained but only in the manner termed undenominational and unsectarian.

Plan III.

The third plan, although capable of a considerable width of application in practice at discretion, yet as a plan to be secured by legal enactment I at once put aside, since it involves the creation of a new State Religion by the method of reduction or excision. As to the first, although the reading of Scripture alone may (as is plain from its common use in Family prayers) be a simple and solemn exercise, it seems to be rejected by the prevailing opinion as a mode of solution for the Problem before us.

There remains the plan that the Bible be read and explained, while formularies are to be forbidden. There is something amiable and attractive in this visible homage to the Scriptures, which all Christians value, without the vehicles of instruction on which they can be divided. It is also to be observed that the adoption of this plan leaves the Board free to act on Plan II if it think fit: by which the rate would be applied to secular teaching only, and freedom & facility might still be given for the separate supply of religious teaching. Again, it is a supplemental provision, to meet what may be called the extreme cases, where the energy of the denominations has failed. This consideration appears to me most weighty in favour of Plan II: but it may also have more relative force in favour of the plan now under consideration. While it is for the present a remote corner of the scheme that we are now dealing with, it is a corner into which, *possibly*, in the course of time, much of it may be driven.

I will now briefly enumerate some objections, to which the plan appears to be open. 1. It seems to guarantee or promise unsectarian instruction, (for why are formularies shut out except for being sectarian?) and yet it does not fulfil the pledge: inasmuch as whereas there is the desire to give denominational or peculiar instruction upon the basis of the Scripture text it can and will be done not only without difficulty but without limit. In truth while Catechisms tend to insure that instruction in religion shall be special & denominational, they *limit* the degree in which it can assume a character of peculiarity. 2. To set up any exclusive text-book whatever in matter of religion *savours* of interference with the perfect freedom of religious teaching, which is a principle of the utmost consequence to the wellbeing of the State. 3. In view of what may be termed the interests of religion, at a period when nearly the whole force of the attack upon religion is directed to the disintegration of the *corpus* or text of Scripture, I greatly doubt the wisdom of attempting to separate it, even in a residuary class of cases, from those accompaniments of moral & practical support, which it derives from the atmosphere, traditions and agency, of the religious bodies associated to maintain and teach it. 4. The adoption of this plan by the local Boards would leave the Roman Catholics no refuge but the Conscience Clause. From the actual benefit of the plan, they are as a body wholly excluded. But, while they may not be more than 5 per Cent of the population, they will supply I apprehend, full 10 per Cent of the children for whom the Rate Schools ought to provide. Further, they are massed together in such a manner that their children are likely to be not infrequently a majority, or even a large majority in Rate

Schools: in which a religious instruction, not according to their views, would be supplied out of rates which they will have to pay. We in their circumstances should not be content with this: and they will not, and cannot. Compulsory attendance, combined with compulsory rating, will give great point & force to their objections. 5. The main objection urged against the Bill as it stands is the possibility of contention in the School Boards. This plan will not remove it. The exclusive application of the rate to the secular instruction, with freedom & facility for voluntary religious teaching, is likely to be more acceptable, or less unacceptable, to large or important sections of opinion: to those who prefer secular instruction, to those who hold firmly and clearly the voluntary principle, to the Roman Catholics, to the prevailing and permanent sentiments of the Church. There seems to me to be as much risk of religious contention in the Boards under this plan, as with the present provisions of the Bill. But the moment that the application of the Rate to religious teaching is forbidden, the main ground of strife, and the *only* ground likely to make a minority tenaciously resist the majority, is removed. 6. We have no experience in the United Kingdom to show that this plan would be desirable. In Scotland the people appear to demand a free discretion for the Local Boards. In Ireland the plan of Scripture Extracts bore a certain resemblance to it:but it is now made clear that those Extracts have gone out of use; while the National System is actually worked, in all but 111 Schools, on the principle of special & free religious instruction outside the times given to secular teaching. In England it works as a *voluntary* system, under the British & Foreign School Society, which I presume looks to the controul of its own Schoolmasters. This throws no light on the working of such a system by Act of Parliament. 7. Lastly, every man who chooses may if he likes agitate against this system if adopted by the Local Board on the principle which was fatal to Church Rate. This may not happen in a large number of Parishes: but Church Rate was not opposed in a very large number of Parishes. If it is likely to end in the exclusive application of the Rate to secular teaching, much inconvenience might be avoided if Parliament were content to begin here, supposing it to be discontented with the Bill as it stands. Of one thing I feel confident: that in debate such a project, if there be disposition to view it critically, would be easy to assail, and not easy to defend.

30. M.

Wrote to Ld Granville—Master of St John's Cambr.—Sir A. Panizzi —Judge Keogh—The Queen 2, & Mem.—and minutes. Saw Sir R. Phillimore—Mr B. Hope cum Mr Walter—Dr Chapman—Mr Ouvry —Mr Ayrton—Mr Glyn—Ld Halifax. Conclave on Ld Lieutenancies. Read Blackie's Lecture[1]—Hayward on Lothair.[2] H of C. $4\frac{1}{2}$-$9\frac{1}{4}$ and $10\frac{1}{2}$-$1\frac{3}{4}$.[3] Attended the Levée.

31. Tu.

Wrote to Ld Stair—Dean of Peterborough—The Queen—& minutes.

[1] J. S. *Blackie, 'On scientific method in the interpretation of popular myths' (1870).
[2] Hayward's review, *Macmillan's Magazine*, xxii. 142 (June 1870).
[3] Spoke on exclusion of strangers: *H* cci. 1645. See 28 May 70.

Dined with the F. Cavendishes. At Christies. Saw Scotts—Mr Glyn
—Mr Candlish—Mr Miall[1]—Ld Stratford de R.—Mr Forster—Mr
Winterbotham—Mr Bruce. H of C. 2¼-7, 9-9.30 & 11¼-1¼.[2] Read
'De l'Unanimité Morale'.[3]

Wed June One 1870. [Walmer Castle, Kent]

Wrote to Mrs Thistlethwayte—and minutes. Read Sir G. Lewis's
Letter. Preparations for departure. Went off at 11.45 to the Derby,
by the S.E. Railway, with Granville, who most kindly arranged everything, including two drives through beautiful country. I was immensely
interested in the scene, and the race. Conversation with P. of Wales—
Admiral Rous[4]—and many more. The race gave me a tremor. We
reached Walmer at 7¾, joining C.G. & the party at Tunbridge.

Th. 2.

Wrote to Sir G. Grey—Mayor of Lpool[5]—Queen (Mem)—Mr Warner—D. of Argyll—and minutes. Read Lewis's Letters—Faraday's
Memoirs.[6] We went to St Margarets Bay, by that grand solitary road
between cliff and sea. C. gallantly bathed. We watched the mackerel
fishing.

To E. WARNER, 2 June 1870.   Add MS 44538, f. 157.

I can assure you that as far as wishes are concerned nothing could be more
acceptable to the Government than your reappearance in the House as member
for Norwich. I find, however, upon inquiry, that Glyn is of opinion that this
very desirable result cannot now be attained. I am not aware that he has authorised Mr. Tillett to make any declaration of our, or his, wishes, for this is a proceeding which often gives offence in a divided constituency.[7] But it naturally
would prevent him from taking any step in a contrary sense: nor could I with
any advantage undertake to correct the information which he receives, & which
he judges with an equally friendly, & a more experienced eye. I am truly glad to
learn from him that another vacancy is likely at an early date, which he considers you would certainly be enabled to fill. Pray remember us kindly to Mrs. W.

[1] 'I mean to see two or three of the hardest-headed Nonconformists and try to ascertain
their real wishes'; Ramm I, i. 100.
[2] Questioned by Winterbotham on civil service: H cci. 1702; he was a prominent nonconformist, advocating Bible reading as the only solution to the education impasse; for this
day's meeting, see A. W. W. Dale, Life of R. W. Dale (1898), 278.
[3] Untraced.
[4] Jockey Club member and public handicapper; see 14 May 42.
[5] Joseph Gibbons Livingston.
[6] H. B. *Jones, The life and letters of ... Faraday (1870).
[7] By-election following a petition; Warner did not stand; J. H. Tillett, liberal, won.

3. Fr.

Wrote to The Queen (Mem)—Mrs Thistlethwayte—Ld Chancellor of Ireland—Mr Ayrton—Mr Glyn—Ld Lyttelton—and minutes. Finished Lewis's letters. Read Faraday's Memoirs—Whist in evg. Walked over to Updown & saw the Jameses. Rode back. Willy's birthday: God bless him.

4. Sat.

Wrote to Archbp of York—Ld Clarendon—The Queen (Mem)—Mr Hammond—and minutes. Read Brewster's Memoirs[1]—Brown on Shakesperian Sonnets[2]—Lewis's Letters (finished)—Annals of an Eventful Life[3]—Faraday's Memoirs. Cut down a tree: missed two rooks with a rifle: visited Ld C[lanwilliam] at Deal Castle & had tea. A party to dinner.

5. Whits.

Walmer Ch mg (with H.C.) and aft. Wrote to Ld Clarendon—Chancr of Exr—Ld R. Cavendish—& minutes. Read Marriott on Catacombs[4] —Blenkinsopp on Development. Tea at Deal Castle where Ld C. gave us a curious account of the Deal Boatmen; sad enough.

6. M.

Wrote to the Viceroy and minutes. Fête in the Gardens. Bp [Wilberforce] of Winchester came. Read Faraday (finished Vol I)—Blenkinsop on Devt—M'Carthy's Transl. of Calderon.[5] Long & late evening conversation.

7. Tu.

Wrote to Ld Clarendon—The Queen—Bp of Brechin—Mr M. Arnold—and minutes. Drove to Shell Ness & rode back. Long conversation with Bp of W. on Education—& afterwards with Granville on that & other subjects. Read Brewster's Memoirs.[6]

[1] Probably M. M. Brewster, *The home life of Sir David Brewster* (1869).
[2] H. Brown, *The sonnets of Shakespeare solved* (1870).
[3] [G. W. *Dasent], *Annals of an eventful life*, 3v. (1870).
[4] W. B. *Marriott, *The testimony of the catacombs* (1870).
[5] See 27 Mar. 70.   [6] See 4 June 70.

To MATTHEW ARNOLD, 7 June 1870.   Add MS 44538, f. 161.

I am greatly obliged by the present of your work[1] which I shall read with particular interest. I cordially agree in what you appear to describe as your main
thesis. Indeed I was upon ground not far apart from it in a book published more
than 30 yrs ago. I admitted that the Church of England was politically intolerant,
& accounted for this by special reference to the circumstances of its Reformation. Hooker's Mary I think in those times tended towards intolerance. But I
maintained that theologically the Church of England was the most tolerant religious body of that age. And all this I still think is sound. I am in hopes it will not
appear to you much otherwise.

I remember making a very weighty list of the notable men preferred by Abp.
Laud, with whom he did not agree. Among them were Hall, Hales, & Chilling-
worth. There are others perhaps, including the very curious case of Goodman,
the Bp. of Gloucester. Could I prevail on you to breakfast with me on Thursday
morning at 10? May I say the 10th or any other (except 23rd) which might suit
you better.[2]

To LORD CLARENDON, foreign secretary,   Clarendon MSS, c. 498.
7 June 1870.

You have the whole tenour of your Greek correspondence in your head much
better than we have, & without doubt it will all come out right.[3] As to the Constitution, I can conceive it perfectly possible to introduce great changes without
diminishing the liberties of the people: but that diminution is, I fear, what Russia & France will desire. I do not say that in no case should it be effected: but
we ought to require a good case to be made. And in any view of the matter, I
feel convinced there is evil to be removed, & good to be done, without directly,
or even substantially, involving the question of popular privileges. I hope whatever else we do, we shall take care to place the balance of receipt & expenditure
in Greece on a sound footing, for without this, the little country never can keep
straight.

8. Wed. [London]

Wrote to Bp of Bath & Wells—Mr Fortescue—Mr Forster—Mr Ayr-
ton—Viceroy of I.—The Queen (Mem)—Ld Granville—Chancr of
Exr—Mr Bruce—Mrs Rumpff—and minutes. Saw Bp of Winchester
—Ld Bessborough—Sir D. Salomons. Left Walmer 10.15. Reached
home at 2. Saw Mrs Th. Saw Isaac & another X. Read M'Carthy's
Calderon.

[1] Almost certainly 'St Paul and Protestantism', sent with a letter on 4 June 1870, Add
MS 44427, f. 3: 'The preface treats of the effect which political dissent has upon practical
religion. . . . Dissent has been due, not to Church persecution only, as is commonly said and
believed, but yet more to the Church's refusal to make more narrow and exact her definitions of doctrine on the points of original sin, election, justification.'
[2] School inspections prevented his coming; Add MS 44427, f. 19.
[3] Replying to Clarendon's charge that Gladstone and Granville were 'overcritical' of a
draft to Lyons on the Greek constitution; 6 June 1870, Add MS 44134, f. 216.

To H. A. BRUCE, home secretary,   Add MS 44538, f. 162.
8 June 1870.

I think with you[1] that we should discuss as soon as possible the question of the Census. This application from Scotland will go far to make the ground taken by the English non-conformists in /60 untenable.[2]

To W. E. FORSTER, vice president,   Add MS 44538, f. 161.
8 June 1870.

Many thanks for your speech.[3] I read it in the Times, where it seemed to be well reported. It is difficult, either for you or me or anyone, to speak or converse at any length, without betraying our personal preferences on this or that point, but I think you both evidently, & successfully endeavoured to avoid committing yourself or the Govt.

We shall have ample opportunity for conversation in London, but the Cabinet will not approach the question again until very hard upon the day of the opening of the discussion. I imagine we shall have perfect warrant for declining any more specific declaration before the Speaker leaves the Chair, if we think fit. Meantime the following seems to me a singular point. The discretion of the Boards as to religious teaching is to be limited, in order to prevent quarrelling. If so, the Boards ought to be either compelled or forbidden to aid denominational schools from the Rate? The latter is impossible. I continue of the opinion, for myself, that *if* we cannot hold the Bill as it is with respect to Rate Schools proper, the only sound course is to limit the application of the *Rate* absolutely to secular purposes. But I am bound to say I entertain some doubt at present whether the *Church party* would prefer this method to the adoption of the Bible as the only text book, with free exposition.

9. Th.

Wrote to Bp of Lichfield—Ld Chancr. Ireland—The Queen—and minutes. Read Wilkinson on Study of Hebrew:[4] Faraday's Memoirs Vol. II. Dined with the Wests. We had a long *éclaircissement* with the new Butler: of doubtful issue. Small breakfast party. Saw Signor Guerzoni[5]—Mr Glyn—Mr Bulwer Lytton—WHG on Ch. preferments—Mr Childers—The Speaker—Tried to find Ld Salisbury. Saw Mr Noble's Studio & his beautiful recumbent statue of the Duchess.[6] H of C. 4½-8½ & 9½-1¼.[7]

[1] Bruce's letter of 7 June 1870, Add MS 44086, f. 151, reported Free Church requests for a religious census.
[2] When they prevented a religious census; see 9 July 60; but none taken 1871.
[3] Forster sent the *Bradford Observer* report of 6 June of meeting with the Bradford education league, Add MS 44157, f. 26.
[4] W. F. Wilkinson, *A plea for the study of Hebrew* (1870).
[5] Giuseppe Guerzoni, poet and biographer of Garibaldi.
[6] Of Sutherland; for a different version, see above, vi. 360.
[7] Spoke on customs: *H* cci. 1816.

10. Fr.

Wrote to Ld Clarendon—Mr C. Villiers—Sir Geo. Grey—The Queen —and minutes. Saw Robertson X. Saw Mr Glyn—Mr Forster—Mr Stansfeld—Mr Childers—Mr West. H. of C. $4\frac{1}{2}$-$8\frac{1}{2}$ and $9\frac{1}{2}$-1.[1] Read Gainsborough's Life[2]—Faraday's Memoirs.

To Sir G. GREY, bart., 10 June 1870.   Add MS 44538, f. 164.

Many thanks for your kindness in writing: will you also be so good as to return my mem. of which I have no other fair copy. I think it will be wise for us to decide nothing more until we are in fuller possession of the views which prevail, & which seem to fluctuate from day to day. The Nonconformist mind moves in the direction of confining the rate to secular instruction; in Rate-founded Schools especially, & to this, if we are again to move as is not unlikely, I personally incline; but I am doubtful whether the Church could be brought to acquiesce, though on this I hope to obtain further information. Winterbotham (who is of that way of thinking) told me he thought that the action of the Government might avail, so far as the N.C. are concerned, to carry any one of these 4 plans:— 1. Confining the rate to secular purposes. 2. Scripture reading. 3. Scripture with Exposition, limited to the [?] undenoml. 4. Scripture with Exposition free.

11. Sat.

Wrote to Dean of Ch Ch—Sol. General—Ld Ashburnham—Watson & Smith—Mr Ayrton—Mr T.B. Potter—Ld Clarendon—Bp of Gloucester—and minutes. Saw Mr Glyn—Ld Halifax—D. of Argyll —Saw Howard X missed Meurice. Dined at Argyll Lodge—Lady Halifax's afterwards. Rode with Helen. Read Faraday—Lancashire Songs (Waugh).[3]

12. Trin.S.

Chapel Royal mg (with H.C.) and aft. Wrote to Mr Childers (2)—and minutes. Saw Ld Spencer: Mr Glyn. Called on J. Wortley: missed Ld Salisbury again. Read Coll. Peripatetica[4]—Bp of Gl. on Revision[5]— Marriott on Catacombs—E. Irving.[6]

[1] Misc. business: *H* cci. 1855.
[2] G. W. Fulcher, *Life of Thomas Gainsborough* (1856).
[3] E. *Waugh, *Lancashire songs* (1863).
[4] *Colloquia peripatetica* [by J. Duncan] (1870).
[5] C. J. *Ellicot, *Considerations on the revision of the English version of the New Testament* (1870).
[6] Possibly from *The prophetical works*, ed. G. Carlyle, 2v. (1867–70).

13. M.

Wrote to Ld Clarendon—Ld de Grey—Mr Hammond—Mrs Thistle-
thwayte—Prof. Jowett—Dr Bateson—The Queen—& minutes.
Saw Ld Salisbury—The Speaker—Mr Glyn—Mr Childers—Mr
Forster—Mr [R.] Peel Dawson—Mr Disraeli—Mr Samuelson—
Chr of Exr—Col. Stepney. Saw two. Dined at Mr West's. H of C. 4½-
8½ and 9½-12¾.[1] Read Faraday.

To LORD CLARENDON, foreign secretary,   Clarendon MSS, c. 498.
13 June 1870.

I have read these interesting letters.[2] Pray consider whether it would not be
well to have a very careful collection & dispassionate review of all the facts that
can be collected or have been already recorded which illustrate the case of
Fenianism in America in its relations to international law. If done, it should be
done with the aid of some men of the temper as well as knowledge of Bernard:
but if *so* done, it might be of great advantage, as it seems to me, in more points
of view than one. In the Alabama case, what an arbiter would probably find
against us is insufficiency or miscarriage of preventive measures. He would have
a nice point to determine in what seems to me to be the American contention,
viz. that every such failure invests the foreign State injured thereby with a claim
for compensation. A case substantially parallel, & in its development stronger &
more varied, might be brought out in the inquiry about Fenianism & the U.S.
Govt?
    [P.S.] Note the great change of tone in the D. Telegraph of today about
Greece.

To Rev. B. JOWETT, 13 June 1870.   Add MS 44538, f. 165.

Individually I attach little importance, & less value, to the reservation of the
Headships.[3] But the difficulty in which we are placed is this; we came under an
engagement, as we thought to two parties: we are now not only not sustained,
but resisted in its fulfilment by one of them: while we have no release from the
other. I hope there will be some communication between the two Universities
on this subject, which may help to clear up the case. If necessary, I shall propose
to postpone the point tonight, indeed I may have no alternative. But I am sorry
for anything which operates as a postponement to the Bill. In recommending Dr.
Scott for Rochester, I anticipated, with my very partial information that you
would obtain an honour to which, irrespective of particular opinions, every-
[one] must feel that you had established undeniable claims by eminent ability,
by high & spotless character, & by selfdenying & unwearied devotion to your
work.[4]

    [1] Questioned on civil service and education; spoke on university tests: *H* cci. 1944.
    [2] Perhaps Thornton to Clarendon, 10 May 1870, Clarendon MSS, c. 481, on Fenianism,
Canada and the U.S.A.
    [3] To continue to have a Test; Jowett had signed a memorial, Add MS 44427, f. 40.
    [4] Gladstone had told G. V. Wellesley (25 May 1870, Add MS 44538, f. 153) that he be-
lieved *Jowett would be elected master of Balliol if *Scott went to Rochester.

14. Tu.

Wrote to Mr Fortescue—The Queen—Scotts—and minutes. Saw
Ld Granville—Mr Forster—Mr Glyn. Read Faraday. Cabinet 1-4¼.
H of C. 4½-6¾. Spoke on Revision of Authorised Version of H.S.[1]
Dined with Mr Tollemache & he drove us down, the whole party, to
the Crystal Palace Fireworks. Saw 3[R].

Cabinet Jun 14. 70 1 PM[2]
√ Kensington Road. Postpone to another year.
  St James's Park Road
√ Buxton's motion. Object.
√ McCullagh Torrens's motion. oppose.[3]
√ Committee on Police Force. Report to be presented: motion not admitted
  now.
√ Mundella's motion for a Commission on Truck. Reserve judgment till debate.
√ Amendments on the Education Bill. Much debated. Accepted. C. of E. ob-
  jected strongly. Goschen approved but anticipated serious party mischief.
  Others saw difficulties but approved.[4]
√ Processions Bill Ireland—approved.

15. Wed.

Wrote to Prof. Jowett—Chancr of Exr—Mrs Th.—Ld Clarendon—
Mr Ayrton—and minutes. Read Faraday—Gk Papers—Jewitts
Sepulchral Remains.[5] H of C. 12½-2½. Spoke on the minority Clause.[6]
Rode with Mary. Saw Ld Shaftesbury—Sir R. Alcock—Mr Glyn (2)
—Ld Granville—Mr Bruce—Chancr of Exr—Mr Forster (3). Dined
at Ld Shaftesbury's. Large evening party after.

With reference to the decision of the Cabinet of yesterday respecting the support
of Voluntary Schools, the Chancellor of the Exchequer suggests that the sum
which that decision would award to them should not be charged upon the Rates
but distributed from the Exchequer.

I have consulted Mr Forster who approves. Ld de Grey is out of town but Mr.
F. is sure he would approve. Ld. Granville is out of town. Mr. Cardwell Mr Bruce
Mr Goschen (& Mr Glyn) approved.

[1] Opposing Buxton's motion for American collaboration for a Revised Version: *H* ccii.
112.   [2] Add MS 44638, f. 83.
[3] On unemployed labour; opposed by *Goschen on 17 June: *H* ccii. 407.
[4] de Grey's note reads: 'Shown to Mr Gladstone after the Cabinet 14 June 70. 1. To
accept Cowper-Temple's amendment [for non-denominational religious instruction in rate-
funded schools]. 2. To render aid to Denominational Schools compulsory upon School
Boards with provision to secure its being applied only to secular instruction and with limitation as to amount. 3. To withdraw the year of Grace but to maintain the power of aiding
now Denominational Schools from local & national resources'; Add MS 43514, f. 33. See
16 June 70.
[5] L. F. W. *Jewitt, *Grave-mounds and their contents: a manual of archaeology* (1870).
[6] Supporting Hardcastle's Bill to abolish the minority clauses of the 1867 Act: *H* ccii. 142.

I am most willing to agree. It is also proposed that Building grants should be discontinued.

I sent this Minute in partial Circulation.[1]

To LORD CLARENDON, foreign secretary,   Clarendon MSS, c. 498.
15 June 1870.

I would avoid any official support of the Italian application to France for the evacuation of Rome by saying that this country had always abstained from mixing in that question: and that we were the more induced to persevere in that policy from being well convinced that the French Govt. is perfectly aware that in this country the occupation of any part of the Pontifical Territories by French troops is regarded with regret, pain & disapproval. Further that those who most strongly entertain these sentiments are generally the persons who most highly value & have most striven to promote the good understanding between France & England. Should France consult us we should readily give our opinion. Thus I have set out my view. The French occupation of Rome & Roman States has been almost a crime: & the French fear to use the power thus given against the madmen of the Council has been altogether a blunder. Such at least is my confession of Faith. While declining the Italian application officially might we not make known at Paris the terms in which we decline?[2]

[P.S.] I sent you a letter from Acton which I think requires notice from me.

To R. LOWE, chancellor of the exchequer,   Add MS 44301, f. 148.
15 June 1870.

I have received your letter, & I entirely appreciate the spirit of it, & of the suggestion it contains.[3] I will not enter into detail, but I can confidently say that *no* agreement can be had on the Education question without sacrifices at the very least of cherished preferences.

Your suggestion is so big in relation to the machinery of the Bill, that I think I had better see Forster on it, as soon as I can get at him. The matter is clearly beyond the sphere of my discretion: but we are not too late for a Cabinet.

16. Th.

17 to breakfast. Wrote to Ld Clarendon—Dr Bateson—Mr Goschen —The Queen—& minutes. Worked much on the subject of Educa-

[1] Initialled and dated 15 June 1870, Add MS 44759, f. 131. Comments noted on it: 'I feel sure that the MAIN danger of the proposal lies in the compulsory application of Local Rates to R.C. Schools—and that this danger is lessened greatly, by giving the needful aid out of the Consol. Fund. Argyll. I approve H[atherle]y. I entirely concur C[larendon]. So do I G[ranville.] I think this proposal avoids a serious danger. I entirely concur in it K[imberley.] C. P. F[ortescue.]'

[2] Clarendon replied on 15 June, Add MS 44134, f. 221, that he would discourage Italy from making an official request.

[3] Lowe to Gladstone, 15 June 1870, Add MS 44301, f. 146, proposed that 'if you must increase the pay to denominational schools you had better take it [the money] from the general Revenue than from the Rates. Increase the Privy Council Grant by one half and the thing is done. . . .' Lowe stressed his constituents' dislike for denominational education, concluding 'much as I value my [cabinet] place I value my seat more'.

tion & the Bill. Saw Mr Forster—Mr Glyn—Dr L. Playfair—Mr Thornton Hunt. H of C. 4½-8¼ and 9½-12¾. Explained the plans of the Govt in modification of the Bill, to an eager and agitated House.[1] Read Life of Faraday—do of Gainsborough—Cobden's Speeches on Education.[2] Exhausting Siroccolike heat.

17. Fr.

Wrote to Ld Shaftesbury—Rev. H. Allon—The Queen—Mrs Thistle-thwayte—Lady Westmoreland—Provost of Oriel—Sec. of King's Coll.—H. Glynne—The Queen—& minutes. Saw Lord Kildare[3]—Mr Glyn—Mr Forster—Lucy Cavendish—Ld Dalhousie—Mr Childers—Mr Whitbread. Saw Oates: who will write home X. H of C. 2-3 and 4½-6½, also 9-1¼.[4] Dined at Panizzi's.

To E. HAWKINS, provost of Oriel, Oxford.   Add MS 44538, f. 168.
17 June 1870. 'Private.'

[First letter:] I thank you for your tract[5] which I shall read with great interest. I cannot wonder at your thinking we go too far, & I shall read respectfully your ever fair & kindly criticism. But there are others who go a great deal further than we do. What we seek is to admit or render admissible all individuals to the honours emoluments, & powers of the University & Colleges where they are no[t] connected with Theology or Holy Orders, & to leave intact the established system except so far as it clashes with the purpose I have mentioned. What they seek is to destroy the established system for the favourite purpose of enthroning what is barbarously called undenominationalism, & the admission of individuals they regard not as the end in view but rather as a consequence. I was glad that in a petition or declaration some time ago the Oxford Liberals disclaimed this extreme purpose. On the contrary I am amazed at the line of conduct they have thought themselves at liberty to pursue with reference to the Headships. It is the first case of the kind that I have known, & I hope it will be the last.
Pray remember us on some other Thursday if you can (not the 23d when we shall be away).

[Second letter:] On reading your tract I am glad to find, or think I find, that I can remove one stumbling block at least out of your way. If I have spoken of free and various teaching as to Religion in the Colleges of Oxford, it is not in the present Colleges. This is to say the Bill is not intended in any manner to affect their official teaching.

[1] Accepting *Cowper-Temple's amendment: H ccii. 226.
[2] Quoted in his speech this day.
[3] Charles William Fitzgerald, 1819-87; liberal M.P. Kildare 1847-52; Baron Kildare 1870; 4th duke of Leinster 1874.
[4] Supply, and unemployed labour (see 14 June 70): H ccii. 407.
[5] Sent by Hawkins on 16 June, Add MS 44206, f. 285; apparently unpublished, see J. W. Burgon, Lives of Twelve Good Men (1891), 218, 231; Hawkins strongly opposed the change. See 21 Mar. 66.

What may be done by particular members of those bodies in their own rooms on their own responsibility we cannot know. But we speak of teaching free & various with reference to the future & as against those who claim that hereafter no 'denominational' college shall be founded in either university. Next to teaching single & authoritative comes (in my judgment) teaching free & various.

It was freedom that brought the Christian Church up to the civil position which she is now unable [sic] to hold, & to guard this freedom is now I think the chief duty of politicians in their direct relations with religion. This is not said polemically, but in reliance on your never failing indulgence.

[P.S.] I congratulate you on having in your (our) new Chancellor a model of political integrity, as well as a most amiable, a most high minded, & a most able man.[1]

To LORD SHAFTESBURY, 17 June 1870.   Add MS 44538, f. 168.

I was not at liberty on Wednesday to speak to you otherwise than in very general terms on the intentions of the Govt. respecting the Education Bill. We have now taken our stand; & I write to say how ready I shall be to communicate with you freely in regard to the prospects & provisions of the measure.[2] I can the better make this tender, because the plan we have adopted is by no means in all its main particulars the one most agreeable to my individual predilections. But I have given it deliberate assent, as a measure due to the desires & convictions of the country, & as one rendering much honour & scope to religion without giving fair ground of objection to those who are so fearful that the State should become entangled in theological controversy.

Energetic objection will I have some fear be taken in some quarters to our proposals; but I believe they will be generally satisfactory to men of moderation. Pray understand that the willingness I have expressed is not meant to convey any request, but only to be turned to account if you find it useful.

18. Sat. [Cassiobury Park, Hertfordshire]

Wrote to Rev Mr Hawley—Mr Ayrton—Chr of Exr—Ld Chancr—The Queen—Ld Granville—Bp of Glos.—and minutes. Cabinet $2\frac{3}{4}$-$5\frac{1}{4}$. Saw Mr Childers—Do cum Sir S. Robinson[3]—Ld Clarendon—Mr Glyn. Off at 5.30 to Cassiobury [Lord Ebury's] where we found a delightful retreat & most kind welcome. Read 'The Bible & the School Fund'.[4]

Cabinet June 18. 70. 2½ PM.[5]
√ Clarendon read commn. respecting measures in Greece: Ld Stratford's notice.
A Paper to be drawn setting forth the shortcomings of Greece for answers, &

[1] i.e. *Salisbury; this letter is in Add MS 44206, f. 289.
[2] Shaftesbury was 'delighted with the amendments'; Add MS 44300, f. 42.
[3] Sir Robert Spencer *Robinson, 1809–89; controller of the navy 1861–71; lord of the admiralty 1868–71; effectively dismissed after a dispute with Childers.
[4] Untraced.
[5] Add MS 44638, f. 88.

conference with the Three Powers, with a view to being commun[icate]d for the Greek Govt. to elicit their views of remedies.

√ Queen's suggestion for the removal of Erskine.[1]

√ Childers mentioned the miscarriage of the transaction with Sir S. Robinson. Mr C[hilders] agreed on our representations to take his departure at once.[2]

√ Colonies. Ld Russell's motion. Poss[ibilities:] 1. Previous question 2. Negative. If pressed[3]

√ Amendments to Irish Land Bill considered.[4]

19. 1 S.Trin.

Watford Churches mg & aft. Wrote to Ld Granville, & minutes. Read Abp Trench on Parables[5]—Bp Ellicott on Revision.

20. M. [London]

Wrote to Ld de Grey—Mrs Th.—The Queen (and Mem.)—Bp of Winchester: & identical letter to 8 other Bishops respecting Land Bill. Reached home 11.45. Smaller & larger conclaves on Land Bill till the House met. Also saw Mr Glyn—Mr Goschen. H of C. $4\frac{1}{2}$-8 and 9-$12\frac{3}{4}$.[6] Read Faraday.

To S. WILBERFORCE, bishop of Winchester,   Wilberforce MSS, d. 38.
20 June 1870.

I venture earnestly to beg that, if you are able to contrive it, you will devote some time to the House of Lords during the Committee on the Irish Land Bill which commences on Thursday next, and that you will give such consideration as you may think fit to the important questions which are likely to be brought under discussion.

On an ordinary question of politics, indeed on any question of mere politics, I should hesitate long before venturing to make to a Prelate of the Church any request urging him to give attention to or take part in the proceedings on a particular measure. But I consider the Irish Land Bill to stand by itself: it really appertains not so much to the wellbeing as to the being of civilised society, for the existence of society can hardly be such as to deserve that name, until the conditions of peace & order, & of mutual goodwill & confidence shall have been more firmly established in Ireland.[7]

[1] *Victoria wished to remove Edward Morris Erskine, d. 1883, British minister at Athens, for mismanaging the Dilessi murder question.

[2] *Robinson objected to the conditions of his service imposed by Order in Council; Add MS 44538, f. 174.

[3] *Russell withdrew his motion for a royal commission on imperial security on 20 June: H ccii. 485.

[4] The Lords had completed their amendments; see Steele, *Irish Land*, 307.

[5] R. C. *Trench, *Notes on the parables of Our Lord* (1841).

[6] Education Bill in cttee.: H ccii. 495.

[7] A circular intended also for the bps. of Salisbury, Bath & Wells, Exeter, Carlisle, Oxford, Chichester, Manchester, and Chester; Wilberforce replied supporting the Bill, Add MS

21. *Tu.*

Wrote to The Queen (& Tel)—Watson & S. (and Telegr.)—Sir S.
Robinson (draft)—Sir W. Heathcote—Mr Delane—Mr Fortescue—
Mr Brewster—Ld Bessborough—Rev Dr Bateson—& minutes. Saw
Rev. Mr M'Coll—Mr Childers—Mr Glyn—Ld Chancr of Ireland—
Mr Trevelyan—Mr Delane—Mr Forster. H of C. 3-6¾ and 9-1¼.
Spoke on Bps Seats in H. of Lords.[1] Saw Davis X. Read Faraday—
Statement respecting St Paul's.[2]

To J. T. DELANE, 21 June 1870.   Add MS 44538, f. 171.

Will you do me the favour to come to my room at the House of Commons
this afternoon at 4.30 & to send me word of your arrival? I make the proposal in
conformity with your permission & name the hour because I hope it may suit
your convenience with reference to the H. of Lds.

22. *Wed.* [*Strawberry Hill, Twickenham*]

Wrote to Robn G.—Ld Bessborough—Abp Manning—and minutes.
Saw Lady Westmoreland. Saw Mr Glyn—Mr Herbert R.A. Read
Robinson on the Drawings[3]—Br Quart Rev. on Plantag. Period[4]—
Jewitt on Sepulchral Remains.[5] Went down to Twickenham for the
dinner & play at Lady Waldegraves. Saw Ld Russell—Ld Spencer—
& others.[6] The Play was well acted, rather low in tone & character.
A Ball followed. I had a night in three periods of excessive heat, then
noise, then light. A very few such would dispose of me.

To ARCHBISHOP H. E. MANNING, 22 June 1870.   Add MS 44249, f. 161.

My sentiments about the Council do not depend on the 'Correspondents' of
any class; they are rooted deep in my nature. But (if that be a compensation)
they are not the sentiments of the majority here. That majority is much better
represented, on this question, by the British Quarterly Review just published
which concludes an article p. 473 with the words 'Thanks be to God for having
permitted Pius ix to summon his Oecumenical Council'.

I have written to Ld Granville about Ld. Beaumont:[7] & am sure he will do
all he can. Should any opportunity offer itself to me, I will gladly use it also.

44345, f. 164 (see Wilberforce, iii. 345) but does not seem to have voted for it; all the
others named did; *H* ccii. 766, 772, 988.

[1] Defending their presence there: *H* ccii. 688.   [2] Untraced.
[3] Sir J. C. *Robinson, *A critical account of the drawings of Michel Angelo and Raffaello
in the University Galleries, Oxford* (1870).
[4] *British Quarterly Review*, li. 362 (April 1870).
[5] See 15 June 70.   [6] See O. Hewett, *Strawberry Fair* (1956), 210.
[7] Not in Ramm; Manning wrote from Rome on 14 June requesting 'work' for Beaumont
and asked about Irish university legislation; Add MS 44249, f. 159.

You ask what we will do for the R.C. University in Dublin. Nothing could be less desirable than that there should be any correspondence between you & me on that subject at present. Already the shadow of the question of Irish Education is cast darkly over the English Bill. Upon that Bill, we have striven as far as we could to serve the interests of the Roman Catholic body, in & by serving the interests of general justice. I must say in honesty that in the general proposals & manifestations throughout the country, while no very enlightened view is taken of justice to the Ch. of England, justice to the R.C's appears except by a very few to be wholly forgotten. It is coolly proposed by a large section that while undenominational education shall be made to reign in Schools funded by the Rate, the Privy Council grants shall remain provisionally until the Schools which they aid can be gradually swallowed up in the so-called National System.

Communications with those who represented your Communion served to show, that their views with reference to the Bill were summed up in seeking adequate provision for the Voluntary Schools, & that there were no terms, which could be proposed for Rate Schools, of a nature to be accepted by them. Mr. Allies told me if they could make sure of one moiety of the School Charges from the State, he thought they could perhaps perform their work: & this moiety will I apprehend now be secured for efficient schools by the proposals of the Govt. While the R.C. interest is most concerned of all, I feel sure we have served the general & comprehensive interests of justice by the new provision. But the business is a very heavy one. Time is against us, so is much prejudice. On the other hand there is a lack of firmly organised opinion, & possibly the weight of the Govt. may in this state of things suffice to carry the Bill.[1]

23. Th. [London]

Wrote to Ld Bessborough—Sir W. Heathcote—The Queen—and minutes. Left at 9½ for town. Cabinet at 11½. To Windsor at 1.45. Audience & Council. H of C. 4.45-8½ and 9.20-2.30.[2] Saw Mr Fortescue—Mr Glyn—Ld de Grey—Ld Kimberley—Mr Hugessen— and others. Read Gainsborough's Life.[3]

Cabinet Thurs Ju 23 11½ AM[4]
√ Univ. Tests Bill. Headships [of colleges] not to be reserved.[5]
O Education Bill. Plural in Cl. 7. Minority vote.[6]
  Irish Land Bill. Various Amendments cons[idere]d. Especially Assignment. Agreed to adopt WEG's 1, 3, 4.

[1] Some in Lathbury, ii. 140.   [2] Education Bill: *H* ccii. 751.
[3] See 10 June 70.   [4] Add MS 44638, f. 89.
[5] For Anglicans only; Gladstone had told the master of St. John's, Cambridge, on 21 June 1870 (Add MS 44538, f. 172): 'I think the restriction on the Headships can hardly be maintained with advantage, but on Thurs. I shall submit the questn. to the Cabinet wh. had cheerfully accorded to the request, as they recd. it at the commencement of the year.' The amndt., secularising Headships of about a quarter of the colleges, was carried by 205: 86: *H* ccii. 1391.
[6] Clause 7 dealt with regulations for conduct of public elementary schools.

24. Fr.

Wrote to Ld Clarendon—Mr Childers—The Queen—Ld E. Fitzmaurice—Mr Fortescue—and minutes. Saw Mr Trevelyan—Mr
Forster—Mr Glyn—Ld Granville—Sir Geo Grey—Ld Bathurst—
Mr Fortescue. H of C. 3-7. Spoke on Education Bill: & voted in
421: 60.[1] Dined with the Thistlethwaytes. Col. N. Sturt then took
me to the last act of The Huguenots[2] at Covent Garden.

25. Sat. [Ashridge Park, Berkhamsted]

Wrote to Ld Chancellor—D. of Sutherland—Robn G.—Sir C.
O'Loghlen—Scotts—Watson & Smith—Rev Dr Rigg—Ld Clarendon—The Queen—Mr Walpole—Mr Hardy[3]—and minutes. Cabinet
2½-5¼. Saw Rev. M. M'Coll—Mr Glyn—Ld Granard. Clarendon was
absent, but we were not alarmed. Went down to Ashridge:[4] with
Lady M. Alford. Delighted with the place, scenery, & party. Read
Döllinger's 'Stammen'[5]—Jewitt's Sepulchral Remains.

Cabinet 10 D. St. Ju 24 [sc. 25] 2½ PM.[6]
○ Fix a day for abandoning bills?
○ Mrs Lloyd's Pension.[7] Postponed. Ld Clarendon absent[8]
√ Week's business: considered.
√ Red River. Riel's Amnesty urged by U.S.—Delay.—Ministry of Canada to
 have an opp[ortunit]y of saying whether they object.[9]
√ Amendment on Scale Clause respecting descent to a lower [?] Class approved.
√ Party Processions Bill. Mr Fortescue to consider further.
√ Dublin City. Writ to issue. Disfranchise the corrupt men.
√ Waterford [election] petition against Baron Hughes. Mr Matthews to be asked
 by Mr Fortescue what course he will pursue.[10]
√ Judicature Bills. Can Not come on at present.
√ Sandon. Parochial Councils Bill. Not oppose introduction.
√ Chambers Repeal of Act of Uniformity. Oppose.
√ Lectionary Bill. Bruce to inquire as to effect wh. a suspension of it wd. pro-
 duce upon trade.
√ Committee on Army Colonels (Anson). Resist.[11]

[1] Defeating H. *Richard's amendt.: *H* ccii. 929.   [2] By Meyerbeer.
[3] Same letter sent to S. H. *Walpole and Gathorne *Hardy telling them of Cabinet decision on Heads of Houses (see 23 June 1870): Add MS 44538, f. 179.
[4] Seat of 3rd Earl Brownlow and his mother, Lady Marion *Alford, connoisseur (see 3
June 43 and 30 Oct. 63n.)
[5] J. J. I. von Döllinger, *Einige Worte über die Unfehlbarkeitsadresse* (1870).
[6] Add MS 44638, f. 90.
[7] Barbara, widow of Edward Lloyd, in debt when murdered by the Greek brigands; see
2 Aug. 70n and Jenkins, *Dilessi murders*, 149.   [8] See 27 June 70.
[9] *Wolseley's expedition withdrew in September 'without bloodshed or political en-
tanglement'; *PP* 1871 xlviii. 99.   [10] On 30 June; *H* cii. 1208.
[11] But on 29 June Cardwell agreed to Anson's motion for a select cttee on colonels in
India: *H* cii. 1168.

√ Ballot Bill. Not decline to support Mr Leatham's 2°R if he means to go no farther and if we do not go on with our own Bill.[1]

To Sir C. M. O'LOGHLEN, Judge Advocate General,   Add MS 44538, f. 174.
25 June 1870.

I am led to suppose by your absence from the Division yesterday, that there may not be a perfectly clear understanding between us as to the obligations of members of the Govt. on these occasions. Yesterday gave occasion of much inconvenience on account of the entertainment at Windsor, but all the members of the Govt., who could be expected to attend, voted in the Division, except yourself. This circumstance would of itself suffice to show the general impression on the subject of official duty, notwithstanding that the invitation to Windsor was a Royal one, & commonly to be regarded as a command. I can say from my own recollection that as far as regards political affairs the Sovereign always permits the claim of the H. of C. to prevail. Forgive my noticing the matter.[2]

26. 2 S.Trin.

Little Gadsden Ch mg and Prayers in Ashridge Chapel aft. Read Irving's Remains[3]—Massey's In Memoriam[4]—Galls Instant Salvation.[5] Walk about the unrivalled Beechwoods: saw the old Manor House.

27. M. [London]

Early Telegrams informed me of the death of Ld Clarendon: an incomparable colleague, a statesman of many gifts, a most loveable and genial man. Peace be with him.[6]
We went to town at 10.45. Arr. 12.40. Wrote to Mr Anderson—Mr Stanley—Ld Sydney—Mr Hammond—Mr Bright—The Queen (2)—and minutes. Saw Mr Hammond—Ld de Grey *cum* Mr Forster—Mr Cardwell—Ld Granville[7]—Mr Glyn—Mr Angerstein—Sir Thos G.—Sir R. Phillimore. H of C. 4¼-8½ and 9½-1. Educn Bill admirably driven by Forster.[8]

[1] On 27 July Gladstone supported Leatham's Ballot Bill, lost by end of session: *H* cciii. 1028.
[2] No reply has been found.
[3] See 12 June 70.
[4] G. Massey, *'In memory of John William Spencer, Earl Brownlow' (a poem)* (1869).
[5] J. Gall, *Instant salvation by the instant acceptance of a mediator and surety* (1864).
[6] Misleading version in Morley, ii. 417.
[7] About to become foreign secretary, the news being kept secret until the cabinet met on 2 July; he received the seals on 6 July; see 2 July 70. Gladstone told Hammond of the appointment on 29 June 'in order to enable you to place yourself in relations with him'; Add MS 44538, f. 178.
[8] *H* ccii. 1006.

To J. BRIGHT, president of the board of trade,   Add MS 43385, f. 81.
27 June 1870.

You will, I know, feel deeply the death of Ld. Clarendon & even amidst the great pressure of business I must write you a line about it. I am afraid his gallant spirit has been fatal to him. He probably counted on the marvellous elasticity of constitution or the force of mental action which have repeatedly seemed to bring him back from the gates of death. On Wed. he was at dinner & evening entertainment at Strawberry Hill, when the heat was excessive. He kept at his work on Thurs: & was in the H. of Lds. on Fri: he was with difficulty restrained from going to Windsor. But on Sat. he wrote me a note saying he had had five days of unchecked Diarrhoea, & could not attend the Cabinet. The family were, I believe, not then seriously alarmed. But yesterday morning his state was so bad that he was almost despaired of. In the afternoon he was better, but did not, I believe, recover consciousness. This morning at six, he died. He is gone where we shall soon follow him. Peace & rest be with him, & joy in a better world. Nothing since the formation of the present Govt. has given me greater pleasure than to observe the rapid & steady formation of friendship between you & him. Late in life, these intimacies are not readily formed. I can scarcely say to which of the two it was more honourable. And now as to politics I will only tell you we have become hopeful about the Education Bill. Your favourite clauses, I believe, in the Land Bill, are not to be mutilated by the Lords: & the Commons will enable us, I have no doubt, to repair the havock in other parts of the Bill, which they have indiscreetly made. Pray take care of yourself, & do not be troubled to write unless it is quite good for you.[1]

28. Tu.

Helen's birthday: God bless her.
    Wrote to W. Phillimore—Watson & S.—Mr Grogan—Mr W. Harcourt—V. Chr James[2]—D. of Sutherland—The Queen (3)—Sir J. Young—Sir T. Gladstone—and minutes. Saw Mr Glyn—Mr Cardwell—Ld Granville—Mr Brand—Ld Bessborough—Mr Forster. Rode with H. H of C. 2½-7 and 9¼-2.[3] Dined with the Thistlethwaytes. Read Faraday.

29. St P.

Wrote to V. Chr James—Lady M. Alford—Mr Hignett—Watsons (Tel.)—Scotts—Mr Childers—Mr Ouvry—Queen (& Mem)—Lord Hyde—Ld Sydney—Ld Granville—Mr Hammond—Mr Cardwell & minutes. Saw Mr Trevelyan—Lord T. Clinton—Mr Glyn—Lord W. Hay—Ld Granville—Count Bernstorff—Mr Grote—Mr Mitford—

[1] Bright replied briefly on 3 July, Add MS 44112, f. 136.
[2] Offering lord justiceship to Sir William Milbourne James, 1807-81; vice-chancellor 1869-70, lord justice from 1870.
[3] Education: *H* ccii. 1090.

Ld Acton. I went to Notting Hill to see Mrs Rumpff and received a sad tale from her which baffled me. Read Sharman Crawford's Pamphlet of 1837 on Ireland.[1] Dined at Ld Houghton's. Saw 4 X.

To E. CARDWELL, war secretary, 29 June 1870.   PRO 30/48/7, f. 59.
'Most Private.'

If you are disposed to take the vacant Red Ribbon,[2] I think that among many good claims yours is very decidedly pre-eminent. Are you inclined to allow me to name you to H.M.?

At the proper time Granville will without doubt take the F.O. It appears to me that Kimberley is his proper successor. If you desired it, without denying your title, I should intreat you to remain for a while in your present heavy charge. On that supposition, what think you of K?[3]

30. Th.

Wrote to Lord T. Clinton—Mr Hammond—Ld Spencer—The Queen (2) (and Mem.)—Ld Kimberley—Mr West—Abp of Canterb.—Watsons—Ld Campbell—Lord W. Hay—Prof. Sedgwick—and minutes. Saw Mr Fortescue—Ld Granville—Ld de Grey—Ld De Tabley—Mr Forster—Bp of Winchester—Mr Glyn—Duke of Argyll—Chancr of Exr—Mr Stansfeld. Dined at Mr Forsters. Rode with Agnes & Gertrude. H of C. $4\frac{1}{4}$–$7\frac{3}{4}$ and $8\frac{1}{2}$–2. With effort, & some pressure, we disposed of the 'religious difficulty' beating Mr Jacob Bright by 259: 132.[4] The Bill I hope is now clear of shoals. Read Faraday.

Friday July One 1870.

Wrote to Messrs Barker & Hignett—Ld Camperdown—Ld Russell —Kildare—Fitzwilliam—R. Grosvenor—Howard of Gl.—Mr Grote—Scotts—Mr Bate—The Queen—and minutes. Saw Mr Hignett *cum* Mr Burnett on the Aston purchase difficulty.[5] Saw Ld Kimberley—Ld Halifax—Mr Forster—& made to them severally my proposals. Ld Halifax took time to consider.[6] Saw Ld Camperdown —Irish Land Bill conclave 12–$1\frac{3}{4}$.—Mr Glyn—Ld Kildare. Dined

---

[1] See 25 July 42.   [2] The civil G.C.B., eventually declined.
[3] 'I believe that his [Kimberley's] views of Colonial questions are in harmony with the policy of your government.' Cardwell to Gladstone, 30 June 1870, Add MS 44119, f. 117.
[4] Figures given in Hansard as 251:130; Bright's amndt. prohibited 'teaching . . . in favour or against the distinctive tenets of any religious denomination'; Gladstone said its effect would be 'to introduce a new kind of State religion'; *H* ccii. 1281.
[5] An addition to the Hawarden estate, with mining interests; see above, Introduction, section X.   [6] See next day's cabinet.

at Sir D. Marjoribanks's house-warming. H of C. 2½–6½.[1] Read Ocean Telegraphy.[2] Saw Reed: &c two less satisfactory X.

To LORD HOWARD of Glossop, 1 July 1870.　　　　　　Add MS 44538, f. 181.
'Most private.'

I received from you & from others very urgent representations as to the bearing of the Education Bill on Roman Catholic interests. Feeling them to be in great measure just, I endeavoured with my colleagues to frame a modification of the measure which should meet the case. This modification we could only support or carry as a whole. One portion of it was fought last night, which was absolutely vital to our carrying the provision as to voluntary schools in which the Roman Catholic body are so deeply interested. We staked upon the whole plan the fate of the Bill & the credit of the Government. We were assailed last night by a powerful adverse movement on the amendment of Mr. Jacob Bright: & in the division out of 33 Irish Roman Catholic members (besides 3 belonging to the Government) 8 were present & voted with the Government or paired, & 25 were absent.[3]

You may well conceive what is our position under circumstances so extraordinary, in reference to representations which you or others may have to make.

2. Sat.

Wrote to Mr Hignett—Mrs Heywood—Ld de Grey—Sir B. Peacock[4] —Sir S. Cotton—The Queen 2 (& Mem)—and minutes. Saw Mr A. Munro—Mr M'Coll—Mr Glyn. Saw Hunt X. Rode with Helen & G. Cabinet 2½–5. Dined at Mr Holfords:[5] & saw the upper region of the house at night in all its glory. Conversation with Sir C. Lindsay[6] & Comte de Paris on Dante and other deep subjects. Read Rio.

D. St. Cabinet Sat July 2. 1870. 2.30 PM[7]
√ New appointments announced[8]
√ ABANDONMENT OF BILLS[9]
　　Glebe loans
　　Party processions—amend, & try.

[1] Education: *H* ccii. 1307.
[2] Probably J. C. Parkinson, *The ocean telegraph to India* (1870).
[3] Howard replied this day, Add MS 44427, f. 152: 'I did all I could . . . to get the Irish members to London. It is most unsatisfactory.'
[4] Sir Barnes *Peacock, 1810–90; kt. and vice-president of legislative council of India 1859; paid member of judicial cttee. of privy council 1872.
[5] Robert Stayner Holford, 1808–92; tory M.P. E. Gloucestershire 1854–72; built Dorchester House for his picture collection.
[6] Sir Coutts Lindsay, 1824–1913; soldier; 2nd bart. 1837.
[7] Add MS 44638, f. 93.
[8] *Granville as foreign secretary, *Kimberley as colonial secretary, *Halifax (not previously in this govt.) as lord privy seal. *Forster remained vice-president of the education cttee., but entered the cabinet.
[9] Statement on a number of these made by Gladstone on 18 July: *H* cciii. 412.

= Inclosures.
√ Army enlistment
= Parl[iamentary] Elections
√ Scotch Bills. = Scots Valuation An early morning for 1. Entail Bill 2. Game.
√ Ecclesiastical Titles
√ Extradition.
√ Ld Chancellor's Bills. Lords.
√ Savings Banks Bills.
= Merchant Ship Bill
√ Stamp Duties Bill—Not to announce on Monday if unopposed.
√ Mines
√ Post Office Bill. Difficulty
= Turnpike Acts Bill. Substitute a continuance Bill.
√ Census Bill. Religious enumeration in I[reland] & Scot[land] only.
= Real estate. Pilotage. Stands over.
√ Irish Marriage.
√ Judicial Committee: Plan: to pay two Indian Judges (retired). Temporary appt. of two Judges £2500 p.a.
√ Address carried by Col Sykes answer agreed on.[1]
√ Nat[ural] Hist Museum. C. of E. to answer Hope. Try S. Kensington again.
√ Alderney Breakwater. Mr Cardwell—Ld de Grey—Halifax—Chanc. of Exchr.—Hartington—Kimberley, and one from the Admiralty.[2]
√ Lectionary Bill: to go on.

List of Bills to be given up: Parl. Elections. Govt will not offer any opp[ositio]n to 2d R. of L[eatham']s Bill—Real Estate—Inclosures—Turnpike Roads (a continuing Bill to pass)—Scotch Valuation—Burgage Tenure—Merchant Shipping Bill.

3. 3 S. Trin.

Chapel Royal mg (with H.C.) & All Saints aft. Wrote to Ld Granville —Mr Childers—Mr Bright—Gen. Church. Saw Ld Lyttelton—Mrs Thistlethwayte X—Bp of Gloucester—Mr West. Read Rio 'Epilogue a l'Art Chretien'[3]—Bp of Gloucester on Revision[4]—'The Blood of Jesus'—Bavaria, M. Arnold, and Pusey Articles in Contemp Rev.[5]

4. M.

Wrote to Watsons (& Tel.)—Sir H. Elliot—Mrs Rumpff[R]—Ly M. Alford—Scotts—Earl Russell—The Queen—and minutes. Saw Mr Niewenhuys—Mr Hignett—D. of Sutherland—Mr Glyn—Scotts— M. Van de Weyer—Mr Cardwell—Mr Cross—Ld Houghton—Sir R.

[1] On 28 June, Col. Sykes had carried a motion (despite a speech against it by Gladstone) for an address for redress of grievances of E.I. officers: *H* cii. 1147.
[2] i.e. for a cabinet cttee., see 9 July 70.
[3] A. F. Rio, *Epilogue à L'Art chrétien*, 2v. (1870).   [4] See 12 June 70.
[5] *Contemporary Review*, xiv. 495, 540, 597 (July 1870).

Phillimore. H of C. 4¼-8¼ and 10¾-1¼. Dined at Stafford House and proposed the health of M. de Lesseps.[1] Spoke on Univ. Tests Bill & Education Bill.[2] Read Faraday——Articles in Baily's Mag.[3]

To EARL RUSSELL, 4 July 1870.   PRO 30/22/16F.

I assure you that Glyn will be most desirous to do anything he can for Amberley.[4] But alas for our poverty of which you can judge when I tell you that for a long long time we have been seeking in vain to get Sir H. Storks into Parliament, to assist Cardwell under his heavy burden, & have been unable to do it. I have again to thank you for your speech at the Warehousemen & Clerks Schools on Sat.[5] It was a great disappointment to us that Sir G. Grey lent the weight of his high authority to that foolish motion of Jacob Bright's,[6] but your judgement on the matter effectually consoles me & the bill is, I hope, now pretty safe. Your testimony on such a subject is of such a weight with the country as no official title could add to. It [is], I imagine, the fact of Mr. Bryce's having given way to Hyde, which disables us now from in any manner questioning his claim.

5. Tu.

Wrote to Ld Chancellor (2)——D. of Argyll——Mr Angerstein——Mr Childers——Col. Ponsonby——Mr Carvell Williams——The Queen——& minutes. Saw Ld De Tabley——Bp of B. & Wells——Mr Glyn——Mr MacColl——Mr Gurdon——Ld Camperdown——Ld Granville. H of C. 2½-7 and 9-1¼.[7] Dined with the Glyns. Read Faraday——Rio's Epilogue.

To J. CARVELL WILLIAMS, 5 July 1870.   Add MS 44427, f. 171.
'Private.'

Regarding your letter as a public one[8] I send an official acknowledgement in reply, but I cannot refrain from writing you a few lines to say how truly I am concerned to find that you see so much cause to object to certain provisions of the Education Bill as amended.

The immediate question at issue is indeed one of fact——is it or is it not proposed to support denominational Education at the public cost? This is the proposition which you maintain in regard to the Elementary Schools & which

---

[1] *The Times*, 5 July 1870, 12d.

[2] And made statement of hours of sitting of the House: *H* ccii. 1368, 1391, 1423.

[3] *Baily's monthly magazine of sports and pastimes, and turf guide*, xviii (July 1870).

[4] Gladstone to Russell, 1 July 1870, Add MS 44538, f. 180, on impossibility of getting Amberley adopted at Brecon.

[5] See *Daily Telegraph*, 4 July 1870.

[6] Bible teaching in schools not to support or deny any denomination position: *H* ccii. 1270.

[7] Spoke on the 'Bombay' and 'Oneida' incident: *H* ccii. 1540.

[8] Not found published; Williams was secretary of the Liberation Society; see 14 May 68.

we deny. I hope our denial will be well tried & tested in that arena of debate of which you would be the last man to question the searching power, & the consequent authority, & this is all that now remains for political discussion. The rest is for private retrospect & reflection & has no connection with the interest of the Government, or the fate of the Bill. But I own to you that the history of these last few months leaves on my mind some melancholy impressions which I hope at some fancied period of future leisure and retirement to study & to interpret.

6. Wed.

Wrote to Ld Granville—Ld Kinnaird—Queen (Tel.)—Mrs Thistlethwayte—Sir W. Tite—Ld Chancr Ireland—Queen (Mem)—Ld Huntington[1]—M. Lavalette and minutes. Saw Depn on Chamn Bills[2]—Baron de Rothschild jun[3]—Ld Granville—Ld de Grey—Ld Halifax—M. Lavalette[4]—D. of Mecklinburg[5]—D. of Cambridge—Prince of Wales—Col. Ponsonby. Saw Mrs C. Rumpff[R]. Concert at B. Palace. Read Revue des Deux M.[6] Attended Council at Windsor & had an audience of the Queen.

√ 1.[7] Civil Lordship of the Admiralty. Ld Camperdown. O 2. Thames Embankment. √ 3. M. de Lesseps. G[rand] C[ross] Star of India.[8] Lange[9] Knighthood. √ 4. Mr Bright. Ld Lothian. √ 5. Mr Forster. Audience. √ 6. Spanish Throne.[10]

7. Th.

Wrote to Ld Camperdown—Mr D.A. Lange—Mr Bruce—M. De Lavalette—The Queen Mem. and Letter—Vicomte De Lesseps (2)—and minutes. Sixteen to breakfast. Saw Bp of Lichfield—Col. Ponsonby—Ld de Grey *cum* Mr Forster—Dr Rigg—Mr Glyn—Mr [J.] B[aldwin] Brown—Mr Allon. H of C. $4\frac{1}{4}$-$8\frac{3}{4}$ and $9\frac{3}{4}$-$2\frac{3}{4}$.[11] Read Faraday. Dined with the Wests.

[1] Francis Theophilus Henry Hastings, 1808-75; 12th earl of Huntington 1828; a liberal.
[2] No report found.
[3] Probably Alfred Charles Rothschild of Tring, 1842-1918; baron of the Austrian Empire; director of the Bank of England 1868-90.
[4] For this talk, see Ramm I, i. 106 and 7 July 70.
[5] See 28 June 43.
[6] *Revue des Deux Mondes*, lxxxviii (July 1870); 'Les hommes d'État de L'Angleterre. William Ewart Gladstone'; see Add MS 44424, f. 230.
[7] Notes for the audience at Windsor, undated; Add MS 44638, f. 98.
[8] Offered to him in next day's letter; Add MS 44538, f. 186.
[9] See 17 July 57.
[10] She recollected Clarendon's comments on the Spanish succession in 1869; see 9 July 70n. and Ramm I, i. 107.
[11] Questions, education: *H* ccii. 1621.

To the MARQUIS DE LA VALETTE,   Add MS 44427, f. 173.[1]
French ambassador, 7 July 1870.

I am sorry that the forced & sudden close of our conversation last night deprived me of the benefit of hearing from your mouth the full statement of the motives which have actuated your Government at this grave juncture in their policy with regard to the throne of Spain.

[2][In the painful & somewhat difficult question which has arisen, I am happy to think that our first efforts are decidedly in the direction which you desire, & which you have pressed upon us. If they do not succeed, be assured they will not have failed from want of Earnestness, & they will, I trust, be found to have been such as will in any contingency warrant our continuing to hold in every quarter the language of moderation & peace.]

If you have found Lord Granville reserved, I am confident it has been because he felt that any hope we might entertain of being able to render useful service would be frustrated unless he made it his first care to approach and ascertain the exact facts in a spirit of perfect calmness; & in any professions he might make, not to go beyond, but to keep within his hopes and his desires to study alike the honour of Friendly Powers, the principles of public law, & the peace of Europe.

I am sure that you will find that however sparing he may have been of assurances often tending to mislead, his conduct & that of the Government he represents will be & I may say has been, conformable to the warm & prolonged sentiments of friendship which have prevailed between our two countries; & has proceeded upon a just estimate of what is due to the susceptibilities of France.

8. Fr.

Wrote to Ld Granville (2)—Ld Lyttelton—The Queen (2)—and minutes. H of C. 2½-7 and 9-1¼.[3] Wrote Draft of reply to Address.[4] Saw Mr Glyn—Mr Buxton—The Speaker—The French Ambassador—The Lord Advocate. Finished Faraday. Rode in evg.

9. Sat. [Chislehurst, Kent]

Wrote to The Queen (2)—Ld Granville—Chancr of Exr—Lady Dinorben—Mr Ayrton—and minutes. Framed answer to Address of H. of C. Saw Ld Granville—Mr Ayrton—Mr Glyn—Sig. Cortchazzi.[5] Cabinet 2¾-6. Dined at Ld Sefton's. Finished M. Challemel Lacours very able Critique.[6] Went at 11 PM down to R. Cavendish.

---

[1] There are several drafts of this letter; this appears to have been the version sent, a fair copy taken from holograph draft.
[2] Passage in [ ] is in the holograph draft, but not in the fair copy.
[3] Questions, and defeat on Address on Thames embankment: *H* ccii. 1752.
[4] See cabinet on 9 July 70.
[5] Possibly F. Cortazzi who lived in Kensington.
[6] Untraced article by P. A. Challemel-Lacour forwarded for the author by W. P. Price, M.P.; see Add MS 44538, f. 197.

Cabinet 10 D. St. Sat Jul 9 2.30 PM[1]
√ Spanish Throne[2]
√ Sir W. Hutt's question. To reply.[3]
√ Oneida Subscription. *No*. Crew U.S. sailors.[4]
√ Alderney [Breakwater] Committee. Mr. Lowe reported. Mr. Hawkshaw to be allowed the sum of £10,000 to try what is practicable.
√ Party Processions. Bill to be withdrawn.
√ Park Road. Mr. Ayrton's comm[unicatio]n approved.
√ Amendments to Irish Land Bill.[5]
√ Lord Chancellor's Bills.
√ Answer to address of H. of C. respecting Embankments Land: adopted.[6]
√ Ld. Stratford's motion on Greece. Previous question.
√ Week's business.

To R. LOWE, chancellor of the exchequer,   Add MS 44538, f. 187.
9 July 1870.

As we have much to do in Cabinet today & little time to do it in——I send you a sketch of answer[7] which it seems to me would place us on strong ground with regard to the address so improperly carried last night by the House of Commons.

We shall have the Law Officers present. I had written out paragraphs pointing more directly to the objectionable character of the address but perhaps these would irritate & may be spared. If you approve of the draft, pray [send it] to the Solicitor General to whom I had an opportunity of speaking last night.

2. Mr. Graves *wishes* to ask publicly (unless we disapprove) whether we will propose any vote in aid of the subscription for the relief of the families of those drowned in the Oneida. We can speak of this today.

10. 4 S. Trin.

Chiselhurst Ch. mg. Conversation with R.C. & Lacaita. Read Union Rev.[8] —Brit. Quarterly Rev.[9]—Symington on Faith[10]—Bp of Winchester's Heroes.[11] Wrote to Ld Granville (2)—Col. Ponsonby—and minutes.

---

[1] Add MS 44638, f. 100.

[2] An undated fragment, not by Gladstone, but docketed by him '2.30 CHT', reads: 'War certain unless the King of Prussia gives way. We have telegraphed to Madrid.' Gladstone to West, 8 July 1870, reads: 'See whether in Lord Clarendon's letters of last autumn to me there is anything about Prince Leopold (Hohenz.) & the throne of Spain.' West's reply, on the same sheet, reads: 'Nothing between May 1869 & Jan. 1870 A. E. W[est].' Add MS 44638, f. 102.

[3] Gladstone answered Hutt on the Spanish throne on 11 July: *H* cciii. 33.

[4] The British Captain of the 'Bombay' was much criticised for not assisting crew of U.S. 'Oneida' after colliding with it in Jan. 1870.

[5] Sent back by the Lords.

[6] On 8 July W. H. *Smith had defeated govt. on office buildings on the Embankment.

[7] Not found in Add MS 44301; see also Gladstone to Cardwell, 12 July 1870, Add MS 44538, f. 190.

[8] *Union Review*, (July 1870).   [9] *British Quarterly Review*, lii (July 1870).

[10] A. J. Symington, *The reasonableness of faith* (1870).   [11] See 20 Mar. 70.

11. M. [London]

Returned to London by the 10.3 train. Wrote to Dean of Waterford
—Bp of Winchr—Lady Jersey—Mr Anderson MP—the Queen (3)
—and minutes. 12–2. Princess Louise came to breakfast: and charmed
all. Two round tables. Some more guests followed: music: luncheon
at 3 tables when the Princess was gone. M. de Lesseps was here & was
presented. Saw Col. Ponsonby—Mr Glyn—The Law Officers—Mr
F. Knowles—Chancr of Exr. Worked further on ansr to Address of
Friday, wh is a nice matter. H of C. 4¼–8 and 8¾–2½.[1]

12. Tu.

Wrote to Col. Ponsonby—Bp of Winchester—The Queen (and Mem.)
—Ld Granville—and minutes. H of C. 2¼–7 and 9¾–2. We disposed
of the Land Bill amendments.[2] Saw Sol. General—Att. General—
Chr of Exr—Mr Stansfeld—Mr Cardwell—Mr Bruce—Mr Goschen
—Ld Granville—Mr Glyn—Dr Clark—who examined me with
care. Read Ocean Telegraphy.[3] Dined at Mr Lefevres.

13. Wed.

Wrote to Ld Granville—Ld Kimberley—Hon A. Gordon—Mrs
Thistlethwayte—Ld Russell—Scotts—Marchss of Lothian—Ld S.
Kerr (Telegr.)[4]—& minutes. Saw Sir W. Heathcote—Count Bernstorff—Mr Glyn—Mr Hodgson—Mr Forster—Ld De Tabley—
Lord Granville. Attended the St Paul's meeting in the City at 3 &
spoke.[5] Read Ocean Telegraphy. Dined at Ld De Tabley's. Fine Arts
party[6] at my house afterwards. With much reluctance I abandoned
the intention of going to Lothian's funeral.

14. Th.

Wrote to Mr Whatman—Ld Bessborough—The Queen (2)—&
minutes. Saw Archbishop of York—Ld Granville—Mr Glyn—Ld
Kimberley—Mr Ayrton—Mr Murphy—Scotts—Chancr of Exr—

---

[1] Spanish throne, education: *H* cciii. 33, 41.
[2] *H* cciii. 118. This day's note on land revenues in Add MS 44759, f. 133.
[3] See 1 July 70.
[4] To Lord Schomberg Henry Kerr, 1833–1900, 9th marquis of Lothian July 1870, regretting, after strong pressure from Granville to stay in London (Ramm I, i. 111), his
inability to attend the funeral of his br. the 8th marquis; Add MS 44427, ff. 175, 193.
[5] Meeting to raise funds to clean and complete St. Paul's, 'a burning reproach to Englishmen': *The Times*, 14 July 1870, 8a.
[6] The Fine Arts Club; see 17 July 61 and above v. lxi.

Mr Fortescue—& others. Saw Mad. Charles[R]. Cabinet 12½-1¾: summoned at an hour's notice. We agreed on Telegrams & answers for this sad business. Dined with the Wests, H of C. 4¼-8¼ and 9¼-5. Answers early in evg.—A great battle with a minority which after 14 divisions we beat.[1]

Cabinet July 14 70 12.30 PM. Summons sent out at 11.30[2]

        (Candidature of Prince Leopold for Spanish Throne.)
Proposals to Prussia & France considered.
Drafts of Telegrams read & approved.
(Finally settled with Lord G[ranville] afterward)[3]
Determined to make general replies in both Houses today to any question wh. may be put.[4]

1.[5] We ought not to interfere between Regent & Minister.
2. We ought not to labour for a combination of Powers.
3. We ought not to admit to France that she will be justified in carrying into effect the threat of immediate war which she has made in the event of failure of efforts to cancel the Candidature.
4. We ought, without reserve or qualification to dissuade Spain from the Candidature a) on general grounds of prudence, & of the *future* opened by the arrangement b) because the secrecy of this project has given just offence, as against the comity[6] of nations.
On the same grounds we might suggest to the K. of Prussia to forbid the acceptance.[7]

15. Fr.

Wrote to Ld Bessborough—The Queen 2—and minutes. H of C. 2¼-6.[8] Saw Count Bernstorff (2)—Lord Granville (ter)—Mr Fortescue —Mr Ayrton—Ld de Grey—Mr Glyn—Mr Cardwell. Dined with the Wests. Virtual declaration of war by France. Read Q.R. on Lothair.[9] Saw three[R].

16. Sat.

Wrote to Ld Huntley[10]—Mr Cardwell—Watsons—Bp of Winchester —Bp of Moray—The Queen—and minutes. Cabinet 12¼-4. Saw Ld

---

[1] Over the ballot clauses for election of school boards: *H* cciii. 301.
[2] Add MS 44638, f. 104. The cabinet met after the publication of the Ems telegram in this day's Continental newspapers, but before news of it reached London; Millman, 193.
[3] See Ramm I, i. 112n. For Gladstone's summary of the decisions, see Guedalla, *Q*, i. 236.   [4] Drafts of answers, all rejected, at Add MS 44638, f. 105.
[5] Undated note, clearly referring to options considered this day; Add MS 44638, f. 103.
[6] This word scrawled.   [7] Bismarck rejected this; Millman, 194.
[8] Note of question from *Disraeli, and answer, in Add MS 44759, f. 136; *H* cciii. 346.
[9] *Quarterly Review*, cxxix. 63 (July 1870).
[10] Successfully offering lordship-in-waiting to Charles Gordon, 1847-1937, 11th marquis of Huntly.

Kimberley—Ld Spencer—Mr Motley—Count Bernstorff—Mr Hammond. Dined at Ld Egerton's. Countess Bernstorff's afterwards. Read Q.R. on Army Admn.[1]

Cabinet D. St Jul 16 12 noon[2]

1. War.

a. Ask HM to allow engag[emen]t for a Council to remain pendent

b. Contraband of war not to be prohibited.

c. Proclamation of neutrality to be framed & held ready. No reference to prohibition of enlistment.

d. Recommendation of Comm[issio]n to obtain from Parliament power to seize ships intended to be employed by Belligerent.

e. Members of the Cabinet to be summoned pro hâc vice to consider questions of neutral right & duty.

f)[3] Lyons to inform us at the first moment of a decl[aration] a [*sc.* of] war, or of actual hostilities.

g) Belligerents to be asked to declare as Russia & Turkey did with reference to interfering as little as may be with commerce of neutrals.

h) thank France for her spontaneous decl[aration] respecting Neutrality of Belgium: & suggest the same to Prussia.

i) Gratuitous issue of charts to be stopped.

j) Sale of old ships of war to be stopped.

k) To be silent officially about Luxemburg but Lyons to try to learn.

l) At request of France undertake to protect French subjects in the German Territory.

m) Prince of Wales—WEG to call respecting his proposal to go to Denmark for the Princess.[4]

n) Cardwell's statement of force. To inquire what could be done in the shortest time.

p) Determined not to stop the visits of foreigners to our military & naval establishments.

q) Military & naval officers to be sent to the respective armies & to the French Baltic fleet.

r) Discharges of workmen in Dockyards: not to be suspended.

2. Irish Land Amendments.

3. Canada. Carnarvon's motion on the use of Regulars in Canada.[5] Previous question if necessary. Complaints of Canada as to Fenianism in U.S. to be put together: for submission to U.S. Govt. Canadian demand for pay[men]t of expenses of raid. Answer to keep the question open.

4. Week's business. Bills to be dropped: Mines Regulation—give up—Savings Bank—Pilotage Bill—Univ. Tests Bill: De Grey to communicate with Ld Salisbury. Retain legal provision as to worship in Chapels &c.

Hosier.[6] Applies to be correspondent. decline

---

[1] *Quarterly Review*, cxxix. 244 (July 1870).

[2] Add MS 44638, f. 106. This meeting lasted over four hours; see Guedalla, *Q*, i. 237.

[3] Rest of the list written on next page, from the bottom upwards.

[4] *Wales brought Alexandra back on the royal yacht.

[5] *Carnarvon withdrew his motion after debate, 22 July 1870: *H* cciii. 703.

[6] *Delane observed on 17 July: 'The two Hoziers were ready to start for the Prussian army last night . . . but they are retained lest the presence of British officers with the Prus-

To E. CARDWELL, war secretary, 16 July 1870.   PRO 30/48/7, f. 74.
'Immediate.'

[First letter:] Can you give me today, ever so roughly, a comparison of our really available regular military force at this time as compared with what it was say in 1859 and 1866—or any other recent years more convenient. By available force, I mean force at home & in the Mediterranean—or the former only.[1]

[Second letter:] I have read the answer you prepared with so much promptitude. If unhappily, which God forbid, we have to act in this war, it will not be with 6 months, nor 3 months, nor even one month's notice: and the real question is supposing an urgent call of honour and duty in an emergency for 15000 or 20000 men, what would you do? What answer would the military authorities make to this question, those of them especially who have brains rather than mere position? Have you *no* fuller battalions than those of 500? At home or in the Mediterranean? If in the latter should they not be brought home?

Childers seemed to offer a handsome subscription of Marines: & the Artillery would count for much in such a case as is most probable. What I should like is to study the means of sending 20000 men to Antwerp with as much promptitude as at the time of the Trent affair we sent 10000 to B.N.A.[2]

17. 5 S. Trin.

Bedfordbury Ch. mg. Surrey[?] aftn & baptism of Mr Goschen's child to which though much too old I stood godfather.[3] Wrote to Ld Granville—Mr Hammond—and minutes. Saw Mrs Th.X. Read Fuller's Thoughts[4]—Perowne on the Psalms.[5]

To E. HAMMOND, 17 July 1870.   Add MS 44538, f. 193.

I presume Ld G. has promised papers immediately. I am not aware of having done it myself. I said when the time should come without definite indication I should not be disposed to regard the promise as irrevocable if policy is the other way.
2. I do not as yet comprehend the force of the objection to putting forward the Duke of Aosta's candidature which primâ facie looks like a means of enabling the French to withdraw their demand of our engagement covering the future.
3. Combined neutrality would never do.

sian army should excite the just susceptibilities of the Emperor.' Dasent, *Delane,* ii. 265. (Sir) Henry Hozier, 1838–1907; see R. S. Churchill, *W. S. Churchill* (1967), ii. 248.

[1] War Office paper on 'Strength of continental armies', & undated printed paper by Cardwell, 'Military Organization', in Add MS 44615, ff. 15, 32, and untitled MS of 24 July 1870 on state of the army, Add MS 44119, f. 134.
[2] Part in Morley, ii. 339.
[3] William Henry, 1870–1943, 2nd s. of G. J. *Goschen.
[4] T. *Fuller, *Good thoughts in bad times* (1645).
[5] See 1 May 70.

18 M.

Wrote to Lord Lieutt[1]—Archbp of Armagh—H.J.G.—Mr Cardwell
—Watts—Abp of Canterb.—Scotts—The Queen: letter, Tel.,[2] &
Mem.—and minutes. Saw Mr Glyn—The Prince of Wales[3]—Ld
Granville—D of St Alban's—Chancr of Exchr—A.R. Hyde (in
Hull)[4]—The Speaker. Rode with Agnes. H of C. 4¼-8¼ and 9-12½.
Read Gainsborough's Life (finished)[5]—Marsh on English Language.[6]

19. Tu.

Lay on my back all day, because of threatenings. Wrote to The Prince
of Wales—The Queen *bis* and Tel.[7]—R. Lawley—Mr Leeman—Mr
Glyn—Ld Granville—Mr Childers—Bp of Lichfield—& minutes.
Saw Baron Rothschild—Ld Granville—Mr Glyn (2)—Mr Cardwell
—Dr Clark (2)—Rev Mr M'Coll—D. of Argyll—Count Bernstorff:
do *cum* G[ranville].[8] Read N.A.Quart.Rev. on Travel[9]—Mr M'Coll's
Ammergau Passionspiel[10]—Stanhope's Hist.[11]

20. Wed.

Wrote to The Queen—Prince of Wales—Ld Spencer—Mr T.B. Potter—Mr Brand—Sig. L. Torrigiani[12]—and minutes. Saw Ld Granville—Mr R. Lawley—Dr Clark—Prince of Wales—and others.
Radcliffe Trust 2¼-4.[13] To Holland House at 4.30. Watts's Studio
6.30: a great sight. Dined at Grillion's. Saw Jacobs: a notable case
with much hope[R].

To H. B. W. BRAND, M.P., 20 July 1870.   Add MS 44538, f. 194.

The prospect you hold out is most attractive: but I am afraid Glyn would not
give his consent. I was a forced absentee from the House yesterday with some
slight inkling of my illness of last year but the 24 hours of complete bodily rest
have set me all right again. I must however look to pretty close attendance until
the end of the Session which there seems to be some disposition to hasten.

The war is a grievous affair & adds much to our cares for to maintain our
neutrality in such a case as this will be a most arduous task. On the face of the

---

[1] i.e. *Spencer.   [2] Arranging next day's Council; Guedalla, *Q,* i. 239.
[3] See 16 July 70.   [4] Apparently *sic*; obscure.   [5] See 10 June 70.
[6] G. P. Marsh, *The origin and history of the English language* (1862).
[7] Statement of military and naval force: Guedalla, *Q,* i. 243.
[8] At this meeting Bernstorff told Gladstone and Granville of the French proposal to
Prussia in 1867 and 1869 to trade S. Germany for Belgium; Gladstone replied that such a
communication was 'an insult to the govt. to which it was made'; Millman, 200.
[9] *North American Review*, cx. 260 (April 1870).   [10] See 5 Feb. 70.
[11] See 21 Mar. 70.   [12] Had sent a book; Add MS 44538, f. 194.
[13] As its chairman; see 25 May 55.

facts France is wrong but as to personal trustworthiness the two moving spirits on the respective sides, Napoleon & Bismarck are nearly on a par.
Poor Glyn is much apprehensive today about a sister in law Mrs. H. Glyn.

21. Th.

Wrote to Ld Granville (2)—Count Bernstorff—The Queen (2)—Mr Phillips—and minutes. Saw Ld Granville—Mr M'Coll—Mr Glyn— Mr A. Gordon—Ld Granville *cum* Mr Hammond—Mr Kendall—Sir Thos G.—Dined with West. Twelve to breakfast. H of C. 4¼-8¼ and 9¼-1½.[1] Read Wilkinson on Forcible Introspection.[2]

22. Fr.

Wrote to Ld Chancellor—Sir T.E. May—H.J.G.—Mr Geo. Pringle —Scotts—Watson & Smith—The Queen—Mr Lambert[3]—Ld Lyttelton—and minutes. Dined with the F. Cavendishes. Saw Bp of Brechin—Mr Fortescue—Mr Glyn—Mr Leeman—Sir R. Palmer— Mr Cardwell[4]—Mr Childers—Mr Stansfeld—Bar. Brunnow—Count Bernstorff—M. Lefevre—R. Lawley. H of C. 2¼-6½. Then to C.s Garden party, & H of C. 9½-1.[5] Read Duchess of Cleveland's Ruby.[6]

To Count A. VON BERNSTORFF, 22 July 1870.   Add MS 44538, f. 195.

My sister 'Mrs. Helen Gladstone' has been residing for some time at the Hotel Disch in Cologne, & she has no one, but her servants, with her. She is naturally desirous to move, at this critical juncture, from a pt. so exposed, & is at the same time apprehensive of obstructions. Would it be too much if I were to ask whether you could kindly pen two or three lines, which she might upon occasion present to any Prussian employé, requesting that any reasonable assistance or facility might be afforded to her movements. With her regular passport, I think a British one, she is of course provided. Unhappily she is an invalid, & moves with considerable difficulty, so as to be in an unusual degree dependent upon those about

[1] Made statements on neutrality and the war, Irish Land Bill amndts., civil estimates; *H* cciii. 645, 665, 679, 691.

[2] J. J. G. Wilkinson, *The forcible introspection of women for the army and navy by the oligarchy, considered physically* (1870).

[3] Asking him to withdraw his motion to increase the Prime Minister's salary from £5000 to £8000; Add MS 44538, f. 196.

[4] On whether to submit increased estimates; Gladstone's note this day, on Cardwell's mem. requesting application to the Commons, reads (PRO 30/48/7, f. 86): 'This is for conversation rather than notes: but it appears to me upon such papers as I have seen that, in case of the great emergency & necessity which alone would bring us into action, we could send 25000 men to Antwerp or elsewhere without any aid from Parliament (I include 5000 marines) and without sending one fivehundred battalion. I do not therefore as yet see the case for going to Parliament.'

[5] Spoke on education: *H* cciii. 744.   [6] Untraced.

her. I hope you may think the circs. excuse the great liberty I have taken whether you can comply with my request or not. God send a speedy deliverance.[1]

To Sir T. E. MAY, Clerk of the Commons,   Add MS 44538, f. 195.
22 July 1870. 'Secret.'

Will you kindly tell me
1. What is the shortest time within which you consider that Parlt. can be summoned on Emergency? (I think the Germans did it last week in 3 or 4 days). 2. What is the shortest time within which votes can be had say (a) for increasing no. of army (b) for vote of credit (c) for Embodying Militia. 3. It is [sic] not the fact that our present rules as to supply are cumbrous, & waste days, & if so would it not be proper before the Prorogation to alter & abridge them.[2]

23. Sat.

Wrote to Ld Acton—Bp of Winchester—Mr Price—Mr Childers— The Queen—and minutes. Saw Mr Cardwell with Sir H. Storks and Sir W. Mansfield 11-12.—Ld Granville—Mr Glyn—Ld Chancellor. Cabinet 2¼-5: stiff. 5-12: Went down to Greenwich to preside at meeting of Cobden Club: spoke at some length, & touched the war as war.[3] Saw M. Laveleye[4]—Mr Bigelow[5]—and others.

Cabinet Sat. Jul 23. 2.30 PM. D. St.[6]
√ 1. Business for the week H of C discussed.
√ 2. Univ. Tests Bill—partially [discussed].
√ 3. Irish Land Bill amendments partially [discussed]
√ 4. Childers made statement of the condition of the Naval Force & Establishments. Proportion to France 3:2—Statements deemed satisfactory.
√ 5. Discussion on condition of the Army—continued for some time & interrupted by the departure of the Chancellor & WEG for the Cobden Club dinner.

24. 6 S. Trin.

After breakfast went to the Coopers[7] for the day, under my wife's orders. The air was charming. Chiselhurst Ch. mg & aft. Read Fuller

[1] Bernstorff arranged her safe passage; Add MS 44427, f. 209.
[2] Reply probably oral, see 25 July 70; see also 28 July 70n.
[3] '. . . among all the wars by which the course of the 19th century has been chequered there is none which might be characterised as a more unspeakable drawback, as more unmixedly sorrowful, more full of every painful association. . . . I do not know what is to be the immediate fate of the ideas of Mr. Cobden . . .'; *The Times*, 25 July 1870, 6c.
[4] Baron Emile Louis Victor de Laveleye, 1822–92, Belgian economist at the dinner; see Gladstone's introductory letter to his 'Protestantism and Catholicism, in their bearing upon liberty and prosperity of nations' (1875), anticipating Weber and Tawney.
[5] John Bigelow, 1817–1911; American editor, diplomatist and free-trader.
[6] Add MS 44638, f. 108.
[7] Probably George Cooper of Widmore House, Bromley, nr. Chislehurst.

—Blenkinsop.[1] Wrote to Mr Fortescue—Ld Granville—Mr Adam
—Mr Cardwell. Back to town at 10.30.

To E. CARDWELL, war secretary, 24 July 1870.   PRO 30/48/7, f. 90.
'Private.'

I return your paper[2] after reading it with much interest. Will you let me have
a copy.

I entirely agree with you that *when* it is 'seriously intended' to send troops to
Antwerp or elsewhere abroad, 'immediate measures must be taken to increase
our force'.

I feel, however, rather uneasy at what seems to me the extreme susceptibility,
on one side of the case, of some members of the Cabinet. I hope it will be
balanced by considering the effect of any forward step by appeal to Parlt., in
compromising the true & entire neutrality of our position, & in disturbing & mis-
directing the mind of the public & of Parliament.

I am afraid I have conveyed to your mind a wrong impression as to the state
of my own. It is only a far outlook which, in my opinion, brings into view as a
possibility the sending a force to Antwerp. Should the day arrive we shall then
be on the very edge of war, with scarcely a hope of not passing onwards into the
abyss.

25. M. St James: marriage day & T.G.s birthday.

Wrote to Watson & Smith—Mr Pringle (2)—Mrs Th.—The Viceroy
—Mr Westall—Michel Chevalier—Sir H. Elliot—Abp of Canterbury
—The Queen (2)—and minutes. Saw Ld Granville—Mr Fortescue
—Mr Hope—Count Bernstorff—The Speaker—Sir T. E. May—Mr
Fawcett—Chancr of Exr. Cabinet 2-3½. H of C. 4¼-8 and 9½-1½.[3]
Dined with the F. Cavendishes. Read Stanhope. The day of the ex-
plosion of the 'Project of Treaty': in the Times.[4]

Cabinet Jul 25 2.30 PM[5]
√ Abp of Canterbury's proposal for a Prayer—decline with due explanations
   for the time.[6]
√ Fortescue. Resolution respecting Baron Hughes. Agreed to.
√ The Treaty in the Times. Answers to any possible questions agreed on[7]

---

[1] See 17 July 70 and 5 June 70.
[2] Paper on preparedness of the army, sent this day; PRO 30/48/7, f. 88 and Add MS
44119, f. 134.
[3] Answered *Disraeli's question on absence of a Blue Book, and the alleged Franco-
Prussian treaty: *H* cciii. 883. *Disraeli's notice of question on the Treaty is at Add MS
44427, f. 224.
[4] The draft treaty with Prussia proposed by France; see 20, 26 July 70; *The Times* (25
July 1870, 9d) did not disclose its source, but assured readers, 'the paper is authentic.'
[5] Add MS 44638, f. 109.
[6] *Tait had proposed a day of prayer for peace; Add MS 44538, f. 198.
[7] Draft answers at Add MS 44638, f. 111.

√ Army Question postponed: *quoad* applications to Parliament—but 'quiet preparation' of Snyders and torpedoes to be carried on at the discretion of the Sec. for War. Amendment of Standing Orders [of the House of Commons] and shortening the time in which Parlt. may be called.

√ Foreign Enlistment Act—Meeting appointed for today. Chancr. of Exr.—Ld Kimberley—Mr Bruce—Ld Halifax—Law Officers—Ld Granville—Forster.[1]

√ Univ. Tests Bill. They may beat us in L[ords] on Headships [of colleges]. We shall acquiesce in Commons: but not guarantee finality.

√ Mr Forster to answer Colebrooke in the sense of intending to have a Scotch Education Bill next year.[2]

√ Irish Land Bill amendments: course settled; Granville empowered.[3]

To M. CHEVALIER, 25 July 1870.   Add MS 44538, f. 198.

We much lamented your absence at the Cobden Club Festival on Sat. when we felt ourselves in the most painful discord with existing circumstances. Even more there did we lament its Cause. I cannot describe to you the sensation of pain, almost of horror which has thrilled through this country from end to end at the outbreak of hostilities, the commencement of the work of blood. I suppose there was a time when England would have said 'let our neighbours, being as they are our rivals waste their energies, their wealth, their precious irrecoverable lives, in destroying one another: they will be the weaker, we shall be, relatively, the stronger'. But we have now at least unlearned that bad philosophy; and the war between France & Prussia saddens the whole face of society, & burdens every man with a personal grief. We do not pretend to be sufficient judges of the merits: I now mean by 'we' those who are in authority, & perhaps in a condition to judge least ill. We cannot divide praise & blame as between parties: it would be impertinent to do so, but if we were entitled, as men in the Church are called to forbid the banns of an ill-assorted marriage, we should forbid this most ill-omened strife. I hope you do not think it unkind that I should write thus. Forgive the weakness[?] of a friend. One of the purposes in life dear to my heart has been to knit together in true amity the people of my own country with those of your great nation. That web of concord is too tender yet, not to suffer under the rude strain of conflicts & concussions even such as we have no material share in. I think that even if I err, I cannot be without a portion of your sympathy: now when the knell of the brave begins to toll. As for us, we have endeavoured to cherish with both the relations of peace & mutual respect. May nothing happen to impair them! If you come over, I shall hope to have early notice of your arrival.

26. Tu.

Wrote to Ld Granville (2)—Mr Cardwell (2)—Mr Thring—Mr Hopwood—The Queen (3)—and minutes. Saw Mr Christie—Mr Glyn —Ld Granville (2). H of C. 2-7 and 9½-1.[4] Much & various work. Saw Davis X. A few to dinner.

[1] See 6 Aug. 70.   [2] This day: *H* cciii. 875.
[3] Final stages of negotiation; Steele, *Irish Land*, 311.
[4] Gave details from *Loftus of the draft treaty: *H* cciii. 955.

To E. CARDWELL, war secretary, 26 July 1870.   PRO 30/48/7, f. 95.

I thank you very much for your frank remark[1]—but are you not, like the rest of our tribe, a little suspicious? I can explain the subject of the observation more fully in conversation; but I will now mention succinctly one or two points. 1. It was by no arrangement of mine that the Cabinet was asked last Saturday to determine whether 10,000 men should be added to the army—it was your doing only—no complaint attaches to it—but you cannot hold me responsible for the effect of a proceeding which I did not know was to arise, & which I thought premature. 2. It was by mere accident that Granville & I, who were much oppressed, & greatly puzzled, by this strange communication of Count Bernstorff's made to us individually & personally, had not on our own personal responsibility consulted you & one or two more upon it on Saturday at two just before the Cabinet— not in the least in anticipation of a military proposal to be then made & decided. 3. It was wholly impossible for us, without much previous consideration, to intercept your proposal when we heard it by at once throwing the information down before the entire body of our Colleagues.

Our possession of it was in truth one of several reasons which made me regret the discussion: but we anticipated, as it turned out, that the Prussians would themselves give the secret to the world, & I believe firmly that the original communication to G. & me was a trap laid for us by Bismarck, who probably thought he would so stir our fears & indignation as to make us become the instruments of the publication. This we had sense enough to avoid, but amidst the tumults of business we had made no further progress, except the intercepted intention I have named, when we were overtaken by the debate you raised.

[P.S.] I think that on any principle except that of indulgent interpretation, Granville would have believed me & I might have believed him, guilty of a trick about the Irish Land Bill. There is really no getting on with any other rule. In this note I speak entirely for myself: & blame no one.

27. Wed.

Wrote to Mr Cardwell—The Queen (Mema & letter)—Bp of Winchester—Sir Thos G.—and minutes. Prince Arthur visited me at one. He was most pleasing. H of C. 2¼-5. Spoke on the Ballot.[2] Saw Mr Phillips—Mr F. Lawley—Mr Glyn—Ld Granville—Saw Mrs Th.— Graham. Dined with the Glyns. Read Dupont White.[3]

To E. CARDWELL, war secretary, 27 July 1870.   PRO 30/48/7, f. 101.

As I may fail to see you today I write to thank you for taking mine so completely in the spirit which should prevail between colleagues & old friends:[4] but

---

[1] Cardwell to Gladstone, 26 July 1870, PRO 30/48/7, f. 93, complained of not being informed about the draft treaty.

[2] Supporting 2°R of Leatham's Bill: *H* cciii. 1028.

[3] C. B. Dupont-White, *Le progrès politique en France* (1868).

[4] Cardwell to Gladstone, 27 July 1870, Add MS 44119, f. 146: 'The misunderstanding seems to have lain in this; viz. that I thought your calling upon Childers [on 23 July] involved a call upon me,—while you thought my proposal wd. not come forward at that Cabinet.'

also to tell you our responsibility is greater than you suppose for it was on the afternoon of *Tuesday*, when I was on my back, that Bernstorff told us of the Treaty though the pressure of business & the puzzle of the subject had prevented us from clearly seeing our way except to that which was the most important thing, viz. not to become Bismarck's cat's paws by taking the responsibility for the publication of the Treaty.

28. Th.

Caught with another threatening in the night prob. from change of wind: kept my bed till the afternoon. Wrote to Mr Hopwood—The Queen (and Mem.)—& minutes. Saw Ld Granville—do cum Ld Halifax—Mr Cardwell—Mr Glyn—Chancr of Exr—Mr Ouvry—Mr Goschen—WHG. Dined with the Wests. H of C. and H. of L. 4¼-8 and 9½-2.[1] Read Stanhope.

29. Fr.

Rose at twelve: pretty well. Wrote to Ld Granville (2)—The Queen (Mem & letter)—Duke of Cambridge—Governor of the Bank—Ld Halifax—Baron Beaulieu (2)—King of the Belgians—Col. Ponsonby and minutes. Saw Duke of Cambridge—Lord Granville (2)—Mr Glyn—Rev Mr M'Coll—Govr of Bank—Govr of Bank *cum* Mr Hodgson—Baron Beaulieu—Ld Halifax—Count Bernstorff. Saw Wilson[R]. H of C. 3½-6 and 9-2.[2] Read Laveleye[3]—Franco Prussian Papers.[4]

To BARON BEAULIEU, Belgian minister,   Add MS 44427, f. 241.
29 July 1870.

It is now past 5, & in order not to lose time, I send this note to urge your Excellency to telegram at once to H.M. that I think a confidential person thoroughly acquainted with the affairs & situation of the Bank should at once be sent over to lay the case before the Governor of the Bank of England, from whom he would meet with a friendly reception, & every disposition to act upon the wish expressed by the King provided it can be done conformably to the essential rules of an Establishment like the Bank. Later this afternoon I will do myself the honour to write to H.M.[5]

[1] *Granville's statement on the situation; moved 1°R of [emergency] Meeting of Parliament Bill: *H* cciii. 1146.
[2] Questioned on inventions: *H* cciii. 1230.
[3] E. L. V. de Laveleye, *Études et essais* (1869).
[4] The second Blue Book on the war was published this day; *PP* 1870 lxx. 101; also E. Hertslet's foreign office mem. on 'supposed' negotiations and the Benedetti initiative; Add MS 44615, f. 49.
[5] Gladstone arranged a meeting with the Bank: Add MS 44427, f. 242.

To LORD HALIFAX, lord privy seal, 29 July 1870.   Hickleton MSS A 4.88.

I own reflection inclines my mind the other way.[1] Arming, in whatever degree, may appease the public mind, but it is only preparing discredit for the future, if it is attended with no measure towards obtaining aid for the defence of Belgium, but only with a conviction that we cannot defend her alone, and that nobody else will help us.

In your general view of the probable disposition of the Powers I agree. But it seems to me that the publication of the nefarious Project of Treaty, has given us an immense advantage at this moment, in respect to the two Belligerents—if only we use it *now*: and that one, or even both, may be morally compelled to enter into engagements, which would give Belgium a new security.

If we arm *without* doing anything else, my opinion is that it will worsen our relations with both belligerents, and that it *may* help to bring about a new con-spiracy between them, in the face of which our arming would run the risk of becoming ridiculous. To that course I can not see my way.

To The O'DONOGHUE, M.P., 29 July 1870.   Add MS 44538, f. 201.

I regret as much, as bitterly as you can do, the tenacity with which the Lords have contended for their final amendments in the Irish Land Bill. It has been such & so applied as to suggest that fear rather than any larger wisdom has been the main cause of the acceptance of the chief provisions of the Bill. We have used every effort of persuasion but in the end have simply had to determine whether to throw over the measure rather than give way to these amendments. On this question we have conferred as we best could with some Irish members in Town, & from the language they have used I am led to believe that you too, while we enter into your feelings would not dissent from our course.

I will send to the Postmaster General your observations on the Post Office Bill.

30. Sat.

Wrote to The Queen—Col. Ponsonby—and minutes. Ld Mayor's dinner: made a peaceful speech to a warlike company.[2] Cabinet 2½-5¾ and the important decisions taken for the 'situation'. Conclave in D St at 12 on Irish Church Charter. At 2 on the War & measures to be taken. Read [blank]

Cabinet July 30. 70. 2½ PM[3]
√ 1. Greece. Ld G[ranville] announced we persevere in the inquiry not with-standing the war. Warn her agt. aggression on others & say she must take the consequences.[4]

[1] Halifax's letter, 29 July, Add MS 44185, f. 29, continued conversation of 28 July, opposed 'our taking any step with other powers', proposed 'some vote for money & men. We shall hardly be allowed by public opinion to do nothing. . . .'
[2] Though his view that 'the ideas that necessarily occur to the mind of an English mini-ster when, unhappily, he arrives at one of those dreadful crises of European affairs are security and neutrality' was cheered, and the speech generally well received; *The Times*, 1 August 1870, 6a.   [3] Add MS 44638, f. 115.
[4] Inquiry into the murders; see Jenkins, *Dilessi murders*, ch. 7.

√ 2. Suggestion unofficial from Sweden that the disputed districts in Schleswig
might be transferred to Denmark through England—& the neutrality of
D[enmark] there upheld. No proceeding nec[essary] at present.
√ 3. The Draft Treaty. Ld Gr[anville] proposed a new engagement with *both*
the belligerents if possible for the protection of Belgium.[1]
4. Defence. Determined to present on Monday a. Vote of Credit for 2 ⋒
b. Vote of 20000 men.

31. 7 S.Trin.

Chapel Royal mg. St Paul's Kn. evg. Saw Turkish Ambassr—Mr Glyn.
Saw Mrs Rumpff—Mrs Jacobs[R]. Went to Argyll Lodge[2] in afternoon. Read Lumby on Crisis in Religion[3]—Blenkinsop on Development—Liano on the R.C. internal feud.[4]

Monday Aug.One 1870.

Wrote to Lady Dinorben—Mr Hammond (2)—Mr Bright—Mr Cardwell—Mr Disraeli—The Queen (2)—Dean of Windsor—M. de Laveleye—Mr Lefroy—and minutes. Read M. Laveleye. Saw Ld Granville
—Mr Glyn—Sir R. Palmer—Mrs Lloyd. H of C. 4¼-8 and 8¾-1½.
Spoke on the War & Defences in answer to Disraeli.[5]

To J. BRIGHT, president of the board of trade,   Add MS 43385, f. 91.
1 August 1870. 'Secret.'

I send you a copy of a letter which I addressed to the Queen on Saturday.[6] It
will partially explain to you our situation: and pressed as I am on every side with
business I shall trust to your kindness to refer to me for any further information.

I may however tell you that although some members of the Cabinet were inclined on the outbreak of this most miserable war to make military preparations,
others, Lord Granville & I among them, by no means shared that disposition:
nor I think was the feeling of Parliament that way inclined.

But the publication of the Treaty has altered all this; and has thrown upon us
the necessity either of doing something fresh to secure Belgium, or else of saying
that under no circumstances would we take any step to secure her from absorption.

This publication has wholly altered the feeling of the House of Commons:
and no Government could at this moment venture to give utterance to such an
intention about Belgium. But neither do we think it would be right, even if it
were safe, to announce that we would in any case stand by with folded arms, &
see actions done which would amount to a total extinction of public right in
Europe.

[1] Signed on 9 August with Prussia, on 11 August with France; see Millman, 203.
[2] The duke of *Argyll's.
[3] J. R. *Lumby, *Early dissent, modern dissent, and the Church of England* (1870).
[4] E. Sant'A. de Liaño, *Die Kirche Gottes und die Bischöfe* (1869).
[5] *H* cciii. 1300.
[6] Add MS 43385, f. 95, giving cabinet decision of 30 July 70; Guedalla, *Q*, i. 248.

We have therefore adopted the double resolution announced in my letter to the Queen: and I hope that in this way we shall prevent all intemperate manifestations of public feeling whether within or beyond the walls of Parliament.

I am glad to say that the first indications on the part of France are in favour of compliance. If both parties agree, a great European danger will be removed to a distance greater than any which it has hitherto been placed: at the same time our liberty with regard to the single handed defence of Belgium will be rather increased than diminished.[1]

To B. DISRAELI, M.P., 1 August 1870.   Add MS 44539, f. 2.

It may be convenient for you to know before the House meets today that we shall lay upon the table, before public business commences, a vote empowering the Government to add 20,000 men to the Army, and a vote of credit in aid of the Naval & Military services for two millions.
We shall propose to take these votes tomorrow.

2. Tu.

Wrote to Mr Hammond—Ld Granville (2)—Mr Morrison—Ld Chancellor (2)—A. Gordon[2]—Ld Chief Baron—The Queen—Ld Kimberley—Abp Manning—and minutes. H of C. 2-7 and 9-3 (half an hour at Mrs Talbots for tea).[3] Saw Mr Glyn—Mr Levy—Ld Granville —Mr Ouvry—Mr Lefevre—Robn G. Read Laveleye.

To LORD HATHERLEY, lord chancellor,   Add MS 44539, f. 3.
2 August 1870.

[First letter:] I am sorry to say that I found last night there would be great opposition to the Judicial Committee Bill.

Perhaps you would communicate with the Attorney General who would give you information better than I can: but it was R. Palmer who most of all alarmed me as to the power of passing the Bill at this late period of the Session.

Palmer did not recognise the necessity of making an immediate provision for the present arrear[?].

[Second letter:] The storm whistles round the heads of other Bills.
1. Palmer *abhors* the wording of the Ecclesiastical Titles Bill as it now stands, & says it would be *better* to leave the law alone till next year. But he approves of your original wording, & thinks we should do wisely to restore it in the Commons, & then leave Cairns to stop the Bill, if he likes, in the Lords. 2. There is a varied & vehement opposition springing up to the Lectionary Bill. On our side

[1] Bright's reply of 3 August, Add MS 44112, f. 142, could not 'sanction our entering into any new engagement for the military defence of Belgium' nor could he support funds 'for supporting the independence of any foreign state', and requested acceptance of his resignation. See 4 Aug. 70. Part in Morley, ii. 341.
[2] Not in *T.A.P.S.*, n.s. li, part 4.
[3] On Mrs. Lloyd's case (see 25 June 70), and Greek affairs: *H* cciii. 1421.

Sir G. Grey, Bouverie, Locke King: on the other side Sandon, Russell Gurney, Smith of Westminster, Collins, & others. Glyn tells us it cannot be carried except by a violent pressure. I fear it must go. The Opposition is founded on divers grounds, & includes largely the uncomfortably late period of the Session. 3. Some of us in the Government think the Foreign Enlistment Bill too strong in its present enactments to be passed hastily: & raise the question whether it would be well to take power *now* simply to seize vessels like the Alexandra or the Rams, & leave the rest of these for consideration hereafter. There is no sign however of great difficulty in passing this Bill with its main provisions as they are.[1]

To ARCHBISHOP H. E. MANNING, 2 August 1870.   Add MS 44249, f. 170.

I shall be happy to see you on any forenoon: on Thurs. at ten you would find two or three friends breakfasting with us, & you would be most welcome.[2] Forgive me if I suggest that perhaps we had better not talk of what has been going on at Rome. Our opinions on the matter are strong on both sides, & are wide as the poles asunder: I am not vain enough to think I can act upon you, & for you to act upon me would tear up the very roots of my being.

3. Wed.

Wrote to The Queen (Mema)—Ld Chancr—Ld Granville—E.H. (name forgotten)[3]—and minutes. H of C. 2½-5.[4] Wrote Mem. on the Dual Engagement.[5] Wrote part Abbozzo[6] of Q. Speech. Saw The Prince of Wales—Ld Granville—do *cum* P. of Wales—Mr Glyn— Mr Motley. Drive with C. Dined with the Granvilles. Saw Mrs Th. X.

4. Th.

10 to breakfast: then lay up for a slight attack. Wrote to Musurus Pacha—Master of the Rolls (Irel.)—Ld T. Clinton—The Queen— Mr Bright—and minutes. Saw Ld Granville—Mr O. Russell—Mr Glyn. Read Laveleye—Ld Stanhope.[7]

To J. BRIGHT, president of the board of trade,   Add MS 43385, f. 99.
4 August 1870.

It will be a great addition to the domestic portion of the griefs of this most unhappy war, if it is to be the cause of a political severance between you and the present administration. To this I know you would justly reply that the claims of conviction are paramount. I hope however that the moment has not quite arrived. The *Votes* asked from the House of Commons were asked so, that no

¹ See 6 Aug. 70.
² Manning, back from Rome, requested a meeting; Add MS 44249, f. 168.
³ Passage in parentheses in pencil.
⁴ Foreign Enlistment Bill in cttee.: *H* cciii. 1502.   ⁵ In Ramm I, i. 120.
⁶ 'Outline'. Add MS 44759, f. 135.   ⁷ See 21 Mar. 70.

one need connect them with the defence of Belgium. Some members of the Cabinet would I believe have objected to our asking them on that ground. There was much audible, & more inaudible, complaint in the House on Monday, of my not having explicitly referred to Belgium. As to the Treaty, Protocol, or Engagement, none such is yet concluded.

> There's many a slip.
> Twixt cup and lip;

and until it is done we cannot be sure it will be done. Now to you as an absent member of the Cabinet having taken no part in the deliberations, I would put it that all you have to guard against is being an accessory after the fact. I hope then, and think, you will be contented to wait for the fact: which will, it is pretty certain, arrive either soon, or not at all. I shall of course await your answer.

What I have thus far written, has been written from your own point of view, and without any attempt to modify or alter it. It would scarcely be fair to entangle you in an argument during your period of rest. But you will I am sure give me credit for good faith when I say, especially on Lord Granville's part & on my own, who are most of all responsible, that we take this step in the interest of peace, and that we believe it to be the one most calculated to remove the danger of the absorption of Belgium. The recommendation set up in opposition to it generally is, that we should simply declare *we* will defend the neutrality of Belgium by arms in case it should be attacked!

Now the sole or singlehanded defence of Belgium would be an enterprise which we incline to think Quixotic, if these two great Military Powers combined against it. That combination is the only serious danger: & this it is which by our proposed engagements we should I hope render improbable to the very last degree.

I add for myself this confession of faith. If the Belgian people desire, on their own account, to join France or any other country, I for one will be no party to taking up arms to prevent it. But that the Belgians, whether they would or not, should 'go plump' down the maw of another country to satisfy dynastic greed is another matter. The accomplishment of such a crime as this implies, would come near to an extinction of Public Right in Europe. And I do not think we could contentedly look on while the sacrifice of freedom & independence was in course of consummation.[1]

5. Fr.

Wrote to Mr G. Kidd—Rev Mr. Kitchin—The Queen—P. of Wales —and minutes. Saw Mr Gurdon (R.B.)—Abp Manning—Mr Brand —Mr Glyn—Ld De Tabley—Ld Granville. Saw White—Robertson —Vernon. (1) & (3) interesting. H of C. 2-6: again at 9: and $11\frac{1}{4}$- $1\frac{3}{4}$.[2] Read Stanhope.

6. Sat. [St. George's Hill, Weybridge]

Wrote to Mrs Vernon—Mr S. Beaumont(2)—Mr Glyn—The Queen (& Mem.)—and minutes. Cabinet 2-5$\frac{1}{2}$. Read Laveleye. Saw Ld de

[1] A postscript adds: 'I wish you had given me a full and good account of your progress but I am sure this wretched war must have retarded it.' Copy in Add MS 44112, f. 144. Part in Morley, ii. 342. See 1 Aug. 70n. Bright replied on 5 August, ibid., f. 147, agreeing to 'act upon your suggestion for the present'.   [2] Defended East India accounts: *H* cciii. 1611.

Grey—Ld Granville—Ld Chancellor. Worked with M. de Lavalette on terms of expln for Treaty.[1] Went at 6.10 to St. George's Hill to visit the Egertons[2] in their very delightful retreat. Finished writing the Speech.

Cabinet Sat Aug. 6. 2 PM[3]

√ For[eign] Enlistment Act—Bill. Amendment respecting 'Storeship'. Words proposed[?] to be omitted. Amend title.[4]
(Judicial Committee Bill—discussed with Chancellor).
√ Commun[icatio]n to M. Lavalette. Granville gave an account of proceedings. Draft framed to meet Lavalette's view.
√ Production of Papers.
√ Queen's Speech. Approved.
√ Denmark. Ld G[ranville]'s explanation.
√ Red River. Indemnity.
√ Red River Amnesty. Require Canadian Govt. explicitly to renounce before we agree to decide.
√ Mr Childers to send a fit person to learn [*sic*] the Scheldt: Mr Cardwell to the Belgian Army & Antwerp.
√ Fleming's salary. £1200 demanded.
√ Eccl[esiastical] Titles Bill as amended. To be dropped if Lord Cairns presses his objection.[5]

7. *8 S.Trin.*

Byfleet Ch & H.C. mg. Wrote to Ld Granville—Mrs C. Rumpff[R]. Read Farrar's Sermon[6]—Lliano's Work (finished)—Blenkinsop on Devt (finished)—Fullers Thoughts. Walk. We were stunned with the military news.[7]

8. *M.* [*London*]

Left our kind hosts at 10¾. Wrote to The Queen—Mr Bright (2)—Mr Glyn—Mr Delane (with proofs)[8]—and minutes. H of C. 3-6½.[9] Saw M. Lavalette—do *cum* Ld Granville—Ld G. *cum* Mr Hammond —Mr Glyn—Att. General—Count Cadorna—Sig. Minghetti—Princess of Wales & P. of Wales.—Mr Fortescue *cum* Sol.Gen.Irel. Dined with the Granvilles. Saw Seymour X. Read Laveleye.

[1] See 30 July 70. Notes in Add MS 44759, f. 144.
[2] Seat near Weybridge, Surrey, of Francis and Lady Louisa Egerton (see 20 Dec. 62, 15 Jan. 70).
[3] Add MS 44638, f. 119.   [4] Bill amended in Lords on 8 August: *H* cciii. 1680.
[5] Bill withdrawn in Lords on 8 August: *H* cciii. 1684.
[6] F. W. *Farrar, 'Righteousness exalteth a nation'. A sermon (on Prov. xiv. 34) (1870).
[7] Defeat of the French at Wörth and Forbach on 6 August.
[8] No copy found; possibly of the treaty with Prussia signed next day.
[9] Made statement on neutrality of Belgium: *H* cciii. 1699.

To J. BRIGHT, president of the board of trade,   Add MS 43385, f. 104.
8 August 1870.

It is now my duty to make known to you that the communications of today
render it morally certain that the intended Treaty with Prussia will be concluded.
And I think that the corresponding engagement with France is within an ace of
certainty. We have taken these steps in the hope & belief that they will very
greatly reduce the dangers, in the Belgian quarter, to the peace of Europe, &
what is even more, the danger of a violation, amounting almost to extinction, of
European law, & public right. If I neither argue with nor intreat you, it is not
from indifference. If you find that the acts we have done do not come into sharp
conflict with your convictions, the announcement will fill me with unmixed joy
& satisfaction. I have told your brother why I refrain from pressing you with
long letters: & how my desire for your continued cooperation is precisely the
same as it was on the day when you first took office.[1]

9. Tu.

$8\frac{3}{4}$-$6\frac{1}{2}$. Went to Osborne, with the Speech. Audience of the Queen.
Saw Sir T. Biddulph—Ld de Grey—Mr Glyn—Sir W. Heathcote
(sworn P.C.)—Mr Helps. Wrote to Lady Skelmersdale—Viceroy of
Ireland—Mr Chambres?[2]—and minutes. Seven to dinner. Read
Laveleye.

Council at Osborne. Aug. 9. 1870.[3]
Another Council?—Speech Par. 7—Leave to change further in call of need—
Captain Vivian—Mr Bright—Minghetti—Ayrton.

10. Wed.

Wrote to The Queen—The Speaker—Mrs Robn (book)—L. Rumpff[4]
—and minutes. Saw Sig. Minghetti—Mr Pringle—Ld Granville—
Mr Glyn—Sir P. Braila—Mr M'Coll—Mr Goschen *cum* Chr of Exr.
Cabinet & House 12-4. Spoke on Belgium & the Treaties.[5] Read
Laveleye—Stanhope—Phillips on Wales.[6] Saw Mrs Th.—Mrs Sey-
mour X.

Cabinet Aug. 10 70. 12 and again at 3.[7]
√ 1. 7th Paragraph of Speech corrected to correspond with the circs.[8]
√ 2. Whether to insist on the presence of our representatives at the inquiry in

[1] Bright replied on 10 August, Add MS 44112, f. 149, that 'nothing more should be said
now of my retirement . . .', but expected to resign on grounds of health if he had not recovered by the November cabinets.
[2] i.e. William Chambers, physician, who had requested an appointment, Add MS 44539,
f. 7.
[3] Add MS 44757, f. 17. Written in ink over pencil jottings.
[4] Relative of the rescue case.
[5] Gave details of the Treaty: *H* cciii. 1776.   [6] See 20 Feb. 70.
[7] Add MS 44638, f. 121.   [8] This day's prorogation speech.

Athens. Yes nem. con. Nothing ulterior can be decided—but *sole* action seemed hardly possible.[1]

√ 3. As to any mediation in the War. We ought to be sure it is desired.

√ 4. Granville announced that an understanding had been established with Italy that either Power shd. communicate to the other before abandoning its neutrality. To be commun[icate]d to Russia with expression of willingness that this shd. be extended. Obligations under Treaties respecting Belgium of course expected.

√ 5. Ld Kimberley to proceed to write what had been approved respecting Red River.

√ 6. Mr Childers mentioned the arrangements as to the Fleets.

To J. BRIGHT, president of the board of trade,   Add MS 43385, f. 110.
10 August 1870. 'Private.'

I have received your letter with great pleasure & I most readily accept your offer.[2] It seems to me that your decision is wise. In fact, & in the view of the public, your ministerial capacity is for the moment suspended. As to the engagement with France, there is no Government in Paris at this moment which, I apprehend, could venture to bind that country. The treaty with N. Germany while it is a temporary, will I hope also remain a Paper Treaty. Should it grow to anything more of course I shall not hold you bound.

I may now without impropriety say that, had you resigned, it was my intention, if the business of the Department permitted, to hold open the office until November in the hope that, by that time, neither health nor politics need offer any obstacle to its resumption. I shall send your letter to the Queen who I am sure will read it with pleasure. But no minister except Lord Granville has been made aware of the correspondence between us, since it happily did not ripen. We shall have difficulty, & shall require courage, in returning to the tone & proceedings of peace. Still I agree that you are right in fixing a time for your decision, though it need not be absolutely immutable. It is much expected that a great battle will take place today. The horror of the whole thing weighs heavily on the heart. I read with much pleasure your improved report of your health. Perhaps a peace would be the best medicine for us all.

11. Th. [*Walmer Castle*]

Wrote to Sir T. Fremantle—The Queen (2)—Mr Bright—Mrs Thistlethwayte—Mrs Darbishire—The King of the Belgians—Mr Glyn—and minutes. A busy morning of preparn among books papers &c. Saw Baron Beaulieu—Mr F. Lawley—Mr Glyn—Mr Gurdon— B. Benjamin—Mr F. Byng—Sig. Minghetti. Off at 4.48 to Granville's hospitable abode at Walmer. Read Gasparin's Letter on the War.[3]

[1] See 29 July 70.
[2] See 8 Aug. 70n.
[3] Count A. E. de Gasparin, *La République neutre d'Alsace* (1870).

To LEOPOLD, King of the Belgians, 11 August 1870.   Add MS 44428, f. 23.

I have received with deep satisfaction, from the hands of Baron Beaulieu, Your Majesty's letter of yesterday.[1] I appreciate the more vividly Your Majesty's goodness in writing it, because I feel that Lord Granville, & that I myself still more, have been compelled to maintain in public our attitude of silence & reserve, while sentiments of warmth were alive within us. These sentiments I at length found yesterday an opportunity of partially expressing in Parliament.

I must own that I was struck with horror by the discovery of the now notorious Project of Treaty. Reflecting much upon it, and in constant communication with Lord Granville, I felt that diplomatic communication relating to it, carried on with the parties, could do nothing but mischief; that at the same time it was impossible to pass it by, & wholly unsatisfactory, as well as dangerous, to meet it with a vague declaration; that amidst many difficulties, the wisest course was to establish a fresh point of departure, & obtain from each Belligerent a new & solemn pledge, at a critical moment, & with a practical application, on any violation of which the world would cry shame.

All this, I doubt not, has been evident to the discerning mind of Your Majesty [which] has appreciated the reasons which led us to act on our responsibility, without attempting to *lean upon* the Power which we were anxious, according to our means, to support. I will only presume to add that the feelings, which in common with the world I entertain towards Your Majesty's personal character, though they could not form the main or proper ground of our national duty, went to make the performance of that duty in every way more agreeable and satisfactory.

12. Fr.

Wrote to Mr Fortescue—The Queen—Sir T.E. May—Mr T.D. Hornby—and minutes. Walk with C. Conferences with Granville. Read Van Praet[2]—Macmillan's Mag. Articles—Longleat.[3]

13. Sat.

Wrote to Scotts—Mrs Th.—Mr Helps—and minutes. Read Van Praet—Longleat. Drive with C: & afternoon tea at Deal Castle. F.O. papers & business.

14. 9 S. Trin.

Walmer Ch mg & evg. Wrote to Mr Sotheran—Archbp Manning—Sir A. Panizzi—and minutes. Conferences on Foreign Affairs: Halifax & Cardwell here.—Saw Count Bernstorff. Read Fuller's Holy Thoughts[4]—Blunt's Hist. Engl Bible.[5]

[1] Add MS 44428, f. 21.
[2] J. Van Praet, *Essais sur l'histoire politique des derniers siècles*, 3v. (1867-84).
[3] E. Lake [Mrs D. Armstrong], *Longleat*, 3v. (1870).
[4] See 17 July 70.   [5] J. H. Blunt, *A plain account of the English Bible* (1870).

To ARCHBISHOP H. E. MANNING, 14 August 1870.   Add MS 44249, f. 178.

I will shew your letter[1] to Granville & I have no doubt he will act conformably with the precedents: though I do not well know what are the steps to which you refer. Have you in view our sending one or more ships of war to Cività Vecchia?[2] Odo Russell has received an appointment in the F.O.: he will soon have a successor & in the meantime Mr Jervoise, a very intelligent man from the F.O., holds the post in Rome. Severn is well meaning; but I fear not very efficient. We have not received any intelligence yet shewing immediate danger; but it is said that the Pope's army is far below its (very considerable) nominal strength, & much gone down in discipline. We look on with awe at the events on the Continent—It is strange to see France overmatched in war as she has been thus far: & the general expectation seems to go with yours.

15. M.

Wrote to Sir C. Locock—Ld Houghton—A. Panizzi—Mr Fortescue —Mr Marlow[3]—Mrs Thistlethwayte—and minutes. Walk with Cardwell to St Margaret's Bay & much political conversation. Read New York World on *Juventus Mundi*[4]—Van Praet Historical Essays —Long Leat.

To C. S. P. FORTESCUE, Irish secretary,   Carlingford MSS CP1/124.
15 August 1870.

Thanks for your satisfactory answer about Maynooth.[5]

We, the conclave here present, (Halifax, Cardwell & mine host) read with some dismay the accounts of the proceedings at Derry.[6] I was in hopes the whole thing was to be stopped by common law, on account of those prospects of danger to the public peace, which have been sadly enough realised.

When do you think of setting to work upon Irish (higher) education? I do not mean by this that there is any violent hurry. But I should like to know whether I may trust to the Report of the Commission on Dublin University to give all needful information concerning it? I have two or three books about the university.

16. Tu.

Wrote to Mr Storr—Mr Ayrton (2)—Mr Helps—The Queen (Mem.) —and minutes. We went [to] Dover: saw the Castle, the Pharos, the old Roman Church, extremely curious. Read Van Praet—Long Leat. Granville went to town.

---

[1] Of 13 August 1870, Add MS 44249, f. 174, suggesting action on behalf of British subjects in view of the 'Garibaldian conspiracy in Rome'.

[2] *Manning replied (15 August 1870, Add MS 44249, f. 180) that he meant contingency plans as drawn up by *Palmerston. See 19 Aug. 70.

[3] Unidentified.

[4] Possibly sent by J. Makins or Meakins; see 18 Aug. 70.

[5] Untraced.   [6] Violence during a procession.

17. Wed.

Wrote to Ld Bathurst—Ld Granville (Telegr.)—and minutes. Read Van Praet—Long Leat—began Vol. 3. Walk with Glyn to St Margarets. Again the voice of politics under the solemn cliff.

18. Th.

Mr Helps announced to me the passing of the Order in Council which makes the new provision for Seaforth Church.[1] At length then I have accomplished in the main this act of honour to my dear Father's memory.

Wrote to Mr J. Breakenridge—Rev. W. Rawson—Mr J. Meakins[2] —Mrs Thistlethwayte—Count Bernstorff—Robn G.—Lady Cowper—The Queen (2)—Mr Pringle—Ld Halifax (Tel)—and minutes. Read Long Leat: got into Vol III. Whist in evening. The Bessboroughs came. 12–3½. Expedition by boat on board the Penelope.[3] We went over her with much interest. If it had been calmer we should have gone also to the Achilles.

To COUNT A. VON BERNSTORFF,   Add MS 44428, f. 43.
Prussian ambassador, 18 August 1870.

I have received your letter dated the 15th:[4] and I have referred to such practical records as I possess of the correspondence between Lord Clarendon on the one side and the North German and French Governments on the other with respect to a ⟨partial modified⟩ manner of disarmament.

In answer to the questions you have put to me I must say first that I do not recollect any reference made during the correspondence to the States of South Germany though I am far from being able to rely absolutely upon my memory. As to the second point, Count Bismarck undoubtedly referred to the actual and possible relations of North Germany with Russia; [and the character of his allusions to the last-named country may be viewed differently perhaps by different persons]:[5] but as his allusions conveyed no imputation dishonourable to Russia or to any person or section within it, I should feel wholly unable to describe them as injurious insinuations.

19. Fr. [London]

Wrote to Abp. Manning[6]—Mr Fortescue—D. of Argyll—Lord

---

[1] Conclusion of negotiations on advowson of St. Thomas, Seaforth.

[2] Had written on *Juventus Mundi*; Add MS 44539, f. 11.

[3] New central battery iron-clad; *Achilles*, an iron-clad broadship, was the first iron-clad built in a govt. yard; see Lord Brassey, *Naval Annual* (1882), 91.

[4] Asking Gladstone to deny truth of Grammont's circular of 3 August on S. Germany and disarmament; Add MS 44428, f. 32.

[5] Section in [ ] deleted in draft and presumably not sent.

[6] Arranging next day's meeting: Add MS 44539, f. 12.

Spencer—Ld Halifax—Mr G. Howell[1]—The Queen—Att. General —and minutes. 2.30-6. Went to town, with West & Glyn. Dined with Panizzi. $11\frac{1}{2}$-$1\frac{1}{4}$. Conclave at Walmer on Honours of various kinds. Saw Ld Halifax—Mr Childers respecting the fleet: also respecting The Pope: & wrote Memorandum.—Chancr of Exchequer. Finished Long Leat: a book full of holes, much too long, of high principle great poetry and feeling, and deep interest of human character and destiny. Saw Mrs Th. after dinner, a long time. I was more & more convinced of her essential purity; but the situation while it excites interest requires reflection.

Defence to repair immediately to Civita Vecchia (and to be relieved at Athens) —Captain's instructions to be sent to Civita Vecchia.

General object—protection in case of need for British subjects and property.

Should the Pontiff request to be taken on board for protection, he is to be received, and treated with all respect.

Should he express a desire to be carried to any particular destination, report it home instantly by telegraph unless further instructions for dealing with such request shall have been received before it is made.[2]

To C. S. P. FORTESCUE, Irish secretary,   Carlingford MSS CP1/125.
19 August 1870.

I return your enclosures:[3] & I hope that before another anniversary comes round we shall be able to make satisfactory arrangements to prevent disorder & bloodshed.

It occurs to me that while information as to the views of the Roman hierarchy on Education, & especially on the higher Education, in Ireland, cannot but be useful, yet in the present state of jealousy about them we cannot use too much caution as to any direct communication or proceeding which might be general. It seems to me that in the main we *know* what we ought to give them whether they will take it or not. As regards the Bill or Bills which it may be requisite to bring in I certainly should not compete with you, for the important duty of conducting them, & *primâ facie* they would fall to the charge of the Sec. for I. Still there are so many considerations which might affect portions of the question of Education in Ireland that it might be well not wholly to close at this early stage the question whether the Education Department should in any manner intervene in the management of such measures.

20. Sat.

Wrote to J. W. Hartley[4]—Lord Granville—Lord Stair—Lord Chancellor—Robn G.—Rev. W. Rawson—Mrs Th.—C.G.—Abp Man-

---

[1] Sent £25 to fund for Edmund *Beales; ibid., f. 13. See 10 Sept. 70.

[2] Initialled and dated 19 August 1870, Add MS 44759, f. 148, but not in diarist's hand.

[3] On the Derry procession, and Irish universities, sent 17 August 1870, Add MS 44122, f. 153.   [4] Had sent a book; Add MS 44539, f. 13.

ning—Hon R. Meade—& minutes. Saw Abp Manning[1]—Mr Pringle (& framed plan)[2]—Deputation on Church Service Books—Mr Burnand—for bust.[3] Saw Mrs C. Rumpff & received from her a most extraordinary account as to her extraction: seemingly incredible, yet not unsupported. Read Country Courtships.[4] Dined with Panizzi: most interesting accounts of Japan from Capt. Stanhope.[5]

21. 10 S.Trin.

Chapel Royal, (to hear Mr D. Gordon);[6] and All Saints aftn. Read Hunt's Hist. of Religious Thought[7]—Phillips on Religion in Wales. Saw W. Hampton—Mr Hammond—Mr Byng—Mr Kusserow.[8] Also saw one X. C.G. came in evg. Dined at Ld Halifax's: saw Ld Stratford. We discussed the Wounded Transit case.[9] Wrote to Mr Hammond— Ld Granville—C.G.

22. M.

Wrote to Mr Burnand—J. Breakenridge—Robn G.—Sir J. Whitworth—Mrs C. Rumpff—The Queen (Mem), & minutes. Dined with Ld Halifax. Saw Graham. Saw Mr Thornton Hunt—Lord Halifax— Mr West—Scotts. Read Country Courtships. Shopping & private business.

23. Tu. [Walmer]

Wrote to Duke of Norfolk—Lord St Germans—Sir J. Young—and minutes. Began Laveleye's L'Autriche et la Prusse.[10] Saw Mr West. Off at 11.45. Reached Walmer at 3. Conversation with Count Apponyi on Hungary—with Granville on Crimea.

[1] Telling him of the arrangements for the Pope, see Ramm I, i. 122.
[2] Developments at St. Thomas, Seaforth.
[3] N. N. *Burnard; see 24–5 July 68; bust untraced.
[4] A. Beale, *Country courtships. A novel*, 3v. (1870).
[5] Charles Scudamore Scudamore Stanhope, captain, R.N., 1858.
[6] *Aberdeen's son; see 21 Dec. 60.
[7] J. Hunt, *Religious thought in England*, 3v. (1870–3).
[8] Herr von Kusserow, secretary in the Prussian embassy, on transit of wounded; see Ramm I, i. 122.
[9] Transit of wounded required Prussian use of railway through Luxembourg and Belgium; Britain recommended approval; *Gleanings* iv. 226.
[10] E. de Laveleye, 'La Prusse et l'Autriche depuis Sadowa' (1870); this prompted Gladstone's famous article; see 26 Aug., 1 Sept. 70.

24. Wed. St Barthol.

Walmer Ch. 11 A.M. Wrote to Chancellor of Exchr—The Queen—
Mr Watson—Mrs Thistlethwayte—Mr West (Telegr.)—and minutes.
Whist in evg. The diplomats are a very pleasant party. Conferences
with G. Read Laveleye—Van Praet Hist. Studies. Drive to Sandwich.
Conversation with Count A[pponyi] on the Council. Read Challemel
Lacour on Sir G. Lewis.[1]

25. Th.

Wrote to Chancr of Exr—Duchess of Somerset—and minutes. Ld G.
drove me to Dover races; saw Col. Dickson[2] & others. Conferences
with Ld G. Conversation with M. Hochschild.[3] Read Laveleye—Van
Praet.

26. Fr.

Wrote to Queen (Mem)—H. Reeve—Mr Watson—Helen—and
minutes. The D. & Dss of Cleveland came. Conferences as usual on
Foreign Affairs. Read Laveleye—Van Praet—Mrs Jerningham.[4]

To H. REEVE, editor of the *Edinburgh Review*,   Add MS 44539, f. 16.
26 August 1870.

Are you open to the tender of an article on M. Laveleye's La Prusse & L'Autriche depuis Sadowa for your Oct. number. You will I trust, & am indeed sure
reply without the smallest ceremony & I consider it likely your arrangements
may have already gone beyond the stage at which it could be introduced. I think
him a political writer of the first class among contemporaries & the book is an
excellent text both upon the war & on the future of Europe as well as upon our
own military organisation & also our civil economy.[5]

27. Sat.

Wrote to G. Glyn—Mr A. Gordon[6]—Sir R. Phillimore—F. Ouvry
—and minutes. Read Ellis's Memoirs[7]—Laveleye's Pr. & Autriche
—Van Praet's Hist. Essays. Conferences as usual.

[1] P. A. Challemel Lacour in *Revue des Deux Mondes*, lxxxviii. 809 (July 1870).
[2] Col. Alexander George Dickson, 1834–89; tory M.P. Dover from 1865.
[3] Baron Carl Frederick Lotharius Hochschild, 1831–98; minister in London for Sweden
and Norway 1866–76.
[4] *Mrs Jerningham's Journal (in verse)* [by Mrs E. A. Hart] (1869).
[5] Reeve accepted the suggestion on 29 Aug.; Add MS 44428, f. 72; see 1 Sept. 70.
[6] Sending him to Ceylon; Add MS 44539, f. 16.
[7] Sir S. B. *Ellis, *Memoirs and services ... from his own memoranda* (1866).

28. S.11 Trin.

Walmer Parish Church mg & shore Ch. aftn. Wrote to Mr Glyn—Mr Reeve. Read Blunt on Engl Bible—Church's St Anselm[1]—Wilson's Pref. to Keble's Letters[2]—Blew on New Lectionary.[3] Conferences as usual. Helen's birthday: God Almighty bless her.

To G. G. GLYN, chief whip, 28 August 1870.   Add MS 44539, f. 16.

These names occur to me as worth Bruce's [attention:] Lord Eversley—Bp. of Carlisle—Dr. Miller (Greenwich)—Sir W. James—Ld Sandon—Count Strzelecki—Dr. Hannah (late Warden of Trinity Coll Perth a very able man).[4] Of these perhaps either of the two first would do well for Chairman but the Head should not be a man deeply committed & I still think the Commission on the contagious diseases act should be large. I remain here in a state of difficult uncertainty as to my movements & partly perhaps seduced by most kind and pleasant entertainment. But it seems likely we may go to London about Tuesday & to Hawarden in the end of the week. The French I think have not done themselves much credit by their stern opposition to sending the wounded through neutral territory and the general aspect becomes more grave from the almost certainty that the Germans, if they hold anything like their present relative position will ask for territory. I hope my daughter makes herself of use. There is really stuff in her if she works & I hope that you & Mrs Glyn see that she prosecutes her Education. I write on her birthday.

29. M.

Wrote to Ld Halifax—D. of Argyll—Ld Bathurst—Ld Kimberley —and minutes. Finished Van Praet's interesting Volume. Conferences as usual. Granville drove us to St Alban's Court.

To LORD KIMBERLEY, colonial secretary,   Add MS 44539, f. 17.
29 August 1870.

I have read your letter[5] & shown it to Granville. Not having your draft before us we understand the case to be 1. That you will have handed over to Canada the Government of Manitoba order & tranquillity prevailing—2. That no new circumstances, vitally affecting the case have arisen. If these things be so there cannot be the least doubt I think that you should persevere nay that to leave the troops now would be an error which might interfere permanently with the

---

[1] R. W. *Church, *St Anselm* (1870).

[2] J. *Keble, *Letters of spiritual counsel and guidance*, ed. R. F. Wilson (1870).

[3] W. J. *Blew, 'On the proposed New Lectionary' (1870).

[4] Bruce to Glyn, 29 August 1870, Add MS 44348, f. 38, encloses long list of those approached for commission on the Contagious Diseases Acts; Eversley declined, bp. of Carlisle accepted; Gladstone's other suggestions not on it.

[5] Of 27 August, Add MS 44224, f. 83: British troops should be withdrawn: the 'Canadians are much more likely to act with discretion and moderation [against the Red River rebellion] if they have to rely on their own resources'.

Establishment of sound & normal relations between Canada & her little but free sister.

Though Italy & in a degree Russia seem to look towards mediation, *we* here see no opening or likelihood at present & feel very strong objection, in which I think you would concur, not only to officious offers, but even to any hasty acceptance of overtures from the parties themselves, as we ought not to begin such a work without a real likelihood of being able to carry it to a satisfactory termination.

30. Tu.

Wrote to Mr Macfie——Mr Childers——Mr Watson——D. of Norfolk—— Mr Glyn——Ld Westminster——Sir J. Kirkland——& minutes. Read Laveleye Vol. 2.——Ellis's Mémoirs. Cards in evening.

To the DUKE OF NORFOLK, 30 August 1870.   Add MS 44539, f. 18.

I thank you for your very frank letter;[1] & I will not apologize for being disappointed at the announcement it makes, since it would be a very bad compliment to you besides belying my own very sincere feelings, if I set no store by your confidence & support. I often feel it a burden to be so much tied down by considerations of party in giving advice as to honours——& it was a great pleasure to me when last year I was able to propose the Garter to Lord de Redcliffe who, after half a century of public service, was able to accept it without fear of being misunderstood. Your half century is (I trust) still before you, & I must in candour state my impression that the public would consider your acceptance of the Garter as implying not by any means a permanent pledge but a present inclination *towards* the party & the Govt: as indeed they may already have thought from so slight a circumstance as your doing me the favour to drive with me on the celebration of the Queen's birthday. I am afraid therefore that if you are not at the least in an open state of mind, but have a bias adverse to the general policy of the Liberal party, I must without hesitation though with much regret refrain from pressing you. Meantime the only aid I can give in the case is by an explicit statement such as I have endeavoured to lay before you. I should be much gratified if on considering it you felt able to reply to my proposal in the affirmative. P.S. Upon reperusing your letter I cannot escape the suspicion that you may have put the case too strongly against acceptance from a sentiment of honour which everyone must appreciate.

31. Wed.

Wrote to Mr Ayrton——Chancr of Exchr——Mr West——Sir D. Salomons ——Col. French——Mr Childers——Mrs Th.——Lord Stratford de R.—— Duke of Edinburgh——Dean of Windsor——& minutes. Conferences as usual. Read Laveleye——Vol. II.

---

[1] Norfolk declined, on political grounds, the Garter offered on 23 August; see Add MSS 44539, f. 15, 44428, ff. 68, 86. See Introduction above, section v.

To LORD STRATFORD DE REDCLIFFE, Add MS 44539, f. 20.
31 August 1870.

The perusal of Mrs Jerningham's journal[1] has given me all the entertainment & satisfaction which your benevolence had anticipated, & provided for. The Authoress for *he* must be a woman is singularly light in hand & easy in her paces.

I shall retaliate by sending you, when I get it back to London, the little book about the Passion Play. We are thinking of London & even Hawarden but still here. I think Russia begins to show uneasiness at the amount of German success. We continue sceptical as to mediation, & well resolved to avoid if we can the commission of any impertinence. The next battle probably already fought must in all likelihood determine much.

Thurs. Sept One 1870.

Wrote to Mr A. Gordon—Mr Cardwell—and minutes. Began to write a projected Article on Prussia & the War for the Edinb. Rev.[2] Read Laveleye—The Motleys[3] came. Conferences as usual.

2. Fr.

Wrote to Duke of Argyll—Dr Hannah—Ld Shaftesbury—Ld Halifax—Mr Helps—and minutes. Continued Article. Read Laveleye—Belly's Déchéance et Liberté[4]—The Motleys came. Whist in evg.

To LORD SHAFTESBURY, 2 September 1870. Add MS 44539, f. 22.

Count Bernstorff having officially brought before the Government the question of the export of arms[5] we shall state our whole view of the case in reply, & I will obtain from Granville a copy of the paper on which you will be able to pass your judgement. While I think we have judged & acted rightly I grant the subject is a very fair one for international consultation. At present there is an unjust inequality if it be true as I have heard it stated that the French have by pressure got the Belgians to agree not to export nor to allow the transit of arms through their territory. I can assure [you] the Govt. has not, at least consciously, been guided by abstract arguments as opposed to moral considerations. To alter our course now at the moment when France is almost crushed, & when Prussia has shown herself independent of foreign supply, would be a proceeding that would carry an awkward appearance of partiality. The international discussion to which I refer would be one having for its object the adoption of a uniform rule if possible.

But I doubt for myself whether it would end in prohibition.

[1] See 26 Aug. 70.

[2] See 23, 26 Aug. 70 and Add MS 44693, f. 1, published as 'Germany, France and England' in *Edinburgh Review*, cxxxii. 554 (October 1870), reprinted in *Gleanings*, iv. 197. Though published anonymously, authorship soon became widely known: see 3 Nov. 70.

[3] J. L. and Mary Motley; see 1 Apr. 69; his govt. had already requested his resignation as minister in London, dismissing him November 1870.

[4] F. Belly, *Déchéance et liberté* (1870).

[5] Shaftesbury wrote on 31 August 1870, Add MS 44300, f. 48, suggesting prohibition of export of rifles.

3. Sat.

Wrote to Mr Fortescue—Ld Spencer—Mr Cardwell—Vestry Clerk of St James's—Mr West—and minutes. Conferences as usual. The news which has been so exciting every day, became overpowering: Macmahon's army has capitulated, the Emperor a prisoner.[1] Continued MS. Read Laveleye. Conversation with Mr O. Russell. Attended the American Circus at Deal with the whole party.

To EARL SPENCER, Irish lord lieutenant,   Add MS 44539, f. 23.
3 September 1870.

Has not the time now arrived when we may again consider the question of releasing the batch of Fenian prisoners whom we still hold in durance?[2] It will be a great advantage to do this, if otherwise proper at a moment when the agitation for their release seems absolutely dead. It would I presume revive hereafter, I suppose that banished from this country as a condition of release, they would be very little able to do mischief & considering how Fenianism has had its root in bad laws there is something of pain & of scandal in prolonging the memory of this outbreak after we have launched our main remedies, unless it be absolutely required by the necessities of public order, of which you will be the proper judge. I have talked the matter over with Granville to whom I have been paying a prolonged visit & I have written to Fortescue on the subject.

4. 12 S.Trin.

Walmer Ch mg with H.C.—Lower Walmer Ch Evg. A long & interesting conversation with Mr Motley on the B.N.A. question—on Bismarck—& on the Fenian prisoners. Wrote to Duke of Argyll—The Mayor of Wells[3]—Ld Shaftesbury—and minutes. Read Church's St Anselm—Lumby on Ch. & Dissent—Work on Angels & Separate State.[4]

5. M.

Wrote to Sir T. Bateson—Ld Spencer—Mr Ouvry—Mr West—Mrs Th.—Ld Houghton—and minutes. Continued MS as well as constant calls of business would allow. Conferences. Read Laveleye. Walked to S. Foreland. Whist in evg.

[1] Fighting at Sedan ended on 1 September, MacMahon and Napoleon capitulated on 2 September.
[2] Spencer replied that it had not, 5 September 1870, Add MS 44306, f. 312.
[3] Letter untraced.
[4] Perhaps W.T.V., *Angels and their ministry* (1869).

To EARL SPENCER, Irish lord lieutenant,   Add MS 44539, f. 24.
5 September 1870.

Since I wrote to you on Saturday I have learnt that the American Govt. has been pressed & driven on by Congress to endeavour to obtain the release of one of the Fenians named Halpin I think if I caught it rightly.

Applications relating to this man are impending & cannot long be withheld. I mention them because the moment of calm being so plainly the proper one for considering the subject this circumstance seems to shew that it is not likely to be much prolonged though measures have been taken to procure a short delay.[1]

6. *Tu.* [*London*]

Off at 2.30 to London. Wrote to M. Michel Chevalier (dft)—Ld Granville—Mr Cardwell & Mr Childers (Tel.)—Mr Bruce—Mrs Rumpff—and minutes. Wrote a little of my Article. Saw Mr Glyn— Ld Granville—Count Strzelecki—Dined with the Wortleys. Saw Anderson[R]. Finished Laveleye.

To the DUKE OF ARGYLL, Indian secretary,   Add MS 44539, f. 25.
6 September 1870.

You think[2] Dodson & Ayrton beneath contempt but say if a man like Sir C. Trevelyan could be got it would be another matter. Neither Glyn, who is here, nor I at all agree in this comparative estimate. Not that I think Ayrton can be recommended without a great deal more consideration but as to the general calibre of the man it is much greater than you seem to think. As to Dodson, I consider him far superior to Trevelyan for such an office. But I do not know whether he could be got. I know nothing of your financial resources in the Civil Service of India, so I will say nothing.

About mediation I quite agree or even go further—I would not now say a word ever so gently. I believe it would do great mischief. As at present advised I see but two really safe grounds for mediation: 1. a drawn battle. 2. The request of both parties.[3]

To M. CHEVALIER, 6 September 1870.   Add MS 44127, f. 79.
'Private.'

I have read with deep sympathy the letter which you addressed to me on the 5th,[4] and which I did not receive in time to answer it by the post of the evening.

My course and language on every occasion since I began to pay any serious attention to the subject of foreign politics, have I hope borne more effectual witness than any words now employed could render, to my earnest desire that the most cordial relations with France should be cherished, for the benefit of our two countries and of Europe.

---

[1] Marginal note by A. West: copy sent to Fortescue.
[2] Argyll wrote on 4 September 1870, Add MS 44101, f. 275, commenting on Gladstone's suggestions for auditor 'I don't like any of the names at all.'
[3] Part in Morley, ii. 344.   [4] Add MS 44127, f. 76.

During the annexation of 1860, I was silent: and on the only standing subject of difference between France & England, I mean the occupation of Rome, in common with other public men of this country, I have maintained a great reserve. From my heart I desire that the two nations may ever be allied to each other & to right. The present war is to us a profound affliction. Our earnest efforts to prevent it are upon record. We have refrained from passing judgment upon it with anything like the freedom so honourable to you, which is exhibited in your letter.

In the negotiations prior to the outbreak, we felt how limited were our powers. They are now confined within much narrower bounds. It is not competent to us to interfere about the war with authority. And if not, then the only course open to us is, to perform, as well as we can, the duties of friendship to both the parties engaged in this tremendous quarrel. But would it be consistent with that principle of friendship, if we were to interpose before a state of things had arrived, in which we could reckon at least with hope on a fundamental approximation of views between the respective sides, and in which the adoption by us of the proposition by one would not form a positive cause of offence to the other? Now it is no less needful, than sad, to acknowledge that, in the ordinary course of things, it is the fortune of war alone which can bring about this approximation. You are aware of the present want of harmony between the public opinion of the two great countries now at war. You will feel how easily we might, even without intending it, transgress the bounds of that respect which we owe at all times to France & Germany, and which we never can owe more strongly than at a moment when both have performed such deeds of valour & endurance. We have already by advice which has been uttered from the Throne of this country, pledged ourselves to watch with anxiety for any opportunities of being useful. We have so watched, and we shall continue so to watch: and shall readily perform any duty, however small & ministerial, which may serve even, if no more, to put the two Governments into communication. We are aware of the vast resources, and of the unabated spirit, of France. We cannot prognosticate what effect the expected siege of Paris may have on the condition of the German armies, and on the awful balance of the war. But our duty in this matter is one dependent upon facts that we cannot controul. It is not indifference, etiquette, or pride, that keeps us back, it is the apprehension of doing actual mischief. And we sorrowfully see that, whether it be in a near or in a distant future the opportunity we should hail with pleasure is not yet in view.[1]

7. Wed.

Wrote to Ld Halifax—Mr Fortescue—Mrs Rumpff—M. Chevalier (corr. & sent)—Mr Bruce—Mr Motley—and minutes. 11½-2. Went to see the Working Men's Exhibition.[2] Inquiries for Meurice: & saw Hunt X. & Rose[R]. Saw Baron Rothschild—Ld Granville—Mr Glyn —Mr Cardwell—Mr Probyn. Read Barkley Britten on Artillery[3]— Stanhope's Hist. Dined with Mr Motley, & had much pleasant conversation.

[1] Part in Morley, ii. 343.
[2] In Islington; see *The Guardian*, 14 Sept. 1870, 1079.
[3] B. Britten, *Our effective artillery. What has been done. What has to be done. What may be done* (1870).

To C. S. P. FORTESCUE, Irish secretary,   Carlingford MSS CP1/130.
7 September 1870. 'Private.'

I receive your letter with pleasure[1] and I quite agree that cases when the offence can justly be judged to bear the essential character of ordinary crime should be omitted.

In consulting as you will no doubt do with the non-Parliamentary advisers of the Irish Government it will I hope be borne in mind what very large considerations of national character are really involved in our pursuing a mild & dignified course so soon as we have made just provision, which has now been done, for the security of life & property. We must clearly not pay too great a regard to merely local opinion but endeavour to carry the question into that larger sphere to which it properly belongs. I do not mean to express any distrust of anyone, but the judgements of men of course depend in some degree on the point of view, which their offices & responsibilities provide for them.[2]

I do not see any daylight as yet in France where there must either be a change of the fortune of the war in her favour, or an abandonment of the Rhine frontier. But on these subjects for the present of course I have no opinion and could do nothing but mischief.
I understand the unhappy Emperor did *fight* at Sedan.

To J. L. MOTLEY, American minister,   Add MS 44428, f. 90.
7 September 1870.

With reference to the suggestion, if such it can be called, which fell from me this evening when I was enjoying your genial hospitality, I would venture to observe: 1. There is a tide of opinion rising in this country on behalf of mediation which, when it reaches a certain point, the Government may find it difficult to withstand. 2. At this moment, we, who alone of the considerable European Powers, are (I think) without any special or separate interest in the matter, are in the rear of the rest, who are far more disposed at once to tender a judgment upon the terms of peace. 3. This judgment, once tendered, would become a formidable fact, & might tend to ulterior consequences. 4. Though it be not the time for official mediation, it may be the time for friendly advice, when personal relations are such as to allow of it. 5. As, on the French side, he would be a good friend to peace, who encouraged France in the notion that without a change in the fortune of war she could escape on easy terms, so on the side of Prussia, he will be a good friend who advises her to be *moderate*, and to be *expeditious*.

Forgive this note, as the words dropped from my lips, I thought it my duty to explain briefly the feeling which prompted them.[3]

8. Th. [*Nottingham*]

C. went off to Hawarden. I in aft. to Nottingham. Wrote to Mr H.M. Thompson—The Queen—Ld Clanricarde—Mr Taylor MP.—and minutes. Saw Ld Granville—Mr Forster—Mrs Rumpff—Baron

[1] Untraced.
[2] Fortescue's reply, 9 September 1870, Add MS 44122, f. 162, opposed releasing 'our Irish republicans' at the start of a French republic.
[3] Motley conveyed Gladstone's views to a friend: Add MS 44428, f. 96.

Rothschild—Count Bernstorff—Mr West—Baron Gudin[1]—Missed M. de Lavalette. Read Country Courtships.[2] 4½-8¼. To Nottingham. Business with Mr Ouvry and Mr Hunt in the Evg.[3]

9. Fr. [London]

Wrote to C.G.—Mr West (Telegr.)—Went over the Park Estate. Saw Children's Hospital & other institutions. Divers calls. Saw Mr Hine— The Mayor—Town Clerk—Chairman of San. Committee—Mr Chapman—& others.[4] 4-5¼. Meeting on the Sewage question—I spoke at some length. Read Country Courtships. Back to London by 6.30 Train. Plenty of boxes awaited me! And the sad news of the 'Captain'.[5] Walked afterwards.

10. Sat.

Wrote to Dowager Dss Somerset—Adm. Dacres—Ld Chancellor— Mr Lingen—C.G.—Mrs B. Osborne—and minutes. Christy Minstrels 8-10¾. Saw Mr Rothschild—Ld Granville—Mr West—Mr Beales. Saw Vernon: & made inquiries. Read Country Courtships—Bp Watson's Speech of 1803.[6]

To LORD HATHERLEY, lord chancellor,   Add MS 44539, f. 27.
10 September 1870.

I received your letter last night having spent the day in Nottingham and on the whole I thought the best thing I could do would be to send for Mr. Beales which I did.[7] I gave him no pledge whatever on your part but merely treated him as substantially a candidate for judicial employment, & spoke of what that involved. He quite agreed that a Judge must effectually separate himself from all ostensible & public proceedings in politics. He is pledged to take the Chair at a meeting tonight when the first resolution to be proposed expresses pleasure at the establishment of the republic in France *on the ground* that it is likely to lead to peace & to the union of the two great nations of France & Germany. He assures me that it will not be a meeting in favour of republicanism as a principle,

[1] Count Charles Gabriel César Gudin, 1798-1874; senator in 2nd Empire.
[2] See 20 Aug. 70.
[3] i.e. on the 5th duke of Newcastle's estate, of which Gladstone was a trustee.
[4] Account of the visit in *The Times*, 10 September 1870, 9e.
[5] H.M.S. *Captain*, an iron-clad turret ship, capsized off Finisterre on 7 September, over 450 crew and observers perishing. At the subsequent court martial, faulty construction and topheaviness as a result of failure to follow the original design were found to be the chief causes of the disaster.
[6] R. *Watson, *The substance of a speech intended to have been spoken in the House of Lords, November 22d, 1803* (1803).
[7] Bright recommended E. *Beales, the radical, for a judgeship; Hatherley worried about the appointment's timing; he was appt. a county court judge; Add MS 44205, f. 122; see 19 Aug. 70.

& that he has taken & will take no part in any movement or declaration of such a character. He considers that he has been able effectually to check any movement in that direction. It appeared to me that there was nothing in his opinions or intentions which need interfere with your propitious mind towards him, & though we would rather that his activity had undergone no revival whatever in connection with these popular meetings, yet it is to be remembered that his interposition has materially served to check any tendency to political excess. I daresay you know that there has recently been a private subscription on his behalf which I believe was demanded by his actual needs.

11. 13 S. Trin.

St Mark's Ham[ilton] Terrace mg. Found Chapel Royal closed in afternoon. Saw Mrs Barber—Mr Wortley. Dined with the Wortleys. Inquiries, &c. Wrote to C.G.—Ld Granville. Saw Mr West—Miss C. Smith. Read Holy Eastern Church[1]—Triumph of Moral Good.[2]

12. M.

Wrote to Ld Halifax—Ld Chancellor—Mr Bright—C.G. (L. & telegr.)—Mr Beales—Ld Kimberley—Mr Fortescue—& minutes. Went to Clar. Road & found Mrs R[umpff] not at home. Saw Ld Hartington—B[aron] Beaulieu—Musurus Bey—Baron Rothschild —Gen. Burnside[3]—Mr Goschen—Mr Motley. Saw Russell X not unhopeful. Read Newman Hall on U.S.—Country Courtships. Dined at D. Dss of Somerset's.

To J. BRIGHT, president of the board of trade,   Add MS 43385, f. 113.
12 September 1870.

I have received with great pleasure your account of yourself, which is highly cheering and satisfactory.[4]

There has not I think been one single day since the Prorogation, on which Granville and I have not been in anxious communication on the subject of the War. Of course I shall summon the Cabinet at the first moment when there shall seem to be for their consideration any substantive question of weight or difficulty, on which a resolution can be taken.

On Saturday at the request of the French we transmitted to the Germans, through Bernstorff, the overture of the new French Government. The reply to this overture may throw some real light upon the question.

Your letter suggests a multitude of interesting considerations—but I am afraid I have not made such rapid or effectual progress towards a conclusion, as you have done.

[1] [J. M. *Neale], *The holy Eastern Church; a popular outline* (1870).
[2] *Complete triumph of moral good over evil* (1870).
[3] Ambrose Everette Burnside, 1824-81; U.S. general and financier; accidentally abroad, acted as intermediary between France and Prussia.
[4] Letter of 11 September 1870, Add MS 44112.

I agree in this important point: it would much please me to know that the Germans had freely agreed to make peace without exacting territory.

Or again that they found the fortunes of war, and the difficulties of a siege of Paris, with the advancing season, such, as that they should be obliged to make peace without exacting territory.

But to 'urge strongly the folly of retaining French territory' upon a nation in arms is a serious matter.

We urged strongly upon Russia much that concerned Poland, upon Germany and Prussia much that concerned Denmark: in neither case with advantage to those whom we sought to protect, in both with a decided loss of our own moral weight.

I am persuaded that a great authority attaches to this country but it requires to be used with strict regard to the nature of the work it is to do, or it may turn like a razor's edge.

Suppose we say to Germany unconditionally 'We object to your taking any portion of French territory.' And suppose Bismarck replied by a summary[?] demand. 'Give me the assurance that what you now say to us, you would have said to France if the fortunes of the war had been precisely reversed.' We should be obliged to confess, that we would not.

We might reason with the Germans, and say that the retention of territory was contrary to their interests. But I suppose they would reply by advising us to give up Gibraltar for ours: or by claiming to be the best and proper judges in the case.

There is one ground of principle which if ascertained has much strength. And that is that the inhabitants of Alsace and Lorraine should not be handed over to Germany against their own will. But the fact is not perhaps easy of ascertainment: and it is remarkable that the French have *not* hitherto put the question on this ground.

I grieve to say that in my view one of the very greatest difficulties in the case is this. No man can say what Government France will give herself, or what after it is established she will do with it, or how while established it will work its foreign policy, (that is to say traffic in the blood of Europe,) for dynastic or other internal purposes.

You will take these few and disjointed remarks, I am sure, as they are meant. Foregone conclusions in the case I have none, except first that it is our duty to lose no opportunity of promoting peace, and secondly that we must not allow either desire of glory, or fear of reproach, or even a very blind impulse of humanity to mislead us into taking for an opportunity what is really not one.

But may it come, & come soon.

To LORD HALIFAX, lord privy seal,   Hickleton MSS A4.88.
12 September 1870.

Downing St. is my safe address & loses nothing as a rule wherever I am. But at present I do not get further from it than my present date.

I fully believe in the reality of the suffering and the excitement you describe[1] & I am very sorry that the conversation of the Prince of Wales should tend to increase either the one or the other.

But believing in their reality I also believe with much sorrow that part is owing

[1] Halifax's letter not in Add MS 44184.

to a system of most unhappy self-indulgence which is growing more marked from year to year. If it goes on unchecked I fear that before ten years are over the consquences will be very serious, probably to the health of the Queen, and perhaps to much beside.

The reality of consequences which flew from causes founded only in the imagination is unhappily a cardinal fact in such cases.

It is very creditable to the Queen, with her strong German sympathies, to desire that the victors should take no territory. I hope her representation may weigh. You, I see, give them Luxembourg and an indemnity (of which it is said Bismarck will himself demand a million: he had 250m[ille] in 1866). Perhaps a fortnight of reflection, exposure and disease before the walls of Paris, if it can hold out, might bring them to this.

13. Tu.

Wrote to C.G.—Lord Granville—Mr Childers—& minutes. Dined at Mr Motley's. Worked a little on MS. Saw Ld Granville (4)—Mr Cartwright—Mr Glyn—Mr Motley—Scotts—Mr Dana. Read Country Courtships. Long conversation with M. Thiers. He seemed *vague* as to purpose.[1]

14. Wed.

Wrote to Ld Spencer—Mr Max Müller—Sir T. Biddulph—M. Michel Chevalier—and minutes. Dined with Dowager Dss of Somerset. Saw Ld Granville—Mr Levy—Mr Cardwell—M. Lavalette—do *cum* M. Rouher—Baron Beaulieu. Read Country Courtships.

To M. CHEVALIER, 14 September 1870. 'Private.'   Add MS 44127, f. 85.

There is little that I need say, with reference to your letter of yesterday,[2] in the way of general remark; & that little I will say briefly.
1. When I spoke of 'offence' I meant no more than this; that we might excite a sentiment which would diminish our power of subsequent usefulness in negotiation.
2. We should view with dissatisfaction the 'domination' of Germany or of any power in Europe: & with a pain & shame that I cannot describe the crushing of France, were such a catastrophe really in view. I do not *think* it is in view, even for the present: and I heartily agree with you that she is certain of her future.
3. You touch a point of great importance in my view when you speak of the Frenchness, so to speak, of Strasburg & Mulhouse. I have been struck with the fact that the French declarations have turned more on the inviolability of the soil of France, than on the attachment of the people of Alsace and North Lorraine

[1] See J. H. Rose, 'The mission of M. Thiers to the neutral powers in 1870', *T.R.H.S.*, xi. 35 (1917) and Ramm I, i. 125. Gladstone told Max Müller next day: 'It would please me much to converse with you on the war were it possible. The "Times" is wrong about Thiers. His purpose is diplomatic & pacific if not very definite.'
[2] Of 12 September 1870, Add MS 44127, f. 81.

to their country. Forgive me if I ask whether it is easy to erect inviolability of soil into an abstract principle, in a country which has made recent annexations? And further whether the promulgation of such an abstract principle, in such circumstances, does not rather throw a difficulty in the way of friends elsewhere?

And now let me assure you that we strive to fulfil the pledge of watching, as we best can from day to day.

The first step in reason seems to be that we should learn the views of the parties to this terrific war. Those of France we know to some extent, but in part only negatively. Of those of North Germany we know nothing. In this state of matters we should very gladly see the two Powers brought together in the person of their proper organs for the purpose of full conference. This direct communication we are striving to effect: & I hope it will not fail through the fault of the Germans: France has already I believe done her part. There is a subject extraneous to the war which is much before my mind. What is to be its result upon the peace of Europe, & what therefore on its military system? Do not think this to be the wanton intrusion of an irrelevant topic. I am satisfied it is in the power of either Belligerent by a right policy in this matter at the present crisis, to attract to itself very powerfully the sympathy of the Nations. Brief letters on vast subjects are liable to much misapprehension; but I trust myself to your friendly & charitable interpretation, & with all my old sentiments towards you & your country.

To EARL SPENCER, Irish lord lieutenant,   Add MS 44539, f. 28.
14 September 1870.

Thank you very much for sending me so full a statement of your views as also for the letter of the Attorney General. I must own, however, that your reasons do not convince me, & Granville who had read the letters is also of my mind. If the Fenian prisoners refuse as Barry says they may, the condition of expatriation, then we stand clear. In my opinion their release belongs to a policy of confidence, their continual confinement to a policy of mistrust & apprehension. Doubtless we cannot put down Fenianism, but surely what we have to do is gradually to estrange the principles of the Irish people especially of the rising generation as they grow up, from that bad cause. Now I think we know from unexceptionable evidence that the sufferings of these Fenians, by which I mean simply their continued imprisonment tend to place in sympathy with them multitudes of men who are not Fenians. It is on these men that I think we should strive to act. What appreciable reinforcements would they form when exported to the Fenians of America? None but even if they did, there would be more than a countervailing advantage in liberating the American Government from its difficulties, strengthening our case for urging on them a course of systematic repression of hostile manifestations & emboldening them to face the clamours that have made them at times slack in their duty.

As to the Republic in France, is it meant that these men are to be prisoners as long as it exists?

Surely only until it is proved harmless; & (I think) that it has been proved already by the total failure of propagandism in Spain & Italy. The difficulty is more likely to be, to prevent the French Republic from becoming ridiculous. At any rate two or three more weeks might be given if necessary to prove this new Government innocuous. Not quite with my goodwill: for among the sad possibilities before us there is this, that it may be succeeded by something really dangerous.

Even before these weeks have passed, I am afraid we shall have at least an application from the U.S. Government which I deeply regret. What I should most seriously deprecate would be allowing the question to stand over until the annual revival of political activity in October or November for I think we cannot expect to escape a new agitation.[1]

15. Th.[2]

All Saints Ch 5 P.M. Wrote to Abp Manning—Mr Fortescue—M. Michel Chevalier—Mr Hammond—Ld Granville—Ld Wolverton— C.G.—& minutes. Saw Mr Motley (2)—M. Thiers—Ld Granville— Count Strzelecki. Dined with the Wortleys. Saw D'Olier.[3] Read Country Courtships.

To ARCHBISHOP H. E. MANNING,   Add MS 44249, f. 196.
15 September 1870. 'Private & Immediate.'

I perceive that the apprehensions expressed in your letter[4] with regard to the independence of the Pope in his spiritual capacity rest upon your general belief that no substitute, efficient in that respect, can be found for the present state of things, or what was a few days ago the present state of things. That opinion of yours I could not hope to shake but from my point of view I think that the intentions of the Italian Government are satisfactory. It appears to me not only that they respect but that they desire the spiritual independence—that they seek to act from principle as well as policy on Cavour's world-famous maxim, *Libera chiesa in libero stato*: that they are quite willing to give or leave to the Pope a mathematical point (which 'hath position but not parts[']) of actual sovereignty by way of special guarantee with perfect security for his freedom of movement on the Italian territory as if it were under his absolute dominion. Further, the question of money has never been a difficulty. I have mentioned only *part* of the offers made.

I learned yesterday by telegram with pleasure that the U. Sec. of State in Rome had requested British mediation.

If in any sense as *amicus curiae* I might offer a suggestion it would be this, to aim at an arrangement with respect to the City of Rome, which shall offer conditions of finality. By this I mean not to leave the Sovereignty of the City in a condition likely to lead to further changes. I hope that Italy might not press the point of making it a Capital; but I doubt the utility of making it a San Marino. I speak now of the City apart from the Leonine. And I speak personally, & individually.[5]

---

[1] See 11 Oct. 70; Spencer remained opposed to release; Add MS 44306, f. 316 ff.
[2] Adams Acton's statue of diarist (see 18 Oct. 66) this day unveiled in St. George's Hall, Liverpool, after a eulogy by T. H. *Huxley; *The Times*, 15 September 1870, 10f.
[3] Probably rescue.   [4] Of 14 September 1870; Add MS 44249, f. 192.
[5] *Manning replied on 16 September, ibid., f. 199, suggesting a guarantee of 'the independence of Rome . . . by the common pact of the European Powers'.

16. Fr.

Wrote to Ld Granville (3)—Mrs Thistlethwayte—Mr Reeve—C.G.
—Mrs Helen Gladstone—Lady Mary Herbert—and minutes. Dined
with Glyn at the Travellers. Saw Ld Granville—M. de Lavalette—Sir
J. Lacaita—Mr West—B. Benjamin (in grief)—Mr Glyn. Went with
a party to the Two Roses. Acting mostly poor: sneers at dissenting
religion bad.[1] Read Country Courtships—La France vaincue.[2] Saw
Casson: a notable person.

17. Sat. [Hawarden]

Off at 8.30 to Hawarden, after seeing S. who told me more of Willy's
Merciful deliverance.[3] Arr. 3.15: found a happy party. Unpacked
books. Read Country Courtships—Descant on Penny Postage.[4] Heard
more of the Escape.

18. 14 S. Trin.

Hn Ch mg: (S. read prayers & administered the Chalice): & evg 6.30.
Wrote to Abp Manning—Ld Granville—Mr Motley—Ld Spencer—
Mr Murray—Mr Anderson MP.—and minutes. Walk and conversa-
tion with S.E.G. Read Evans on Marriage[5]—Wyatt on Ritualism[6]—
Basil Jones's Sermons.[7]

To J. L. MOTLEY, American minister,   Add MS 44539, f. 32.
18 September 1870. 'Private.'

When I saw you at Walmer I think my language may have conveyed to you an
expectation of the nearly immediate release of our Fenian Culprits. Though my
mind is not altered, I have found more difficulty than I anticipated, & now fear
there may be some delay.[8] Though it will not I trust be very long, yet I think it
affects the question as I put it before you & I therefore send this explanation
that you may act as you judge fit with reference to the general merits of the case.
Though I must go back to London on Tuesday evening, I hope within a week
later or thereabouts to pay a more stable[?] visit here. If you should after that
be moving northwards I hope you will bear in mind that Chester lies conveniently

---

[1] By James *Albery, at the Vaudeville, with *Irving; Gladstone tried to get his secretary
to start a campaign of protest; see West, *Recollections*, i. 366.
[2] Untraced.
[3] A climbing accident while in Switzerland with Stephen Gladstone; Catherine Gladstone
to diarist, 15 September 1870, Hawn P: '. . . earnestly hoping these mountain escapades are
at an end, surely Willy has had enough now.'
[4] X. A. P. [John Peace], *A descant on the penny postage* (1841).
[5] H. D. Evans, *A treatise on the Christian doctrine of marriage* (1870).
[6] Perhaps W. E. Wyatt, *The Christian altar* (1846).   [7] See 6 Feb. 70.
[8] See *Spencer's opposition, Add MS 44306, f. 316 and 14 Sept. 70.

for almost all directions. About Oct 1-10 would be a time very acceptable here but pray consult your own convenience.

19.

Wrote to A. E. West—Ld Granville (Telegr.)—J. Watson & Smith—and minutes. Church 8½ A.M. Worked on MS. Read Lanfrey's Essays.[1] Worked on re-arranging books in my library. In aft. we cut down a thick ash & had tea with Mrs Potter.[2] Music in evg.

20. Tu. [London]

Ch. 8½ AM. Wrote to Sir T.G.—Ld Granville—Dr Brewer MP[3]—and minutes. Conversation with C. Lacaita respecting Herbert. Read Lanfrey. Arranging papers: discussed house plans with C. Off at [blank, to London].

[The inside back cover contains:—]

The French.

Qui veut les bien maitriser doit les caresser grandement, leur donner modestement, leur pardonner rarement, et ne leur faire tort aucunement.

Pamphlet of the day: in
Capefigue's Richelieu &c. III. 92.[4]

Un homme de capacité attend que les titres arrivent a une position dejà faite: il se garde de prendre les hochets avant les réalités.

Ibid. 325. (1624.)

Le cardinal [Richelieu] appelait l'unité de pouvoir, mais matériellement.

Ibid. (1638) [vi] p. 5.

---

[1] P. Lanfrey, *Études et portraits politiques* (1864).
[2] Elizabeth, born in Hesse, wife of Benjamin Potter, a local farmer; see 19 Nov. 70.
[3] William Brewer, d. 1881; physician and liberal M.P. Colchester 1868-74.
[4] J. B. H. R. Capefigue, 'Pamphlet contre Marie 1619' in *Richelieu, Mazarin, La Fronde et le règne de Louis XIV*, vol. iii (1835-6); 'i. Anyone who wants to master them must be lavish with attentions, modest with gifts, sparing with forgiveness, and on no account do them wrong. ii. An able man waits for titles to arrive when his position is already established; he is careful not to take baubles before realities. iii. The cardinal called for unity of power, but materially. iv. As they age, men's whole characters become marked with greater obstinacy. v. They try grandeur and magnanimity to win thanks for all the harm they do not do.'

Les caractères entiers, lorsqu'ils vieillissent, s'empreignent d'un plus dur entêtement.

ibid p. 34.

Ils essaient la grandeur, la magnanimité, pour qu'on les remercie de tout le mal qu'ils ne font pas.[1]

ibid p. 40.

[At the bottom left hand corner, in pencil:—]

36 NUH	2 Franklin
7 Cavour	51 John

[End of Volume XXVII]

[1] See p. 363, n. 4.

[VOLUME XXVIII]¹

[The inside front cover contains:—]

PRIVATE. NO. 28.

SEPT 21.70–JUNE 15. 72.

ἀσθενέστατον γὰρ ὄν
φύσει, μεγίστοις οἰκονομεῖται πράγμασιν.²
Menander ap. Plut. Consl. (p. 103 Reiske)

[And in faint pencil, left hand side, between dates and quotation:—]

Worcd Socks	Rev A Lanfrey
Fl. waistcoats	Write Rumpff
£5 from April & June	Juvenal.
Tulk Hist	

Hawarden—London
Wedn. Sept. 21—1870.

Wrote to Kath. Gladstone—Mr Cardwell—Mr Reeve—Mich. Cheva-lier—C.G.—Mr Parker—& minutes. Worked on MS. Saw Ld Gran-ville—Mr Glyn—Mr Rothschild—Count Strzelecki. Saw Casson X: hope is there. Read Lanfrey. Dined with the Wortleys.

To E. CARDWELL, war secretary, 21 September 1870.   PRO 30/48/7, f. 127.

When I saw you last I made a suggestion about Col. Walker, on which you were I think disposed to act. Something was said about Capt. Hozier. I know not what may be the proper instrumentality, but it appears to me that we ought if we can to obtain the fullest & most accurate accounts of the whole of the Prus-sian military system, both at rest & in action. Probably there are books which contain the former of these. It would be important to know them and I should

¹ Lambeth MS 1442.
² Menander fr. 740. 13–14 Körte: '[Man is an animal] which, though the weakest of all by nature, yet achieves the mightiest things.'

myself be very glad to be guided to the sources of information. Perhaps a Digest could be prepared for the Cabinet.

Col. Walker ought to be sedulously employed in preparing a perfect account of the system in action, in all its various Depts: or if he requires aid should it not be supplied. I assume his competence, as it would have been a gross error to appoint any other than a really able and accomplished soldier to the office he holds. In speaking of such reports I do not, of course, include such subjects as may have been already fully investigated. The great reform needed with us I take to be in regard to officers, & I suppose the Prussian solution of this difficult problem to be one of the best parts of their system.[1]

To M. CHEVALIER, 21 September 1870.   Add MS 44539, f. 33.
'Private.'

I trust that you received duly my two letters of last week:[2] and I am now in possession of yours of the 18th[3] to which I must be content to make only a very brief reply. As regards your first proposition I do not think the public opinion of this country desires that we should remain passive or indifferent to what is going on upon the Continent: but on the contrary that we should avail ourselves of any opportunity to be useful. Indeed many seem so oversanguine as to suppose that it is in our power at any moment by the friendly influence of reasoning to solve the problem which has brought together in the shock of battle the two greatest military powers of Europe. As regards your second proposition I have not seen or heard of a single person who believes France to be a nation in decay. It has been a surfeit of strength & fame that have brought upon her this terrible disaster. But I think the belief of Englishmen in her prospective greatness is as firm & as entire as your own, or as their knowledge of what she has been in the past. I take due notice of your suggestion that Parliament should be summoned & it coincides with the recommendation of Sir H. Bulwer, a high diplomatic authority in the Times of today. Government, however, in this country, only summons the Parliament when it has something to propose to that assembly, & if it departed from that rule, it might seem to be evading its proper responsibility. You will have seen that we are not asleep: but all that has hitherto offered, has been within our own force. God send us a happy & honourable peace.

22. Th.

Wrote to C.G.—and minutes. Visited the Bowden party. Worked on MS. Saw Ld Granville—Sir Jas Lacaita (2)—Archbp Manning—Mr Reeve—Mr Glyn—Mr Delane. Read Lanfrey: and D. Baxter on National Debts.[4] Saw MP at the Prince of Wales.[5] Play poor, *most* of the acting also poor.

[1] Cardwell replied that Walker's reports were as yet inadequate, and that he was preparing views on purchase abolition and officer education; 22 Sept., Add MS 44119, f. 151. (Sir) Charles Pyndar Beauchamp Walker, 1817-94; military attaché at Berlin 1865-77; directed military education 1878-84.   [2] See 6 and 14 Sept. 70.   [3] Add MS 44127, f. 88.
[4] R. D. *Baxter, 'National debts . . . read before the British Association' (1870).
[5] Also known as the Scala, showing 'cup and saucer' dramas.

23. Fr.

Wrote to Mr Cardwell—L. Rumpff—Ld Granville—Mr Glyn—C.G.
—& minutes. Read Ed.Rev. on Bismarck.[1] Worked on revising MS.
Went over the Govt Telegraphic Establishment. Saw Mrs Barber. Saw
Mr Scudamore—Mr Bagehot—Mr Glyn—Ld Granville—Sir A.
Spearman—Sir D. Salomons. Went to Sadler's Wells & saw Hamlet
acted with much talent by Mr Pennington.[2] Read Ed. Rev (69) on
Bismarck—Sallust.

To E. CARDWELL, war secretary, 23 September 1870.   Add MS 44539, f. 34.

Many thanks for your packet.[3] I hope you will take full time & not allow
yourself to be hurried by any influence without or within. I quite agree in the
four distinctions[4] you lay down between our system or rather our case & that of
Prussia. It is not servile copying that we want; but real study. I earnestly hope
you will make a full & careful study of the whole Prussian system of officering.
Here is our greatest difficulty: & I own I do not believe that any mere improvement of the Education of our officers will suffice to meet the case. Why should
not we take largely in this vital point from the Prussian system.

To H. REEVE, editor of the *Edinburgh Review*,   Add MS 44539, f. 34.
23 September 1870.

I send a further batch. But I have broken faith, & I must ask until tomorrow
for the rest which I have not been able to look over. The first part of the article
consists in a review of the positions of Prussia & Austria; the second in an
account of the transactions preceding the war, & a general notice of its events.
The third is prospective.[5]

24. Sat. [Stanmore Park, Middlesex]

Wrote to Mr Childers—Ld Granville—Mr Reeve—Mrs Th.—C.G.
—Viscss Brimont Bressac—and minutes. Finished revising MS. Saw
Mr Ayrton—Mr Reeve—Mr West. Off at 5.15 to Ld Wolverton's.
Saw Mr Merritt—Dr Butler—And Mr Woolner's fine collection of
pictures. Read Alison on Army Organisation.[6]

[1] [F. H. Geffcken] in *Edinburgh Review*, cxxx. 417 (October 1869).
[2] W. H. Pennington, 1831?–1923; had fought at Balaclava; became Gladstone's favourite tragedian.
[3] See 21 Sept. 70n.
[4] Ibid.; conscription, no colonial army, threat of France on the immediate frontier, and 'her people are not employed in Creative[?] pursuits in the peculiar degree that our people are'.
[5] Reeve replied on 28 Sept. urging including a passage on Alsace and Lorraine; Add MS 44428, f. 119.
[6] Sir A. *Alison, *On army organisation* (1869).

25. 15 S.Trin.

Parish Ch. mg and evg. Saw Mr West—Dr Bernays.[1] Wrote to Granville.[2] Wrote Mem. on the Bismarck Mem.[3] Read Triumph of Moral Good—Keble's Letters. This is a very Christian family.

The Chancellor of the North German Confederation announces, in his memorandum of the [blank]th current, the intention of the Confederation to demand from France, as a condition of peace, the cession of Alsace and a portion of Lorraine, countries inhabited by more than $1\frac{1}{4}$ million of inhabitants.

In signifying this intention as a matter of fact, he likewise states the ground on which the demand is to be enforced. It is not to be for the mere augmentation of German Territory: nor is it to be for the purpose of improving the facilities for an attack by Germany upon France. It is to be a defensive acquisition exclusively, and is simply to make it more difficult for France to attack Germany.

Avoiding all collateral and secondary matters, the British Government feels itself required, by the communication it has received, to consider briefly

1. Who it is that makes the demand?
2. What it is that is demanded?
3. Why it is that the demand is made?

As respects the first:—

The demand of a belligerent people, expressed by its constituted organ, must be taken as the authentic expression of its will.

But this expression may vary greatly in moral weight and authority, according as it may in given cases express the free and ascertained sentiment of the nation, or on the other hand only the sentiment of those who, thinking in accordance with the governing power, are allowed to speak their minds, while others who differ are put to silence by the action of the Government.

In order that we may give to the demand announced by the Chancellor of the Confederation its full moral weight, we must absolutely assume that the formation and expression of opinion upon that demand in Germany are free: that the public enunciation of the opinion opposite to that of the Government, besides encountering no hindrances, entails no legal penalties to person property or otherwise, more than that of an opinion coinciding with that of the Government. Otherwise we could not tell whether this condition is one really desired by the German nation, or whether it only represents the opinion which is held by persons in authority, and is supported by the greatest degree of physical force.

2. The thing that is demanded is, that a country with its inhabitants shall be transferred from France to Germany. More than a million and a quarter of men who, with their ancestors for several generations, have known France for their country, are henceforth to be severed from France, and to take Germany for their country in its stead.

[1] Leopold John Bernays, rector of Great Stanmore.

[2] Wrongly dated, as 24 September, in Ramm I, i. 131, on Bismarck's circular dispatch of 13 September forwarded by Bernstorff on 22 September (see *PP* 1871 lxxi. 105) which regarded the cession of French fortresses 'on our south west frontier' (i.e. effectively Alsace and Lorraine) as the essential preliminary to peace: 'If the paper be not withdrawn, it appears to me as at present advised, that we might examine it & comment upon it to the effect of the memorandum herewith.'

[3] Granville Papers, PRO 29/58, copy in Add MS 44759, f. 151, printed in H. Temperley and L. M. Penson, *Foundations of British Foreign Policy* (1938), 324. See 30 Sept., 23 Nov. 70 and introduction above, vol. vii, section III.

The transfer of the allegiance and citizenship, of no small part of the heart and life, of human beings from one sovereignty to another, without any reference to their own consent, has been a great reproach to some former transactions in Europe; has led to many wars and disturbances; is hard to reconcile with considerations of equity; and is repulsive to the sense of modern civilization.

All these considerations would apply with enhanced force, if there were any sort of foundation for a rumour, which has gained some currency, that it was intended to constitute and govern the territory of Alsace and Lorraine, after cession, not for itself, nor upon terms of perfect equality (whether incorporated or not) with the rest of Germany, but in some special and artificial manner, on behalf of Germany as a whole, and in a state of qualified civil or political inferiority.

The British Government must therefore presume it to be a *sous-entendu* in the memorandum of Count Bismarck, that the transfer of Alsace and a portion of Lorraine to Germany is only to take place upon its being ascertained to be conformable to the wishes of the population of those districts.

3. Thirdly and lastly, with reference to the reason, for which, and for which alone according to the Chancellor's memorandum, the transfer is to take place.

It needs no argument to shew that according to the common opinion a river is a bad strategic frontier, and that Metz and Strasburg afford to the French great facilities for the invasion of Germany.

It is however natural[1] to ask whether, were the fortresses of Alsace and Lorraine in the hands of Germany, they might not afford considerable facilities for the invasion of France by Germans?

It is difficult to carry the conviction to mankind in general, that any one country, whatever it may be called, is by a special charter of Nature exempt under all circumstances from all temptation to political excess: however freely it may be admitted on the other hand, that Germany is entitled to take ample securities against France, and that this cannot be done without materially impairing her rights and powers.

It would appear, however, that no greater harm ought now to be inflicted upon France, than is sufficient to meet the demand of Germany for ample security.

If then there is a method of proceeding which, with less of injury, and of future danger, to France, would give to Germany in substance the same guarantees against France as the appropriation of French territory, it would seem that that much ought to be preferred to such appropriation.

It seems to be worth while to consider, whether the military neutralization of the territory in question, and the destruction of all its fortresses, would not, without its being withdrawn from French allegiance attain the object of giving security to Germany.

The base of any military operations to be effected against Germany must then lie in France west of the proposed frontier, just as much as if the territory were transferred to Germany.

The exercise of civil Government from Paris in Alsace and Lorraine could not it is apprehended, be made to subserve the purposes of military aggression.

The disadvantages to France would be great. It may be uncertain whether she would submit to them. But the question now is why should the German demand extend beyond the condition of a military neutralization, of an interposition between the two countries of a space strategically void and exempt, and this wholly at the expense of France.

[1] Thus in Gladstone's draft; Temperley and Penson have 'rational'.

There may be other more eligible methods of proceeding: or there may be a perfect answer to the question which has been put. But as at present advised the demand of the Chancellor seems to have been pushed, and if so then inadvertently without doubt, beyond the scope of the argument on which it is founded, and within the true limits of which they cannot doubt it would if necessary according to reason, be reduced.

26. M. [London]

Back to London $10\frac{1}{2}$-$11\frac{1}{2}$. Wrote to Sir D. Salomons (Telegr.)—Abp of Canterbury—Ld Granville—Ld Spencer—Bp of Winchester—Herbert G.—Rev Dr Hannah (cancd)—and minutes. Saw Mr Merritt—Mr [blank]—Mr [blank] (candidates for Shrewsbury)[1]—Vicomtesse Brimont Bressac—Mrs Rumpff. Dined with the Wortleys. Saw two X.

To EARL SPENCER, Irish lord lieutenant,   Add MS 44539, f. 36.
26 September 1870.

There will be a Cabinet on Friday. It was summoned in order to consider the position of the Provisional Government in France with reference to the Elections which were to have been held on Oct. 1. Unhappily these are now postponed. But it may still be right that the Cabinet should be held. You will probably communicate with Fortescue about the Fenians and look to him to state your views. It is with much reluctance that I find myself entertaining strongly and clearly an opposite conviction to yours, but though I have this strong and clear conviction I am sensible of what is due to you, and I shall not as my own conclusion endeavour to press it to extremes, while I hope that if it should prove as may or may not be the case to be the view of the Cabinet, you will on your side give due weight to such a circumstance. I am painfully at a loss to comprehend the rejection of the armistice, offered on such moderate terms, and the postponement of the French elections.

To S. WILBERFORCE, bishop of Winchester,   Wilberforce MSS d. 38.
26 September 1870. 'Private.'

The answer *ad hominem* to Guizot's letter is but too obvious & conclusive. 'You said the war was wrong but as a Frenchman you must support it. You know that if it had been successful France would have demanded territory, and got it. Such was her desire for it (under Napoleon) that she took as the price for successful aid even from a friend. She cannot now plead the doctrine of inviolability.' It is most sad & piteous. The failure of French diplomacy & French mind in this war is unhappily quite as conspicuous as the failure in arms. Of course I cannot make through you any communication to M. Guizot. But were I in your place I should suggest to him that the best chance as matters now stand of keeping Alsace

---

[1] Unclear what is meant here; the by-election for the vacant Shrewsbury seat had been on 21 September, Charles Cecil Cotes, 1846-98 (liberal M.P. Shrewsbury from 1874) losing the seat to a tory.

& Lorraine would be to plead the sentiments of the people of those provinces & to work the question on that basis rather than on the principle of inviolability, an appeal to which, as between France & Europe, has but little force.[1]

We shall I think be here in Nov. & might be in a condition then to profit by your very welcome invitation. I am one of those who have upon the whole witnessed with extreme pain & dissatisfaction the proceedings about the mixed Communion: and I am not sanguine as to the point of the Revision.

27. Tu.

Wrote to Mr West—Ld Granville (2)—C.G.—The Queen (Mem)— Lord Spencer—& minutes. Read Lanfrey. Saw Deputn of Working Men on Recognition & Mediation[2]—Abp Manning—Ld Granville —The Rothschilds. Worked on my room. Saw C. Mills who will go home to Manchester: Olga X. Dined with the Bernstorffs. Conversation with Count B.—Mad B.—Delane—Houghton.

28. Wed.

Wrote to C.G.—Ld Granville (2)—Mr Bright—Dean of Wells—Mrs Th.—and minutes. Saw Reeves X hopeful. Read Lanfrey—Natal Council Report. Dined with the Wortleys. Saw Ld Granville—Bp of Winchester. Tea with Dowager Dss of Somerset. Worked on order in my room.

29. St Michael

At St M.Magd.Paddn. 7 P.M. Wrote to Sir D. Salomons—Ld Spencer —C.G.—Ld Stratford de Redcliffe—and minutes. Read Lanfrey. Saw Ld E. Bruce—Mr Moses[3]—Mr West—Ld Granville (2). Went with A. West to dine with his Rev. brother:[4] & after service went over the Church Institute &c. Home at 11.

[1] Wilberforce stayed with Guizot in Normandy in July, and forwarded his letter on the war (also printed in *The Times*) on 23 September 1870, Add MS 44345, f. 173, Wilberforce, iii. 354.

[2] Deputation led by Allan, Howell and Applegarth from the Labour Representation League, requesting immediate British recognition of the French republican government and mediation to prevent annexation: *The Times*, 28 September 1870, 9e. Gladstone denied 'any dynastic influence' was delaying recognition, and promised to acknowledge 'any Government chosen by the people of France'; on annexation he said 'The terms of peace involve questions too grave for me to give an opinion at present, but I suppose the great objection is to the transference of the people from one Power to another without their consent.'

[3] Possibly John Moses, curate of Woollavington.

[4] Richard Temple West, 1827?–93; student of Christ Church, 1848–75; vicar of St. Mary Magdalen, Paddington 1865. For this visit see West, *Recollections*, i. 366.

30. Fr.

Wrote to Ld Granville—Mr Reeve—Mr Glyn—Mr Maclaren—C.G.
—Mr D. Robertson—The Queen—and minutes. Saw Ld Granville
—Mr Woolner—Ld Halifax—Sir J. Lacaita—D. of Argyll—Mr
Motley. Cabinet 2¼-6. I failed in my two objects 1. an effort to speak
with the other neutral Powers against the transfer of A. & L. without
reference to the populations 2 (Immediate) release of Fenian prisoners. Read Lanfrey. Dined with Baron L. Rothschild.

Cabinet Sept. 30. 70. 2 PM[1]
√ Alternative plans of Ld G[ranville] & WEG. for treating the Memo. of Oct.
[*sc.* Sept.] 13 deposited by Count Bernstorff & the application of the Defence
Government of France for active intervention of the neutral Powers.[2] Plan of
Ld G[ranville] adopted.
√ Decided however in writing an acknt. to Bernstorff, to reserve expressly our
opinions on the matter of the Mem. of O. [*sc.* S] 13.[3]
2. Release of remaining Fenian prisoners (except those not merely political
offenders) recommended by WEG.[4] Decided to postpone until after some
(agrarian) experience of the short days.
3. Argyll submitted Indian Railway Guage [*sic*] Question. Remitted to him &
his Dept.
NB absent from this Cabinet: Lord Chancellor—Mr Bright—Ld de Grey—
Mr Childers.

Sept. 30[5]
1. No sole action. 2. No offer to negotiate. 3. No proceeding without Russia
as well as the other principal Powers. 4. No active intervention. On these
G[ranville] & WEG are agreed.

Appeal of Govt. of National Defence to the Neutral Powers.
Recite that by direction of Count Bismarck, the North German Ambassador
made known to Ld Granville the Circular of Sept. 13 in which it is set forth that
an acquisition of French Territory will be necessary for the safety of Germany.
That in the official report by M. Jules Favre of his interviews with Count Bismarck, Count B. is stated to have said, speaking of the population of the territory
to be acquired 'Je sais fort bien qu'ils ne veulent pas de nous. Ils nous imposeront
une rude corvée.'
That the French Government of National Defence have involved the aid of
the neutral Powers against the claims of North Germany.
That on the [blank] of Septr. M. Jules Favre declared that France would yield
neither an inch of her territory nor a stone of her fortresses: and that this declaration was repeated by M. [blank] on the [blank] of the same month.
France is entitled to ask for communication among the Neutral Powers on the

---

[1] Add MS 44638, f. 123.   [2] See 25 Sept. 70.
[3] *Granville told Bernstorff: 'It does not appear that any observations which occur to us
would at the present moment be of any practical effect.' *PP* lxxi. 125.
[4] See 3, 5 Sept. 70.   [5] Add MS 44638, f. 125.

subject of her appeal. The British Govt. has taken this appeal into cons[idera-tio]n accordingly.[1]

The neutral Powers are invited to declare, in answer to the appeal, that they, viewing with grief the prolongation of this sanguinary war, believe that both the parties to it might be disposed to pay some degree of regard to the general and impartial opinion of friendly Powers; and are anxious, even though they cannot undertake to propose the terms of an arrangement, yet at once offer suggestions which might tend to narrow the distance between the declarations & claims of the respective Belligerents.

They therefore state, in answer to the Government of National Defence, that they do not think that in the present or any proximate state of the fortunes of war the declaration of the [blank] and [blank] of September can as it stands be entertained. They are of opinion on the other hand, without laying down a general or abstract rule, that under the actual circumstances of the case the transference of Alsace and a portion of Lorraine from being part of France to become part of Germany, without any regard had to the wishes of the inhabitants (if not, according to M. Favre's report, in presumed opposition to them) could constitute a deviation from the most recent and approved examples, and could be a measure, in itself retrogressive, painful to the general sentiment of Europe and likely to cause future troubles, involving possible danger to the general peace. That regard being had to the Circular of the 13th,[2] and to the official communication of its contents to [certain of][3] the Neutral Powers, this Declaration of the Neutral Powers parties hereto be made known to the Government of North Germany.[4]

To H. REEVE, editor of the *Edinburgh Review*,   Add MS 44539, f. 39.
30 September 1870. 'Most Private.'

Can you look in upon me tomorrow forenoon? I am extremely glad you are pleased with the Article. I hope you think we can reckon on keeping the authorship absolutely secret.[5] Clearly something should be said on the terms of peace —& this is what I should like to consider with you tomorrow.[6] It might be worth considering whether *you* should touch this part of the subject rather than me.

Saturday Oct One 70. [*Hawarden*]

Wrote to Sir R. Palmer—Sir W. Tite—Sir S. Adair—Mr Bright— Mr Headlam—Mr Reeve—Mrs Jacobs—C.G. (Telegr.)—Mrs Reeves —M. Arles Dufour—Mr Cardwell—Ld Lyons—and minutes. Saw Ld Granville—Duke of Argyll—Mr Reeve—S.E.G. Saw invalids—

[1] 'Consider that they wd. not be justified in proposing "action intervention" ' added in the margin.

[2] Bernstorff's circular demanding annexation; see 25 Sept. 70.

[3] Diarist's square brackets.

[4] Docketed by diarist: 'Proposed by WEG (rough) to Cabinet'. Initialled and dated 30 September 1870; Add MS 44759, f. 166. See Ramm I, i. 135n.

[5] *Reeve replied on 3 October, Add MS 44428, f. 135: '. . . I have cautioned Longman to be *absolutely secret*.'

[6] See para. 60 of the *Edinburgh Review* article, in *Gleanings*, iv. 241.

Mr Byng—Mr Wortley—Hampton. Read Lanfrey. Packing books & arr. for departure. Off by the 9.15 P.M.—Hn at 3.15.

To J. BRIGHT, president of the board of trade,   Add MS 44539, f. 40.
1 October 1870. 'Private.'

Having written you some time ago a dissuasive letter about France,[1] & assuming that you have received & read M. J. Favre's detailed report of his conferences with Ct. Bismarck, I send for your private perusal the inclosed mem.[2] which I proposed to the Cabinet yesterday, but could not induce them to adopt. It presupposes the concurrence of the Neutral Powers. They agreed in the opinions, but did not think the expression of them timely. My opinion certainly is that the transfer of territory & inhabitants by mere force calls for the reprobation of Europe, & that Europe is entitled to utter it, & can utter it with good effect. The release of the Fenian prisoners also stands over. I am going to Hawarden tonight. Could you pay us a visit there? You would be most welcome.

2. S.16 Trin.

Ch mg (with H.C.) and evg. Wrote to Mr Gurdon—Read Triumph of Moral Good—Bp Moberly's Charge[3]—and other works.

3. M.

Wrote to Mr Gurdon—F.O. (Telegr.)—and [blank]. Arranged some books. Ch. 8½ A.M. Read Cic. de Nat[ura] Deorum—Max Müller Science of Reln[4]—Randolph's Praelectiones[5]—Our Father's Care.[6] Cutting down trees in aftn. Saw Mr Burnett.

4. Tu.

Wrote to Mr Fortescue—Mr Cardwell—Ld Granville—Mr Max Müller—& minutes. Conversation with Mr G. Williams[7]—Mr [H. R.] Sandbach—Sir J. Lacaita. Attended the distribution of Prizes to the Volunteers.[8] Read Cic. de Nat Deorum—Col. Chesney on Army Orgn[9]—Max Müller on Religion. Ch. 8½ AM.

[1] See 12 Sept. 70.   [2] See 25 Sept. 70.
[3] G. *Moberly, 'Primary charge to the clergy' (1870).
[4] F. Max *Müller, *Introduction to the science of religion* (1870).
[5] J. Randolph, *Praelectiones Academicae in Homerum* (1870).
[6] M. *Sewell, *'Our father's care'. A ballad* (1870 ed).
[7] George *Williams (see 21 Dec. 39), at Hawarden on Eastern Churches Association affairs, with particular reference to maltreatment of the abp. of Syra and Tenos by the Sultan; see Matthew, 'Vaticanism', 426 and Gladstone to Sir H. Elliot, 5 October 1870, Add MS 44539, f. 44. Gladstone also got permission for Williams to consult foreign office papers; to O. *Russell, 7 October 1870, ibid. f. 45.   [8] *The Times*, 5 October 1870, 11d.
[9] C. C. Chesney and H. Reeve, *The military resources of Prussia and France, and recent changes in the art of war* (1870).

To E. CARDWELL, war secretary, 4 October 1870.   PRO 30/48/7, f. 137.

I thank you for your note. In Alison's little book on the British Army (of which you sent me a copy,[1] with 'Northbrook, from the author' within) it is recommended that in order to facilitate dealing with the question of purchase a rule should be laid down (p. 68) that no officer shall receive money for a commission which he has not purchased. Would not this be very advantageous if practicable? And is it practicable? At once?

I suppose that promotion from the ranks ought sometimes to occur. But to promote not only to pay & station, but to a property seems absurd. Is it not also absurd that the Queen should have power not only to give her Pages an appointment but to endow them with a considerable sum which is to be eventually as it appears at the public charge. We shall not forget your kind invitation.

Wed. 5.

Ch. 8½ A.M. Wrote to Ld Granville—Mr Hammond (tel. & letter)—Ld Bury—The Queen—Mr Headlam—Mrs Th.—Sir H. Elliot—and minutes. Saw Mr Williams on the case of the Abp of Syros. Read Chesney & Reeve on Army Organisation. Tree cutting in aftn. Large party.

6. Th.

Ch. 8½ AM. Wrote to Baron M. Rothschild—Bp [H.] M'Kenzie—Scotts—Mr H. Reeve—and minutes. Read Cic. de Nat. Deorum—Chesney & Reeve. Walk with Mr Parker: promised him some R.B.[2] Whist in evg.

7. Fr.

Wrote to Ld Granville—Rev W. Rawson—Watsons—Lady M. Alford—Robn G.—Mr O. Russell—Mr Barker—Bp M'Kenzie—Mr Rowsell—Bp of Down—and minutes. Felling trees with W. Corrected revises.[3] Dined at the Rectory. Read Chesney & Reeve.—Malmesbury Correspondence.[4] Ch. 8½ AM.

8. Sat.

Ch. 8½ AM. Wrote to Ld Granville (2)—The Queen (2 Memoranda)—Mr Cardwell—Mr Gurdon—Mr Max Müller—Mr Reeve—Baron Beaulieu—Mr Hammond (Tel.)—and minutes. Conversation with

---

[1] See 24 Sept. 70; Add MS 44119, f. 151.
[2] J. H. *Parker, the publisher; see 12 Aug. 62.
[3] Of the *Edinburgh* article; see 1 Sept. 70.
[4] *A series of letters of the first Earl of Malmesbury*, 2v. (1870).

Mr [Edmund] Venables on Cathedrals.[1] Read Cic. de Nat. Deorum
—Chesney and Reeve—Voltaire Siècle Louis XIV.[2] Saw Mr Blom-
field.[3]

To E. CARDWELL, war secretary, 8 October 1870.   PRO 30/48/7, f. 139.

I presume we ought not to decide on any scheme for the abolition of purchase, until we have acquired a pretty clear & full notion of the system which is
to follow, & the advantages which are to be attained. In short that the question
of the method of officering the army, reserves, & volunteers, will have to be
fully considered first in all its parts, as we must not abolish purchase on speculation. Now this is an enormous business, requiring I apprehend much preliminary
study of the methods pursued elsewhere, particularly that of the Prussians. I give
you credit for as rapid powers of work as any man: but you will have surpassed
my estimate if in this view of the subject you are able soon to send me in print
a scheme for the abolition of purchase.

Though I would not dissuade you from using the present, & though on the
contrary I trust as well as believe you will turn every moment to the best account,
yet I have the impression that our measures respecting the army cannot well be
decided on by the cabinet, any more than by Parliament & the country, until
after peace is made: so much will depend upon not only the *terms*, but upon the
effect to follow as respects the system of armament in Europe. I think that if
a *moderate* peace be concluded, we have a good chance of rational measures, i.e.
disarmament & economy.

Doubtless H.M. would have to be consulted before the Cabinet: but not I
hope until all is in substance ready & pretty complete.[4]

To F. Max MÜLLER, 8 October 1870.   Max Müller MSS, d. 170.

I need hardly tell you that your letter deeply disappoints me,[5] if I am to interpret it as contending that Alsace and part of Lorraine may properly be annexed
to Germany without any previous proof either 1. that the inhabitants generally
are favourable, or not averse to such annexation; or 2. that the military security
which Germany after what has happened is entitled to demand, can be had by
no other means; or 3. that the fortresses, which have been a menace and a danger
to Germany, will be no menace and no danger to France. Of course I will not
pursue the argument. But upon your closing paragraph, I will say that I entirely
concur in the feeling it expresses. My main specific, however, for maintaining
good will between two nations is that each of them should pursue a policy which
the other can regard as honourable & just.

[1] See 20 Aug. 64.
[2] F. M. A. de Voltaire, *Le siècle de Louis XIV*, 2v. (1751).
[3] The Chester canon; see 14 Sept. 49.
[4] Cardwell sent a summary of army reform proposals on 10 October; Add MS 44119,
f. 157.
[5] Gladstone told Müller on 4 October (Max Müller MSS, d. 170): 'I want to ask you
what we are to think of the Alsace and Lorraine question'; Müller replied on 6 October, Add
MS 44251, f. 288 supporting annexation, as he did in letters to *The Times* (reprinted in
Letters on the war (1871)); see D. Schreuder, 'Gladstone as "troublemaker"', *Journal of
British Studies*, xvii. 125.

The recollections of the Crimean War, & of the Danish proceedings, have not been very favourable to the intimacy you so properly desire; but they were well nigh effaced in a sense of the gross injustice suffered by Germany in the outset of the present quarrel. I wish we may have a fair start for the future.

I send you herewith an account we have received of some proceedings of a public meeting at Munich on the 23rd. I send a curious account, also, of a conversation in Alsace, from the D. News of today.

9. 17 S. Trin.

Ch. 11 AM and 6½ PM. Wrote to Queen (Mem)—Duke of Argyll—Rn G (Card)[1]—Abp Manning—Mr Glyn—Ld Granville—Mrs Th. —and minutes. Read Manning's Sermon[2]—Keble's Letters—Peter on Ch. & Dissent[3]—Jackson's Right & Wrong Serm.[4]—Jewel & Harding on H.E. with Mr Venables;[5] also S. Aug. Conversation with Mr Venables. Worked up the Seaforth Church case and prepared do accounts for tomorrow.

10. M.

Ch. 8½ AM. Wrote to Mr G. Tallents—Ld Spencer—Mr Ouvry—Ld Granville—& minutes. Read Cic. de Nat.D. Off at 11 to Liverpool and Seaforth. Saw Robn G.—J. Breakenridge—Rev. W. Rawson—Mr Keith. Went over Seaforth House, & the Church: arranged a plan for dividing the sittings: attended & addressed a meeting of the Congregation in the Schoolhouse about the new arrangements, which seemed to please. Dined at Courthey: & back, by Lpool and Chester to Hn at midnight.

11. Tu.

Ch. 8½ A.M. Wrote to Ld Granville (2)—The Queen (and Memm.)—Mr Gurdon (Telegr.)—Mr Hugessen—Lady S. Vane [Tempest]—Mr Cardwell—Mr Ouvry—Mr Fortescue—Helen—Rev. Dr Hannah—and minutes. Saw Mr Burnett. Finished draft of arrangement for Seaforth Church.[6] Cut down an Ash with WHG. Read Cic. de N.D.—Voltaire's Louis XIV.[7]

[1] i.e. a post card.
[2] H. E. *Manning, 'Rome the capital of Christendom; a sermon [on Matth. xxvii. 24]' (1870).
[3] R. G. Peter, 'A letter to churchmen and dissenters' (1870).
[4] W. Jackson, 'Right and wrong. A sermon' (1870).
[5] J. *Jewel, *A defense [against M. Hardinge] of the Apologie of the Churche of Englande* (1570).
[6] Add MS 44759, f. 235.   [7] See 8 Oct. 70.

To C. S. P. FORTESCUE, Irish secretary,   Add MS 44539, f. 50.
11 October 1870.

With reference to our conversation in the Cabinet about Fenian prisoners,[1] please to give directions that the reports made monthly of agrarian outrages in Ireland be supplied to me from July last to September, and thereafter monthly as they are made up, until we have disposed of this matter. I should like them to include a comparison with the months of 1868 & 1869.

12. Wed.

Ch. 8½ A.M. Wrote to Mr Gurdon (Tel.)—Mr Hammond (Three Telegrams)—The Queen (2)—Chr of Exr—Ld Granville—Sir R. Palmer—Mayor of Liverpool—and minutes. Saw Mr Burnett. Kibbled an ash with W. Finished Cic. de Nat. Deorum. Read Voltaire's Louis XIV. Today, Agnes & Willy, with some intervention from me, deciphered our first cipher Telegram: without instruction it is not easy.

To ARCHBISHOP H. E. MANNING, 12 October 1870.   Add MS 44539, f. 51.

Before replying to your letter of the 8th,[2] it was necessary that I should communicate with Ld. G: & neither of us are precisely aware to what Cardinal Antonelli refers when he speaks (of) 'the willingness of the Government to offer mediation in the question of Rome'. In another big matter we have rather been holding language to the effect that the mediation of a third power should proceed upon the request of both the parties, but here there is a request from neither: & to define a distinct basis for mediation, for which nobody would be responsible but ourselves, would be a further step which I think would be contrary to all rule. It is of course open to the Pope & his advisers to decline making terms with the Italian Government, but I do not see how, while they hold that language, others could make terms for them. The present course of affairs evidently goes to throw the whole discretion of dealing with the case more & more into the hands of the Italian Government, & I have no means of knowing *now* to what extent they may be disposed to court the aid or recognise the title of other Powers. Many thanks for your inclosures.

13. Th.

Ch. 8½ AM. Wrote to Mr Hammond Tel.—Ld Granville Tel.—Abp Manning—Robn G.—Mr West—Ld Halifax—& minutes. Read Voltaire Louis XIV. Wrote a lengthened Memorandum on Military Organisation.

[1] See 30 Sept. 70.
[2] Add MS 44249, f. 212 and f. 216 reporting Antonelli's views and that *Lothair* was sold in Rome 'some hours after the capitulation. This is a glory for the Leader of H.M.'s Tory Opposition.'

Army questions.

It appears to me that, if we are to submit to Parliament any plan of changes in the Army which is to involve the abolition of Purchase, and thereby as a preliminary and absolute condition to impose on the State a burden (as I understand) of several millions, it will be justly expected that such a plan shall deal with all the great military questions recently opened or not yet settled, consequently that, if in the nature of things it cannot be final yet it shall aim at disposing of those questions according to the best lights of our present knowledge and experience, and shall therefore be complete and definitive.

In this view it seems to me that the question of Home defence cannot be treated without a preliminary consideration of the questions of India and Colonial defence, which have such important bearings upon the term, and the other conditions, of service at home.

The following remarks relate exclusively to the *personnel* of the Queen's forces.

I. First with regard to India. It seems incumbent upon us at this time to review the decision of Lord Palmerston's Government some nine or ten years ago which brought about the consolidation of the (old) Queen's and Indian armies.[1] That decision, if not reversed, will probably be corroborated by the effect of such measures as are now in view.

A three years service is incompatible, as I understand and can readily believe, with the exigencies of the Indian service. But if such a term be one desirable for the army at home, it would surely be a very great disadvantage to have in the same arm of the same army, applicable to one & the same regiment in its entirety, at various periods according to its turn for India, two terms of service, involving probably other differences, as conditions of enlistment. Is this avoidable?

Has the new system worked well, in a military sense, for the army? It is I apprehend costly to India. Is it not also in effect costly to the Imperial Exchequer? Are the exigencies of home and Indian Defence really so far reconcileable, as to render it a good permanent system to supply both by one Army?

If we are ever to separate the armies, cannot it best be done at the time when we are readjusting the method of officering, which might otherwise for India have to undergo a double change before arriving at its ultimate settlement.

If a Queen's Indian Army were constituted, might it not be fixed, with present experience, at such a number as to suffice for that country, so that no call should be made upon the home army except under extraordinary & rare circumstances, as well as on terms of extra pay, which ought to be fixed high; perhaps limited to occasions of war? or if operative at other times, with option to the soldier of passing into the Reserve?

The question of the Indian army is here raised generally, and without reference to any special arms, as for example the artillery, or the corps of Engineers. The natural term of service, so to call it, in these Corps, might not offer the same impediments to union of the two systems as serve to exist particularly in the case of infantry.

II. Secondly with regard to the Colonies.

This appears to be the time for considering whether it may be possible to arrive at a view of what may be considered as in ordinary circumstances their permanent military establishment: so that we may know what draft they will commonly make upon the army, and how far these needs will be likely to interfere with what would otherwise be the best system of service. Much has been done well, but tentatively: should we not now think of a system.

[1] See 27 Jan. and 2 May 60.

I put this question broadly; is it not possible to get rid of all drafts upon the regular army for Colonial purposes, in ordinary circumstances, except in the four cases of Malta—Gibraltar—Halifax—Bermuda. Would it not be possible to make sufficient provision for other places by one or more of the following means 1. Small bodies of pensioners or others, specially remunerated as caretakers of stores and fortifications, in cases where there is no standing necessity for a real military force. Such I suppose to be some of the West Indian Islands, Saint Helena & probably the Mauritius. 2. The aid of marines, in cases where we have a naval force at hand. Such I suppose to be Hong Kong. 3. The use of corps strictly local, which might or might not be governed by local authority: but to which, *if* it were in any case desirable on Imperial grounds, we might contribute in material or in money, perhaps for a time, from the Imperial Exchequer. I am aware of no reason why the Cape Colony which I suppose to present the most difficult case, should not be managed on this principle.

I suggest that it would be well to know the practice, in this matter, of the French: who, I have been told, regulate the defence of their old colonies in the West Indies so as to dispense with, or greatly reduce, the demand upon the regular army. It must not be forgotten that the system of supplying Colonial Service by the British Army has been considerably supported by the notion, that it was among the best means of inducing Parliament to maintain a considerable standing army in time of peace. If the suggestions here made are practicable, I suppose the ordinary Colonial demand on the regular army would scarcely exceed 12000 men of the infantry.

III. Thirdly with respect to Home defence; as to rank & file.

I will assume for the moment that three years will be chosen as the regular term of infantry service: That the engagement will include a subsequent enrolment in the reserve, which under one name or another will extend over a longer term of years: That there will be a reserve, properly so called, i.e. a body of men available for filling up the ranks of the army in time of war like the Prussian reserve: and liable in case of need to the discharge of all army duties: and that there will also be another reserve force, available only, as a rule, for defence at home.

Now would it not be a great military advantage to bring this latter body into the closest possible *relation* to the regular army?

Is not the relation of the Prussian Landwehr to the Army a better relation in the main than that of our Militia: and if so might not our Militia be cast more nearly into the form of the Landwehr?

The men would then pass on into the Militia after a certain time of service first in the Army and then in the Army Reserve. I hope with reference to this part of the subject, that pains will be taken to ascertain exactly, through competent persons, the actual working merits of the Prussian army, and Landwehr, respectively. M. Laveleye contends,[1] and seems to show that the Landwehr, both officers and men, is not less efficient than the Army in actual service. The passing on of Army Reserve Men into the Militia would not of necessity put an end to direct enlistment for that force, if it be desirable to retain a proportion of that element. Another point for close examination would be the Prussian system as to re-engagement, in comparison with the French. The Prussians I think do not admit them as to rank and file: while they have been encouraged in France.

The close association of the army and militia would be highly favourable to the extension and systematic application in the Army of that local principle, which appears to be so highly approved by experience in Germany.

[1] See 23 Aug. 70.

If the total engagement of the soldier were for nine years in three periods of three years each, and if the total number of our *infantry* were no more than 60,000, including 12,000 in the Colonies, there would be in this country a body of 150,000 trained *infantry* soldiers independent of all volunteers, of cavalry, and of Artillery.

IV. Home Defence: Officers. The most difficult of all the questions standing for consideration I presume to be that which concerns the supply of officers. Here in particular I hope the Prussian system both as it was fixed in 1813, and as it is now, will be carefully borne in mind, in so far particularly as it may serve to dispose of the difficulty of class. Without doubt the investigation of this portion of the question will include the following among other points: training, appointment & promotion, tenure, numbers, pay. As to the appointment of Officers, if purchase is to be done away, discretion will probably be substituted. Of this discretion, no mere paper rules will prevent the abuse: while the principle of Seniority, which might check it materially will probably be allowed only a limited scope, lest it should in its turn introduce other evils. The only effectual security against abuse will in my opinion be an accurate and close adjustment between work, pay, and privileges. There are no abuses in the appointment of men to be private soldiers, or to be non-commissioned officers: because when duties, emoluments, & advantages are duly balanced, the system becomes self-working. Surely the position of the officers should be similarly regulated. Hitherto, however it may have been the fashion to complain of slender pay, such has been the disproportion of the emoluments, including a lottery of sinecures in prospect, to the real ordinary burden of duty, that the large overgrowth of advantage has expressed itself in extra regulation prices of commissions: and the nation perhaps not improperly, will now have to redeem the value it has itself given to its own officers by an outlay of several millions of public money.

It seems to me, then, that if purchase is abolished, it will be necessary to consider whether pay should not be reduced; and whether sinecures, either avowed or virtual, should not be greatly cut down. A statement of the comparative pay of officers in the different European armies will be of great value for considering this matter: especially in the case of Prussia where the class of officers is highly aristocratic. Besides pay, other advantages, actual & prospective, must of course also be compared.

As this country has a vast leisured and wealthy class, and as it derives advantage therefrom in an unpaid magistracy and Parliament, so the same constitution of our society should be borne in mind when we proceed to readjust the system of officering for the army. That description of labour, important as it is, should not be dear but cheap.

The present tenure of Commissions I doubt not will be fully considered, in such a way as to prevent effectually for the future the growth of vested interests in them: to provide for officering the reserve and voluntary or irregular forces with men trained in the army, either in whole or in part, I hope in great part, as may be necessary: and to diminish that class of the unemployed which exists under the present halfpay system: a class whose position, burdensome enough to the public, is far from enviable, or calculated to produce contentment, in many cases, as respects its own members. The numbers of our officers in relation to men will doubtless be compared with those of the best foreign armies.

But no subject, I suppose, can be of more vital importance than the training of officers, and here the accumulation of difficulties is enormous. We know how hard it is to bring the youth of this country in the highest order up to any tolerable standard of instruction; and this, although we have the highest inducements and most magnificent establishments for Education in the world, & our teachers are not second to any in knowledge, ability, or zeal. Now, that portion of our youth who go into the army, are certainly & must be on the whole below the average in avidity for knowledge. Yet they have hitherto when mere boys been separated from their schoolfellows, prematurely installed in the privileges of manhood, & surrounded with all the dangers of idleness. Is their introduction to the Army in such extreme youth desirable? I assume that the best methods of instruction will now be provided for them. But, even with compulsory attendance upon this teaching, there will be much difficulty in making it an effective training. The greatest difficulty of all in truth is this: to redeem the officer's life from idleness in time of peace. Something may more readily be done towards this with the soldier, as he is a person dependent on his labour for his bread, by allowing him to work for his own benefit. But, with the growing wealth of this country, we must calculate on having at all times a high proportion of officers who are relatively wealthy, & whose example will in a great degree set the tone, and so sway the rest. There is nothing in my mind to equal the difficulties of this military problem. When war comes, we demand from commanders & from all officers, almost more than the utmost faculties of mind and body can supply: but this profession is, in time of peace, apt to fall as much below the ordinary standard of need for continuous energetic exertion, as in war it must rise above that standard.

We should have the best establishments, teachers, discipline, rewards, punishments; and yet all will not suffice. Why should we not employ at least one other powerful auxiliary, which has the highest countenance abroad; why should we not make all our young cadets learn a soldier's business in the ranks while carefully guarding him against any conditions of duty and service which might be incompatible with a just consideration for his station. Here again we should obtain some test of physical qualifications which of course must not be forgotten amidst the efforts to secure mental knowledge and development.[1]

14. Frid.

Ch. 8½ AM. Wrote to Mr Gurdon (Tel.)—Abp Manning—Mr Hammond—Mr Cardwell—Ld Granville (letter & Tel.)—& minutes. Cut tree with Willy. Tea at Mrs Potter's: & conversation about her exiled father. Music in evg. Read Siècle de Louis XIV.

To E. CARDWELL, war secretary, 14 October 1870.　　　PRO 30/48/7, f. 151.

I sent off yesterday a Mem. to be copied & sent on to you which this note ought to have accompanied & introduced: but its purpose is really to do little more than say that while I am too much interested on [sic] the subject to be without ideas & desires regarding it, & while I think it may be convenient to you to be acquainted with them at the outset, I am sensible that from my want of acquaintance with military administration they may be not only crude, but in particular points wholly wide of the mark.

[1] Initialled and dated 13 October 1870; Add MS 44759, f. 169. Gladstone docketed it: 'Make copy forthwith and send it to Mr. Cardwell with my note [of next day]'.

I am however also anxious that we should not as a Government approach the question too soon. I do not trust the nation for any calm judgment in the moment of a war. Decisions now must be taken if taken at all with some reference to a state of the public mind which is excited & unbalanced in no small degree. And it is probable that this terrific struggle will be over in ample time to enable the Cabinet to deliberate between the Pacification, & the Session. But I do not mean by this to recommend delay in the preparation of plans.[1]

15. Sat.

Ch. 8½ AM. Wrote to Ld Granville (& Tel.)—Mr Hammond (& Tel.)—Lady S. Vane—and minutes. Music mg & Tree cutting. Arranging books. Read Siecle de Louis XIV.

16. 18 S.Trin.

H.C. mg (with H.C.) [sic] and evg: when Mr Peel preached very well. Wrote to Ld Granville—Mrs Thistlethwayte—Ld Kimberley—Scotts—& minutes. Read Keble's Letters[2]—Triumph of Moral Good.

To LORD KIMBERLEY, colonial secretary,   Add MS 44539, f. 56.
16 October 1870.

The question of the Gold Coast[3] appears to be for me at this time a very narrow one, after the Convention of 1867 & the subsequent correspondence. I think there would be nothing unreasonable, as the Dutch appear to be the asking and we the giving party, in requiring them to take the 24m[ille] on the security of the Colonial Revenues; but the matter is not worth vexing them or stopping a good cluster of arrangements, & if Lowe does not object I do not.

17. M.

Ch. 8½ AM. Wrote to Ld Granville (1. and Tel.)—Mr Gurdon (1. and Tel.)—Chancellor of Exchequer—Mr Forster[4]—The Queen—The Lord Mayor—and minutes. Saw Mr Burnett. Singing, forenoon & evg. Cut an ash with W. Arranging books. Read Siecle de Louis XIV—Ed.Rev. on Cox's Angevins.[5]

---

[1] Cardwell responded favourably (16 October 1870, Add MS 44119, f. 161), promising verbal analysis.

[2] See 28 Aug. 70.

[3] Responding to Kimberley's mem., sent 14 October, Add MS 44224, f. 88.

[4] On the creeds and the Education Act, in Lathbury, ii. 141.

[5] *Edinburgh Review*, cxxxii. 154 (July 1870).

18. St Luke. Tu.

Agnes's birthday: God crown her with all blessings. Church 11 AM. Wrote to Abp Manning—Adm. Hornby—Ld Granville Tel.—Mr Thistlethwayte—Mrs Thistlethwayte—Mr Forster—& minutes. Arranging books. Made Catalogue of my books on Shakespeare. Read Voltaire, Siècle. Music forenoon & evg. Saw Mr Barker sen—& jun.

To ARCHBISHOP H. E. MANNING,   Add MS 44249, f. 236.
18 October 1870.

I thank you for your letter[1] and The Tablet. You put in a new view the suggestion you had made, which is not as I now understand it one of mediation at all but it is to be a request or overture from us to the Italian Government to maintain the status quo provisionally and await the decision of Europe, not only on the proper guarantees for the independence of the Pope but on the Civil Government of the City of Rome and its appended provinces. Such a suggestion would of course be disregarded by the Italian Government who plead the Plebiscite.

Now however little we may in this country be blind to the possible defects of that method we could not without overturning the convictions of the vast majority of our population plead against it the doctrine that Europe, or that the Roman Catholic body in Europe were for their own religious objects entitled to dispose of the civil interests of the people of the Roman States. I do not therefore see how we could act upon your suggestions.[2]

19. Wed. [London]

Off at 8¼. Reached C.H.T. at 3. Saw Ld Granville—Mr Hammond *cum* do—Mr Hugessen. Wrote to Duke of Argyll—Lord Mayor—Mr Ayrton—The Queen—C.G.—and minutes. Dined with Mrs Th. Saw two[R]. Read Q.R.[3]—Mrs Montagu's Essay[4]—Dean of Chester on Races.[5]

20. Th.

Wrote to C.G.—The Queen—and minutes. Dined at Count Apponyi's. Saw Rev. S.E. G[ladstone]—Mr Levy—Mr Childers—Ld Granville —Mr Helps—Do *cum* Count Apponyi—Count Cadorna. Saw Davidson. Cabinet 3–6. We took important resolutions: unanimously. Read Innes on W.E.G.[6]

---

[1] Of 16 October 1870, Add MS 44249, f. 230.
[2] Manning apparently did not reply.
[3] *Quarterly Review*, cxxix (October 1870).
[4] E. *Montagu, *An essay on the writings and genius of Shakespeare* (1769).
[5] J. S. *Howson, probably 'The history of the Mediterranean. A lecture' (1849).
[6] A. Taylor Innes had sent his 'Mr Gladstone in transition', *Contemporary Review*, xv. 630 (November 1870); Add MS 44428, f. 164.

Cabinet Oct. 20. 70. 3 PM[1]

√ Granville detailed circs. & read draft of dispatch to Bismarck. Correlative Tell. to Tours (& dispatch St Petersburg[)] discussed, corrected, & agreed to.[2] Cabinet probably on Monday.

21. Fr.

Wrote to Sir J. Sinclair—Earl of Devon—Mr Knowles—C.G.—Mr Forster—Dowager Duchess of S[omerset]—Ly Holland—and minutes. Saw Reeve. Saw Ld Halifax—do *cum* Ld Granville—Mr Motley—Mr Glyn. Dined with Mrs Th. & went to see Amy Robsart: wonderful but defectively expressed. How Shakespearian![3] Read Q.R. on Palmerston—and on Prevost Paradol.[4]

To Sir J. G. T. SINCLAIR, M.P., 21 October 1870.   Add MS 44539, f. 59.

I thank you for the papers[5] you have sent me & I shall hope further to profit by their interesting contents. With regard to Alsace and Lorraine I am not aware on what particular ground you rest the observation that I am hostile to the transfer. I have no abstract or general opinion on the transfer of territory apart from the wishes & attachments of the inhabitants. You will have observed however the very ominous fact that Count Bismarck, when criticizing and correcting M. Jules Favre's report of their interviews, made no objection to that part of the statement which represented him as admitting the thoroughly French inclinations of the people of Alsace and Lorraine, and as intending to consider them.

22. Sat.

Wrote to E. Cardwell—Duke of Argyll (2)—C.G.—Mr Hammond—Mr Anderson—Mr Maguire MP.—& minutes. Dined (as did S. and H.) with Dowager Duchess of Somerset. Saw Netherlands Minister—Mr Ayrton—C. Villiers—Belgian Minister. Read Q.R. on British Army—On Terms of Peace[6]—Lanfrey's Essays.

To E. CARDWELL, war secretary, 22 October 1870.   PRO 30/48/7, f. 166.

As the method of giving the least trouble I send back your paper[7] with some marginal notes. I do not presume to *form* an opinion about the single or dual

[1] Add MS 44638, f. 126.
[2] Granville sent Bismarck a copy of his despatch to Loftus, relating British pressure on France for an armistice and admitting Prussia's 'two moral causes', self defence and 'right of a great country to constitute itself in the way most conducive to the full development of its resources'; *PP* 1871, lxxi. 174.
[3] At Drury Lane.   [4] *Quarterly Review*, cxxix. 327, 369 (October 1870).
[5] Not found.
[6] *Quarterly Review*, cxxix. 392, 540 [G. R. Gleig] on military inefficiency, [*Salisbury] on the peace.
[7] On 'Military Organization', Add MS 44615, f. 33.

Queen's Army, much less to press it; but I note down what occurs to me because this is the best time to raise all the points. I have read Q.R. on the army: I dislike the article in general, but it has some very good particulars I think.

23. 18 S. Trin.

Chapel Royal mg & aft. Wrote to Mr Hammond—C.G. Saw Mr Hammond—do *cum* Ld Granville—Ld De Tabley—Ld R. Cavendish—Sig. Pellegrini[1]—Dr Rock.[2] Saw Mrs Th. Dined at Holland House: where I was much pleased with the Duchess of Manchester.[3] Plenty of mind in her. Read Fuller's Thoughts[4]—B. Gould Devt of Belief.[5]

24. M.

Wrote to Ld Granville—Mr Ouvry—Sir S.R. Glynne—Mr H. Reeve—Miss O. Barry[6]—Adm. Hornby—Mr Parker—C.G.—& minutes. Saw Ld Granville—Ld Halifax—Count Bernstorff. Dined with the Wortleys. Saw Terry: there is hope[R]. Read Lanfrey.

To Sir S. R. GLYNNE, 24 October 1870.   Hawarden MSS.

Thanks for your letter.[7] The moment is critical. You will now have to determine whether you will attempt to establish a Welsh training of a high order for Wales. The Dissenters are ready to cooperate. I cannot now speak for the Government with reference to a Welsh University: but I can say for myself that although all my prejudices were in an opposite direction reflection and inquiry have convinced me 1. that the measure is fair and just. 2. that it will be eminently beneficial to the Church. Get her once fairly into the open intellectual field with the Dissenters, & she is sure to hold her own.

It seems to me however that it would be unwise to propose to found a Welsh University anywhere but in a thoroughly well chosen situation. Is Llampeter such a situation? And if it is not would not the disadvantage of proposing it be aggravated by Dissenting jealousies? Could not the Theological College easily enough be moved? And might not the building probably be employed for one of the Schools likely to be formed under the Endowed Schools Act of 1869?

I am much pleased with your account of the Bishop, very sorry to have missed him.

25. Tu.

Wrote to Mr Maguire—Ld Lyttelton[8]—C.G.—and minutes. Haymarket Theatre evg. The Rivals. Saw Ld Halifax—Mr M'Coll—Ld

---

[1] Unidentified.   [2] Daniel Rock, 1799–1871; Roman catholic controversialist.
[3] *Hartington's mistress; see 6 Dec. 68.   [4] See 17 July 70.
[5] See 12 Dec. 69.   [6] Octavia Barry, of St. Ives; see Add MS 44539, f. 61.
[7] Of 23 Oct., Hawn P: bp. J. Watson of St. Asaph 'anxious to engage in plans which may have the effect of raising the tone & education of the Welsh Class [*sic*]'; Glynne himself feared 'it may be a dangerous experiment'.   [8] On education, in Lathbury, ii. 141.

Granville—Count Cadorna—Mr Childers—Mrs Th. Read St Simon 1709[1]—Sismondi Hist. Français[2]—Lanfrey.

26. Wed. [*Bowden Park, Wiltshire*]

Wrote to Mr Cardwell—Ld Houghton—C. Mills—Mrs Jacob. $1\frac{1}{2}$-$6\frac{1}{2}$ Off with Stephy to Bowden Park[3] where we found a large and happy party. Travelled with Tom. Read Gibson's Life.[4]—V. Fitzgerald on Suez Canal[5] &c.

To E. CARDWELL, war secretary,   PRO 30/48/7, f. 168.
26 October 1870.

There is some misapprehension between us, doubtless with me, as to the equation. Hitherto you have recruited without any distinction between Home & Indian service. Now you are to make a distinction where there is to be a liability to Indian service, or a certainty of it, for I am not sure which it is. I presume that men will engage for 3 years on different terms from those which would be necessary for six. All this will clear itself in conversation: with other points, among them this, that I have presumed you will hereafter, for certainty's sake, include reserve service in the conditions of the original engagement. And this that my marginal note as to officers or a portion of them seems to me to leave quite apart the solution of the difficulty which arises as to the men.

But I have received your packet[6] as I am about to start for Wiltshire where I hope to read it carefully before my return tomorrow. No fresh news: expectations doubtful as before.

27. Th. [*London*]

Holy Communion at $8\frac{1}{2}$. The marriage $11\frac{1}{2}$. The entertainment at one. All went well, and looked happily. A notable comparison with the Funeral visit.[7] I returned thanks on behalf of Kate. Wrote (Tel.) to Ld Granville: and minutes. Much conversation with T.G. With Col. M'Clay[8] on Australian meat. $2\frac{1}{2}$-$6\frac{3}{4}$. We returned to London. Read Life of Bewick[9]—Holyoake on Pictures[10]—Malmesbury Correspondence.

[1] *Mémoires complets et authentiques du Duc de Saint-Simon sur le siècle de Louis XIV et la Régence*, vol. vii (1829).
[2] J. C. L. Simonde de Sismondi, *Histoire des Français*, 31 v. (1821-44).
[3] Seat of his deceased br. J. N. Gladstone, for the marriage of his niece, Kate, to Rev. W. C. *Lake; see 4 Mar. 40.
[4] *Life of J. Gibson*, ed. Lady *Eastlake (1870).
[5] W. F. Vesey Fitzgerald, *The Suez Canal, the Eastern Question and Abyssinia* (1867).
[6] Add MS 44119, f. 116. See 22 Oct. 70.   [7] See 12 Feb. 63.
[8] Probably (Sir) George MacLeay, 1809-91, Australian legislator settled in England; kt. 1875.
[9] *Memoir of Thomas *Bewick, written by himself* (1862); see 2 July 73.
[10] G. J. Holyoake, 'The good of going to Paris to see the Exhibition; a letter to Willis Chater' (1867).

28. Fr.

Wrote to Mr Fortescue—Vestry Clerk of St Martin's—St James's—
Ld Granville—Robn G.—Mr Hammond—Chancr of Exr—&
minutes. Saw Mrs Jacobs: who perseveres—Saw The Office Keeper
—on his retirement. He wept. Dined with Mrs Th: a party of nine.
Read Life of Bewick—Helps in Contemp. Rev.[1]—Torcy's Memoirs:[2]
& other works of French Hist. to ascertain the negotiations of 1709–
10 about Alsace and Strasburg.[3]

To E. HAMMOND, 28 October 1870.   Add MS 44539, f. 63.

With regard to Sir H. Elliot's reference in his letter[4] of the 16th to a passage
in one he had received from me, I presume he could not at the date when he
wrote have received a communication lately made to him (I do not know the
precise date) by Ld. Granville with respect to the Turkish or Eastern question.
If you think any explanation of my meaning is requisite for Sir H. Elliot's information, here it is. He looks at the question of Turkey from within the Empire,
I looked at it from without. Within I do not doubt that it is mended, without
attempting to determine the degree; and the policy pursued in Servia for which
the Porte deserves great honour, is both a good omen, & a cause of strength,
I believe in the particular province. But without the case is very different, if we
take as I suppose we must, the *malveillance* of Russia for granted. France may be
considered as out of the case; in this country the whole policy of the Crimean
war is now almost universally, & very unduly depreciated; and the idea of another
armed intervention on behalf of Turkey, whether sole or with allies, is ridiculed.
Austria, I presume has a good will to Turkey; lest which she has her own troubles
to look after she may have that good will converted by her territorial interests,
and almost necessities, into one very different. Of North Germany, I suppose no
one would say more than that she may be friendly, or may not; and if she were
friendly the only means of action would be by a direct conflict with Russia on
the frontier. On the whole, as I conclude, Turkey has been habituated to look to
external aid, and there is now no prospect of it on which any sane man can rely.
The question then arises can she rely for her European Empire on the attachment of her own subjects, and if she cannot, what can she further do to bring
that attachment up to the mark which may settle in her favour the question of
life and death. This is what I mean by the most critical moment of the existence
of the Sultan's Empire; for in the Crimean war the Turk was but a secondary
party, he now runs the chance of being not only primary but sole. This hurried
sketch is necessarily void of due reserves & explanations.

[1] *Contemporary Review*, xv. 440 (October 1870).

[2] J. B. Colbert, Marquis de Torcy, *Memoirs*, 2v. (1757).

[3] The issue over Strasburg and Alsace in 1709 was how much Louis XIV could be made
to give up to get the peace he desperately needed; see G. M. Trevelyan, *England under
Queen Anne* (1930), ii, ch. 19.

[4] See Ramm I, i. 152–3. Granville requested it be withheld 'till we have settled our Turkish policy in the Cabinet'.

29. Sat.

Wrote to Agnes G.—Mrs Molyneux—C.G.—Mr Hammond—Mr Grogan—Mr Ayrton—Mr Tupper—& minutes. Read Torcy's Memoirs—Malmesbury Corresp.—Pamphlets. Saw Casson X.— S.E.G.—Mr West. Dined with the Wortleys.

30. 19 S. Trin.

Chapel Royal mg & St Peter's Kennington L. 6.30 PM. Wrote to C.G. —Ld Kimberley—Bp of Cape Town[1]—Saw Mr Forster M.P.—Mr West—W. Hampton—considerably sunk, yet not as on the eve of death. Read Maclaren's Speech—Fuller's Thoughts—Sermon by Ignatius—Macduff, Shepherd and his Flock—Cowper Life[2] & some Poems. Tea with S. & H.

31. M.

Wrote to General Fox—J. Watson & Smith—Chr of Exchr—Mr Fortescue—& minutes. Dined at Duchess of Somerset's. C.G. came. Read Schmidt[3]—Malmesbury Corresp. Saw Mr Childers—Mr Goschen—Gen. Burnside[4]—S.E.G.—Duc de Grammont (Dss of S.s)— Dr Evans—Dr Jackson—U.S. Minister. Between 12 & 1 I was called downstairs by Dr Jackson to see our old servant and friend Hampton die. It was doubtful whether he was wholly sensible. His wife & two sons were by him. I read the prayers. He departed in great peace: the fierceness of the last Enemy was controuled. God be with him.

Tues. Nov. 1. All Saints.

Wrote to Ld Granville (Tel.)—The Queen (Mem)—Mr Eykyn[5]— Mr Burnett—and minutes. 3-6$\frac{1}{2}$. Presided & spoke at the closing of the Workmen's International Exhibition.[6] Dined at Lady Herbert's. Saw Count Strzelecki—Mr Motley—Professor Pierce.[7] Read Schmidt —Malmesbury Corresp.

[1] R. *Gray, threatening resignation; the affair referred to Kimberley; Add MS 44539, f. 66.
[2] Probably *The life of William Cowper. With selections from his correspondence* [R. B. *Seeley] (1855).
[3] W. A. Schmidt, *Elsass und Lothringen* (1870 ed.). [4] See 12 Sept. 70.
[5] Roger Eyckyn, 1826-96; liberal M.P. Windsor 1866-74.
[6] At the Agricultural Hall, Islington; *The Times*, 2 November 1870, 7d.
[7] Benjamin Peirce, 1809-80; American astronomer; about financing observation of the eclipse in December 1870; see next day's letter to Motley, Add MSS 44539, f. 66, 44428, f. 184.

2. Wed.

Wrote to The Queen—Mr Motley—Mr Cardwell—Mrs Strahan—
Surv. of Taxes—and minutes. Cabinet 3½-6. Dined at Baron L.
Rothschilds. Discussed the limits of the power of the Franc to bor-
row. Saw Ld Granville—Chancr of Exchr—Mr M'Coll. Read Schmidt
—Malmesbury Corr.—Cardwell's War Papers.

November 2. 70. 3½ PM Cabinet.[1]
1. WEG stated general purpose. Survey of business for the Session. But the Burnside Report first.
2. Granville reported his interview with Gen. Burnside.[2]
3. Whether to convey to Lyons our opinion of the French refusal—no result.
Granville to put a construction on Lyons' words to Chaudordy.[3]
4. Armistice dispatch to Berlin if pub. in Germany to be repub. here.[4]
5. Turkey. Treaty of 1856. Papers to be circulated; Hammond's Mem. & Granville's letter.[5]
6. Ten subjects of legislation indicated.
  Class I:[6] 1) Univ. Tests 2) Eccl. Titles 3) Secret Voting 4) Chancellor's Bill I.
  5) Chancellor's Bill II. 6) Landed Successions.[7] 6) Licensing System. 7) Local
  Rating. 8) Education.[8] 9) Scotch Measures. 9) Trades Union Bill[9] 10) Transfer
  of Land Bill.
  Class II: 1) Irish Education—no decision to introduce. 2) County Boards.
  3) Metropolis Local Government—notice not to be given. 4) Paper Currency.
  5) Recasting the Death-Duties. 6) Military organisation (10). Ten subjects
  marked.
[7.] Licensing Bill to be a[mende]d.
8. Comm. on Secret Voting Bill appt: Hartington—de Grey—Forster—Childers
—Att. General. And certain provisions of the Bill considered.
9. Childers stated the course he proposed to take respecting the Captain. And
proposed a Royal Commn. on construction of Iron Ship.[10]
Chancr. of Exr.—Eclipse grant (Dec 22).

To E. CARDWELL, war secretary,   PRO 30/48/7, f. 171.
2 November 1870.

  It is rather hard upon you to be detained so late, but I can readily believe that
you cannot well help it. I observe that you say nothing of the severity of the
accident which has caused the delay. Of course military matters will stand over in
the Cabinet until you come. I have read your able papers upon Military Organization, and there are, as you would expect, a variety of points on which I should
desire further satisfaction & information. But what I am desirous to ask of you

---

[1] Add MS 44638, f. 128.
[2] Attempts to mediate between Versailles and Paris to arrange elections for constituent
assembly; see CAB/A/40, f. 69.
[3] See *PP* 1871, lxxi. 215 ff. Jean, comte of Chaudordy, 1826-99; French delegate for
foreign affairs at Tours 1870-1, later ambassador.   [4] See 20 Oct. 70n.
[5] See Ramm I, i. 153 and 28 Oct. 70.   [6] On next sheet, f. 129.
[7] This item bracketed, and subsequent items renumbered.
[8] This item in pencil.   [9] This item promoted from 11.
[10] This became the Dufferin commission on ship design, *PP* 1872 xiv.

now is, that you would cause documents to be prepared showing the methods adopted in the best European armies especially the North German, as to the great question of officers, in all its main points, among them those mentioned in the memorandum which I sent you.[1]

I will only now make a few cursory remarks. 1. Your total of 510,000 (though I am not certain whether this applies to Home Services only), increased by Navy and Navy Reserve to near 600,000, seems to me large. I doubt whether it is necessary, or wise, that, in our position, so large a number of persons should be bound to handling arms more or less every year. The Volunteer Force seems to be growing into a serious difficulty. I am much pleased with what you say of its Artillery: but, taking it as a whole, can you make it fit for action, & is it desirable for Parliament to spend large sums upon any force not fit for action. 2. As respects Officers, I hope you do not mean to pass by the consideration of many questions not touched in your papers. Meantime, among suggestions raised by it [sic], I wish it to be considered 1. Whether your excellent principle of supplying Line Officers for Auxiliary forces cannot be carried below the grade of Field Officers. 2. Whether we are really right in treating all Officers as if they were to be Officers for life, and whether our system might not include provisions under which Officers like men might after short terms pass into a reserve & discharge a *terminable* service.

These matters will probably be more simply and easily disposed of, as far as you and I are concerned, in conversation than on paper.

3. Th.

Wrote to Mr H. Reeve—Sir T. Bazley—The Queen—Dr L. Playfair —Ld De Tabley—Sir C. Trevelyan—Mr Hammond—& minutes. Dined at Mr Forster's and went (taking Harry) to the Play: Mids.N. Dream, indifferently acted, at the Globe, Long Acre. Saw Ld Halifax —Ld Granville—Ld Kimberley—and others. Read Schmidt— Malmesbury Corresp.

To H. REEVE, editor of the *Edinburgh Review*,   Add MS 44539, f. 66.
3 November 1870. 'Most Private.'

What shall we do about the little paragraph which has unfortunately crept into the Daily News,[2] & which in the enclosed note Mr. Arnold drives home? Shall we talk the matter over or have you a formula or *recipe* for such cases? Acknowledgment I think is on general grounds most objectionable, as it leaves one forever at the mercy of every & any querist.[3]

[1] See 13 Oct. 70.
[2] *Daily News*, 3 November 1870, 5: 'Mr Gladstone is, we understand, the author of the article. . . .'
[3] Reeve replied on 4 November, Add MS 44428, f. 174: '. . . By us the secret has been carefully kept. . . . The only formula I can recommend is that the Editor of the Review is alone responsible for what appears in it. In such cases, silence is the only remedy. . . .' Gladstone prepared an anonymous statement, neither accepting nor denying authorship, which Reeve sent to Delane on 7 November, Add MS 44428, f. 185; Delane set it in type, but withdrew it at the last moment; ibid., f. 190.

4. Fr.

Wrote to Watsons (Dent.)—Mr A.T. Innes—The Queen—Wm Gladstone—and minutes. Read Schmidt (finished)—Malmesbury Corresp. 10¼-12¼. C. & I went to Hampton's funeral at the Brompton
cemetery.[1] Stephen read the Service. All was calm & consolatory.
Cabinet 2½-6. Dined at Duchess of Somerset's. Saw Baron Beaulieu
—General Burnside—Ld Granville.

Cabinet Nov. 4. [1870] 2½ PM[2]

√ 1. Information from Ld Granville brought up to date: & drafts approved.

√ 2. Ld. G[ranville] to express regret for having referred in Dispatch to the
pressure of France upon the Italian Govt. for assistance.

√ 3. Granville. To draft a letter pointing out to Turkey the lessons[?] which
flow from the present state of Europe i.e. to adopt any practicable means for
strengthening the attachment of her subjects.[3]

4. D[itt]o as to Treaty of 1856. If Brunnow[4] opens the question? to try to
make him show his cards, give no pledge, make much of the gravity of the
proposition and assure him that we are determined on one thing viz. no word
no blow, & v[ice] v[ersa].

5. Add Glyn to Committee on Secret Voting.

6. Proposed Telegram of Hammond to Lyons, to exhort[?] Provisional Govt.
—not adopted.

7. Licensing System. Bruce's Bill discussed—are all liquors to be dealt with
alike?

8. Childers: proposes to place the Inquiry respecting [iron] ships under
authority of Admiralty: a Committee scientific & professional on construction.[5]

5. Sat.

Wrote to Ld Granville—Mr Fortescue—The Queen—Ld Ed. Clin-
ton—and minutes. Saw Ld Granville—Mrs Stoddart—Ld Halifax
—Lady S. Vane—Mr Childers—Abp Manning—Mrs Gordon—Mr
Cardwell—Mr M'Coll—Mr Gurdon—Mr Glyn. Dined at Ld Gran-
ville's: Seized with nausea in aftn, and felt the head weak. Read 'The
Intt of Europe in the Conditions of Peace'.[6]

To C. S. P. FORTESCUE, Irish secretary,   Carlingford MSS CP1/140.
5 November 1870.

I have read & return your inclosures.[7] It will be a great misfortune if we do
not get rid of this Fenian question before the agitation commences. For if we do

---

[1] See 31 Oct. 70.   [2] Add MS 44638, f. 132.

[3] Never despatched; see Ramm I, i. 154n.

[4] Russian ambassador.   [5] But see 2 Nov. 70n.

[6] *The interest of Europe in the conditions of peace. By a member of the British Legislature* (1870).

[7] Untraced; see 11 Oct. 70?

not, on the one hand the grace will be lost, on the other hand the anti-Irish & ultra-Conservative feeling will utter a much louder condemnation after the noise of discussion has once begun.

As respects the condition of quitting the country, I look upon that as a most valuable element, for I cannot pretend to hope for much amendment, as a general rule, in the prisoners themselves. As to discrimination I presume it is only contemplated in cases when the offence partakes of the character of ordinary crime. To such discrimination, I trust, that Mr. Brodrick's remarks are not, or not fully applicable.

6. 20 S. Trin.

Kept my bed till two: read the Service: Chapel Royal aftn. Saw Mrs Thistlethwayte. Dined at Lady Herbert's and discussed the Stodhert case.[1] Read Union Review (all)[2]—Stanley in Contemp. Rev.—Dr Jacob in do[3]—Bewick's Life, (on religion: very interesting, & typical).[4]

7. M.

Wrote to Mrs Stodhert—Ld De Tabley—Duke of Argyll—Sir J. Sinclair—Ld Lyons—Mr Maguire—Mrs Th.—Mr C. Downing—Mr Reeve—The Queen—and minutes. Saw Mr Fortescue—Ld Granville —Ld Halifax—Mr Childers—Mr Ouvry—Mr Wetherall—Mr M'Coll —Ld Lyttelton—Mr Reeve (2)—Dr A. Clark. Dined at Ld Lyttelton's. Read Malmesbury Corr. Saw Russell.

Cabinet Nov. 7. 70. 2½ PM[5]
√ 1. Failure of Armistice reported. No further step appeared practicable at present.
√ 2. Report on Secret Voting Bill.[6] *Not* for absolute secrecy. As to throwing necessary expenses on the Constituencies to be further cons[idere]d.
√ 3. Argyll's plan for an Engineering College for India sanctioned *sub modo*.[7]
√ 4. Bruce. Water Supply of London
√ 5. Water Companies & Supply Bill, authorised to be prepared. Notices to be given.

To LORD LYONS, ambassador in Paris,   Add MS 44539, f. 68.
7 November 1870.

I have seen your letter of the 5th to Granville in which you notice that in a note to him I had expressed a hope you would not allow the French to suppose we

---

[1] A widow, engaged to Lord A. S. Pelham-Clinton; see 29 Oct. 64n.
[2] *Union Review* (November 1870).
[3] *Contemporary Review*, xv. 524, 567 (November 1870).
[4] See 27 Oct. 70.   [5] Add MS 44638, f. 135.
[6] By the cabinet cttee.; see 2 Nov. 70.
[7] See *Argyll to Gladstone, 20 October 1870, Add MS 44101, f. 303.

adopted their view as to integrity of territory. I do not recollect the exact words
to which you may refer but I write a line lest I should by chance have conveyed
a false impression. At an earlier stage of this tremendous controversy, the French
took their stand upon inviolability of soil. That ground always seemed to me
quite untenable in the case of a country which had made recent annexations.
The French also declared that they would surrender neither an inch of their
territory nor a stone of their fortresses. This appeared to me an extravagant
proposition, & what is more important, I venture to say it was thought unreasonable by my Colleagues & by the country generally. It is possible that my note
may have referred to *either* of these views on the part of France. But I am very
sorry if I have conveyed to you on my own part, or by implication on the part
of anyone else, the belief that we approved of or were in our own minds indifferent, to the transfer of Alsatians & Lorrainers from France to Germany against
their will. On this subject I for one entirely concur with the opinions which you
have so admirably expressed in your letter: & I should be to the last degree
reluctant to be a party not only to stimulating a German demand of this kind,
but even advising or promoting a compliance with it on the part of the French.
All this you will see is quite distinct from, & consistent with the desire which
you & which we all entertain that the Defence Government of France should
not suddenly deal in abstract declarations, & with a full approval of your reti-
cence as to the conditions of peace. On the failure of the armistice I think the
Cabinet will disperse as having nothing more to consider in the present or any
proximate circumstances. I cannot help feeling doubtful whether the Prussians
do not lose *more* than the French by the unhappy failure of the negotiations. We
are all more grieved at the failure than surprised.[1]

8. Tu.

Wrote to The Queen——Rev Dr Hannah——Mr Ouvry——Bp of Manches-
ter——Mr Maguire——Sir S. Robinson——Robn G.——and minutes. Saw
Mr Glyn——Ld Granville——do *cum* Mr Cardwell——Count de Sartiges.
Dined at Lady Herbert's. Saw one[R]. Read Malmesbury Corresp.
Wrote Mem. on Turkey.[2]

To J. FRASER, bishop of Manchester,   Add MS 44539, f. 70.
8 November 1870.

You know the difficulties which beset the Sunday & Public House question in
Parliament. I should desire to act in the same spirit as heretofore in encountering
them.[3]

We are engaged in the formation of a Licensing Bill: and I have great hopes it
may be such as you are likely to approve. In your estimate of the gravity of the

---

[1] Lyons replied, 14 November 1870, Add MS 44428, f. 200: 'I do not think that at any
time I misunderstood your sentiments respecting French territory.' Granville resented such
direct contacts with ambassadors; Ramm I, i. 153. In Newton, *Lyons*, i. 334.
[2] Given in Ramm I, i. 154 as a letter, recorded in Add MS 44539, f. 70 as a mem. See
also Temperley and Penson, *Foundations of British Foreign Policy*, 331.
[3] *Fraser had written on 5 November, Add MS 44428, f. 178, urging licensing reform:
'I had no idea of the extent of the ravages of intemperance till I came into Lancashire.'

question with my very inferior means of judgment I concur. Ten years are I hope far from being the furthest term of your Episcopal action as they are certainly much beyond the period for which I can think of continuing a political life now in its 39th year. But I am too well pleased as to Manchester with the present to speculate much on a remote future.

9. Wed.

Wrote to Mr Fortescue—Ld Granville—Mr Reeve—and minutes. Read Malmesbury Corresp. and Q.R. on German songs.[1] Saw Mr Glyn —Ld De Tabley—Mr Lefevre—Ld Granville. 6¼-11. To Lord Mayor's Dinner. Returned thanks for Ministers; not to my satisfaction.[2]

10. Th.

Wrote to The Queen—Mr Gourley—Mr Reeve—and minutes. Read Malmesbury Corresp. Cabinet 2¾-6¼. Saw Ld Granville—Dr Hervey —Mr M'Coll—Mr Grogan—Mr Glyn. Dined with the Nevilles: saw Cols Freemantle and Stephenson. At Granville's for more conversation afterwards.

Cabinet 1870. Nov. 10. 3 PM[3]
√ Licensing Bill. Further cons[idere]d.
Fenian Prisoners ⎱ postponed
Army Organization ⎰
√ Armistice Telegrams to Prussia.
√ Russian announcement respecting Treaty of 1856.[4] Decided to write[?] a *sole* reply: protesting, leaving door open, & pointing to a collective judgement of the Powers. Dispatch to be drafted accordingly. Buchanan to maintain reserve until instructed.
√ Odo Russell: to be sent to Prussian Headquarters with Disp. in ansr. to Russia.
√ Granville. America. Can we conciliate by any boon? Will prepare material for cons[ideration].

Nov. 10. 70.[5]
To object to the renunciation of the Treaty. To keep the door open as to the Question. To remind Russia to consider of the proper mode of bringing her desire under the consideration of the European powers collectively.

[1] *Quarterly Review*, cxxix. 485 (October 1870).
[2] *The Times*, 10 November 1870, 3d; calling for a peace on 'principles agreeable to the ideas and to the just sense of modern civilization'. [3] Add MS 44638, f. 140.
[4] In a despatch of 9 November, Gortschakoff, the Russian foreign minister, renounced the covenants of 1856 restricting Russian rights in the Black Sea. Gladstone's mem., based on the notes below, formed the basis for Granville's despatch, is in Ramm I, i. 154 and Temperley and Penson, *Foundations of British Foreign Policy*, 331.
[5] Add MS 44638, f. 141.

To H. REEVE, editor of the *Edinburgh Review*,   Add MS 44539, f. 71.
10 November 1870.

I will send M. Guizot's letter[1] to Ld Granville. He seems to have been mis-informed as to the exact scope of the suggestion of the Neutral Powers for an armistice. We at least expressed an opinion that the prohibition of elections in Alsace and Lorraine if enforced, need not commit or compromise France which would assist her title by sending out the writs. It would have been a[n] act of *force majeure*, not defeating the main purpose of the armistice. As to victualling, nothing was said by the neutral Powers, so far as my knowledge goes. I lament that it could not have been made the subject of a safe and moderate compromise: for the approach of winter gave the Prussians something to say upon the subject. As to an Assembly, for one I much regretted that the convocation of it was ever postponed. Among its purposes, these three were perhaps the main ones. 1. To give authority to the Defense Government 2. To facilitate any dealings, to which the Prussians might be inclined, for peace 3+ To facilitate any proceedings of the neutral Powers in the same sense, as their difficulty in this respect, should all other circumstances favour their actions, would still be extreme from their not knowing the authoritative judgment of the French nation. The first object has been in a degree gained by the Paris vote: the others remain as they were. One other end; it is not a little remarkable that Bismarck should have been relaxed somewhat as to elections in Alsace and Lorraine, since the Burnside messages. I suppose it was because he saw that prohibition of elections in a given district as German might prematurely commit Germany as to the territorial claims she should make. He may have preferred to retain his liberty, and keep in reserve the threat of using it. I am glad Guizot gives you the article. Ld G. has seen his letter. Should you quote or make use of my No 3 marked +, please do not treat as mine.

11. Fr.

Wrote to Ld de Grey—Sir H. Bulwer—Mr Rawson—Mr M. Muller —The Queen (& Mem.)—Ld Kimberley—& minutes. Read Malmesb. Corresp.—Mullinow on Dublin Univ.[2] Saw Mr Watson (from Athens)[3] —Mr Cardwell—Mr Glyn—Mr Fortescue·(2)—Chr of Exr—Ld Granville—Ld Kimberley—Adm. Englefield.[4] Dined at Sir H. Holland's. Cabinet $2\frac{1}{4}$–$5\frac{1}{4}$.

Cabinet Nov. 11. 70. 2 PM[5]
√ Dispatch respecting Treaty of 1856 read, corrected, & approved.
√ Fenian prisoners (in connection with Report of Commission) committed for Treason Felony: case to be [blank]
Kimberley—De Grey—Lowe—against release.
Hartington (app[arentl]y)

[1] Sent to Granville on 21 November and subsequently mislaid, see Ramm I, i. 164. See 26 Sept. 70 for an earlier letter.
[2] Untraced.
[3] Robert Grant Watson, d. 1892, secretary of the British legation in Athens, though he knew no Greek; see Jenkins, *The Dilessi Murders*, 85.
[4] *Sc.* Inglefield.   [5] Add MS 44638, f. 144.

Others seemed neutral. Bruce was among the Fors.

√ Cardwell mentioned that he had measures in preparation.[1]

√ London Govt. Bill. Decision maintained: No Bill.

√ As to relieving Local Taxation a) New local Taxes b) Take *charge* on Consol[idated] Fund c) Surrender a tax. C. of E. to recoup himself. Plan c. preferred. Present charges to be revised.[2]

12. Sat. [*Hawarden*]

Wrote to Chancr of Exr—Sec.Eccl. Commn—Ld Brougham—Mrs Milman—Rev S.E.G.—Abp Manning—Robn G.—Sir C. O'Loghlen —Ld E. Clinton—Rev Mr Christie—& minutes. $4\frac{1}{2}$–$11\frac{1}{4}$. To H[awarde]n alone. Saw Mr Pringle—Mr Hope jun.—Mr Gurdon—Mr Ouvry —Ld Granville—Mr Bruce. Read Malmesbury Corr.—Palmerston's Life.[3]

13. 22 S. Trin.

Ch. mg & aft. Wrote to Ld Lyttelton—Ld Granville—Mr Motley— C.G.—& minutes. Read Abp of York's Charge[4]—Triumph of Moral Good[5]—Acton's Sendschreiben & reply[6]—Bp of Ratisbon's Pastoral.[7]

To J. L. MOTLEY, 13 November 1870. 'Private.'   Add MS 44539, f. 74.

I am happy to inform you that the matter of the Fenian prisoners is now in principle disposed of & that only certain inquiries remain to be conducted before it actually takes effect. Before three weeks at the outside are over I trust they will be out. As we cannot bargain with them upon conduct & as they are generally 'irreconcilables', they will not as a rule be allowed to remain in the United Kingdom. We have reason to be satisfied thus far with the reception & working of our Land Bill in Ireland.

14. M.

Wrote to Mr Gurdon—Sec.Eccl. Commn—Mr Reeve—Mary G.— W.H.G. Walk to Bickley. Read Voltaire Louis XIV—Palmerston's

[1] See ibid., f. 145, which reads, in Gladstone's hand, '1. Scale of force 2. Conscription 3. Remove Vol[unteer] officers from Ld. Lieut. 4. Purchase.'

[2] i.e. to make over the house tax to local authorities, as proposed by Goschen's 1871 Bill; see G. J. Goschen, *Local Taxation* (1872), 205.

[3] W. H. L. E. *Bulwer, Baron Dalling and Bulwer, *The Life of . . . Viscount Palmerston*, 3v. (1870–4); quoted in mem. at 23 Nov. 70.

[4] W. *Thompson, 'Seven years. A charge' (1870).   [5] See 11 Sept. 70.

[6] Lord Acton, 'Sendschreiben an einen deutschen Bischof des Vaticanischen Concils . . . September 1870' (1870).

[7] I. Senestrey, 'Hirtenworte . . . über die Beschlüsse des Vaticanischen Concils' (1870).

Life—Bp of Ratisbon's Letter (finished)—Grant's Home Politics.[1]
Ch. 8½ AM.

15. Tu.

Ch. 8¼ A.M. Wrote to Govr of Labuan[2]—Chancr of Exr—Mr L.
Turner—Abp of Canterb.—Scotts—Mr Gurdon—Mr Reeve—Bp
of Cape Town—Robn G.—C.G. Read Xtn Observer on Ritual
Commn—Voltaire's Louis XIV (finished)—Life of Palmerston. Mr
Burnett dined. Conversation on business afr. Then whist.

16. Wed.

Ch. 8¼ AM. Wrote to Mr Anderson—Ld Granville and Tel.—Mr
Bright—Ly Herbert—Ld Belper—The Queen—C.G.—Mr Gurdon
(Tel.)—and minutes. Read Palmerston's Life—Mr Grant's Book
(finished)—Mr. Müller's Chips Vol III.[3] Visited half a score of the
Aston cottages with Mr Burnett and Mr Thompson.

To J. BRIGHT, president of the board of trade,   Add MS 43385, f. 123.
16 November 1870. 'Private.'

I think it probable you will like, notwithstanding your judicious abstinence
from public cares, to know authentically the pith of what has happened about
the Treaty of 1856. It is as follows. Russia has *announced* that she holds herself
free as to the portions of the Treaty that affect her Sovereignty, in consequence
of certain acts, by which she alleges that the Treaty has already been broken. We
have replied (1) That she is not competent as a single Power, to make such a
declaration, consistently with the rules which determine the nature of Treaties.
(2) That if she had suggested a review of the Treaty, to decide whether any change
was desirable, this we would not have refused to consider with the Consignatory
Powers.

On the other great subject, that of the war, it is now too plain that its horrors
are prolonged only on account of the conflicting views of the parties with reference to Alsace & Lorraine. England I think can never contemplate with satisfaction the transference of unwilling populations from one country of Europe to
another. That these populations are unwilling seems to be quite clear. The question I think will soon arise whether we can continue silent altogether on this
subject. In different modes & degrees, both Russia & Italy appear to have spoken
disapprovingly.

The accounts from Ireland are generally good, & the cases of the Fenian
prisoners are under examination, with a view to the very early liberation of all
those who can be regarded as purely *political* offenders.

---

[1] D. Grant, *Home politics, or the growth of trade considered in its relation to labour,
pauperism and emigration* (1870).
[2] J. Pope Hennessy, thanking him for a flattering letter; Add MS 44539, f. 74.
[3] See 19 Oct. 68.

[P.S.] Pray do not interpret this letter as meant to draw an answer. I think you will not be displeased with its contents.[1]

17. Th.

Wrote to Chancr of Exr (2)—Ld Granville—Ld E. Bruce—Mr Hammond—Mr T. Hughes—Mr Anderson—Ld Halifax—and minutes. Ch. $8\frac{1}{2}$ AM. In afternoon went out to chop ivy off trees. C.G. arrived 11 P.M. Domestic conversation till late. Read Palmerston's Life—Max Müller's Chips—Rossignol, Métaux de l'Antiquité.[2]

18. Fr.

Ch. $8\frac{1}{2}$ AM. Wrote to Mr Cardwell (2)—Ld Granville (& cipher Tel.) —Mr Motley—Sir E. Sabine—M. de Laveleye—and minutes. Cut down a birch in afternoon. Read Life of Palmerston (II)—Max Müller's Chips.

To E. CARDWELL, war secretary, 18 November 1870.   Add MS 44539, f. 79.

This is certainly an astounding proposal[3] & my first impressions are strongly against it. First I think the Foreign Min. should have been first applied to, & the C. of Ex. & the Admiralty are all more concerned than you. But this is of small importance. The plan appears to me to place the British Government in a thoroughly false position. I believe we should greatly offend both Powers now at War by assuming the initiative proposed. We should assert by anticipation the failure of Trochu's plans of offence by defence. We should proceed upon the supposed poverty & exhaustion of the N. W. districts of France which have never been touched. We should arouse in the suspicious mind of Prussia the idea that we used this strange scheme as a cover & meant to cooperate with the enemy. If France is exhausted (& it is very doubtful whether there are more mouths in the country now than there were 6 months ago, at any rate the difference is trifling) what about Belgium, which can supply her with no sea transport [sic] & continuous rail? There seems to me to be three things worthy of consideration. 1. We might go to Bismarck *founding ourselves on his starvation Circular* & offer to place at his disposal with the consent of France our Government machinery & stores with a view to making provision for a calamity which *he* treats as certain & proximate. 2. We might instruct Lyons cautiously to acquaint the Government at Tours of the manner in which we had suggested that Bismarck should act upon his own published anticipations, & might express our willingness to be made use of if the French Government should at any time think it desirable. 3. We might communicate with the Belgian Government, who will know much more about the supplies of food in, to & from the North of France than we do,

---

[1] Bright wrote next day to resign because of ill-health: Add MS 44112, f. 161 and Trevelyan, *Bright*, 417. See 19 Nov. 70.

[2] J. P. Rossignol, *Les métaux dans l'antiquité* (1863).

[3] That Britain prepare to victual Paris on surrender; see Ramm I, i. 159.

& see whether they could in case of need act either jointly or alone. I have thus given my first very adverse impressions. But as strange times may demand strange measures, I speak with all submission; I am willing to be overruled after argument by the judgement of colleagues upon the grand scheme—& the three suggestions which I have proposed to substitute would of course be in the first place for Granville's consideration.[1]

19. Sat.

Ch. 8½ AM. Wrote to Ld Westminster—Ld Granville (2 & Tel.)—Dean of Chichester (Tel.)—Mr G. Glyn—W.H.G.—Ld Kimberley —and minutes. Went with C. to visit Mrs Potter's refugee Father & nephew.[2] Read Palmerston's Life—Max Müller Vol III—F.O. Memoranda on Treaty of 1856.[3]

To J. BRIGHT, president of the board of trade,   Add MS 43385, f. 132.
19 November 1870. 'Most Private.'

I have received, yesterday and today, your three letters.[4] I cannot touch the subject of your quitting us, but with a heavy heart. If you go, you will leave a void that cannot be filled. Still, in the main, I feel the force of the motives which have acted on your mind; and I withdraw all substantial protest against your resignation. Nevertheless I shall, with your permission, hold it in reserve for a very short time, and write to you again about it when I go up to London, which I believe will be some time within the next seven days. The ground on which I ask this permission is that your retirement at this moment would infallibly be construed as a split on the Russian question. This I think you would not desire: and it will not be difficult by a very short delay to avoid the mischief, which would really be a serious one. Of course care will be taken, if you do not dissent from my proposal, that you are not committed to any step you would be likely to disapprove.

Individually I have a second motive acting on me, though the one I have named is the main one. I wish you not to be dissociated from us (officially) while we have in hand, for it is still partially in hand, the business of shortening the horrors of the war by means of an armistice.

I rejoice that you agree in our protest against the lawless law of self-liberation from treaties: and I trust you will find our mode of following up that protest to be temperate.

The Queen when she hears of your approaching departure will I am sure be much concerned. But even when our official connection shall end the friendships it has generated or confirmed will I am sure remain.

[1] Granville informed; ibid.
[2] Of the German-born villager; see 19 Sept. 70.
[3] Mema. by E. Hammond, dated 24 October, printed 1 November, on 'Russia, Turkey and the treaties of 1856' deploring conciliation, and by E. Hertslet, dated and printed 18 November, on 'Prince Gortchakoff's Circular'; Add MS 44615, ff. 87, 93.
[4] Of 17 and 18 November, arguing that Britain should yield to Russia on the Black Sea clauses, and asking that his resignation be now accepted; Add MS 44112, ff. 157, 161, 163.

20. 23 S. Trin.

Confined to house & bed all day to remove i.e. dispel a cough. Morning service by myself. Wrote to Ld Granville—Mrs Thistlethwayte—and minutes. Read M. Müller's Bunsen[1]—N.B. Review on Vatican Council[2]—Triumph of Moral Good.[3]

21. M.

Rose at one. Wrote to Mr Harington—Ld Spencer—Mary G.—Ld Granville—and minutes. Out for a few minutes in the sun. Wrote part Mem. on Alsace and Lorraine. Read Rossignol, Metaux de l'Antiquité—M. Müller's Chips—Palmerston's Life.

22. Tu.

Rose at 11: cough I hope gone. Wrote to Ld Granville—Dean of Chichester (Tel.)—Queen (letter & Mem.)—Chancr of Exr—Mr Gurdon—Ld Bessborough—Mrs Thistlethwayte—and minutes. Wrote (part) Mem. on Alsace & Lorraine. Read Rossignol—Max Müller's Chips—Palmerston (finished Vol. II).

23. Wed.

Up at noon: & really well. Wrote to The Queen (2)—Ld Granville—Mr Plowden[4]—Dr Vaughan—Mr Gurdon (Tel.)—and minutes. Concluded Mem. on Alsace and Lorraine.[5] Read Rossignol—Ed. Rev. on Sir J. Lubbock.[6]

Alsace and German Lorraine.

It is admitted that Germany has received, in the infliction of the present war, an injury from France about the magnitude of which there can be no doubt.

It is known that France is willing to grant to Germany a pecuniary compensation, and that Germany in her present mood not only declines to accept such a

---

[1] F. Max *Müller, 'Bunsen 1868', in *Chips from a German workshop*, iii (1870).

[2] *North British Review*, liii. 183 (October 1870); by *Acton.

[3] See 11 Sept. 70.

[4] Gladstone declined to give him an honour for 'services rendered nearly 40 years back'.

[5] Initialled and dated 23 November 1870, Add MS 44759, f. 191; docketed 'To be copied'. Copied headed 'Private and confidential' at ibid., f. 203. Printed, with a number of phrases omitted, in P. Knaplund, *Gladstone's Foreign Policy* (1935), appendix I. Gladstone sent the mem. to *Argyll on 25 November, asking him for 'judgment on the enclosed paper. It is not meant to be an extravagant statement of the case of Alsace and Lorraine' (Add MS 44539, f. 83), and to *Granville some time before 5 December (see Ramm I, i. 173).

[6] *Edinburgh Review*, cxxxii. 439 (October 1870).

compensation as a sufficient atonement for the wrong done, but insists upon the annexation of territory.

In general terms the demand of Germany is compensation for the past, & security for the future: nor can any objection be taken in limine[1] to such a claim. But it should be observed that there are certain conditions attaching to the course of human affairs by which demands of this kind are practically limited, and neither between individuals nor between nations does it commonly appear that when a wrong has been inflicted, either the compensation obtained for the past or the security taken for the future is complete.

The arguments which have been used for the severance of Alsace & (part of) Lorraine from France, and for their annexation to Germany are as follows

1. That the French, had the fortune of war been in their favour, would have appropriated territory now German without resistance or objection from the Neutral Powers.

2. That the population of the Provinces is German by blood & language.

3. That Europe, not having assisted Germany in the attainment of the results of the war, has no right to prevent her from profiting by the fruit of labours & sacrifices altogether her own.

4. That the German people unanimously demand these provinces.

5. That they are necessary in a strategical point of view for the future defensibility of the German frontier.

6. That as France cannot be expected to be friendly or pacific in time to come, the Germans must seek their security in the reduction of her power.

7. That European wars, in which one of the parties gets the upper hand, commonly close with severance & annexation of territory.

8. That as the Germans are not an aggressive people, France will incur no risk from their possessing the strongly fortified places of Metz & Strasbourg.

Finally it is well to remark that one argument, most summary & drastic in its character, has not been employed to justify this annexation——that is, the supposed right of the conqueror to do what he will with the territory, as with the other possessions, of the conquered.

It is felt that in our day this argument of naked force does not command, but repels, the mind & conscience of Europe.

Answers. 1. It is probably true that France if successful would have proceeded, or endeavoured, to annex territory.

It is most improbable however that she could have annexed the Rhenish Provinces without complaint or resistance.

When she annexed the small acquisitions of Savoy & Nice in 1860, even *they* all but produced a quarrel with England.

Yet they were ostensibly willing to become French.

Is it likely that England would have been silent had France annexed much larger countries, inhabited by palpably unwilling populations?

Even if silent she would have been radically & thoroughly estranged.

2. In a question of disannexation, it is not blood & language but will, conviction, & attachment which are to be principally regarded.

3. Quite independently of participation in a conflict to which she is indebted for nothing but uneasiness, interruption of industry & no inconsiderable amount of military charge entailed on Neutral States, Europe has an unquestionable title to object to any arrangements which tend to lower the principles & throw back

---

[1] On the threshold; at the very outset.

the usages of international conduct, or to endanger the peace of the future: if the proposed annexation be liable to either of these objections—[1]

4. The desire of the German people cannot be so declared as to be beyond dispute because the expression of opinion is not altogether free. But this unanimity, if it existed, tho' an important element in the case, cannot of itself absolutely decide the question either of right or prudence.

5. This has never been proved or even argued, but simply asserted. Venetia, with magnificent fortresses, was not found a security to Austria in 1866. The aversion of the people was a standing cause of danger. Austria is safer towards Italy with her present unprotected (or less protected) frontier: & would have been safer in 1866 with an attached people, & with no fortresses at all in Italy. Several alternative methods of proceeding have been proposed though not by authority, among them are these—

(a) That Alsace & German Lorraine should be erected into a Neutral State under European guarantee. France & Germany would then be separated by a line of neutral States from the Alps to the North Sea.

(b) That Alsace & Lorraine should continue to be under the dominion of France, but that all fortresses in them should be demolished, & that France should not be entitled to keep in them any military force beyond their local proportion of her standing army unless & until they are invaded by a Foreign Power. German occupation to continue until the demolition is completed & the indemnity paid.

There may be serious objections to these, or to any mode of settlement founded upon the admission of the German claim to something in the nature of territorial security; but such objections can hardly be taken on the ground that they would give Germany less security than the possession of a disaffected territory which would be a perpetual focus of machination for an enemy.

Germany would by either of these arrangements have a tract which would be neutralised for military purposes, interposed between her & France, & this tract would be supplied at the cost of France.

6. If the security of Germany is to be found in the weakening ie. the permanent weakening of France, then France, to attain such an end must be weakened considerably—But Alsace & German Lorraine are taken to represent only about 1/25 of her population. A deduction of four per cent from her force in men & territory, leaving ninety six per cent behind, is much more likely to exasperate, & to drive into violent courses, than to deter from such courses.

7. This is untrue. France herself affords the proof—she has been worsted in several wars of the 18th & 19th centuries, especially in the War of the Succession, & in the final issue of the Revolutionary war. At the close of the War of the Succession it was the feeling of Spain, not the strength of France that kept Philip V on the throne. In 1709 & 1710 when France was at the last extremity, the surrender of Alsace was at length tendered. But Alsace though possessed by France was hardly at that time to be considered as *French*; both because the rights conveyed by the Treaty of Munster were only limited & qualified rights, not those of full Sovereignty, & because these rights themselves had never ceased to be in contest, especially until the peace of Ryswick. But the very small turn of the tide in favour of France before the peace was enough to secure to her the continued possession of Alsace at the close of the war.

Perhaps the decision of Europe in 1815 is itself the strongest precedent

[1] Marginal note opposite this point reads: 'See Ld Palmerston's Life Vol 1, p. 224, with reference to a war between Russia and Turkey'; see 12 Nov. 70.

against the allegation——for not only was France at that time worsted, but she was exhausted: & further as all Europe was against her, there was a power of enforcing new arrangements against her, such as Germany single handed certainly does not possess. And Germany at the time was loud in her demands for Alsace & German Lorraine. It was the weight of England & Russia the two most powerful enemies of France, whom alone she had failed to conquer at any period of the war, that prevailed against the German demand. No one can doubt that this decision was agreeable to the sense of Europe, which may be thought to have had a stronger case against the France of 1815 than Germany has against the France of 1870, for surely the French *nation* was much more responsible for the wars of Napoleon the First than for the war of 1870.

8. No people whatever can assert for itself that absolute exemption from national passion & frailty, which this argument assumes: & it is difficult to suppose that it can have much currency even in Germany. It is needless therefore to discuss the point historically.

Further as it is admitted by the highest German Authorities that Alsace & German Lorraine are French in feeling, it may surely be contended that to tear them from France, & to chain them to Germany, would not be a security but a danger to Germany herself, from the fixed sentiment of the population.

This is a question on which Germany cannot claim an exclusive right of judgment: for whatever endangers the peace between France & Germany, endangers, as we now see & feel, the peace of Europe. Europe therefore has a right to an opinion about it. There is another form of danger to that country arising out of the proposed arrangement which ought also to be borne in mind. The aggrandisement of Germany by consolidation from within her own territories, is not a matter of which other countries are entitled to take any hostile cognisance. But so soon as Germany begins the work of aggrandisement by the annexation of territory taken from a neighbour, she steps out of her own bounds, & comes upon a ground where every country is entitled to challenge & discuss the title, & is competent by the general rules of public right if it shall think fit, to consider whether the aggrandisement thus acquired in the shape of territory which had belonged to another power, ought or ought not to be curtailed. It was on this principle of resistance to territorial aggrandisement not actual but simply apprehended that the great Powers of Europe in 1853 sought to abridge the rights & powers of Russia.

But over & above the question of danger to Germany this violent severance & annexation of an unwilling population would be a measure of a nature entirely retrogressive with reference to the public practice of Europe. After the peace of 1815, various populations were attached for the first time to various countries without any assurance of their favourable inclination to the connection.[1] But in none of these cases were they known to be averse, & in none of them were the annexed populations severed from another State to which they were known to be attached. In those instances, when at a later period, the population showed their aversion to what had been done, it has eventually been undone: & in other cases of a different class where dynasties or Governments were set up by European authority against the national feeling, they have one & all been overturned. The result has been the gradual growth of a conviction, by no means associated with mere democratic leanings, that the operations of the Treaty of Vienna (due no doubt to the extraordinary condition of Europe at the time) should not be

---

[1] Marginal note reads 'Venetia——The Rhenish Provinces——Belgium'.

repeated, & that, in questions of annexation at least, much regard ought to be had to the known[1] inclination of the people.

Consequently, for more than half a century, there cannot be said, among many territorial changes to have been one, in which a population has been unwillingly severed from one country & annexed to another. If the Schleswig annexation has been (thus far) pushed beyond what was due, this is a question of exactitude in drawing a line, rather than an admitted variation from the rule, since there is (I presume) no doubt that by far the greater part of the Schleswig Holstein population have in becoming German, found the fulfilment of their own desire.

On the other hand the Protectorate of the Ionian Islands was relinquished by Her Majesty & those Islands were annexed to Greece, in deference to the popular wish, expressed by the legislative assembly. This example indeed goes far beyond what is necessary for the present purpose: it was a voluntary surrender of established & lawful right, whereas the present argument is intended only to deprecate the violent invasion of such rights from without.

In the case of Savoy & Nice the transfer of allegiance was effected with the consent of the government & by the vote of the population.

In the case of the separate Italian States generally it was by similar votes that they attached themselves to the Italian Kingdom.

Reference might also be made to the manner in which the people of the Danubian Principalities were consulted, under the auspices of the Great Powers of Europe, with respect to the political arrangements to be adopted in those Provinces. These acts may be said to form a series. They are no longer mere isolated precedents. They go near to constitute one of those European usages, which, when sufficiently ascertained, become the basis of public international law, & they appear moreover to be founded on natural equity, at least to this extent, that whatever be the right, or want of right, to disturb established relations, at least it is equitable not to break them up & effect a transfer of a whole population from one nationality to another in defiance of the attachments & desires which they entertain. The violence done in the case of Alsace & Lorraine would indeed be extraordinary. For there the proposal is that the people of those districts should become not only the friends of their enemies, but the enemies of their friends: & this at a time when the greatest political authority of Germany declares that the present war must very speedily be followed by another between the same belligerents, & when the laws which regulate the military organisation of Germany would make the mass of the able bodied population of these provinces in whatever rank of life soldiers, or liable to become soldiers against the very armies in which they have now been serving.

But on the other hand it must be admitted that Germany, exercising the self-command & prudence necessary for the abandonment of this extreme claim, would raise herself thereby to a remarkable height of moral dignity, & would acquire a claim to the lasting gratitude of Europe.

24. Th. [London]

Off at 8.20 to London. Much conversation with an intelligent German, from Crewe onwards. Revised Mem. on Alsace & Lorraine. Saw Ld

---

[1] 'or reasonable' deleted.

Granville——Mr Childers. Dined at Ld Granville's. Saw Perry[R].
Wrote to C.G.——Lady Salisbury——& minutes.

25. *Fr.*

Wrote to Ld Granville——M. Chevalier——Ld Chichester——Bns L.
Rothschild——D. of Argyll——Mr Stansfeld——The Queen——Mary G.
——C.G.——Abp of Canterbury——& minutes. S. and Harry breakfasted. Saw Lady Matheson[1]——Thos Turner——Mr Glyn——Mr Cardwell——Mr M'Coll——Mrs Th.——Ld Chancellor——Ld de Grey——Chancr
of Exr——Mr Meade. Saw Casson X. Dined with Lady Herbert.

Cabinet N. 25. 70. 3.30 PM.[2]
√ Russian answer: draft Mem to be prepared & consd. on Monday.
√ Answer to Mr Dease   }
            Dr Vaughan   } WEG obtained general indications[3]
√ Instruction to Odo Russell respecting Russian Question agreed on: to go by
   Telegram.
√ Suez Canal. Childers desires an understanding as to Suez Canal. Precis of
   papers to be prepared.
√ Cardwell. The revictualling of Paris.[4]
   Next Cabinet Monday 2 PM.

To M. CHEVALIER, 25 November 1870.   Add MS 44539, f. 84.
'Private.'

   I need not assure you that I have read with deep interest your letter received
yesterday[5] on the deep tragedy of the day & on the diplomatic outrage which
has been committed by the Russian Government.
   You will not I am sure expect from me a full or detailed reply upon points of
such delicacy, and of such vast weight as those which you have touched. I will
only say on one main head that we have not in our hands the proof of such a
concert as you believe to exist between Russia and Prussia; & on a point which is
personal, that I fear you ascribe to me opportunities as well as faculties which
I do not possess. But I must not pass over that weighty announcement, which is
contained in your P.S.[6] Speaking for myself alone I can assure you it gives me a
profound satisfaction. For a long time, I have been impressed with the belief
that duty & policy alike recommended, even independently of the armistice, the
convocation of a National Assembly.
   Frenchmen naturally & properly absorbed in the business of Defence may

---

   [1] Mary Jane, wife of Sir James Matheson, bart., of Jardine, Matheson.
   [2] Add MS 44638, f. 147.
   [3] Edmund Gerald Dease (1829-1904; liberal M.P. Queen's Co. 1870-80) and H. H.
*Vaughan had protested at the suppression of the pope's temporal power (Add MS 44428,
ff. 205, 226). For Gladstone's response see 30 Nov. 70.
   [4] See 18 Nov. 70.
   [5] Add MS 44127, f. 93, accusing Russia of a second Tilsit.
   [6] Calling of a National Assembly.

also naturally have omitted to realise to themselves what it is for the Neutrals who as such of course are friends, that France should not have an organ entitled to say for her what she desires and what she means. Whether, when such an organ is in action, Neutrals can do anything to restore peace or towards restoring it, must depend upon many circumstances; but its existence is at least a *condition sine quâ non.* For how is it *possible* either to urge upon France that to which she cannot say Aye or No, or to ask on her behalf that which there are no means of *knowing* she desires. I regretted the intervention from Paris against the order from Tours: but I say all this with due reserve, & as to yourself, for I know from experience how difficult & hazardous it is to give any opinion upon the conduct or policy to be adopted in a foreign country & without either control or responsibility on the part of the person giving it. Still I do not dissemble the opinion that probably until the Convocation of an Assembly no fruitful proceedings will begin with a view to the termination of this awful war.

26. Sat. [Hatfield]

Wrote to Ld Granville—Chancr of Exr—Mr M'Coll—Archdn of Meath—Mary G.—Ld Kimberley—C.G.—Mr Dease (dft)—Mr Bruce—Mr Fortescue—& minutes. Wrote Notes for reply to Russia: *before* the case had improved.[1] Saw Mr Levy—Mr Glyn—Mr Glyn *cum* Ld Granville—Ld Granville. Went down by the 5.25 to Hatfield.[2] Most kindly received: & had much conversation pol.eccl. & philol. with Mr Probart.[3] Read Elwin's Introduction to Pope.[4]

To C. S. P. FORTESCUE, Irish secretary,   Carlingford MSS CP 1/149.
26 November 1870.

I think it is understood between us that when you have ascertained all the necessary points about Fenian prisoners you will let me know before proceeding to any actual step, & you will perhaps advise at the same time as to any letter which it may be right to indite for publication at the time of release.

I write this now because the *hope* of a war growing out of the Russian business has, so Bruce reports, to a certain extent & not unnaturally revived the Fenian organisation which was so dispirited a few weeks ago.[5]

I do not myself pay great regard to this circumstance but others may.

I am able to add that the Russian question looks better today than it has yet done. Gortschakoff is willing that a conference shall meet in *London*: & Prussia is we believe sincerely active in endeavouring to compose the affair.

[1] In Ramm I, i. 168.
[2] Marquis of Salisbury's seat.
[3] Unidentified; not a member of the household.
[4] W. *Elwin, *The works of A. Pope. With introductions* (1871).
[5] Fortescue replied, 27 November 1870, Add MS 44122, f. 171: 'the idea of war is very popular here, not merely among Fenians who hope for calamity to England, but among the R. Catholic people generally . . .'.

27. Advent S.

Hatfield Ch & H.C. mg. Hatfield Chapel aft. at 6, a careful & seemly service: rare in private Chapels. Read Manning on the Council[1]—Maguire's Pius IX.[2] Much conversation.

28. M. [London]

Returned to town at 11. Wrote to Mr Fortescue—Ld Kimberley—The Queen—Dr Vaughan—C.G.—Ld Spencer—Mr Glyn—Mr Ouvry—Mr Bright—and minutes. Read Elwin. Saw Ld Granville—Ld Halifax—Mr M'Coll—Chancr of Exr. Cabinet $2\frac{1}{4}$-$5\frac{1}{4}$. Saw the Wortleys: Sir F. Doyle. Dined at Mr Thistlethwayte's & then went to Dean Stanley's to meet Père Hyacinthe.[3] He is much to be felt for.

Cabinet Nov. 28/70. 2 PM.[4]

√ 1. Ld Granville proposes to send Sir J. Rose[5] to U.S. to start from himself the notion of a Commission for discussion of points in difference & putting them in train. Approved: wait a few days to be out of the Russian difficulty.

√ 2. Gortschakoff Circular. Telegrams & letters read. Draft dispatch read & approved.[6]

√ 3. Argyll. Interception[?] of Indian Officers from promotion to be Major Generals. Action on report of Comm[ittee] or agt. it suspended—for. till Parlt. meets.[7]

√ 4. Goschen. Consolidation of Rates. Ratepaying clauses to be abolished.[8]

To J. BRIGHT, president of the board of trade,   Add MS 43385, f. 137.
28 November 1870. 'Private.'

Prussia appears to be exerting herself honestly & actively for the settlement of the Russian difficulty & there seems now to be a great likelihood of a Conference to consider it in a free & becoming manner. In a few days, therefore, I may find myself without any title longer to postpone an event very painful to me. When the time arrives I should like to have not only your sanction to an announcement that your retirement has for its *sole* motive the speedier & more complete re-establishment of your health, but even, if you think fit to have that

---

[1] H. E. *Manning, 'The Vatican Council and its definitions, a pastoral letter' (1870).

[2] J. F. *Maguire, *Pontificate of Pius the Ninth* [3rd ed. of *Rome and its ruler*] (1870).

[3] Charles Jean Marie Loyson, known as Père Hyacinthe, 1827-1912, formerly French Roman Catholic priest; married and founded his own ecumenical church, with a branch in London; considerably helped by Gladstone; see Matthew, 'Vaticanism', 439.

[4] Add MS 44638, f. 150.

[5] Sir John Rose, 1820-88; Canadian finance minister 1867-9, then banker in London, cr. bart. 1872. Rose met Fish on 9 January 1871, to propose an arbitration, without a British admission of liability; see Cook, *The Alabama Claims*, 154.

[6] Accepting conference if no decisions predetermined; PRO FO 181/478.

[7] Royal commission appointed 30 January 1871; *London Gazette*, 3 February 1871.

[8] Proposed in the 1871 bill; see G. J. Goschen, *Local taxation* (1872), 192.

announcement made in words either selected, or at least approved, by yourself.[1] Please to let me know how this strikes you. You will forgive my anxiety that the concord which has so happily marked your relations with your colleagues all along shall not be even in appearance impaired when the time arrives for their ceasing to call you by that name. The Queen writes that she is deeply concerned to hear of your meditated resignation; she thinks back with pleasure to the opportunity she has had of personal relations with you, & hopes she may still be able to see you when your health permits it.

To C. S. P. FORTESCUE, Irish secretary,   Carlingford MSS CP 1/152.
28 November 1870.

I am glad to say the prospects of the Russian question have further improved; & no time should be lost in getting all preliminaries into order so that if, as may now be rather confidently hoped, that matter is put into a pacific train, we may be in a condition to proceed at once to *the release*, as the Viceroy appears much to desire.[2]

Prussia accepts our basis for a conference and will certainly do all she can to settle the business at St. Petersburgh.

29. Tu. [*Windsor*]

Wrote to Ld Monck—Archdn Stopford—Mr Max Müller—and minutes. Off at 12.45 to Windsor. Audience of the Queen & Council. Saw Mr Cardwell—Mr M'Coll—Dean of Windsor—Prince Christian —Princess Helena.[3] Read Elwin & Pope—Bewick's Life. St George's Chapel 4.30.

30. St Andrew [*London*]

Castle Prayers. Off at 10 to town. Wrote to Mr Lefevre—Mr Otway —Mr Bass—Sir H. Johnstone—C.G.—The Queen (1. & Mem.)— Mr Glyn—M.G.—and minutes. Saw Ld Granville—Mr M'Coll—Ld Chancr—Mrs Th. (2). Cabinet 1¼-5. Read Bewick's Life (finished). Dined with Royal Society. Returned thanks for health.[4] Conversation with Sir H. Holland—Prof. Huxley.[5]

Cabinet Nov. 30. 1 PM[6]
√ Ld Granville's recitals. Conversations with Baron Brunnow. Conversation on

---

[1] Bright wrote on 28 November, Add MS 44112, f. 169, agreeing, but declining to write the announcement himself. See 11 Dec. 70.
[2] Gladstone, on 9 December 1870, Add MS 44122, f. 179, now certain of the conference, instructed release of Fenians to proceed.
[3] For both, see 25 May 46n.   [4] *The Times*, 1 December 1870, 5c.
[5] Thomas Henry *Huxley, 1825-95; scientist; on Contagious Diseases Royal Commission 1870-1; later in violent controversy with diarist on the bible; see 2 Sept. 70.
[6] Add MS 44638, f. 151.

Conference. Immediate? On French interposition. May [French] Defence
Govt. be recognised?[1]
√ Cardwell Army Estimates. 107m[ille] men in the Country—120m Militia—
35 Pensioners & Reserve—160 Volunteers—13 Yeomanry—120 Fortresses
—120 on foot—60 Reserve forces: & batteries in reserve.
Augmentation of 20,000. Distributed: Infantry 11m.—Cavalry 3 to 4—Artil-
lery 4 to 5. Militia Commissions. Conscription—none. Volunteers basis of.
√ Childers proposed 61000 for the Navy. Reserve will be larger. agreed.
√ French Govt. at Tours must refer to Govt. at Paris. Decided not to postpone
proceeding on this account only unless some strong reason should emerge.
√ Granville proposed Ld Cowley as 2d Plenipo[tentiary] should there be two.

To E. G. DEASE, M.P., 30 November 1870.   Add MS 44428, f. 236.[2]

Sir, I have the honour to acknowledge the receipt of your letter of the 15th
inst.[3] transmitting a memorial from the inhabitants of Stradbally, in which you
state that they express their desire that Her Majesty's Government may see fit to
use 'such diplomatic intervention as may secure to the Pope the continuance of
such a temporal Sovereignty as will protect him in the discharge of his spiritual
duties, together with an adequate income'. The memorial itself is couched in
larger or less definite language, but I do not doubt that I am to recognise you as
the best expositor of the feelings it is intended to express.

In reply I have to state that Her Majesty's Government have not, during the
various changes which have marked the reign of the present Pope, interfered, nor
have they now proposed to interfere, with the Civil Government of the city of
Rome or the surrounding country.

But Her Majesty's Government consider all that relates to the adequate support of the dignity of the Pope, and to his personal freedom and independence
in the discharge of his spiritual functions, to be legitimate matter for their notice.

Indeed, without waiting for the occurrence of an actual necessity, they have
during the uncertainties of the last few months taken upon themselves to make
provisions which would have tended to afford any necessary protection to the
person of the Sovereign Pontiff.

The subjects to which I have adverted will continue to have their careful
attention; although they have had great satisfaction in observing that the Italian
Government has declared in the most explicit manner its desire and intention to
respect and defend the Pope's freedom and independence, and to take care that
adequate provision shall be forthcoming for the due support of his dignity.

To A. J. OTWAY, M.P., 30 November 1870.   Add MS 44539, f. 87.

I need hardly say it is with very great regret that I learned from your letter
there was a disagreement between you & the Government on such a question as
the grave controversy in which Prince Gortchakoff recently involved us.[4]

[1] The French govt., by then under Thiers, was not recognised until 18 February 1871.
[2] Printed in *The Times*, 8 December 1870, 10b. Edmund Gerald Dease, 1829–1904;
liberal M.P. Queen's Co. 1870–80; a Roman catholic.   [3] Add MS 44428, f. 205.
[4] Otway wrote on 27 November, Add MS 44428, f. 224, anticipating 'humiliation or
war' as a result of British policy on the restructuring of the 1856 treaty of Paris; he resigned
as under-sec. for foreign affairs; Gladstone had already, on 25 November, suggested Lord
Enfield (see 25 June 63) as his successor; Add MS 44539, f. 87.

That it should have led to the consequences which Granville announced to me I could not wonder; since you are yourself the legitimate & only judge of what is required by your public character & by your convictions. You will however I am sure allow me to say how agreeable to me have been at all times our official relations, & how I regret their termination, while I feel assured that in an altered capacity you will continue to render to the country loyal & able service.

Thurs. Dec.One. 1870.

Wrote to Mrs Thistlethwayte—Ld Kimberley—Mr Murray—Mary G. —C.G.—and minutes. Dined at Mr Goschen's. Saw Mr M'Coll—Mr Mundella—Mr Aldis *cum* Mr Robinson—Ld Granville (2)—Gen. Burnside. Saw Gould & Graham. X. Read Gouvt Republicain—Detuyat to K. of Prussia[1]—and other tracts.

To Sir J. D. COLERIDGE, solicitor general,   Add MS 44539, f. 88.
1 December 1870.

Please to read the enclosed [resolution]. I have seen Mr. Aldis with Mr. Robinson of Cambridge this forenoon: I have pointed out to them that their resolution if practically pushed & adopted by the promoters of the University Tests Bill generally will entirely change the position of the question, release the Government & everyone else from all pledges & expectations & establish a new start. I also told him that what the Cabinet had thought of was to introduce & press the Bill at the very earliest period of the session, with a confident hope of its passing into law. Lastly I advised communication between Nonconformists & Academical Promoters both in Oxford & Cambridge that we might know before the Queen's speech what is really meant by those outside the walls & whether the Bill of last year will be taken as a boon worth having or not. This tone I hope you will approve.[2]

2. Fr. [Hawarden]

Wrote to Lady Herbert—The Queen Mem.—Mr Fortescue—Ld Halifax—and minutes. Saw Mr West. 10.30–6.30 to Hawarden: picked up Mary on the way & had mischances. Read Pope's Poems— Ovid—Military Educn Reports.

3. Sat.

Ch. 8½ A.M. Wrote to Gen. Burnside[3]—Ld Granville—2, one secret —Mr Rawson—The Queen—Mr Bruce—and minutes. Cut a tree

---

[1] Neither traced.

[2] Coleridge approved, adding this was 'what I told Salisbury his course in the Lords would certainly provoke'; 2 December, Add MS 44138, f. 107.

[3] Proposing he should visit Hawarden; Add MS 44539, f. 90. He signed the visitors' book on 10 Dec., but Gladstone does not mention his visit.

with Willy. Worked on arranging books. Read School Geography[1]—Tomkins & Jencken on Roman Law[2]—Browne's Poems.[3] Cut a tree with Willy.

To H. A. BRUCE, home secretary, 3 December 1870.   Aberdare MSS.

I was anxious to speak to you at our last Cabinet about the Commission on the Contagious Diseases Acts, but you had left the room before I found an opportunity. I am very fearful of the consequences of the delay which has taken place in starting the enquiry. No doubt it has been due to the difficulty you have experienced in forming the Commission of right materials. But when popular feeling is excited, due allowances for executive difficulties are refused & I am fearful lest attempts should be made, if the tide continues to rise, to discredit the Commission altogether. To prevent any such evil it is highly desirable that the Commission should not only have met but have made some considerable progress before the beginning of the Session. They (the opponents) will be entitled to require that the report should appear about Easter so as to allow the Government time to legislate if they think fit, & so as to allow the opponents of the Acts time to take any measures they please. To this extent their claim will be very strong as they were baulked by the proposal of a Commission in their operations of last Session.

4. 2 S.Adv.

Ch. mg. with H.C. and evg. Wrote to Viceroy of Ireland—Sol. General—The Queen—Rev Mr Rawson—Ld Halifax—Rev Mr Wilkinson—Mr Kirk MP—and minutes. Read Milnes's Letters to a Preb.[4]—Triumph of Moral Good (finished).[5] Arr. a few books.

To Sir J. D. COLERIDGE, solicitor general,   Add MS 44539, f. 90.
4 December 1870.

Many thanks for your letter. I gathered from my two friends on Thursday that they had little expectation of support from the Camb. Univ. Liberals for their new proposition. If you have already had communication with Salisbury on the subject of your Bill, could [you] not as from yourself discuss the matter with him in its present phase. In 1854 I was most anxious to cut off non-resident fellows but could not get one human being in the University to support me. I think the proposal will be a skilful counter-stroke. For me individually it would be beyond anything odious, I am almost tempted to say it would be impossible, after my long connection with Oxford to go into a new controversy on the basis of what will be taken & alleged to be an absolute secularisation of the Colleges; as well as a reversal of what was deliberately considered & sanctioned in the Parliamentary legislation of '54 & '56. I incline to think that that work is work

---

[1] Probably J. Guy, *School geography* (1869 ed.).
[2] F. Tomkins and H. D. Jencken, *A compendium of the modern Roman Law* (1870).
[3] W. *Browne, *Works*, ed. W. C. *Hazlitt (1868).
[4] Untraced.
[5] See 11 Sept. 70.

for others not for me——I think also that the proceeding is much too abrupt &
violent as regards the H. of Lords, which cannot be said yet to have had even one
perfectly fair opportunity of considering the measure of last year. I am, with
you, not *certain* that the measure would be inadmissible with the rider you think
Salisbury will attack (and if he attacks he will carry it) but should wish to consider this further. My confidence in Salisbury's honour is such that I should not
be in the least afraid of discussing the matter with him personally, if any good
should seem likely to come of it. But I am certain the Cabinet will be most
reluctant to open a new controversy on the subject. I shall read your inclosure
with much interest.[1]

5. M.

Wrote to Mrs Milman[2]——Mr Graves MP——Ld Granville——and minutes.
Worked over 5 hours in arranging books. Church 8½ AM. Large party.
Whist in evg. Read Ovid's Fasti.

6. Tu.

Ch. 8½ AM. Wrote to Bp Gillooly[3]——Ld Granville (2)——Lady Her-
bert——Mr Monsell——Chancr of Exr——Mr Cardwell——& minutes.
Wrote Mem. on Baron Brunnow's Mem. respecting the Conference.[4]
Read Coleridge's Address[5]——Ovid Fasti——Br[oad] Ch. Rector on
Prosecutions for Heresy.[6] The annual ball took place in the evening.
Saw Lady Westminster, Mr Barker, Mr Bate. Conversation with Ld
Meath[7] on Irish Church.

To R. LOWE, chancellor of the exchequer,   Add MS 44539, f. 92.
6 December 1870.

Granville spoke to me about the F.O. and [civil service] competition, some
months ago. He said, I thought justly that it would be invidious if he were at
once to reverse Clarendon's very decided & probably very notorious judgement
in the matter.[8] But I never understood that he meant to lay down the system of

[1] No reply traced; see 2 Dec. 70. See Ward, *Victorian Oxford*, 260 and Morley, ii. 313.
[2] Mary Ann, *née* Cockell, widow of H. H. *Milman; she had sent one of her husband's
books; Add MS 44539, f. 92.
[3] Lawrence Gillooly, d. 1895; bp. of Elphin from 1858; sending copy of his letter to
Dease (see 30 Nov. 70) as a reply to an address on the pope's temporal power from the
Roman catholics of Sligo; see Add MSS 44539, f. 93 and 44428, f. 239.
[4] In Ramm I, i. 177.
[5] J. D. *Coleridge, 'Inaugural address delivered to the members of the Philosophical
Institution, Edinburgh' (1870).
[6] *Prosecutions for heresy; their demoralizing influence* (1870).
[7] See 23 July 38n.
[8] Excluding foreign office from open competition rules; Lowe's letter untraced; see
Ramm I, i. 177.

nomination for the permanent government of the office. If that is done, I think it most probable that the H. of C. will run in upon us by an address to the Crown. I will write to him to this effect. When we have his answer we can consider whether to write anything to Bruce, whose case for a delay, is not, apparently so strong.

7. Wed.

Ch. 8½ AM. Wrote to Ld Granville—Ld Sydney—Mr Bruce—Ld Halifax—Mr West—Gen. Burnside—Mr Salisbury—and minutes. We felled an ash in aft. Worked on books. Read Prevost Paradol's Nouvelle France[1]—Dame Europa's School.[2] Large party still here, with changes. Mr Hayward came.

8. Th.

Ch. 8¼ AM. Wrote to Ld Granville—Mr Freshfield—Bp of London —Mr West—Bp Staley—and minutes. Worked on books. Walk with Hayward. Read Prevost Paradol.

9. Frid.

Ch. 8½ AM. Wrote to Ld Granville—The Speaker—Mr Rawson— Mr Fortescue—Mr West—The Queen—and minutes. Reviewed & sent off to Dublin the Fenian-release letter.[3] Worked on my books. Read Ovid Fasti B. II—La Nouvelle France. Mr M. Müller & Sir F. Peel came.[4]

10. Sat.

Ch. 8½ AM. Wrote to Ld Granville (2)—Mr Chadwick—Mr Reeve— Mr Lingen—Mr Dixon—and minutes. C.G. after consideration went off to nurse Herbert. Walk with Mr M. Müller. Read Guizot's Letter[5] —Life of a Clergyman[6]—La Nouvelle France.

To G. DIXON, M.P., 10 December 1870.   Add MS 44539, f. 97.

We have fully considered the subject of the reprovisioning of Paris,[7] & the judgement of the Government is against our moving in the matter on our own

---

[1] L. A. Prévost-Paradol, *La France nouvelle* (1868).
[2] [H. W. Pullen], *The fight at Dame Europa's school* (1870).
[3] Preparing for the public announcement; see 15 Dec. 70.
[4] As did Burnside; see 3 Dec. 70n.   [5] See 24 Jan. 71?
[6] Perhaps R. Gee, '*From Sunday to Sunday*' . . . *the weekday life and labours of a country clergyman* (1865).
[7] See 25 Nov. 70. Dixon's letter untraced.

responsibility. I feel certain that the reasons are conclusive. A joint application from the two Belligerents might at least place the question in a new position.

11. 3 S.Adv.

Ch mg & evg. Wrote to Duke of Argyll—Dr Guthrie[1]—Mr Bright —Ld Halifax—Robn G.—C.G.—and minutes. Read Olliff's Letter to King of Prussia[2]—Johnson's Tracts on Julian & Constantius[3]— Westcott on the Resurrection[4]—Manning's Pastoral Letter—Chadwick on Xty & Paganism.[5]

To J. BRIGHT, president of the board of trade,   Add MS 43385, f. 141.
11 December 1870.

The Conference on Russian matters is now, we think, sure & can hardly end in anything but an adjustment. The Fenians will I hope be released within two or three days. The time is therefore come for considering your permissive resignation. Now, encouraged by what I have recently heard of your health, I am about to put a question to you. But I beg that if you think it likely to worry you, you will make no scruple of at once putting it aside, because your health is our first care in this correspondence, as it should be yours. Once ⟨more⟩ then let me submit to you a new view of the case. Could you prudently try the experiment of continuance in the following form: a. attending Cabinets. b. appearing occasionally at convenient hours in the H. of C. & c. allowing all ordinary office business to be disposed of for you. Might not a short trial of this either show the practicability of going further, or at worst prove, without harm done, the expediency of drawing back. It would give us all great pleasure if your answer to this could be affirmative: but as I have said we cannot wish to purchase that pleasure at the cost of mischief to you.[6] A prudent adjustment of American questions, & of the questions concerning defence at home, are likely to be the next principal cares, I think, of the Cabinet.

12. M.

Ch. 8½ AM. Wrote to Ld Granville (2)—Mr Bruce (tel.)—The Queen —Mr West (Tel.)—C.G.—Ld Kimberley—Mrs Th.—Mr Fortescue —and minutes. Worked on books. Walk in the snow with Ld E. Fitzmaurice & others. Read Hors de Paris[7]—A. de la Gueronniere[8]—La Nouvelle France. Music in evg: with my rusty voice!

[1] On the pope's temporal power; Lathbury, ii. 54, Add MS 44539, f. 97.
[2] E. Pétavel-Olliff, 'Lettre à S.M. le Roi de Prusse par un Ministre Protestant' (1870).
[3] S. *Johnson, *Julian the Apostate* (1682); *Constantius the Apostate* (1683).
[4] See 21 Oct. 66.
[5] J. *Chadwick, *Christianity versus Paganism. Seven letters* (1870).
[6] Bright replied on 14 December, Add MS 44112, f. 171, declining the suggestion; draft paragraph for announcement of resignation in ibid., f. 175. See 16 Dec. 70.
[7] Untraced.
[8] L. E. A. de la Gueronnière, *Aux électeurs de France. Le vote du 8 Mai* (1870).

13. Tu.

Ch. 8½ AM. Wrote to Granville (& 2 Telegr.)—Mr Cardwell—Lady Herbert—Viceroy of Irel.—Mr Lowe—Ld Belper—C.G.—and minutes. Read La Nouv. France—and other works. Cut down an Oak with C. Lyttelton. Much disturbed by the Luxemburg papers—the note of the 3d came.[1]

14. Wed. [London]

Wrote to C.G.—Mr Fortescue—Ld Granville—and minutes. Off at 8 to Liverpool & C[ourt] Hey for my niece Annie's marriage.[2] It was all very genial. Stephy officiated so well.—I proposed the healths at the banquet. Off again at 3 for London. Arr. 10 P.M. Long conversation with Granville. Saw two[R]. Saw Tom: suffering a good deal.

15. Th.

Wrote to The Queen—Ld Granville—Mr Motley—Mr Fortescue—C.G.—Mr M'C. Downing—The Speaker—D. of Argyll—and minutes. Saw Ld Granville—Mr West—Mr G. Glyn—Sir R. Phillimore—Mr Levy. Cabinet 2½–7¼. Dined with the Wests. Saw one X.

Cabinet Dec. 15. 70. 3 PM[3]
√ Luxembourg. Dispatch read, amended, & approved: on Count Bismarck's Circular of the 3d. To be dispatched by us, without an anterior concert.[4]
√ Railway accidents. Queen's letter. Suggestions: difficulty.[5]
√ Fenian Convicts. Form read by Mr Bruce & approved.[6]
√ Letter to Prot[estant] Defence Assocn.—minute for. Approved: & the question discussed.[7]
√ Naval Estimates. Building. Long discussion. No addition except the 400m already agreed on.
√ Russian Question. Proposed Invitation—Speech—Protocol—considered.
√ Anglo-American Committee. Prospectus read. Govt. shd. not as such interfere—however well we may wish.[8]

[1] Bismarck's circular to the signatories of the 1867 Luxemburg Treaty, accusing Luxemburg of breaking neutrality; Ramm I, i. 185n.
[2] Anne, da. of Robertson Gladstone, m. Edward John Thornewill, Liverpool corn merchant.
[3] Add MS 44638, f. 153.
[4] See notes to cabinet, 17 Dec. 70.
[5] See Guedalla, *Q,* i. 266.
[6] Gladstone's letter of 16 December, to Sir William Carroll, leader of the petition for release of the Fenians, informing him of their release and perpetual deportation, printed in *The Guardian,* 21 Dec. 1870, 1481.
[7] Probably the Church Defence Institution; letter untraced, but see 10 Dec. 71, 28 Dec. 72.
[8] Untraced; presumably a cttee. promoting good relations.

16. Frid.

Wrote to Mr Bright—The Speaker[1]—W.H.G.—The Queen (Mem)—C.G.—Mr Fortescue—Ld Halifax—Mr Max Müller—and minutes. Saw Sol. General—Sir R. Phillimore—D. & Duchess of Argyll—Mr West—Ld Halifax—Mr Glyn—Mr Meade—Mr Cardwell—M. Tissot[2]—Ld Granville (2). Dined at the Granville's. Saw Hamilton X & another: also Gould, to give a book. Read Luxemburg u. Preussen.[3]

To J. BRIGHT, president of the board of trade, Add MS 43385, f. 145.
16 December 1870.

I have no choice to give way to your judgement & to the forcible considerations which you urge. I do not wish to make you responsible for the inclosed Paragraph;[4] but if there is anything in it which grates upon you, or if you notice any palpable defect, please to correct it. Perhaps as a free man you may some day give me a little outline of your views about France. The transfer of European populations against their will from one country to another is a measure of which I abhor the idea. With best wishes that you may obtain the good for which we pay a heavy price.

17. Sat.

Wrote to Mr Motley—Sir R. Blennerhassett[5]—Mr Bruce—Mr Fortescue[6]—Mr Tomline—Mrs Nimmo—T.S. Gladstone—Mr Melvill—C.G.—The Queen—P[rince]ss Christian—and minutes. Saw Mr Glyn—Rev. S.E.G.—Ld Halifax—Mr Parratt & conclave—Mr Forster—Ld Granville (2)—Bp of London. Saw Mrs Barber. Dined at J. Wortleys. Finished La Nouvelle France.

Cabinet. D. 17 70. Sat. 1 PM[7]
√ Telegram from Ld Lyons on the 3 things required by the Paris Govt. To be commun[icate]d through Bernstorff.[8]
√ Dispatch to Berlin in answer to Bismarck.[9] Bernstorff's opinion proposed to be recited.

[1] Unsuccessfully recommending *West for a Commons' clerkship; in West, Recollections, i. 373; the missing name there is 'Milman', see Add MS 44539, f. 102.
[2] Charles Joseph Tissot, 1828-84; secretary to French embassy in London 1867-71; ambassador in London 1882-4.
[3] Untraced. [4] See 11 Dec. 70n.
[5] Sir Rowland *Blennerhassett, 1839-1909; liberal M.P. Galway 1865-74, Kerry 1874-85; journalist and prominent Roman catholic.
[6] Offering him the board of trade and a peerage; he eventually declined the latter; Add MS 44539, f. 103, in O. Hewett, Strawberry Fair (1956), 216.
[7] Add MS 44638, f. 154.
[8] On Luxemburg and Bismarck's circular that it be no longer regarded as neutral: PRO FO 27/1796.
[9] Expressing great concern about Bismarck's circular, hoping it is merely cautionary; PRO FO 64/244.

√ Difficulties from Brunnow respecting the documents from the Conference. Agreed to reduce the Invitation: admit the proposed paragraph of B[runnow]'s Speech, with modification if possible: our insistence to be on the Protocol of solemn act.

√ Mr Bright's resignation. Offer to Fortescue. Mentioned.[1]

√ Cabinet agreed to abandon the Tripartite Treaty (Ottoman) if requested by the Porte.

√ to warn France about 'blockade' of French Ports.

√ Kimberley. Respecting withdrawal of the residue of the garrison of Quebec: one battalion and two batteries. No winter clothing for 107[?] to be put in the Estimates.

Mr Ayrton submitted plans for the new War Office.

18. 4 S.Adv.

Ch. Royal mg and St James evg. Wrote to Mrs Thistlethwayte——Mr Liddell[2]——Sir Thos G.——C.G.——& minutes. Read Thos a Kempis——Orby Shipley Vol. on the Cardinal Virtues[3]——L'Allemagne et la Belgique.[4] Went to Richmond & saw Ld Russell: a long & friendly interview & conversation. Dined with Ld Abingdon.

19. M. [Hawarden]

Wrote to Mr Bright——Sir P. Braila——Mr Fortescue——Dean of Windsor ——and minutes. Saw Mr Freshfield——Mr G. Glyn——Ld Granville (at Windsor). Off at 10.30 to Windsor. Saw C.G.——Herbert, looking thin but not unhealthy——E. Coleridge——Off to Chester at 3, and home at 10¾. Read Dana.[5]

20. Tu.

Wrote to The Viceroy——Mr West (Tel.)——A. Kinnaird——Mr Childers ——Sir J. Gray——Ld Enfield[6]——Mr Bennett——Ld A. Clinton——C.G. ——Col. Ponsonby (Tel)——and minutes. Mr Motley arrived: & other

---

[1] *Fortescue formally succeeded *Bright as president of the board of trade on 14 January 1871. Draft for newspapers of *Bright's resignation in Add MS 44759, f. 240.

[2] Arthur Thomas Liddell (1837–1919; 5th Baron Ravensworth 1904) had written about the Fenian prisoners and the Channel Islands; see Gladstone's reply in Add MS 44539, f. 104.

[3] O. *Shipley, The four Cardinal virtues considered in relation to the public and private life of Catholics (1870).

[4] L'Allemagne et la Belgique pendant et après la guerre de 1870 (1870).

[5] R. H. Dana, Two years before the mast. A personal narrative of life at sea (1841); see 13 Jan. 71.

[6] Offering him the undersecretaryship at the foreign office on Otway's resignation; Add MS 44539, f. 105. See 30 Nov. 70.

guests. Read Steane's Appeal[1]—Dana's Before the Mast—Bp Doyle's Essay on R C Claims.[2] Church 8½ A.M. Cut down an Ash with Harry.

To H. C. E. CHILDERS, first lord,   Add MS 44539, f. 105.
20 December 1870.

I think the transposition of charge from the great ironships to the Anti-Alabamas & Harbour Defences is decidedly good: & the scale (as I understand) of charge is to remain the same as when the matter has been heretofore discussed. If I am right in all this I think you will be perfectly safe in proceeding as your letter of yesterday proposes.[3]

21. St Thos. Wed.

Ch. 11 AM. Wrote to Ld Granville—Mr Davison MP—Ld Strafford—Mr West (and Telegram)—Chancr of Exr—Mr Ayrton—The Speaker—Mr Melvill—The Ld Chancellor—and minutes. Read Dubois Reymond's Lecture:[4] & other Tracts on the War. Much conversation with Mr Motley: & Gen. Wilbraham.[5]

To R. LOWE, chancellor of the exchequer,   Add MS 44539, f. 107.
21 December 1870. 'Private.'

1. The B. of T. has already been offered to Fortescue who I think will accept it. All that can be done therefore will be to discuss after his appointment the change you suggest, which for some reasons I should much like.[6]
2. There is much also in your suggestion as to the Irish Secretaryship: but there are some reasons against making the change at this moment which I will explain when we meet & of which I think you will feel the force. If however the office has to be disposed of the question of salary may be named as one open to consideration, & thus our liberty may be preserved.
3. Now for your very *ladylike* P.S. If we require taxes I doubt whether you will be able to manage otherwise than by the everlasting & most commonplace penny [on income tax]. There is however the question whether fiscal reasons may not render it wise to put forward your currency plan if this would fill the gap. In no case will you be able I think to make Ireland fill the gap, without giving her something in the nature of an equivalent, such as a Railway plan.
4. On that subject I send you a short memo from Halifax. On first hearing of the subject, he had been very averse.

[1] E. Steane, *The evangelical alliance and religious liberty* (1864); on Russian Lutherans.
[2] J. Doyle, *An essay on the Catholic claims* (1826).
[3] Add MS 44128, proposing shift of emphasis from ironclads to 'anti-Alabamas' and coastal and harbour defences.
[4] E. H. Du Bois-Reymond, 'Über den deutschen Krieg' (1870).
[5] (Sir) Richard Wilbraham, 1811-1900; governed military hospitals 1861-70; major-general 1866; K.C.B. 1873.
[6] Lowe proposed on 20 December 1870, Add MS 44301, f. 164, the transfer of the commercial treaty department of the board of trade to the foreign office. See 30 July 69. He also stated the Irish secretary's salary was 'excessive', and asked advice on new taxes.

5. I shall be very glad if we can induce Cardwell & the Cabinet to postpone, wholly or mainly, the acceleration of the ports & their armaments. There never was a time perhaps for 30 years past when the likelihood of our wanting them was so small.

6. I am acquainted generally with the effect of the Swiss [army] system but I have not seen the paper to which you refer. It may be adapted to their position as a little country girt about on every side by big ones: but surely it would not be needful or wise, I doubt if it would be popular for us to adopt such a system. What we want I suppose to be a small army, large proportionate reserves, & a pretty liberal allowance of auxiliary forces. Towards these ends I think Cardwell is working. But I see no objection to your suggestion about drill in assisted schools, & much good in it. There are others of your ideas which Cardwell has in hand.

22. Th.

Ch. 8½ A.M. Wrote to Mr West (& Tel.)——Bp of Winchester——Mr Ayrton——Chancr of Exr——C.G.——Mr Johnson——Mrs ODonovan Rossa——Sir C. Trevelyan——and minutes. Read Doyle's Essay[1]—— Dana's Before the Mast——Laveleye on Future of France[2]——Villages around Metz.[3] Conversation with Mr Temple on Ch., Disestabl., & Education. Walk with Mr Motley: who went.

To R. LOWE, chancellor of the exchequer,   Add MS 44539, f. 109.
22 December 1870.

Yesterday in my reference to your currency plan as a measure of procuring revenue, I omitted to notice that I was uncertain at what rate your new supply of notes could be put out and therefore the profit from them realised but I fear this would take too much time to allow of any sudden realisation beyond a limited amount.[4]

2. In our first programme so to call it, of business for the session we have not given a positive place to the Land laws. Now if the determination of the Dissenters should be to make a fresh start on University Tests, & if they put the question in such a position as to prevent our dealing with it, might we perhaps put the question of Land Laws (which stood over from last Session) in its place. I do not attach a first rate importance to the practical result, but it is certainly right & may even be called urgent that they should be dealt with.

23.

Ch. 8½ A.M. Wrote to Ld Granville (& Tel.)——Mr Fortescue (2, & Tel.)——Mr West (Tels. 2)——Mr Cardwell——Mr Bruce——The Queen

[1] See 20 Dec. 70.
[2] E. L. V. de Laveleye, 'The future of France', *Fortnightly Review*, xiv. 615 (December 1870).
[3] R. S. Watson, *The villages around Metz* (1870).
[4] *Lowe replied agreeing; 26 December 1870, Add MS 44301, f. 170.

(and Mem.)—M'Carthy Downing—Ld Hartington[1]—C.G.—Mrs Thistlethwayte—Mr Reichlingen[2]—and minutes. Saw Mr Burnett. Read Lear's Calabria[3]—Dana's 2 Years bef. the Mast. Conversation with Mr Temple.

To E. CARDWELL, 23 December 1870. *'Private.'*   Add MS 44539, f. 110.

It is the old story:[4] the profession wants to make hay when the sun shines. At no time for perhaps 30 years, have our harbours been so safe. We are preparing torpedoes & harbour defence vessels in unusual numbers & for one I know of no reason for also setting about forts at such a time. Lord Russell is an historian: but what *are* the innocent & peaceful nations who as he says have been destroyed or assailed by their less happy neighbours out of sheer envy of their prosperity? Christmas wishes.

24. Xm.Eve.

Ch 8½ AM. Wrote to Mr West (& Tel.)—Ld Granville—W.H.G.—Messrs Freshfield—Mr Lingen—Mr Corderey[5]—Ld de Grey—Ld Chancr—Chr of Exr—Mr Hugessen—C.G.—and minutes. Wrote Mem. on St Thomas Seaforth Arbitration.[6] Saw Mr Burnett—Mr H. Thompson—Mr Glyn (who came in evg). Read Dana—Lear's Calabria.

Will my colleagues kindly give me their opinions whether I may authorise Dr. Guthrie to publish the part of my letter to him No. IV which is with brackets.
    Glyn is disposed to think it would be useful on the R.C. side—while Guthrie denies[?] it from another question. He fears losing *Mallow* through my letter.[7]

25. Sund. & Xmas D.

Ch mg with H.C., and evg. Wrote to Mr Fortescue—Mr M'C. Downing —C.G.—Ld Granville—Ld Halifax—Dr Candlish[8]—and minutes.

[1] Offering him the Irish secretaryship in succession to *Fortescue; see Holland, i. 80 and 29 Dec. 70.
[2] Asking Frédéric Reitlinger, J. Favre's secretary and envoy of the French govt., to Hawarden; Add MS 44539, f. 110. See 28 Dec. 70.
[3] E. *Lear, *Journals of a landscape painter in Southern Calabria* (1852).
[4] Suggestion of engineers for widespread harbour fortifications; Add MS 44119, f. 179.
[5] Edward Cordery had sent a work; Add MS 44539, f. 112; see 12 Jan. 71.
[6] Add MS 44615, f. 145.
[7] Initialled and dated 16 December [1870], Add MS 44759, f. 241. Cabinet opinion overwhelmingly favoured a parliamentary explanation of the letter to Dease (see 30 Nov. 70) rather than publication of the explanation of it to Guthrie. The liberals had just held Mallow in two 1870 by-elections.
[8] Robert Smith *Candlish, 1806–73; free church leader; on his letter to *Guthrie, see 11 Dec. 70. Add MS 44539, f. 113.

Read Littledale's Lecture[1]—Bp of Carlisle's Pastoral[2]—Lord's Visions of Paradise.[3]

26. M. St Stephen.

Ch. 11 AM. Wrote to Rev. Mr West—Ld Hartington (and Tel.)—Mr Ayrton—A.E. West (Tel)—Hn Postmaster—C.G.—and minutes. Read Dana's Two Years—Doyle's Essay on R.C. Claims—Blackie's War Songs of the Germans.[4]

27. Tu. St John.

Ch 11 AM. Wrote to Ld Granville—The Queen—Ld de Grey—Mr West (Tel)—C.G.—and minutes. Felled a tree with Stephy. Mr Reitlinger came: conversation in evg. Read Dana—Finished Doyle's Essay —Read Ovid's Consolatio.

28. Wed. Holy Innocents.

All the forenoon occupied with Mr Reitlinger in an animated conversation on France and the War.[5] Wrote to Lord Granville—Ld Kimberley?—Mr Hammond—The Queen—Mr Fortescue—C.G.—Mr Cardwell—Mr Bruce—Mr Hamilton—Mr Reeve—and minutes. Read Dana's Two Years—Duke of Argyll's Iona[6]—and [blank]. Felled a tree. Function & address in the Orphanage.

To LORD KIMBERLEY, colonial secretary,   Add MS 44539, f. 118.
28 December 1870. 'Private.'

If Hartington accepts as I hope he will the I.O.[7] we shall have the P.O. empty. It may be right to offer this to Monsell (it does not carry the Cabinet). If so I hope you will not dislike having your U. Secsp. offered to Hugessen. He is a good speaker, & a clever fellow, & he would I think discharge the duties perfectly well in Parliament, but his shoulders are not quite broad enough for the present very heavy work of the H.O. & Bruce really needs a greater amount of practical assistance than from some cause or another he seems able to supply in the Department. It would be a great convenience [if] you could telegraph,[8] without names about the arrangement.

[1] R. F. *Littledale, 'Tradition; a lecture' (1870).
[2] H. *Goodwin, 'The first year of my episcopate. A pastoral letter' (1870).
[3] D. N. Lord, Visions of Paradise. An epic Vol. I (1867).
[4] J. S. Blackie, War Songs of the Germans with historical illustrations (1870).
[5] Long account to *Granville in Ramm I, i. 194.
[6] See 12 Jan. 71.
[7] Vacant through Fortescue's move to the board of trade.   [8] Untraced.

29. Th.

Ch. 8½ A.M. Telegrams to Ld Hartington—Ld Granville—Ld Spencer. Wrote to Mr Max Müller—Sir R. Phillimore—Ld Granville—Robn G.—C.G.—& minutes. Read Ovid, Fasti—Smith's Dict. on Ovid[1]—Lear's Calabria. Ld Hartington came. Saw Mr Burnett—Mr Glyn—on Minist. changes, which we discussed at great length.[2]

My birthday was troubled with anxieties about the last named subject. It should have been given to reflection, to thankfulness, above all to penitence & the cultivation of a deep humility. Of *that* grace at least surely I have *cause* to be secure, enough & overmuch.

The sentiment has deepened in my mind that my life can attain neither its just balance nor its true basis till it shall please God to give me a lawful opportunity of escape from the present course of daily excess which is for me inseparable from my place & calling. May He be so pleased.

To F. Max MÜLLER, 29 December 1870.   Max Müller MSS, d. 170.

After having expressed to you my apprehensions about the Luxembourg question, it would not be right that I should absolutely avail myself of your kind permission to waive answering your very interesting letter;[3] although it opens so many topics of importance that the only way to deal with it satisfactorily would be when you are so well disposed as to be ready to pay us another visit.

We have had no answer to our representation on the Luxembourg case, owing doubtless to our having sent it by Berlin, but all we have heard tends to form & confirm the hope that the reply when it arrives will completely sever the Treaty of 1867.[4] If it does so, we shall not too curiously dispute on the scope of the mere words of the recent Circular. There is no doubt that military urgency might justify, in given circumstances, a Power actually at war in taking into its own hands provisionally the determination of certain questions, which could only be finally disposed of by a joint authority.

There is no doubt as to the present current of feeling in this country. What it may be before the end of the war will depend on the circumstances of the war itself, and of the peace: and I am one of the few who as yet do not feel at all certain what these will be.

With regard to the general question of the relations between Germany and England, I cordially adhere to the spirit and intention of that letter of Sir R. Peel's in 1841, which Bunsen showed me, on his receiving it, with a warmth of

---

[1] See 10 Oct. 56n.

[2] *Hartington had refused the Irish secretaryship (see 23 Dec. 70); Gladstone told *Granville this day 'I fear I must be very rude to him. I cannot think of any other member of the Cabinet, or even of Govt, who cd possibly be transferred . . .' (Ramm I, i. 197); Hartington accepted while at Hawarden. Gladstone then moved *Monsell to the Post Office, outside the Cabinet, and made *Hugessen colonial undersecretary, A. W. *Peel parlt. secretary at the board of trade, G. Shaw *Lefevre home undersecretary.

[3] On Luxemburg, 28 December, Add MS 44251, f. 299.

[4] Treaty of 11 May 1867 on Luxemburg: *PP* 1871 lxxiv. 449.

pleasure that I never can forget.[1] At that very time, Sir R. Peel with Lord Aberdeen was doing all in his power to cultivate the French alliance. This he did in the interest of peace. It was always an essential condition of that alliance that it should cease to operate if either party entered upon aggressive schemes of its own. I do not mean a spoken or written condition, but an inherent one. France would consider it idle and cruel to talk of it at all, at this particular moment. The possibility of its action hereafter will much depend upon her adopting a pacific temper and policy. Whether she will do this will I think depend on the circumstances under which the war closes. Such conduct at any rate as that of last July will not I think recur: and I freely admit that Europe is a debtor to Germany for having put it out of the question.

30. Fr.

Ch. 8½ AM. Telegrams to Mr West—Ld Granville—Ld Spencer—Wrote to Ld Granville—Mr Stansfeld—Mr Monsell—Sir Thos G.—Mr Reeve—Mr Fortescue—C.G.—and minutes. Sir F. Doyle came: a friend of near 50 years: I believe now my oldest in the world. And a right good one. Read Lear—Dana.

Note conv[ersation] with Ld Hartington D. 30.[2]
No satisfactory arrangement *possible*—from within or without the Cabinet. No example of such a refusal. Necessary to consult the Cabinet. Probably there may be other changes, but I must go to town to consult Colleagues; perhaps call the Cabinet. Effect uncertain: but it will be to radicalise the Governt. Claim not perpetual.[3] His ulterior future.

31. Sat.

Ch. 8½ AM. Wrote to Duchess of Argyll—Mr Fortescue—C.G.—Mr Hugessen—Mr West—Mr Lefevre—Mr Childers—and minutes. Read Quintil. B X—Ovid's Fasti—Lear's Calabria (finished). Conversation with Doyle. Conclave with the Mining Tenants Crossley & Co. We cut down a great tree: it fell ill, by misdirection & bulk: on arm of the Ch. man.

[1] Probably Peel to Bunsen, 10 October 1841, hoping for 'the union and welfare of the German race'; *Bunsen Memoirs* (1868) i. 622.
[2] Misplaced at Add MS 44760, f. 213; dated 1872? by Morley, but clearly refers to this visit; see 29 Dec. 70. Hartington told his father, 31 December 1870, Chatsworth MSS 340. 450: 'I suppose you won't be much surprised to hear that I was bullied into accepting . . . he explained that . . . if I didn't agree . . . [he] must go to consult possibly the Cabinet itself, wh. would probably renew his requests. Of course I could not stand this, so shut up altogether. Gladstone however acknowledged that I could not be expected to stay long in the place, and the residence in Ireland to be reduced to the least proportion.'
[3] This phrase in pencil.

And so falls the curtain on this great year. What revolutions: what crimes: what sorrows: what hopes, refined in the fire, the fire seven times heated. All this out of me. And in me one hope ever gathering that the time may soon arrive when I may in rest & peace care for my soul aright.

Hawarden Jan. 1. 1871. Sunday Circumcision

Ch. mg & H.C.—also evg. Wrote to Mrs Thistlethwayte—Ld Gran-
ville—Mr Goschen—Sir J. Lacaita—Rev W. Goalen—Dr Candlish
—C.G.—and minutes. Read Leighton's Poems[1]—Mr Dale on the
H Eucharist[2]—Tracts. Conversation with Doyle.

2. M.

Ch. 8½ AM. Wrote to Messrs Freshfield—Ld Granville—C.G.—Mr
A. Gordon[3]—Mr Bright—Mr Glyn (Tel.)—and minutes. Cut a tree
with W. & H. Read I Volghi Pelasgici.[4] Arranged Letters. Walk &
conversation with Doyle: among other things on the present posture
of belief. Conversation with Archd. Ffoulkes and with Mr Johnson.

3. Tu.

Overslept myself: a shame! Telegrams to Mr Goschen—Ld Granville.
Wrote to Vsse Brimont-Bressac—Bp of St Andrews—Mr Hopwood
—Chancr of Exr—C.G.—Ld Granville—Mr Gurdon—Mrs Helen
G.—The Queen—Mr Fortescue—Mr Ayrton—Mr Tilley[5]—Mr
Glyn—Miss Marsh—and minutes. This day I broke down all my
arrears by 3.30. In evg came a Messr. Wrote to the Queen (Mem)—
Ld Granville (2)—Mr Hugessen—Ld C. Paget—and minutes. Worked
on accounts. Read Dana.[6]

To R. LOWE, chancellor of the exchequer,   Add MS 44539, f. 121.
3 January 1871.

1. I send you a letter from Tilley with copy of my reply.
2. I send on your suggestion about the Board of Trade[7] to Fortescue with a
recommendation from myself. Will you not find it difficult to effect a compulsory redemption of Land Tax? Probably however you have ascertained your
ground at Somerset House.

[1] W. *Leighton, Poems (1870).
[2] R. W. *Dale, The doctrine of the real presence and of the Lord's Supper (1870).
[3] In T.A.P.S., new series li, part iv. 55.
[4] A. Oliari, Dei Volghi Pelasgici (1870).
[5] See 10 Dec. 52; this letter, on army postage, forwarded to *Lowe; Add MS 44539,
f. 121.
[6] See 19 Dec. 70.
[7] Lowe successfully recommended, 2 January, Add MS 44301, f. 176, transferring the
Board's treaty jurisdiction to the foreign office, and proposed to redeem the land tax to
fund the redemption of army purchase.

4. It seems to me that to found a separate Fund with reference to Purchase would be open to objection on Parliamentary grounds, & would be a retrogressive step in Finance. But I shall be very glad to cooperate with you, should circumstances continue pretty favourable, in keeping the estimates down. Certainly as regards danger, we are, I believe, safer from invasion than we have been for thirty years: & the risk was never great. Will you speak to Cardwell on this subject? The Lord Chancellor would like to see you on the subject of the Law Officers' Fees on Ecclesiastical Commissioners[?] Orders.

5. Of your Currency plan in its main outline I am an ardent supporter: but pray do not suppose it is one of the measures which ought to be introduced with the specific view of returning a fading popularity. Class interests are still too strong in Parliament to give hope that in the debates on such a Bill its public advantage will be allowed to silence particular outcry. The bills on Land would as far as the party are concerned be more likely to *tell* in our favour. Pray continue to give them a cherishing hand, to which I know you are well disposed. You apologise for length, but length is relative: & so estimated your letters are never long. No one can so well stand the judgment on 'every idle word'.

4. Wed.

Ch. 8½ AM. Telegrams to Mr Gurdon——Mr Cardwell——Ld Granville. Wrote to Ld Granville——Mr Cardwell——C.G.——T.S. Gladstone——and minutes. Saw Mr Burnett. Worked again on accounts. Felled a tree with W. Read Dana——Trevelyan.[1]

5. Th.

Ch. 8½ AM. Telegrams to Mr Hugessen——Ld Granville (2)——Mr Gurdon——Mr Cardwell. Wrote to Messrs Freshfield——Ld Granville——Mr Glyn——Mr Cardwell——Mr Gurdon——Ld Halifax——C.G.——Mr Breakenridge——Mr Courtenay——Mr Lefevre——and minutes. Saw Mr Burnett. Felled a tree: with Harry. Read Dana——Trevelyan (finished)——Macrobius.[2]

6. Fr. Epiphany

Ch. 11 AM. C's birthday: all blessings be on her more & more.

Wrote to Ld Granville (& Tel)——Dr Buchanan——Mr Adam——Mr G.E. Street——Mr A. Peel——Hon A. Gordon[3]——C.G.——and minutes. Gave a dinner at Q[ueen's] F[erry] Hotel to the Aston Tenantry some 70 large & (chiefly) small & addressed them on the proper conditions of the important relation established between us. They were

[1] Probably Sir G. O. *Trevelyan, *Speeches on army reform* (1870).
[2] Probably G. F. C. Schoemann, *Commentatio Macrobiana* (1871).
[3] In *T.A.P.S.*, new series li, part iv. 55.

most hearty.[1] Saw Mr Burnett. Read Dana. Finished Blackie on German Songs & Wars.[2] Tea at the Rectory.

To W. P. ADAM, M.P., 6 January 1871. 'Private.'   Add MS 44539, f. 126.

I write to express the extreme concern with which I find it will not be in my power to turn the vacancy created by the retirement of Mr. Bright to account in any opening which I could ask you to fill. It is necessary to fill the vacancy in the official corps on this occasion from the Radical qr., & I am afraid the office you hold would not be available for an offer. Much do I wish it were otherwise for I am confident that the zeal & ability you have shown in your present irksome office would be exerted with advantage to the Govt., & the public in some distinctly administrative post. I hope some other opportunity may speedily arrive.[3]

7. Sat.

Ch. 8½ AM. Wrote to The Queen (& Mem)—Ld Granville—Mr Gurdon—Mr Kinnaird—C.G.—Mr Hibbert—Sir T. Biddulph—Mrs Thistlethwayte—Mr [F. T.] Chamberlain (Certif.)—and minutes. Read Macrobius—Blackie (finished)—Letters on the War—Dana (finished) a noble book.[4] Felled a tree with Harry. Saw the Potters.

8. 1 S.Epiph.

Ch mg & evg. Wrote to Mayor of Bristol—Mr Macknight—C.G.—Mr Childers—The Queen—Herbert J.G.—Ld Granville (Telegr.)—and minutes. Read Robertson & Hergenrother AntiJanus[5]—Macduff M. of Olives.[6]

To T. MACKNIGHT, 8 January 1871.   Add MS 44539, f. 127.

I thank you much for your letter,[7] & for the article which handles its subject so wisely & well, unless it be open to the objection, as it may that it is too favourable to me personally.

As to the Pope's temporal Power & the letter to Mr Dease, there is little doubt from which side the real objection will ultimately proceed. My opinions are unchanged. The report that we were framing a bill on Education such as you describe is wholly without warrant of any kind.

[1] The Aston estate, soon in turmoil, see 9 June 74.   [2] See 26 Dec. 70.
[3] Adam replied contentedly on 11 January; Add MS 44095, f. 6; but on 26 July 1873 he complained at being passed over for chief whip 'after more than *eight years*' as whip; ibid., f. 10.   [4] See 13 Jan. 71.
[5] J. A. G. Hergenroether, tr. J. B. Robertson, *Anti-Janus* (1870).
[6] J. R. Macduff, *Memories of Olivet* (1868).
[7] Not traced; Macknight edited the *Northern Whig* and was attempting to improve the govt's. image in Ulster; see Macknight to Gladstone, 22 Feb. 1871, Add MS 44429, f. 249.

9. M.

Ch. 8½ AM. Wrote to Ld Granville—The Queen—Mrs Barber—Mr G. Glyn—Scotts—Mr Clay (Tel)—C.G.—Chancr of Exr—and minutes. We dined at the Rectory. Read Macrobius—What a chapter on Slaves! Xty working in a Pagan.[1] Read Thucyd B.I. Tried a little my trochaics in the 11th Odyssey. We worked the snowplough.

10. Tu.

Ch. 8½ AM. Wrote to Mrs Thistlethwayte—Mr West (Tel.)—Chancr of Exr—Mr Monsell—Bp of London—Abp of Canterb.—Robn G. —Bp of Winchester—C.G.—Mr Cowper Temple—Comte A. de Gasparin[2]—Mr Macfie MP.—Lady Kimberley[3]—& minutes. Busied with all my preparations for departure: but arrested them on a Tel. from Glyn at 8 P.M.[4] Read Stigand on Sieges of Paris.[5]

To R. A. MACFIE, M.P., 10 January 1871.   Add MS 44539, f. 130.

It is impossible to read without a deep interest the letter of M. Benard which you have been kind enough to send me.[6] We, who witness with the deepest pain the continued & increasing horrors of the War must not be surprised if in that agony—for such it is though it is an agony of heroism—in which the people of Paris fight for their country, our motives, and even our acts, are not always correctly apprehended.

There is no request before us as from the French Government for recognition. There never has been any since the mission of M. Thiers, several months ago, very shortly indeed after the Government was formed. Yet, for every practical purpose we have proceeded towards and with them just as if their origin had been the most formal in the world, and never by word or act have we implied that they were not entitled in the highest degree to our sympathy & respect.[7]

To A. C. TAIT, Archbishop of Canterbury,   Tait MSS, 88, f. 100.
10 January 1871.

I have received with much pleasure the account contained in your letter of the 27th[8] of the great progress which you have made, & which I trust may be continued. The letter itself & the enclosure addressed to the Bishop of London

[1] See 5 Jan. 71.
[2] A. E. de Gasparin had sent his *Appel au patriotisme et au bon sens* (1871), on Alsace; Add MS 44539, f. 130.
[3] Florence, *née* Fitzgibbon, m. 1847 1st earl of Kimberley and d. 1895; promising to bear in mind her request for a govt. post for Lord Bury; Add MS 44539, f. 129.
[4] Not found.
[5] W. Stigand, 'French unity', *Contemporary Review*, xvi. 321 (January 1871).
[6] Not found. Perhaps from Théodore A. N. Benard, 1808-73; French journalist.
[7] Published, without Macfie's name, in *The Globe* and *The Times*, 1 Feb. 1871, 11e.
[8] From San Remo, Add MS 44330, f. 168, with enclosure to bp. of London on ritualism.

shall at once be brought under the notice of my colleagues who I am sure will consider them in the spirit of cooperation for all useful purposes.

The Bishop of Winchester has written to me with reference to the Clergy Resignation, & he will have my best assistance in any attempt to extricate the Bill from controversy & to pass it in some form generally approved.

The present plethora of legislative matter will make it difficult for the Government to charge itself during the present year with any contested question in Church matters.[1] In another year it is quite possible that the same difficulty might not be felt. The circumstances of the two last years were exceptional, & caused to some extent a block in the ordinary business of the State. The plan of working in the House of Commons through some distinguished independent member, on certain subjects, is well worthy of consideration. By the same post with Your Grace's letter I have received one relating to the same subject from the Bishop of London.

11. Wed.

Ch. 8½ A.M. Telegrams to Mr West—Mr Glyn—Mrs Thistlethwayte. Wrote to Messrs Freshfield—Dr Bennett[2]—Mr Childers—A. Beresford Hope—Mr West—Mr Hammond—Mr Bruce—Count Cadorna —C.G.—and minutes. Tried some correction of my version of the shield [of Achilles]. Read Copleston on Æschylus[3]—Hope on Irish Church[4]—Gasparin on Alsace.[5] Kibbled a tree with Harry. Saw Mr Burnett.

To Dr W. C. BENNETT, 11 January 1871.   Add MS 44539, f. 131.

I have to thank you for your prompt & obliging intimation of the result of the meeting at Greenwich,[6] & also for the energetic & successful part which you appear personally to have taken in the management of the proceedings. I was also greatly obliged by your giving to Mr. Glyn your views on the question whether it was expedient for me to visit the Borough at the present juncture.

12. Th.

Ch. 8½ AM. Wrote to Bp of London—Ld Granville—Ld Spencer— Mr Cardwell—C.G.—and minutes. Felled a tree with Harry. Read

[1] Tait was annoyed at delays in ecclesiastical legislation; Marsh, *Victorian church*, 103.
[2] Dr. W. C. Bennett, liberal organiser in Greenwich; on 9 January 'one of the wildest scenes witnessed of late in a public building' characterised the meeting held to defend Gladstone against demands for his resignation; *The Times*, 10 Jan. 1871, 12f.
[3] R. S. Copleston, *Aeschylus* (1870).
[4] A. J. Beresford Hope, *The Irish Church and its formularies* (1870).
[5] See 10 Jan. 71.
[6] Bennett's account untraced; Gurdon told F. H. Hill, editor of the *Daily News* (9 Jan. 1871, Add MS 44429, f. 22) that Gladstone's visit there was postponed 'on account of the local question of which the opposite party seem to make a free use'.

Duke of A.s Iona[1]—Cordery's Iliad.[2] Worked on correcting 'The Shield'. We had tea with Ellen Griffiths: a feast.

To EARL SPENCER, Irish lord lieutenant,   Add MS 44539, f. 133.
12 January 1871.

I think you were quite right to hold firm & energetic language in Westmeath,[3] & I am very glad to find it was well received. At the same time I hope we are far from the necessity as yet of new exceptional legislation though if we had come to it there are other things I should like to try or at least to sift & weigh before reverting to such an expedient as the suspension of the Habeas Corpus Act. On that subject, it is worth while to look at the first of Ld. Russell's published volumes of Speeches. I will circulate your letter & address among my Colleagues.[4] I think I may congratulate you individually on the successful issue of the conversation with Hartington.

13. Fr.

Ch. 8½ A.M. Telegrams to Dr Hook (2)—Ld Granville—Wrote to Ld Granville—Mr Dana—Chancr of Exr—Mr Bruce—Mr Rathbone— Mr West—Mr Parratt—Mrs Potter—Mr Chamberlain—and minutes. Saw Mrs Outram, the widow. Felled a tree with W. & H. Wrote out fair my corrections of the version of the Shield. Read Ov. Fasti B. II. finished—Iona (finished)—Beale on Disease Germs[5] and. . . .

To R. H. DANA, 13 January 1871.   Add MS 44539, f. 137.

At the time when you were so good as to send me your book 'Two Years before the Mast', & even when I had the pleasure of meeting you at Mr. Motley's, tho' very sensible of your kindness, I was not fully aware of the value of the Gift. It was still among my innumerable arrears. But I have been fortunate enough lately to find or steal time for reading it, & I cannot omit to convey to you the tribute of my admiration, though I know that in so doing I only add a stone to the heap. This sentiment, which is kindled by the whole strain of the book reaches its climax with the patriotic passage at the close. I trust it will have a permanent place in literature, & this not only in your own country but at least in mine also.[6]

To W. RATHBONE, M.P., 13 January 1871.   Add MS 44539, f. 135.

Your letter[7] can require no apology. The intention of the Government so far as it has been matured, was to reintroduce the University Tests Bill of last year

---

[1] G. D. *Campbell, duke of Argyll, 'Iona', reprinted from *Good Words* (1870).
[2] *The Iliad*, tr. J. G. Cordery, 2 v. (1871).
[3] Spencer's report of 10 January 1871 of his visit to Westmeath, Add MS 44307, f. 1.
[4] Their comments at Add MS 44760, ff. 3-5.
[5] L. S. *Beale, *Disease germs; their real nature* (1870).
[6] Dana's grateful reply of 11 Feb. 1871 is at Add MS 44429, f. 198.
[7] Untraced.

in the first week after the assembling of Parliament and to avail themselves of the less crowded period of the Session for sending it to the House of Lords at a very early period.

They attach much value to the measure. They think the controversy with regard to it has been exhausted; & much as they regretted its rejection by the House of Lords they remember that it occurred near the close of a Session which had already been one of great legislative labour, and they have hoped that the vote would not be repeated when the measure should be presented say in the month of March, under far more favourable circumstances, & after that house has had the opportunity of obtaining by its Committee, the information of which it conceived itself to stand in need.

In this state of things I learned that a portion of the active promoters of the measure were disposed to extend & alter its provisions by introducing clauses for the abolition of Clerical fellowships & offices in the Colleges; which now rest upon conditions determined by the Commissioners appointed by Parliament in 1854 & 1856. The new aspect which would thus be given to the measure renders the resolution of the Government inapplicable, if the disposition which has been indicated to me should prove to be at all general among the promoters of the movement against the Tests. I understand it to be the object of the projected meeting in Liverpool to support & recommend the measure as it stood last year which abolishes every denominational disability in the Colleges. You cannot I think go wrong in stating that the Government are ready to proceed upon the intention which I described at the outset of this letter, should they have reason to believe that in so doing they would act conformably to the views & receive the general support of those who were last year friendly to the Bill.

14. Sat. [London]

Off at 8¾. Reached London C.H.T. before 3. Wrote to Sir Geo. Grey —Sir H. Rawlinson—Scotts—and minutes. Worked much post in the train. Found Herbert looking well, but still on the sofa. Saw Ld Granville—Mr Cardwell[1]—Dr Clark—A. Kinnaird—Lord Tenterden.[2] Dined at Granville's: and conversation till near midnight. Read Gasparin's Alsace Neutre.

15. 2 S.Epiph.

Chapel Royal with C. mg & aft. Wrote to Dean of Chichester—and minutes. Saw Ld Granville—Mr Monsell—Mr Bruce—Dined with J. Wortley. Putting things away. Read Union Review[3]—Oliphant's St Francis[4]—Goulburn's Personal Rel.[5]

[1] Meeting to discuss army estimates; Add MS 44539, f. 135. See 20 Jan. 71.
[2] Charles Stuart Aubrey *Abbott, 1834–82; 3rd Baron Tenterden 1870; sec. to commissioners in Washington February–May 1871; subsequently in foreign office.
[3] *Union Review* (January 1871).
[4] M. O. *Oliphant, *Francis of Assisi* (1868).   [5] See 28 May 65.

16. M.

Wrote to Mr C. Williams[1]—Ld Hartington—Dr Ellis[2]—Mr Stanhope—Mrs Barton—Mrs Hamilton—and minutes. Saw Duke of Argyll—Ld Granville—Mr Ellis—Mr Stanhope—Mr West. Saw Chester X. Dined at [blank]. Read the Abn Correspondence of 1813.[3]

17. Tu.

Wrote to the Queen Mem.—Ld Granville—Mr Kinnaird—Dean Hook—and minutes. Saw Mr Cardwell $10\frac{1}{2}$–$12\frac{1}{2}$. on Military affairs.—Charterhouse Governors' Meeting $1\frac{1}{4}$–4. to elect a Master. (Dr Currey).[4] Saw Bp of London—Saw L. Sinclair now Barton—Sad, and touching[R]. Dined with J. Wortley. Read Aberdeen Correspondence.

18. Wed.

Wrote to Ld Lyttelton—Dr Payne Smith—The Speaker—Mrs Barton—Mr Glyn (Telegr)—Ld Sydney—Sol. General—Ld Bowmont[5]—Dean of Waterford—Mr [S.] Morley[6]—The Queen—& minutes. Saw Archbishop of York—Sir R. Phillimore—Mr Baxter—F. Rogers—Scotts—D. Salomons—Mr Kinnaird *cum* Mr Chambers[7]—Mr Miall & Univ. Test Depn.[8] Dined at Ld Granville's. Read Abn Correspondence—[Gasparin's] Alsace Neutre.

To J. E. DENISON, the Speaker, 18 January 1871.   Add MS 44539, f. 138.

Will you kindly consider & mature your plans upon the subject of a Committee on the business of the H. of C. which we promised last year to propose. By the time you come up, you will I daresay be prepared to give me the benefit of

---

[1] i.e. J. Carvell *Williams; forwarding his letter to Rathbone (see 13 Jan. 71), and requesting a deputation be not sent; Add MS 44539, f. 136. See 18 Jan. 71.

[2] Robert Ellis, physician attending *Childers, who wished to resign through ill-health; Childers to have four weeks off; Add MS 44539, f. 136. *The Times*, 19 January 1871, wrongly reported his resignation.

[3] Further instalment of proofs of A. *Gordon's ed. of his father's correspondence; see Conacher, *The Aberdeen Coalition*, 567; see Add MS 44539, ff. 144–7.

[4] George Currey, 1816–85; grammarian and master of Charterhouse from 1871.

[5] James Henry Robert Innes-Ker, 1839–92; styled marquis of Bowmont; liberal M.P. Roxburgh 1870–4; 7th duke of Roxburgh 1879. Asking him to move the Address; he refused, Add MS 44539, f. 138.

[6] Asking him to second the Address.

[7] They expressed liberal anxiety about the supposed anti-Protestantism of Gladstone's letter to Dease (see 30 Nov. 70); see *The Times*, 23 Jan. 1871, 8a.

[8] No report found.

your judgment. Sir G. Grey writes, & I think wisely that the Commee. should be appointed early.

I have not yet read the article in the Edinburgh Review.[1]

To VISCOUNT SYDNEY, lord chamberlain,   Add MS 44539, f. 138.
18 January 1871.

I am assured that the idle & foolish language of a very few individuals, so disrespectful & disloyal towards the Queen, is not at all likely to find expression or countenance on such a national occasion as will be offered by the meeting of Parliament. Please to let me know if you think the Queen intends by your letter to approve of its being announced that she proposes to open Parliament. I will pay attention to the honour[?] to which you refer.[2]

19. Th.

Wrote to The Queen—Mrs Childers (Tel.)—Mr Bruce—Lady Aveland—Mr Kinnaird—Mrs Childers[3]—Mr Hardcastle—The Queen (Tel)—Mr Cardwell—& minutes. Saw Mr Moffatt—Mr Ayrton—Mr Goschen—Ld Halifax—Mr West (2)—Mr M'Coll—Mr Levy—Ld Granville. Cabinet 3½-6¾. Dined with Sir W. Farquhar. Saw Graham: now at home: promised a book[R]. Read Gasparin's Alsace —finished—M. Chevalier on the Neutral Powers.[4]

Cabinet Jan 19. 71. 3.30 PM[5]
√ Letter to Mr Dease. Kinnaird's inquiry.[6]
√ Univ. Tests—Deputation. Expected letter.
√ Conference: account of, & directions as to equivalents. Kimberley, Fortescue, Halifax, Forster—to assist Ld Granville in regard to Danube commission.[7]
√ Recognition of French Govt. Adhere to present course but in terms wh. wd. not preclude our changing it.
√ Protest agt. the Bombardment of Paris.
√ Volunteers contumaciously determining to attend officially on Jules Favre agt. prohibition to be dismissed.

To E. CARDWELL, war secretary, 19 January 1871.   Add MS 44539, f. 140.

I enclose a note from Lowe just received.[8] This proposal has been a perfect bombshell to me. It is the sudden proposal as a wing to a vast measure of army

[1] [E. Knatchbull-Hugessen], 'Business of the House of Commons', *Edinburgh Review*, cxxxiii. 57 (January 1871).
[2] Sydney's letter untraced.
[3] Arranging with Emily, wife of H. C. E. *Childers, for visit this day of *Halifax to coordinate denial of *The Times'* statement of Childers' resignation; Add MS 44539, f. 139.
[4] Untraced article by M. Chevalier.
[5] Add MS 44639, f. 2.   [6] See 30 Nov. 70, 18 Jan. 71n.
[7] European commission on Danube navigation; F.O.C.P. 1911, 1913; see 28 Jan. 71.
[8] Not found, but see 3 Jan. 71.

change, of a measure the most destructive to our finance that has been either adopted or suggested in my time. To have been for near ten years the finance minister of this country, & to end my career with a loan in aid of the annual expenditure for the redemption of Commissions is not possible. Had I known of this some time ago I would have tried to get up the case: at the present moment you may well believe it is for me as impossible as it is to assent to the proposal which comes before me under circumstances so strange & unexpected. If the proposal did not require an almost immediate decision, I would readily undertake to examine it as soon as I could, but it would be idle to give any such pledge in the present stage of foreign affairs, & of the preparation of legislative measures.

[P.S.] I do not admit as far as I understand the case that Goschen's plans can or should be crippled, or that we are about to enter as matter of course, on a period of increased military charge. But if we were it would be more not less necessary to keep the increase under the view of Parliament from year to year.

20. Fr.

Wrote to Rev. H. Glynne—A. Kinnaird—Ld Granville—Rev H. Glynne—Mr Kinnaird—Rev J. L. Ross—Bss Rothschild—The Queen—Mr S. Morley—& minutes. Saw Mr Baxter—Mr Cardwell 11-1.—Ld Granville—Ld Halifax. Cabinet 3¼-7 on the military plans. Read Abn Correspondence.

Cabinet Jan 20. 71. 3 PM[1]
√ Mr Cardwell: Abolition of purchase. Army Estimates increase 3 ₥ perhaps a trifle more. And other points[2]
√ Mr Forster: Committee on Scots Educn. Bill: Duke of Argyll, Mr Bruce, Mr Forster, Mr Forster [*sic*]
√ Peers Bankrupts Bill: also for Commons. Chancellor to prepare an outline.

21. Sat.

Wrote to Mr D. Gordon—Mr W.E. Forster—Sir Geo. Grey—Ld M. of Dublin—Mr Glyn—Canon Mozley—Bp of Moray—Mr Cardwell —Mr Childers—and minutes. Dined with Gen. Fox. Read Abn Corrsp.—Testament d'Eumolpe.[3] Saw Baron Rothschild—Duke of Cambridge[4]—Mr Carvell Williams—Sir J. Lacaita—C. Cadorna— Mr Merivale. Saw Hamilton[R].

---

[1] Add MS 44639, f. 3.
[2] Probably the duke of *Cambridge; see *Cardwell to Gladstone, 9 and 17 January 1871, Add MS 44119, ff. 202-7.
[3] *Sic*; untraced.
[4] On siting of new War Office; Add MS 44539, f. 141.

To G. G. GLYN, chief whip, 21 January 1871.   Add MS 44348, f. 81.
'Very Private.'

I hope Mrs Glyn is now very greatly restored: & if so as the Cabinet meets on Wednesday & perhaps also Thursday or Friday for Bills, I shall be very glad if you can be in Town at the time.

Bowmont declines in a kind note: Morley ponders.

Are you sure of your Private Secretary's due reserve? All the recent appointments prematurely appeared cut and dried in the Observer. I understand the Editor had been for half an hour with Mr C[lay] on the previous day. The Queen complains loudly, & had desired me to enquire, which I should have done before but for domestic troubles.[1]

22. 3 S.Epiph.

Whitehall Chapel mg. Ch. Royal aft., both times with Harry. Wrote to C.G.—Ld Granville—Mrs Barton—and minutes. Called on Sir R. Murchison—Saw Ld Granville (2)—Saw V. Stewart. Read B. Brown First Principles[2]—B. Scuile, Religion & Science.[3] Dined with the Farquhars.

23. M.

Wrote to Ld Granville—Mr K. Hodgson *cum* Mr Morley—Mrs Conynghame[4]—Mr Tupper—Ld Hartington—C.G.—Abp of Canterb.—Mr Rawson—Mr Hamilton of Dalzell[5]—and minutes. Took Harry into the City for his start in commerce.[6] Saw Mr Ouvry—Ld Granville—Mr Goschen *cum* Chr of Exr—D. of Sutherland *cum* Mr Pender—Mr Brand. Dined with the Farquhars. Read Letters of A Stabr[7]—Dyson Wood on Hamlet[8]—Q.R. on RigVeda.[9]

To A. C. TAIT, archbishop of Canterbury,   Tait MSS 91, f. 10.
23 January 1871.

I have only this morning received your Grace's letter of the 14th;[10] and I am apprehensive, not only of difficulties about the Athanasian Creed but of diffi-

[1] Glyn replied, Add MS 44348, f. 84, 'I do not suspect Clay. . . .'.
[2] J. B. *Brown, *First principles of ecclesiastical truth* (1871).
[3] Untraced.
[4] Jane St. Maur Blanche, *née* Stanhope, m. 1854 3rd Marquis Conyngham; on a request for a position; Add MS 44539, f. 142.
[5] Asking John Glencairn Carter-Hamilton (1829-1900, liberal M.P. S. Lanark 1868-74, 1880-6, cr. Baron 1886) to propose the Address; Add MS 44539, f. 143.
[6] In the office of James Wyllie, the London branch of Gladstone, Wyllie and Co., the Calcutta traders; see I. Thomas, *Gladstone of Hawarden* (1936), 39.
[7] Word smudged.
[8] W. D. Wood, *Hamlet from a psychological point of view* (1870).
[9] *Quarterly Review*, cxxix. 182 (July 1870).
[10] Add MS 44330; Marsh, *Victorian church*, 44.

culties which the Athanasian Creed may impart into the whole question of legislation on the Report of the Ritual Commission. I am indeed inclined to regret that that portion of Your Grace's Letter[1] which referred to the Creed was published before some kind of partial agreement had been arrived at as to the course to be pursued.

What the Government are unable to do is to charge themselves with a heavy ecclesiastical controversy on the occasion of a Session which promises to fall short of none of the preceding ones in the severity of the labours imposed upon them. It is not that they grudge or limit their own exertions but that when already charged with more than they can hope to do, there is a point at which they cannot properly make fresh additions.

The first question therefore which they will ask is what is the legislation which is most likely to be adopted with something like general consent. Unhappily the Commission has made a recommendation so damaged by Dissents as to be destitute of all authority. Dean Stanley recommends that the use of the Creed be permissive. Without doubt a moderate suggestion but would it fulfil the condition I have described of attaining general adhesion of Clergy & Laity?

We shall however I can assure Your Grace look at the question with the anxious desire to find some method of settlement by which that condition will be fulfilled. In the meantime I will send your Grace's letter at once to the Chancellor & Home Secretary.

24. Tu.

Wrote to Mr Burnett—The Queen Mema (2)—Mr Douglas Gordon —Mr Reeve—Ld Chancellor—and minutes. Conclave at F.O. $3\frac{1}{2}$–5 on Telegr. to be sent to Sir E. Thornton.[2] Saw Ld Granville—Mr M'Coll—Ld Greville. Read Abn Correspondence—Guizot's Letter[3] —Ed.Rev. on France.[4]

To H. REEVE, editor of the *Edinburgh Review*,   Add MS 44539, f. 144.
24 January 1871.

I have just received & on receiving read M. Guizot's letter:[5] an extraordinary effort & achievement for a brain so long in active exercise. My first duty is to make it known to my Colleagues & this leads me to ask whether I rightly infer from your note that it will appear *immediately* in the public journals?[6] For it will be more readily perused there than in the close though very remarkable MS.

[1] Tait to bp. of London on church legislation, 27 December 1870, published in *The Guardian*, 11 January 1871, 37.
[2] The crisis of the 'Alabama' negotiations; see Cook, *The Alabama Claims*, 164.
[3] Guizot had sent (via H. Reeve, Add MS 44429, f. 86) an enormous letter, printed in *The Times*, 26 Jan. 1871, 4a, calling for British protests against Germany.
[4] *Edinburgh Review*, cxxxiii. 1 (January 1871); by H. *Reeve.
[5] Forwarded this day unopened by Reeve, but with statement of its imminent publication; Add MS 44429, f. 86.
[6] Reeve's second letter this day states the letter will be in next day's *Times*; ibid., f. 103.

25. Wed. Conversion of St Paul.

Wrote to Mr Cardwell—The Queen—and minutes. Cabinet $2\frac{3}{4}$-$6\frac{1}{4}$.
Saw A. Cooper: satisfactory[R]. Wrote Sessional Circular: Mem. on
Seaforth Church.[1] Saw Mr Glyn on legislation of the Session. Saw
W.H.G.—Mr M'Coll—Bp of Winchester—Ld Halifax—Mr Glyn.
Dined at Mr Hankey's: principally a City party. Read Rescue Soc.s
Report—Aberdeen Correspondence.

Cabinet Jan. 25. 71. 2. 30 PM[2]
√ Case of Mr Otway & the Turkish papers discussed.
  Consideration of Bills.
  1. Univ. Tests. WEG. Letter of the Ch[ancello]r read.[3] 2. Eccl.
  Titles. Select Comm[ittee] on Wording. 3. Army Organization.   √ Class
  First day when estimates can be moved. 4. Secret Voting. 5.   I
  Trades Union Bill.
√ On Secret Voting Bill. Glyn called in. Scrutiny.
  Trades Union Bill. To be taken early. [Proposer] To be named in Cabinet.[4]
  Scotch Education. Speech. To be named in Cabinet.
√ Second order of Bills. Scotch Educn. Licensing. Local Rating. (Death Duties)
√ Third Order. Bills to be considered of if circumstances permit.
  I. 1. Univ. Tests. WEG? 2. Eccl. Titles. 3. Army Organization. 4 Secret Voting:
  Scrutiny? 5. Trades Union. 6, 7. Chancellor's Bills.
  II Scotch Education. Licensing. Local Rating. (Death Duties).
  III Landed Successions. Transfer of Land. Currency. Ritual Commission. Re-
  demption of Land Tax.
  Lords: Vagrancy—Parl. Bankruptcy.—W[est] I[ndian] Federation.

26. Th.

Wrote to Sol. General—The Viceroy—Mr Bruce—The Queen
(Mem.)—Mr Lefevre—Dean of Lichfield—Mr Hammond—Dr
Miller—Mr Hamilton MP.—Bp of Lincoln—L. Barton[R]—and
minutes. Saw Ld de Grey—Mr Glyn—Ld Granville—Dr A. Clark.
Failed to find Hastings—Wilkinson[R]. Read Aberdeen Corresp.—
Ed.Rev. on Military Forces.[5]

To EARL SPENCER, Irish lord lieutenant,   Add MS 44539, f. 144.
26 January 1871. 'Private.'

I will recommend Lisgar for the Lord Lieutenancy of Cavan.
I am sure you will forgive me if, while I fully appreciate the motive, I regret
that you should be disposed to consider, & to recommend upon the state of

---

[1] Undated, in Add MS 44759, f. 245; and see ibid., 44429, f. 82.
[2] Add MS 44639, f. 4.
[3] Probably from *Salisbury, chancellor of Oxford university from 1869, who strongly
opposed repeal of the tests; see Cecil, *Salisbury*, ii. 21.
[4] See 28 Jan. 71.   [5] *Edinburgh Review*, cxxxiii. 207 (January 1871).

Ireland apart from the Chief Secretary. Is he not after all officially your natural coadjutor as well as personally one whose fresh & impartial mind would be likely to be of use. It seems to me that the working of our Government at large depends on nothing so much as on this that we are all of us commonly restrained from giving way to influences derived from one quarter or one side of a subject & constrained to make our own minds the meeting point (no pleasant process) on all influences from wheresoever derived that bear upon it. Forgive this little dose of doctrine.

It occurred to me that the St Patrick might stand over till the adjustment of the Fees was fully decided on.

27. Fr.

Wrote to Sir D. Salomons—The Queen (1. and telegr.)—Ld Granville—Mr Rawson—T.S. Gladstone—Bp of Manchester—Ld Chancellor—& minutes. Saw Mr Bruce—Mr Glyn—Ld Granville—Sir R. Phillimore. Nine to dinner.

Went to see Mrs Barton.[1] She asked me 3 questions. 1. Did I advise her to marry Mr D.? 2. Wd I give her away? 3. What ansr shd I make to Mr Larkins or any one inquiring about her. I replied (1) I shd be a bad adviser; & why. (2) No: it wd be in me dishonest. (3.) I shd reply that, taking all in all, I had a sincere regard for her: and say nothing more. Read Abn Correspondence—Bradlaugh on Land.[2]

28. Sat.

Wrote to Mr M'Clure—Rev. J. Baldwin Brown—Rev. W.M. Mayow—Lord Kimberley—Mr Max Müller—The Queen (2)—Ld Salisbury[3]—and minutes. Read Traité de Paix[4]—Aberdeen Correspondence. Saw Mr Ayrton—Ld Granville—do *cum* D. of Argyll—Ld Halifax—Mr Glyn—Ld Lyttelton. Dined with the Lytteltons.

Cabinet Ja 28. 71. 2.30[5]

√ Chancellors Bills—to come in in H. of C. in concert with Law Officers.
√ Guizot Letter to WEG—only mention.[6]
√ Conference.[7] *Etats Riverains* in reference to the access to the Black Sea. Turkey refuses the phrase. We cannot carry pressure to extremes. Perhaps put off Tuesday's meeting. Let Austria try what she can do.

[1] i.e. L. Sinclair; see 8 Aug. 66, 17 Jan. 71 and above, v. lxi.
[2] C. *Bradlaugh, The land, the people, the coming struggle* (1871).
[3] Gladstone this day sent Gasparin's pamphlet (see 10 Jan. 71) to *Max Müller and *Salisbury; Add MS 44539, f. 146. See 30 Jan. 71.
[4] J. Vila y Pons, *Le traité de paix* (1871).
[5] Add MS 44639, f. 6. [6] See 24 Jan. 71.
[7] On the Black Sea, which opened in London on 17 January 1871. The session was postponed; see Ramm I, i. 214n. and 19 Jan. 71.

√ Bruce. Trades Union Bill explained: provisions discussed. It is to be circulated. Principle to prevent violence; & in all economic matters the law to take
no part.[1]

√ U.S. demand for a previous understanding that there shall be a money payment.[2]

√ Greek proposal unsatisfactory (with reference to further prosecutions).[3]

√ Cardwell mentioned Hartington's wishes a. for the immediate provision of
a retirement to follow the abolition of purchase b. for the earlier use of conscription to provide trained men. Stand over.

√ Shall India bear a share of the cost of redeeming purchase?[4] Argyll urged it
should *not*. Conversation. Decision postponed.

√ Cardwell mentioned the controversy between Col. Hamley & Mr Gleig.[5] Inconvenience of the connection of such officers with the Press. Mild caution
to be given.

29. 4 S.Epiph.

Ch. Royal mg & aft. Saw Ld Granville—Sir Walter James. Wrote to
Duchess of Newcastle—Hon. A. Gordon—Lord Lisgar—minutes.
Read Mosaic Theory[6]—Baldwin Brown First Principles—Goodsir
on Pagan Inspiration &c.[7]

30. M.

Wrote to The Queen (Mem)—Mr Maclaren—The Speaker—Sir S.
Robinson[8]—Sir E. May—Mr Max Müller—M. Guizot—Mr Waterfield[9]—Mr Cardwell—Sir T. Biddulph—Scotts—Mr Kinnaird—&
minutes. Saw Mr M'Coll—Ld Halifax—Mr Forster—Ld Granville
—Mrs Th. Read Hist. of Rickmansworth[10]—Aberdeen Correspondence. Dined at home. Conversation with Harry on his work, wh he
at the moment feels rather severe.

[1] Draft of the bill in Add MS 44616; in Gladstone's hand, the number of persons consti-
tuting a picket is reduced from six to three—reduced to one in the Act.

[2] Arranged for Britain to propose a commission on Canadian/U.S. disputes, and that the
U.S. should agree, provided the 'Alabama' claims were included; Cook, *The Alabama Claims*,
166.

[3] In the Greek murders affair; F.O.C.P. 1896, 1914.   [4] See 11 Feb. 71.

[5] Row on war requisitions in *The Times*, 27 Jan. 1871, 11a.

[6] Perhaps J. Hamilton, *Moses, the man of God* (1871).

[7] J. T. Goodsir, *Seven homilies on ethnic inspiration* (1871).

[8] Gladstone's correspondence (30 Jan.–12 Feb. 1871) with Robinson on his dismissal by
Childers, printed in *The Times*, 16 Feb. 1871, 10e.

[9] O. Waterfield, apparently a publisher; Gladstone encouraged publication of the Aberdeen correspondence of 1813 and suggested improvements (see 16 Jan. 71): 'I have now
read near 400 pages': Add MS 44539, f. 148.

[10] Untraced.

To F. Max MÜLLER, 30 January 1871.   Max Müller MSS, d. 170.

I think that your letter[1] is alike noteworthy for its clear intelligence, and for its high and just moral sense. The former is rare enough in the world. The latter in such times & circumstances as those which have fallen upon Germany, is of necessity much rarer still. I should think it uncertain whether Gasparin's pamphlet[2] has reached Count Bismarck: perhaps I should say it is improbable. I wish it could.

You put to me a fair question: could Count Gasparin persuade the Great Powers to guarantee the neutrality of Alsace, if France & Germany had put the question into his hands?

I will try to give you a fair answer. You will not think it less fair because it is individual and unofficial: for a man must be a wretch indeed, who could speak, at this most solemn juncture, otherwise than from the bottom of his heart.

First then I agree with you in disapproving the declaration, or reputed declaration, of Lord Derby (then Stanley) in 1867, about the Luxembourg guarantee.[3] I have in Parliament, & in my present office, declined or expressly foreborne to recognise that guarantee. Secondly, as to the main question. It is great. It is difficult. But I should not despair. I may add I should desire to find it practicable; for I think it would be a condition fair to both parties and one on which Germany would have an absolute title to insist. I say this, well knowing that guarantees may be for us very real things; an opinion, of the strength of which we gave some evidence in the month of July last with reference to Belgium.

I will add a few words. There are some great countries in Europe, whose foreign policy is not yet determined for them in a pacific sense by circumstances wholly or partly independent of their will. But this, which is one, is not now the only country falling into that category. Italy, for the purposes of this question, is nearly in the same position as England. And Austria is likewise, I conceive, now in the same position, with reference to all questions unless they be Eastern. There is therefore much material to count upon and to work with.

Some of the most excusable errors ever committed have also been the most ruinous in their consequences. Such was, I should say, our going, or Mr Pitt's going, to war in 1793. The smallest, in the *forum* of conscience, they are the greatest in the vast theatre of action. May your country, justly indignant, and justly exultant, be preserved from committing one of *these* errors.

[P.S.] With reference to a rumour which has reached me, let me assure you that I had nothing whatever to do with the letters of your antagonist Scrutator [M. MacColl] beyond casually supplying the author, on chancing to see him, with a single reference about hankerings after Alsace and Lorraine. I at the same time supplied him with a notable one of French hankering after the Rhine.

31. Tu.

Wrote to Bp of Peterborough—Mr Baxter—Mr Barker—Sir S. Robinson—Ld Halifax—& minutes. Received Deputation of Irish Schoolmasters.[4] Saw Monsignor Stonor—Mr Stansfield [*sic*]—Miss Wyse—Chancr of Exchr—Mr Fortescue. Eleven to dinner. Read

[1] Of 29 January 1871, Add MS 44251, f. 303, on Gasparin.   [2] See 28 Jan. 71n.
[3] On 9 May 1867 at the Luxemburg conference; Millman, 89.
[4] See *The Times*, 1 Feb. 1871, 6d.

Abn Correspondence—Divers pamphlets on the War—Hist of Rickmansworth.

Wed. Feb. One. 1871.

Wrote to Ld Granville—Sir H. Campbell—The Queen (2)—Miss
Wyse—Mr Milbank—and minutes. Cabinet 2½-5. Saw Mr Reitlinger
—Ld Vernon—D. of Argyll—Mr Cardwell—Mrs Th. Lay up in evg
on account of growing cold. Read Abn Corresp.—Hist Rickmansworth
(finished).

Cabinet Wed. Feb. 1. 71. 2½ PM[1]
√ Message to U.S. Agree to Telegram rec[eive]d yesty.[2]
√ Message to Paris respecting revictualling—agreed to.[3]
√ Conference.[4] Austrian proposal—bad. Articles as drafted distinguished non-
   riverain Powers to be surrendered on the ground of Turkish objection. Q[uer]y
   whether to keep the Art. I as it now is—or take the Turkish propos[itio]n to
   have a discretion to let in [to the Black Sea ships of] the Puissances Armies
   or Alliées. Allow the 2 Danube vessels to be (optionally) large instead of small
   —if not objected to.
√ Formation of Commission for U.S. questions. Granville to see Derby.[5] prob.
   ask Sir G. Grey.
   Forster to take the Ballot Bill.

2. Th.

Kept my bed all day. Saw only Mr West & W.H.G. on business. Also
Dr Clark. Wrote Circular on C.B.s[6]—To Sir S. Robinson—Ld Granville—& minutes. Read Abn Corresp. finished—Motley & Fish Corresp. do.[7]

3. Fr.

In bed still but improving. Saw Mr West—WHG—Dr Clark—Ld
Granville in evg. Wrote to Ld Granville (2)—D. of Norfolk—Scotts
—Sir C. Trevelyan—and minutes. Read Q.R. on Lessons of the War

---

[1] Add MS 44639, f. 8.
[2] Consolidating agreement for the commission; see Cook, *The Alabama Claims*, 166 and
28 Jan. 71.
[3] British aid to be supplied on joint French and German request; Ramm I, i. 213.
[4] See Ramm I, i. 214.
[5] The British commissioners were: de Grey, Thornton, M. Bernard, Northcote, and Sir
John MacDonald, prime minister of Canada, with Tenterden as secretary. Derby and Sir
G. Grey declined.
[6] Pointing out that there were 29 vacancies in the Companionship of the Bath, and asking for names; Add MS 44760, f. 6.
[7] Motley's 'End of a mission', Fish's reply, published 9 January; A. Nevins, *Hamilton
Fish* (1937), 457.

—do on Invasion of France[1]—Mr H. Terrell's 'Was Shakespeare a Lawyer?'.[2]

4. Sat.

Up at 4 P.M. Wrote to Ld Granville—Sir S. Robinson—Mr West— and minutes. The Wests dined: & a pretty full family party. Saw Mr West (2)—Dr Clark. Read Q.R. on Bismarck—on Irish Chancellors.[3] Spent the available time of aft. & evg. in drawing the first draft of the Queen's Speech.[4]

5. S. Septuag.

Kept my bed till the same hour. Read the morning service alone. Saw Ld Granville—Dr Clark. Wrote to Sir S. Robinson. . . .[5] Wrote also to Ld Normanby—Ld Granville—& minute. Read Life of St Francis[6]—Hyacinthe's Appel[7]—Bolling's Sermon[8]—B. Brown's First Principles.

6. M.

Wrote to Ld Hartington—Duke of Norfolk—Robn G.—The Queen (2 & 2 Mema)—Attorney General—and minutes. Saw Ld Granville —Ld Hartington—Ld de Grey—Ld Chancellor *cum* Mr Bruce & Ld de Grey—Mr Hamilton *cum* Mr Morley—Mr Glyn. Cabinet $2\frac{1}{2}$-$6\frac{3}{4}$. Dined at Ld de Grey's to choose the Sheriffs. A spirited debate, afterwards, on Pondicherry.[9] Saw two. Gave 4/-[R].

1871. Cabinet February 6. 2. 30 PM.[10]
Draft of [Queen's] speech: considered & corrected.
Comm[issio]n for U.S. considered & decided. Ld de Grey—Sir E. Thornton— Sir J. Macdonald. Text of instructions (to them) considered & corrected.[11] Further consideration remitted to Ld Granville & others.
Sale of Old Ships at Admty: not to be resumed during Armistice.

[1] *Quarterly Review*, cxxx. 256, 122 (January 1871).
[2] [H. Terrell], *Was Shakespeare a lawyer?* (1871).
[3] *Quarterly Review*, cxxx. 71, 164 (January 1871).   [4] Draft untraced.
[5] Rest of sentence added at foot of page.   [6] See 15 Jan. 71.
[7] C. J. M. Loyson, Père Hyacinthe, 'France et Allemagne, discours' (1871).
[8] E. J. Bolling, 'Religious zeal foolishness to the world. A sermon' (1870).
[9] Still capital of French India; its annexation by Britain pressed for in some quarters; see 16 Feb. 71.
[10] Add MS 44639, f. 10.
[11] Dated 9 February 1871, F.O.C.P., 2028.

To the DUKE OF NORFOLK, 6 February 1871.   Add MS 44539, f. 152.

I have to acknowledge the receipt of your letter;[1] & I need not say that any opinion proceeding from you & the gentlemen who would have accompanied you is received with much respect by the Government. I need hardly add that no religious antipathies will influence the policy of the administration with regard to the Roman question. But I understand your letter as an intimation that the views conveyed in my letter to Mr Dease[2] are not thought sufficient. When you speak of the re-establishment of the Pope's temporal Power, I do not know whether you mean a reestablishment in conformity with or one independent of & if necessary in opposition to the will of those who were lately his subjects. If the latter, I certainly could not promise that it would receive from the British Government any degree of countenance.[3]

7. Tu.

Wrote to Mrs Hampden[4]—The Viceroy—Mr Bruce—D. of Devonshire—and minutes. Educ.Comm. of P.C. 2¾-5. Read divers pamphlets. Saw Mr Hamilton—Mr Glyn—Mr Ayrton—Bp of London—Ld Northbrook—Lord Advocate—Mr Goschen. Dined with the Wests.

To Mrs HAMPDEN, 7 February 1871.   Add MS 44539, f. 153.

I shall value very much, & shall peruse with great interest, the volume you have been kind enough to send me. Bp. Hampden examined me in the Schools at Oxford with an ability & kindness I have never forgotten: & his name is appreciated in my memory with a lesson[?] which has acted upon my after life. Accept my best thanks.

To EARL SPENCER, Irish lord lieutenant,   Add MS 44539, f. 152.
7 February 1871. 'Private.'

I saw Hartington yesterday forenoon; & I have this day received your letter,[5] but I do not yet feel able to realise to myself fully either the purport or the grounds of the recommendation which I understand you to make, & which in your letter to Bruce[6] you will probably have defined. It was not possible in framing the Speech, to omit a reference to the general & happy contrast offered by the present state of Ireland with that of 12 months back. Exceptions however will be referred to in a way which will reserve the liberty of the Cabinet. Meantime I will frankly state that in my opinion the answer you offer to Ld.

[1] Stressing importance to English Roman catholics of restoration of the Pope's 'temporal sovereignty'; Add MS 44429, f. 176.
[2] See 30 Nov. 70.
[3] Norfolk's reply of 9 Feb. expressed alarm at Gladstone's reliance on Italian govt.'s declaration; ibid., f. 192.
[4] R. D. *Hampden's widow had sent her da.'s ed. of his Memoirs (1871).
[5] Add MS 44307, f. 11; suspension of Habeas Corpus essential—'utter collapse of the Law' in Westmeath; printed for cabinet.
[6] See 9 Feb. 71.

Russell's argument on the use of Habeas Corpus Suspension Acts for the purposes of police as compared with cases of danger from abroad is not sufficient. I will state my grounds

1. Laws are made for the internal government of a society, & cannot of themselves determine action proceeding from foreign states & countries. A case therefore of danger from abroad seems of itself to be *presumptively* more or less taken out of their scope & hence the facility with which the idea of suspending Habeas Corpus is entertained in the presence of such dangers. 2. Another consideration seems yet more important. Danger from abroad is commonly an acute, not a chronic, evil. It is therefore appropriately met by a temporary suspension. The danger passes in a short time, & ordinary law resumes its course, as the measure of exception has fulfilled its work. But the application of this view wholly fails, when we attempt to use such a method of remedy for internal mischiefs of a chronic, not an acute, character. You take away the guarantees of liberty. You incarcerate without charge or trial those whom you suppose to be guilty, let us say those who are guilty. How long are they to remain in prison? In the case of foreign danger, every day presumably brings you towards the end of your crisis. But here there is no crisis. Your imprisonment cannot convert, & may not have great power over these obstinately wicked men by intimidating. When are they to be let out? Is it to be supposed that Parliament will consent to a series of renewals of the extreme remedy? If not, why are we to expect improved conduct from them on their liberation? They will know they have this advantage, that the remedy asked by the Government is one which will not gain but *lose* credit: every time it is asked for afresh, from the nature of the case, Parliament will be less willing to give it. I do not state these things as foreclosing the case, but only by way of remark.

Your letter to Bruce will, I have no doubt, at once be printed for the Cabinet with the one you have addressed to me in order that it may be early & easily considered. You will probably have sent us comparative tables of crime in Ireland for this & former winters, month by month. If not, I think they should be supplied.

8. Wed.

Wrote to Ld Granville—Watsons—and minutes. Attended the Council at Windsor: & had an audience of the Queen.[1] Saw the Lord Mayor—Mr M'Coll—Robn G.—Ld de Grey—Mr Glyn—Mr Hayward—Ld Granville—Baron Brunnow—Ld Lyttelton—Baron Beaulieu—Chancr of Exr—D. of Cambridge—D. of Argyll—Col. Ponsonby—Dean of Windsor. Official dinner: read the Queen's Speech before it. Found the printing very defective. Evening party afterwards.

9. Th.

Wrote to Ld Churchill—Viceroy of Ireland—Mr Boxall—Queen (& Mem)—Mrs Th.—and minutes. H of C. $1\frac{3}{4}$-$2\frac{3}{4}$ and $4\frac{1}{4}$-9. Spoke 1 h

[1] On peace terms, and Princess Louise's dowry; see Victoria's diary in *LQV*, 2nd series ii. 119.

in ans. to Disraeli.[1] Saw Ld Granville—The Speaker—Mr Glyn.
Dined with Sir W. James. Read Alsace & Lorraine by Mr Solling.[2]
Saw Jacob: & others[R].

To EARL SPENCER, Irish lord lieutenant,   Add MS 44539, f. 154.
9 February 1871. 'Private.'

I received yesterday, & have read this morning your important letter to
Bruce.[3] At present I will only trouble you for a moment on three points.
1. I have asked for copies of the papers showing the State of agrarian crime in
Ireland as part of the evidence necessary to come before the Cabinet in this
matter. *If* you think any further & more minute comparison will be desirable in
order to bring out the case specially in what you now consider to be the disturbed
districts, will you kindly have it prepared & sent.
2. Your belief that you can secure the peace of these districts by the arrest of 8
or 10 persons is of great moment. Still it is an opinion & Parlt would & ought,
probably, to require it to be sustained by evidence & argument.
3. I do not perceive in your letter any description of the definite proposition
you desire to make under the terms 'suspension of the Habeas Corpus Act'? For
what time? Within what limits? To be applicable to all persons indiscriminately,
at the discretion of the Government (as I apprehend is usual) within those limits?
I will add that it might be well if the Attorney General for Ireland were to go to
work & hunt for cases of precedents in which peculiar evils of peculiar districts
or classes have been brought before Parliament through previous committees or
otherwise, with a view to special remedies in the interest of peace & order. I
apprehend such instances might possibly be found & if it is indeed felt to be
necessary to move might lighten the difficulty & obviate mischief of various
kinds. The object as you will see of these brief notices is that we should approach the consideration of a very critical question with every advantage the
case admits of.

10. Fr.

Wrote to Bp of London—The Queen—and Mem—Mr Kinnaird—
Sir H. Verney—Mr Hammond—Mr Boxall—and minutes. Dined at
Lady Molesworths. Saw Mr Boxall[4]—Mr M'Coll—Mr Glyn—Ld
Granville—Ld de Grey: to say goodbye & discuss.[5] Conversation
with Duc d'Aumale—Sir W. Mansfield.—Sir H. Seymour. H. of C.
4¼-7. Brought in the Univ. Tests Bill.[6] Read Sollings Alsace et Lorraine (finished): & other War Tracts.

---

[1] *H* cciv. 96.   [2] G. Solling, *L'Alsace et la Lorraine* (1871).
[3] Of 6 February 1871, printed version in Add MS 44307, f. 23.
[4] Saw (Sir) W. *Boxall (see 12 May 70) on resignation of his directorship of the National
Gallery which he withdrew; reappointed for five years on 2 March; Add MS 44539, ff. 154,
159.
[5] Off to Washington as commissioner; see 6 Feb. 71n.   [6] *H* cciv. 146.

11 Sat. [Windsor]

Wrote to Ld Hartington—Mr Cardwell—Mr Reeve—Dr Liddon—
Dr Briscoe—Adm. Collier—Mr Cardwell—Mr Draper[1]—and
minutes. Cabinet 2½-4½. Saw Mr Glyn—Ld Hartington—Mr Cardwell—Mr Kingsley. Off to Windsor at 5 with C. & with *two* daugh-
ters, a great kindness of the Queen. Saw H.M. after dining with her:
& spoke out much about Alsace & Lorraine.[2] Read Rape of the
Lock[3]—Bp Hampden's Memoirs.[4]

Cabinet Feb. 11 71. 2.30[5]
√ Conference. Admission to the Black Sea. Discretion to Ld Granville to take
   1. the Italian proposal and failing this 2. The status quo preferred by Granville, Forster.
√ Col. Fielding.[6] Forwards his explanation. We hope it will be thought there
   was no intended breach of neutrality: of no immediate annoyance as he is
   now come home.
√ A. Herbert's question. considered.[7]
√ Smith's question: on Ritual Commission.[8]
√ India. Price of redemption of purchase money. Not to be charged. *But* ulterior
   measure to be considered. WEG went to W[indsor] at 4.30.

To E. CARDWELL, war secretary, 11 February 1871.   PRO 30/48/8, f. 16.

1. I suppose the Cabinet will today seal the question of compulsion.
2. With regard to purchase; have not the E[ast] I[ndia] Government a much
better case in equity upon some other points? For instance perhaps upon
depôts? If we concede, should we not concede to these, where they really have
something to say upon principle, & so make the thing as to money as broad as it
is long? I have the fear that if we grant English money on grounds of policy,
plausible pleas to a like effect will be likely to crop up hereafter, & inconvenient
to deal with. Further, Lowe has an idea, which I very much like that we should put
a price on this gift—that the provisions to secure economy in Indian Administration are weak, weak in India & perhaps not stronger here; & that a great boon
would be conferred upon India if some agent connected with the Treasury here
were empowered under a well-considered system to check Indian charge; within
some such limits, referably to subject matter, as in England, but not with a decisive power. This would very much strengthen the hold of Parliament, in the
interest of India, over the Indian Office. I do not think that a British Treasury
would have sanctioned the Ball [*sic*] in 1868: although it was a measure in relief
of England. Some of the Indian functionaries might not like this: but we have

[1] John William Draper, 1811–82; American scientist, had sent his *History of the Ameri-*
can civil war, 3 v. (1871); Add MS 44539, f. 157.
[2] Victoria greatly regretted the growth of anti-Prussian feeling; Millman, 217n.
[3] By *Pope, in W. W. *Elwin's ed. of his *Works*, 10v. (1871 ff.).
[4] See 7 Feb. 71n.   [5] Add MS 44639, f. 11.
[6] (Sir) Percy Robert Basil Feilding, 1827–1904, col. in Coldstream Guards.
[7] A. *Herbert's question on 13 February on role of the concert; Gladstone answered;
H cciv. 171.
[8] W. H. *Smith's question on progress to legislation; stone-walled; *H* cciv. 317.

them at an advantage, when they are asking money from us, if we give them
that, & something to boot which may secure yet further effect for their own
benevolent wishes on behalf of India. Pray communicate with Lowe on this: if
the principle is agreed to, a Committee of Cabinet might deal with the detail.
3. I should not like to exclude Ireland; but am not so well able as you are to
judge whether the absence of Volunteers there makes it necessary.
[P.S.] You have seen the Pondicherry Telegram today. What an illustration of
Indian poverty, & Indian thrift!

12. Sexa S.

Castle Chapel 10 & 12 AM. St Georges 4½ P.M. Saw The Queen: P.
Louise—Dean of Windsor—Pr. Christian—Mr Johnson & Mr &
Miss Evans at Eton. Wrote to Ld Granville—The Queen (Mem.)—Mr
West. Read Bp Hampden—St Alban's Case[1]—Ethnic Inspiration.[2]

13. M. [London]

Off to London after C[astle] prayers, and breakfast. Wrote to Ld
Hartington—Mr Reeve—Bp of Gloucester—The Queen 1. and Tel
—and minutes. Saw Bp of Winchester—Mr Goschen *cum* Mr Bruce
—Mr Glyn—Mr C. Gore—Ld Granville—Mr Bouverie—Ld H. Len-
nox. 12 to dinner. House of C. 4½-8 and 9½-11. Spoke on P. Louise's
Marriage provision: & other matters.[3] Read the Rape of the Lock,
Elwin thereon. It is wonderful, though perhaps not perfect.

14. Tu.

Wrote to Pr. Christian—Ld Granville—Mr Stephenson—Ld E. Clinton—Mr Robinson—The Queen—Rev. Dr Miller—and minutes.
H of C. 4½-7.[4] Dined at the Club. Read Elwin's Pope. Saw Mr Cartwright—Abp Manning—Mr M'Coll—Mr Cardwell—Mr Glyn—Ld
Hartington[5]—Mr Lingen—Ld Granville—Scotts—Ld Stanhope.

15. Wed.

Wrote to The Queen (2)—Ld Granville—Mr Boxall—Mr Cardwell
—Sir S. Robinson—Ld Bessborough—Robn G.—and minutes.
Cabinet 2¾-6½. Saw Ld C. Paget—Sir S. Northcote—Mr Glyn—Mr
Forster—Ld Halifax—Mr Bruce—C. Apponyi—Baron Brunnow

---

[1] Perhaps *St Alban's Holborn, By a layman* (1871).   [2] See 29 Jan. 71.
[3] Select cttee. on business of the House: *H* cciv. 182.
[4] Trades Union Bill and Ecclesiastical Titles Act Repeal Bill brought in: *H* cciv. 257.
[5] Meeting arranged to discuss next day's proposals; Add MS 44539, f. 157.

—Ld Acton—Count Bernstorff—C. Cadorna. Dined at Count Apponyi's. Evening party at home. Read La Guerre ou la Paix.[1]

Cabinet Feb. 15. 71—2½ PM.[2]

√ Ld Granville's Tel[egram] for immed. recognition of French Govt. when formed—approved.

√ Limitation to the subject of the Conference not to be exacted as condition *previous* to entrance of Plenipotentiary. Opinion that it cd. only [*sic*].

√ Ld Hartington's proposal for 3 Counties in Ireland to suspend the Habeas Corpus.

√ Determined to hear this opinion—& Col. Wood with local head of Constabulary to come over.[3]

√ Letter from Chaudordy to Tissot[4] invoking 1. prompt recognition of new French Govt. 2. Good Offices as to terms of peace. The first *aye*. The second: we do nothing, but shall listen with respect to what Assembly may say.

√ Army Bill: 'great emergency' agreed to.[5]

√ Words as to D. of Cambridge.

√ Baby Farming. No Bill.

Fortifications of Paris.

16. Th.

Wrote to D. of Devonshire—Ld Hartington—Robn G.—M. Mich. Chevalier—The Speaker—Chancr of Exchr—Sir W. Mansfield—The Queen (2 Telegr.)—& minutes. Saw Mr Gurdon—Chr of Exr —Mr Bruce *cum* Mr Rathbone—Ld Halifax—Mr Glyn—Ld Granville—W.H.G. At Christie's. H. of C. 4½–9. Cardwell had a signal & merited success with his statement on the army.[6] Read Elwin's Pope. Dined with the Wests. Saw Russell & another X.

To M. CHEVALIER, 16 February 1871.   Add MS 44539, f. 160.
'Private.'

Thank you for your interesting letter which I have read with much attention.[7] I am not able to see the evidences of a new Tilsit in the circumstances you mention.

The Gortschakoff note was to none more inconvenient than to the Germans. And in the proceedings of Prince Charles in Roumania I see no more judging by all the information we receive from the East, than evidence of his folly & mismanagement. We are now approaching the most interesting & critical of all the epochs of the War. In a few days we shall I hope have a French Plenipotentiary in London: & I shall be very glad indeed that whatever may be done in the Eastern questions France should have her share in it. But what is far more

[1] Perhaps E. Terrel des Chênes, 'Paix ou guerre' (1871).   [2] Add MS 44639, f. 12.
[3] See 18 Feb. 71.   [4] Charles Joseph Tissot, 1828–84.
[5] Cardwell used the phrase in next day's statement, referring to compulsory service.
[6] *H* cciv. 327. Gladstone then moved monies for Princess Louise's dowry, opposed by several radicals; ibid. 359.   [7] Not found.

important, we shall then know the real German conditions, & the manner in which they may be received by the representative body of the French nation. I will not anticipate the grave & difficult questions that may then arise. I will only say I can assure you it is not Pondicherry, or the ships which weigh upon my mind. And as to the indemnity, which must be heavy, there is a sort of natural limit to the sum which can be raised within a given time, & to the time which any calculating people would be content to agree upon for the payment. The truly heavy & menacing subject is the question of territory; or rather the question of the human beings who inhabit it.

As to Pondicherry I am ashamed of the susceptibilities, which appear to me almost insane, of a portion of my countrymen.

17. Sat. [recte Friday]

Wrote to Ld Lyttelton—Sir W. James—Mr Hart R.A.[1]—The Queen Mema & letter—Rev Mr Evans—and minutes. H. of C. 4½-12¼. Spoke on the War, in fear & trembling: & on other matters.[2] Saw Ld Granville—Capt. Hozier[3]—Mr Glyn. Read Elwin's Pope—Draper's Hist. Amn Civil War.[4]

18. Sat.

Wrote to Ld Enfield—Ld Spencer—Robn G.—Ld Granville—Mr Aldis—Dr Lightfoot—T.S. Gladstone—The Queen—and minutes. Dined with the Speaker. Saw Mr Glyn—S.E.G.—Ld Granville— Att.Gen. Ireland—Ld Advocate. Read Elwin's Pope—Hampden's Memoirs.

Cabinet Feb. 18. 71.[5]
√ Indian Committee. Joint.
   Dease Letter.
   Army Bill, Estimate—which? On Thursday.
√ 2 hours on communication with neutrals in anticipation of an application from France. Letter of Granville to B[aron] Brunnow framed.[6]
√ Irish functionaries called in & examined as to Ribbonism. Committee to be appointed to hear the case: suspension of H[abeas] C[orpus] to follow if the case is made good—in that country.[7]
√ Forster proposes to reserve the Question in the Ballot Bill as to prevention of improper candidatures.

[1] Solomon Alexander Hart, 1806–81; artist; had applied to direct the National Gallery; Add MS 44539, f. 160.
[2] On A. *Herbert's motion for a concert of neutral powers 'to obtain moderate terms of peace'; his speech persuaded Herbert to withdraw the motion; *H* cciv. 396.
[3] See 16 July 70.   [4] See 11 Feb. 71n.
[5] Add MS 44639, f. 16.
[6] The letter asked Brunnow to inquire whether Britain and Russia could examine a French appeal to the neutrals; see Ramm I, i. 221. See 20 Feb. 71.
[7] i.e. the Westmeath cttee., see 2 Mar. 71.

To LORD ENFIELD, foreign office undersecretary,   PRO FO 391/24.
18 February 1871.

I cannot conceive a greater disgrace than a war between China and some great
European Power growing out of proceedings such as those suspected or alleged
on the part of missionaries in that country & especially on the part of Roman
Catholic missionaries. The Chinese authorities seem to me to be honest in the
matter, & would probably be glad of a thorough investigation of the facts. Would
it be possible to make this investigation in China itself by a Joint Commission
composed of Chinese Functionaries & of Diplomatic agents of the Powers principally concerned, say France England & America. Such a man as Mr. Robertson[1] of Canton, who is (apparently) the essence of good sense in these matters,
would represent us well. I do not know him but have been a close observer of his
letters. I wish you would speak to Mr Hammond, who knows this matter so
thoroughly. The reports herewith, containing opinions from such high authorities
as to the certainty of a war should matters continue without a check make me
feel the occasion serious. The facts once established by *authority*, the question
would not be so difficult to deal with according to the rules of justice & policy.[2]

19. Quinqua S.

Chapel Royal mg. St And. Wells St aft. Saw Sir R. Phillimore—Ld
Bessborough—Ld Lyttelton—Ld Granville. Dined at Sir R. Phillimore's. Wrote to Ld Hartington. Read Bp Hampden (finished)—Abp
of Syra's Report[3]—La Moda, Appello &c.[4]—Abp Manning's Lent
Letter.[5]

20. M.

Wrote to Duke of Argyll—Ld Granville—The Speaker—Ld Enfield
—H.N.G.—Ld Hartington—Mr Dumaresq—and minutes. H of C.
$4\frac{1}{2}$-$7\frac{3}{4}$ and again at $9\frac{3}{4}$.[6] Twelve to dinner. Saw Adm. Sir S. Dacres—
Mr Glyn—Ld Granville—Mr Baring—Baron A. Rothschild. Read
Draper's Hist—Appeal of German Liberals.[7]

Feb. 20 [1871][8]
On the important question of the letter to Brunnow (& other Neutrals)[9] my Col-
leagues according to speech leaned as follows. Much against: Cardwell, Lowe.
Against: Hartington, Goschen. Proposed by: WEG. Much for: Chancellor, Forster,
Fortescue. For: Kimberley. For, rather varying: Granville. Assented at last:
Argyll. Rather for: Halifax. Silent: Bruce.

[1] (Sir) Daniel Brooke Robertson, 1810–81, consul at Canton; kt. 1872.
[2] Enfield's letter untraced.
[3] Of his visit (see 10 Jan. 70), printed in *Occasional Papers of the Eastern Church Association, number xiv* (1872).
[4] Untraced.   [5] H. E. *Manning, 'Modern society; a pastoral for Lent' (1871).
[6] Spoke on University Tests repeal: *H* cciv. 501.
[7] Either *Wahlaufruf der Deutschen Fortschrittspartei* or *Wahlaufruf der Nationallibera-
len Partei*, both published Jan. 1871.
[8] Add MS 44639, f. 17.   [9] See 18 Feb. 71.

21. Tu.

Wrote to The Queen (2)—The Ld Mayor—Ld Bessborough—and minutes. Saw Chancr of Exchequer—Sol. General—Ld Hartington —Baron Brunnow NB—Ld Granville—Ld Halifax—Sir Walter James—Mr Glyn. H of C. $4\frac{1}{2}$-$7\frac{1}{2}$ and $8\frac{1}{2}$-12.[1] Dined at Sir W. James's. Attended the Queen's Court in aft. Arranging drawers &c.

22. Ash Wed.

Chapel Royal at noon. Bp of L. preached well. Wrote to Bp of Chester—Mr Hugh Mason[2]—Mr Mozley—Ld Halifax—D. of Grafton —Princess Louise—and minutes. Read Jowett's Plato[3]—Draper's Hist. War in U.S.—Playfair's Inosculation of Science.[4] Saw Ld Granville—Mr Glyn—Ld Overstone—Mr Richmond—F. Lawley.

23. Th.

Wrote to Duke of Norfolk—The Queen (Mem. & 2 letters)—Ld Hartington—and minutes. H of C. $4\frac{1}{2}$-$8\frac{1}{4}$ and $9\frac{1}{4}$-$12\frac{1}{4}$.[5] Dined in D.St. Saw Sir H. Bulwer—Ld Chancellor of Ireland—Mr M'Coll— Mr Glyn—Ld Lyttelton—Ld A. Hervey—Mr Roundell—Chr of Exchr. Read Draper's Hist.—Elwin's Pope.

24. Fr.

Wrote to Mr Max Muller—Ld Enfield—Ld Granville—The Queen —& minutes. Dined with Lady James. Read Elwin's Pope. Wrote Mem. (in forenoon) on Olympian religion.[6] Saw three[R]. Saw Mr E. Deutsch—Mr Glyn (3)—Mr West. Ld Granville came at 2.30 with the French Appeal. We considered the matter & hastily summoned the Cabinet. He wrote for further particulars & I made a draft of dispatch to the French Ambassador.[7] The Cabinet sat over an hour. H of C. $5\frac{1}{4}$-$8\frac{1}{4}$ and $9\frac{1}{4}$-$10\frac{1}{4}$. Spoke in answer to D., and about the messages to Versailles.[8]

---

[1] Deb. on his letter to Dease (see 30 Nov. 70), introduced by W. Johnston, who successfully moved, against diarist's opposition, that a copy of the letter be laid before the House; *H* cciv. 646.

[2] See 20 June 68. [3] *Dialogues of Plato*, tr. B. *Jowett (1871).

[4] L. *Playfair, *The inosculation of the arts and sciences* (1870).

[5] Moved for a select cttee. on Indian finance, spoke on University Tests; *H* cciv. 763, 778.

[6] Untraced. [7] Ibid. [8] *H* cciv. 854.

D. St. Cabinet at 3.45 precisely this day. WEG. F.24. 71[1]

√ Appeal from French Govt. on the amount of indemnity[2] demanded by the Germans considered. draft framed: subject to review on receipt of certain further particulars for which Ld Granville had written to Duc de Broglie.
Letter to German Govt. to be framed in conformity herewith.
This summons only went out from D. St. at 3 or a little before. Ministers who attended—from the beginning—WEG, Ld Granville, Ld Chr., Chr. of Exr., Ld Kimberley, Mr Fortescue, Ld Hartington, Mr Bruce, Mr Forster, Mr Goschen, Ld Halifax. D. of Argyll—Mr Cardwell came in later.

To F. Max MÜLLER, 24 February 1871.   Max Müller MSS, d. 170.

I hope to write tomorrow on the question you have kindly put to me with respect to my letter of 1864.[3]
You will see that the brief proceedings last night on the University Tests' Bill define in some degree the intentions of the Government. We shall I hope give heed to the further prosecution of the question concerning the Endowments when the Tests' Bill is disposed of, if not before.
But the foreign world interferes very much for us at this time with the domestic world. We are still without certain news of the peace. I cannot wonder that your communication of the Gasparin pamphlet produced no fruit.[4] For the policy studiously pursued by Count Bismarck has been to shut out all foreign interference or even suggestion as to the peace. I do not question his title to act for himself in this manner. The neutrals need not acquiesce in it unless they please; but apparently they will or may please. I am afraid the result will be, that Germany, crowned with glory & confident in her strength, will start on her new career to encounter the difficulties of the future without the sympathies of Europe: which in my opinion no nation, not even we in our sea-girt spot, can afford to lose. I would your larger spirit might prevail.
[P.S.] When you say you would take away all 'protection' from Theology at Oxford, I do not understand you to mean of necessity that you would abolish all offices of religious worship or teaching.

25. Sat.

Wrote to Ld Hartington—Mr Fortescue—Mr O. Russell—Bp of Oxford—Mr Reeve—Mr M. Müller—M. Tissot—Lady James— The Queen (2, and Mem.)—and minutes. Saw S.E.G. (the Judgement)[5]—Mr Glyn—M. Tissot—The French Ambassador—Baron L. de Rothschild—Baron Brunnow—Ld Granville—Mr Forster.

[1] Add MS 44639, f. 26. This summons, circulated in a box, was subsequently used to record the agenda.
[2] Germany claimed 6 milliard francs; Granville's despatches in *PP* 1871 lxx. 323.
[3] Gladstone to Max Müller, 28 September 1864, of vast length, on Homeric mythology; Max Müller MSS, d. 170. See 26 Feb. 71n.
[4] See 30 Jan. 71.
[5] The *Purchas judgment by the judicial cttee. of the privy council, on ritualism, delivered on 23 Feb.; copy apparently circulated to cabinet, with annotations, in Add MS 44616, f. 48. See 18 Apr. 56.

Attended the Levee at 2. Cabinet 3-6. 14 to dinner: Cabinet Mins Ladies Fr Ambr & M. Tissot.

Cabinet 1871. Feb. 25. 3 PM.[1]
√ Ld Hartington's motion discussed & course determined.[2]
√ Granville related what had happened on the subject of yesterday's Cabinet.
√ Ld Advocate to be a P[rivy] C[ouncillor].
√ Reduction of Indian Native Army Expenditure—Army.
  Salary Sec[retary] Educn. Committee.
  'Local legislation Ireland Bill' (not to come on next Monday)[3]

To C. S. P. FORTESCUE, president of the   Add MS 44539, f. 166.
board of trade, 25 February 1871.

Unless my memory deceives me Disraeli in a grand flight of oratory assailed us last year about our allowing murder to stalk about unchecked in Ireland. Can you track this? It might be well to hold it in hand on Monday. You will I daresay be ready to speak on Hartington's motion if needful.[4]

To Odo RUSSELL, 25 February 1871.   Add MS 44539, f. 165.

I see from a letter of yours to Granville that you have been informed that I snubbed you in the H. of C. on the 17th. Mr Disraeli confirmed this last night by saying that 'I threw you over' which I denied. You will form your own judgment upon the matter when you see the reports, & we can then communicate further.[5] But in our debate last night the question assumed rather large dimensions. Mr Disraeli coolly contended you had acquainted Ct. Bismarck that we should with or without allies go to war for the neutralisation of the Black Sea. On examining the passage closely, with some aid from Mr Fortescue, I came to two conclusions —To the first positively, that you spoke of the question in its present state meaning thereby under the Gortschakoff note, from the apparent bearings[?] of this we had then in no way been extricated—on this I need not trouble you with any question. To the second conclusion I came with less certainty. It was this that in giving the words 'which I had frankly proved to him' and those which follow to the end of the sentence you are quoting Count Bismarck & not yourself asserting that you had frankly proved to him &c. On this question I should be very glad if you would favour me with as explicit an answer as you can give: & such an answer, provided you can make it such, as I can use publicly should occasion arise.

I may add I do not think the point vital: for the words 'in its present state' suffice for all that is necessary.

---

[1] Add MS 44639, f. 27.
[2] *Hartington had given notice on 23 February of a motion for a secret cttee. on Westmeath; *Disraeli had given prior notice of a question on its procedure: *H* cciv. 762, 945.
[3] Private members' bill 1°R on 16 February, delayed until 3 May; *H* ccvi. 124.
[4] No reply found.
[5] Russell, on a mission to the German army at Versailles, withdrew the charge after seeing *The Times*' report and offered to resign if he had compromised the govt.; to Gladstone, from Versailles, 27 Feb. 1871, Add MS 44429, f. 279.

26. 1 S.Lent.

Chapel Royal at 12. Bp of Exeter preached a really noble Sermon.
Ch.R. again in aft. Saw Ld Granville—Mr Glyn—Ld Vernon—Mr
Levy. Wrote to Mr Max Müller—Mrs Thistlethwayte—Ld Harting-
ton—Sir J. Hay—Bp of London—Dr Liddon—Mr Forster . . . &
minutes. Conversation with Herbert[1] on his future life. Read Life of
St Francis—B. Brown's First Principles—Stanley on Ath. Creed[2]—
Judgment in the Purchas Case.[3]

To F. Max MÜLLER, 26 February 1871.   Max Müller MSS, d. 170.

It will be a great honour to me if in your new edition you take any notice or
use any part of my letter, returned herewith.[4] Pray do with it as you please. In
reading it over I have very slightly modified in pencil one or two expressions.
Since writing it & particularly in 1867–8 I made some progress in the subject &
I may send you a memo of my conclusions in outline, which will not take more
than half a minute to read.

Many thanks for the interesting letter from Abeken which I have shown to
Lord Granville.[5] I think I could answer him about moral courage: but I gladly
refrain. In truth I am more concerned at what he says about Alsace and German
Lorraine. It discloses a deep & wide difference between English & ruling German
ideas on the first principles of free Polity.

[P.S.] I am distracted by the *most* conflicting accounts & rumours with
reference to Peace.

27. M.

Wrote to Mr Disraeli[6]—The German Ambassador—Dean of Windsor
—Mr Westell—Mr [blank]—Ld Hartington—Pss Louise—Master
of Balliol—Mr Richmond—Ld Halifax—Mr Macnamara—The
Queen—& minutes. Dined with Lady James. Saw Ld Granville—Mr
Fortescue—Mr Glyn—Chr of Exr—Conclave on Solicitorship of
Treasury.[7] H of C. $4\frac{1}{2}$–8 and 9–12.[8] Read Harold Erle.[9]

---

[1] Nearing end of his time at Eton.
[2] A. P. Stanley (1871).   [3] See 25 Feb. 71.
[4] See 24 Feb. 71n, printed in F. Max Müller, *Lectures on the science of language* (6th
ed., 1871) ii. 440–4.
[5] See Schreuder, xvii. 125 (9 Oct. 70n) and Add MS 44251, f. 313.
[6] Declining *Disraeli's request for immediate discussion of *Hartington's Westmeath
motion, but agreeing to it after the Scottish Education Bill this evening; Add MS 44539,
f. 167. See Add MS 44429, f. 266, and *H* cciv. 944 for the question and reply.
[7] Offered unsuccessfully to Henry Tyrwhitt Jones Macnamara, 1820–77, Add MS 44539,
f. 170; J. Gray appointed, see 6, 15 Mar. 71.
[8] Scottish Education, Ireland: *H* cciv. 946, 989.
[9] [W. A. Gibbs], *Harold Erle. A biography* (1871).

To B. JOWETT, Master of Balliol,   Add MS 44539, f. 168.
27 February 1871.

    I scarcely know how to thank you for having presented me with your impor-
tant & attractive work:[1] for I feel that I shall certainly, among those whom you
may have selected for the honour, be the least worthy of it. It will however be
my misfortune rather than my fault, if I do not turn it to account for my own
advantage. You will have observed our proceedings on the Tests Bill. I am hopeful as to its fate in the House of Lords; though I have no title to speak of what is
to befall it there. But I think it will be our duty either immediately or very
shortly to consider what step should be taken on the subject of the tenure &
incidents of College offices. Mr Roundell desires a Commission on Revenues:[2]
if this is appointed I think it should be statutory. I daresay you have considered
& will consider the subject. Pray remember our breakfasts on Thursdays at 10
after Easter, & sometimes kindly give us notice: they are an institution, which
has now survived the storms & vicissitudes of nearly a quarter of a century.

28. Tu.

Wrote to Mr Cardwell—Prof. M. Müller—Bp of Chester—Ld Hartington—Mr Boxall—J. Breakenridge—Robn G.—The Queen—&
minutes. Dined with Lady James. Read Harold Erle. Saw Mr M'Coll
—Mr Glyn—Mr Richmond—S.E.G.—D. of Devonshire—Dr Armstrong.[3] H of C. 4½-8 and 9-1.[4]

To F. Max MÜLLER, 28 February 1871.   Max Müller MSS, d. 170.

    I am truly sorry if I have committed an Error in showing Abeken's letter to
Ld. Granville:[5] but the truth is that the Foreign sec. & the First Lord are, especially in times like these, as man & wife, of the best type, as to intercommunica-
tion of all intelligence of interest. Every thing that I see goes to him if it be
worthwhile and I believe also *vice versa*. But you may, I think, rely on its not
going farther. And I hope I need not say that whatever I may read in the letter
as to public & political tendencies of the nation, it contains nothing calculated
to alter in the least my old sentiments of respect & regard for the man.

Wed. Mch One 1871

Wrote to Mr Max Müller—Ld Chancellor—Ld Halifax (2)—Bp of
Winchester—Mrs Greenwood[6]—Mr [H.] B. Samuelson—& minutes.
Dined at Argyll Lodge. Lady Marg. Beaumont's afterwards.[7] Saw Mrs

---

    [1] See 22 Feb. 71.   [2] Eventually the Cleveland Commission.
    [3] Alexander Armstrong, admiralty physician; about Childers' health.
    [4] *H* cciv. 1017.
    [5] See 26 Feb. 71; Max Müller wrote that he had marked the letter 'private'; Add MS
44251, f. 317.
    [6] Consoling the widow of John Greenwood, 1800-71, treasury solicitor; Add MS 44539,
f. 170.
    [7] Lady Margaret, da. of 1st marquis of Clanricarde, m. 1856 W. *Beaumont (see 24 May
53) and d. 1888.

Gould—Mrs Terry. Saw Dr Armstrong—Mr Gurdon (R.B.)—Mr Glyn—Saw Mr Steegmann[1]—Ld Chancellor. 2–3¼. Conclave on Admty Succession.[2] Saw Count Szecken.[3] Read Harold Erle—Ld Palmerston et La Belgique.[4]

To F. Max MÜLLER, 1 March 1871.   Max Müller MSS, d. 170.

The keynote to my opinions on the peace is to be found in a remark which I hazarded in a former letter & which embodies a conclusion drawn by me from all I know of history; namely this that the most fatal & (in their sequel) most gigantic errors of men are also frequently the most excusable & the least gratuitous. They are committed when a strong impetus of right carries them up to a certain point, & a residue of that impetus, drawn from the contact with human passion & infirmity, pushes them beyond it. They vault into the saddle, they fall on the other side. The instance most commonly present to my mind is the error of England in entering the Revolutionary War in 1793. Slow sometimes to go in, she is slower yet to come out. And if she had then held her hand, if she could have held her hand, the course of the Revolution & the fate of Europe would in all likelihood have been widely different. There might have been no Napoleon. There might have been no Sedan.

Thanks for the Fellowship papers which I shall read with care.

2. Th.

Wrote to The Queen (2)—Lady Mansfield—Miss Wyse—and minutes. Dined at Mr West's. A short drive with C. Read Contemp. Rev. on Native Races.[5] Saw Ld Granville—Mr Glyn—Both these with Ld Halifax & Mr Cardwell, on the debate tonight, & on Admiralty arrangements. Saw C. of E. and Rev Mr White—Mr Hodgson. H of C. 4½–8½ and 9½–1½. Spoke at length on the Westmeath Committee wh was carried by 81.[7]

3. Fr.

Wrote to Ld Chancellor—Ld Granville (2)—Ld Halifax—Rev S.E.G.—The Queen (2), & minutes. H of C. 4½–9¾ and 10¾–1¾.[8] Conclave at 5½ in my room, on placing the Statues.[9] Read Miss Wyse's Introdn to her Uncle's Book.[10] Saw Mr Glyn (2)—Ld Halifax—Mr

---

[1] Unidentified.

[2] *Childers was too ill to continue; *Goschen officially succeeded him on 9 March; changes circulated to cabinet on 5 March 1871; Add MS 44760, f. 10.

[3] Count Anton Szecsen von Temerin, Austrian plenipotentiary at the Black Sea conference.

[4] Perhaps untraced article by T. Juste, Palmerston's biographer 1873.

[5] *Contemporary Review*, xvi. 537 (March 1871).   [6] Business untraced.

[7] *H* cciv. 1179.   [8] Siege of Paris: *H* cciv. 1296.

[9] Of Peel, Palmerston, and Derby; sketches in Add MS 44639; mem. asking for further information on positioning, in Add MS 44760, f. 11.

[10] Sir T. *Wyse, *Impressions of Greece* (1871) with his niece's introduction.

Boxall—Ld Granville—Chancr of Exr—Mr Beresford Hope—The
Speaker—Mr Childers—Mr Ayrton—Baron N. Rothschild.[1]

4. Sat.

Wrote to Mr O. Russell—Ly Waldegrave—Mr Stansfeld—Mr Locke
King—Mr Goschen—Bp of Winchester—The Queen—and minutes.
Dined at Granville's F.O. Royal & Dipl. dinner: 1400 afterwards. All
so well arranged. Read [blank]. Saw S.E.G.—Col. W. Patten—Mr
Glyn—Mr Goschen—Ld Hartington—D. of Argyll—Ld Chancellor
—Ld Granville—Conclave on vacant office,[2] G. H[alifa]x & E.
C[ardwell]. Cabinet 3-5¾. Saw Mlle de Rosny[R].

Cabinet Mch. 4. 71. 2½.[3]
√ As to amendment of Order for Westmeath Committee by consent: yes.
√ As to the list of members for it—considered.
√ Granville recited conversation with Broglie.
√ Rothschild overture with ref. to guaranteeing some part of present War-
   instalment for France. Not to be entertained.[4]
√ Papers respecting peace to be got ready for presentation by inquiries from O.
   Russell & Bernstorff as to receipt of Tel[egram] of Friday 24th.
√ Salisbury's motion on Guarantees. Ld G's frame of reply. Decline to admit
   impotence: avoid detail.[5]
√ Kimberley. Univ. Tests Bill to be read 2° as soon as we like.
√ Dilke's motion—conversation on. If Conference closes or is near it we may
   ask him to postpone.[6]
√ Game Laws. 2R. M'Lagan's Bill. Not to object. Propose reference of Bills
   including our own to a Committee.[7]
√ Mr Forster. Salary of Sir F. Sandford. £1800 to the office, £200 to him.
   Bethnal Green Museum.

To Odo RUSSELL, 4 March 1871.   Add MS 44539, f. 171.

I have received your letter of the 27th & read your despatch of the same date.
I think they leave nothing to desire.[8] It would have been unwarrantable on our
part to send instructions to any agent abroad to use the word war in his argument on the Gortschakoff note. But it was perfectly warrantable in you or any
other person communicating in a diplomatic character with one of the other
Powers, to make use of it. In this sense I meant to speak when I said (as I am
correctly reported in the 'Times') that not the 'slightest blame' attached to you.
We will however consider what more can best be said & in what way. I do not

[1] Nathan Mayer de Rothschild, 1840–1915; liberal M.P. Aylesbury 1865–85; cr. Baron
1885; see next day's cabinet.   [2] See 1 Mar. 71n.
[3] Add MS 44639, f. 28.   [4] See also Ramm I, i. 226.   [5] See *H* cciv. 1360.
[6] *Dilke's motion postponed until 30 March, when defeated: *H* ccv. 894.
[7] Five Bills on Scottish Game Laws, including one govt. bill, were introduced in February; all were dropped. Peter Maclagan, 1823–1900; liberal M.P. Linlithgow 1865–1900.
[8] See 25 Feb. 71n.

know in what way Disraeli will sustain his doctrine of 'throwing over' but efforts will be made to hit us for that in the hope of driving us into a confession that *we* threatened war.

I am glad to think that after such a sacrifice of domestic comfort prolonged through so considerable a period you are about to be relieved from your arduous labour. You have certainly bewitched the Pan Teutonic Royalty & Bismarck himself.

5. 2 S.L.

Chapel Royal mg with HC. All Souls Evg. Wrote to The Queen—Col. Ponsonby. Saw Mr Stansfeld (2)[1]—Mr Baxter—Mr Goschen—Mr Glyn—Mr West—Ld Halifax. Read Union Rev. Mch[2]—Mr Capes in Contemp.Rev.[3]—B. Brown's First Principles[4]—Oakeley's Priest on the Mission.[5]

6. M.

Wrote to Mr Tyrrwhitt[6]—Ld R. Cavendish—Mrs Norton—Sir R. Phillimore—Col. [A. G.] Dickson—The Queen (Mema 2 & letter) —Ld Hartington—Mr Adam—& minutes. Saw Mr Kersley[7]—Ld Granville—Mr Glyn—Conclave on Solrship—Mr Ayrton—Mr Forster—Chancr of Exr—Comte de Paris—and minutes. H of C. 4½-8¼ and 9¾-1.[8] Read Harold Erle. Dined at Lady James's & secured 3 drawings of W. Brooks.[9]

7. Tu.

Wrote to Mr Ayrton—Mr Plimsoll—Mr Forster—Mr Ellis—Dr A. Clark—Ld Granville—the Queen—& minutes. Saw D. of Argyll—Ld Granville—Mr Bryce—Ld A. Hervey—Mr Glyn—Sir A. Buchanan —Dr A. Clark—Capt. Herbert—Ld Advocate. Attended the breakfast after Lady Ailsa's marriage.[10] Visited Fisher's, & Christie's. Dined at Ld Lyttelton's. H. of C. 4½-8 and 11-12.[11]

[1] Offered, and accepted, presidency of poor law board in the cabinet, *Goschen to retain control of local taxation legislation already launched; Add MS 44539, f. 171.

[2] *Union Review* (March 1871).

[3] *Contemporary Review*, xvi. 519 (March 1871).   [4] See 17 July 66.

[5] F. *Oakeley, *The priest on the mission. A course of lectures* (1871).

[6] Robert Philip Tyrwitt, 1798-1886, police magistrate at Marlborough St., hearing the Kersley case.

[7] Benjamin Kersley, house carpenter in Carlton House Terrace, charged with indecent exposure in a Hyde Park urinal; on 8 March Gladstone gave character evidence for him; he was discharged; *The Times*, 9 Mar. 1871, 11f.

[8] Spoke on Westmeath: *H* cciv. 1389.

[9] Warwick Brookes, 1806-82; artist in Manchester.

[10] Archibald Kennedy, 1847-1938, 3rd marquis of Ailsa, a tory, m. this day Evelyn Stuart, da. of 12th Lord Blantyre; she d. 1888.

[11] Questioned by *Disraeli on alleged Russo-Prussian treaty: *H* cciv. 1501.

8. Wed.

Wrote to Chancr of Exr—M.F. Tupper—S.E.G.—Mlle de Rosny—
Mr Bruce—and minutes. Fourteen to dinner: suddenly got up for
the two sisters. Saw Mlle de Rosny X. Saw Baron A. Rothschild—Mr
Glyn—Robn G.—Read Harold Erle—Droits de l'Allemagne sur
L'Alsace et L[orraine].[1]

Putting together what I hear I am inclined to fear that the heavy cost of the abolition of Purchase should cause many of the Liberals to hesitate as to giving it
real & persevering support, when they connect it with the large increase in the
Estimates decided on by the Cabinet while the war was raging.
    Col. Napier Sturt advised, last night, that the Estimates should if possible be
reduced, very much for the purpose of helping onwards the abolition of Purchase.
    Glyn I think shares this view but is of opinion that the reduction, to have a
sensibly good effect, must not be less than a million.
    Will you two meet Glyn here tomorrow Thursday at 3 to consider this matter?
(or at some other hour if that time be inconvenient).[2]

9. Th.

Wrote to Ld Kimberley—Ld Granville (2)—V[ice] C[hancellor]
Stuart—Mr Tupper—Mlle de Rosny—Ld Chancr—Ld Halifax—
Sir T. Biddulph—The Queen—and minutes. Saw Baron L. de Roths-
child—Mr Stansfeld *cum* Mr Glyn—Conclave on Mil. Estimates—
Mlle de Rosny—Mr Glyn (2)—Mr Forster. Attended Sale at Fisher's.
Dined with the Wests. H of C. 4½-8¼ and 9½-1.[3] Read Harold Erle
(finished).[4]

10. Fr.

Wrote to Ld Kimberley—Bp of Winchester—Ld Granville—The
Queen—and minutes. H of C. 4½-8 and 9¼-1.[5] Visited Christie's.
Saw Mr M'Coll—Mr Forster—Mr Glyn—Mr J. Russell—Mr Lowe.
Read Draper's Hist.[6]

To S. WILBERFORCE, bishop of Winchester,   Wilberforce MSS, d. 38.
10 March 1871.
    A reference to me as head of the Government, in an executive office only,
upon the Purchas question which has been in a judicial course,[7] is *telum imbelle*

[1] H. C. L. von Sybel, *Les droits de l'Allemagne sur l'Alsace et la Lorraine* (1871).
[2] Circulated to Granville, Cardwell, and Glyn; initialled and dated 8 March 1871, Add
MS 44760, f. 15.
[3] Requested *Dilke to postpone his motion; see 4 Mar. 71. Intervened on Westmeath:
H cciv. 1751.
[4] See 27 Feb. 71.   [5] Questions: *H* cciv. 1767.   [6] See 11 Feb. 71.
[7] See 25 February 71n; request sent by Wilberforce on 9 March; Add MS 44345, f. 194.

sine ictu,[1] & beside the point, when it states only opinions & feelings: & no one, in so referring, has pointed out any step that I could properly take, or submit to the Cabinet. It could only be upon grounds of law, duly stated & attested, & capable of being carried to legal issue, that so far as I can see any cause for consideration could arise nor am I able to say what the result of such consideration might be as I am up to this time wholly in the dark. There must be a Council soon for the new appointments, & in the regular course the judgments would be confirmed at it.

11. Sat.

Wrote to Sir W. Mansfield—Sir H. Bulwer[2]—Ld Chancellor (2)—Mr J. Watson—the Queen—& minutes. Saw The French Ambassador—Mr M'Coll—Mr Glyn—The Lord Chancellor—Ld Granville—Prince of Wales. Read Vericour on History:[3] Jesse's London.[4] Cabinet 2½-6. Dined with Ld Granville to meet the P. of Wales.

[*Cabinet*] *10 D. ST. Mch. 11. 71. 2½ PM*[5]
√ Reception of the poorer English from France.
√ Mr Goschen stated the outline of his Local Rating Bill which was considered & approved.
√ Telegram from U.S. on Alabama case considered—Telegram in reply agreed to.[6]
√ Weeks business considered & arrangements made.

To LORD HATHERLEY, lord chancellor,   Add MS 44539, f. 176.
11 March 1871. 'Private.'

1. Last time I saw you I spoke of prospects of obedience to the recent [Purchas] Judgment. What has reached me since *looks* much otherwise. Our case is this: a Bishop commonly considered to be 'Low' never looked upon as 'High' has I am told informed those interested that he cannot enforce the Judgment. All this however I state merely for fear I should have misled you in any degree.
2. What is more to the purpose is this. I understand the matters at issue are to be raised again forthwith in some sort of friendly suit; in order to raise an argument to the effect that the Judgment is in contumacy to former judgments. Would this or would it not, if any judicial process have been instituted, have a bearing on the question whether the Judgment ought at once to be confirmed by O[rder] in C[ouncil]. Perhaps we can speak together today.[7] Also about V. C. Stuart.

[1] 'A feeble weapon thrown without effect'; *Aeneid* 2. 544.
[2] Offering *Mansfield and *Bulwer peerages; Add MS 44539, f. 176.
[3] R. De Véricour, *Historical analysis of Christian civilization* (1850).
[4] J. H. *Jesse, *London; its celebrated characters and remarkable places*, 3 v. (1871).
[5] Add MS 44639, f. 33.   [6] See Cook, *The Alabama Claims*, 172.
[7] Purchas petitioned the Privy Council for a rehearing; Add MS 44205, f. 172.

12. 3 S.Lent.

Chapel Royal mg. St James's evg. Dined with Sir W. James, now partially convalescent. Saw Mr Glyn. Walk with C. Read Life of St Francis: & a number of Sermons & Tracts.

13. M.

Wrote to D. of Argyll—Mr Buxton—The Queen—and minutes. H of C. 4½-8 and 9-1¼.[1] Read Sir T. Wyse's Impressions of Greece.[2] Saw Ld Granville—Mr J. Russell—Mr Adam—Mr Glyn (2)—Mr Bruce—Mr Lefevre—Mr Winterbotham.

To C. BUXTON, M.P., 13 March 1871.   Add MS 44539, f. 177.

I owe you many thanks for your note[3] but I cannot do less in return than state to you the difficulties we feel about your motion as a subject for discussion at the present time. We think the irritated & inflamed state of mind in the two countries recently at war has two effects bearing upon it, & both of them unfavourably. First a statement of severities exercised, & the reception by the Government of that statement in whatever way they may receive it, can hardly fail to give fresh offence to minds singularly susceptible & jealous with regard to all we say or do. Secondly a discussion of that kind cannot do good, & may do harm with reference to the pending negotiations for peace.

An appeal to us has already been made to watch those negotiations & any slight chance there may be of our finding an opening for good as unprejudiced parties must become much slighter if we are now to set about canvassing the transactions of the War in the manner proposed. In truth I think we should find ourselves bound to silence on the main points of the question. Frankly stating to you these difficulties I must leave them to your consideration.

14. Tu.

Wrote to Ld Chancellor—Mr Scudamore—Ld A. Hervey—The Queen—& minutes. H of C. 4½-8¼ & 9½-12½.[4] Saw Me de Rosny[R]. Saw Mr Pennington—Mr Glyn—do *cum* Ld Hartington—Miss Burdett Coutts. Read Life of Joan of Arc[5]—Tour to Caaba & Charing Cross.[6]

15. Wed.

Wrote to Ld Kimberley—Ld Chancellor—Dean of Ch.Ch.—Mr Gray—& minutes.—Scotts. Dined with the Ellices. Evening party at

---

[1] Questioned on Westmeath, and spoke on Army Bill timetable: *H* cciv. 1874, 1967.
[2] See 3 Mar. 71.   [3] Not found; see next day's note.
[4] Got Buxton's motion on war postponed: *H* cciv. 1983.
[5] Probably D. W. Bartlett, *The life of Joan of Arc* (1855).   [6] Untraced.

home. Saw Bp of Winchester—Mr Beresford Hope *cum* do—Duke of Argyll—Mr Glyn (2)—Mr Blount[1]—Sir R. Palmer—Ld Granville —Sir A. Buchanan. Read M. Bernard on Neutrality of G. Britain.[2]

16. Th.

Wrote to Mr Cardwell (2)—Mr A.B. Hope—Watsons—The Queen (3)—Ld Chancellor—Mrs Thistlethwayte—and minutes. Cabinet 2-4½. Saw Mr Winterbotham—Mr Glyn—Ld Granville—Mr Cardwell—Mr Lowe. H of C. 4½-8¼ and 9½-3¼. An untoward night of obstructive divisions.[3] Read Sir T. Wyse—Bernard.

Cabinet 10 D. St. Mch. 16. 71. 2 PM[4]
Telegram from U.S. with draft of the terms considered. Law Officers called in.[5]

To E. CARDWELL, war secretary, 16 March 1871.   PRO 30/48/8, f. 29.
'Private.'

With reference to your number of men I wish to submit to you the following idea. If you keep it up, what is to prevent 'militarism', with which you are at war, from discouraging & obstructing the passage of men into the reserve?

But if you diminish the numbers will not the choice lie between the reserve and discharge instead of between the reserve & the ranks and will they not prefer the reserve to discharge as decidedly as they would prefer the ranks to the reserve?

To LORD HATHERLEY, lord chancellor,   Add MS 44539, f. 180.
16 March 1871.

Lowe has told me about your labours on the telegram which I do not doubt will prove satisfactory. I feel however that the operation of carrying back into the past as *international* law that which we do not believe to have been such at the time is a highly conventional [*sic*] & artificial process & one open to a great deal of criticism in debate. Now I would submit for your consideration this modification of the manner of proceeding. It presupposes the adoption of your *resserrements*[6] of the three propositions. 1. At the beginning for 'A neutral Power is' substitute 'the British Govt. was', 2. Add a fourth proposition 'We consent that the foregoing rule shall be held to be international law for the future'.

[1] Probably Walter Aston Edward Blount, 1807-94, Norroy herald.

[2] M. *Bernard, *The neutrality of Great Britain during the American civil war* (1870); a defence by one of the commissioners in Washington.

[3] Series of adjournment motions on the Army Regulation Bill: *H* ccv. 150.

[4] Add MS 44639, f. 35.

[5] Crisis in Washington over San Juan island, the Americans obliquely bidding for the cession of British Colombia; see Cook, *The Alabama Claims*, 174. America had also submitted a new set of rules on neutrality; ibid. 180.

[6] Reading uncertain; if *sic*, then 'contractions'.

I think that the advantages of this change would be 1. It gets rid of what is palpably artificial & conventional[?] in the proceeding. 2. It admits the obligation which the Americans want to establish 3. It leaves to us the scope for a rather more elastic argument.

If you think it worthwhile pray mention this to Palmer.[1]

17. Fr.

Wrote to Ld Granville—Mrs Lindsay—The Queen (2)—and minutes. Read Miss Wynn's Letters.[2] Saw Ld Granville—Mr Glyn (2)—Mr Richards [sc. Richard?] cum Mr O. Morgan. Cabinet 2-4¾. U.S. H of C. 4¾-8 and 9-12¼. Spoke on Army Regulation Bill.[3]

Cabinet. Mc. 17. 71. 2 PM[4]
√ Answer to Commissioners in U.S.[5]
√ Sir S. Robinson.
√ Military Estimates. Mundella's Motion.
√ Game Laws Wed.
√ Candlish. Abyssinian motion.[6]
√ Royston. Friday. Haviland Burke. Park Commrs.[7]

18. Sat. [Windsor]

Wrote to Chancr of Exr—The Queen (Mema)—and minutes. Read C. Wynn L. & Journals. Saw Sir R. Blennerhassett—Mr Glyn—Rev. S.E.G.—Ld Granville—Mr Milnes Gaskell. Called on Mrs Th. & divers, on my way to Paddn. Off at five for the Deanery at Windsor. Saw Sir T. Biddulph.

To R. LOWE, chancellor of the exchequer,   Add MS 44539, f. 179.
18 March 1871.

Glyn tells me that the tone of our debates on reduction in Army Estimates will be materially affected not only by the amount of expenditure, but by the answer to the question, can it probably or can it not be met without extra taxation? I think it would be well if you could put *your* figures provisionally into a form which would enable us to judge in some degree whether we have any good hopes in this respect. No vital matter, or even grave matter of policy, could be allowed to turn upon such a const[ructio]n, but it might just turn the scale on

---

[1] Hatherley next day suggested modifications; Add MS 44205, f. 175.
[2] *Extracts from the letters and diaries of Charlotte Williams *Wynn* (1871).
[3] H ccv. 245.   [4] Add MS 44639, f. 39.
[5] Granville to High Commissioners, 17 March 1871, PRO/FO/5/1299, declining to regard the four articles on neutrality as actually in existence in 1861-5, but agreeing that the arbitrator should assume Britain had undertaken to act in their spirit; see Cook, *The Alabama Claims*, 182; *Argyll's notes at Add MS 44639, f. 40.
[6] Withdrawn.   [7] See *H* ccv. 606.

certain points of reduction, in the Estimates. I shall be happy to see you if you like on Monday at 12, but I think it would be well if you could see Cardwell in the interval should you have anything material to lay before him. The Cabinet is not, I think, tied by any final resolutions.

19. 4 S.Lent.

Eton Chapel mg & evg: much interest in the sight of that living mass of hope and promise. Saw Col. Ponsonby—Dean Stanley—Walk & much conversation with the Dean on the [Purchas] Judgment, Promotions, & the like. Wrote to Ld Chancellor—The Queen—Mr Gurdon—and minutes. Read C. Wynn, much, & slow.

To LORD HATHERLEY, lord chancellor,   Add MS 44539, f. 180.
19 March 1871.

I troubled you rather unreasonably with the papers about Ewelme Rectory but all this you draw upon yourself by your unbounded readiness to take trouble. The first is a simple one. At present the Rectory is by Act given to the University & attached to the Regius Professorship of Divinity therein. It is thought they should be severed. What arrangement is fairest as between the Crown & the University? I [suggest?] this; that the Crown should take the advowson but should be bound to present a member of the University. They say this is not usual. But they do not convince me it is not right. I can easily consult the Solicitor General—one opinion will embolden me to proceed; but it must be by act.
P.S. I have received your note but I own I do not like either of the methods suggested by you, but I will speak to you on the subject.[1]
The option I think lies between my method & *simple transfer* to the Crown. Practically no one but an Oxford man would be presented to a living of that kind historically connected with the University.

20. M. [London]

Wrote to Sir W. Mansfield—The Qu. (1. & Mem)—Mrs Th—and minutes. Finished Miss Wynn's remarkable Memorial. Read Joan of Arc. Back to C.H.T. at 11.30. H of C. $4\frac{1}{2}$–$8\frac{1}{2}$ and $9\frac{3}{4}$–$11\frac{1}{4}$.[2] Saw Depn Chambers of Commerce.[3] Saw Chancr of Exchr—Mr Cardwell—Mr Goschen.

[1] Of 18 March, Add MS 44205, f. 177, suggesting 'the medium of alternate presentation or of presenting in the proportion of 1 to 2 by the Crown'. See 22 Mar. 71.
[2] Spoke on army promotion: *H* ccv. 297.
[3] He declined the dpn.'s call for a Minister of Commerce; *The Times*, 21 Mar. 1871, 11d; *The Economist*, 25 Mar. 1871, 341.

21. Tu.

Wrote to Col. Wright—The Queen (1. & Mem.)—and minutes. $10\frac{1}{2}$–$4\frac{1}{2}$. To Windsor for the marriage.[1] The Qu. & Princess L. very gracious: the spectacle beautiful: some things should have been otherwise. Cabinet in G.W.R. carriage on the way back: to consider the Telegram on the U.S. fourth Article.[2] Saw the Chancellor—Ld Halifax (2)—Mr Goschen—Ld Granville—Ld Sydney. H of C. $4\frac{3}{4}$–$7\frac{3}{4}$ and $8\frac{3}{4}$–$12\frac{1}{2}$. Spoke on Harbours of Refuge.[3] Read Joan of Arc. Saw three. Dined at No 21 [Carlton Gardens].[4]

22. Wed.

Wrote to Ld Dufferin—Ld Granville—Mr M'Coll—Mr Mundella—Mr Thring—Prof. Fraser—Mr F. E. Weatherly[5]—and minutes. Read Hist. of The Campbells.[6] Dined at Mr Lowes. A curious conversation with Mrs L. Saw Dr Clark *cum* Mr P. Hewitt.[7] Saw Granville & others at the Levee on return Tel. to US. Saw Mr Glyn—W.H.G.—Count Bernstorff—Deputation on Scots Educ. Bill.[8] Speaker's Levee in evg. Then a large evening party at home.

To A. J. MUNDELLA, M.P., 22 March 1871.   Mundella MSS.

I thank you for your kind note.[9] I think your demand was one which if you thought proper you were fully entitled to make, and one which it was our duty to give way to if this could be done without prejudice to the public service. This was the case: subject to the understanding that we take the vote tomorrow night. We must not therefore mind a little opposition bluster, which merely indicates the absence of substantial grounds of attack.[10]

To H. THRING, parliamentary draftsman,   Add MS 44332, f. 57.
22 March 1871.

I have now fully considered the Ewelme case & the result is that I have to ask you to prepare a Bill to detach the living from the Professorship, leaving the Advowson with the Crown, but only for the presentation of a person such as might be appt. to the Regius Professorship of Divinity.[11] The object is to leave all

---

[1] Of Princess Louise to Argyll's son, the marquis of Lorne.
[2] Britain attempted to restructure the fourth article of the American proposals (see 17 Mar. 71), to avoid parliamentary hostility; for the original, this cabinet's proposal, and the final version of 4 April, see Cook, *The Alabama Claims*, 180–4, and 1 Apr. 71.
[3] *H* ccv. 389.   [4] Lord F. Cavendish's.
[5] Had sent his poems, *Muriel, the sea king's daughter* (1870); Add MS 44539, f. 182.
[6] *The House of Argyll and the collateral branches of the Clan Campbell* (1871).
[7] i.e. P.G. *Hewett; see 9 Aug. 61:   [8] No report found.   [9] Not found.
[10] Mundella moved on 23 March for no increase in the Army Estimates.
[11] Sundry copies of the Bill in Add MS 44616.

parties (except holders) as nearly as possible in their present position. Please to consider the best form of expression. I presume that the living & Professorship are not yet vacant but this Mr Gurdon can ascertain at the H.O.

23. Th.

Wrote to Dr Sternd. Bennett—Mr Benedict—Dr Elvey[1]—Ld Kimberley—Mrs Weldon—Mrs Davidson—Watson & S.—The Queen —& minutes. Saw Mrs Blake X. Saw Mr Goschen—Mr Glyn—Mrs Young—Ld Granville. Read Muriel. H of C. $4\frac{1}{2}$-8 and $9\frac{1}{4}$-$2\frac{1}{4}$. Spoke on Military Expenditure.[2]

24. Fr.

Wrote to Ld Lyttelton—The Queen—and minutes. $12\frac{3}{4}$-5. To Windsor for the Council. Audience of H.M. Saw P.M.Gen. *cum* Ld O'Hagan—Mr Glyn—Mr M'Coll—Ld Granville. H. of C. 5-$8\frac{1}{4}$ and $9\frac{1}{2}$-$12\frac{1}{4}$.[3] Read Joan of Arc.[4]

25. Sat. Annunciation

Wrote to Col. French—Ld Granville—Mr Weatherly—The Queen —Mr Hope Scott—Mr Ayrton—and minutes. Cabinet $2\frac{1}{2}$-$5\frac{1}{2}$. Breakfasted at Grillion's. Saw Exhibn of British Artists. Received the Burmese Deputn with whom I was much pleased.[5] Saw Baron. L. Rothschild—Ld Halifax—Mr Glyn. Dined at the Lord Chancellor's. Read Joan of Arc—Prof. Bryce's Lecture.[6]

Cabinet March 25. 71. 2½ PM[7]
√ Week's business. considered.
√ Westmeath committee. State of evidence before.
√ Bill for Federation of the Leeward Islands: to be introduced.[8]
√ Canada. Fenian Raids Compensation. Conditional ultimate power of entertaining the subject to be sent to Ld de Grey.[9]

[1] He offered knighthoods to the musicians Sterndale *Bennett (see 5 Mar. 69), Julius *Benedict, 1804-85, and George Job *Elvey, 1816-94.
[2] Opposing *Mundella's motion that the army could be efficient without increased estimates, which was beaten in 294:91; *H* ccv. 482.
[3] Questioned on London republicanism: *H* ccv. 574.   [4] See 14 Mar. 71.
[5] He accepted, after the India Office urged its diplomatic advisability, 'a gold decoration of honor, set with precious stones' brought by the chief secretary of the king of Burma; brief mention in *The Times*, 27 Mar. 1871, 12d. See Add MS 44430, ff. 41, 59, 69, 96.
[6] Probably J. *Bryce's inaugural 'Academical study of Civil Law'.
[7] Add MS 44639, f. 42.   [8] On 9 May.
[9] i.e. as leader of the British commissioners in Washington.

√ Telegram on its way from America. Cabinet may have to meet on Monday.[1]
√ Licensing Bill—application of the monies forthcoming considered.
√ Indian Colonels Promotion considered.

To J. R. HOPE-SCOTT, 25 March 1871.   Add MS 44539, f. 183.

We have often thought & sometimes (from the Duke of Norfolk) heard of you since your great affliction: & I learn with pleasure that you now find yourself able to make the effort necessary for applying yourself to what I trust you will find a healthful & genial employment.

You offer me a double temptation to which I yield with but too much readiness. I am glad of anything which associates my name with yours; & I feel it a great honour to be marked out in the public view by your selection of me as a loyal admirer of Scott, towards whom, both as a writer and as a man, I cannot help entertaining feelings perhaps (though this is saying much) even bordering upon excess.

Honesty binds me to wish you could do better for your purpose, but if you do not think any other plan desirable I accept your proposal with thanks.[2]

26. 5 S.Lent.

Chapel Royal mg. St James's evg. Sick &c. calls—Mr Byng, J.S. Wortley, Ly Lyttelton. Dined with the Phillimores. Wrote to Mrs Th. Read Blunt on Ch. of E.[3]—Beard on Religious Thought[4]—Coleridge's Letter to Liddon[5]—Bodington's Sermon.[6] Herbert drove in open carriage.[7]

27. M.

Wrote to Bp of Winchester—Padin Woon—Duke of Devonshire—Mr Childers—A. Baillie Cochrane—Mrs Th.—Mr T.B. Potter—Me de Rosny[R]—The Queen (letter & Mem.) H of C $4\frac{1}{2}$-$6\frac{1}{2}$, $7\frac{1}{4}$-$8\frac{1}{4}$, and $9\frac{1}{2}$-$12\frac{1}{4}$.[8] Saw Mr Dickinson—Ld Granville—Mr Glyn—Sir F. Crossley—Scotts—Mr Bruce—Mr Baxter. Princess of Wales came, to tea & music: I was summoned from H of C. Cabinet 2-$4\frac{1}{2}$. Read Joan of Arc.

Cabinet March 27/71. 2 PM[9]
√ Benefices Resignation Bill.

---

[1] *Granville requested Monday rather than Sunday; Add MS 44639, f. 43.
[2] Hope-Scott dedicated his abridgment of Lockhart's *Scott* to Gladstone; Ornsby, ii. 240.
[3] J. H. *Blunt, 'The condition and prospects of the Church of England' (1871).
[4] J. R. *Beard, *The progress of religious thought* (1861).
[5] Sir J. T. *Coleridge, 'Remarks [on *Purchas]' (1871).
[6] Untraced; probably by Charles Bodington.   [7] i.e. recovered from illness.
[8] Navy estimates; *H* ccv. 689.   [9] Add MS 44639, f. 44.

√ Dilke's Vote of Censure. Counter-motion by Rylands.[1]
√ Terms of reply to Telegram from Commissioners in U.S.[2]

28. Tu.

Wrote to Ld Chancellor—Dean Ramsay—Mr Read MP—Archdn Bickersteth—Mrs Cooper—Mr Weld Blundell—The Queen—Lady Phillimore—& minutes. Saw Mr M'Coll—Mr Hardy—Mr Glyn—Mr Gregory—Ld Granville—Mr Dowse. H of C. $4\frac{1}{2}$-$8\frac{1}{4}$ and $9\frac{1}{2}$-1.[3] Dined with Sir W. James. Read Joan of Arc—Wrigley on Railways.[4] Visited Christie's & Phillips's.[5] Saw Me de Rosny[R].

To T. J. WELD BLUNDELL, 28 March 1871.   Add MS 44539, f. 185.
'Private.'

The matter contained in the inclosure to your letter[6] is altogether new to me, & I have no sufficient means of deciding upon its credibility; but on the whole, & speaking for myself, I am inclined to be sceptical. Sella is a man of ability, not to say of honour, & I should not well know how to reconcile the hypothesis, which would treat the statement, with[7] either description of him. Were I to presume to offer a friendly suggestion to the friends of 'Papal independence', it would be this: that they are strong, as long as they resist an interference of the Civil Power in the sphere of religion, but weak as long as under the phrase they intend to convey a supposed title to govern a people against its will & by coercion. Such an assumption the future certainly will not sanction: & the attempt to obtain it will violently & ruinously react upon the interests of religion. I do not here refer to the interests of the Italian Government or of Italy in the matter: but I observe a great indisposition to admit that the people of Rome & the Roman states have political rights, & I am certain that no system which proceeds on such a basis will endure.

29. Wed.

Wrote to Mr Ouvry—Sir T. Biddulph—Robn G.—and minutes. Read Draper's History. Saw Mr Glyn—Chancr of Exr—Mr Gurdon —Mr Eykyn—Ld Chancellor. Attended the opening of the Albert Hall: a splendid spectacle, & great acoustical effects.[8] H. of C. $2\frac{1}{4}$-$5\frac{1}{2}$. Spoke on Lord Sandon's Bill.[9] Dined with Mr Glyn. Saw Mrs Th— Russell—Grey—D'Oliva.[10]

[1] Peter Rylands' (1820-87, liberal (unionist) M.P. Warrington 1868-74, Burnley from 1876) motion supported govt., against *Dilke's motion of censure on Black Sea conference; Rylands began his speech saying 'the Government had not in any way accepted his Amendment'; see 30 Mar. 71.
[2] See 21 Mar. 71n.   [3] Defence, and Trades Unions Bill: *H* ccv. 808.
[4] T. Wrigley, 'Look before you leap! Railway accidents: their cause and cure' (1871).
[5] Auction rooms.   [6] Not found.   [7] This and next word smudged.
[8] *The Times*, 30 Mar. 1871, 9d, found the echo gave 'a mocking emphasis which at another time would have been amusing'.
[9] Sandon's Parochial Councils Bill: *H* ccv. 866.   [10] Probably rescue.

30. Th.

Wrote to Ld Granville—Sir S. Northcote—Ld Chancellor—Mr Chambres—Abp Manning—The Queen—C.G.—and minutes. Dined with Meriel Talbot 8¼-9¼. Saw Mr M'Coll—Mr O. Russell[1]—Mr Glyn —Mr Gurdon (RB)—W.H.G. (livings)—Duke of Argyll—Ld Lorne —Mr Jessel—Sol. General—Mr Forster—Ld Hartington. H of C. 4½-8¼ and 9¼-2. Saved speaking on the Dilke motion.[2]

31 Fr.

Wrote to Ld Granville—Chancr of Exchr—Scotts—Ld Kimberley —C.G.—and minutes. H of C. 4½-8 and 9½-11½.[3] Read Brougham's Life.[4] Saw B. Benjamin—Mr West—Ld Granville—Mr Glyn—Mr Cardwell—Sir J. Lacaita—Mr Forster. Visited Mrs Th—late X.

To R. LOWE, chancellor of the exchequer,   Add MS 44539, f. 187.
31 March 1871.

I have not the least objection to your consulting the Cabinet but I will state frankly my own opinion about bringing forward your bill on currency.[5] There are two strong reasons for it: one its excellence: the other the advantage of obtaining the money it would yield.

But there are yet stronger ones against it. We have filled up our time for the Session even to cramming; we have given pledges as to other measures which cannot be set aside; I have never known a Bill which more manifestly than yours required to be treated as paramount: it is only by such treatment that the adverse interests could be confounded & dispersed: your measure brought forward next month would instantly produce a Park Lane jumble & block of business: it might greatly damage others of our plans: It could not be carried & by not being carried would infallibly be in a greater or less degree discredited. Had I my personal choice I would gladly (so much do I value it) substitute it for one, or perhaps more than one, of our actual plans. But this you will agree we are not free to do.

Sat.Ap.One.1871.

Wrote to Sir T. Biddulph—Watsons (2)—Mr Levy—The Queen— C.G.—and minutes. Saw Ld Granville—Mr Glyn—Mr M'Coll. Cabinet 12-2¼. Went down to Chiselhurst to write my name at the

[1] Summoned to give details on Black Sea Conference for *Dilke's motion; Add MS 44539, f. 185.
[2] Rylands moved, then withdrew his amhdt. (see 27 Mar. 71); Dilke's censure motion was negatived without dividing; *H* ccv. 976.
[3] Spoke on Cochrane's motion (withdrawn) that Germany be pressed to reduce severity of the peace terms: *H* ccv. 1002.
[4] *The life and times of Henry, Lord Brougham, written by himself*, 3v. (1871).
[5] Lowe wanted cabinet permission to make the currency plan part of the budget; Add MS 44301, f. 187.

lodge for the Ex-Emperor.[1] Visited Mr [Thomas] Woolner's Studio to see his fine Virgilia; & some pictures. Dined with Panizzi: much talk on Italian & other matters. Saw Fredez[R]. Read Reasons for returning to the Church of England.[2]

Cabinet Ap. 1. 71. 12 o'clock[3]

√ U.S. High Commission. Fisheries. Ask for Sir J. M[acdonald's] & Commissioners views to be sent by post. Advise introduction of money price.[4]

√ Alabama. Amendments in Art. IV upon ·the new version agreed on. After 'having been' insert the following words 'fitted out armed or equipped as above it being understood that these words may include the case of a ship …[']'[5]

√ San Juan. 'middle channel'.

In drafting these four articles our proposal is to acknowledge not an *international law* in force at the time of the sailing of the Alabama, but an equitable obligation incumbent upon Great Britain to execute faithfully her non municipal law for the benefit of a friendly Power.

Therefore we cannot admit for the settlement of the Alabama question any objection going beyond the terms of our municipal law as it then stood. But our municipal law only forbad 'arming, equipping and fitting out'. Therefore we cannot honourably acknowledge any obligation, retrospectively, with respect to any 'special adaptation' except such as included in 'arming, equipping, or fitting out'.[6]

To E. LEVY[-LAWSON], 1 April 1871. 'Private.'   Add MS 44539, f. 188.

If you see occasion to refer in the D[aily] T[elegraph] to my explanation delivered last night, respecting the step taken by the Government at the time when the preliminaries of peace were signed, you will I am sure avoid the strange error of the Morning Post which overlooks the undoubted transmission of our representation through Bernstorff to Bismarck apparently 30 or 36 hours before the Preliminaries were signed. The Times is nearer the mark. But I apprehend that Mr O Russell's first representation was made some hours before that act took place.

2. Palm S.

Chapel Royal mg, & H.C.—St George's evg. Dined with G. Glyn. Finished the remarkable book of 'Reasons'. Wrote to H.N. Gladstone (his birthday)—Mr H.A. Bruce—Mrs Th.—Sir S.R. Glynne—C.G. Read Massari on the Freedom of the Church (Speeches).[7]

---

[1] i.e. Napoleon III.   [2] [By J. M. Capes] (1871).   [3] Add MS 44639, f. 48.
[4] Gladstone's draft telegram in ibid. f. 50.   [5] See 21 Mar. 71.
[6] Holograph note, undated, possibly circulated before the cabinet; Add MS 44639, f. 47.
[7] G. Massari, *Garanzie per la libertà della Chiesa* (1871).

3. M.

Wrote to Mr Helps—Mr Pim MP—Scotts—Mr Blackburn[1]—Mr
Ayrton—The Queen 1. & M.—C.G.—Chancr of Exr (2)—S.R.G.
—Sir S. Northcote—Ld de Grey (2). Visited the French Exhibn.
Meeting of Commn of Exhib. 51 at Marlborough House at 12. H of C
$4\frac{1}{2}$-8 and $9\frac{1}{2}$-$1\frac{1}{4}$.[2] Saw Ld Hartington—Mr Glyn—Lady Gordon—
Col. Scott—Mr Goschen—Mr Gurdon—Lady Gordon—Mrs Th.—
Chancr of Exr. Dined with the James's.

To EARL DE GREY, lord president,   Add MS 43514, f. 78.
3 April 1871. 'Private & Confidential.'

I daresay you envy the Lords, who adjourned for three weeks or thereabouts
on Friday. Today I have received your letter of March 21, for which many
thanks.[3]

The construction which you with knowledge put upon Sumner's removal is
that which I had conjecturally attached to it. It did not raise my spirits.

We must not expect you in so multiform a business to make progress on all
points at once. It will be progress made on any one, which will be a lever to help
the others forward.

I shall be sorry if you have to spend your final residuum of strength on San
Juan because it will be given to a merely colonial rather than a British purpose.
But only *so far* sorry. The course of events may make that the right thing to do.
But in real importance Alabama is A & the fisheries B, as I at least apprehend.

On Saturday we sent to you a telegram which I hope may a little gladden you
in the midst of your hard work with the skinflints on your *front & flank*.

I wrote an answer to a letter of Northcote, which goes by the same mail as
this. It explains the sort of considerations which have been passing through my
mind, & to a great extent through the minds of others. But I sincerely hope
that the whole affair may be one of retrospect before this reaches you—& the
letter not worth your reading. Granville concurred in my sending it, though
it is by way of exception, as he had adopted the rule of silence for himself, (and
I think wisely under the circumstances): indeed I think it was arranged in the
Cabinet.

You are certainly well put together as a Commission, and I must say markedly
from the head downwards. I am glad you appreciate Northcote so warmly. It is
I assure you reciprocal. He is an excellent man. If you get so *thick* with him as to
become inseparable, you must bring him, & not go to him.

I am glad to report *well* of the humour of the H. of C., & the position of
the Government. The two assaults (purchase & Dilke) have each ended in egre-
gious *fiascoes* and the Westmeath imbroglio was cleared by a speech from
Dowse, excellent in argument, & in humour (punitive humour however) incomparable.

---

[1] Involved in the Irish Church Fund; see Add MS 44539, f. 196.
[2] Spoke on ballot: *H* ccv. 1060.
[3] Add MS 44286, f. 110: 'I am convinced that the removal of Sumner [from the Senate's
foreign relations cttee.] was a serious blunder.'

To R. LOWE, chancellor of the exchequer,   Add MS 44539, f. 191.
3 April 1871. 'Immediate.'

It is my opinion as Cardwell & Granville know, that even this year we ought, on the whole, to have cut a million off our estimates. Next year in the absence of new circumstances & causes requiring expenditure, we ought to take off *not less* than two. And as the normal increment of our income is over $1\frac{1}{2}$ million, & as you are going to augment that by new taxes, I feel no apprehension in consequence of the figures you give me. Still it might not be ill if Goschen in surrendering the house tax in principle, & while declaring the *intention* to give it up for 1872/73 were also to point out parenthetically that state considerations are paramount, & that the pledge as to *time* of surrender could not therefore be absolute.

To Sir S. NORTHCOTE, 3 April 1871.   Add MS 50014, f. 222.
'Confidential.'

[First letter:] The enclosed is my reply to the letter you kindly wrote me. I could not send it without showing it, to Granville & the Chancellor particularly. Hence it was delayed until Saturday, when the considerations it contains entered much into our deliberations. We then sent off a telegram which I hope may enable you to close the Alabama discussion, at least if the U.S. Commissioners will give any *quo* for our *quid*. The whole affair is retrospective, but it may serve in some degree as comment on an important decision. I write briefly to de Grey. [P.S.] Poor France keeps descending out of the lowest deep into a lower deep. We have neither news, nor daylight.

[Second letter:] I thank you very much for your interesting letter[1] and I have also seen letters from de Grey to Granville & from Mr M. Bernard to Granville, which came by the same opportunity. It gives me the utmost pleasure to receive your warm & valuable testimony to the manner in which de Grey is doing his share of the work.

We have felt, and you must have felt also, the difficulties entailed by our being virtually restricted to Telegraphic communication. Where the exact force of the words, & their intention, are matters of such nicety & importance, it is a sad loss that we cannot transmit or receive simultaneously an effectual comment.

I am glad however to perceive, that the distance between us & the Americans is gradually being narrowed on the Alabama question. It is a matter of the first importance, in all cases of this kind, that each party should be able to place himself in the position of the other, & comprehend in some degree what that other means & wants. I think that what *we* for ourselves, in the Cabinet, mean & want is, first & foremost, not to be committed to abandoning the ground of argument, as to international law, which was maintained by the British Government, on the advice of its jurists, in & after 1862.

With regard to the proposal that we should consent to be tried by rules which did not exist, through the medium of a friendly fiction, I would observe that it would be far better even to give in (in my opinion) than to resort to an evidently artificial method of proceeding with the effect of thereby veiling a proceeding

[1] Of 17 March, from Washington, praising de Grey, and commenting adversely on the U.S. constitution; Add MS 44217, f. 115.

that we do not like to avow. I should say in a matter like this avoid above all things what is artificial.

It is a great concession to America to allow an arbitrator to decide whether we did or did not duly execute the provisions of our own municipal law. That concession we have already made in agreeing that the British Government was, in 1862, bound to use due diligence & so forth. Thus far we leave it open to the Americans to urge their own view of international law; & we meet them by steps forward, to the extent to which they can succeed in sustaining that view from our own municipal law of that date. But there is this difficulty in *adding* terms to the terms of our municipal law: that we seem then either to fall into the capital error of renouncing our old line of argument as to international law, or else to adopt the arbitrary & fictive procedure of allowing ourselves to be tried by rules that in our belief did not exist. This of course applies to the addition of the words 'specially adapted in whole or in part' to the words of our old Foreign Enlistment Act.

What then, placing ourselves at the American point of view, can we conceive them reasonably to require, which is not sufficiently covered by those words (of the Act)? And I suppose that what they may reasonably require is to be secured against the doctrine which prevailed in opposition to the Crown in the case of the Alexandra; & which I understand to have been that equipping could include nothing except what was separate from the fabric of the ship and attached to her or put into her after her building was complete.

We might, with perfect consistency & honour, shut out that doctrine, by incorporating in the Articles a declaration that we do not give to the word equip so narrow a construction but leave it to the Arbiter to consider what else, besides things moveable & separate, may enter into equipment.

One word more. These articles are intended, so far as two nations can make them, to become rules of international law for the future. If so they ought to be as clear as possible. Would not the words 'Specially adapted in whole or in part' be either the subject of infinite contention as to their meaning, or else intolerably rigid? For instance in time of war *bonâ fide* merchant ships often carry guns for their defence; they may have their decks strengthened in consequence. Would not this be a special adaptation in whole or in part? & ought this to stop a ship?

I have said so much on this subject that I must not touch on the remainder of your letter. I have expressed only my own opinion, except where I have referred to others—there is therefore I trust nothing that can mislead or perplex in my efforts to explain. If I ask you to show this to Lord de Grey in particular, it is only because there should be no thread however slight of communication which is not under his eye: & because, if difficulty still remains, I presume we shall seek the first means of remedy in allowing a little time for fuller interchange of ideas both among ourselves & with our American friends.[1]

4. Tu. [Hawarden]

Wrote to The Queen—Miss Burdett Coutts—C.G.—Mr Hammond —Ld Granville—and minutes. Dined with Glyn. Huge trouble about the sweeps. Saw M. de Sommerard[2]—Mr Glyn—Mr Russell—The

---

[1] Dated 30 March, but sent this day.
[2] Esmond du Sommerard, 1817-85, French archaeologist, in London arranging an exhibition.

Burmese party—Mr Hammond—Sir A. Spearman. Held a quasi Cabinet on de Grey's Telegrams: & reported our opinion to Granville by 'the wire'.[1] H of C. 2¼-3.[2] Read Joan of Arc—Brougham's Autobiography. Packing & preparing. Off by mail to Hn. Arrived 4.15 A.M.

To EARL DE GREY, lord president,   Add MS 43514, f. 81.
4 April 1871.

I write to apologise for having in my letter of this morning included by implication Sir J. Macdonald in the general & irreverent phrase of Skin-flints. Undoubtedly the Cabinet, without any doubt, did on Saturday adopt Sir John Macdonald's view, except it be as to the perpetuity of the transfer for money which we did not feel ourselves able to dispose of. It seems to me that we should lay a foundation of great and just complaint against us in Canada were we to fasten upon her a plan in which the privilege of fishery, which is in the nature of a property, was to be given up as an equivalent for reduction in the American Tariff, which, according to our constant declarations & established principles of action, are beneficial indeed to other countries but are most of all beneficial to the Americans themselves.

Undoubtedly when you went from hence we were under the impression that the U.S. Government were prepared to deal with this subject by the way of a money payment. I do not know that we should be justified in saying they were ready to do this in any other way except as a condition of the transfer in perpetuity. But I do not understand this to be the point now specially at issue.

5. Wed.

Church 11 A.M. and 7 P.M. Wrote to Prof. Max Müller—Chancr of Exr—C.G.—Mr J. Miller. Read Coplestone's Reply to Calumnies of Ed.Rev.[3]—Helps's Life of Cortes[4]—Plutarch de Superstitione. Arranging my things. Examined accounts with reference to the state of my property in the Metrop.Distr. Railway.

6. Th.

Ch. 11 A.M. & 7 P.M. Wrote to Ld Granville (2)—Mr Wickens—Mr West—& minutes. Saw Mr Burnett. C.G. & Herbert came: he much improved in healthy appearance. Read Plut. de Superst.—Coplestone's

---

[1] Final agreement of Washington articles; Cook, *The Alabama Claims*, 184.
[2] Misc. business and adjournment for Easter: *H* ccv. 1180.
[3] See 4 Aug. 40.
[4] A. *Helps, *The Life of Hernando Cortes* (1871); sent by the author; Add MS 44539, f. 191.

Reply—Life of Cortes—Bp of St David's on Greece & Assyria[1]—
Fottrell's Inaugural Address.[2]

7. Good Friday.

Church (H.C.) 11 A.M. and 7 P.M. Wrote to Ld Chancellor—Ld
Granville (letter & Tel.)—The Queen—Ld Normanby—Miss Watson
—Mr Stansfeld—Chr of Exchr—and minutes. Read Life of St Fran-
cis[3]—Reville's Essays[4]—Dr Monsell's Hymns[5]—Morgan's Hymns of
Lat.Ch.[6]

8. Easter Eve.

Church 8.30 A.M. and 7 P.M. Wrote to Ld Granville (L. & Tel.)—
Mrs Th.—and minutes. Saw Miss Goalen. We felled a tree: & in-
spected others. Read Preller's Gr.Mythol.[7]—Caulfeild's Poems[8]—
Coplestone's Reply to Ed.Rev.—Plutarch respecting Woman's Virtue.[9]

9. Easter Day.

Church 8.30 AM H.C.—11 A.M.—7 P.M. Wrote to Mr Ayrton—Mr
West Tel.—Mr Bass—and minutes. Read Th. Parker's Life[10]—St
Francis of Assisi—Divers Sermons & Tracts.

10. Easter M.

Ch. 8½ AM. Wrote to Mr A. Strahan—Ld Granville (3 Telegr.)—Mr
G.E. Street—Ch. of Exr—Mr Acland MP.—Mrs Th.—and minutes.
Examined some Homeric translations. Read Plutarch's Consolatio—
Coplestone's Replies—Helps's Life of Cortes. Saw Mr Burnett. We
felled a beech.

To A. STRAHAN, publisher of *Good Words*,   Add MS 44539, f. 196.
10 April 1871.

You have lately published a small work entitled 'Reasons for returning to the
Church of England' which I have read with the utmost interest. So much so

---

[1] C. *Thirlwall, *A history of Greece*, 8v. (1835-47).
[2] Sir G. Fottrell, 'Inaugural address' (1871); to the Catholic university in Dublin.
[3] See 15 Jan. 71.   [4] H. Reville, *Essais de critique religieuse* (1860).
[5] J. S. B. *Monsell, *Hymns of love and praise for the Church's year* (1863).
[6] D. T. Morgan, *Hymns and other poetry of the Latin Church* (1870?).
[7] See 22 Nov. 67.   [8] S. F. A. Caulfeild, *Avenele and other poems* (1870).
[9] 'Mulierum virtutes', one of Plutarch's *Moralia*.   [10] See 22 Dec. 69.

indeed that I cannot help writing to you to express the hope that it is meeting with that attention from the public which it well deserves. Only the fact of its wanting a name can prevent its being widely read, & this I trust *may* not.

Had I been a free man, I should have been much disposed to write upon the book: but this I am not equal to undertaking in my present condition. But I have been very sorry to have declined or passed by your suggestions & I have been half tempted to send you some very old verses of mine for consideration, if only to show that it was not from want of will. I would not however do this without your wishing it & if I do send them I hope you will submit them to some *severe* judge.[1]

11. Tu.

Ch. 8½ A.M. Wrote to Mr Odo Russell—Mrs Th.—Ld R. Gower MP. —Chancr of Exr—Mr Cardwell—Ld Devon—Sir A. Gordon—Mr Goschen—Mr Bennett[2]—and minutes. Read Plut. Consolatio— Finished Coplestone's Tract—Sir M. Lopez's speech.[3] We felled a tree. In evg I set to work on an Inscription for the Monument of the dear Duchess of Sutherland.[4]

To R. LOWE, chancellor of the exchequer,   Add MS 44539, f. 198.
11 April 1871.

1. I think you are right in resorting to the Income tax, & likewise in trying to avoid the 2d penny if possible.
2. Of your items the most difficult is that of the death duties; I am not sure that I fully comprehend your plan. But I would give no *aggregate* relief to personal property; would lay no more on land than a fair equivalent for the relief it is about to get by the relinquishment of the House duty; & would temper but not abolish the consanguinity Scale. I doubt the necessity of lowering the 10%. I have a strong impression that you would fail in the proposal to raise land (I mean *virtually* to raise it for in the very large majority of instances, I believe it pays only *one*) to three. I cannot give an opinion on the getting rid of all questions as to predecessor & successor if it means more than that they would naturally disappear with the abolition of the scale which is doubtless true. I am not clear that the Cabinet would agree to abolish the scale: indeed I think it would not.
3. The lucifer matches I hope & think you would carry but I have little information & that old. I advise that on this & on gas Glyn be consulted as to the feeling in the H. of C. I am sceptical as to the ultimate revenue of 1ₘ̃: but I have no present alarms about 1872. 3. Your motto[5] will doubtless help.
4. I have always looked on gas as a tax that would be freely given in case of war. I do not feel sure as to its acceptance; but there is much to be said for it.

---

[1] Strahan responded enthusiastically, on 11 Apr. 1871; Add MS 44430, f. 117. See 16 Apr. 71.
[2] John G. Bennett, relative of diarist's widowed cousin and co-translator, Anne R. Bennett, who had apostasised; Hawn P. See 8 June 71.
[3] Sir L. M. Lopes, 'Speech on local taxation' (1871).
[4] See Add MSS 44431, f. 228; 44760, f. 24.
[5] 'ex luce lucellum', to be stamped on each match box.

5. We ought I think certainly to try the reduction of interest on the old S[avings] B[anks] monies.

Perhaps we can talk over these matters on Monday at H. of C. during the army estimates.

12. Wed.

Wrote to Ld R. Gower—Ld Granville (2, and Tel.)—Ld Cowper— Ld Lyttelton—Bp of Winchester—and minutes. Read Life of Cortes —Consolatio of Plutarch (finished). We felled a good oak. Ch. 8½ AM. Saw Aston Colliery Lessees—Mr Burnett. Further considered & finished draft of Inscription: also made an English Version.

13. Th.

Ch. 8½ A.M. Wrote to Ld Granville (1. & Tel)—Chancr of Exr—Mrs Th.—Mr Roundell—Mr Strahan—Mr Lambert—Mr S. Smith—Ld Halifax—Mr A.B. Hope—and minutes. Began Plut[arch] de Defectu Oraculorum. Read Life of Cortes Vol. 2.—We walked in woods & park.

To LORD HALIFAX, lord privy seal, 13 April 1871.   Add MS 44540, f. 4.

I find upon inquiry that H.M. is likely to be at Osborne until about May 5. & then a short fortnight only at Windsor before Balmoral.

In that fortnight we should require a Council for the Queen wishes Prince Arthur to be sworn a P.C. upon his coming of age which seems perfectly proper. It would not be desirable to raise the question of the provision for him during the Queen's absence.

That question is ugly, & had it been in[1] able hands would have been uglier. We now begin to see the first results in a practical form of the Queen's retirement from London, which has grown to be, to so serious an extent a retirement from business. Our affairs in America seem to march; but I think our excellent Commissioners a little over anxious to settle.

To Sidney SMITH, liberal agent, 13 April 1871.   Add MS 44540, f. 3.
'Private.'

My opinions on the minority clause[2] are still in unison with yours, & I feel as much as ever the hardships inflicted on the City of London, from which it has however been for the time relieved by a casualty. But looking back to the experience of last year, I am very doubtful whether the present attempt to stir the question is likely to lead to any advantageous result, & I think the Government will very likely have to reserve its 'liberty of action'.

It is a great matter that those members of it, who approved the minority clause in 1867 have since waived their own individual opinions.

---

[1] 'Less' omitted by copyist?   [2] Of the 1867 Reform Act.

14. Frid.

Ch. 8½ AM. Wrote to Ld Granville (1. & tel.)—Chancr of Exr—The Queen—Mr Cardwell—Ld Sydney—Mr Samuelson—Scotts—Mr Richard MP—Ld A. Hervey—& minutes. S. & I felled a stout oak. We had our tea in the open. Read Plut. de Def.Orac.—Life of Cortes.

To Henry RICHARD, M.P., 14 April 1871.   Add MS 44430, f. 132.

I have received your letter of the 8th with its inclosures relating to the proposed college at Aberystwith [*sic*].[1]

The spirit with which that undertaking has been set about is without doubt most honourable to its promoters.

The subject however of the interview which I had the pleasure of holding with you and Mr Osborne Morgan, I think during the last Session, was a different though a kindred one.

I then, speaking for myself individually, expressed a desire that the Government might, by a general cooperation from Wales, find itself in a condition to promote the higher education of the Welsh people in their own country, by the formation and endowment as far as necessary from public sources of a Welsh University. This desire I still entertain though I do not venture to form as yet a final opinion on the question.

Such an University would afford encouragement and support to Welsh Colleges by its examinations and degrees. If it were found allowable and expedient to endow it with some Exhibitions or Scholarships, and with Fellowships of reward (as distinguished from the Life and teaching Fellowships of the older Universities) which would more directly assist the Colleges [*sic*].

But I do not see how the Government could assist any particular Colleges without raising great difficulties. 1. I incline to think that if such assistance were given it must be on the footing of the Act of 1845 for establishing the Queen's Colleges. But the plan of the Aberystwith College is altogether different. 2. The plan adopted raises again that religious difficulty which ample experience has shown us it is so much easier to raise than to lay. The State has never adopted the principle of giving aid from the Exchequer to Colleges on the ground of their teaching only an 'undenominational religion' and you were one of those who in the discussions of last year on Education appeared to feel, as I felt, that this basis affords no real or unequivocal means of escape. 3. The Chancellor of the Exchequer and the Government have declined aid to Owen's College in Manchester[2] notwithstanding the large sums provided for it by voluntary means: and were aid to be granted to Aberystwith, not only that but a number of other like applications would have to be encountered.

The fact is that when I carefully defined my expression of opinion last year as my own & nothing more, it was because I felt by no means sure whether I should be able to induce the Finance Minister & my other colleagues to share the views I am so much inclined to entertain respecting a Welsh University intended to meet the wants of the middle class and of the industrious and aspiring youth in whom Wales honourably abounds. But even if my own ideas extended beyond this subject, which I am bound to own that they do not I should still see no

---

[1] Add MS 44430, f. 100.   [2] See 10 and 24 Apr. 69.

likelihood of a movement of the Government as a whole or of Parliament in the sense indicated by the papers you have sent me.[1]

15. Sat.

Ch. 8½ AM. Wrote to Ld Granville (Tel.)—Mr Odo Russell (Tel)—Sir J. Lacaita—Mr Lowe—Mr Cardwell—Ld Lyttelton—Mr Jacob Bright—Ld R. Gower—Mr Ayrton—and minutes. Saw Rev. Mr Chamberlayne. Herbert & I kibbled the oak of yesterday. Read Plut. de Orac.Def. (finished)—Life of Cortes (finished).

To Jacob BRIGHT,[2] M.P., 15 April 1871. 'Private.'   Add MS 44540, f. 6.

I am sure it would not be expedient that I should receive the proposed deputation of Ladies on the subject of the woman suffrage.[3] I do not say this in a spirit of indiscriminating hostility to all the claims now made on the part of women: but I consider that the Deputation would tend to connect the argument with associations, which would not be beneficial to it.

I might take a broader ground, & reply in the negative for that my time does not allow me to become the object of deputations merely demonstrative, & that neither am I able to discuss with advantage orally a subject which, so far as Parliament is concerned, has not passed beyond its initiatory stage, & to which I could do much more justice by studying the argument in the form of a written communication.

16. 1 S.E.

Ch. 11 A.M. with H.C. and 7 P.M. Visited the Potters[4] with C. Wrote to Mr J. C. Williams—Ld R. Gower—Mr Burnett—Ld A. Hervey—Sir R. Phillimore—& minutes. Corrected proof of my Verses for Good Words.[5] Read Buchanan's Teuton[6]—Miss Phillimore on Paradiso[7]—Mrs Oliphant's St Francis (finished).

17. M. [London]

Off at 8.10 with WHG. for London. Reached C.H.T. at 3. Wrote to Mr St George Burke[8]—Mr A. Strahan—Rev F. Morse—Dr Payne Smith

[1] Despite Gladstone's refusal, Aberystwyth opened 1872; see K. O. Morgan, *Wales in British Politics*, 47.

[2] A leading protagonist of women's suffrage.

[3] Request untraced; see 3 May 71.   [4] See 19 Sept., 19 Nov. 70.

[5] 'On an infant who was born, baptized, and died on the same day', verses composed 12 July 1836, *Good Words* (1871), 365.

[6] R. W. *Buchanan, 'The Teuton monologue', *Poetical Works* (1884-1901); Gladstone gave him civil list pension 1870.

[7] C. M. Phillimore, 'Dante's "Paradise" ', *St Paul's Magazine*, viii. 63 (April 1871).

[8] See 13 July 44.

—Mr Blunt—Ld Granville (2)—C.G.—The Queen—Mrs Th.—and minutes. Saw The Lord Justice Clerk—Chancr of Exr (on Budget, etc.)—Sir J. Pakington—Mr Glyn—Sol. General—Ld Elcho—Sir T.E. May—Mr A. Kinnaird. Saw Mrs Th—wonder. H. of C. $4\frac{1}{2}$-$12\frac{1}{4}$.[1] —But dined (2 h) with Sir T.E. May. Began Evidence before Public Business Committee.[2]

Cabinet Ap. 17. 71. 2 PM.[3]
√ Westmeath Committee's Report.[4]
√ Public Business Committee's Recommendations.
√ U.S. High Commission.
√ Budget.[5]

18. Tu.

Wrote to Sir T. Brinckman—The Queen (2)—Mr Monsell—C.G.— & minutes. Read Westmeath Report—Brougham's Autobiography.[6] Saw Mr Lambert—Ld Dalhousie—Ld Granville—Mr Glyn—Mr Goschen—Ld Hartn. H of C. $4\frac{1}{2}$-8 and $9\frac{1}{4}$-$12\frac{1}{2}$. Spoke on Sunday Labour motion, & on Sir S. Robinson. We could not allow this proposal to be withdrawn.[7] Dined with the J. Talbots. Cabinet 2-$4\frac{1}{2}$.

Cabinet 2 PM. Ap. 18. 71.[8]
On American negotiation. √ Alabama. √ Fisheries. Telegrams answered & framed.

19. Wed.

Wrote to Chr of Exr—Abp of Canterbury—Mr Baxter[9]—Bp of Winchester—C.G.—Ld Lyttelton—Mr [W. T.] Bullock—Bp of Exeter—Mr Disraeli—Ld Granville—The Queen—Mr Fortescue (2)[10]—and minutes. Saw D. of Sutherland *cum* Mr Loch—Ld Granville—Sir R. Phillimore—Chancr of Exr. Cabinet 2-$5\frac{3}{4}$, Dined with Mr Foster at the Garrick Club: we then went to the French

[1] Army estimates: *H* ccv. 1180.
[2] Reported 28 March, *PP* 1871 ix. 1; he answered Gathorne *Hardy's question on it next day; *H* ccv. 1242.
[3] Add MS 44639, f. 51. Appears to read *sic* as to date and time; perhaps that held on 27 April 1871 at 12.30; no cabinet mentioned in *The Times* as held this day.
[4] See 22 Apr. 71. Report in *PP* 1871 xiii. 547.
[5] See 19 Apr. 71.   [6] See 31 Mar. 71.
[7] Gladstone justified his conduct in the dismissal of Sir S. *Robinson as third lord of the admiralty, in the aftermath of the 'Captain' affair; he prevented Lord H. Lennox withdrawing his motion for a cttee. which was beaten in 104 : 153; *H* ccv. 1320.
[8] Add MS 44639, f. 52.   [9] As next note.
[10] First letter, complaining at his absence from the division on Lennox' motion last night: 'I am sure you did not happen to notice . . . [it] was a vote of confidence, & the issue one of life or death'; Add MS 44540, f. 11.

play: paid rather much (10/6) and perhaps distinctly heard little, with a good deal of effort.[1] Read Westmeath Evidence—Q.R. on Civil Pensions.[2]

Cabinet Ap. 19. 71. 2 PM.[3]

    U.S. negotiation. Telegram to Commissioners allowing them to propose 'civil war' and fall back on 'the years 186-'.[4]

√ Budget. 1. Duty on Lucifer matches. Agreed to.[5] 2. Alteration of death duties. 3. Raise Income Tax from 4d in the £ to £2.4 or $2\frac{1}{2}$ per Cent. Agreed to. Deficit 2713m[ille]. Incr[ease]

               Death duties 300m.
               Matches   500m.

√ Ld de Grey's No 79. answer agreed to—approach to be given at the proper time.

√ Mauritius Fortifications. Action postponed. Perfect liberty reserved.

√ Westmeath Committee.

Mr. Goschen: 1. Can you not make even a shot at the amount of benefit, which the *land* derive (through farmhouses &c.) from remission of House Tax? [I will try but I should think those who levy the House Tax ought to have the best information]

2. Have you seen the letter from me to you in Pall Mall Gazette? Can you account for this impudent forgery? [No! Most scandalous but I presume they meant it for a joke. They had something like it once before].[6]

To B. DISRAELI, M.P., 19 April 1871,   Hughenden MSS, Box 129.
'Private & Confidential.'

    Considering that one of your leading political friends[7] is engaged in the important negotiations at Washington for which we are responsible, I think it due to you and to those who act with you (and I am sorry it did not happen to strike me sooner) to state that we cannot either adopt or account for the statements which have appeared on this side of the water with reference to the settlement of what are termed the Alabama Claims. Those statements, as far as they have met my eye, are as a whole premature, and are in some important particulars inaccurate.

To C. S. P. FORTESCUE, president of the   Carlingford MSS CP 1/168.
board of trade, 19 April 1871. 'Night'.

    I thank you for your frank explanation;[8] and, as the matter has gone by, it is happily as needless, as it would be disagreeable, to raise it into a question of practical difference.

    [1] *Nos Intimes* at the Charing Cross Theatre.
    [2] *Quarterly Review*, cxxx. 407 (April 1871).   [3] Add MS 44639, f. 53.
    [4] Further details of the neutrality agreement; see 21 Mar. 71.
    [5] An ill-fated proposal; for Gladstone's warning, see 11 Apr. 71.
    [6] Note, with *Goschen's replies in [ ], pushed across the cabinet table; Add MS 44639, f. 54. *Pall Mall Gazette*, 18 April 1871, 11.   [7] i.e. Northcote.
    [8] Of his abstaining on Lennox' motion, knowing the govt. safe, 19 April 1871, Add MS 44122, f. 228.

But I should not act frankly by you if I did not state it, without hesitation, as a general & prospective proposition, that, without reference to the likelihood or unlikelihood of defeat, there can upon motions which must from their nature be votes of confidence, be but one rule for members of the Government, & that is to give the votes themselves which at the same time the Government with less strong title is asking from the members of their party.

20. Th.

Wrote to Dean of ChCh—Mr Baxter—Duke of Argyll—M. Wolowski—Miss Wood[1]—Mr T.B. Potter—Ld Kimberley—The Queen—& minutes. H of C. $4\frac{1}{2}$-$8\frac{1}{4}$ and $9\frac{1}{4}$-$12\frac{1}{2}$.[2] Saw Sir A. Spearman—Mr MacColl—Mr Glyn—Ld A. Hervey—Ld Granville—P.M. General—Mr Hardy—Mrs Th. late: more wonder X. Read Westmeath Evidence.

To the DUKE OF ARGYLL, Indian secretary,   Add MS 44540, f. 12.
20 April 1871.

Lowe's argument about the Death duties question seemed to carry the Cabinet without any hesitation on its part. The imposition as far as it regards land is very mild. Its ultimate effect in accord[?] with the *scale* will be 1. To levy under Succession duty *one half* of the min. Ests. of 1853. 2. To get additional Income from *realty*, probably of £200,000 or something more, & from *personalty* of certainly over £500,000.

Even independently of your wish, & still & much more with your wish, Cliveden could not be refused were we free: but I doubt whether my wife can leave Hawarden until Saturday morning—in the evening we dine with the Egertons: & I am afraid a visit could hardly be made out with any satisfaction under these circumstances. Indeed I gather that my wife has written in this sense, in reply to a most kind letter from Lady W[estminster].

21. Fr.

Wrote to Abp of Canterbury—Ld Granville—Ld R. Gower—Dean Ramsay—Ld Lyttelton—Mrs Hope—Mr Bowie[3]—The Queen—& minutes. Saw Ld R. Cavendish—Ld Granville—Mr Glyn. Read Westmeath Evidence. H of C. $4\frac{1}{2}$-$8\frac{1}{2}$ and $9\frac{1}{2}$-$1\frac{1}{4}$.[4]

[1] On Queen's instructions, sending condolence on d. of her relative, John Robert Davison, liberal M.P. Durham; Add MS 44540, f. 12.
[2] *Lowe's budget: *H* ccv. 1391.
[3] Declining Henry Bowie's invitation to address the Philosophical Institute; Add MS 44540, f. 13.
[4] Spoke on 1856 Paris declaration: *H* ccv. 1499.

22. *Sat.*

Wrote to Ld Salisbury—Ld Moncreiff—The Queen—& minutes. Cabinet 2¾-6: chiefly on Westmeath. Saw Ld Moncreiff—Mr Glyn —Mr West—W.H.G.—Ld Stratford de Redcliffe. Dined with the Egertons. Duchess of Marlborough's after. Read Westmeath Evidence.

Cabinet Sat. Ap. 22. 2.30 PM[1]

√ Westmeath. Decided to bring in, within the limits of the late inquiry, a Bill to empower L[or]d L[ieutenan]t to proclaim susp[ension of] Habeas Corpus —to endure for two years—up to July 1. 73.[2]

√ U.S. Telegrams. as to San Juan. Telegram of Gr[anville] Kim[berley] & G[ladstone]. as to British Claims. We do not know why to another Commission. Tel. 89—Articles amended.

Mr. Stuart to go temporarily to Athens *vice* Erskine on leave.

√ Finance: Monday. C. of E. to speak.

√ Univ. Tests. Salisbury's Resolutions shall be opposed.[3] WEG. to see him if possible.[4]

23. *2 S.E.*

York St Chapel to hear Mr Capes,[5] who was much affected. Chapel Royal in aft. Saw Mr Glyn—Mr West—Mrs Th. Read Nomad on Ref. Reformed[6]—Field's Autobiography[7]—Hawkins's Sermon[8]— Divers Tracts. Wrote to Mr Cardwell—Mr Fortescue—& minutes.

24. *M.*

Wrote to Chancr of Exr—The Queen—Ld Halifax—Mrs Th.—Mr Warwick Brookes—& minutes. Saw Archdn Harrison—Capt. Harris —Mr Glyn—M. Wolowski. Dean of Ch.Ch & Depn on Revised Version[9]—Dean & Dr Cartmell[10] on Univ. Tests. Dined with the F. Cavendishes. H of C. 4½-8 and 9-1¼. Spoke on White's motion respecting Budget & voted in 257:230.[11] A help to future economy. Read Crabb's Tales.[12]

---

[1] Add MS 44639, f. 56.   [2] Introduced on 27 April in the Lords.
[3] For *Salisbury's hostility, see Cecil, *Salisbury*, ii. 19.   [4] See 25 Apr. 71.
[5] John Moore Capes, 1812-89; maverick, blind Anglican priest; see 1 and 10 Apr. 71.
[6] *The Reformation reformed, by a Nomad* (1871).
[7] Perhaps J. Mullaly, *The laying of the cable . . . with biographical sketches of C. W. Field* (1858).
[8] E. *Hawkins, 'The duty of weighing the relative importance of questions' (1871).
[9] No report found; the Revised Version was in preparation.
[10] James Cartmell, 1829-81; master of Christ's, Cambridge, from 1849.
[11] James White, liberal M.P., moved retrenchment resolution; *H* ccv. 1659.
[12] G. *Crabbe, *Tales* [in verse] (1812).

To R. LOWE, chancellor of the exchequer,   Add MS 44540, f. 15.
24 April 1871. 'Most private.'

I have new *doubts* about the question whether matches should be dealt with
in a separate Bill—
1. It is not easy summarily to smother the demand for a reasonable time in a
case where such allegations are made about displacement of labour, unless you
can meet them with a very clear confutation; or with strong evidence as to the
effect of the present system of match manufacture in the loss of property by
fire (This last is the point, on good evidence of which I think your best chance
of carrying the measure may probably depend).
2. Suppose that by pressure & with some difficulty we put this proposal as a
separate proposal through the Commons—We then send it to the Lds, & the Lds
throw it out. We ought not to place the H. of C. in the condition to receive,
through our agency & influence, such a slap in the face. But the Lords cannot
on account of it throw out a Tax Bill in which it is entirely an item. Please to
consider this.[1]

25. Tu.

Wrote to Mr Crossfield—Ld Kimberley—Mr C. Gore—The Queen
—and minutes. Saw Ld Lyttelton—Ld Salisbury[2]—Mr Glyn—Ld
Kimberley—Mr Goschen—Ld Halifax. Cabinet at 3.30.[3] H of C.
4.30–8 and 9–10$\frac{3}{4}$.[4] Saw Hamilton X. Read Crabb's Tales.

To LORD KIMBERLEY, colonial secretary,   Add MS 44540, f. 16.
25 April 1871. 'Private.'

I told Salisbury *inter alia* that No 2 of his resolutions, even in a negative form
would not be accepted by the H. of C. I said we deprecated any widening of the
area of the Bill as dangerous. But that if he pressed it, I thought it might be possible to adopt his No 3 & No 7 provided No 3 were clearly understood (& this he
understands) to cover No 7, & provided No 7 ran somewhat as follows: 'That no
Fellow unless he shall have become & continued to be a Tutor or other officer
of his College, shall be one of the Governing Body of such college, until he shall
have been a Fellow for 5 years, & shall have been elected into the said Body.' I
only however reserved this as a matter open to cons[ideratio]n.

26. Wed.

Wrote to Ld Granville—Mr Parratt—Canon Trevor—Ld Halifax—
Mr Childers—Robn G.—& minutes. Attended Levee at 2 PM. Saw

[1] No reply traced.
[2] Meeting arranged on University Tests; 'I am afraid from your language, that it will be
to hear an unfavourable opinion of my resolutions'; Salisbury to Gladstone, 23 Apr. 1871,
Add MS 44430, f. 150. See 30 June 71.
[3] No agenda found; it decided 'to desist from pressing the proposal of the duty on
matches'; Gladstone to Victoria, CAB A41.
[4] Questioned by *Dilke on matchmakers' demonstration; *Lowe then announced withdrawal of the proposed match tax; *H* ccv. 1684.

Ld Lyttelton—Mr M'Coll—Mr Glyn (2)—Mr Gurdon—WHG.— Ld Granville—Chancr of Exr—Mr Forster—Ct Cadorna. Clar. Trustees met here at 3. At the last gasp of the Trust, its work being all but done.[1] Dined with the Forsters. Read Crabb's Tales.

To H. C. E. CHILDERS, M.P., 26 April 1871.   Add MS 44540, f. 17.

I must write a line to say how glad I am to hear of your progress,[2] & all your old colleagues will share the feeling, though we have now lost the hope of immediately profiting by what I hope is to be your early recovery. Of the S. Robinson question we all thought we got free as satisfactorily as a case of the kind admits, where a Govt. fights with hands tied behind its back against assailants who hit fou[l] & left handed friends who do not know when they get up within a mile or two how far their tongues will carry them. For you there is in the H[ouse] a genuine sentiment of respect & gratitude.

No subject on which you could touch is to me more interesting than all that relates at this moment to Dr. Döllinger. I do not quite understand his being able wholly to avoid churches, but perhaps he can have in private the offices of religion. The Hungarian bishops as a body are, I suppose, those alone to whom we must look as having in their hands the best interests of the Latin Church.

I can well understand that the awful disorganisation of France, while it is influencing[?] Germany as to the indemnity, is playing her game as to the still weighty question of territory. You will have seen that we are in a little rough water about the Budget. The real cause lies in the Expenditure. Disraeli has given notice of a motion of general condemnation, which may help us out into smoother water.

To LORD HALIFAX, lord privy seal, 26 April 1871.   Add MS 44540, f. 16.
'Private.'

I understand it to be the opinion of the Cabinet yesterday that whatever concession we were to make upon the Budget in the way of withdrawals was to be made yesterday, & at one stroke, not successively. In this view your letter[3] would have wholly a retrospective character. I do not know whether you would advise that now when Lowe by direction of the Cabinet has announced his intention to proceed tomorrow he should be asked to announce a change of that intention. At the same time, there is no disputing the general truth of your remarks; & the knowledge obtained by Glyn last night has altered his calculations about the death duties simply for the worse, so that if that question be fought alone, instead of 'doubtful' as I yesterday reported it, we are pretty *certain* of defeat. Dizzy has however put down a notice of a general condemnation which may bring us out of the affair. Should Dizzy change his front it may untie our hands a little & enable us to change ours.

---

[1] The Radcliffe Trust; see 16 July 58.
[2] Childers to Gladstone, 22 April 1871, Nuremberg, Add MS 44128, f. 215, reporting two talks with Döllinger.
[3] Not found.

27. Th.

Wrote to The Queen—Mr Hammond—& minutes. Cabinet 12.30-2.[1]
Abn Memorial Committee met here at 2 & made arrangements. 3-4.
Royal Academy: Prince of Wales's party. H of C. 4½-8¼ and 9¼-12¼.
Made the explanations on the Budget.[2] Dined with the Wests. First
breakfast party at home. Saw Ld Salisbury—Ld Granville *cum* Mr
Brand and Mr Glyn. Began Mr Maguire's Novel.[3]

28. Fr.

Wrote to Ld Granville—Mrs Th.—Mrs Bennett—Mrs Begbie—Mr
Ouvry—The Queen—and minutes. H of C. 4½-8 and 9-12½. Wrote
Mem. on U.S. Negotiation. Saw Rev Mr M'Coll—Mr Monsell—Mr
Glyn—Ld Granville—Mr Ayrton—Mrs Hope—Mr Morrison—Mr
C. Howard. Read Lanfrey's 'Essais'[4]—Maguire's Novel. We were de-
feated on Cowper Temple's motion with circumstances of much
indignity.[5]

1. Rebellion is (I apprehend) forcible resistance of subject persons or communities to lawful authority: and the question whether the resort to force by the
Southern States of America in 1861 was a rebellion or not depends entirely on
their prior position in reference to the Federal Power. If the States were up to
that date Sovereign States, united by a tie properly Federal, as a large & perhaps
the weightiest portion of American Statesmen have held, then the Act of War
was not an Act of rebellion, any more than was the recent Circular of Prince
Gortschakoff. If on the other hand the States were not Sovereign States then, as
(I believe) they are not now, then the Act was an Act of rebellion. What have we
to do with the decision of this question? And what has it to do with the present
negotiation? No more, it must be answered, than the question of the use of the
term has to do with the moral merits or demerits of the war.
2. On the question thus absolutely irrelevant, opinion is much divided in this
country. Not that the point has been accurately examined except by a few: but
sides were taken strongly and sharply, and the controversy would be revived by
the needless & wanton provocation which the use of such a word offers.
3. It has now been ascertained that the British Govt. advisedly and uniformly
refrained from the employment of this word during the struggle: and it does not
appear creditable, or consistent with due respect to those, who then conducted
the correspondence & the controversy with America, or to this country as represented by their acts, to depart from their phraseology upon a point when the
departure will be reasonably construed to be a repudiation.

[1] No agenda found. Perhaps that printed at 17 Apr. 71, though the time does not fit.
[2] He announced 2d. on income tax to replace withdrawn match tax: *H* ccv. 1780.
[3] J. F. *Maguire, The next generation [a novel]*, 3v. (1871).
[4] See 19 Sept. 70.
[5] Defeated in 96 : 197 on motion on Epping Forest of W. F. Cowper-Temple, a whig,
moved despite diarist's appeal for withdrawal; *H* ccv. 1867.

4. Still less is it agreeable to the dignity of this country that as long as the Southern States were maintaining the conflict with a prospect of success, & with a probability that we might in the future have to deal with them as an independent Power, we should uniformly abstain from affixing to them the political stigma implied in the word rebellion: but when they are trampled under foot we do the act which, it could be said with some appearance of reason, we were too timid or too selfish to do while there was anything to be lost by it.

5. If the Americans, acting in the spirit of the Orangemen, wish to place on record some impression disagreeable to a portion of their fellow countrymen, they might call them retrospectively the 'so-called Southern States' as this phrase was used during the controversy by the British Government to avoid the affirmation of a title which it was not our business either to deny or affirm.

6. I cannot go so near to imputing sheer insolence to the American Commissioners as not to believe that they would be perfectly satisfied, if not with the alternative just suggested, with placing the word rebellion in the Treaty so as to show distinctly that it was part of their allegations, or else with our recording in a protocol that we accepted the American description of an American court, and did not take upon ourselves to pronounce any judgment on a question of political rights under the American constitution as it stood prior to 1861.[1]

29. Sat.

Wrote to Mr Morrison[2]—Chancr of Exr—Ld Lyttelton—Archbp of York—Bp of London—Bp of Winchester—Mr Macfie—Mr Burnett —Robn G.—Prof. Lightfoot—Mr Phipps—Watson (Tel)—and minutes. Saw Mr West—Mr M'Coll—Duke of Argyll—Mr Glyn— Ld Halifax—Ld Chancellor—Bp of Winchester—Bp of London. Saw Mrs Th.—who goes on Monday. It was the climax of our communications. May the great Friend ever help her. 2-5. Visited the Academy Exhibn with much interest and delight. Attended the dinner: & spoke to the Toast of Ministers.[3]

To LORD LYTTELTON, 29 April 1871.   Add MS 44540, f. 19.
'Private and Confidential.'

Seeing that Charles voted in the majority last night on Cowper Temple's motion, I beg you to read a description contained in the leading article of the 'Standard' this morning,[4] which is substantially true, & to say that in my judgment a motion carried under circumstances of such indignity is very like a notice to quit, & might raise if repeated, questions of gravity for which the supporters of such motions had better be prepared. Pray do not suppose I write for the purpose of drawing forth any explanation.

[1] Initialled and dated 28 April 1871; Add MS 44616, f. 149.
[2] Walter Morrison, 1836-?; liberal (unionist) M.P. Plymouth 1861-74, Skipton 1886-1900; had sent a memorial on women's disabilities; Add MS 44540, f. 19.
[3] On purchase of *Peel's pictures; *The Times*, 1 May 1871, 6.
[4] 'The minority of 101 last night is nothing less than a catastrophe . . . [Gladstone's] hold on the Liberal party is growing weaker and weaker'; *The Standard*, 29 April 1871.

30. 3 S.E.

Ch. Royal mg—York St Chapel aft. for Mr Capes: but I slept too much. Wrote to Mr Cardwell—Mr Stansfeld. Saw Ld Granville—Mr Glyn. Read Liddon & Pusey's letters[1]—Lightfoot on Revision[2]—O. Shipley on the Judgment[3]—Stanley, Capes, & Bavarian Catholic in Contemp.Rev.[4]

London Monday May One 1871. St Ph. & St. James

Wrote to Ld Hartington—Bp of Winchester—Ld Granville (2)—The Queen—& minutes. Read Q.R. on Ch. & Nonconformy[5]—Maguire's Novel. Wrote Mem. on Greek Affairs. Saw Mr Glyn—Chancr of Exr —Ld Devon *cum* Mr Forbes—Ld Granville—Divers of Cabinet on U.S. Telegr. Eleven to dinner at home. H of C. $4\frac{1}{2}$–8 and 9–$1\frac{3}{4}$. Spoke on Smith's motion & voted in 335 : 250.[6]

2. Tu.

Wrote to Sir D. Salomons—Ld Granville—Mr Peek MP[7]—Mr Cardwell—Mr Bate—Rev Mr Church—H.J.G.—Mrs Th.—& minutes. H of C. $4\frac{1}{2}$–$7\frac{3}{4}$. Turned the corner of an awkward *little* attack.[8] Saw Ld Granville—The O'Conor Don—Mr Glyn—Mr Goschen— Bp of Winchester. Dined at Bp of Winchester's, to meet the Heywoods. Read Q.R. on Records—Macmillan on Ireland & H of C.[9]— Maguire.

To E. CARDWELL, war secretary, 2 May 1871.   PRO 30/48/8, f. 64.

1. I wrote to you in the recess[10] suggesting that returns or statements should be prepared comparing minutely in all the essential points the case of the officers of the German or Prussian Army with that of our own. I do not know whether you have been able to procure anything of this kind.
2. I want now to ask for something which is entirely within our reach, & to ascertain exactly the proportion of temporary officers, who do not make the

---

[1] H. P. *Liddon, 'The Purchas Judgment . . . together with a letter by E. B. Pusey' (1871).
[2] J. B. *Lightfoot, *On a fresh revision of the English New Testament* (1871).
[3] O. *Shipley, *Secular judgments in spiritual matters* (1871).
[4] *Contemporary Review*, xvi. 486 (February 1871); xvi. 519, 505 (March 1871).
[5] *Quarterly Review*, cxxx. 432 (April 1871).
[6] W. H. *Smith opposed the increase in income tax: *H* ccv. 2011.
[7] (Sir) Henry William Peek, 1825–98; tory M.P. Surrey 1868–84; cr. bart. 1874.
[8] On postage charges; *H* ccvi. 61.
[9] *Macmillan's Magazine*, xxiv. 32 (May 1871).
[10] On 23 April 1871, PRO 30/48/8, f. 51. And see 11 May 1870.

army a profession, to life officers, or those who do, & who become the proper subjects of retirement.[1]

It is difficult to suggest the form of a return for this purpose, & I do not doubt your Department has it all. I am desirous to become well acquainted with the facts. It appears to me to be a grave subject for consideration whether that system of temporary officership, which we now keep alive at the option of the individual, might not be advantageously changed into one for the benefit of the State; & whether a permanent Commission carrying title to retirement might not be earned after a period of probation & upon adequate proofs of merit.

To Sir D. SALOMONS, M.P., 2 May 1871.   Add MS 44540, f. 22.

The subject of the Contagious Diseases Acts will have from me a full & careful consideration: but I could not with advantage receive any deputation[2] on the subject until the Commission reports & the report is in my hands. Only thus should I be in a condition to see that the points of the case were duly raised or to explain myself properly to the Deputation.

3. Wed.

Wrote to Sir T. Biddulph—Ld Chancellor—Col. Scott—Mr Fortescue—The Queen—Ld Granville—Watsons—and minutes. Read Maguire. Saw Mr Goschen—Mr Glyn—Ld Lyttelton—Mr G. Hardy —6-7 Abp of Y. Bp of L. Bp of W. on Lectionary Bill—Ld Halifax —Dined at Grillion's—Lady O. Fitzgerald's after-d. Saw Russell: Terry yesterday, an interesting case[R]. H of C. 12½-3. Spoke on Women's Disabilities Bill.[3] Sat to Mr Dickinson's Photographer in Langham Pl(?)

4. Th.

16 to breakfast. Wrote to Sir F. Rogers—Watsons (Tel)—Ld Kimberley—The Queen—& minutes. H of C. 4½-8¼ & 9½-1¾. Spoke on Torrens's m. & voted in 294:248.[4] Saw Dean of Canterbury—Mr Newman Hall—Mr West—Ld Granville—Mr Glyn—WHG (Dewsbury)[5]—Mr Roundell *cum* Prof. Bryce—Bp of Winchester. Dined with Mr Fortescue. Read Maguire. Visited Maclean's Gallery.

[1] Sent on 9 May 1871, Add MS 44119, f. 234.
[2] Apparently suggested by Salomons, but no letter found.
[3] Stating govt. offered no view of it; personally opposing it, but ambiguously: *H* ccvi. 88. Bill defeated in 151:220.
[4] Defending the revised budget, which then passed: *H* ccvi. 222.
[5] On its vacant living; Add MS 44540, f. 31.

5. Fr.

Wrote to Miss Burdett Coutts—Duke of Argyll—The Queen—Rev.
Sir Gilbert Lewis—and minutes. Read Maguire—Lanfrey. Eleven to
dinner. Saw Mrs Young's Landlady—Blake.[1] Visited Christie's. Saw
Mr Glyn—Mr Goschen. H of C. $4\frac{1}{2}$-$8\frac{1}{2}$ and $9\frac{1}{2}$-$1\frac{1}{4}$.[2] Visited N. Gallery to see the Peel collection: with much delight.[3]

6. Sat. [Windsor]

Wrote to Mr Heron[4]—Rev. Coker Adams[5]—The Queen—Mr W.D.
Christie—Mrs Th. Read Maguire. Arranging papers. Saw Mr Gurdon
—Bp of Winchester—Mr West—Dean of Westmr—Mr Glyn—Ld
Stanhope—Mr Cardwell—Ld Chancellor—Mr Forster—Ld Gran-
ville—D. of Argyll—Ld Sydney. Cabinet $2\frac{1}{2}$-6. Dined with the D. of
Cambridge. Went down by 10.45 to Windsor with Pr. Arthur & Lt.
Picard.[6]

Cabinet May 6. 71. 2.30 PM.[7]
√ Order of business—announce on Monday.[8]
√ Budget—disposed of?[9]
√ Westmeath—morning sitting on Friday & till through?
⎰ Trades' Unions.
⎱ Univ. Tests.
⎰ Eccl. Titles.
√ Army Bill—all Govt. rights as far as possible.
√ Ballot Bill—to follow.
√ Scotch Education—to follow.
√ Licensing Bill—New Bill. To be pressed to an issue. Cabinet Committee?[10]
√ Local Rating Bill—give up contested parts H[ouse] Tax[11]
Chancellor's Bills? Postpone our judgment? desirable to elicit Parl. opinion?
√ Game Bills—to *one* Committee?
√ Prayer Book & Lectionary?
√ Public Business Resolutions—morning sitting after Westmeath Bill?[12]
√ Registration Bill—Mr Bruce to settle.[13]

[1] Rescue work.
[2] Questioned on China and taxation, then Poor Law deb.: *H* ccvi. 271.
[3] The fine collection of Sir R. *Peel, 2nd bart., given to the National Gallery.
[4] Denis Caulfield Heron, 1826–81; lawyer and liberal M.P. Tipperary 1870–4.
[5] Cadwallader Coker Adams, vicar of Shilton from 1852.
[6] Lieut. Pickard, Prince Arthur's aide.
[7] Add MS 44639, f. 57.   [8] *H* ccvi. 399.
[9] Overoptimistic; because of technical anomalies, the re-committed Income Tax Bill had
to be withdrawn on 11 May.
[10] See Add MS 44639, f. 59: Halifax, Hartington, Bruce, Lowe, Stansfeld, Kimberley.
[11] Bill withdrawn on 8 May.
[12] Proposed and accepted on 12 May 1871: *H* ccvi. 696.
[13] Two liberal private member bills to improve the registration system were introduced
in May, withdrawn at the session's end.

√ Univ. Tests Bill. Ld Kimberley. Proposed amendments of Ld Salisbury answered in detail.
Scotland. Schemes for charitable institutions. Commission proposed by Mr Bruce: no.[1]
As to losses of Captain's officers.

7. 4 S.E.

Castle Chapel 10 & 12. St George's 4.30.—'Hear my prayer':[2] most beautiful. Wrote to C.G. Saw H.M. aft.—& dined. Conversation with P. Leopold. Conversation with Ld Alfred Paget[3] respecting the Crown. Long walk with the Dean:[4] also conversation in evg, very much about the Crown. Read Union Review—Macmillan on Darwin —Tracts on Purchas Judgment and other subjects.

8. M. [London]

Went up at 10.20 with Prince Arthur. Saw Mr Pandeli Ralli[5]—Mr J. Russell—Mr Glyn—Ld Granville. Wrote to The Queen 2, & Mem . . . and minutes. At Christie's. Read Maguire—Pictura Picturae.[6] 10 to dinner. H of C. $4\frac{1}{2}$-8 and $9\frac{1}{2}$-2: also in H. of L.[7]

9. Tu.

Wrote to Mr Disraeli—Sir A. Gordon—Watsons—Prince Arthur— Ld Lyttelton—Sir H. Elliot—The Queen—and minutes. H of C. $4\frac{1}{4}$-$8\frac{1}{4}$ and $9\frac{1}{2}$-$12\frac{3}{4}$. Spoke against Mr Miall's motion.[8] Saw Mr M'Coll —Mr Glyn—Miss Burdett Coutts—Mrs Brown—Mrs Th. Attended Meeting Trustees N. Portrait Gallery. Read Maguire.

To B. DISRAELI, M.P., 9 May 1871.　　　　　　Hughenden MSS, Box 129.

I have just received the authentic intimation that the Treaty with America has been signed.

I am not at this moment in possession, with certainty, of its continuous text; but when I receive it, no time will be lost in sending it to you.

[1] See Add MS 44639, f. 66 for Bruce's circular on it.
[2] Probably Mendelssohn's version.
[3] Lord Alfred Henry Paget, 1816-88, 5th s. of 1st marquis of Anglesea; Victoria's chief equerry and clerk marshall.　　　　　　[4] i.e. *Wellesley.
[5] Pandeli Ralli, 1845-1928, merchant and liberal M.P. Bridport 1875-80, Wallingford 1880-5.
[6] C. Reade, Pictura picturae; a poem (1871).
[7] In the Commons, Army Regulation Bill, in the Lords, Salisbury's amndt. to University Tests Bill passed, three bps. voting with govt., nine against: H ccvi. 383.
[8] *Miall's motion for abolition of established churches defeated: H ccvi. 559.

Meantime I need hardly guard you against accepting fully accounts which may appear in the newspaper Telegrams. I read today for example that no claims on account of the Fenian Raids will be admitted. The meaning I believe simply to be not that they have been abandoned, nor that they have been the subject of any formal act, but that they are not included in the Treaty, and will stand for such separate consideration as they may deserve.

The general basis is, settlement by arbitration: a good & significant precedent, I trust, for us, & for mankind.

To Sir H. G. ELLIOT, ambassador to Turkey,   Add MS 44540, f. 27.
9 May 1871.

I thank you very much for your letter of the 1st,[1] & for the kind interest you have taken in the matter of the Archbishop of Chios. What I have heard of him through private channels leads me to believe that he is really a good man. The clouds of the Session here appear to clear, & we have just heard of the signature of our treaty in America: but I fear the cares of your special post do not offer much hope of diminution. Although Granville got us in the very best manner out of the Black Sea business, & although there is, I believe, nothing irrational or dangerous in the main alterat[ion] made, it is impossible I think to dream of ever reposing the slightest confidence either in Gortschakoff, or in his Government unless it should shake off the evil association connected with his name. And Austria would be more than human, if after what she has suffered elsewhere, she were entirely to forswear glancing eastwards. Our great desire must be that neither the one, nor the other, may have any opportunities offered them. In this view I earnestly look for the maintenance of what I take to be the only effectual barrier namely a firm union, founded on common interest, between the Porte & its dependent provinces. I trust the danger of any cause or pretext for Turkish interference in the Principality is passing by, for nothing I am persuaded can be so dangerous to Turkey, or will so effectually serve the purpose of any ambitious power. Though I have a great respect for the memory of the Patriarch whose ashes are whether actually or vicariously to be removed, I suppose it cannot be denied that there is a design to turn him to account for political objects. But the Greeks have received, or are about to receive, on the occasion of Mr. Stuart's going to Athens, a large & drastic dose of good advice from Granville, & I trust they may profit by it. Pray remember us kindly to Ldy. E. I have never got over my compunctions at having for a moment failed to recollect her when we met at Marlborough House, & I had the pleasure of being her neighbour.

10. Wed.

Wrote to Ld Chancellor (2)—Dean of Westminster—Ld Lyttelton —Ex[ecut]or of Mr Briscoe[2]—Ld Stanhope—Miss Coutts—Sir R. Phillimore—Sir J. Matheson—Mr Glyn—Abp of Canterbury— The Queen (Mem). Saw Ld A. Loftus—Col. Hogg—Robn G.—Mr Glyn—Mr Russell—Ld Granville—Sir R. Phillimore. At Christie's. Visited Sir R. Murchison. Dined at Ld Halifax's. Mad. Bernstorff's

[1] Not found.
[2] F. C. Wilkinson, who had sent Briscoe's tr. of St. Mark; Add MS 44540, f. 26.

afterwards. Saw Ld Russell—Gen. Budeau[1]—Count Bernstorff—Ld Lytton. Saw Mr Th.—There, is a subject of perplexity to me. Read Maguire.

11. Th.

Eighteen to breakfast. Saw Bp Moriarty—Mr Glyn—Miss Burdett Coutts—Mr Ouvry—Mr Stansfeld. Read Maguire. Dined with the Wests. Wrote to The Queen (2, & Mem.)—Mr Fortescue—Ld Granville—Ld Kimberley—Mr Cardwell—Mrs Th. (2)—& minutes. H. of C. $4\frac{1}{4}$-$8\frac{1}{4}$ and $9\frac{1}{4}$-$12\frac{1}{4}$.[2]

To E. CARDWELL, war secretary, 11 May 1871.   PRO 30/48/8, f. 67.

The higher officers of the Prussian Army are I believe few, actively employed, chosen by severe selection, and well paid. An excellent system. Ours I imagine to be the reverse in all points; but sinecure & indirect emolument are brought in to meet the fourth point, where the class is *primâ facie* the sufferer & not the public. But I apprehend that the aggregate pay of the whole number of officers for say 50000 or 100000 men in the Prussian Army is far less than in ours.

Cannot a table comparing them accurately be drawn?[3] My belief is that we are *relatively* unjust to the higher officers & the men who make the army their profession.

The little that I know impresses me painfully not only as to the intelligence but as to the spirit & morale of the administrative arrangements of our army. [P.S.] Genl. Walker's letter[4] is *much* above the level of those I had previously seen.

To LORD KIMBERLEY, colonial secretary,   Add MS 44540, f. 27.
11 May 1871.

If, as appears,[5] the parties be willing, & the resolution of the Legislature of the Cape unequivocal, I do not object to the proposed annexation of the Diamond Field, while I regret the necessity which brings it about; but I think it should be mentioned in the Cabinet on Saturday. I suggest inserting the word 'entire' in the Colonial pledge.

12. Fr.

Wrote to Bp of Rochester—Dr Liddon—Duke of Argyll—Mr Hubbard—The Queen—and minutes. Read Mr Roundell on Agrarm in

[1] *Sic.* General Adam Badeau, American consul general in London.
[2] Spoke on the re-committed Income Tax Bill, which was withdrawn; *H* ccvi. 634.
[3] See 2 May 71n.   [4] See 21 Sept. 70.
[5] Responding to draft dispatch and Kimberley's letter of 11 May, Add MS 44224, f. 126, annexing the diamond fields 'on certain conditions'.

Fortn. Review[1]—Lanfrey. Saw Mr Glyn—Mr Joseph—Mr West—Ld Lyttelton—Bp. of Chester. H of C. $2\frac{1}{4}$-7 and 9-$1\frac{1}{4}$.[2] Dined with the Jameses.

13. Sat. [Chislehurst]

Wrote to Sir J. Pakington—Bp Moriarty—Mr J. Russell—A.W. Peel—Miss Burdett Coutts—The Queen—& minutes. Saw Sir R. Phillimore—Mr Gurdon—Mr Glyn—Mr Angerstein—Scotts. At Phillips's. At Christie's. Cabinet $2\frac{1}{2}$-$4\frac{1}{2}$. Off at 5.5 to R. Cavendish's pleasant home at Chiselhurst. Read Ed.Rev. on Ld Broughton's Reminiscences.[3]

Cabinet May 13. 71. 2½ PM.[4]
War Office Plans St James's Park.
√ Univ. Tests. Lords Amendments reviewed & course determined.[5]
√ Open air Statues near Houses of Parliament. Discussed generally.
√ Muntz's motion. To be revised as fatal to the plan.[6]
√ Appeal for the Irish College. agree to postponement of Ld C's motion. to learn all the facts.[7]
√ Ld. Russell's motion respecting American negotiation on Monday. Not to be debated on our side.[8]
√ Annexation of the Cape Diamond Fields.[9]
√ Cumulative Educational Vote Bill. Not to agree.

14. 5 S.E.

Chiselhurst Ch mg & aft. Saw Capt. Galton. We left our names for the Ex-Emperor.[10] Read The Speaker's Bible Intr. &c.[11]—Oxenham on Atonement, & on Development[12]—The beautiful 'Mirror for Monks'.[13]

15. M. [London]

Off to London at 10.45. Wrote to Ld Bessborough—Miss Burdett Coutts—Scotts—A. Kinnaird—Ld Stanhope—The Queen—and

[1] *Fortnightly Review*, xv. 580 (May 1871).   [2] Misc. business; *H* ccvi. 716.
[3] *Edinburgh Review*, cxxxiii. 287 (April 1871).   [4] Add MS 44639, f.60.
[5] Commons' alterations to the Lords amndts. were sent back 13 June, the govt. eventually beating Salisbury in 129:89; *H* ccvi. 1971.
[6] Muntz failed to alter Cardwell's purchase abolition plan; *H* ccvi. 811.
[7] Apparently never moved.
[8] Russell's motion delayed until 12 June; *H* ccvi. 1823.
[9] Colony of Grinqualand West, containing the Kimberley diamond fields, constituted 27 October 1871; see letter to Kimberley, 11 May 70, and 14 Dec. 71.
[10] i.e. Napoleon III.
[11] *The Holy Bible according to the Authorized Version A.D. 1611* (1871).
[12] H. N. *Oxenham, *The Catholic doctrine of the atonement* (1865).
[13] F. L. Blosius, *A Mirrour for monkes*, probably 1871 ed. by J. D. *Coleridge.

minutes. H of C. $4\frac{1}{4}$-$8\frac{1}{4}$ and 9-$12\frac{1}{4}$.[1] Saw Ld Granville—Mr Glyn—Chancr of Exchr. Read Maguire (finished): as a novel it is almost null[2]—Lanfrey's Etudes (finished)[3]—'Heathen Chinee'[4] &c.

16. Tu.

Wrote to Ld Kimberley (2)—Mr Bruce—H. Glynne—Mr J. Russell. H of C. $2\frac{1}{2}$-7 and at 9.[5] Dined with the F. Cavendishes. Saw Mr M'Coll—Dr A. Clark—Mr Russell—Mr Glyn—Ld Halifax—D. of Devonshire. Read Christie's Shaftesbury[6]—Bowyer & Rome papers.

To LORD KIMBERLEY, colonial secretary,   Add MS 44540, f. 31.
16 May 1871.

[7]Do I understand the prayer now in your hands to be this, that New Zealand (for instance) may admit free shoes made in Sydney & tax at any rate she pleases shoes made in Northampton? If this be so I think the matter requires a good deal of consideration & should not be settled without being fully brought home to the public mind here in the first instance. My impression is that the original concession of power to colonies simply to tax our productions & favour their own was originally made without being observed as much on this side the water as would have been desirable.

It was a pretty strong measure. The advance upon it now proposed, if I apprehend it rightly, brings us near the *reductio ad absurdum* of colonial connection, & the people of this country should have an opportunity of passing an opinion upon it.

17. Wed.

Wrote to Ld Granville—The Queen—Ld R. Gower (2)—Ld Lyttelton—Watsons (Tel.). Saw Mr Glyn—Col. Ponsonby—Abp Manning & Bp Danell[8]—Nonconformist Deputation[9]—Mr J. Russell. Music at home in aftn. Luncheon at 15 G. Square.[10] $10\frac{1}{2}$-2. Went to Windsor & had an audience of HM. Read Crabbe's Poems[11]—Mill on Land Tenure.[12] Dined with the Cowpers. Duchess of Marlborough's concert afterwards.

---

[1] Questioned on income tax; *H* ccvi. 810.   [2] See 27 Apr. 71.
[3] See 28 Apr. 71.   [4] B. Harte, *That Heathen Chinee and other poems* (1871).
[5] Ireland; *H* ccvi. 875.
[6] W. D. *Christie, *A life of Anthony Ashley Cooper, 1st earl of Shaftesbury*, 2v. (1871).
[7] Reply to Kimberley's letter forwarding H. T. Holland's mem. on Australian differential tariffs; see Knaplund, *Imperial Policy*, 107, Add MS 44224, f. 132, and 29 Dec. 71.
[8] James Danell, 1821–81; R.C. bp. of Southwark from 1871.
[9] On school fees and university tests, led by T. B. Potter; *Daily Telegraph*, 18 May 1871,3.
[10] Mrs Thistlethwayte.   [11] *Poetical works* (1829).
[12] J. S. *Mill, *Chapters and speeches on the Irish land question* (1870).

18. Ascension Day. Th.

Chapel Royal & H.C. 12–2. Wrote to Bp of Winchester—Sol. General
—The Queen—C.S. Parker—Dr Liddon—Ld Chancellor—Ld Bessborough—Abp Manning—Ld M. of Dublin & Sir J. Gray—The
Queen—& minutes. Saw Ld Granville—Mr Glyn. H of C. 4¼–8½ and
9½–1½.[1] Read The Battle of Dorking.[2]

19. Frid.

Wrote to Ly Waldegrave—Dean of Canterbury—Queen Tel.—Dean
of Windsor—Mr Hammond—and minutes. Saw Mr Glyn—Mr West
—Dr Clark. Confined to bed all day by a slight dysenteric attack.
Read Masson's Life of Milton[3]—Palgrave's Poems.[4]

20. Sat.

Got up at one: and gave the Birthday dinner. Evening party afterwards. Cabinet 2½–4½. Saw Mr Glyn—Dr Liddon—Ld Chancellor—
Ld Granville. Wrote to The Queen (L. & Tel.)—Bp of Winchr—and
minutes. Read Masson's Milton.

Cabinet May 20. 2½ PM[5]
√ Business of the House. Course considered. Prayer Book & Lectionary Bill.[6]
√ U.S. Treaty. Void, if Canadian Parlt. refuse? Apparently not.
√ closing words of Rule II. 'renewal or augment[atio]n of supplies or arms'.[7]
   Determined not to ask now for any explanatory declaration.
√ Papers to be laid [before parliament:] Treaty Instructions & Protocols.[8]
√ Week's business considered.

To S. WILBERFORCE, bishop of Winchester,   Wilberforce MSS, d. 38.
20 May 1871. *'Private.'*

   I do not think myself authorised to commit the Govt.[9] but I should advise
our keeping within the limits the Calendar unless we have from the Bishops as
a body the assurance that the adoption of some motion on the Athanasian Creed
like that of Mr. Chambers, which remits penalties on those who substitute the

---

[1] Income Tax; *H* ccvi. 964.
[2] By Sir G. T. *Chesney, *Blackwood's Edinburgh Magazine*, cix (May 1871), reprinted as
a pamphlet; story of a successful foreign invasion, written to encourage development of the
Volunteers. For Gladstone's reaction, see 24 May 71.
[3] D. *Masson, *The life of John Milton* (1859).
[4] F. T. *Palgrave, *Lyrical poems* (1871).
[5] Add MS 44639, f. 62.   [6] Recommitted in Commons on 15 June; *H* ccvii. 103.
[7] *PP* 1871 lxx. 49; in article vi of the Treaty of Washington, not quite so worded.
[8] Ibid., 25–58.
[9] Wilberforce sent letters from Pusey and (Sir) Thomas Chambers, 1814–91, liberal M.P.
Marylebone 1865–85, recorder of London 1878; Add MS 44345, f. 198.

Apostles Creed for it, would be acceptable to the Church in general. I should under all circumstances be glad to receive such an assurance but we must not mistake the desire of a thing for its possession.

21. S.aft Asc.

Chapel Royal mg & aft. Dined at Mr Heywood's. Wrote to Mr Disraeli. Saw Ld Bessborough. Read Stoddart on Liturgy[1]—Lightfoot on Revision[2]—Memoir of Ap Ithel[3]—Miss Young's Biographies.[4]

To B. DISRAELI, M.P., 21 May 1871.   Add MS 44540, f. 35.

I send you an authentic copy of the Treaty with the U.S. as it has been actually signed which I have just received from the Foreign Office.

22. M.

Wrote to Ld A. Hervey—Pr. of Wales—Sir W. Anderson—Mrs Cobden—D. of Sutherland—Mr Cardwell—Dr Angus—Mr J.C. Williams —Bp of Winchr—G.S. Lyttelton—Mr Jowett—Ld Granville—Ld Kimberley—The Queen—& minutes. Saw Mr Stephenson—Mr Monsell—Mr Gurdon—Mr West—Mr Glyn. Luncheon at Mrs Th.s. H of C. $4\frac{1}{4}$-8 and 9-$1\frac{3}{4}$.[5] Eight to dinner. Read Christie's Shaftesbury.[6] Visited Mr Noble's Studio.[7]

To E. CARDWELL, war secretary, 22 May 1871.   PRO 30/48/8, f. 73.

I am disposed to think we ought to make an effort to put the Civil Branch of the Bath on the footing originally intended; and that for this purpose we might adopt a rule of the nature of that which I enclose. If you agree with me I will submit it to the Queen.

'That except in the case of persons advanced in life, or for service of a character distinctly special, the honour of a K.C.B., in the Civil branch of the order be henceforward conferred only upon persons who shall already have received the honour of C.B.'[8]

To LORD KIMBERLEY, colonial secretary,   Add MS 44540, f. 35.
22 May 1871.

I infer, I hope rightly, from your silence that your serious anxiety of Saturday has been relieved. I do not see any answer to your argument. But I believe

[1] See 25 June 65.   [2] See 30 Apr. 71.   [3] Untraced.
[4] Possibly C. *Yonge, *Journal of the Lady Beatrix Graham* (1871).
[5] Question on Ecclesiastical Titles; then Army Regulation Bill: *H* ccvi. 1117.
[6] See 16 May 71.   [7] See 20 Mar. 54.
[8] Cardwell replied (23 May 1871, PRO 30/48/8, f. 74): 'I think the rule is a good one, with the exception you have made.'

the system has grown up unknown to the public of this country. I myself was not aware of it as an intercolonial system. It is astounding, in conjunction with the ordinary notion of the Colonial System. If we assent to this further development we should take care that we make it an assent of the country & not merely of the Executive.

By all means name it to the Cabinet when you think the matter rife [*sc.* ripe?].

Can it not be made the subject of a grave preliminary statement & review in correspondence which might be laid before Parliament?[1]

To J. CARVELL WILLIAMS, secretary of the   New York Public Library.
Liberation Society, 22 May 1871. 'Private.'

I need not say that I am gratified with the earlier part of your letter.[2] As regards the latter part, am I to understand it to be your opinion that having now presumably obtained, & at any rate being determined to obtain, from the House of Lords, a complete abolition of Tests in the Universities (except as to the faculty of divinity) we ought to refuse to qualify the surrender which at length is made by any concession whatever?

In the House of Commons our Speaker appoints a Chaplain whom we pay to provide us with daily worship at the commencement of our proceedings. This usage is maintained & this pay provided without objection from any person of any religious profession whatever. Now I should be well content like you to have left this subject out of the Bill: but would it be easy for the Govt., considering (for example) the circumstances to which I have referred, to take very high ground in objecting to it? And would it not be a very serious responsibility for us on account of a matter such as this to keep still alive this one among our many controversies, when we appear to have a reasonable opportunity of closing it?

23. Tu.

Wrote to The Queen (2)—Archbp of York (2)—Mr Lowe—Ld Granville. Saw Mr Stephenson—Ld Granville—Mr Forster—Ld A. Hervey—Mr Glyn—Sir W. Anderson—Mr Cardwell. Wrote Reams agt Lords' Amendments. Benefices' Resignation Committee 12-1½.[3] H of C. 2-7 and 9¾-11¾. Disposed I hope finally of the Univ. Tests Bill.[4] Read Masson's Milton.

24. Wed.

Wrote to Mr Repington—Watsons—Mr West—Ld Wrottesley[5]—& minutes. By Glyn's advice, I did not go to the Derby. Saw six[R].

[1] See Knaplund, *Imperial Policy*, 108 and Add MS 44224, f. 137.
[2] Of 22 May 1871, Add MS 44430, f. 241; the first part praised the govt.'s determination, the latter objected to religious instruction in college chapels.
[3] He was a member till his resignation on 7 June 1871; *PP* 1871 vii. 169.
[4] Cttee. set up to draw up reasons to be reported to Lords: *H* ccvi. 1209.
[5] Offering him the Lord Lieutenancy of Staffordshire, which he eventually accepted; see 29 June 71. Add MS 44540, f. 37.

Saw Mr West—Ld G. Hamilton. Missed the Argylls at C. Hill. Music at home in aftn. Gavard[1] came. Dined at Ld Brownlow's. Devonshire House afterwards. Read Macdowall's Parisiana.[2] Working up 'arrears' of disorder.

To Colonel C. H. W. A'COURT-REPINGTON, Add MS 44540, f. 37.
24 May 1871.

 Yes, I had read the article & I must own I think it mad, without at all questioning your proposition[3] that we must depend mainly (as here) on a regularly trained army, a proposition on which all the plans of the Government have been founded. The article is mischievous as well as mad, heaping together a mass of impossible or incredible suppositions & sending forth to the world the idea that this country is so degraded in intelligence as to bring them within the range of reasonable anticipation. I am afraid you have been sconced to the extent of half a crown; many thanks for your kindness in sending me the number which I return.

25. Th.

16 to breakfast. Wrote to Sec.Eccl. Commn—Mr Ward Hunt—The Speaker—The Queen—& minutes. Saw Lady de Grey—to announce.[4] Read Masson's Milton. Luncheon at 15 G[rosvenor] S[quare]. Saw Ld A. Hervey—Mr Baillie Cochrane—Mr Glyn—Mr Acland—Mr Forster *cum* Mr Goschen—Mr Cardwell—Chr of Exr. H of C. $4\frac{1}{4}$-$8\frac{3}{4}$ and $9\frac{1}{2}$-$12\frac{1}{2}$.[5]

26. Fr. [*Panshanger*]

Wrote to The Queen Mem. & L.—Sir J. Matheson—Mr Ward Hunt —Lady C. Denison—and minutes. H. of C. $2\frac{1}{2}$-$5\frac{1}{2}$. Spoke on Westmeath Bill.[6] Saw Ld Portman—Mr Gavard—Mr Glyn—Ld Granville—Mr D. Robertson. Off at 5.35 to Panshanger: where we had a pleasant evg with Ld & Lady C[owper] & H.C. Read Morgan on Tenure of Fellowships[7]—Palgrave's Poems.[8]

 [1] Charles Gavard, first secretary in the French embassy in London 1871-3.
 [2] By C. J. F. S. Macdowall (1871).
 [3] In an untraced letter. *The Battle of Dorking*, see 18 May 71.
 [4] Probably the marquisate on her husband's return from America.
 [5] Answered questions, then Army Regulation Bill: *H* ccvi. 1267.
 [6] *H* ccvi. 1335.
 [7] H. A. Morgan, *The tenure of fellowships* (1871).
 [8] See 19 May 71.

27. Sat.

Wrote to The Queen—Canon Trevor—Mr Todd[1]—Miss Burdett Coutts—Mr Cardwell (2)—Sir W. Boxall—and minutes. Walk with the Cowpers C. & H. Read Rogers Speech respecting Greek in Education[2]—Lubbock Origin of Civilisation.[3]

To E. CARDWELL, war secretary,   PRO 30/48/8, ff. 75, 82.
27 May 1871.

[First letter:] I cannot send without a word of apology this intolerably long letter which represents the upshot of my thought on the present position of the Purchase question. I might have written much more: and on the other hand I may sum up all in one short sentence: I want air, light, elbow room, $\pi o\hat{v}$ $\sigma\tau\hat{\omega}$,[4] for the public in its prospective dealing with the officers of the army.

May our fortifications prove as difficult of capture as our officers: & we are safe enough.

[Second letter:] [5]Can we not secure for the public some vantage ground from which to operate on the officers of the future with a real command of the situation? And is it not possible so to choose this vantage ground as to make it the means of effectually setting aside the formidable complaint of 'inequality'?

My answer will involve the removal of what appears to be nothing less than a palpable absurdity; namely the system under which, upon the issue to a lad of (I believe) 16 or 18 years old of a first Commission, we, without ever establishing for the state the command of a life-service or of service for a definite term, constitute at once on behalf of the lad, a life-claim. And I suggest that we should attach to commissions of first entry *into* the army a temporary character. A great number of temporary or term-officers you have now, & you must have hereafter. Why are they to be such at their own pleasure only? Why so, especially when we consider the arduous capabilities & demands of this profession & the enormous difficulty of knowing at 18 who will be the good officer & who will not? Why should not the first Commissions as a rule be for ten years? Why should the State only after experience invest with a life-claim for promotion & retirement those only who shall by service have shown what they are? You thus get rid of a mass of those, who would cumber the ranks. You thus remove at once the whole argument of inequality, which now presses & even threatens. You thus make a Selection not only possible but necessary: for you can renew the Commissions of only so many as are required for the higher ranks of the Army & the rest disappear *ipso facto*: in short you substitute so far a *self-acting* process for one which will offer a new temptation & require a new effort of public virtue on every occasion of a promotion: and Selection among life officers will be far easier, when once this great barrier has been passed. You at the least must simplify & reduce the question of retirement. You obtain a period of ten years, during which you may with an unquestionable title be maturing and elaborating prospective arrangements for the very men now about entering your

---

[1] Reading uncertain; perhaps Charles John Todd, a lieutenant of the City.
[2] Untraced.
[3] J. *Lubbock, *The origin of civilization and the primitive condition of man* (1870).
[4] Where I may stand; a base to work from.
[5] Follows extensive analysis of officers' recruitment.

army. Above all you establish practically, palpably, & at once, by an effectual sample, that title of the public to reconsider throughout the whole of the particulars that will determine the position of the officers of the future, which I much fear may, unless we take some further security, be found apt to resolve itself in thin air.

Great difficulties of details may exist; some difficulties even I can see but they appear perfectly surmountable. The principle may be unsound; but to me, one-eyed as I am, it appears salutary, even apart from present use. I confess myself, at any rate, to be far from satisfied as to the security of our position if & when the Parliamentary victory is consummated: & most desirous that some effectual means may be found for imparting to it further strength.

28. Whits.

Parish Ch mg: (near 2 miles) and H.C. Wrote to Mr Cardwell—D. of Argyll—Mr Glyn—Ld Lyttelton. Read Speaker's Bible—Lubbock on Primitive Marriage &c.—Lightfoot on Revision.[1] Without any notice during the day, I was seized at night with shivering & a sharp attack of bowel-complaint.

29 M.

My attack was severe thro' the night & day; I had C.s admirable nursing & the usual remedy; at night Dr Clark to whom we had sent for instructions came down himself, & staid through the night. For these 24 hours, the intervals were hardly two. I found myself for the first time unable to do business, or even to read: I could hardly dictate to Helen one short & necessary letter for Robertson [Gladstone].

30. Tu.

An improvement today: but the process was not complete. I could read: & went to work upon Shakespeare's Henry IV. Also I wrote a number of minutes for letters. Dr Clark went away at eleven. I saw Ld C[owper] & Mr O. Russell in evg.

31. Wed.

Dr Clark returned at an early hour: the fever not having gone off he forbade me to rise. I wrote minutes: and letters to Mr Cardwell—Ld Spencer—Mr Hammond—Mr Glyn: all by dictation. Finished Henry IV (P. 2) and began Henry V. Saw Ld Tankerville.

[1] See 30 Apr. 71.

To G. G. GLYN, chief whip, 31 May 1871.   Add MS 44540, f. 46.

Dr. Clark will not allow me on account of some degree of fever to come up tomorrow. I expect to come up on Saturday & though he wishes me to stay here till Monday I should not like to be away from the Cabinet. 1st: With regard to the prayer-book Bill I suppose I ought not to be absent from the discussion, please therefore let it stand over to next week at whatever time Cardwell may think best for his Army Bill—all this if Bruce approves. 2nd. As respects the amendments in the Westmeath Bill which involves England. If there is any prospect of difficulty about this it will be well to consult the Chancellor & perhaps Cardwell could bring the house to assist in looking to it. I do not understand the law of the case well enough to give a positive opinion.

Thurs. June One 1871.

Wrote to J. Watson & Smith—Ld Hartington—Freshfields—Mr Cardwell—The Queen—Ld Granville (Tel.) West came down—& assisted me. After dinner I dressed & went to the drawingroom. Read Henry V—Henry VI P.1—O'Shaughnessy's Poems.[1]

2. Fr.

Hartington & Barry came down & we discussed, & rejected, the extension Clause for the Westmeath Bill.[2] Worked with West. Wrote to Glyn. Dr Clark came 3°. Came down to dinner. Read Henry VI. II and III.

3. Sat.

Cardwell & Glyn came down to see me. We dealt especially with the case of the Duke of Cambridge.[3] Business with West: minutes. Wrote to Scotts—Mr Richmond. Got down to luncheon. Read Richard III.

4. Trin S.

Parish Ch. mg. Rain stopped me in aft. Read Lightfoot on Revision —Proctor on Astronomy[4]—Vance Smith on Bibl. Theol.[5] Down to breakfast.

---

[1] A. W. E. *O'Shaughnessy, An epic of women and other poems (1870).
[2] i.e. that the Irish Lord Lieutenant's writ should run in England and Scotland; the govt. had agreed to prepare clauses, but did not do so; H ccvi. 1779.
[3] His views on purchase abolition.
[4] R. A. *Proctor, Lessons in elementary astronomy (1871).
[5] G. V. *Smith, The Bible and popular theology (1871).

5. M. [*London*]

Wrote to Prince of Wales—Mrs Thistlethwayte—The Queen—&
minutes. Off at 11 from this most kind refuge. We went up together.
Read Huxley's Lay Sermons.[1] Home at one—transacting business
on the way, from K. Cross. Saw Duke of Cambridge—do *cum* Mr
Cardwell—Sir S. Northcote—Mr Glyn (2). H of C. $4\frac{1}{4}$-$8\frac{1}{4}$ and $9\frac{1}{2}$-
$2\frac{3}{4}$. The divisions of this evening gave us the victory as to morning
sittings & will I hope carry our Bills through the House.[2]

6. Tu.

Wrote to Mr Monsell—Dean of Lichfield—The Queen—Abp of
Canterbury—Mr Levy—Duke of Cambridge—Sir W. Fairbairn—
Mr Stephenson. H. of C. $4\frac{1}{4}$-8.[3] Read Masson's Milton.[4] Saw Ld de
Grey[5]—Mr Glyn—Mr Work—Sir H. Storks. Eight to dinner. Saw
Russell—& another[R].

To A. C. TAIT, archbishop of Canterbury,   Add MS 44540, f. 49.
6 June 1871.

1. In consequence of the pressure of time I had made known before receiving
Your Grace's letter of the 2d[6] both (I think) to the Archbishop of York & the
Bishop of Winchester that the Government would resist any amendment to the
Prayerbook & Lectionary Bill of a nature to carry it beyond the limits of the
Calendar.
2. I would propose with Your Grace's approval to introduce a Bill at some suit-
able period for the purpose of enacting permanently the Episcopal Resignations
Act of 1869. It seems to me however that the proportion of 1/3d of the
Revenue is rather high in the case of the sees of higher income & that it might
advantageously be altered to 1/4th. Perhaps Your Grace will kindly favour me
with your judgment upon this subject when it may be convenient.
[P.S.] I enclose a letter on the point of Pensions from the Archb. of York. But
I have told his Grace that there never had been a suggestion made for the abso-
lute equalisation of Episcopal Pensions.

7. Wed.

Wrote to Watsons—Ld Chancellor—The Queen—Ld Kimberley—
Ld Granville—Mr Maguire—Sir J. Hudson—Mr Cardwell, & minutes.
Saw Mr Glyn—Ld Granville—Ld Chancr—Ly Herbert (respecting
her son)—Belgian Minister. Luncheon at 15 G.S. & saw Mrs Th.

[1] T. H. *Huxley, Lay sermons, addresses and reviews* (1870).
[2] *H* ccvi. 1595; majorities of 71.
[3] Manning of the navy: *H* ccvi. 1604.   [4] See 19 May 71.
[5] Offered him a marquisate on his return from Washington; Ramm I, ii. 249.
[6] On the Lectionary Bill consultations, Add MS 44330, f. 179.

later: when she told me the singular story of her birth. Saw the Jerichau Pictures.[1] Read Masson's Milton. Saw Mad. Jerichau's works.
Saw Rochdale Deputation.[2] Dined with the Herberts: & an evening
party at home.

To Sir J. HUDSON, 7 June 1871.   Add MS 44540, f. 50.
'Private & confidl.'

As our friend Lacaita tells me he is to leave Florence soon after the 11th, I
answer his letter to you. With respect to a conference it certainly was my personal opinion that the idea was not *unconditionally* inadmissible, & that if the predetermined & clearly expressed basis of the proposal to be made to Italy if any-
[thing] excluded absolutely the reversal of the Roman Plebiscite, so that the
question should go only to guarantees other than the restoration of Temporal
Power, it was perfectly possible that it might be worked into a measure favourable
to Italy, to peace, & to international right: I have not heard any argument on this
question which has destroyed the elements of this opinion in my mind. But I
have never stated nor breathed it to the best of my recollection unless to Granville, to Lacaita, & especially to Cadorna, to whom I said more of it than to anybody else, telling him he might rest assured I should take all the care in my
power that it should never become in any manner through *me* a cause of embarrassment to the Italian Government. This I shall strictly & carefully bear in
mind. Even so much I should not have said had the whole matter been clearly
a *res peracta* never to revive. But there is an awful longevity & pertinacity in the
mischievous opinion prevalent among Ultramontanes in all countries & I should
be too glad to see any barrier erected *by consent of Europe* against the mischief
which they will certainly try to do. Chambord has already sounded the trumpet
in this sense. I hope the Italians are not going to be aggressionisti in Africa.

8. Th.

Small breakf. party. Wrote to Mrs Bennett—Mr Parsons—Mr Kinnaird—The Queen (Mem. & 2 letters)—Mr Bruce—& minutes. H of
C. $4\frac{1}{4}$-$8\frac{1}{4}$ and $9\frac{1}{2}$-1.[3] Read Ld Acton's Lecture.[4] Saw Bp of Winchester—Mr Newton (B.M.)—Mr Bruce—Mr Glyn—Ld Granville—Mr
W. Hunt—Scotts. Dined with the Wests.

To Mrs. A. R. BENNETT, 8 June 1871.   Add MS 44431, f. 8.

I am very sensible of your kindness and of Dora's in writing to me on the sad
subject to which your letters relate.[5] I am afraid the only thing I can say on the

[1] Pictures by Anna Maria Elizabeth Jerichau-Baumann, 1819-81; Danish painter; exhibited in London. See *Art Journal* (1871), x. 165.
[2] No report found; 'To the Potterians I have proposed an interview as resistance is in
vain. And those Lanc. Radicals are a good set & give less trouble than anybody'; to Glyn,
28 May 1871, Add MS 44540, f. 45.
[3] Spoke in row over counting out of the House; then Army Regulation Bill: *H* ccvi.
1686.
[4] Lord Acton, 'The war of 1870. A lecture' (1871).
[5] His cousin and *quondam* literary collaborator (see 13 Sept. 27, 27 Nov. 50n), who

subject of her letter without giving pain is to beg you to assure her from me of my earnest hope that the Almighty may rule and overrule all things for her good.

The termination of any literary relations between us is viewed by you as I could wish. It is really not a matter of principle but of prudence. In the situation which I hold I am absurdly and yet not unnaturally (or rather, for not unintelligible reasons,) held responsible for the religious colour & proceedings of any & every one connected with me: & even denounced by various bodies calling themselves Protestant Associations because I refuse to answer their inquiries whether I have been reconciled to the Church of Rome. The imputations themselves are pointless & worthless: but they are used to cripple me in the discharge of duty & on this account it is a duty not only not to give them warrant but even plea.

The consolations to which you refer in the midst of these sad differences are not to be forgotten, indeed they are even more & more to be cherished. As far as matter of religion proper is concerned, they reach a long way. But you cannot fail to know the double sting of the particular class of cases now in question. It is on the one side the proselytizing, disturbing, undermining influence: it is on the other (yet more serious) the attitude of the dominant party in the Roman Church with reference to history, experience, thought, to the family & the State, & to freedom, and the frightful & seemingly hopeless aggravation of that attitude by the proceedings of last year. To these things there is, unhappily, & yet happily, no parallel in the religious world.

9. Fr.

Wrote to Bp of Winchester—Rev. W.M. Goalen—The Queen, and minutes. H of C. 2¼-7, 9-9½, and 10-11¾.[1] Saw Mr West—Ld Lyttelton—Mr Glyn—Sir W. James—Mr Forster—Ld Granville—Mr M'C Downing—Mr Cardwell—Mr Levy. Dined with the Jameses. Read Christie's Life of Shaftesbury.[2]

10. Sat.

Wrote to Archdn Ffoulkes—Mr Maguire—The Queen—Ld Granville —Sir S. Northcote—& minutes. Saw Mr Glyn (2)—Ld Granville. Cabinet 2½-6¾. Saw Mr Phillips's reproductions in jewellery. Dined with the F. Cavendishes: long conversation with W. Lyttelton on 'comprehension'.[3] Saw Mrs Terry—A. Hamilton X. Read Masson's Milton—Fawcett on Pauperism.[4]

had recently become a Roman catholic. Gladstone had earlier broken off any prospective collaboration; Add MS 44430, f. 169.

[1] Spoke on Westmeath Bill: *H* ccvi. 1791.
[2] See 16 May 71.
[3] See D.L.F.C., ii. 100.
[4] H. *Fawcett, *Pauperism; its causes and remedies* (1871).

1871. Cabinet 10 June. 2½ PM[1]

√ Honours for the [U.S. High] Commissioners: announced to the Cabinet—
Secret till after Debate.[2]

√ Sir R. Palmer's Questions for Monday. Substance of answer agreed on.[3]

√ Fishery Articles: discontent in B.N.A.: not confined to maritime Provinces.
Instructions to Admiralty Vessels for executing the Treaty to remain suspended: to keep order & protect Canadians if attacked by an armed force: no
more. Repeal of Imperial Act of prohibition to stand over.[4]

√ Intention of France to send [communard] prisoners to New Caledonia. Not
to inquire. Ascertain the facts.

√ Non-inclusion of the Fenian Raid claims,[5] conversation upon. It was impossible. It remains open.
Cardwell explained the situation as to the Army Bill.

11. S. 1 S. Trin & St Barnabas.

Chapel Royal mg Crown St Evg. Wrote to Ld de Grey—Mr Hammond.
Saw Ld Bessborough—Mr Glyn. Read Ullathorne's C. Hierarchy[6]—
Vance Smith Bible & Pop. Theology[7]—O'Shaughnessy's Poems—
Aitken's Letter to W.E.G.[8]—Allies on the See of St Peter.[9]

12. M.

Wrote to Mr Cardwell—Rev. R. Aitken—Mr Forster—Mr E. Saun-
ders—The Queen (& Mema)—Abp of Canterbury—Capt. Cole—
Sir G. Lewis—Ld Lyttelton—Bp of Winchester—Ld Eliot[10]—Ld
Bessborough—& minutes. Saw Duke of Argyll—Mr Glyn—Sir A.
Panizzi. 2½-4. Went to B. Museum to see the Castellani Collection
and the Missal. H of C. 4¼-8 and 9-2: Army Bill, & a crisis.[11] Read
Masson's Milton.

To LORD ELIOT, 12 June 1871. 'Private.'   Add MS 44540, f. 54.

I hope we may count on your taking a favourable view of the form in which
we have sent the University Tests Bill back to the House of Lords; & therefore

[1] Add MS 44639, f. 63.
[2] Privy councillorships etc. for them. *Northcote declined the G.C.B.
[3] On neutral ports: *H* ccvi. 1903.
[4] Fisheries were also raised on 12 June by *Russell in his attack on the Washington
treaty: *H* ccvi. 1823.
[5] i.e. in the Washington treaty.
[6] W. B. *Ullathorne, *History of the restoration of the Catholic hierarchy in England*
(1871).   [7] See 4 June 71.
[8] R. *Aitken, 'Church reform spiritually considered. A letter to . . . Gladstone' (1871).
[9] See 4 Oct. 50, 11 Feb. 66.
[10] William Gordon Cornwallis Eliot, 1829-81; diplomat; liberal M.P. Devonport 1866-8;
summoned to Lords as Lord Eliot 1870; 4th earl of St. Germans 1877.
[11] Govt. announcement of pruning of the Bill: *H* ccvi. 1906.

on your assistance in saving it tomorrow from being further disturbed. We have brought the Bill to a form more favourable to the Church than I had recently thought possible. It can never take a milder form. This has been brought about by the free use of all legitimate influence, & by compromising for the sake of the object in view, our credit with 4/5ths at least of our supporters. I have myself laboured to the uttermost in this matter but if we *now* fail I cannot look forward to renewing these efforts that have been made for I would hardly expect my party to tolerate them again though of course I might retire from the position I hold or leave perhaps the question alone.[1]

To W. E. FORSTER, vice president, 12 June 1871.   Add MS 44540, f. 53.

I have received the Nonconformist memorial (with your marginal notes) on Clause 25 of the Education Act & I send it in Circulation. If it were expedient to raise the point—which I take not to be the case at present—what would you say to adding to the limitations placed upon the payments which may be made to the Voluntary Schools this one other viz. that the rate may not exceed the actual or estimated charge upon the rates for children of the same age in the Board Schools of the place.

13. Tu.

Wrote to Mr T.M. Gibson—Sir H. Moncreiff—The Queen—Ld Advocate—Sir W. Russell—Prof. Goldwin Smith—Col. Ponsonby—& minutes. H of C. 2¼-7 and 11½-2.[2] Saw Mr Glyn—Mr Forster—Ld Granville—Chancr of Exr—D. of Richmond—D. of Edinburgh. We dined at Marlborough House. Read Masson's Milton—Gregory & Liddon's Letter.[3]

To GOLDWIN SMITH, 13 June 1871.   Add MS 44540, f. 55.

Though I am sorry for the circumstances which made you a mere observer of the recent negotiations & of American opinion concerning them, I am truly glad of the result. Upon the whole I think, considering the infirmity of human nature, the reception of the late treaty on the two sides of the water has been what was most to be desired in the practical interests of peace & goodwill. It is certainly a great honour to the two Anglo-Saxon countries that they should first have rendered such a striking homage to the value of arbitration as a means of settling international disputes.

---

[1] Eliot replied on 14 June: 'I cannot but look on it as a serious attack on the Church ... I thought it best to abstain'; Add MS 44431, f. 30.
[2] Army: *H* ccvi. 1985.
[3] R. *Gregory and H. P. *Liddon, 'The Purchas Judgment' (1871).

14. Wed.

Wrote to Mr E. Saunders—Mr Newton—Ld Chancellor—Chancr of
Exr—& minutes. H of C. at 1.[1] Sat to Mr Dickinson.[2] Saw Sir T.
Biddulph—Mr Glyn (2)—Mr Forster—Ld de Grey. Read Masson's
Milton. Luncheon at 15 G.S. 15 to dinner: evg party afterwards with
Music: G. D. Vladimir[3] & Duke of Edinburgh came.

15. Th.

Wrote to Watsons—Earl of Dudley—Mr W.E. Jelf[4]—D. of Argyll
—Mr Fawcett—The Queen—& minutes. H. of C. $4\frac{1}{4}$-$8\frac{1}{4}$ & $9\frac{1}{2}$-$2\frac{1}{2}$.
Army & Prayerbook Bills: the latter we just managed to work
through.[5] Saw Ld Granville—Chancr of Exr—Mr Glyn. Mr Fowler
took Glyn & me to the City to see the works of M.D. Cannon St Station: a Chaos wh is to be Kosmos upon July 1.[6] Read Fawcett on
Pauperism.[7] Princess Louise & the Argyll House party with others
came to breakfast.[8]

To the EARL OF DUDLEY, 15 June 1871.   Add MS 44540, f. 57.
'Private.'

The Lord Lieutenancy of Staffordshire is virtually vacant.[9] I remember with
pleasure our political sympathies as adherents of Sir R. Peel, & your great kindness with respect to me; & it is an object of sincere desire to me that you should
succeed to the Ld Lieutenancy, if you are willing to do so, under my advice to
the Queen. Standing as I now do in relation with the entire Liberal party, &
bound to them by gratitude & duty, I hope I might be able to acquaint any political friend that he might feel confident the proposal I now make had been made
to one not unfavourably disposed towards them as regards the general objects of
their political action, reasonably understood. I am sure that Granville, both as
leading the House of Lords, & as a Staffordshire man, will much desire that the
arrangement I now suggest should take effect. Should you, as I hope may be the
case, accede to it, I must ask you to consider it as private until I shall have written to the Queen.

[1] Endowed Schools Bill: H ccvii. 1.
[2] Lowes Cato *Dickinson, 1819-1908. Sitting for the group portrait of the cabinet,
illustrated in this volume; an individual portrait was exhibited at Royal Academy 1875,
presented to Liverpool college.
[3] Grand Duke Vladimir, 1847-1909, s. of Alexander II, br. of Alexander III.
[4] Offering him living of Ewelme; he declined it; Add MS 44540, f. 56.
[5] H ccvii. 119.
[6] The Mansion House section of the Metropolitan District Line; see 1 July 71.
[7] See 10 June 71.   [8] Princess Louise was on her honeymoon with Lorne.
[9] Already declined by Wrottesley, see 24 May 71; Dudley refused, as did Hatherton;
Wrottesley eventually accepted.

16 Fr.

Wrote to Ld Devon—The Queen 2 and Mem.—and minutes. 11 to dinner. Family. H of C. 2¼-7 and 9½-12½.[1] Read Christie's Life of Ld Shaftesbury. Saw Mr Glyn—Duke of Edinburgh—Chancr of Exr.

17. Sat. [*Chislehurst*]

Wrote to Mr Murphy MP—Watsons—The Queen—Scotts—G. Burnett—& minutes. Cabinet 2¼-5¾. Saw Mr Glyn—Mr Cardwell. Off at 5.55 to Chislehurst.[2] A restful evening. Read Ed.Rev. on the case of the Chorizontes.[3]

Cabinet Jun 17/71. 2 PM.[4]
√ Universities Commission. The Govt. desire to bring out the facts by a Voluntary Commission, if possible.[5]
√ Constitution Hill. Model—see Note.[6]
√ Torrens' Clause in Army Bill.[7]
√ Intercolonial Duties. In assenting, record regret; & wait answer before Bill. Agreed to the proposal of Ld. K[imberley] in principle.[8]
√ Mr Fowler's Contagious Diseases Acts Bill. Introduce in silence.
√ Ld Chancellor's plan for strengthening the Judicial Comm[ittee of the privy council]. Approved: with reserve of further consideration as to appointing two new Puisne Judges.[9]
√ Granville. Dispatch from Lyons. answer not to bind. to listen. indisposed to retrogressive negotiation: but shall proceed in a friendly spirit.[10]

18. 2 S.Trin.

Chiselhurst Ch mg (with H.C.) and aft. Read Rawlinson's Lecture[11]—Philarète, Consecn Sermon[12]—Pusey, Serm. on H. Eucharist[13]—

[1] Spoke on parliamentary notices: *H* ccvii. 144.   [2] Lord Frederick *Cavendish's.
[3] *Edinburgh Review*, cxxxiii. 358 (April 1871).   [4] Add MS 44639, f. 64.
[5] Became the Cleveland commission on Oxford and Cambridge property: *PP* 1873 xxxvii. See 20 June 71.
[6] To open Constitution Hill to members of both Houses in the Session; Add MS 44639, f. 65. Debated on 23 June; *H* ccvii. 502.
[7] W. M. Torrens, after debate on 19 June, withdrew his clause to make 20 the minimum overseas army age: *H* ccvii. 225.
[8] Kimberley reluctantly followed Gladstone's line of hostility to extension of the system; see 16, 22 May and Knaplund, *Imperial policy*, 108.
[9] A requirement already raised by Gladstone to Hatherley; Add MS 44540, f. 56. The Act passed on 21 August as 34 & 35 Vict. c. 91.
[10] Italian developments, see Lyons' dispatch of 15 June: PRO FO 27/1866.
[11] G. *Rawlinson, *The alleged historical difficulties of the Old and New Testaments* (1871).
[12] Filaret, Metropolitan of Moscow, sermon in A. P. *Stanley, *Essays chiefly on questions of Church and State* (1870), 496.
[13] E. B. *Pusey, ' "This is My Body." A sermon' (1871).

Wilkinson on Parables[1]—Manning's Pastoral Letter[2]—& other Tracts. Much conversation with Dr Liddon—Mr Williams—Dr Clark.

19. M. [*London*]

Wrote to Mr M. Gaskell—Archd. Harrison (Tel.)—Sir Thos G.—D. of Devonshire—Sir Wm Tibb—The Queen (and Mem.)—and minutes. Came up from Chiselhurst before 12. H. of C. $4\frac{1}{4}$–8 and $9\frac{1}{4}$–$1\frac{1}{2}$.[3] Dined with the Jameses. Saw Ld Advocate—Mr Glyn—Mr Cardwell—Mr Bruce—Sir W. James. Read Christie's Shaftesbury— Erckmann Chatrian Le Sous-Maitre.[4] Scotch Educ. Bill Depn. 3.30.[5]

20. Tu.

Wrote to The Queen 2 & Mem.—Ld Kimberley—Robn G. (2)—Ld Granville—Mr Reeve (2)—Watsons—Mr O'Shaughnessy—Mr Henchman—& minutes. H of C. $2\frac{1}{2}$–7 and 9–$2\frac{1}{4}$.[6] 10 to dinner. Read Masson's Milton. Saw Mr Niewenhuys—D of Devonshire—Mr Forster—Mr Gibson—Mr Glyn.

To A. HELPS, 20 June 1871.   Add MS 44540, f. 59.

It has been thought expedient to look over the names most prominent & most honourably known in the several Departments with a view to tenders of C.B: & it has also been determined that, except in certain limited categories, no one shall hereafter receive the civil K.C.B. who has not passed the threshold of the C.B.

Under these circumstances I hope you will be disposed to accept a C.B. which I have H.M.'s permission to propose to you.

To H. G. LIDDELL, Dean of Christ Church,   Add MS 44540, f. 59.
Oxford, 20 June 1871.

The Government are desirous to obtain a full statement of the revenues of the Universities and Colleges of Oxford and Cambridge, for the information of the Parliament & of the public. This would I presume best be done by means of a Commission: & a Commission issued by the Crown would be the most convenient instrument; but such a Commission could not act *in invitis*, & we should be glad to know whether, as was the case with the Public Schools, undistinguished bodies concerned in this instance would give their voluntary aid to the Commission or

[1] J. B. Wilkinson, 'Instructions on the parables of Our Lord and Saviour Jesus Christ' (1870).
[2] See 19 Feb. 71.
[3] Army: *H* ccvii. 237.
[4] Erckmann-Chatrian, *Histoire d'un Sous-Maître* (1871).
[5] No report found.
[6] Questioned on army; then Supply: *H* ccvii. 309.

whether we should have to invoke the assistance of Parliament. Can you give me any aid or advice as to obtaining in the most trustworthy form a reply to this question? I have not as yet addressed any communication to Cambridge on this subject but I need not place you under any restraint as to the use to be made of this preliminary note.[1]

21. Wed.

Wrote to Dean of Ch.Ch.—Ld Hatherton—The Queen—Bp of Winchester—Mr Helps—and minutes. Conclave of Bps at St Thomas's at 12.45. Saw also Bp of Winchester—Bp of London—Abp of York —Archdn Harrison—Chr of Exr—Mr Glyn—Mr Kinnaird. H of C. at 1.30. Luncheon at 15 G.S. Saw Mr Richards [sc. Richard] & others on Welsh College.[2] $4\frac{1}{2}$-$6\frac{1}{2}$. Conclave in D St on the anxious subject of Royalties & Residence in Ireland.[3] Nineteen to dinner. A notable conversation in the Park alcove. Read Guinnard's Patagonia.[4]

22. Th.

Wrote to The Queen—Ld Justice Christian—and minutes. Eleven (strangers) to breakf. Saw Archdn Harrison—Mr Glyn. Saw Mrs Russell X. Read Lowe's Speech of Ju. 2.[5]—Ld Justice Christian's Judgment[6]—Grote's Sp. of 1835 on Ballot.[7] H. of C. $4\frac{1}{4}$-$8\frac{1}{4}$ and $9\frac{3}{4}$-$1\frac{3}{4}$.[8]

23. Fr.

Wrote to Gen. Garibaldi—Duchess of Argyll—Dean of Windsor— Ld Sydney—The Queen—& minutes. Saw Mr A. Joseph—Mr M'Coll —Mr Bruce—Abp of Canterbury (2)—Mr Glyn—Bp of Winchester —Abp of York—Sir T. Biddulph. Attended the Queen's Garden Party. H of C. $2\frac{1}{4}$-$5\frac{1}{4}$ and 9-$12\frac{3}{4}$.[9] Dined with Mr Glyn. Read Note sur l'Organisation Militaire[10]—Grote on Ballot (1833).

[1] Liddell stressed the difficulties of assessing opinion in the vacation, offered none, suggested Salisbury, as chancellor, be informed; 24 June, Add MS 44236, f. 333; diarist docketed he would do this. See 17, 30 June 71.

[2] See 14 Apr. 71.

[3] Revival of the 1868-9 plan, see 22 Dec. 68; Kimberley, *Journal*, 24.

[4] A. Guinnard, *Three years slavery among the Patagonians* (1871).

[5] R. *Lowe, 'The National Debt. Speech ... on the 2nd June 1871' (1871).

[6] Gladstone had asked Jonathan Christian (1811-87, Irish lord justice of appeal 1867-78) for a copy of his judgment of 9 June 1871, questioning validity of 1870 Land Act; Add MS 44540, f. 60. See 24 June 71 and *PP* 1871 iii. 9.

[7] G. *Grote, 'Speech delivered ... on moving for the introduction of the vote by ballot at elections' (1833).

[8] Spoke on the Elections [i.e. Ballot] Bill: *H* ccvii. 404.

[9] Questioned on the pope, and Constitution Hill; *H* ccvii. 500.   [10] Untraced.

To GENERAL GARIBALDI,[1] 23 June 1871.   Add MS 44431, f. 49.
'Particulier.'

J'ai recu votre lettre du 7me passè[2] après quelques delais, et j'ai fait des recherches a Paris quant aux faits. On nous écrit que M. Rochefort, prisonnier à Versailles, attend encore son procès. Quant a nous autres, nous n'avons, comme Gouvernement Britanniques, aucun droit d'ingérence. Ce qui nous manque absolument c'est le *locus standi*; et si nous l'essayions sans titre incontestable nous pouvions il me semble faire du mal plûtot [*sic*] que du bien a M. Rochefort lui même. Dejà une grande partie du corps diplomatique a Paris a constaté plusieurs faits importants a [*sc.* en] faveur de M. Paschal Grousset, mais nous nous trouvâmes a même d'agir pour son conte [*sc.* compte] parce qu'il il s'étoit interessé avec beaucoup d'empressement pour les étrangers des diverses nations a Paris pendant la guerre civile, et ils en avaient beaucoup profité. J'espère comme individu que le Gouvernement Français mettra de la douceur a tout ce qu'il leur reste a faire, et je crois qu'après tout ce qui est arrivé jusqu'a ce moment c'est fort probable.

24 St.J. Baptist [*Windsor*].

Wrote to Archbishop of Canterbury—Sir H. Holland—Robn G.—Watsons—Mr Westell—Chancr of Exr—Dean Ramsay—T.M. Gladstone—and minutes. Saw Mr Glyn—Abp of Canty. Cabinet 2¼-5¼. Garden party. Off to Windsor before 6. We dined with H.M. Conversation with Bp of Peterborough on Lectionary Bill. Read Memoir of Miss Austen.[3]

Cabinet Jun. 24. 2 PM[4]
√ Meeting of party on Ballot Bill. Liberty to call if desired.[5]
√ Irish National Schoolmasters. Grant of 18 m. for this year.
√ + Lectionary Bill. Case stated by WEG—Cardwell & Lowe will speak to Locke King.
√ Christian's Judgment. Cairns's Bill to go forward if conv.[6]
√ Zanzibar Slave Trade: Gilpin's motion. Consent of H. of C.[7]
√ Nawab of Tonk. Judicial Committee. Resist.[8]
√ Royal Residence in Ireland—opened generally.
√ Fenian claims. Nothing to be said at present to Macdonald.[9]
√ Tichborne case: Chancr. to consider whether to bring in a Bill to enable court to go on continuously, & decide.[10]

[1] Begins 'Mon cher General Garibaldi', ends 'Croyes moi avec beaucoup d'égards, votre sincère ami'; docketed 'Copy on signed sheet.' Diarist's eccentric accents retained.
[2] Add MS 44431, f. 47.
[3] J. E. A. Leigh, *A memoir of Jane Austen* (1870).
[4] Add MS 44639, f. 67.   [5] See 6 July 71.
[6] Christian's judgment (see 22 June 71) questioned legality of 1870 Land Act; Cairns' amending bill passed with govt. support (34 & 35 Vict. c. 92).
[7] For select cttee. on E. African slave trade; passed; *PP* 1871 xii. 1.
[8] Successfully: *H* ccvii. 1139 (4 July 1871).   [9] See 10 June 71.
[10] Tichborne trial began 11 May 1871; govt. announced bill to enable continuous sittings, but never introduced; *H* ccvii. 961, 995; court sat till 7 July, adjourned till 7 November.

+ I announced that I cd. not bind myself as to carrying forward the Bill if changes in the body of the Calendar i.e. Prayer Book were made by H. of C.[1]

25. 3 S. Trin.

Castle Chapel at 10 & 12: Parish Ch. at 6½. Long conversation with H.M. Wrote Memm of the part on residence in Ireland. We dined with the Queen. Saw Col. Ponsonby—Dean of Windsor. Read Grindle on Supremacy[2]—Wordsworth's Sermon[3] and divers Tracts.

I have had a long and interesting conversation with the Queen today on the subject of 'Royal Residence in Ireland'.

She began with some apparent disinclination to the subject, was disposed to disparage Ireland & the Irish; said so much had been done for them already, more than for Scotland or for England; and threw out the opinion that, though there might be occasional visits of one or another member of the Royal Family, yet, if any thing more or systematic were attempted, it would lead to false hopes, exactions, & other inconveniences. She quoted Lord Dufferin once or twice as leaning more or less towards her views of Ireland; & thought want of personal security was a serious impediment to Royal visits on any considerable scale.

I first opened the 'minor plan', of a Royal residence, to be provided by Parliamentary vote, with a grant to meet some portion of the expence of living there. I stated that I had nothing of a definite character to propose on the part of the Cabinet; but I described what had taken place during the last few years in Parliament with reference to the question, & how it had grown at length into the shape of a regular notice of motion on which a good deal of interest appeared to be concentrated. I pointed out that the subject had been touched generally both by the late & the present Government as one not unworthy to be entertained: and I repeatedly pressed upon this consideration that it was to be regarded by no means as an exclusively Irish question, but as likely to be of great utility in strengthening the throne under circumstances which require all that can be done in that sense, if indeed we can make it a new means of putting forward the Royal Family in the visible discharge of public duty. The desirableness & necessity of any plan likely to have this effect the Queen readily admitted. The plan, however, did not seem to find favour with her, & especially she anticipated me in declaring rather positively

[1] A view characteristic of Gladstone's anti-Erastianism.
[2] E. S. Grindle, *This church and realm* (1871).
[3] C. *Wordsworth, 'A plea for the diocese of Maritzburg, Natal' (1871).

that it would not do for the Prince of Wales. She mentioned considerations of health, of time, of character; was afraid of his being identified with Ireland, of his being surrounded with flatterers, & was doubtful of his disposition to act steadily upon any plan that might be laid down, and other matters.

I quoted with some emphasis the opinions of Ld Spencer & Ld Bessborough with reference to a plan of this kind, and I pleaded much in favour of the Prince of Wales; dwelling on the difficulties of his position, which he might have been better able to encounter if he had been endowed with the gifts and character of his Father, but which it really was hard for a commoner man to cope with. I contended that, if duty were found for him, he might show or acquire a disposition to do it. I admitted that, if anything serious were to be undertaken, it must be the subject of a regular understanding with him, and that the continuance of the arrangement with him must depend upon the manner in which he might set about its execution. She contended that he would not like it. This however was in the next stage of the conversation.

I pressed a good deal the general gravity of the subject, while speaking for the most part in my own name & only referring occasionally to the Government, in order to avoid giving too definite a character to the discussion, and to use it as a means of ascertaining in what direction it was best to move. I referred to the fact that there were various modes of proceeding: and she, giving way a little, began to entertain the matter more favourably, & said that it had been once recommended to her, by some person, that Prince Arthur should go to Ireland as Lord Lieutenant.

This gave me an excellent opportunity of opening the larger scheme, as the small one had had all the fair play I could obtain for it, and had not been very successful. Without giving up the case for the Prince of Wales, I said that of course any member of the Royal Family going to Dublin to represent Her Majesty must stand wholly detached from the Ministry of the day & from political responsibility. But she thought he ought to be kept cognisant of business, & should have the opportunity of forming and giving opinions on it confidentially: so that in fact I found H.M. at this point quite on the same line of thought with myself. However, without dwelling very specially upon this part of the case, we pursued the subject generally from the more extended point of view. I referred to what had taken place under the Government of Lord Russell, and observed that the Irish Department must be reconstituted, and a Cabinet minister of well defined station and attributes appointed to discharge with adequate authority the administrative duties of the Lord Lieutenant. She said that liberal time must be allowed for visits & duties in this country, but did not think four or even six months too much to contemplate as the portion of the year to be given to Ireland. It was in dealing with this part of the case that when she said the Prince of Wales would not like it, I pointed out that he would receive, by a plan of this kind, an assistance to his income which might be acceptable.

In fact, though it was all dragging, so to speak, while we were on the smaller plan, the Queen talked with content and freedom and a good deal of approval of the abolition of the Lord Lieutenancy, and the substitution of a Royal representation of the Sovereign. The whole matter seemed to have become congenial to her. But I was careful to explain that though it would probably be my duty to report something very shortly, from the Cabinet, of a more substantive character, I did not seek to commit her to anything now said but merely to break ground upon the case.

As the conversation went on, two circumstances happened which gave it a more favourable turn with respect also to the Prince of Wales. First it occurred to her that residence in Dublin, & duties assumed there, might interfere with the military career of Prince Arthur. And secondly, she said she should like to speak in great confidence to one or two persons: to Sir Thos. Biddulph & perhaps to the Dean of Windsor. I told her I had already conversed with the Dean: and had found him very much impressed with the advantages of the plan and particularly in reference to the Prince of Wales. Whether from these or other causes I know not, but undoubtedly the Queen very much relented on this, the point with respect to which she had been stiff, and ended with freely allowing that it was a fair subject for consideration. The upshot of the whole conversation then was, as to the smaller plan, adverse; she said it would not work: as to the larger plan, decidedly favourable: as to the Prince of Wales, quite open.

The Queen entirely agreed that, if a scheme of this kind were to be adopted, the execution should follow promptly on the announcement, and that the proper time would be the opening of the new Session.[1]

26. M. [London]

Wrote to Ld Granville—Sir E. Cust—Ld Ripon—The Queen—& minutes. Came up (10.20) with Prince Arthur who was agreeable & sensible as always. Saw Mrs Russell[R]—Sir G. Grey—Saw Mr Glyn

---

[1] Marked 'Most Private'; initialled and dated 25 June 1871; Add MS 44760, f. 40.

—Chancr of Exr. H. of C. $4\frac{1}{4}$-$8\frac{1}{2}$ and $9\frac{1}{2}$-2.[1] Read Journal in S. of France[2]—Masson's Milton.

27. Tu.

Wrote to Mr Ayrton—Nawab Nazim[3]—Capt. S. Osborne—Chancr of Exr—The Queen—and minutes. Fifteen to dinner: young folk. Saw Mr M'Coll—Ld Spencer—Mr Thring—Mr Glyn—Ld Halifax (2)—Mr Jowett. Luncheon at 15 G.S. & saw Mrs Th. H of C. $3\frac{1}{2}$-7 and 9-$10\frac{1}{2}$.[4] Read Masson's Milton (finished V.2)—Christie's Shaftesbury.

28. Wed.

Wrote to Mr Westell—Bp of Lichfield—Capt. Galton—The Queen Mem.—Sir Thos G.—Mrs H.G.—G.G. Glyn—Ld Kimberley—and minutes. Read 'Inside Paris'.[5] Saw Sir J. Hudson & Sir J. Lacaita— Ld Granville—Mr Glyn—Mr Prescott Hewitt—Ld Northbrook— Mad. Kanshy[6] & Col. [C.] N. Sturt. Took my niece Mary to Mr Watts's Studio. Lady Curtis's garden-party afterwards. Dined with Sir D. Marjoribanks. Saw Howard X.

29. Th.

Wrote to Watson's—Mrs Howard—The Queen—Ld Wrottesley[7]— and minutes. Saw Rev. Dr Lightfoot—Archdn Harrison—Mr Glyn —Ld Polwarth[8]—Ly Waldegrave (Ireland)—Mr E. Hamilton. Read Mr Jevons on the Match Tax.[9] H of C. $4\frac{1}{4}$-8 and $9\frac{1}{4}$-$3\frac{1}{4}$. Spoke on Ballot & voted in 324:230 with mind satisfied & as to feeling a lingering reluctance.[10]

---

[1] Answered questions; then Elections Bill in cttee.; *H* ccvii. 561.
[2] Perhaps N. W. Senior, *Journals kept in Italy and France from 1848 to 1852*, 2v. (1871).
[3] Nawab of Bengal; see 24 June 71.   [4] Supply; *H* ccvii. 648.
[5] *Inside Paris during the siege. By an Oxford graduate* [D. A. Bingham] (1871).
[6] Name smudged.
[7] Thanking him for accepting 'at a sacrifice of your own inclination' the Staffordshire lord lieutenancy; see 24 May, 15 June 71 and Add MS 44540, f. 63.
[8] Walter Hugh Scott, 1838-1920; 8th Baron Polwarth 1867; Scottish representative peer 1882.
[9] W. S. *Jevons, *The match tax: a problem in finance* (1871), defending *Lowe's defeated proposal.
[10] Misdated in Morley, ii. 368; *H* ccvii. 827.

30. Fr.

Wrote to D. of Devonshire—Ld Salisbury—Archdn Ady[1]—Messrs
R.G. Hill & T. Lamb[2]—Bp of Manchester—Mr Hope—The Queen
—Robn G.—Rev. W. Goalen—and minutes. Saw Dean of Ch Ch
(V.C. of Oxf)[3]—Mr Glyn—Mr Moffatt. H. of C. 2½-7: dined with
Mr Glyn and H of C. 9-1½.[4] Read Lady Susan.[5]

To LORD SALISBURY, 30 June 1871.   Add MS 44540, f. 63.

You may perhaps remember that in our conversation, now some time ago,[6]
on the University Tests Bill, I expressed the hope that it might probably be the
end, if not of legislation, yet of conflict in Parliament, about the Universities, &
at the same time stated that, after it should have been passed, the Government
would be desirous of obtaining for Parliament & the country through a Commission an accurate statement of the Revenues of the Universities & the Colleges.
Since the passing of the Bill, the Govt. has considered the matter; & the question
with which they wish now to deal is whether the Commission should be from
the Crown or Statutory. I hear from the Vice Chancellor Dean, to whom I
addressed a preliminary inquiry, that there might be some differences of opinion
on this subject & this being so & the Long Vacation having now commenced, I
presume the matter must stand over until the Oct. term. I shall be very glad at
any time to communicate with you on the subject, should you think it advantageous. We certainly should not wish to bring about any appearance of aggression
or risk of collision. In the case however of the Public Schools when Ld Palmerston's Government made inquiry from the governing bodies as to their preference
between the two kinds of Commission, the reply was decidedly in favour of one
from the Crown. Possibly we may deem it right to proceed by way of formal
inquiry at the time I have mentioned.[7]

[1] William Brice Ady, 1816–82; archdeacon of Colchester from 1864.
[2] Thanking Irish farmers for an address supporting the 1870 Land Act; Add MS 44540,
f. 64.
[3] On the Oxford commission; see 20 June 71.
[4] Army Regulation Bill finished in cttee.: *H* ccvii. 938.
[5] See 24 June 68n; the 2nd ed. (1871) contains *Lady Susan and fragments of two other
unfinished tales by Miss Austen.*
[6] See 25 Apr. 71.
[7] Salisbury replied on 2 July 1871, Add MS 44431, f. 83: 'I see no objection whatever
to the proposed Commission, and I have no doubt that it will work without serious friction,
whether it is appointed by the Crown, or by Statute. . . .' See 17, 20 June 71.

WHERE WAS HE?
1869-June 1871

The following list shows where the diarist was each night; he continued at each place named until he moved on to the next. Names of the owners of great houses have been given in brackets on the first mention of the house.

1 January 1869	Hagley	26 October	London
2 January	Hawarden	6 November	Grove Park, Watford (Clarendon)
22 January	London (Carlton House Terrace)	8 November	London
23 January	Osborne	13 November	Windsor
25 January	London	15 November	London
30 January	Pembroke Lodge, Richmond (Lord Russell)	16 November	Windsor
		17 November	London
		19 November	Hawarden
1 February	London	6 December	London
20 March	Latimer (Chesham)	11 December	Boveridge, Dorset (Mrs. Thistle-thwayte)
22 March	London		
25 March	Wilton (Pembroke)		
1 April	London	13 December	London
12 June	Dufferin Lodge, Highgate (G. G. Glyn)	21 December	Hawarden
		15 January 1870	Hagley
14 June	London	20 January	London
26 June	Windsor	9 April	Windsor
28 June	London	11 April	London
3 July	Dufferin Lodge, Highgate	12 April	Hawarden
		25 April	London
5 July	London	1 June	Walmer Castle
24 July	Chislehurst (Lord R. Cavendish)	8 June	London
		18 June	Cassiobury Park, Hertfordshire (Ebury)
30 July	London		
10 August	Walmer, Kent (Granville)	20 June	London
4 September	London	22 June	Strawberry Hill (Fortescue & Lady Waldegrave)
6 September	Raby Castle (Cleveland)		
10 September	Balmoral	23 June	London
25 September	Fasque (Sir T. Gladstone)	25 June	Ashridge, Berkhamstead (Alford)
27 September	Camperdown, Forfarshire (Camperdown)	27 June	London
		9 July	Chislehurst
		11 July	London
29 September	Carlisle	6 August	St. George's, Weybridge (Egerton)
30 September	Hawarden		
14 October	Chester	8 August	London
16 October	Hawarden	11 August	Walmer Castle

19 August	London	2 December	Hawarden
23 August	Walmer Castle	14 December	London
6 September	London	19 December	Hawarden
8 September	Nottingham		
9 September	London	14 January 1871	London
17 September	Hawarden	12 February	Windsor
20 September	London	13 February	London
24 September	Stanmore Park,	18 March	Windsor
	Middlesex (Wolver-	20 March	London
	ton)	4 April	Hawarden
26 September	London	17 April	London
1 October	Hawarden	6 May	Windsor
19 October	London	8 May	London
26 October	Bowden Park, Wilt-	13 May	Chislehurst
	shire (J. Gladstone)	15 May	London
27 October	London	26 May	Panshanger (Cow-
12 November	Hawarden		per)
24 November	London	5 June	London
26 November	Hatfield (Salisbury)	17 June	Chislehurst
28 November	London	19 June	London
29 November	Windsor	24 June	Windsor
30 November	London	26 June	London

LIST OF LETTERS BY CORRESPONDENT,
PUBLISHED IN VOLUME VII

Note on editing of letters

Wherever possible the holograph of the letter is the version quoted. In most cases the holograph was sent to the recipient and a copy made and kept by the secretaries. Most of the holographs, therefore, are not in the Gladstone Papers, but in the papers of the recipient. The collection from which the version printed is taken can be seen from the reference printed at the head of each letter. Collections in the Public Record Office and the British Library are not differentiated by name. In certain cases Gladstone would keep the holograph and instruct the secretaries to copy the text of the letter onto a sheet which he had already signed (see, e.g., letter to G. Howell at 1 December 1871); sometimes the whole of the holograph has not survived, and has been supplemented from the secretary's copy; such cases have been indicated in the footnotes. Most of the letters by Gladstone preserved in the Gladstone Papers in the British Library (Add MSS 44086-44835) are, for the years of his premierships, copies made by the secretaries. Any reference number from the Special and General Correspondence (Add MSS 44086-44526, in which copies of certain, usually longer, letters are interleaved with the letters of the correspondents), should be taken to refer to a copy unless the contrary is indicated, and all letters taken from the Letter Books (Add MSS 44527-44551) are copies, though Gladstone sometimes corrected these copies himself, as he did those preserved in the Special and General Correspondence. Occasionally, the date of a letter differs by a day or so from Gladstone's diary note of it (see 20-21 June 71); such letters have been placed at the dates on them. The secretaries often used standard abbreviations when copying; these have usually been filled out, but where there is doubt as to the meaning, square brackets have been used; where the version printed is the holograph, Gladstone's abbreviations have been preserved. An ampersand has on occasion been used. Considerations of space have meant that it has not always been possible to reproduce exactly Gladstone's sometimes expansive lay-out, paragraphing, and punctuation. In making their copies, the secretaries very rarely followed Gladstone's paragraphing, as students of Lathbury will know. Similar considerations have also prevented extensive quotation from the letters of Gladstone's correspondents; the substance of these letters, when they have been found in the British Library or the Hawarden collections, or elsewhere, has been indicated in the footnotes where appropriate. In a surprisingly large number of cases the correspondent's letter, either as precursor or reply, has not been found; it would have been wearisome to have included a footnote, 'untraced', on each occasion of such an absence. It is interesting to note that Lathbury and Guedalla worked primarily from these copies in the Gladstone Papers, and that the Gladstone side of the correspondence in Guedalla's *The Queen and Mr. Gladstone* is taken from the drafts which Gladstone made for his letters, not from the letters as the Queen received them.

The owners of collections in private hands or on deposit in libraries who made access possible are very much to be thanked, and in particular the Earl of Clarendon and the Duke of Devonshire. Unfortunately, access to the Argyll,

Spencer, and Kimberley Papers, for the purpose of preparing these volumes for publication, was not possible; the Lowe Papers proved to be little more than a bundle of mementoes.